Modules

```
MODULE Identifier;
    Import
    ...
    Declaration
    ...
BEGIN
    StatementSequence
END Identifier.
```
Program module

```
DEFINITION MODULE Identifier;
    Import
    ...
    Definition
    ...

END Identifier.
```
Definition module

```
MODULE Identifier;
    Import
    ...
    Export
    Declaration
    ...
BEGIN
    StatementSequence
END Identifier;
```
Local module

```
IMPLEMENTATION MODULE
    Identifier;
    Import
    ...
    Declaration
    ...
BEGIN
    StatementSequence
END Identifier.
```
Implementation module

(Shaded portions are optional; constructs followed by . . . may be repeated.)

Reserved Words

AND	ELSIF	LOOP	REPEAT
ARRAY	END	MOD	RETURN
BEGIN	EXIT	MODULE	SET
BY	EXPORT	NOT	THEN
CASE	FOR	OF	TO
CONST	FROM	OR	TYPE
DEFINITION	IF	POINTER	UNTIL
DIV	IMPLEMENTATION	PROCEDURE	VAR
DO	IMPORT	QUALIFIED	WHILE
ELSE	IN	RECORD	WITH

An Introduction to Computer Science with
Modula-2

J. Mack Adams
New Mexico State University

Philippe J. Gabrini
Université du Québec à Montréal

Barry L. Kurtz
New Mexico State University

D. C. Heath and Company
Lexington, Massachusetts   Toronto

Cover: © Henry Ries

Copyright © 1988 by D. C. Heath and Company.
All rights reserved. No part of this publication may be reproduced or transmitted in any form or by any means, electronic or mechanical, including photocopy, recording, or any information storage or retrieval system, without permission in writing from the publisher.
Published simultaneously in Canada.
Printed in the United States of America.
International Standard Book Number: 0-669-12171-1
Library of Congress Catalog Card Number: 87-81175

10 9 8 7 6 5 4 3 2 1

To the students in our introductory course
in computer science at
New Mexico State University.
          J. Mack

à mes femmes Anne-Marie, Karine, Céline,
Audrey, sans oublier Némésis.
          Philippe

To my courageous brother Mike.
          Barry

Preface

An Introduction to Computer Science with Modula-2 is intended for a first course in computer science for students who are majoring or minoring in this discipline. Although no assumptions are made as to any previous programming experience, the majority of students will have been exposed to computers and will have taken high school mathematics courses, including algebra and geometry.

The book's main objectives are to provide students with a substantive introduction to computer science, to give them a thorough understanding of the basic concepts of this discipline, and to teach them problem solving with computers using the Modula-2 programming language. The book stresses problem-solving and software engineering principles from the start since we feel that the best place to acquire a good methodology is in the very first computer science course.

Although the text is aimed at students seriously interested in computer science and other sciences, the book's presentation is not overly formal. We firmly believe Samuel Johnson's assertion:

> Example is always more efficacious than precept.

Thus, our general approach is to introduce a topic using a few good examples followed by a more formal treatment. For deep topics, this approach takes what is commonly known as a spiral presentation. For example, recursion is introduced early in the text as a special case of the divide-and-conquer problem-solving strategy, using simple examples and recurrence relations. The goals of this introduction are to make sure students are comfortable with recursive (inductive) formulations and to see how such formulations can be implemented almost mechanically as recursive programs. This introduction is not intended to explain how recursive programs are executed. The execution process is explained in a later chapter, using the simple examples from the introduction and more complex examples. In still later chapters, recursion is used to develop searching and sorting programs, including Quicksort. The spiral approach is also used for information hiding and the treatment of program verification using assertions.

The text uses the Modula-2 programming language. We have chosen Modula-2 because it is a modern language that facilitates the introduction of many basic concepts of computer science. Niklaus Wirth, who designed the Pascal programming language for academic purposes, recognized the limits of Pascal. He designed and experimented with Modula, a programming language that introduced the concept of the module. This led to the definition of Modula-2 in the late seventies as the sole computer language for the Lilith microcomputer. Modula-2 incorporates high-level abstraction and features for dealing with very large programs and features for dealing with machine-dependent characteristics. Modula-2 is likely to replace Pascal in computer science curricula because of its suitability for implementing concepts such as information hiding. We chose Modula-2 over Ada, another modern programming language, because Ada is much less concise and less suitable for an introductory course. Using the best available language in a first course seemed eminently sensible as it enabled us to give greater emphasis to concepts and to spend less time on the idiosyncrasies of the programming language.

This text was wholly conceived and written as a Modula-2 textbook. It is not a rewritten Pascal text; since its inception, the book has focused on using the new features of Modula-2 to introduce the basic concepts of computer science. Features that are growing in importance in introductory computer science courses have been used throughout the text. These include:

- *software engineering principles* (problem-solving methodology, top-down design, structure charts, modular design charts, testing strategies, program documentation)
- *modularization* (early use of procedures and external modules)
- *information hiding and abstract data types*
- *early introduction of recursion* and continued use throughout the text
- *introduction to program correctness using assertions as comments*
- *introduction to analysis of algorithms*
- *introduction to numerical analysis*
- *introduction to concurrency*
- *an overview of selected topics in computer science*

To promote understanding of these features, the text includes numerous examples drawn from numerical, nonnumerical, and graphical sources. Many chapters include complete case studies that offer the student a chance to follow a problem through the problem-solving process from definition to documentation. Exercises and programming problems at the end of each chapter reinforce the student's grasp of newly introduced concepts. Difficult exercises are noted with an asterisk (*).

As with any course involving programming, laboratory work is extremely important. A seven-disk software support package exists for institutions equipped with microcomputer labs. This tutorial package runs on IBM PCs and compatible systems. Documentation for this package is found in an Instructor's Guide available from the publisher. Also included in the Instructor's Guide are answers to selected exercises and over 95 transparency masters.

Preface

At New Mexico State University, we have used the text for more than two years in our first course for computer science majors (a 15-week semester). We cover all of Chapters 1 through 13 and selected topics in Chapters 14 through 16, depending on the instructor's interests. Chapter 17 is usually given as a reading assignment, with only a short general discussion in class. The later chapters can be skipped completely for a course based on a shorter term, or they may be supplemented to provide adequate material for two short terms.

Chapter Outline

Chapter 1 features a general introduction to computers and introduces a six-step method for solving problems with a computer. It illustrates the first steps of the method by defining algorithms for various examples using pseudocode and by introducing the four basic structures of programming: sequencing, selection, repetition, and invocation.

Chapter 2 introduces the first Modula-2 program, describes its syntax in some detail, and introduces input and output statements as well as program debugging. The introduction to input and output leads to a natural presentation of external modules and how to import items from them.

Chapter 3 discusses parameterless procedures as a means of modularizing solutions, and then covers procedures with parameters. Function procedures are also introduced. Even though we have only the assignment statement and input/output calls, we develop simple, yet meaningful, examples.

Chapter 4 introduces control structures for iteration: LOOP, WHILE, REPEAT and FOR. Control structures for simple selection precede the presentation of the IF statement, while the combination of these control structures creates a discussion of nested statements. Simple examples support each presentation.

Chapter 5 introduces recursion as a special case of the powerful problem-solving strategy, divide-and-conquer. Once again, simple examples illustrate the concept. A study of multiple selection introduces the ELSIF clause and the CASE statement; the study also compares the various methods available for multiple selection.

Chapter 6 discusses the details of numeric and BOOLEAN data types and introduces subrange and record data types. Through this early introduction of subranges and records, we can cover more interesting examples. An extremely important topic, the introduction of abstract data types and the definition of external modules as a means to implement abstract data types, ends the chapter.

Chapter 7 pauses in the introduction of new Modula-2 syntactic topics to discuss program structure. This discussion includes explanations of the rules of scope and nested procedures. Recursion is revisited, with emphasis placed on the execution of recursive calls. Also presented are the information hiding principle and some of Modula-2's hiding techniques.

Chapter 8 reviews in more detail the six-step problem-solving method first introduced in Chapter 1. We also introduce our first case study, a complete programming example using the methodology just reviewed. The next six chapters all contain complete case studies.

Chapter 9 details the character and string data types. The treatment of the string data type leads to the introduction of one-dimensional arrays. The discussion expands to include multidimensional arrays and open array parameters.

Chapter 10 reviews input and output topics and offers a more general view of standard I/O modules. Other topics include file systems and graphic systems.

Chapter 11 gives a complete coverage of modules. First, we see a more formal presentation of external modules. Next, modular design charts are introduced as design tools. A discussion of separate compilation of modules follows, and local modules are covered as well.

Chapter 12 reviews the array data type and offers more information on the record type, then discusses combining these two types. We are introduced to searching algorithms: linear and binary search, with an informal discussion of the efficiency of the algorithms. Finally, we explore the set data type and some of its applications.

Chapter 13 continues the discussion of analysis of algorithms by developing and analyzing several sorting algorithms, including Quicksort. The case study in this chapter builds on the Quicksort example.

Chapter 14 introduces the field of numerical analysis. It discusses the representation of numerical values as well as computer arithmetic. We see some common numerical methods: series approximation, numerical integration, and random numbers. The examples used help introduce the procedure type and illustrate local modules.

Chapter 15 completes our presentation of abstract data types by using the Strings module as an example and by showing how information hiding can be achieved using opaque types. Dynamic data structures and the pointer data type are introduced, then used to illustrate opaque type implementation, as well as linked lists and trees.

Chapter 16 introduces the concept of concurrency in a simple way, by means of simple examples. The chapter ends with a more general discussion of concurrency based on the producer-consumer problem.

Chapter 17 gives a brief overview of important fields of computer science as an introduction for the beginning computer scientist. The chapter aims to give a better understanding of computer science as a whole. Topics include computer architecture and operating systems, programming languages and artificial intelligence.

Acknowledgments

We would like to acknowledge the contributions of the following reviewers: Thomas J. Ahlborn, West Chester University; John Beidler, University of Scranton; Andrew Black, University of Washington; J. Glenn Brookshear, Marquette University; Steven C. Bruell, University of Iowa; Henry A. Etlinger, Rochester Institute of Technology; Michael Hennessy, University of Oregon; John J. Leeson, University of Central Florida; Barry Levine, San Francisco State University; Timothy Long, Ohio State University; C. Dianne Martin, George Washington University; James C. Miller, Bradley University; Larry Neal, East Tennessee State University; Arnold M. Ostebee, St. Olaf College; Jeff Parker, Boston College; James F. Peters III, St. John's University; Richard F. Sincovec, University of Colorado, Colorado Springs; and Lynn R. Ziegler, Michigan

Technological University. Their critical assessments of different versions of the text sometimes had a negative effect on our egos, but definitely had a positive effect on the text. Colleagues and students have also contributed much to the text, and we would particularly like to acknowledge two of these contributions. A discussion with Joe Pfeiffer completely changed our approach to concurrency and improved the presentation a great deal. The work of David Corgan on the Instructor's Guide and the software that accompanies the text was invaluable. We are also indebted to Jeff Brumfield of the University of Texas, whose ideas on the presentation of programming language syntax influenced the syntax diagrams on the inside covers. Last, but definitely not least, we thank Tony Hoare for his story on the discovery of Quicksort.

We want to thank our editor, Karin Ellison, who has been the driving force behind this project and without whom the book would not be what it is. Thanks are also due Jonas Weisel, who tackled the huge task of smoothing out the style differences of three authors; Jill Hobbs and all the D.C. Heath people; and the hundreds of introductory computer science students who endured several different versions of the text.

Finally, we must note that without the availability of BITNET, we would probably have been unable to continue the collaboration that made this effort possible.

J. Mack Adams
Philippe J. Gabrini
Barry L. Kurtz

Contents

Introduction 1

- 0.1 A Brief History of the Computer *2*
- 0.2 Computers and Computer Programming: An Overview *4*
- 0.3 A General Approach to Problem Solving *6*

1 · Problem Solving and Algorithms 8

- 1.1 Problem Solving with a Computer *8*
  - Define the Problem *9*
  - Design a Solution *9*
  - Refine the Solution *10*
  - Develop a Testing Strategy *11*
  - Code and Test the Program *12*
  - Complete the Documentation *13*
  - Overview of the Problem-Solving Method *13*
- 1.2 A Graphical Algorithm *14*
- 1.3 A Numerical Algorithm *17*
- 1.4 Character String Algorithms *23*
  - Counting Words in a Line of Text *23*
  - Counting Words in a Paragraph *27*
- 1.5 Sequencing, Repetition, Selection, and Invocation *29*
  - SUMMARY *30*
  - EXERCISES *30*

2 · Introduction to Modula-2   33

- 2.1 From Algorithms to Programs   *34*
  - The Programming Environment   *34*
  - Program Implementation   *34*
  - Program Syntax, Data Types, and Library Modules   *36*
  - Four Program Examples with Simple Input and Ouput   *40*
- 2.2 Testing and Debugging Programs   *48*
  - Compilation Time Errors   *48*
  - Run Time Errors   *52*
  - Semantic Errors   *52*
  - Redirecting Input and Output   *53*
  - SUMMARY   *54*
  - EXERCISES AND PROGRAMMING PROBLEMS   *55*

3 · Procedures and Functions   57

- 3.1 Procedures and Value Parameters   *58*
  - Declaring and Invoking Procedures   *58*
  - Procedures with a Single Parameter   *61*
  - Procedures with Local Declarations   *63*
  - Procedures with Several Parameters   *66*
- 3.2 Functions   *70*
- 3.3 Variable Parameters   *72*
- 3.4 The Use of Value and Variable Parameters   *74*
  - SUMMARY   *75*
  - EXERCISES AND PROGRAMMING PROBLEMS   *75*

4 · Control Structures   78

- 4.1 Iteration   *79*
  - The LOOP Statement   *79*
  - The WHILE Statement   *80*
  - The FOR Statement   *82*
  - A Programming Example with a Loop and an Arithmetic Expression   *84*
  - The REPEAT Statement   *87*
  - A Comparative Summary of LOOP, WHILE, FOR, and REPEAT   *88*
- 4.2 Simple Selection   *90*
  - One-Branch IF Statement   *91*
  - Two-Branch IF Statement   *93*
- 4.3 Using and Debugging Nested Control Structures   *95*
  - Nested IFs   *95*
  - Nesting IFs within a Loop   *96*
  - Nested Loops   *97*
  - A Procedure with Nested Control Structures   *98*
  - Debugging Nested Control Structures   *101*
  - SUMMARY   *102*
  - EXERCISES AND PROGRAMMING PROBLEMS   *103*

5 · Recursion and Multiple Selection — 106

- 5.1 Recursion *107*
  - Efficiency of Recursive Algorithms *112*
  - Mathematical Induction and Recursion *116*
- 5.2 Multiple Selection *117*
  - IF Statements with ELSIF Parts *118*
  - The CASE Statement *121*
  - A Programming Example of the CASE Statement *123*
  - Improvement of Recursion's Efficiency with Multiple Selection *125*
  - A Comparison of Methods for Multiple Selection *126*
- SUMMARY *128*
- EXERCISES AND PROGRAMMING PROBLEMS *128*

6 · Data Types — 132

- 6.1 A Conceptual View of Data Types *133*
- 6.2 Numeric Data Types *133*
  - Operations, Expressions, and Standard Procedures *133*
  - A Programming Example *137*
- 6.3 BOOLEAN Data Type *139*
  - Boolean Variables, Operations, and Expressions *140*
  - Evaluation of Boolean Expressions *142*
  - Complex Boolean Expressions, Nested IF Statements, Decision Tables, and Decision Trees *145*
- 6.4 Subrange Types *148*
- 6.5 Records *150*
- 6.6 An Introduction to Abstract Data Types and External Modules *152*
  - Defining the Point Data Type *153*
  - Defining a Module *154*
  - Using the Points Module *156*
- SUMMARY *157*
- EXERCISES AND PROGRAMMING PROBLEMS *158*

7 · Program Structure — 161

- 7.1 The Structure of Modula-2 Programs *162*
  - Local Environments of Procedures *162*
  - Rules of Scope *164*
  - Scoping and Parameter Passing *167*
- 7.2 Nested Procedures *169*
- 7.3 Recursive Procedures *175*
- 7.4 The Principle of Information Hiding Applied to Program Structure *184*
  - Problem Decomposition as a Key to Design *184*
  - Access to Nonlocal Identifiers *187*
  - Shared Components and Information Hiding *187*
- SUMMARY *188*
- EXERCISES AND PROGRAMMING PROBLEMS *189*

8 · Problem Solving and Program Development — 194

- 8.1 The Problem-Solving Method Revisited   *195*
  - Define the Problem   *195*
  - Design a Solution   *195*
  - Refine the Solution   *197*
  - Develop a Testing Strategy   *198*
  - Program Coding, Programming Style, and Testing   *200*
  - Complete the Documentation   *202*
  - Summary of the Problem-Solving Method   *203*
- 8.2 Application of the Problem-Solving Method   *203*
  - Design   *203*
  - Implementation   *210*
  - Maintenance   *217*
- SUMMARY   *217*
- EXERCISES AND PROGRAMMING PROBLEMS   *218*

9 · Characters, Strings, and Arrays — 221

- 9.1 Character Data Type   *222*
  - Character Representation   *222*
  - Character Operations   *223*
  - A Program Example   *224*
- 9.2 Enumeration Data Types   *226*
  - Simple and Structured Data Types   *226*
  - Examples of Enumeration Types   *226*
- 9.3 String Data Type   *228*
  - Access to Characters in a String   *229*
  - Two Programming Examples   *229*
- 9.4 Arrays   *232*
  - One-Dimensional Arrays   *232*
  - The STRING Data Type as an Array   *237*
  - Multidimensional Arrays   *238*
  - Open Array Parameters   *240*
- 9.5 Case Study: Stylistic Analysis of Text   *242*
  - Design   *243*
  - Implementation   *250*
  - Maintenance   *254*
- SUMMARY   *255*
- EXERCISES AND PROGRAMMING PROBLEMS   *256*

10 · Input and Output Revisited — 258

- 10.1 Sequential Input and Output   *259*
- 10.2 Legible Input and Output   *260*
  - Character Data   *261*
  - Numeric Data   *262*
  - Review of Input and Output Redirection   *264*

10.3 Multiple Input/Output Streams *265*
  Interaction with the User and Input/Output Redirection *265*
  The Library Module Terminal *266*
  A Programming Example *267*
10.4 Files *270*
10.5 Graphical Screen-Oriented Output *273*
10.6 Case Study: Merging Sorted Files *274*
  Design *274*
  Implementation *279*
  SUMMARY *281*
  EXERCISES AND PROGRAMMING PROBLEMS *282*

11 · Modules 284

11.1 Programming Languages and the Software Crisis *285*
11.2 Development of External Modules *287*
  Definition Module *287*
  Implementation Module *289*
11.3 Strings: A Sample External Module *290*
  The Strings Definition Module *290*
  Using the Strings Module *295*
  The Strings Implementation Module *298*
11.4 Modular Design Charts *300*
11.5 Separate Compilation of Modules *302*
11.6 Local Modules *303*
  Declaration of Local Modules *303*
  Using Local Modules *307*
11.7 Case Study: Line Justification *311*
  Design *311*
  Implementation *318*
  SUMMARY *324*
  EXERCISES AND PROGRAMMING PROBLEMS *325*

12 · Arrays of Records, Searching, and Sets 327

12.1 Arrays of Records *328*
12.2 Abbreviation of Field Selectors with the WITH Statement *330*
12.3 Variant Records *332*
12.4 Searching *335*
  Linear Search *335*
  Binary Search *338*
  A Library Module Using Linear and Binary Search *343*
12.5 Sets *345*
  SET Types *345*
  Operations *346*
  Applications *347*

12.6 Case Study: Doña Ana's Restaurant   *349*
    Design   *349*
    Implementation   *355*
  SUMMARY   *361*
  EXERCISES AND PROGRAMMING PROBLEMS   *362*

13 · Sorting and Analysis of Algorithms   *364*

13.1 Simple Sorting Algorithms   *365*
    Selection Sort   *365*
    An Introduction to Proving a Program Correct   *368*
    Insertion Sort   *369*
    Program Correctness Revisited   *372*

13.2 Elementary Analysis of Algorithms   *373*
    The Big-*O* Notation   *373*
    Complexity Classes   *376*

13.3 Quicksort   *377*

13.4 Case Study: Sorting into Three Parts   *382*
    Design   *382*
    Implementation   *388*
    Complexity Analysis   *390*
    Application to Quicksort   *391*
  SUMMARY   *391*
  EXERCISES AND PROGRAMMING PROBLEMS   *392*

14 · Numerical Methods   *394*

14.1 Computer Arithmetic   *395*
    An Aside on Fixed Point Numbers   *397*

14.2 The Binary Number System   *397*

14.3 Internal Representations of Numeric Values   *399*

14.4 Series Approximations   *401*
    An Aside on Polynomial Evaluation   *403*

14.5 Numerical Integration and Procedure Types   *404*

14.6 Random Numbers   *407*

14.7 Case Study: Finding a Root of an Equation   *411*
    Design   *411*
    Implementation   *414*
  SUMMARY   *417*
  EXERCISES AND PROGRAMMING PROBLEMS   *417*

15 · Abstract Data Types and Dynamic Data Structures   *420*

15.1 Abstract Data Types   *420*
    Strings   *421*

Opaque Types   *422*
15.2   Dynamic Data Structures and Pointers   *424*
    Static Structures   *425*
    Dynamic Structures   *425*
    Opaque Strings Implementation   *430*
    Linked Lists   *431*
    Binary Trees   *434*
    SUMMARY   *438*
    EXERCISES AND PROGRAMMING PROBLEMS   *438*

16 · Concurrency   442

16.1   Concurrent Processing and Multiprocessing   *442*
16.2   Concurrency in Modula-2   *443*
16.3   The Producer-Consumer Problem   *452*
    SUMMARY   *457*
    EXERCISES AND PROGRAMMING PROBLEMS   *457*

17 · An Overview of Selected Topics in Computer Science   459

17.1   Computer Architecture and Operating Systems   *459*
    Evolution of Computer Architecture   *460*
    Evolution of Operating Systems   *462*
17.2   Programming Languages   *465*
    Evolution of Programming Languages   *466*
    Formal Definition of Programming Language Syntax   *467*
    Formal Definition of Programming Language Semantics   *468*
    Program Verification: An Example   *469*
17.3   Artificial Intelligence   *472*
    Selected Areas of Artificial Intelligence Research   *472*
    A Sample Problem: The Eight Puzzle   *475*
    SUMMARY   *480*

Appendix A   Decimal and Octal Representation for the ASCII Character Set   *A1*
Appendix B   Modula-2 Syntax (Using EBNF)   *A2*
Appendix C   Modula-2 Syntax Diagrams   *A9*
Appendix D   Standard Procedures and Functions   *A22*
Appendix E   Standard Modules (InOut, RealInOut, MathLib0) and System Dependencies   *A23*
Appendix F   Nonstandard Modules (Strings, TurtleGraphics, SYSTEM, Storage, FileSystem)   *A30*
Answers to Selected Exercises   *A43*
Index   *A83*

Introduction

Tools drive the subsequent evolution of the mind.
JOSEPH BRONOWSKI (*THE ASCENT OF MAN*)

In some sense the computer is the most powerful tool ever developed. This power comes from the fact that the computer is a tool of the mind. Computers enhance and even extend our mental capabilities rather than our physical faculties. Unlike other important tools in our history, which had applications in only a few areas like industry and transportation, the computer can be used nearly anywhere that people use their minds. It can perform enormous volumes of calculations quickly and accurately—whatever the subject. Indeed many of our technological accomplishments would have been impossible without computers. The CAT scanner, which allows sophisticated medical diagnosis, is a good example, and similar instances can be found in almost every field of science and engineering. Computers are also contributing in other areas such as business and education, enabling management to process the mountains of data necessary for the day-to-day operations of a large company and providing computer-assisted instruction in the classroom.

Another way of describing the computer's wide applicability is to say that computers do not address any particular need but instead give us the means to solve problems. Thus this text will help you understand how to analyze problems and use computers effectively to reach solutions.

The problem-solving process will involve learning a programming language with which you can command the computer to perform desired actions. The language you use will have a substantial effect on your thought process—its expressiveness will enhance your problem-solving capabilities and its limitations will hinder them. As a result, the language has been chosen very carefully. We have chosen a small but powerful language called Modula-2 because it is simple and consistent, and yet quite powerful. Also, as the name implies, it facilitates solving large problems in a modular way using solutions, called modules, of smaller problems.

Before embarking on a detailed discussion of problem solving with Modula-2, however, we'll take a few pages here in this Introduction to set the stage. First, we'll explore a brief history of computer evolution. We'll see how scientists, searching for solutions to diverse problems, developed increasingly sophisticated machine technologies, which led to the modern computer. This history, however short, will give us a sense of how advances in computer development are motivated by the need to solve problems.

Next, we'll discuss what we mean by a computer. We will describe its basic parts and introduce the terminology needed for subsequent discussions.

Finally, we'll preview the problem-solving process itself—that is, quite apart from any computer-related application—and begin to lay out an approach that can be applied to problem solving with a computer.

0.1 A Brief History of the Computer

Let's begin our history with some of the earliest landmarks in the invention of an automatic calculating device:

- 1642—the French mathematician Blaise Pascal designed the first mechanical adding machine.
- 1694—the German mathematician Gottfried Wilhelm von Leibniz created a mechanical calculator capable of performing both addition and multiplication.
- 1801—the Frenchman Joseph Jacquard developed a loom for weaving cloth in which the patterns in the cloth were controlled by punched cards (essentially a special-purpose computer whose control was determined by the holes punched in the cards).
- Mid-1800s—the English mathematician Charles Babbage designed an "analytical engine." A forerunner of the modern computer, the machine could not be built due to the inadequate technology of that era.

Each of these four events was a significant step in the development of calculating devices that could operate in an increasingly automatic way. The operations of Pascal's and Leibniz's calculators were carried out by mechanical devices such as gears, and each operation was specified by the user at the time it was to be done. In other words, an entire sequence of operations, now called a *program,* could not be specified in advance. Jacquard's loom, however, was controlled by instructions external to the machine and read from punched cards. Thus, the loom could be programmed to execute an entire sequence of instructions. Because punched cards controlled the loom's operation, the pattern woven into the cloth could be changed by changing the cards. Babbage extended this concept by using punched cards for entering both data and instructions. The full implementation of Babbage's ideas was not feasible with the technology of that time, though, and the further advancement of automatic computing devices awaited the development of electrical and subsequently electronic devices.

The first electrically powered automatic computer was the Harvard Mark I, which became operational in 1944. The Mark I used electromechanical relays, or mechanical switches that are opened and closed by electromagnets. This effective use of electrical devices in computers opened the way for a flood of significant advances based on electronics.

The ENIAC, which became operational in 1945, was the first completely electronic computer, using vacuum tubes as electronic switching devices rather than electromechanical relays. It was developed by J. Presper Eckert and John Mauchly for the U.S. Army to do computation of trajectories of artillery shells. The machine turned out to be massive, containing nearly 20,000 vacuum tubes and weighing a whopping 30 tons. It had a memory unit for data, but the instructions that made up the programs came in the form of cables between plug boards. Thus the construction of computer programs was as much a physical as a mental activity. Subsequent developments sought a more effective means of specifying programs.

Eckert and Mauchly, and, independently, a prominent mathematician named John von Neumann worked out the concept of the *stored program*. The stored program concept involves storing the instructions constituting a program in the computer memory along with the data. This innovation made programming primarily a mental pursuit—considerably more appropriate for using a tool whose primary purpose is to assist in problem solving. However, the languages used for programming had a numeric form, and so the mental work necessary to create even a relatively small program was considerable.

The first computers to adopt the stored program concept were a prototype of the Ferranti Mark I (1948) at the University of Manchester, the EDSAC (1949) at the University of Cambridge, and the EDVAC (1950) in the U.S. These machines can be considered the forerunners of the early commercial computers, which became available in the 1950s. Computers of this period are called *first-generation computers*. They used vacuum tubes and were bulky, unreliable, and expensive by today's standards. During this time, researchers began to experiment with rudimentary symbolic languages, which eased the effort of writing programs.

In the early 1960s the size of computers shrank with the advent of transistors, electronic switching devices much smaller than vacuum tubes. Transistors characterized *second-generation computers*, making them less costly, faster, and more reliable. The 1960s was also a time of intense development of software (programs controlling the operation of computers). More sophisticated symbolic programming languages, as well as the first operating systems (programs to organize the computer's resources and make them available to the users), were designed.

Later in the 1960s came *third-generation computers,* which were even faster and less expensive. These devices used integrated circuits that consisted of small silicon chips, each containing hundreds of switches. Also, operating systems became more sophisticated, allowing more than one task to be processed at a time by "time sharing" a computer's resources.

Fourth-generation computers in the 1970s used large-scale integrated (LSI) circuits, with thousands of switches on a chip. LSI made it possible to have the central processing unit of small computers, called microcomputers, completely contained in a single silicon chip. The 1970s also saw the beginning of computer networks (interconnection of independent computers over communication lines).

The development of computer networks has been even more extensive in the 1980s, ranging from small local area networks to worldwide networks. Microcomputer development has also been intense, using very large-scale integrated (VLSI) circuits, which provide hundreds of thousands of switches on a chip.

The rapid growth that has occurred in less than half a century hardly shows signs of abating. Along the way it has spawned a new science concerned with computer acquisition, organization, and processing of data. This field, computer science, ranges from abstract mathematical theories, which form its foundation, to very concrete techniques for the development of complex computer-based systems.

0.2 Computers and Computer Programming: An Overview

To use a machine, we do not need to understand all its construction details. When we drive a car, we do not need to know how the engine or its fuel injection system works. Similarly, when we use a computer to solve a problem, we do not have to know the intricacies of its electronic circuits. However, we do need to know a few general things, which will help us understand some of the concepts in programming.

Most computers, big or small, have the same basic capabilities: they can accept (read) data from an external device and store it for later use, they can manipulate the stored data by performing the instructions that constitute a program, and they can display (write) results on an external device. Also, they must be able to control the order in which these operations are done. Thus a computer can be represented in a very general way by the diagram in Figure 0.1, where arrows represent the flow of data. Figure 0.1 depicts a computer as a collection of five components: input devices, memory, arithmetic-logic unit, control unit, and output devices. This rather generalized depiction will be adequate for our description of a computer's operation.

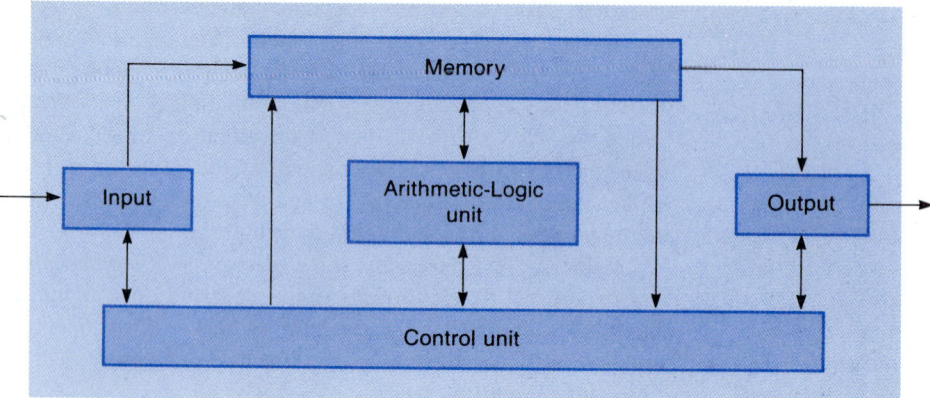

Figure 0.1
A Simple Computer

Data may be read from input devices, such as keyboards or text scanners, and stored in memory. Data may also be transferred from memory to output devices, such as screen displays or printers.

Computer memory can also hold programs (recall the stored program concept), and these programs may be read from the input devices. Generally, there are at least two types of memory: secondary memory usually consisting of magnetic disks, and main memory consisting of silicon chips. Secondary memory may also be considered to be an input or output device, because the results from one program may be written on secondary storage and used as input data for another program. This is often done in large jobs, where the intermediate results are of no particular interest to the user.

The contents of main memory are directly accessible by the arithmetic-logic unit, which performs the actual computations by executing instructions of a program stored in main memory. The instructions are directly interpreted by the machine, and so they are called *machine language* instructions. The control unit controls the operation of the other components. Together the control unit and the arithmetic-logic unit constitute what is commonly called the central processing unit (CPU), or simply processor.

Collectively, the physical devices that make up the five components are called the computer *hardware*. The operations to be performed by the hardware are specified by lists of instructions, called programs, or the *software*.

One of the most important software items is called the *operating system,* which is a group of programs supplied with your computer hardware to make it easier for you to write and use your own programs. We usually interact with the computer through the operating system rather than directly with the hardware. Operating systems will be discussed in greater detail in Chapter 2, when you will start to develop your own programs. Meanwhile we will discuss programming in a very general way.

Creating computer programs, or programming, can be thought of as a form of communication—communication between a human and a computer, where the human defines the tasks to be executed by the computer. More specifically, a program is a list of instructions describing actions for a computer to perform in order to accomplish some task. Programming is the act of creating these instructions.

We must be very careful to distinguish between the act of creating a program and the computer's action when it executes the instructions of the program. Creating a program is done initially on paper, and then, when we decide the program is what we want, it is entered into the computer and converted to the form of machine language instructions, which are executed to produce the desired output. Figure 0.2 is a very general view of program execution as a process to apply to some input in order to produce some output. The input may come in a variety of forms, such as numbers or alphabetic characters. It may come from many sources, such as humans, instruments, or other computers. Similarly, output may have many forms, such as numeric or character data, signals to control equipment, or movement of a robot arm. In this introductory course we will concentrate on numeric and character data from human input sources and output in a form suitable for human interpretation (text or graphics).

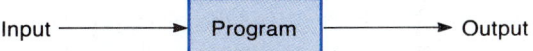

Figure 0.2
Action of a Program

Computer programming has too often been equated with the actual writing of code—the lists of instructions given to the computer for execution. There is much more than that to computer programming. Programming encompasses all the steps necessary to solve a problem on a computer: defining the problem, designing a solution, choosing or developing methods (called *algorithms* in computer science) for the solution, translating these algorithms into a form acceptable to the computer (coding), testing the program, documenting (describing) the program, and maintaining (changing) the program. While the coding process may be difficult, the formulation of an unambiguous and correct way to solve a problem is much more challenging. Computer programming is first and foremost problem solving.

0.3 A General Approach to Problem Solving

Problem solving has been described by the mathematician George Polya, one of the greatest teachers of problem solving, as a four-step process:

1. understand the problem
2. devise a plan
3. carry out the plan
4. look back

Understanding the problem can be a very difficult first step, but some general guidelines are helpful. You can ask yourself the following questions whenever you are having trouble with this step. What information are you given? What is the unknown, or what are you required to find? Is the information given sufficient to determine the unknown? The last question leads naturally to the beginning of the next step.

Devising a plan for solving a problem involves finding the relationship between the information and the unknown. When computers are used, this is a relationship between the input data and the output data, and is eventually put in the form of a computer program. For nontrivial problems, considerable thought must be given to discovering the relationship between input and output, and a program should not be attempted until this thought process has been carefully carried out. Again some guidelines may be suggested. Do you know how to solve a similar problem? Can you reformulate the problem so that it resembles a similar problem? Can you restrict the problem so that it can be solved, and, if so, can the solution be generalized to remove the restriction? Has previous work been done that will help you solve the problem?

When you have settled on a plan that seems capable of solving the problem, you should carry it out as systematically as possible. Each part of the plan should be checked as it is done. With a computer, this means that the creation of the program should be carried out faithfully according to the plan. If you feel that some aspect of the solution is unsound, you should return to the previous step and revise your plan rather than trying to make corrections without appreciating the effects of the corrections on other parts of the plan.

Finally, when you have carried out the plan, you should examine the results to ensure their validity to as great an extent as possible. In the case of a computer program this means that the output obtained from executing the program should be scrutinized and checked by some other means if possible.

With this Introduction we've tried to view the computer within the context of problem solving—to see the computer as an instrument for helping us solve problems. The computer's power as a tool derives from this capability, and the history of its development is a search for a device that will aid us in finding solutions. The parts of a computer work together to transform input data into the desired output data. Finally, Polya's simple scheme gives us the basic foundation for addressing problem solving systematically.

We're ready now to begin exploring the process of problem solving with a computer. We'll start in Chapter 1 with an elaboration of Polya's approach to problem solving specifically adapted for programming.

1 Problem Solving and Algorithms

In this chapter you will:

- be introduced to a six-step problem-solving method
- learn about refining general solutions into more detailed solutions
- discover four fundamental techniques for controlling the order in which a computation is done

In the preceding Introduction we described George Polya's general four-step problem-solving plan. In this chapter we will extend Polya's plan to a six-step approach that is aimed more specifically at solving problems with a computer. To illustrate this method, we will work through three examples: a graphical problem, a numeric problem, and a text-processing problem. The examples, in turn, will introduce us to the four basic ways of ordering instructions: sequencing, repetition, selection, and invocation. These four structures will be important tools for programming throughout this book.

1.1 Problem Solving with a Computer

In most cases there is no single correct way to solve a problem. Often when several people are faced with the same problem, each individual reaches a solution in a very personal way. The subsequent solution approaches, which may be equally valid, may also be quite different. In this chapter we will describe a general problem-solving method for programming that can be adapted to suit each person's own style. The important point here is that the individual must adopt some sort of systematic method to attack a problem. Otherwise, if a person follows no particular method during programming, he or she may hasten to write code without adequate preparation. Such an ad hoc approach usually causes difficulties later in the process. Good preparation before coding, on the other hand, leads to easier coding and more efficient testing of the code.

Our general problem-solving method begins with the basic framework of George Polya's approach, described in the Introduction. But here, to accommodate the concept of solving problems with a computer, we've expanded the process to six steps:

1. define the problem
2. design a solution
3. refine the solution
4. develop a testing strategy
5. code and test the program
6. complete the documentation

We will discuss each of these steps in the following sections.

Define the Problem

To solve a problem we have to understand it well. This initial step is a crucial one. In fact, when users define a problem, they usually must work in conjunction with the computer scientist to make sure both parties understand the problem. The dialogue between user and computer scientist should clarify the original problem formulation and precisely define the input data and desired output.

Design a Solution

After the problem has been defined, we should try to develop the outline of a solution. An effective way to start is by breaking the problem into smaller subproblems, which is a version of the familiar "divide and conquer" strategy. The structure of a solution is based on this decomposition, and so we will often refer to this step as *structural design*.

To illustrate the generality of this step, let's consider a noncomputer problem such as changing a flat tire. We can decompose this problem into four subproblems: jack up the car, take off the wheel, mount the spare wheel, and jack down the car. In turn, the subproblems can themselves be divided until we obtain very simple subproblems. One of the goals of this step is the construction of a chart that illustrates the structure of our solution (Figure 1.1). Such charts are called *structure charts*, because they give the structural components of the solution and the general relationship between the

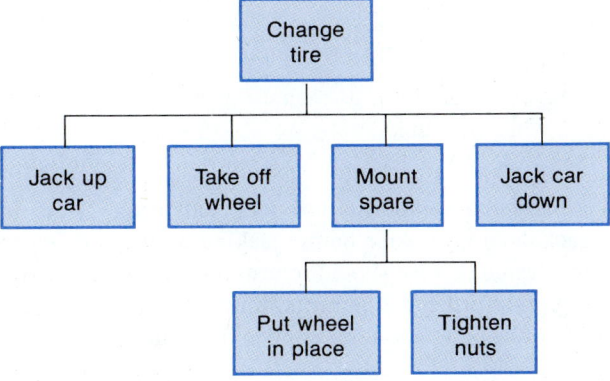

Figure 1.1
Structure Chart

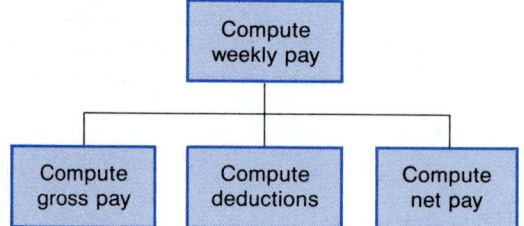

Figure 1.2
Payroll Structure Chart

components. The box at the top of the chart represents the entire solution, the boxes at the next level represent the major components of the solution, and so on.

Another simpler example is the computation of the weekly net pay of an employee. We will assume that the values for pay rate, hours worked, and tax rate are already known. The computation could be broken into three smaller steps as illustrated by the structure chart of Figure 1.2.

Refine the Solution

The preceding step leads us to a very high-level solution: an outline of the solution consisting of various subtasks, without the details of how these subtasks are accomplished. Thus we must refine our solution by developing reasonably detailed methods to do these tasks. We may find methods in the computing literature or develop our own methods. If we can find methods, we should use them, even if some adaptation is necessary. Otherwise, we must develop our own methods by describing the data and the manipulations to be performed on the data in very precise English, using common mathematical notation where applicable. This description is called a *pseudocode solution*. Pseudocode provides an outline for the final solution. Pseudocode uses concise imperative sentences. As a language, it is simpler than English. But it also is not tied to any particular programming language, such as Modula-2, so it can be easily understood and adapted to various languages. For example, pseudocode for the task "Take off wheel" might be

> For all nuts on wheel
>   loosen nut
>   unscrew it
>   take it off
> Take the wheel from its mounting
> Put wheel in trunk

This particular solution is not quite satisfactory since untightening the nuts can (and in fact should) be done before jacking up the car. In essence we have exposed a flaw in the design and we should return to the design step and correct this flaw before proceeding with further refinements. Since such a discovery is a common occurrence, we should not be reluctant to redesign if flaws are encountered in refining the solution.

Our example of refinement also illustrates another common situation: the level of detail of a refinement may not be sufficient. In this example the unscrewing of a nut could lead to another set of pseudocode instructions. In other words we may have to refine the solution successively until we have enough detail to avoid misunderstanding. This step, therefore, is sometimes called *stepwise refinement*.

To refine the solution for computing net pay, we need more information about the input data and the method by which gross pay and deductions are to be computed. For now, let's make the simple assumptions that input data include hourly rate and hours worked, and that gross pay is computed on an hourly basis. We also assume that there is a single standard deduction of 18 percent. The pseudocode version of our computation could then be written as follows:

> Set gross pay to hourly rate $\times$ hours worked
> Set deductions to 0.18 $\times$ gross pay
> Set net pay to gross pay $-$ deductions

We use the verb *set* to associate a computed value with a particular name.

Notice the difference between the pseudocode for our two examples. For instance, the steps involved in putting the wheel in the trunk may involve a considerable amount of judgment if a circumstance arises, such as the trunk being full. In the other example, all the steps in the net pay computation are precisely defined. When a method is composed of precisely defined steps that solve the problem, the method is known as an *algorithm* for the problem's solution. An algorithm, therefore, is a series of unambiguous steps used to solve a problem or, more formally, a sequence of operations that, when executed, will produce a result in finite time. If a method involves some judgment or interpretation, however, the method is a *heuristic process*. Algorithmic methods can be implemented on computers, but heuristic processes have not been amenable to such implementation. In recent years much research has been done on the possibility of implementing heuristic processes on computers. This research is part of a field called artificial intelligence, which seeks to develop computers to perform functions normally associated with human intelligence such as reasoning and intuition. For our purposes here, though, we will deal with algorithms.

Develop a Testing Strategy

In the previous step we wrote detailed pseudocode algorithms that will be the basis for computer programs. When these programs are run on the computer, we expect that they will provide correct solutions for our problems. However, it is absolutely essential that we run the programs with a wide variety of input data, called *test cases,* to give us confidence that the programs will give correct results for all cases. To do this, we should develop a broad assortment of test cases: normal input values, extreme input values that test the limits of the program, and input values that test special aspects of the program. For example, test cases for computation of net pay should include input data with minimum and maximum hourly pay rates, zero hours worked, the maximum number of hours allowed, and so on. Expected results should be specified for all test cases.

We need to develop test cases before we code a program, for the following reasons:

1. The test cases can be used to check our algorithms on paper for possible errors. If detected, these errors can be corrected before effort has been spent on coding an unsound solution.
2. The pressures of completing a program may cause us to test less objectively after the program has been coded.

Code and Test the Program

The next step in our problem-solving strategy is to prepare the program and test it using our test cases. As we have previously observed, to get a computer to do the operations we want, we must code the appropriate instructions in a language acceptable to the computer. We call such languages *programming languages*. We use the pseudocode from a previous step as a blueprint for coding, and ideally we would like the process of translating from pseudocode to programming language to be almost mechanical. Unfortunately, the limitations of our programming languages make this ideal currently unattainable, and so the coding step can be quite challenging. However, some languages make the coding step easier than others. Some of the most commonly used languages are FORTRAN, COBOL, LISP, C, Pascal, Modula-2, and Ada. We have chosen to use Modula-2 (a descendant of Pascal), because it is fairly simple but quite powerful.

The algorithm we developed earlier for the computation of net pay can easily be converted to Modula-2 as follows:

```
GrossPay := Rate * Hours;
Deduction := 0.18 * GrossPay;
NetPay := GrossPay - Deduction;
```

Notice that := corresponds to "set" in pseudocode and that multiplication is denoted by an asterisk. Most programming languages have a specialized notation similar to this. Names, such as GrossPay, are called *variables* and can be thought of as names of locations in computer memory where values can be stored. This Modula-2 program segment would constitute only part of a program to do a payroll. We will see many complete programs in subsequent chapters.

As we code the algorithms, we must test them using the strategy developed in the previous step. The programs must be run, therefore, with trial data for each test case, and the results have to be analyzed. This analysis can lead us to revise our algorithms or even to go back to the design step to revise our design. Such a backward step is discouraging, but it may be the best course of action if our programs have become overly complex and still do not perform correctly.

As stated previously, the data for our test cases must be defined in a systematic way to make sure that the most important cases are tested. For instance, for the net pay computation, we should use normal values for the pay rate and the number of hours worked, such as the following:

$4.50   38 hours   expected result $140.22

We should also establish minimum and maximum values for both pay rate and hours worked and make sure that, for values outside these extremes, the program produces an error message rather than computing meaningless results. The process of detecting whether input data are outside the allowable ranges is called *data validation*.

Complete the Documentation

Documentation consists of the descriptions of the steps in the problem-solving process, including explanations of critical design decisions and subtle points in the implementation. Documentation should actually take place throughout the preceding steps to record the work being done. The final documentation should contain not only a printed listing of the program but also descriptions of the program design and the testing that the program has undergone.

The program itself should be made very readable by formatting it attractively and including explanations of the parts that are especially complex. Most of the explanations can be included in the program as comments, but sometimes lengthy explanations and references to appropriate texts or papers are more appropriately placed in a separate document. All this documentation will be very helpful if the program must be changed at a later date to correct a subtle error or to improve it in some way. Such changes are called *program maintenance*. After each change the documentation should be updated to facilitate subsequent changes.

Finally, the documentation should also include instructions for running the program. For simple programs these instructions are usually relatively short and may be given in a comment at the beginning of the program. For more complex programs, which will be used by people unfamiliar with computer programming, it may be necessary to prepare a detailed document, called a *user's manual*. The user's manual should describe how to use the program and how to interpret results.

Overview of the Problem-Solving Method

The problem-solving steps described in the preceding sections are not necessarily strictly sequential: several of them overlap or might be repeated depending on the results of later steps. Documentation takes place throughout the process. Also, the boundaries between steps are not sharply defined. For example, it may be difficult to distinguish between the final stages of designing a solution and the beginning of refining that solution. Thus the refinement step is often called *detailed design*. Even the boundary between problem definition and the first stages of design may be fuzzy, since design decisions may emerge as the problem is more carefully defined.

The problem definition may be neither obvious nor easy. Often the person with the problem may be unable to state the problem precisely and unambiguously. This inability may be due to a lack of technical background or simply a somewhat vague perception of the problem. In any event the computer scientist must work with the user to make the problem more precise and to determine whether a computer solution is feasible. If a solution does seem feasible, the computer scientist must then develop precise written specifications of input data, output data, needed processing (without details), and sometimes performance requirements, such as speed of execution.

The initial phases of definition and design are essential to the whole process; without them the coding and testing phase grows longer and less systematic. In the following sections, we will illustrate steps 1, 2, and 3 of the method by developing some simple algorithms. Because the problems are simple, steps 1 and 2 will be uncharacteristically brief.

1.2 A Graphical Algorithm

As a simple example, we will consider the drawing of a square on a computer terminal screen. Before we start writing the algorithm, let's look at a similar example so we're sure we understand the problem. You are at a street corner and want to walk around the block, as shown in Figure 1.3. The arrowhead here indicates your initial position and direction.

A solution can easily be designed using two commands

> walk straight ahead to the next corner
> turn left

Thus our structural design is extremely simple, consisting of two one-command components. Because the structure is so simple, we do not need to draw a structure chart.

The first stage of the detailed design is also simple, as shown by the following algorithm.

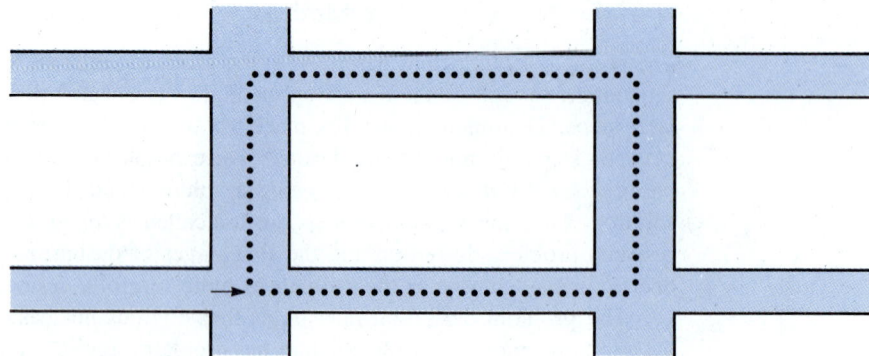

Figure 1.3
A Walk Around the Block

> walk straight ahead to the next corner
> turn left
> walk straight ahead to the next corner
> turn left
> walk straight ahead to the next corner
> turn left
> walk straight ahead to the next corner
> turn left

The last "turn left" will ensure that you are facing in the same direction as when you started, which is desirable for graphical algorithms.

This algorithm can be the basis for a solution to our original problem, but further refinements will depend on the computer we are using. We will assume that our computer has a

- graphic screen with rectangular coordinates
- graphic cursor (rectangular spot or arrow on the screen) that has a position and a heading (direction)
- command that moves the graphic cursor and produces a line
- command that changes the direction of the graphic cursor

With the commands, we can write a somewhat more appropriate algorithm for our original problem of drawing a square.

> Square
>   move along the side
>   turn left
>   move along the side
>   turn left
>   move along the side
>   turn left
>   move along the side
>   turn left
> End Square

This solution works if we know precisely what is meant by "move along the side" and "turn left." In fact, we need to be more precise when specifying the various actions to be performed because the computer will execute only those actions that it is given and it has no idea of what we really intended. Instead of saying "move along the side," we have to indicate a distance corresponding to the length of the side of our square; the exact distance depends on our computer's screen and the size of the square. Let's use 100 units; "Move along the side" will then become "move 100." We also have to be more precise when specifying the turn to the left. For a square the angle must be 90 degrees; our refined pseudocode algorithm is

```
Square
    move 100
    turn left 90
    move 100
    turn left 90
    move 100
    turn left 90
    move 100
    turn left 90
End Square
```

We could simplify the turn instruction if we agree that a positive angle will mean a turn to the left (counterclockwise) and a negative angle a turn to the right (clockwise). Our turn instruction would then become "turn 90."

The simple problem described here has introduced an important concept in designing algorithms: the sequencing of instructions. *Sequencing* is the first of four ways of interpreting pseudocode that we'll study in this chapter. It is sometimes called a *control structure* because it controls the order in which instructions are done. In sequencing, the instructions of the pseudocode algorithm are executed one after the other successively, as illustrated in Figure 1.4. Charts of this nature, which are called *flow charts*, indicate the order in which instructions are executed. Note that flow charts have quite a different purpose than structure charts, which serve only to show the primary structural components, not the order of execution.

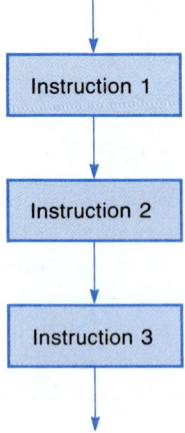

Figure 1.4
A Sequence of Instructions

1.3 A Numerical Algorithm

Let's now consider an example involving numeric computations. Such computations are common in scientific and engineering applications. We want to develop an algorithm to compute the sum of integers from 0 to any nonnegative integer, call it N, given as input. The definition of the problem seems adequately precise, but we still might want to reformulate it in a somewhat different way to confirm our understanding of what is given and what is required (see Figure 1.5).

The design of a solution is fairly simple, but it still requires a bit of thought. Our first idea may be that additions must be done. However, any further work requires some knowledge of the tools we will use to solve the problem. Because we intend to use a computer, we need information about the way computers do addition. Most computers have an operation to add two values, and we can express this operation in pseudocode by a statement of the form

> Set S to A + B

where we have used S for the name of the sum and A and B as the names of the values to be summed.

Now we might observe that we have broken our problem into N subproblems, since there are N additions to be performed. With this in mind, we can proceed to the detailed design phase. To give a more detailed solution, we must next specify the order in which the additions are to be performed. The choice is somewhat arbitrary, and we will chose a left-to-right order, which leads us to a first pseudocode version of our algorithm:

> Sum of Integers
>   Read N
>   Set Sum to 0
>   Add to Sum each number from 1 to N
>   Print "The sum is" Sum
> End Sum of Integers

In this solution, N is called an input variable, because it will have a value entered by the user of the algorithm. The Read instruction will accept the value from the user. Similarly, Sum is called an output variable, because it is the result displayed for the user by the Print instruction. As observed earlier, we can think of a variable as a name for a location in the computer's memory where a value can be stored.

Figure 1.5
A Summation Algorithm

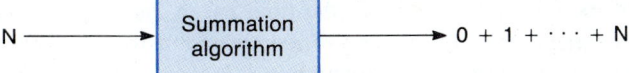

We should now improve this solution by defining more precisely the step of adding to the sum. Since we want to do one addition at a time, the adding operation must be done repeatedly. At this point we need some general information about how to specify that operations are to be done repeatedly using a computer. The computer will need to know precisely which operations must be executed repeatedly and when to stop the repetition. In our pseudocode we will use the word "Loop" at the beginning of a sequence of instructions to be repeated, and the words "End loop" at the end of the sequence. We will specify when the repetition is to terminate by using a command of the form

> Exit if condition

When this command is executed, the specified condition will be checked. If it is true, the repetition will terminate; otherwise it will continue. We will allow this command to be placed anywhere in the list of instructions that form the loop so that we can terminate the repetition at any point we choose. On termination, the instruction following "End loop" is executed. Using these features, we do a refinement of our first solution.

> Sum of Integers
>   Read N
>   Set Sum to 0
>   Loop
>   Exit if all numbers have been added
>   Add appropriate number to Sum
>   End loop
>   Print "The sum is" Sum
> End Sum of Integers

Thus the repeated execution of a sequence of instructions is called *repetition, looping,* or *iteration*. Like sequencing, repetition is a control structure that establishes the order of execution of instructions of the pseudocode algorithm. The basic form of the Loop instruction is

> Loop
>   List of instructions
>   Exit if condition
>   List of instructions
> End loop

In some cases the initial list of instructions may be empty so that the exit test is at the top of the loop. In other cases the final list of instructions may be empty, so the exit test is at the bottom of the loop. The indented instructions below the word "Loop" are repeated as long as the exit condition is not true, as illustrated by the flow chart in

A Numerical Algorithm

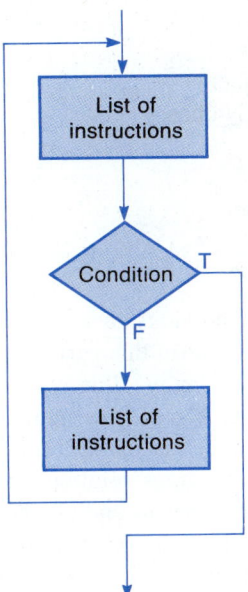

Figure 1.6
Flow Chart of a Loop

Figure 1.6. The diamond represents the condition to be tested and indicates the path to follow when the condition is true (T) or false (F). When the condition is true, the loop is terminated and execution continues with any instructions following the end of the loop. As we have noted, one of the lists of instructions may be empty, as in Sum of Integers, where the first list is empty.

Thus far in this algorithm we have used both sequencing and repetition, which are important control structures used in the design of algorithms. For our summation algorithm, we need to be still more precise. In particular, we need to specify the Exit condition more carefully, as well as the statement "Add appropriate number to Sum." Both of these instructions can be accomplished by using a variable that ranges over the numbers to be added (that is, 0 to N). We set the variable to 0 initially, and we successively increment by 1 through subsequent values to be added until the variable reaches the last number, N. This variable will indicate the number of iterations that have been completed, as well as specify the numbers to be added, so it can also be used for the termination condition. We will name this variable Number and use it for our third refinement of a solution. This refinement will also contain two very important comments, enclosed in braces, which specify exactly what we have accomplished at the positions where the comments appear.

	Sum of Integers
(1)	Read N
(2)	Set Sum to 0
(3)	Set Number to 0
	Loop
	$\{ \text{Sum} = 0 + 1 + \cdots + \text{Number} \}$

(4)   Exit if Number = N
(5)   Set Number to Number + 1
(6)   Set Sum to Sum + Number
        End loop
        { Sum = 0 + 1 + ⋯ + N }
(7)   Print "The sum is" Sum
(8)   End Sum of Integers

This solution is more precise than the previous ones, because there is no ambiguity in the interpretation of each step. Notice that in this particular instance of a loop the list of instructions before the exit test is empty. This algorithm will work for any nonnegative integer: check the case when N = 0. The numbers appearing to the left of the solution will be used only to aid in the discussion of the algorithm.

The Read instruction (line 1 in the previous solution) causes: (1) a value to be accepted from the keyboard when the user types it, and (2) the value to be assigned to the variable N. We can illustrate a variable by a box labeled with the variable name. The contents of the box will be the value of the variable. Assuming that 3 is entered by the user, we have

Instructions like "Set Sum to 0" and "Set Number to 0" are called *assignments* since they assign a value to a variable. In this instance the results of the assignment are

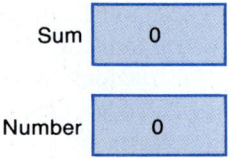

Notice the similarity between the assignment (Set) instruction and the Read instruction: both give values to variables. In the assignment the value is supplied by an expression within the program; in the Read the value is supplied from an external source (the user in this case).

After these assignments to Sum and Number, the loop is entered. Notice that the comment asserts that Sum = 0 + ⋯ + Number, which is correct because both Sum and Number are 0. We will call this comment a *loop invariant*, because, as we shall see, it is true whenever execution reaches the point at which the comment is located.

The first instruction in the loop is the Exit statement, and because Number is not equal to the value of N, the loop is not terminated. The assignment instruction, "Set Number to Number + 1", will, therefore, be executed. This instruction causes Number to have the value 0 + 1, or simply 1, which replaces the previous value. Next, the instruction "Set Sum to Sum + Number" is done. To do this, Number is added to the old value of Sum to determine the new value to be assigned to Sum. This new value replaces the old value of Sum. So we now have

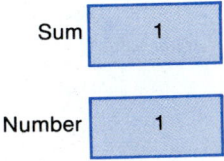

We are now at the bottom of the list of instructions that form the loop, so execution resumes at the top of the loop. Notice that the loop invariant is still true because Sum equals $0 + 1$, when Number is 1.

If the value of N is greater than 1, more repetitions will be done; otherwise, the loop will terminate because the condition Number = N will be true. Notice that the comment in braces always accurately indicates the current value of Sum when execution has reached that point in the loop. This point is illustrated in Table 1.1. Also notice that the comment immediately after End loop follows directly from the comment in the loop, because the loop terminates exactly when Number = N. As you can see, these comments help to ensure that the algorithm performs the desired computation. However, we should always check the correctness of an algorithm as many ways as possible; thus the development of a testing strategy is the next step in our problem-solving methodology.

For such a simple problem, we need specify only that the algorithm be tested on boundary cases—that is, the largest and smallest possible values for N and some typical cases. The smallest possible value is 0, but we have not specified the largest possible value. In fact, our algorithm should work for any positive value, no matter how large, as evidenced by the argument in the previous paragraph, which did not depend on the value of N. Unfortunately, any computer program based on the algorithm will have a limit on the values that can be represented. As a result, part of the specification of a testing strategy will depend on the computer and the programming language used to implement the algorithm. For now we will be content with checking the algorithm on a "typical" case, say N = 3. We can do this checking by a manual simulation of the execution of the algorithm, as we started doing earlier. This simulation leads to the

TABLE 1.1   **Iterations and Comment**

Iterations Completed (Value of Number)	Comment
0	Sum = 0
1	Sum = 0 + 1
.	.
.	.
.	.
N	Sum = 0 + 1 + $\cdots$ + N

TABLE 1.2 Trace of Sum of Integers Algorithm

Instruction	N	Sum	Number	Condition
1	3	—	—	—
2	3	0	—	—
3	3	0	0	—
4	3	0	0	false
5	3	0	1	—
6	3	1	1	—
4	3	1	1	false
5	3	1	2	—
6	3	3	2	—
4	3	3	2	false
5	3	3	3	—
6	3	6	3	—
4	3	6	3	true
7	prints "The sum is 6"			
8	stops			

production of a *trace* of its execution, indicating the instructions executed and their effect on the data. We can produce a trace of our summation algorithm using the instruction numbers (see Table 1.2). This trace of the algorithm shows that the algorithm works for N = 3.

The Sum of Integers algorithm is expressed in pseudocode and must be translated into a programming language to be run on a computer. The following program shows the corresponding Modula-2 program for this algorithm. This program serves to illustrate what a Modula-2 program looks like; Modula-2 programs will be discussed in the following chapters. You should, however, notice the similarities with pseudocode.

```
MODULE SumOfIntegers;
(* Program to add a series of numbers 0 + 1 + . . . + N,
   where a nonnegative integer N is given as input
                     J. M. Adams, January 1988 *)

FROM InOut IMPORT ReadCard, WriteCard,
                  WriteString, WriteLn;

VAR Number, N, Sum: CARDINAL;

BEGIN
  WriteString( "Please enter the last number of the series: " );
  ReadCard( N ); WriteLn;
  Sum := 0;
  Number := 0;
  LOOP
     (* Sum = 0 + 1 + . . . + Number *)
     IF Number = N THEN
       EXIT;
     END;
```

```
      Number := Number + 1;
      Sum := Sum + Number;
    END; (* LOOP *)
    (* Sum = 0 + 1 + · · · + N *)
    WriteString( "The sum of the series is " );
    WriteCard( Sum, 6 );
    WriteLn;
END SumOfIntegers.
```

As a final observation, we should note that there is another way to express the sum for which this program was written

$$0 + 1 + 2 + \cdots + N = \frac{N(N + 1)}{2}$$

This formula would have made our program development much easier, since we would not have had to use a loop. The point of this observation is that some mathematical knowledge can sometimes make programming much easier. We can use this formula to verify some of the results obtained when the program is run. For instance, if we use 15 as the value for N, we know the program should print 120.

Incidentally, the formula just shown will be useful when we analyze algorithms in later chapters, so you might want to verify it on a few test cases and even prove it if you know about mathematical induction.

1.4 Character String Algorithms

Thus far we have discussed algorithms dealing with graphical and numerical applications. Another important form of data is a sequence of characters, called a *string*. In numerous applications, users must process character strings such as names of students or employees, names of books, and so on. We will consider a typical application in the following sections.

Counting Words in a Line of Text

Let's take as an example the problem of counting the number of words in a paragraph. Given our knowledge of written language, this problem is fairly easy to understand, but it needs to be sharpened up a bit. In particular, we will assume that a paragraph is a sequence of lines and that each line is represented by a character string with no leading spaces.

When doing our structural design, we could observe that the solution would be reasonably straightforward if we could solve the subproblem of counting the words in a single line of text. Thus the general structure of our solution will be based on a single powerful component, which we will call Process Line.

For our detailed design, we first formulate a pseudocode solution for Process Line, which uses a variable called Word Count.

> Process Line
>   Loop
>   Exit if the line is empty
>   Set Word Count to Word Count + 1
>   Remove the first word from the line
>   End loop
> End Process Line

This solution is not very satisfactory because we have not specified what constitutes a word. Actually this was a defect in the definition of the problem, but it is not uncommon to discover such defects after design is under way. When defects are discovered, they must be rectified before proceeding.

For our problem, we will say that two successive words are separated by exactly one space, but the last word of a line will not be followed by any spaces. Our next solution will be based on this expanded definition of the problem.

> Process Line
>   Loop
>   Exit if the line is empty
>   Set Word Count to Word Count + 1
>   Delete all characters up to and including the first space
>   End loop
> End Process Line

We still have not specified how to find a space (the word boundary) nor how to delete characters. Our solution should also work if we have to deal with an empty line. In order to specify how to test for an empty line and how to search for a space, we need more tools.

Let us introduce some common instructions for processing character strings. These instructions will have a form similar to the instructions we used in our graphic example: they will have the name of a command followed by one or more values on which the command operates. The character string values will be surrounded by double quotes to distinguish them from the other characters in the instruction. We will need three instructions:

1. **Length string**—Returns the number of characters in the string; 0 means the string is empty.

   EXAMPLE 1 Length "hello" will return 5, because the string within double quotes has five characters.

   EXAMPLE 2 Length "How are you?" will return 12, since spaces are counted.

   EXAMPLE 3 Length "" will return 0, since "" denotes the string with no characters.

2. **Pos string1, string2**—Finds the position of the first occurrence of string1 within string2. If found, the position of the first matching character is returned. Character positions start with 0, for the first character in the string, and go up to the length of the string minus 1, for the last character. If string1 is not found within string2, the length of string2 is returned.

   EXAMPLE 1 Pos "How", "How are you?" returns 0, since the match starts on the first character.

   EXAMPLE 2 Pos " ", "How are you?" returns 3, which is the position of the first space.

   EXAMPLE 3 Pos "how", "How are you?" returns 12, the length of the the string "How are you?", since the string "how" was not found. The case (upper or lower) of the characters makes a difference.

3. **Delete string, start, count**—Deletes from the string the number of characters indicated by count starting at the position indicated by start.

   EXAMPLE 1 If string contains "How are you?", Delete string,0,3 will change the value of string to " are you?"

   EXAMPLE 2 If string contains "How are you?", Delete string,3,5 will change the value of string to "Howyou?"

Pos and Delete will allow us to find and remove words. We will use Length to determine when we have removed all the words. With these tools our previous version of the algorithm becomes

```
        Process Line
            Loop
(1)             Exit if Length Line = 0
(2)             Set Word Count to Word Count + 1
(3)             Set Blank Position to Pos " ",Line
(4)             If a blank is found then
(5)                 Delete Line,0,Blank Position + 1
                Else
(6)                 Delete Line,0,Length Line
                End if
            End loop
        End Process Line
```

In this solution we have introduced a third control structure, *selection*. Like sequencing and repetition, selection controls the order of execution of the instructions in an algorithm. Specifically, selection makes it possible to choose between alternative courses of action depending on a condition, which, in this case, is either true or false. The choice is specified by the If instruction.

```
If condition then
    first list of instructions
Else
    second list of instructions
End if
```

If the condition is true, the first list of instructions is executed and the second list of instructions is skipped. If the condition is false, the first list of instructions is skipped

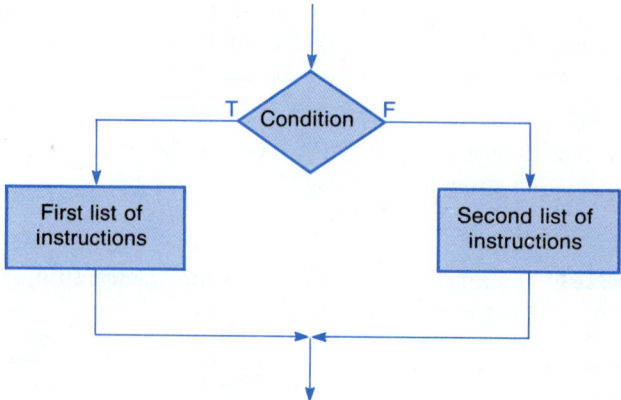

Figure 1.7
Selection

Character String Algorithms

TABLE 1.3 Trace of Process Line Algorithm

Instruction	Word Count	Line	Length Line	Blank Position	Condition
1	0	"How are you?"	12	—	false
2	1	"How are you?"	12	—	—
3	1	"How are you?"	12	3	—
4	1	"How are you?"	12	3	true
5	1	"are you?"	8	3	—
1	1	"are you?"	8	3	false
2	2	"are you?"	8	3	—
3	2	"are you?"	8	3	—
4	2	"are you?"	8	3	true
5	2	"you?"	4	3	—
1	2	"you?"	4	3	false
2	3	"you?"	4	3	—
3	3	"you?"	4	4	—
4	3	"you?"	4	4	false
6	3	""	0	4	—
1	3	""	0	4	true

and the second list of instructions is executed. Figure 1.7 illustrates selection by means of a flow chart, in which the diamond contains the condition. The diamond has two paths, labeled T and F—one for each value of the condition. The instructions executed are selected depending on the value of the condition: the first list of instructions is selected for execution if the condition is "true" and the second list is selected if the condition is "false." After the appropriate list of instructions has been executed, execution continues with the instructions following the entire If instruction.

Our last solution is fairly complex and requires closer examination. Notice that we have introduced variables that can be assigned string values. In this case we assume that Line was assigned the string value of the line to be processed. Supposing that Line has the value "How are you?" and Word Count is 0, let us trace the execution of this algorithm in Table 1.3.

At this point, to make sure you understand this algorithm, check it with other values for the variable Line. This algorithm assumes one space separating words. Trace the algorithm when there are additional spaces, such as the sentence "Hello   World!". Does the algorithm still work correctly?

Counting Words in a Paragraph

The algorithm developed in the previous section processes a line, but our original problem was to process a whole paragraph. However, we can apply the solution repeatedly for each line in the paragraph.

> Process Text
>   Get the sequence of lines
>   Set Word Count to 0

>   Loop
>   Get next line
>   Exit if no lines left in text
>   Process Line
>   End loop
>   Print Word Count
> End Process Text

This solution could be refined further, but we would need to know more about the form of the text to be processed. Notice that this algorithm illustrates the fact that one algorithm can use another one. We call this operation *invocation,* and it joins sequencing, repetition, and selection as the fourth control structure described in this chapter. In invocation the algorithm invokes (or calls) a second algorithm and completely executes it before returning to the first algorithm. Without being able to specify all the needed details, we can still produce a pseudocode solution to the original problem.

> Process Text
>   Get the sequence of lines
>   Set Word Count to 0
>   Loop
>   Get next line
>   Exit if no lines left in text
>   Process Line
>   End loop
>   Print Word Count
> End Process Text
>
> Process Line
>   Loop
>   Exit if Length Line = 0
>   Set Word Count to Word Count + 1
>   Set Blank Position to Pos " ",Line
>   If Blank found then
>   Delete Line,0,Blank Position + 1
>   Else
>   Delete Line,0,Length Line
>   End if
>   End loop
> End Process Line

For most problems we will find that decomposition of the task into smaller tasks is essential for good design. The corresponding solution is usually said to be modular (composed of several parts, or modules), and often it will involve the invocation of one algorithm by another. Note again that we have started each algorithm by its name and that we have ended it by End followed by its name. This format is an appropriate way to identify each algorithm.

1.5 Sequencing, Repetition, Selection, and Invocation

In our examples in the preceding sections we have introduced four fundamental control structures used in developing algorithms. They determine the order in which instructions of an algorithm are executed. That is, they determine the *flow of control* that a computer would take in executing a program based on the algorithms. These control structures are thus fundamental to programming languages as well as pseudocode algorithms. Here we briefly review their definitions and their basic formats.

SEQUENCING A list of instructions is executed in order from top to bottom unless a selection, repetition, or invocation construct dictates otherwise.

REPETITION Repetitions have the form

```
Loop
    list of instructions
    Exit if condition
    list of instructions
End loop
```

The indented lists of instructions are executed until the condition is true.

SELECTION Selections have the form

```
If condition then
    first list of instructions
Else
    second list of instructions
End if
```

If the condition is true, the first list of instructions is executed; otherwise the second list of instructions is executed.

INVOCATION One algorithm invokes, or calls, a second algorithm by specifying the name of the second algorithm. When this is done, the second algorithm is completely executed before control is returned to the first algorithm.

In Chapter 2, we will study sequencing of Modula-2 statements and look at program structure as a whole. In Chapter 3, we will learn about defining and invoking Modula-2 procedures. Methods of repetition and selection in Modula-2 will be introduced in Chapter 4.

SUMMARY

An effective general problem-solving approach for computer programming problems has the following six steps:

1. define the problem
2. design a solution
3. refine the solution
4. develop a testing strategy
5. code and test the program
6. complete the documentation

We must carefully define the problem at the start in order to know what input will be needed and what output will be desired. We design the solution by dividing it into smaller subproblems. This process of subdivision can be illustrated in a structure chart. The next step is to begin refining the solution so that the instructions are more precise. We write the solution first in pseudocode, a language of concise, imperative sentences that bridges the gap between English and a specific programming language. When the solution consists of precisely defined instructions specifying a finite process, it is known as an algorithm. Algorithmic solutions can be implemented on a computer. Next, we develop a testing strategy and then translate the pseudocode—we code the program in a language acceptable to the computer. Finally, we document the program by describing the program's design and testing.

As we refine a solution, we can make it more concise and accurate by using a number of control structures that establish the order of execution of the instructions. These structures are sequencing, repetition, selection, and invocation:

1. In sequencing, the instructions are executed one after another successively.
2. Repetition causes a list of instructions to be done over and over until a certain condition is met.
3. Selection allows us to choose between two courses of action depending on a particular condition.
4. With invocation one algorithm invokes a second, and the second algorithm is completely executed before returning to the first algorithm.

In this chapter we have emphasized the first three steps in our problem-solving method, which are critical in the solution of large problems. In the next few chapters we will concentrate on the coding and testing step on smaller problems in order that you can become familiar with Modula-2. We will then discuss problems of increasing size and complexity, which will require the full power of our problem-solving method.

EXERCISES

1. Give your own English language description of the concept of an algorithm.
2. Design a solution for each of the following problems. Do you think you could refine the solutions into algorithms?
    (a) making a phone call from a pay phone
    (b) cooking an omelette

(c) planning a birthday party
(d) finding a spouse

3. Write an algorithm that determines the number of gallons of paint needed to apply two coats on a given area. The paint can be purchased only in gallon containers, and a gallon of paint covers 300 square feet.

4. Euclid's algorithm for determining the greatest common divisor of two integers can be described as follows:

    Divide the larger of two positive integers by the smaller one. Then divide the divisor by the remainder. Continue this process of dividing the last divisor by the last remainder until the division is exact. The final divisor is the greatest common divisor of the original two positive integers.

    Give a pseudocode version of this algorithm.

5. List some tasks that you think cannot be solved with algorithms, and indicate why not, for each task.

6. An ambiguous sentence is one that can be interpreted in more than one way. For example, "She hit the woman with the purse" can be interpreted as hitting with the purse or hitting a woman who had a purse. Give two more ambiguous sentences, and explain why they are ambiguous. Modify the sentences so that they are not ambiguous.

7. Write an algorithm to balance your checking account.

8. Write an algorithm to calculate your grade point average.

9. Develop an algorithm that will draw an equilateral triangle, whose side length is determined by the value of an input variable. Use the graphics commands introduced in Section 1.2.

10. Trace the execution of the Sum of Integers algorithm with the input values 0 and 4.

11. Trace the execution of the Process Line algorithm with the following values of Line:

    ```
    ""  (i.e. no characters)
    "Hello"
    "Go now!"
    ```

12. Develop an algorithm to read and print a series of nonzero values. The algorithm should stop on a zero value and not print it. It should then print the number of values printed.

13. Develop an algorithm to print the series of numbers 3, 6, 9, 12, . . . , 99.

14. In grade 3, Audrey was asked to add the numbers 0, 1, 2, 3, . . . , 100. She did it in less than a minute and obviously did not do 100 additions. Define the fast algorithm she used.

15. Develop an algorithm to read four numbers and then print the largest of the four.

16. Mrs. Nogaro has a grocery bill that looks like this:

10.66	T
3.45	N
8.00	N
14.92	T
15.15	T
7.32	N
.	
.	
0.00	F

The last item signals the end of input. Develop an algorithm to compute a subtotal of the taxable items (T) and a subtotal of the nontaxable items (N); the algorithm should also compute the tax due (5.25 percent of taxable subtotal) and the total amount due.

17. Develop an algorithm that reads in two triplets of numbers (month, day, year) representing two dates, and determines which date is the most recent.

18. Develop an algorithm which reads three numbers and finds if one of the numbers is the sum of the other two.

19. Develop an algorithm that will compute the speed of the runners (in meters per second) in a 1500-meter race. The input will consist of pairs of numbers (minutes, seconds) giving the time of a runner; for each pair the algorithm should print the two numbers as well as the corresponding speed. Sample input: (3,34) (3,42) (3,50) (4,0) (0,0). Note that the last item is used to indicate end of input.

20. Governor Peter Minuit of the Dutch West India Co. bought Manhattan island in 1626 from an Indian tribe for items valued at $24.00. Develop an algorithm to compute how much money the tribe would have now if they had invested this sum at a yearly interest rate of 6 percent compounded annually.

21. Develop an algorithm to produce a table indicating for five tank sizes (10 gallons, 15 gallons, 20 gallons, 25 gallons, 30 gallons) how far a car can drive based on five rates of gas consumption (15 mpg, 20 mpg, 25 mpg, 30 mpg, 35 mpg).

22. Develop an algorithm to determine whether or not a number N is prime. A prime number can be divided only by itself or by 1.

23. Develop an algorithm to count the number of occurrences of the letter *I* in a text.

24. Develop an algorithm to count the number of sentences in a text.

25. Develop an algorithm to read in a text and print it out on paper in a maximum width of k columns. Words are separated by blanks and cannot be split between two lines. For instance, if k was 20, this text would be printed as

```
Develop an algorithm
to read in a text
and print it out on
paper in a maximum
width of k columns.
. . . . . . . . .
```

To develop this algorithm, you will need the string operation Copy

```
Copy(Source, Start, Count, Destination)
```

which copies Count characters from the Source string starting at character position Start into the Destination string.

2 Introduction to Modula-2

In this chapter you will:

- be introduced to the elementary rules of grammar for Modula-2
- learn to prepare, compile, execute, and debug Modula-2 programs
- find out how to use procedures obtained from library modules
- learn to declare variables of simple standard data types
- learn about basic input and output of data

Moving from the development of algorithms, which we covered in Chapter 1, to their realization as computer programs is one of the most exciting aspects of problem solving with computers. With programs our mental creations take a more concrete form, so that the results of executing the algorithms can be seen and assessed. We are actually able to see the geometric figures that an algorithm was designed to draw. We obtain numerical results from a program based on a computational algorithm. We can observe the changes in textual characters produced by programs based on a text manipulation algorithm. Often the results are not quite what we expect, but the process of finding and correcting errors is a necessary aspect of problem-solving.

    This chapter describes how to write, compile, execute, and debug simple programs. We begin with a brief look at the computer software that allows us to write programs and an overview of the programming process. Then we explain the basic features of the Modula-2 language and the rules governing the writing of programs. To learn a language, you must program with it. Thus the main teaching tool here will be examples of Modula-2 programs. All the programs in the text have been run with one implementation of Modula-2, but implementations of Modula-2 have slight differences. We will point out the major differences as we discuss the programs.

2.1 From Algorithms to Programs

To take the step from an algorithm to a program, we must learn how to use the computer software and programming environment available to us. Much of this software is helpful, and we will discuss the more essential items in the following section. But apart from software, we will quickly concentrate on the most important item, the programming language used to implement an algorithm. Since we are using the Modula-2 language, we will give you its grammatical rules and introduce its most basic features. These features are of two forms: declarations and statements. *Declarations* allow us to define the objects we need to work with, and *statements* allow us to specify operations on or with these objects. Note the distinction between declarations and statements:

- Declarations specify objects.
- Statements specify actions.

The Programming Environment

Most computers are delivered with software designed to help you use the hardware. If a computer were delivered with only hardware and no software, it would be very difficult to use. As we mentioned in the Introduction, one of the most essential pieces of software is the operating system. An operating system is a program that controls other useful programs, which you can use to help prepare and run your own programs. There are many different operating systems in use, but our discussion of programming will not depend on the peculiarities of any specific system.

The programs controlled by the operating system usually include editors, file systems, and compilers. *Editors* enable you to enter the text of your programs. *File systems* allow you to retain your programs for future use, much as you use a file cabinet to keep track of written documents. *Compilers* make it possible for your programs to be run on the computer by translating your programs into a language the computer can execute. Without this translation you would have the very tedious task of writing your programs in machine language, using binary codes as instructions. With a compiler you can write programs in a high-level language, such as Modula-2, which is much closer to English and mathematics than machine language. We assume that you have a compiler for the Modula-2 programming language available on your computer. The compiler might not be quite the same as the one we have used for the programs in the text, but the differences are usually minor.

Program Implementation

Now that we have an idea of the environment in which you will implement your Modula-2 programs, let's get an overview of implementation. After completing the design of a program, the basic steps in the coding and testing stage of our problem-solving method are:

1. coding the program
2. entering the program, using an editor
3. translating the program to machine language, using a compiler

4. executing the machine language program on the computer hardware with the appropriate input test data to obtain output
5. inspecting the results for correctness

These steps are illustrated in Figure 2.1.

After an algorithm has been designed, it can be implemented, first by coding the program and then using an editor to create a file containing the program. A program that is not written in machine language cannot be directly executed by the hardware to produce the desired results. It must first be translated (compiled) from a programming language, like Modula-2, to machine language. Then the machine language program may be executed to produce results, or output, using any input data that the program may need for the computation.

When you have written a program in Modula-2, it probably cannot be executed alone. Most programs must use other existing programs to perform specific tasks like

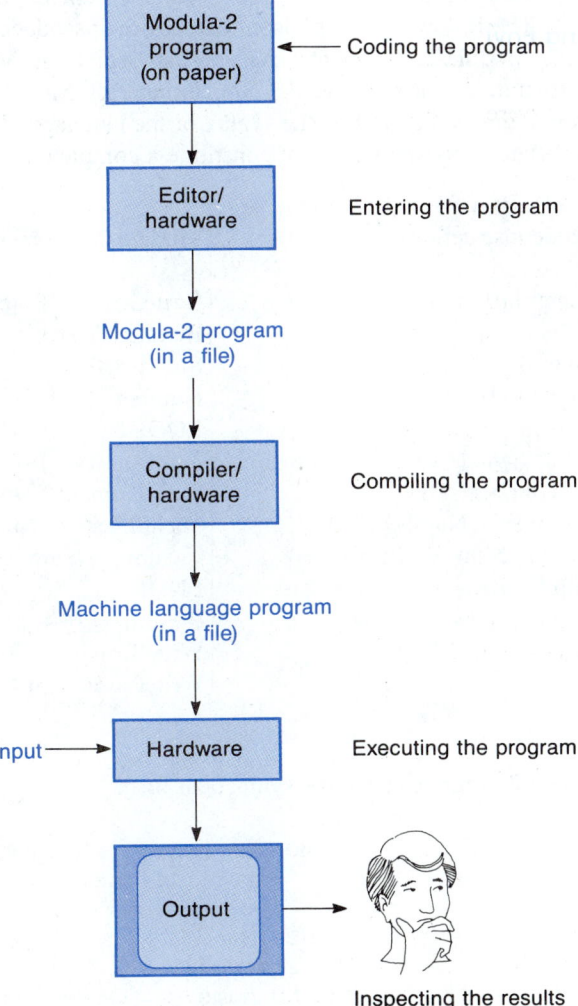

Figure 2.1
Implementation of a Program

the input of data, or the output of results, or the computation of common mathematical functions. This means that, before your program can be executed, it must be connected to the other programs it uses. Some systems will do this automatically, pulling the needed programs out of *library modules* that have been created by programmers in order to make them available to others. Other systems require a separate step, called *linking,* to accomplish this.

Program Syntax, Data Types, and Library Modules

Learning a programming language entails learning its *syntax* (grammatical rules) as well as its *semantics* (meaning of the various statements in the language). In this section we'll discuss the syntactic and semantic features of a simple Modula-2 program and, based on this example, we'll begin to develop rules of the syntax and semantics of Modula-2.

Let's recall the pseudocode solution for the sum of integers problem given in Chapter 1. The following comparison matches the pseudocode solution with the corresponding Modula-2 statements. As you can see, these Modula-2 statements have similar structure to our pseudocode. Notice that each Modula-2 statement is ended by a semicolon; this is required by the syntax of the language. As we will see shortly, the Modula-2 statements shown do not constitute a complete program.

Pseudocode instructions	Modula-2 statements
Print "Enter last number"	WriteString("Enter last number");
Read N	ReadCard(N);
Set Sum to 0	Sum := 0;
Set Number to 0	Number := 0;
Loop	LOOP
{ Sum = 0 + 1 + · · · + Number }	(* Sum = 0 + 1 + + Number *)
Exit if Number = N	IF Number = N THEN EXIT END;
Set Number to Number + 1	Number := Number + 1;
Set Sum to Sum + Number	Sum := Sum + Number;
End Loop	END;
{ Sum = 0 + 1 + · · · + N }	(* Sum = 0 + 1 + · · · + N *)
Print "The sum is " Sum	WriteString("The sum is ");
	WriteCard(Sum,6);

Modula-2 programs have the syntactical form

```
MODULE name;
  import lists
  declarations
BEGIN
  statements
END name.
```

The words MODULE, BEGIN, and END are *reserved words* in Modula-2. They are used by the compiler to recognize different parts of the program, and so they must not be used in any other context in the program. In most implementations all reserved words must be in uppercase. You will find a list of reserved words in Appendix B.

Let's use the Modula-2 statements that we just listed to create a complete program conforming to this syntax. We'll identify the parts of this syntax here and then we'll define the various elements and explain their role in the following sections. Our program has a first line containing the module name and then there follows an import list, declarations, BEGIN, the statements corresponding to our pseudocode, and END. We have also added some comments as documentation.

```
                    MODULE SumOfIntegers;
    comment         (* Program to add a series of numbers
                         1 + 2 + 3 + 4 + 5 + · · · + N, where N is given as input
                                    J. M. Adams,  January 1988 *)

    import list     FROM InOut IMPORT ReadCard, WriteCard,
                                     WriteString, WriteLn;

    declaration     VAR Number, N, Sum: CARDINAL;

                    BEGIN
                      WriteString( "Enter last number of series " );
                      ReadCard( N ); WriteLn;
                      Sum := 0;
                      Number := 0;
                      LOOP
                         (* Sum = 0 + 1 + · · · + Number *)
                         IF Number = N THEN
                           EXIT;
    statements        END; (* IF *)
      and             Number := Number + 1;
    comments          Sum := Sum + Number;
                      END; (* LOOP *)
                      (* Sum = 0 + 1 + · · · + N *)
                      WriteString( "The sum is " );
                      WriteCard( Sum, 6 );
                      WriteLn;
                    END SumOfIntegers.
```

The author of the program chose a suggestive name for the module and placed it after the reserved word MODULE. The same name was placed after the reserved word END and followed by a period indicating the end of the program. These formats are required by Modula-2 syntax.

In Modula-2, names are often called *identifiers* and may consist of a letter followed by any number of letters or digits. The case (upper or lower) of the letters in an identifier is significant, because the compiler distinguishes between uppercase and lowercase letters. For example, the identifier SumOfIntegers is not the same as the identifier SUMOFINTEGERS or sumofintegers. Usually, we will capitalize the first word of each part, as in SumOfIntegers, to get a more readable identifier. In addition to naming modules, identifiers can be used to name variables—objects with values that may vary during program execution. Each variable should have a unique name. The identifiers Number, N, and Sum in the SumOfIntegers program are variables.

Comments may be included almost anywhere in a program, providing that they are enclosed between the delimiters (∗ and ∗). Comments are only for explanatory purposes and have no effect on program execution; they are ignored by the compiler. The first comment in our example indicates the program objectives, identifies the program author, and gives the date the program was written. The other comments are assertions about the variable Sum.

Import Lists The *import lists* in a program contain identifiers that name objects used in the program but whose declarations occur in other modules. In this example the objects are ReadCard, WriteCard, WriteString, and WriteLn, which are small pieces of programs, called *procedures,* for performing input and output. Objects can also be *constants* (names associated with fixed values), *types* (which specify the range of acceptable values of a variable), and *variables* (named memory locations that can store values).

In general, every import list must have the syntactical form

```
FROM name of module IMPORT list of identifiers;
```

where FROM and IMPORT are reserved words and "list of identifiers" contains the names of objects, separated by commas, which are defined in the module specified by "name of module." This module must have been created previously, or, like InOut, be a library module that is part of your Modula-2 system. These imported objects have been declared in module "name of module" and will not have to be declared again in the importing module. For example, in the import list

```
FROM InOut IMPORT ReadCard, WriteCard,
                  WriteString, WriteLn;
```

WriteString is a procedure declared in the module InOut, so it may be imported from that module and then used in statements in the SumOfIntegers program.

Declarations Declarations are required for every object that is not imported from another module. Each variable used in the program must be declared in order to reserve enough space in computer memory to store its value. The declaration also serves to help anyone reading the program understand the nature of the variable. Other objects, such as procedures, which we will study in the next chapter, can also be declared. The declarations in SumOfIntegers consist only of a declaration of variables, since no other objects are needed in the program. In this case the three variables are of the same type, CARDINAL. The identifier CARDINAL is a *standard type* (built into the language) whose values are the nonnegative integers.

TABLE 2.1 **Modula-2 Basic Types**

Type	Description	Examples of Values
INTEGER	Values are integers.	123 0 −345
CARDINAL	Values are nonnegative integers.	98 0 12678
REAL	Values are numbers that may have a fractional part.	12.34 0.0 −12.34 0.000054 6.023E23
CHAR	Values are single characters. Constant values are enclosed in quotes.	'A' 'a' ';'
BOOLEAN	Values are TRUE or FALSE	TRUE FALSE
STRING	Values are sequences of characters. Constants are enclosed in quotes. (nonstandard type)	"Any Such Thing" "abc" "Tax Rate: 12% "

In general, the syntax of variable declarations is

```
VAR list of identifiers: type;
    list of identifiers: type;
           .
           .
           .
```

VAR is a reserved word and can be followed by as many of these variable declarations as you wish. Each variable declaration must be ended by a semicolon. Within a declaration a colon is used to separate the list of identifiers from the type specification of that list. The declaration

```
VAR Number, N, Sum: CARDINAL;
```

declares the variables Number, N, and Sum to all be of type CARDINAL.

Table 2.1 presents the basic types we will use in the first chapters. All those types are standard types in Modula-2, except for STRING, but strings are available in most implementations.

Note that REAL values can be expressed in two forms. The first form is the usual decimal notation. The second form is called scientific notation and uses the letter E to indicate a power of ten by which the preceding number is multiplied.

$$6.023E23 \text{ represents } 6.023 \times 10^{23}$$

Statements   The statements between BEGIN and END in a Modula-2 program constitute the instructions to solve the problem for which the program was designed. The reserved words BEGIN and END themselves are not statements. Instead they are similar to parentheses, because they serve only to group statements rather than to cause an action to be performed. Several identifiers may appear in a statement to represent objects used by the statement. Each different object has a unique name and must have been declared or imported.

The statements in a program or a procedure may be of several different kinds. In the program SumOfIntegers the statements that contain := are *assignment statements*, which cause a value to be assigned to a variable. They correspond to the pseudocode instruction Set in Chapter 1. Other statements in the program are the IF statement and the LOOP statement, which are easily identified by the reserved words IF and LOOP. The program contains statements that invoke procedures; for instance, ReadCard(N) invokes the procedure ReadCard imported from InOut.

The syntax of an assignment statement is

```
variable name := expression;
```

where := is a rather strange reserved "word" referred to as *assignment*. The variable name must be an identifier that has been previously declared, and the expression must result in a value of the same type as the variable name. For example, in the statement

```
Sum := Sum + Number;
```

since the variables Sum and Number have been declared to be of type CARDINAL, the expression on the right is of type CARDINAL, which is also the type of variable Sum on the left. Type consistency is very important in Modula-2—much more so than in most older languages.

In this chapter all the expressions on the right-hand sides of assignment statements will be simple arithmetic expressions that will look very much like ordinary algebraic expressions of mathematics, except that multiplication will be denoted by an asterisk. We will have more to say about expressions in subsequent chapters.

Other statements, such as the LOOP statement, have a somewhat more complicated syntax that will be discussed as the statements are introduced in the following chapters.

Four Program Examples with Simple Input and Output

Now that you know the structure of a Modula-2 program, we will discuss some very simple programs. These examples will help you become familiar with Modula-2 syntax. Also, the programs will show you how to use parts of programs, called procedures, by importing them at the beginning of a program and using statements to invoke them. All the examples use procedures imported from library modules. We will give brief explanations of these procedures, but we *strongly encourage* you to look at their declarations in Appendices E and F to become familiar with the library modules containing the procedures. The library modules are your most powerful tools at the implementation stage of problem solving, and your success in implementation will depend directly on your knowledge of these tools. After we see examples of using procedures from library modules, we will give more details on the modules themselves.

The first programs we will discuss are extremely simple and use only assignment statements and *calls* (invocations) of imported procedures. Because these programs are used to illustrate implementation of algorithms in Modula-2, we will not go through a full development according to our problem-solving methodology.

EXAMPLE 1 *Multiplying Two Integers*

For the first example we will explain a program that simply computes the product of two integers. Our program will query the user in the same manner as the sample Modula-2 program shown earlier in this chapter. It will prompt the user for each input value and then compute and display the result. Since this program is so short, we will omit showing the pseudocode solution.

```
MODULE Multiply;
(* A program to compute the product of two integers.
                        J. M. Adams    January 1988 *)

FROM InOut IMPORT ReadInt, WriteInt, WriteLn, WriteString;

VAR Operand1, Operand2, Product: INTEGER;

BEGIN
  WriteString( "Enter an integer: " );
  ReadInt( Operand1 ); WriteLn;
  WriteString( "Enter another integer: " );
  ReadInt( Operand2 ); WriteLn;
  Product := Operand1 * Operand2;
  WriteString( "The product is " );
  WriteInt( Product, 6 ); WriteLn;
END Multiply.
```

Our program uses three variables: Operand1, Operand2, and Product. These variables must have integer values as declared on the line beginning with VAR. All the statements in the program, except the one that does the computation, use procedures imported from the standard module InOut. The Modula-2 system includes a number of *standard modules,* which are collections of predefined procedures available for programmers to use. As suggested by the module name, the procedures from InOut are used for input and output (reading of input values and writing of results). The statements between BEGIN and END that invoke procedures are just the procedure names (for example, ReadInt), usually followed by information enclosed in parentheses, which is needed by each procedure. Such statements are referred to as *procedure calls,* and the items in parentheses following the procedure names are referred to as *arguments* or *parameters*. Parameters are the objects with which the procedures do their work. For instance, WriteString is a procedure that will display a string of characters given as an argument (in the first call "Enter an integer: "). In this program we have used the WriteString procedure to prompt the user for input and to label the result. Most of the calls to the WriteString procedure use sequences of characters surrounded by quotes, called *string constants,* as parameters. These constants are used to specify small pieces of text that do not vary during execution of the program.

The next procedure call, ReadInt, accepts an integer value entered from the keyboard. That value is assigned to the variable that is the argument of ReadInt (Operand1 in the first call to ReadInt). The input of an integer may be ended by pressing any nonnumeric key; it is quite common for users to use the space bar or the return key. In order not to have all the prompts and input values on the same line, we have included the call to WriteLn after ReadInt. WriteLn simply causes subsequent output to appear on the next line of the display device. Some procedures, such as WriteLn, have no parameters.

A call of the WriteInt procedure causes the integer value specified by its first parameter to be displayed in a space, often called a *field,* whose width in characters is specified by the second parameter. So the WriteInt statement in this example causes the value of the variable Product to be displayed in a space that is six characters wide. If the number does not require six digits, spaces are placed to the left of the value.

The computation in this example is specified in the assignment statement

```
Product := Operand1 * Operand2;
```

The right side of this assignment statement is an arithmetic expression. Since an asterisk denotes mutiplication, this statement causes the values of the variables Operand1 and Operand2 to be multiplied and the resulting value to be assigned to the variable Product. Values for Operand1 and Operand2 have been read by the ReadInt statements that preceded this assignment.

Execution of our program would have displayed something like this (the values typed by the user have been underlined for emphasis):

```
Enter an integer: 12
Enter another integer: 24
The product is    288
```

EXAMPLE 2 *Converting Degrees to Radians*

For our next example we will develop a program for converting from an angle in degrees to an angle in radians. The conversion can be done by multiplying by $\pi/180$. Since the conversion factor is a constant, we can declare it as a constant in our Modula-2 program. The proper syntax for constant declarations is

```
CONST name of constant = constant expression;
      name of constant = constant expression;
                       .
                       .
                       .
```

where CONST is a reserved word. The names of constants are identifiers and must follow the syntax rule for identifiers stated earlier. The form of constant expressions depends on the types of constants we wish to specify. For our examples we will limit ourselves to numeric and string constants. The specification of integer values means only whole numbers. The specification of a real value must include a decimal point, which is used to distinguish it from an integer value. If the whole number part is zero, it must be entered, as in 0.05. Numeric constant expressions are written as mathematical expressions and use arithmetic operators, other constants, and numbers. Since some Modula-2 implementations have restrictions, such as allowing only real constants rather than real expressions, you must check your implementation for any such restrictions. As we learned in the last example, string constant expressions are simply sequences of characters enclosed in quotes. Note that each constant definition must be terminated with a semicolon. As with the syntax for variable declarations, you may define as many constants as you wish.

The following program does the desired conversion from degrees to radians:

```
MODULE ConvertAngle;
(* A program to convert an angle in degrees to
   an angle in radians.
                    J. M. Adams    January 1988 *)

FROM InOut IMPORT WriteString, WriteLn;
FROM RealInOut IMPORT ReadReal, FWriteReal;

CONST Pi = 3.14159;
      ConversionFactor = Pi / 180.0;

VAR Degrees, Radians: REAL;

BEGIN
  WriteString( "Enter an angle in degrees: " );
  ReadReal( Degrees ); WriteLn;
  Radians := ConversionFactor * Degrees;
  WriteString( "The angle in radians is: " );
  FWriteReal( Radians, 8, 5 ); WriteLn;
END ConvertAngle.
```

Since our angles may contain a fractional part, two variables of type REAL have been used in this example. To do the input and output of the values of these variables, we have imported and used the procedures ReadReal and FWriteReal, which are quite similar to their counterparts ReadInt and WriteInt for type INTEGER. Note, however, that they are imported from a different module, RealInOut.

The actual conversion from degrees to radians is done by the assignment statement, which involves a multiplication in the arithmetic expression on its right-hand side. Another arithmetic expression occurs in the definition of the constant ConversionFactor, which uses the common notation of / for division of real numbers. In general, a constant of any type may be defined by an expression involving operations and constants of that type. Whenever you have to use constant values, you should define them using the CONST declaration.

The execution of our program will display the following (the parts entered by the user are underlined):

```
Enter an angle in degrees: 30
The angle in radians is:  0.52831
```

Note that the output format of a real value is implementation dependent. We have shown a procedure FWriteReal that prints a real number in decimal notation. The second parameter is the total field width, while the third parameter is the number of decimal digits to be displayed. Your system might use a different format, consisting of a different number of digits or using an exponent.

EXAMPLE 3 *Drawing a Square*

Our next example will be a simple program to draw a square with sides of length 100.

The pseudocode version of the program developed in Chapter 1 is

> Square
>   move 100
>   turn left 90
>   move 100
>   turn left 90
>   move 100
>   turn left 90
>   move 100
>   turn left 90
> End Square

We assume you have a Modula-2 library that makes it possible to draw lines on the screen. It may not be the same as our library file, but it is probably similar enough to enable you to adapt the graphical programs we will present. If your system has no graphical capabilities, you should still be able to understand the examples presented in the text.

Our version of Modula-2 allows you to draw simple graphical figures using what is called a "Turtle." The Turtle is depicted as an arrowhead that starts in the middle of the screen facing to the right. You can make it move or change directions by calling the procedures Move and Turn with the appropriate parameters. These procedures must be imported from a module called TurtleGraphics, described in Appendix F. Using TurtleGraphics, we can write a Modula-2 program based on the preceding pseudocode.

```
MODULE Square;
(* Program to draw a square with side length 100
   using TurtleGraphics.
              J. M. Adams    January 1988 *)

FROM TurtleGraphics IMPORT Move, Turn, TurtleStop;
```

```
BEGIN
   Move( 100 );
   Turn( 90 );
   Move( 100 );
   Turn( 90 );
   Move( 100 );
   Turn( 90 );
   Move( 100 );
   Turn( 90 );
   (* The Turtle has the same position and direction as it had
      at the beginning of the program. *)
   TurtleStop; (* Keeps display on screen until return is pressed *)
END Square.
```

Note that this program uses no variables, which is perfectly acceptable but rather unusual. The statements in the program are all calls to procedures that were imported from the module TurtleGraphics. A call to Move causes the Turtle to move by an amount specified by the parameter given in the call and to draw a line as it moves. If the parameter is positive, the Turtle moves in the direction it is currently facing. If the parameter is negative, the Turtle moves backward. The parameters of the Move statement may be different for computers with different screens. Our TurtleGraphics programs have been designed for microcomputers with a graphics card and are implementation dependent. The dependencies, such as screen size, are given in comments in the library module TurtleGraphics in Appendix F. A call to Turn has a parameter that specifies a change in the Turtle's direction. The parameter specifies a turning angle in degrees. A positive value causes a counterclockwise turn, and a negative value causes a clockwise turn. Figure 2.2 shows the result of the program execution.

As a final observation about our Square program, notice that after the last Move, the Turtle is back at its original position but does not have its original orientation. The

Figure 2.2
Execution of Square Program

final Turn is done to return the Turtle to its original orientation. Returning the Turtle to its original position and orientation makes it easier to keep track of the Turtle if more figures are to be drawn. In order to keep the square on the screen, we use a call to the procedure TurtleStop. This procedure suspends the program until the return key is pressed.

EXAMPLE 4 *Manipulating Strings*

Our final example involves a simple manipulation of two strings. The following program accepts two strings as input, concatenates the two strings (builds a new string by appending one string to the end of the other), and displays the result. For example, if you enter the three-character string "abc" first and then the two-character string "xy," the result will be the five-character string "abcxy."

```
MODULE Concatenate;
(* A program to append one string to another.
                      J.M. Adams      January 1988 *)

FROM InOut IMPORT WriteString, WriteLn, ReadString;
FROM Strings IMPORT STRING, Concat;

VAR S1, S2, BigS: STRING;

BEGIN
  WriteString( "Enter a string: " );
  ReadString( S1 ); WriteLn;
  WriteString( "Enter another string: " );
  ReadString( S2 ); WriteLn;
  Concat( S1, S2, BigS );
  WriteString( "The concatenated strings are: " );
  WriteString( BigS ); WriteLn;
END Concatenate.
```

This program uses three variables whose values must be strings, as indicated by the word STRING in the declaration. STRING is a type that was imported from the module Strings. This importation was necessary because STRING is not a standard type in Modula-2. It is declared in the module Strings and must be imported from the module along with any nonstandard string procedures that are needed. In this program we need only the string procedure Concat, which does precisely what we want. Concat appends the value of the second parameter to the value of the first parameter and stores the result in the third parameter. The reading of a string by ReadString is terminated by typing a space; strings S1 and S2, therefore, will not contain any space characters. The module Strings contains many other useful string procedures, which are described in Appendix F.

Execution of our program displays

```
Enter a string: supercalifragil
Enter another string: isticexpialidocious
The concatenated strings are: supercalifragilisticexpialidocious
```

Library Modules The preceding examples illustrate how you can use existing programs by importing them from modules that may be available. Most versions of Modula-2 are supplied with several useful modules that are called library modules. InOut and RealInOut are library modules and other library modules for the version of Modula-2 used in this text are given in Appendices E and F. Appendix E includes standard modules, such as InOut, which will be very similar in most implementations. Appendix F includes nonstandard modules, such as Strings and TurtleGraphics, which may not be available in some implementations and may vary considerably among the implementations in which they are available. Later you will be shown how to develop modules that can be used by others, so that they can build upon your work just as you have built on the work of others. The ability to develop and share modules is one of the most important features of Modula-2, since it enables us to save a great deal of effort in developing programs. Thus, it would be a good idea for you to start becoming familiar with the library modules for your version of Modula-2.

Each library module has two parts: a *definition module* describing the objects available for import and an *implementation module,* which contains all the details that completely define the objects. The definition modules given in Appendices E and F contain all the information needed to use the objects in the module, although the information is rather terse. For example, a portion of the definition module for RealInout of one implementation is

```
DEFINITION MODULE RealInOut;

..............................................

PROCEDURE WriteReal( x: REAL; FieldLength: CARDINAL );
(* Write the REAL value of x in scientific notation in a space
   FieldLength characters wide. *)
..............................................
```

This tells you that WriteReal is a procedure that may be imported to display real values in scientific notation, but it does not give the details of the format of the display. The details of the format can be obtained from documents describing the implementation, or simply by writing and running a small program containing a few WriteReal statements such as

```
WriteReal( 3.1415, 15 );
```

which should cause the indicated five-digit approximation of π to be displayed in scientific notation in a space of width 15.

Because the term *module* has been used in so many different ways, we should clarify the relationship between the ways we have used the term and one of its nontechnical meanings. The nontechnical meaning that is closest to our usage is: a detachable section with a separate purpose. Our library modules are clearly detachable components, since they may be used by any program. Furthermore, library modules are themselves composed of two separate components—definition and implementation modules. A further decomposition is possible: library modules usually contain procedures, which are themselves separate components. Thus, procedures are modules, in the nontechnical sense of the word, but not in our technical usage relating to Modula-2. To make matters worse, even our programs begin with the reserved word MODULE. The important thing about all of these "modules" is the relationship between them. Programs may use library modules that contain procedures. A library module is defined by two parts: a definition module and an implementation module.

2.2 Testing and Debugging Programs

Once a program is written, we must compile it. Usually we have to correct a few syntax errors and then compile the program again before being able to run it. Such recompilations are normal since we may be careless in either typing the program or applying the language rules of Modula-2. Once these errors are removed and the program is compiled successfully, we run it with some test data. We must then check the results to see if they are correct. If the results are incorrect, we have a different kind of error, which must also be removed before our program can be used. This section describes the various kinds of error that can arise and explains how to detect and correct them. Generally errors are called *bugs* and finding errors is called *debugging*. The entire debugging process is illustrated in Figure 2.3, which is an elaboration of Figure 2.1.

Compilation Time Errors

Compilation time errors are detected by the compiler in the process of translating source code in a high-level language into machine code. The compiler detects syntax errors and gives an error message for each one. Generally, these errors are easy to find and correct.

Some compilation time errors are caused by the violation of the syntax of a single statement. For example, consider the variable declaration

```
VAR A,B INTEGER;
```

This declaration would result in an error since the colon separating the variable list and the type is missing.

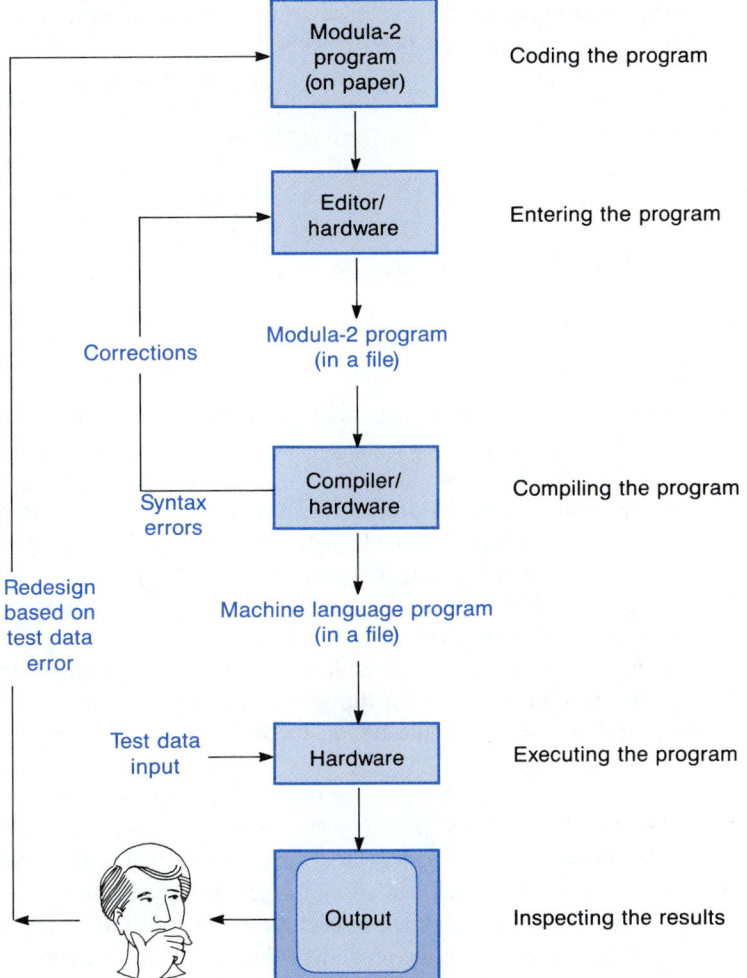

Figure 2.3
Implementation of a Program: An Elaboration

Some compilation time errors occur between statements. Consider

```
CONST PI = 3.14159
      E  = 2.71828;
```

Both declarations are correct, but there is no semicolon ending the first declaration. A missing semicolon will produce an error on one of the subsequent lines. Sometimes, to find and correct an error, you must look at the lines preceding the one on which the error message occurred.

Modula-2 is a *strongly typed* language—that is, the type expected and the type provided must match. Actually, strong typing does not always require an exact match but only type compatibility, which we will discuss in Chapter 6. Until then, exact matching of types will serve our purposes. As examples, consider

```
            VAR A,B:  INTEGER;
                X,Y:  REAL;
            BEGIN
              A := -5;
              X := 5.0;
              B := X;
              Y := A;
               .   .
               .   .
               .   .
```

The first two assignment statements are correct: a constant integer value is assigned to an integer variable, and a constant real value is assigned to a real variable. However, the third assignment attempts to assign a real value to an integer variable; this move will result in a compilation time error indicating a type mismatch. The fourth assignment also has a type mismatch since an integer is being assigned to a real variable. In Chapter 6 we will see how to avoid this type of error.

Type mismatches can also be caused by parameters in procedure calls. The parameters used in a procedure call should be of the same type expected by the procedure; the expected types are specified in the procedure declaration as you can see by looking at the procedures shown in the library modules given in Appendices E and F. For instance, in library module InOut, the information given for the procedure Write is

```
            Write( ch: CHAR );
```

which indicates that the procedure must be supplied with a parameter of type CHAR. If a variable R has been declared of type REAL, then a call like Write(R) will result in a type mismatch. Correcting such problems is simple: it is sufficient to change the actual parameter or use the procedure WriteReal. As you can see, type mismatches can occur in many situations. We will discuss this issue in greater detail in Chapter 6.

Another common compilation time error is the failure to declare an object. The object could be a variable, constant, procedure, or any other named object. Often this kind of error is the result of mistyping the identifier. This is particularly true in Modula-2 since the case of letters is important. For example,

```
          CONST PI = 3.14159;
          VAR Radius, Circumference: REAL;
          BEGIN
            Radius := 5.0;
            Circumference := 2.0 * Pi * radius;
             .   .
             .   .
             .   .
```

The last line contains two errors. Can you spot them?

All the errors discussed so far are called *syntax errors,* because they involve some violation of the Modula-2 syntax rules. Type mismatch and undeclared identifier errors are not violations of the syntax of a single statement; rather, they involve the relationship between a statement and the rest of the program. Programming languages are *context sensitive*—that is, the syntactic correctness of a statement may depend on other parts of the program in which the statement is embedded. In other words, the syntax of Modula-2 is not completely specified by the syntax rules given for each statement.

Sometimes an error message will appear on a line below the actual violation of syntax that caused the error, as we saw in the example with a missing semicolon. In a more extreme case which follows, the error message will appear after the last line of the program and will probably indicate an unexpected end of program. See if you can spot the error before reading the explanation below the program.

```
MODULE Concatenate;
(* A program to append one string to another.

FROM InOut IMPORT WriteString, ReadString, WriteLn;
FROM Strings IMPORT STRING, Concat;

VAR S1, S2, BigS: STRING;

BEGIN
   WriteString( "Enter a string: " );
   ReadString( S1 ); WriteLn;
   WriteString( "Enter another string: " );
   ReadString( S2 ); WriteLn;
   Concat( S1, S2, BigS );
   WriteString( "The concatenated strings are: " );
   WriteString( BigS ); WriteLn;
END Concatenate.
```

The cause of this error is in the second line of the program: the comment at the top of the program does not have the end of comment delimiter, *). As a result, the remainder of the program was ignored by the compiler since it considered all remaining statements to be part of the comment. The compiler detected this error only when the end of the file containing the program was reached.

Once a compiler detects an error, it will print an appropriate error message and may attempt to continue and find other errors. However, in some cases this is not feasible and subsequent errors are ignored. The program Concatenate, just shown, would be an example of masking additional errors. Even if the program had many syntax errors, the compiler would ignore all such errors because it considers the program to be part of a comment.

In other cases many additional spurious error messages may be generated when only one error has actually been made. Detecting spurious error messages is more difficult. As a rule, for any errors following the first error, if you cannot spot the error condition quickly, then fix the initial error and try recompiling the program. Sometimes you will be surprised to find that many of the other error messages will go away.

The appropriateness of compilation time error messages varies greatly between compilers and we can only hope that your compiler is one of the better ones.

Run Time Errors

Not all programming errors are detected at compilation time. As you will soon find out, you can write and compile a program, but it may not run properly. Two types of errors may occur: *run time errors,* which will cause the program to terminate abnormally, or "crash," and *semantic errors,* where the program does not perform the desired task.

Run time errors often occur when a data value is not of the proper type. If a program involves reading data from an external source, such as the keyboard or a data file, there is no way the compiler can do type checking on data that has not yet been read. Another possibility is that the data supplied result in an illegal operation. Consider the following program.

```
MODULE Sharing;
(* Compute allowances from available money
                  B. Kurtz    January 1988     *)

FROM InOut IMPORT WriteString, WriteLn;
FROM RealInOut IMPORT ReadReal, FWriteReal;

VAR TotalMoney, Allowance, NumberOfChildren: REAL;

BEGIN
   WriteString( "How much money is available for allowances? " );
   ReadReal( TotalMoney ); WriteLn;
   WriteString( "How many children?" );
   ReadReal( NumberOfChildren ); WriteLn;
   Allowance := TotalMoney / NumberOfChildren;
   WriteString( "If divided equally, each child would receive $ " );
   FWriteReal( Allowance, 6, 2 ); WriteLn;
END Sharing.
```

Normally, this program would run as expected. However, if the number of children was specified as 0.0, this input would result in a run time error of attempting to divide by zero. Other erroneous input might cause run time errors, but the exact error indication may be dependent on the system. For example, suppose the user entered "two" in response to number of children. Some systems would give a type mismatch run time error, while others might assign the value of 0.0 to NumberOfChildren and end up with the divide-by-zero error.

Semantic Errors

The final type of error is a semantic error: the program does not solve the problem the programmer intended. These errors are often the most difficult to track down since the compiler and operating system provide no direct support for detecting them. Consider the statement

$$\text{Radius} := \text{Circumference} / 2.0 * \text{Pi};$$

The variable names indicate the programmer's intent, but the value of the Radius calculated will be incorrect. The expression will be evaluated from left to right, resulting in a value equivalent to (Circumference / 2.0) * Pi, although the correct expression is Circumference / (2.0 * Pi). We will study arithmetic expressions in more detail in Chapter 6.

This kind of error is often difficult to detect since the program will seem to be working and producing results. Sometimes the results are obviously not what is expected—that is, they are very small or very large values. Other times the results "look" normal and may even have an attractive appearance displayed on the screen or printed on paper in an orderly manner. Test case results *must* be checked for correctness, which means doing the computations in some other way, usually by hand, and comparing the results of those computations with the results displayed by the program. If they differ, the program has an error, which you will have to track down. One way of finding such an error would be to insert extra debugging statements at various places in the program. For instance, statements like

```
WriteString( "Intermediate price:   " ); WriteCard( Price,5 ); WriteLn;
```

can be added to the regular statements of the program. These debugging statements will produce a series of messages that will enable the programmer to trace program execution and examine variable values. It might be necessary to add or delete some of the extra print statements as you narrow down the location of the bug.

A few systems provide *interactive debuggers* that allow the programmer to specify statements where the program should stop execution. When the program stops, the programmer can examine variable values or carry out other actions, including resumption of program execution.

Redirecting Input and Output

The process of debugging a program usually requires several cycles of program compilation and program execution. If a program requires interaction with a user, it can become quite laborious to enter the same test data again and again. Fortunately, Modula-2 provides a facility, called input redirection, which allows the test data to be read from a file. The editor can be used to enter the data into the test file, and then this file can be used to supply the necessary interaction with the program.

Input redirection is done by the procedure OpenInput imported from InOut. Here is a sample call to this procedure:

$$\text{OpenInput("dat")}$$

This procedure *closes,* or makes unavailable, the standard input device, which is typically the keyboard, requests a file name, and *opens* this file for the source of input data. The form of the file name is implementation dependent; normally it is in the form required by the operating system for file names. The string parameter is used to complete the name given with a default extension (implementation dependent). For instance, with the call just shown, if the user answers the prompt with a name ending with a period, as in "Grades.", then the system will add "dat" to the name to obtain the complete file name "Grades.dat". If the name given does not end with a period, the default extension is not used. This is an implementation-dependent feature. If the procedure is successful, subsequent input will be read from this input file. The standard input device can be reinstated as the input source by calling the procedure CloseInput, as follows:

```
CloseInput;
```

This parameterless procedure is imported from InOut.

The standard output device is usually a computer terminal, but sometimes we need to save results for additional processing, such as printing them out. The procedure OpenOutput, imported from InOut, can be used to redirect output. Here is a sample call:

```
OpenOutput( "out" );
```

This procedure is similar to the OpenInput procedure. It closes the standard output device, usually the display screen, and opens the file whose name is supplied by the user. The string parameter is a default extension and is appended to any file name ending with a period. If the procedure is successful, subsequent output will be sent to the specified file. The standard device can be reinstated by calling CloseOutput, imported from InOut, as follows:

```
CloseOutput;
```

SUMMARY

As we move from the writing of algorithms to the creation of actual programs, our ideas begin to take concrete shape and we are able to see the results of our labor.

The computer's programming environment helps us to develop working programs. The operating system usually supports software for editing, compiling, and executing programs. The file system helps keep track of documents and make copies of documents. The standard steps of program implementation follow the sequence of coding, entering, compiling, and executing the program, and then inspecting the results. Modula-2 programs often cannot be executed alone but must import other programs from library modules to perform specific tasks. Library modules consist of two parts: a definition module, which describes what can be imported, and an implementation module, which contains the details that define the objects.

Part of learning Modula-2 is becoming familiar with its syntax and semantics. For instance, reserved words—such as MODULE, BEGIN, and END are used to set off parts of the program so they can be recognized by the compiler. Identifiers, consisting of a letter followed by letters and/or digits, name modules, procedures, and variables. Comments explain parts of the program but are ignored by the compiler. Modula-2 also makes use of import lists. Such lists contain identifiers that name objects used in the program but declared in other modules. Declarations, which define the objects, are required for every object that is not imported from another module. Statements specify the actions to be done with objects. For example, an assignment statement assigns a value to a variable.

As a convenience Modula-2 offers a number of library modules containing collections of predefined procedures. Procedures are small program segments and statements that invoke procedures are known as procedure calls. These calls are followed by items in parentheses called parameters.

After a program has been written, we must compile and execute it. As we do so, a number of different errors are liable to arise. Compilation time (syntax) errors are detected by the compiler during translation of the source code into machine code. After removing syntax errors and compiling, run time errors may occur, causing the program to stop prematurely. Finally, other semantic errors may occur when the program does not solve the problem the programmer intended. Debugging a program is the act of finding and correcting all these different kinds of errors.

You have the basic information about Modula-2 necessary to write some useful programs. If you have studied the library modules and can make good use of them, your programs may be quite powerful. Your skill will come from doing, as much as from reading, so experiment and use what you have learned as much as you can.

EXERCISES

1. Indicate the valid identifiers:

Y	4Square
CUST-2	Employee52
Invoice	Cost@Discount
Mile#	ValidData
Miles Per Gallon	C2H5OH

2. Write a constant declaration for YardsPerMile, LitersPerGallon, and RadiansToDegrees.

3. Choose variable identifiers and write the VAR declarations for year of study, grade point average, and student status.

4. Write the statements that will print the following message: "Computer Science is good for your health!"

5. Using appendices E and F, determine the types of the parameters of the following procedures: WriteCard, WriteReal, Concat, and MoveTo.

6. Indicate the errors in the following two statements:

   $$A \; + \; B \; := \; C;$$
   $$CONST \; Z \; := \; 3;$$

7. What is printed by the execution of the following program?

   ```
   MODULE Trial;

   FROM InOut IMPORT WriteCard, WriteString, WriteLn;

   VAR X, Y: CARDINAL;

   BEGIN
     WriteString( "The results are: " );
     X := 128;
     Y := 32;
     WriteCard( X, 3 );
     WriteLn;
     WriteCard( Y, 3 );
     WriteLn;
     WriteCard( 2, 2 );
     WriteString( " numbers printed" );
     WriteLn;
   END Trial.
   ```

8. Alter the program given in Example 1 to read in two integers and then compute and output their sum, difference, and product.

9. Alter the program given in Example 3 to draw the square in a clockwise rather than counterclockwise direction.

10. Alter the program in Example 4 to concatenate the input strings so that the second string entered appears first.

PROGRAMMING PROBLEMS

11. Enter and run the program of Example 1.

12. Enter and run the program of Example 2.

13. If you have TurtleGraphics, enter and run the program of Example 3.

14. Find out about the available string operations in your implementation. Then adapt, enter, and run the program of Example 4.

15. Write a program to "display" the following "square" made up of asterisks:

    ```
    *****
    *   *
    *   *
    *   *
    *****
    ```

16. Write a program to read a price and then compute a 5 percent tax on that price as well as the total price. The program will display results in the following form:

    ```
    Enter price (for example: 9.95): 25.50
    Tax on 25.50 is 1.27, total cost is 26.77.
    ```

3 Procedures and Functions

In this chapter you will:

- declare and invoke your own procedures
- use parameters for passing data to and from procedures
- declare and use local variables within procedures
- declare and invoke functions

In Chapter 2, we saw that it was convenient to import small pieces of programs, called procedures, from library modules. Procedures help us develop well-structured programs. This makes it possible to apply a "divide and conquer" strategy: each part of the solution, which may be implemented by a procedure, solves a subproblem of the original problem. Often the desired procedures are not available from library modules, so the programmer must develop new procedures.

This chapter begins by describing the syntax of simple procedures. Then we show how value parameters are used to transmit information into a procedure and, consequently, make the procedure more useful. We explore several examples using value parameters. We can also declare functions—procedures that return values. A brief section describes the syntax for functions and shows how functions are called. Finally, we look at variable parameters. With variable parameters, we transmit information into and out of procedures. Throughout the chapter, examples help us appreciate the role procedures play in program development.

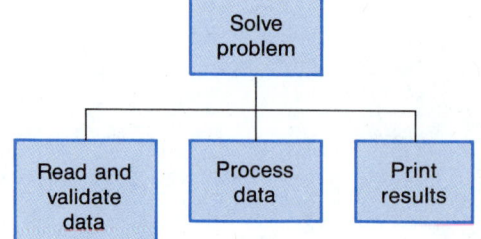

Figure 3.1
Solution Structure Chart

3.1 Procedures and Value Parameters

When developing programs to solve substantive problems, we need to divide the problem into parts and use relatively small program segments, called procedures, to solve each part. As we saw in Chapter 1, the division of the problem is usually shown by a structure chart. For example, many problems have a structure chart similar to Figure 3.1.

According to this chart, our solution has a main program (upper box) and three subparts (lower boxes). If we want to implement a solution with this structure, we may make each part of the structure chart a procedure, resulting in a very simple main program structure.

```
BEGIN (* SolveProblem *)
   ReadAndValidateData;
   ProcessData;
   PrintResults;
END SolveProblem.
```

ReadAndValidateData, ProcessData, and PrintResults are *procedure invocations*, or *calls* that cause the procedure to be executed. The procedures themselves must be defined in the declaration part of the program, similar to our declaration of constants or variables.

In some sense, procedures can be considered new commands to be used in a program. If appropriate procedures are available in existing modules, they should be imported. If they are not available, however, you must develop the procedures yourself.

In this section we introduce simple procedures and then develop more powerful procedures by using value parameters. We also show how procedures can have local declarations. These discussions are accompanied by several programming samples.

Declaring and Invoking Procedures

Since procedures are actually small program segments, their structure is very similar to programs. Indeed the main differences between a procedure and a program are that their headings are different and the procedure does not have import lists.

To get a picture of these differences, let's look at the syntax of simple procedure declarations

```
PROCEDURE name;
   declarations
BEGIN
   statements
END name;
```

where PROCEDURE, BEGIN, and END are reserved words. You may choose the name for the procedure, as you did with programs, and that name must also appear after the END that terminates the declaration of the procedure. Declarations may be given within the procedure declaration itself for any objects that are needed only by the statements in the procedure. The syntax of these declarations is exactly the same as for programs. You may even include other procedures in the declaration part, if you want to define a procedure that is only used within the statements between BEGIN and END. Procedures declared within other procedures are said to be *nested* (see in Chapter 7). Note that the entire procedure declaration must be terminated by a semicolon.

EXAMPLE 1 Drawing a Spruce Tree

To illustrate the development of a program with a declared procedure, let's develop a program to draw the spruce tree in Figure 3.2.

```
   *
  ***
 *****
*******
   *
  ***
 *****
*******
   *
  ***
 *****
*******
```

Figure 3.2
Spruce Tree

When considering a design, you might naturally think of a structure with three components, as illustrated in Figure 3.3. However, with a little more reflection, you would observe that the same thing should be done three times. Thus a structure with one component will suffice, as shown in Figure 3.4.

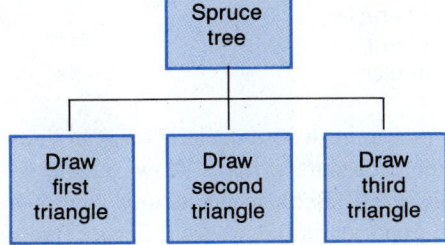

Figure 3.3
First Structure Chart for Spruce Tree

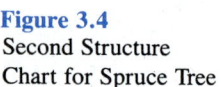
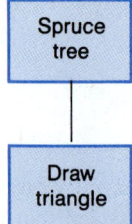

Figure 3.4
Second Structure Chart for Spruce Tree

A pseudocode solution, based on this structure is

> Spruce Tree
>   draw triangle
>   draw triangle
>   draw triangle
> End Spruce Tree

The drawing of a triangle can easily be done by writing strings with the appropriate number of asterisks. Based on the pseudocode, therefore, we can write the following program using a procedure called DrawTriangle. The numbers to the left of the program, which are not really part of the program itself, will be used in our explanation of the program.

```
(1)    MODULE SpruceTree;
(2)    (* Program to draw spruce tree figure.
                 P. Gabrini    January 1988 *)

(3)    FROM InOut IMPORT WriteString, WriteLn;

(4)    PROCEDURE DrawTriangle;
(5)    (* Procedure to draw a triangle of asterisks *)
(6)    BEGIN
(7)       WriteString( "   *" ); WriteLn;
(8)       WriteString( "  ***" ); WriteLn;
(9)       WriteString( " *****" ); WriteLn;
(10)      WriteString( "*******" ); WriteLn;
(11)   END DrawTriangle;

(12)   BEGIN (* SpruceTree *)
(13)      DrawTriangle;
(14)      DrawTriangle;
(15)      DrawTriangle;
(16)   END SpruceTree.
```

DrawTriangle is a procedure whose declaration is in lines 4 through 11. The declaration conforms to the procedure syntax. DrawTriangle is particularly simple and contains no declarations itself. Because procedures cannot have import lists, WriteString and WriteLn are imported in the program SpruceTree.

Having declared a procedure, we can call the procedure by using its name as a statement in the main program. Thus the SpruceTree program has three calls (invocations) to the DrawTriangle procedure on lines 13, 14, and 15. As you can see, the WriteString and WriteLn statements are also calls to procedures, which have been imported from the module InOut. WriteString has a parameter, too, which makes it more powerful. In the next section we'll see how to define our own procedures with parameters.

Procedures with a Single Parameter

Procedure WriteString, imported from standard module InOut, is very useful because the same procedure can produce different results based on its input. Input to a procedure is achieved through the use of parameters. You'll recall from Chapter 2 that parameters are the objects with which the procedures do their work. To declare procedures with parameters, we must generalize the first line, or *heading,* of the syntax for procedures. The syntax for the heading becomes

```
PROCEDURE name( formal parameter list );
```

The formal parameter list is similar to the variable declarations in a program: it lists identifiers and their types. A *formal parameter* (also called *dummy parameter*) is an identifier standing for a value that will be supplied to the procedure when it is called. The actual value that is specified in a procedure call is appropriately referred to as an *actual parameter.* The following example demonstrates the format for using formal and actual parameters with procedures.

EXAMPLE 2   *Drawing an Irregular Sawtooth*

In this example we will develop a program to draw the irregular sawtooth in Figure 3.5 using TurtleGraphics. We can see that this figure is simply a sequence of four equilateral triangles of various sizes. So, as in the previous example, the structure of our solution can be a main program and a single procedure, which draws an equilateral triangle of a specified size.

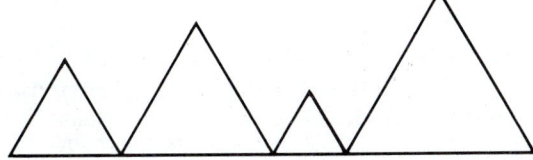

Figure 3.5
Irregular Sawtooth

A procedure to draw an equilateral triangle, using TurtleGraphics would be

```
PROCEDURE DrawTriangle;
(* Draw an equilateral triangle using TurtleGraphics *)

BEGIN
  Move( 40 );
  Turn( 120 );
  Move( 40 );
  Turn( 120 );
  Move( 40 );
  Turn( 120 ); (* Return Turtle to its starting direction. *)
END DrawTriangle;
```

To accomplish our original goal, we need to alter the declaration of this DrawTriangle procedure so that it will draw a triangle of a size determined by a parameter. Then the various calls to DrawTriangle in the main program will include an actual parameter indicating the size of the desired triangle. The complete program looks like this:

```
MODULE IrregularSawtooth;
(* Program to draw an irregular sawtooth figure.
            J. M. Adams      January 1988 *)

FROM TurtleGraphics IMPORT Move, Turn, TurtleStop;

PROCEDURE DrawTriangle(Size: CARDINAL);
(* Draw an equilateral triangle using TurtleGraphics *)

BEGIN
  Move(Size);
  Turn(120);
  Move(Size);
  Turn(120);
  Move(Size);
  Turn(120); (* Return Turtle to its starting direction. *)
END DrawTriangle;

BEGIN (* IrregularSawtooth *)
  DrawTriangle(30);
  Move(30);
  DrawTriangle(40);
  Move(40);
  DrawTriangle(20);
  Move(20);
  DrawTriangle(50);
  TurtleStop;   (* Hold display until return is pressed. *)
END IrregularSawtooth.
```

The declaration of the DrawTriangle procedure now specifies a parameter, Size, which appears in parentheses after the name of the procedure. Size is a formal parameter that will hold a cardinal value. As before, the actual choice of the name is up to us, but it should be meaningful. The calls to DrawTriangle must now supply actual values, such as 30, 40, 20, and 50, as in the program just shown. In our program the actual parameters are all nonnegative integers, as required by the type specification for Size, CARDINAL, in the heading of the declaration of DrawTriangle. A type specification is always required for formal parameters, and the types of the actual parameters must match this specification.

Let's examine in detail a call to a procedure. As shown in Figure 3.6, when the call DrawTriangle(30) is executed, the number 30 replaces the formal parameter Size in the definition of procedure DrawTriangle.

```
                                              Formal
Declaration Heading   PROCEDURE DrawTriangle ( Size: CARDINAL );

Call                            DrawTriangle( 30 );
                                              Actual
```

Figure 3.6 Formal and Actual Parameters

Then the statements of the procedure are executed. Thus the call has the same effect as if the following statements were executed:

```
Size := 30;
Move( Size );
Turn( 120 );
Move( Size );
Turn( 120 );
Move( Size );
Turn( 120 );
```

Procedures with Local Declarations

A procedure is very much like a program. Before proceeding with more examples of value parameters, we will explore some of these similarities. In particular, a procedure has a declaration part where objects can be declared as they would be in a program. We say that these objects are *local* to the procedure and that their *scope* is the procedure. These objects, therefore, can be referenced *only* within the procedure, not from the main program itself. To illustrate this point, let's take another example of a procedure with a single parameter.

EXAMPLE 3 *Drawing a Bar Chart*

Let's develop a program to display simple bar charts with four bars, such as the following:

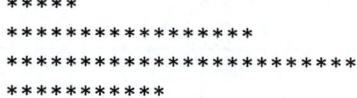

Our program will accept as input four integers and display bars with the number of asterisks indicated by the input. The input for the chart shown here would be the integers 5, 17, 24, and 11.

Assuming we had a procedure to draw a bar with a specified number of asterisks, the first version of our program could be written in pseudocode as follows:

> BarChart
>   Read input values i, j, k, l
>   Draw bar of length i
>   Draw bar of length j
>   Draw bar of length k
>   Draw bar of length l
> End BarChart

Since input can be accomplished using the procedures introduced in the previous chapter, we will concentrate on developing a procedure to draw a bar. Once we have such a procedure, we can simply call it four times in the program to draw a bar chart.

One possibility for displaying a string of asterisks is to write a string with the desired number of asterisks. This observation leads to the following pseudocode version of the desired procedure:

> DrawBar
>   Form a string with the desired number of asterisks
>   Write the string
> End DrawBar

Writing a string poses no problems, since we can import a procedure to do this, as was done in the examples of the previous section. But the first pseudocode statement seems to pose two problems:

1. obtaining the "desired number of asterisks"
2. forming the string

The first problem can be solved by providing the procedure with a parameter through which the "desired number" can be supplied each time the procedure is called. A refined pseudocode version of the procedure could then be formulated as

> DrawBar(n)
>   Form a string with n asterisks
>   Write the string
> End DrawBar

At this stage our detailed design is complete. We should, however, develop a test strategy. Such testing was unnecessary for the two previous examples, because testing consisted merely of compiling and executing the programs to see if they produced the desired result. In this example, though, since the result depends on the input data, we must work out a testing strategy. Test cases should include some typical input values within the allowable range. They should also include the boundary values—that is, the upper and lower limits—of the allowable range, because they are potential problem areas for most algorithms. We will have much more to say about testing strategy in Chapter 8.

We still have to solve the problem of forming the string. One solution is to create a very long string of asterisks and then choose a portion of this string of the desired length. Fortunately we can accomplish this task fairly easily by creating a string constant consisting of many asterisks and copying the desired number of asterisks from the string. We will assume our bar chart will never have a bar longer than 40, and then we can use a string constant of 40 asterisks. Since an appropriate copy operation is available from the Strings module (a nonstandard module given in Appendix F), we do not have to define it in our program. Using this approach, we can write the following Modula-2 program:

```
MODULE BarChart;
(* Program to draw a bar chart with 4 bars.  Each bar may
   be no longer than 40 units.
                              J. M. Adams    January 1988 *)

FROM InOut IMPORT ReadCard, WriteString, WriteLn;
FROM Strings IMPORT STRING, Copy;

VAR i, j, k, l: CARDINAL;

PROCEDURE DrawBar(n: CARDINAL);

CONST Asterisks = "****************************************";
VAR Bar: STRING;

BEGIN (* DrawBar *)
  Copy(Asterisks, 0, n, Bar);
  WriteString(Bar);
  WriteLn;
END DrawBar;
```

```
BEGIN (* BarChart *)
  WriteString("Enter four positive integers"); WriteLn;
  ReadCard(i); WriteLn;
  ReadCard(j); WriteLn;
  ReadCard(k); WriteLn;
  ReadCard(l); WriteLn;
  WriteLn;
  DrawBar(i);
  DrawBar(j);
  DrawBar(k);
  DrawBar(l);
END BarChart.
```

The main program reads in the data values; the WriteLn after each ReadCard helps visually separate the data for the user. The main program then calls DrawBar four times, once for each input value. The call to the Copy procedure in the declaration of DrawBar causes a substring of length n to be copied from Asterisks starting at position 0, the first position of the string. This substring then becomes the value of Bar. Thus Copy is ideally suited for forming the string we want. After forming Bar, it is displayed by the call to the procedure WriteString. Finally, WriteLn moves the cursor to the next line.

Note that the variable Bar is declared within the procedure and is a *local variable* of DrawBar. We can also say that Bar is local to DrawBar, or that the scope of Bar is DrawBar. This terminology is important, and the concept of locality and scoping will be developed more fully as we need more sophisticated features of Modula-2. Since Bar is local to DrawBar, it may be referenced only within the declaration of DrawBar, not in the main program. In other words, the name Bar cannot be used outside DrawBar, and any attempt to do so will cause a compilation error. This limited access is desirable because Bar is needed only within the procedure DrawBar. We can protect it from inadvertent changes outside DrawBar by making it a local variable. The constant Asterisks is also local to DrawBar and can be used only in that procedure. As a final remark, we note that variables such as i, j, k, and l, which are declared in the main program, are called *global variables,* since they are accessible throughout the program. We will study the accessibility of objects in more detail in Chapter 7.

Our program should be tested with input values between 1 and 40, and also with the boundary values of 0 and 40. The results of the program for input values outside the acceptable range are not specified and will produce various results. A negative value should produce a type error, and values greater than 40 will depend on the implementation of procedure Copy. As your programming skills develop, you will learn how to validate the input data to provide predictable performance on erroneous data.

Procedures with Several Parameters

Often we need procedures that have more than one parameter. Recall procedures WriteCard, WriteInt, and FWriteReal, which were used in previous examples. The first two required two parameters—one to indicate the value to write, and a second to indicate the width of the field in which the value will be written. FWriteReal required a third parameter indicating the number of decimal digits to be written. We can declare procedures with more than one parameter by including a list of formal parameters with their type specifications in the heading of the declaration of the procedure. The formal parameter specifications are separated by semicolons. More precisely, the syntax of a simple formal parameter list in the declaration of a procedure is

```
list of identifiers: type; list of identifiers: type; . . .
```

As an example, consider the formal parameter list in the heading

```
PROCEDURE DisplayTitle( Text: STRING; NumBlanks: CARDINAL );
```

This example has two lists of identifiers, but each list consists only of a single name. Notice the similarity of the syntax of the parameter list to the syntax for the declaration of variables. Later we will need slightly more elaborate formal parameter lists, but these lists will do for now.

As with a single parameter, calls to procedures with multiple parameters must match the declaration. Calls to procedures with more than one parameter must specify a list of actual parameters separated by commas, and there must be as many actual parameters as there are formal parameters in the definition. Also, the actual parameters *must* be in the same order and of the same type as that specified for the corresponding formal parameters, as illustrated by the example

```
DisplayTitle( "This is a Title", 2 );
```

If these conditions are not met, a compilation error will occur. The following examples illustrate such errors:

```
DisplayTitle( 2, "This is a Title" ); (* parameters of the wrong type *)
WriteCard( Number ); (* the second parameter for field width is missing *)
```

Parameters that appear in a formal parameter list of the kind whose syntax has just been described are called *value parameters*. When the program is executed, they pass values *from* the calling program *to* the procedure containing the formal parameter list in its declaration. Furthermore, any change made to such a parameter within the procedure has *no* effect on the corresponding actual parameter in the calling program. Consequently, a value parameter is used to transmit data in one direction only. Later in the chapter we will introduce another kind of parameter, called a variable parameter, which can be used to transmit data in both directions.

EXAMPLE 4 *Displaying Variable Size Titles*

Let's now develop a procedure to print titles in boxes of asterisks, so that the boxes have a variable size. For instance, the title "Procedures and Value Parameters" could be printed as:

```
*****************************************
*      Procedures and Value Parameters   *
*****************************************
```

or as

```
***************************************************
*            Procedures and Value Parameters       *
***************************************************
```

and the title "Results" could be printed as

```
*************                    *****************
*  Results  *        or as       *    Results    *
*************                    *****************
```

Our procedure will need two parameters: the title to be printed, which is a string of characters, and the number of spaces which should precede the title in the box. Our pseudocode solution will be

> Display Title (Text, Number of Blanks)
>   Calculate the box width
>   Print a line of asterisks for the top of the box
>   Print "*", Blanks, Text, Blanks, "*"
>   Print a line of asterisks for the bottom of the box
> End Display Title

We still have to be more precise about computing the width of the box and about forming strings of asterisks and blanks of the right size. We know how to form strings of the right size from our previous example, using Copy. To compute the size of the box, we will need the number of characters in the string. We can get this number by calling the procedure Length, which can be imported from the Strings module. We also have to add twice the number of blanks for padding on each side and two more for the asterisk characters at the box edge. Using variables named Width, Box Side, and Blank String, we can refine our previous pseudocode solution to

> Display Title (Text, Number of Blanks)
>   Set Width to Length(Text) + 2 * Number of Blanks + 2
>   Set Box Side to a string with Width asterisks
>   Set Blank String to a string with Number of Blanks spaces
>   Print Box Side
>   Print "*", Blank String, Text, Blank String, "*"
>   Print Box Side
> End Display Title

The corresponding Modula-2 procedure is given as part of a program that tests it, using input and output redirection. Notice that the program must import the procedures needed by DisplayTitle because a procedure cannot have an import list. Also note that the maximum box size is 42, the length of the Asterisks string constant. Thus we must require that the titles to be displayed are no longer than 40 characters.

```
MODULE CheckTitles;
(* Module to check procedure DisplayTitle
            P. Gabrini   January 1988 *)

FROM InOut IMPORT WriteString, WriteLn, OpenInput,
                 OpenOutput, CloseInput, CloseOutput;
FROM Strings IMPORT STRING, Copy, Length;

PROCEDURE DisplayTitle(Text: STRING; NumBlanks: CARDINAL);
(* Display a title in a box of asterisks *)
CONST Asterisks = "******************************************";
      Blanks    = "                                          ";

VAR Width: CARDINAL;
    BoxSide, BlankString: STRING;

BEGIN
  Width := Length(Text) + 2 * NumBlanks + 2;
  Copy(Asterisks, 0, Width, BoxSide);
  Copy(Blanks, 0, NumBlanks, BlankString);
  WriteString(BoxSide); WriteLn;
  WriteString("*"); WriteString(BlankString);
  WriteString(Text); WriteString(BlankString);
  WriteString("*"); WriteLn;
  WriteString(BoxSide); WriteLn;
END DisplayTitle;

VAR Argument: STRING;

BEGIN (* CheckTitles *)
  OpenInput("");
  OpenOutput("");
  ReadString(Argument);
  DisplayTitle(Argument, 2);
  WriteLn; WriteLn;
  DisplayTitle(Argument, 6);
  WriteLn; WriteLn;
  ReadString(Argument);
  DisplayTitle(Argument, 2);
  WriteLn; WriteLn;
  DisplayTitle(Argument, 4);
  CloseInput;
  CloseOutput;
END CheckTitles.
```

If the program is executed with the input file

```
Procedures and Value Parameters
Results
```

the output will be the four boxes given previously as examples.

The procedure Length, imported from module Strings, gives the number of characters in a string. For example, Length("Results") will return 7. The width of the title box is equal to the length of the string plus twice the number of blanks plus 2 because we print an asterisk and the blanks in front of the title as well as the blanks and an asterisk behind the title.

3.2 Functions

The previous example, DisplayTitle, used the procedure Length to compute the length of a string. Modula-2 procedures such as these, which return a value to the calling program, are called *function procedures,* or simply *functions*. In this section we will develop a program with a declared function procedure. The declarations of function procedures must have the following syntax, which is very close to the syntax we have seen for procedures.

```
PROCEDURE name( formal parameter list ): type;
declarations
BEGIN
   statements
END name;
```

There are two differences between procedure declarations and function procedure declarations: the type at the end of the heading of the declaration indicates the type of the value that the function procedure will return when it is called, and the statements in the declaration must always contain at least one return statement.

A return statement has the syntax

```
RETURN expression;
```

The expression must result in the same type as the function type. The expression can involve constants, variables, built-in operations, or other function calls provided the final result is of the appropriate type. When this statement is executed, the value of the expression is returned by the function, and program control returns to the place of the function call. The function call must be part of an expression expecting a value of this type. Most functions will have parameters, but in the rare instance that a function does not have any parameters, the parentheses are still required, both in the declaration and the function call.

To illustrate the definition and use of functions, let's modify one of the examples from Chapter 2—the angle conversion program ConvertAngle. Our alteration will use a function procedure that returns a value of type REAL:

```
MODULE AngleConversion;
(* A program to convert an angle in degrees to
   an angle in radians
                         J. M. Adams    January 1988 *)

FROM InOut IMPORT WriteString, WriteLn;
FROM RealInOut IMPORT ReadReal, WriteReal;

VAR Degrees, Radians: REAL;

PROCEDURE ConvertAngle( Angle: REAL ): REAL;
(* Convert an angle from degrees to radians *)
CONST Pi = 3.14159;
      ConversionFactor = Pi / 180.0;

BEGIN
  RETURN ConversionFactor * Angle
END ConvertAngle;

BEGIN (* AngleConversion *)
  WriteString( "Enter an angle in degrees: " );
  ReadReal( Degrees ); WriteLn;
  Radians := ConvertAngle( Degrees );
  WriteString( "The angle in radians is: " );
  WriteReal( Radians, 12 ); WriteLn;
END AngleConversion.
```

ConvertAngle is a function procedure that expects one parameter of type REAL, as indicated by its parameter list (Angle: REAL). It also returns a value of type REAL, as indicated by the :REAL following the parameter list. The procedure consists only of a RETURN statement. Since a call to ConvertAngle returns a value of type REAL, the call itself must be part of a REAL expression. In this example the call is the entire expression on the right-hand side of an assignment statement.

We should note one important difference between function calls and procedure calls: a function call *must* appear in a place in the program where an expression is allowed, whereas a procedure call must appear in a place where a statement is allowed. Since the execution of a function returns a value, we must be sure that this value will be used at the point where it is returned. On the other hand, a procedure call does not explicitly return a value but simply accomplishes some action and thus has the same nature as a statement.

You may have noticed that a function procedure is very similar to a function in mathematics, but there is one very important distinction: a mathematical function only produces a single value for each function call, whereas a function procedure may have other effects as well as producing a value. For example, a function procedure could alter the value of a global variable or cause values to be written on an output device. Such actions, called *side effects,* are not generally considered to be good programming style. Nevertheless, side effects are possible, and consequently, the relationship between function procedures and mathematical functions is not exact.

3.3 Variable Parameters

Often we need procedures that return more than one value to the calling program. Since a function procedure can only return a single value, a function will not suffice for this task. However, we can use a kind of parameter that can be used to transmit values from the calling program to the procedure or transmit values from the procedure back to the calling program or do both. Such parameters are called *variable parameters*. We can specify parameters of this kind by preceding them with the reserved word VAR in the formal parameter list of the declaration of the procedure.

In general we can have as many variable parameters as we wish, and they can be interspersed with value parameters. As a result, a generalization of our syntax for formal parameter list is needed:

```
[VAR] list of identifiers: type;
[VAR] list of identifiers: type;
          .
          .
          .
```

where [VAR] means that the reserved word VAR is optional. We will use square brackets to enclose optional syntactic components, which means the components appear zero or one time. VAR should be used when the list of identifiers that immediately follows it consists only of variable parameters. It should not be used when the list contains value parameters. Actual parameters corresponding to formal variable parameters *must* be variables, because it must be possible to assign values to them.

To illustrate variable parameters, let's develop a procedure that does a simple decomposition of a string. Given a string representing a person's name in the form of the last name followed by a comma followed by the first name, the procedure will return a string representing the first name and another string representing the last name. A pseudocode version of the procedure is

> SplitNames
>   Find the position of the comma
>   Return the substring before the comma as the last name
>   Return the substring following the comma as the first name
> End SplitNames

To implement this solution, we need to know the position of the comma. Fortunately, the module Strings contains a function procedure called Pos that will do this, as we have already seen in Chapter 1. If S and T are strings, the call Pos(S, T) will cause a search of the string T for a substring matching the string S and return the position of the leftmost match in T or the length of T if no match is found (string manipulation procedures are implementation-dependent, so check your implementation for exact definitions). Using Pos, we can write our procedure, assuming that a comma will always be present in the input string.

To obtain the substring preceding the comma and the one following the comma, we can use the Copy procedure introduced earlier in this chapter. The Copy procedure must be used with care. Remember that the first parameter of Copy specifies the initial string, the second parameter the position of the first character to copy, the third parameter the number of characters to copy, and the last parameter the resulting string. To copy the last name, we start with the first character in the string, at position 0, and copy all characters up to, but not including, the comma. The character before the comma is at position CommaPos − 1; therefore, if we desire to copy all characters from position 0 to position CommaPos − 1, the number of characters is CommaPos. For the first name, we want to start at the position just beyond the comma—namely, CommaPos + 1. The last character in a FullName is located at the position designated by Length(FullName) − 1, so the number of characters beyond the comma is given by Length(FullName) − CommaPos − 1.

The procedure is shown here embedded in a test program:

```
MODULE TestNames;
(* Program to determine the names in a string
          J. M. Adams    January 1988 *)

FROM InOut IMPORT WriteString, WriteLn, ReadString;
FROM Strings IMPORT STRING, Copy, Pos, Length;

PROCEDURE SplitNames(FullName: STRING;
                     VAR FirstName, LastName: STRING);
VAR CommaPos: CARDINAL;

BEGIN
  CommaPos := Pos(",", FullName);
  Copy(FullName, 0, CommaPos, LastName);
  Copy(FullName, CommaPos + 1,
       Length(FullName) - CommaPos - 1, FirstName)
END SplitNames;

VAR Full, First, Last: STRING;

BEGIN (* TestNames *)
  WriteString("Enter a name in the form: last name,first name");
  WriteLn;
  ReadString(Full); WriteLn;
  SplitNames(Full, First, Last);
  WriteString("The first name is: ");
  WriteString(First); WriteLn;
  WriteString("The last name is: ");
  WriteString(Last); WriteLn;
END TestNames.
```

The first parameter of SplitNames is a value parameter, which is used to transmit the full name from the test program to the procedure. The second and third parameters are variable parameters, which transmit the first and last names back to the calling program.

In this case the variable parameters are used to pass information just one way—from the procedure to the calling test program. Figure 3.7 shows the correspondence between actual and formal parameters established by the call: SplitNames(Full, First, Last).

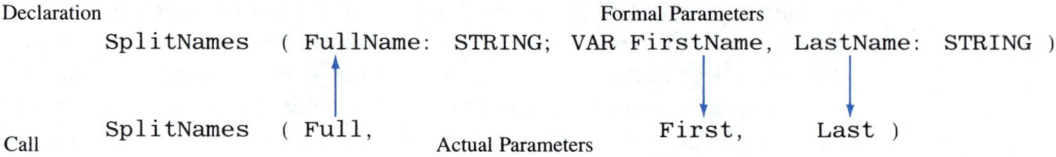

Figure 3.7   Correspondence Between Actual and Formal Parameters

3.4 The Use of Value and Variable Parameters

Note that the actual parameter for a value parameter may be any expression of the expected type, but the actual parameter for a variable parameter may only be a variable. Unlike the result of a function that replaces the function call, the result that is passed back to the calling program through a variable parameter must be assigned to a variable. Since only variables may be assigned values, the actual parameter corresponding to a variable parameter must be a variable and cannot be an expression other than a variable (such as A + B) because it is impossible to assign a value to such an expression. With some further reflection about value and variable parameters, you might notice that we could do without value parameters entirely! The value of any expression that was to be used as a value parameter could first be assigned to a temporary variable, and the temporary variable could then be used as the actual parameter rather than the expression. Why then does Modula-2 have both value and variable parameters? The answer is related to one of the most common problems in developing and maintaining correct programs.

A frequent error in program development and maintenance is inadvertently changing the value of a variable during program execution. Such errors can be extremely hard to locate, since the program may run to completion and might even give results that look reasonable. It is very important, therefore, that we try to avoid such errors by programming in a very disciplined manner: if we do not intend for a value to be changed, we should protect it from change. Modula-2 provides several means of protection. For example, if a value should never be changed, it may be protected in Modula-2 by declaring it to be a constant.

Extending the protectionist philosophy to parameters gives us the answer to our question about the inclusion of value parameters in Modula-2. If a parameter of a procedure is intended *only* for transmission of a value *to* the procedure, it should be a value parameter so that a change of that parameter within the procedure does not change the value of the corresponding actual parameter. Variable parameters are used when the transmission of a value *from* a procedure is required.

SUMMARY

One of the best ways of solving any problem is to divide it into smaller, independent parts and solve each part separately; we do this when we develop structure charts. To follow this approach in programming, we can divide the program into small segments called procedures. Whenever possible, procedures should be imported from library modules; if they're not available, though, we have to develop them ourselves. Like all the objects that are not imported by our program, our procedures must be declared. Once they are declared, they can be used, and this is done by calling, or invoking, them.

The syntax of procedures is similar to the syntax of programs, except that their headings are different and they do not have import lists. Communication between a calling program and a procedure is established with two lists of identifiers: the formal parameter list in the procedure heading and the actual parameter list in the call. A formal parameter is an identifier that stands for a value to be supplied to the procedure when it is called. The actual value specified in the procedure call is known as the actual parameter. The elements of both lists of parameters must match in number, position, and type. Function procedures are special procedures that return a value to the calling program, and, as a result of this, a function call is an expression, whereas a procedure call is a statement.

Objects declared in a procedure are said to be local to the procedure; they can be referenced only within the procedure. Objects declared in the main program are said to be global because they can be accessed throughout the program.

Value parameters are used to transmit values from the calling program to the called procedure. Function procedures return a value to the calling program. Variable parameters may be used to transmit values into and out of procedures.

EXERCISES

1. Write a function procedure RadToDeg that converts an angle in radians to an angle in degrees.
2. Trace the TestNames program using your own last and first names as a test case. Suggest some other test cases to check that the operation of the program is correct.
3. Write a new DrawTriangle procedure that displays a triangle as illustrated here and whose size is specified by a parameter.

The triangle will always take up five lines. The middle line will have a number of asterisks equal to the parameter value. Lines 2 and 4 will have a number of asterisks equal to half the value of the parameter (parameter DIV 2).

4. Write a SailingFlags pseudocode program that uses the procedure developed in Exercise 3 to print a figure with triangles of various sizes, as shown here:

```
*
* *
* * * *
* *
*
*
* * * * * *
* * * * * * * * * * *
* * * * * *
*
*
* * * *
* * * * * * * *
* * * *
*
```

PROGRAMMING PROBLEMS

5. Write a Modula-2 procedure to display on the left side of the screen a solid rectangle of asterisks with a length four lines high, and a width specified by a parameter. Develop an interactive test program for the procedure that prompts the user for the width of the desired rectangle and then calls the procedure.

6. Alter the procedure written for Problem 5 to display the rectangle of asterisks starting in a column specified by a second parameter to the procedure. Also, alter the test program to prompt for the column as well as the width.

7. Implement your sailing flag procedure from Exercise 4 along with a test program.

8. The text has a ConvertAngle procedure that goes from degrees to radians, and in Exercise 1 you developed a procedure RadToDeg to convert from radians to degrees. Include both procedures in the same test program, which should prompt for an angle in degrees, print the same angle in radians, and then use the result to convert back to degrees to print the final value.

9. Develop a function procedure to convert yards to meters (1 yard = 0.914 meters) and an interactive program to test the procedure.

10. Write a procedure that will decompose a string representing a simple arithmetic expression of a sum of two terms and return the first term and the second term. For example, given "first+second," it will return "first" as the first term and "second" as the second. Also write an interactive test program.

Since it is very hard to approximate the drawing of the following figures by displaying characters, do Problems 11, 12, and 13 only if your computing system has TurtleGraphics.

11. Write a Modula-2 program to draw an irregular mesa, similar to the one shown here.

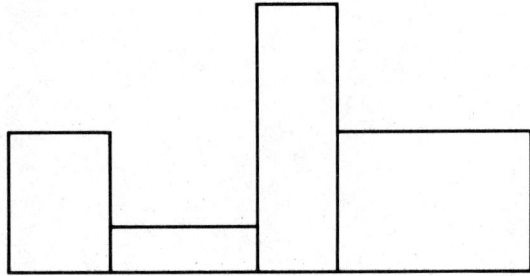

12. Write a Modula-2 program to draw a windmill figure like the one shown here.

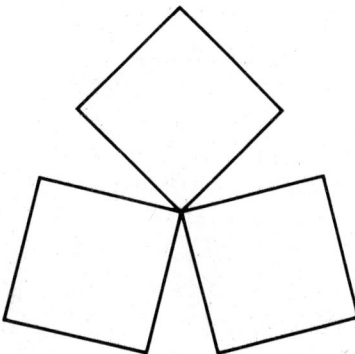

13. Write a Modula-2 program to draw a five-pointed star, similar to the one shown here.

4 Control Structures

In this chapter you will:

- learn about the characteristics and uses of the Modula-2 statements LOOP, WHILE, FOR, and REPEAT for implementing iteration, or the repeating of a sequence of statements
- learn how to use the IF statement to implement selection, the choice between alternative statement sequences
- see how these statements can be combined to solve complex problems

Thus far the programs that we've described have executed their statements in sequence one after another. A fundamental aspect of programming languages like Modula-2, however, is the ability to change the sequential order in which statements are usually executed. Changing this sequential order gives the programs real power because it enables them to accomplish certain repetitive tasks or to choose between alternative tasks. As we explained in Chapter 1, statements that allow us to control the order of execution are called control structures. In this chapter we'll look at two of the primary control structures in Modula-2: iteration and selection.

Iteration is the repetition of a group of statements. Our discussion will start with the basic iterative statement, LOOP, which is similar to the Loop in pseudocode. Then we'll examine three special forms of looping that occur frequently and have their own statements: WHILE, FOR, and REPEAT. A comparison of these looping statements will show what they have in common and how they differ.

Selection, the choice between alternatives, is implemented in Modula-2 by the IF statement. Here we'll see two forms. The one-branch IF statement (IF . . . THEN) allows the choice of whether to execute a group of statements or to skip them. The two-branch IF statement (IF . . . THEN . . . ELSE) allows a choice between two alternative groups of statements.

Finally, this chapter describes nested control structures, such as IFs within LOOPs or LOOPs within LOOPs. Such combinations of control structures enable us to solve complex problems. We'll explain how these structures are designed and then debugged if errors arise.

4.1 Iteration

We will start our discussion of control structures with statements that permit us to execute a group of statements repeatedly. After examining the LOOP statement, which we have already seen in pseudocode, we introduce three other looping structures: WHILE, FOR, and REPEAT. Since these four statements all perform repetition, we will briefly compare them to emphasize similarities and differences.

The LOOP Statement

One of our first examples of a simple Modula-2 program in Chapter 1, SumOfIntegers, contained a *LOOP statement*. By using LOOP, we can cause a group of statements to be executed repetitively. In the SumOfIntegers program we used a LOOP statement to generate the sequence of integers and to maintain a running total. We have modified our pseudocode solution in Chapter 1 to add to the running total before incrementing the number; therefore, we initialize Number to be 1.

```
Sum := 0;
Number := 1;
LOOP
   IF Number > N THEN
     EXIT;
   END; (* IF *)
   Sum := Sum + Number;
   Number := Number + 1;
END;   (* LOOP *)
```

We can summarize the execution of this LOOP statement by saying that as long as Number is less than or equal to N, the two assignment statements will be executed. Since Number is initialized to 1, these two statements are executed for values of Number from 1 to N, or precisely N times.

The syntax of the LOOP statement is

```
LOOP
    statement;
    statement;
         .
         .
         .
END;
```

LOOP and END are reserved words, and the statements between them are to be executed repetitively. When the END is encountered, control is transferred back to the top of the loop. The statements between LOOP and END are collectively called the *loop body*. The body of a LOOP statement usually contains at least one EXIT statement. The EXIT statement causes the body of the loop to cease executing; without it, there would be no way to terminate the repetition. For instance, the execution of the loop

```
LOOP
    WriteString( "Forever" );  WriteLn;
END;  (* LOOP *)
```

would print an endless sequence of "Forever" messages.

The EXIT statement is usually controlled by an IF statement, as was done in the LOOP statement in the SumOfIntegers program. The IF statement will be discussed in greater detail later in this chapter. For now it is sufficient to observe that the IF statement in our earlier example causes a condition to be tested (Number > N), and if the condition is true, the EXIT will be performed. Such a test for exit (end of repetition) can be placed anywhere in the body of the loop. Whenever the EXIT statement is executed, the rest of the statements in the body of the loop are skipped, and execution continues with the statement immediately following the END of the LOOP.

The WHILE Statement

In the LOOP statement used in the SumOfIntegers program, we tested for the exit condition at the beginning of the loop. Since this situation occurs frequently in programming, Modula-2 has another statement for repetition, the *WHILE statement*. The WHILE statement is a shorter way of writing loops where the test for iteration is at the beginning of the loop. In our SumOfIntegers example the LOOP statement can be replaced with an equivalent WHILE statement:

```
Sum := 0;                              Sum := 0;
Number := 1;                           Number := 1;
LOOP                                   WHILE Number <= N DO
  IF Number > N THEN                     Sum := Sum + Number;
    EXIT;                                Number := Number + 1;
  END;  (* IF *)                       END;  (* WHILE *)
  Sum := Sum + Number;
  Number := Number + 1;
END;    (* LOOP *)
```

The condition in the WHILE loop is Number <= N, which is the test for loop entry. It is the logical negation of LOOP exit condition Number > N. In this example the WHILE is shorter and more readable than the corresponding LOOP statement.

The syntax of the WHILE statement is

```
WHILE condition DO
   statement;
   statement;
      .
      .
      .
   END;
```

Figure 4.1 illustrates this control structure by means of a flow chart. The WHILE statement has a built-in test of the condition that occurs between the reserved words WHILE and DO. The statements between DO and END (the body of the loop) are executed only if this condition is true. In the WHILE statement the condition is a test for *entering* the loop; exit from the WHILE loop is done when the repetition condition is false. This test is the opposite of the LOOP statement, where the condition in the IF statement is a test for exiting the loop, and the loop is exited if the condition is true.

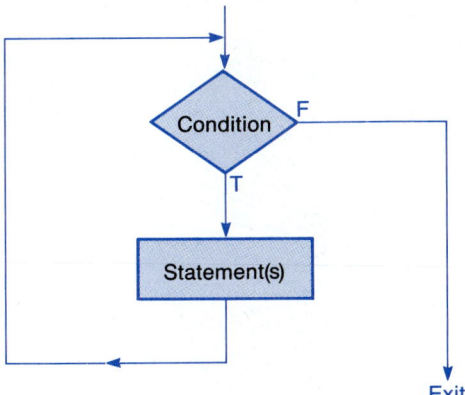

Figure 4.1
WHILE Statement

For another example of a WHILE statement, consider the following Mystery program. Before reading the explanation given after the program, see if you can determine what the program does. Note that this is a program without any input.

```
MODULE Mystery;
(* Program to draw a ?????? using TurtleGraphics *)

FROM TurtleGraphics IMPORT Move, Turn, TurtleStop;

VAR L: CARDINAL;
```

```
BEGIN
  L := 9;
  WHILE L < 200 DO
    Move( L );
    Turn( 89 );
    L := L + 3;
  END;       (* WHILE *)
  TurtleStop;           (* Hold screen *)
END Mystery.
```

The program draws a figure similar to a spiral. Since it is made of increasingly longer line segments with sharp corners between each segment, the figure is not smooth. However, as the figure is drawn, you see four fairly smooth spirals appearing as secondary curves form from the corners of the primary figure! Thus, we might rename the program SpiralGalaxy (see Figure 4.2).

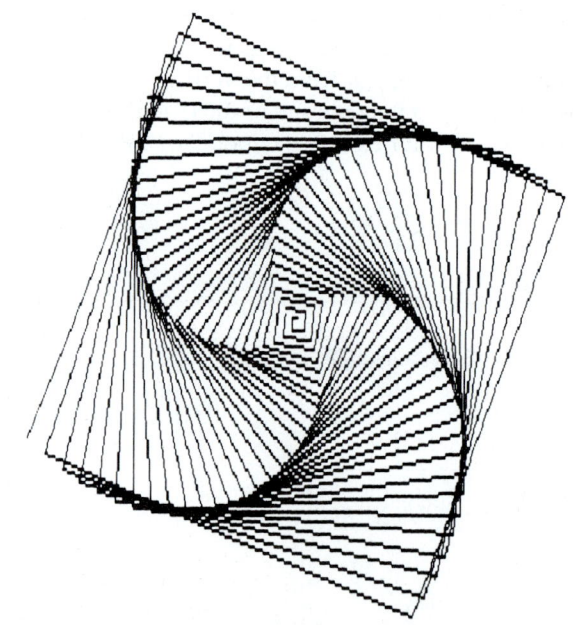

Figure 4.2 Output of SpiralGalaxy

The FOR Statement

Like most other languages, Modula-2 has an iterative control structure that is convenient for dealing with problems where the number of iterations is known at the time the loop is entered. This structure is the *FOR statement*.

The LOOP and WHILE statements test a logical condition to see if the loop should be exited. Such a configuration is called *indefinite iteration* since the number of times the loop will execute is not known in advance. However, in some situations the number of repetitions is known; this circumstance is called *definite iteration*. In the previous example, SumOfIntegers, the number of repetitions is known to be N. We can therefore use a FOR loop instead of a WHILE loop.

SEC. 4.1 Iteration

```
            Sum    := 0;                        Sum    := 0;
            Number := 1;                        FOR Number := 1 to N DO
            WHILE Number <= N DO                   Sum := Sum + Number;
               Sum    := Sum + Number;          END; (* FOR *)
               Number := Number + 1;
            END; (* WHILE *)
```

Notice that the FOR statement eliminated two statements—the initialization of Number by assignment (Number : = 1) and the incrementation of Number (Number : = Number + 1). Both these tasks are done automatically by the FOR statement.

The syntax of the FOR statement is

```
FOR identifier := expression TO expression [BY constant expression] DO
   statements;
           .
           .
           .
   END;
```

where the brackets indicate that "BY expression" is optional. The FOR, : = , TO, DO, BY, and END are reserved words. The identifier after FOR is called the *loop control variable,* which can be of any scalar type (that is, simple and ordered) other than REAL. The first expression is the starting value assigned to the loop control variable; the second expression is the final value. These expressions must be of the same type as the loop control variable. Each time the loop executes, the loop control variable is advanced to the next value. When the final value is exceeded, the loop is exited.

Let's examine the simple example

```
            FOR Count := 1 TO 5 DO
               WriteCard( Count, 3 );
            END;   (* FOR *)
```

The loop body will be executed exactly five times; the loop control variable, Count, will take on successive values 1, 2, 3, 4, and 5, which will be printed on a single line. The loop control variable should not be changed by any statement within the loop body. Also, the value of the loop control variable is unpredictable after the loop is exited. Finally, if the initial and final expressions involve variables, their values should not be changed in the loop body.

It is also possible to provide an increment value other than 1 in a FOR loop, as illustrated by the example

```
FOR Scan := 2 TO 8 BY 2 DO
   WriteString( "Counting up: " );  WriteCard( Scan, 3 );  WriteLn;
END;   (* FOR *)
```

The body of this loop will be executed four times with Scan taking on the values of 2, 4, 6, and 8, values which will be printed on four different lines preceded by "Counting up: ". The expression after BY must be a constant expression—that is, it cannot contain variables or function calls. However, its value can be negative, as in

```
FOR Scan := 8 TO 2 BY -2 DO
  WriteString( "Counting down: " ); WriteCard( Scan, 3 ); WriteLn;
END;    (* FOR *)
```

The body of this loop will be executed four times with Scan taking on the values of 8, 6, 4, and 2, which will be printed on four different lines, preceded by "Counting down: ".

We can also simplify our SpiralGalaxy program:

```
L := 9;                         FOR L := 9 TO 200 BY 3 DO
WHILE L < 200 DO                  Move( L );
  Move( L );                      Turn( 89 );
  Turn( 89 );                   END;    (* FOR *)
  L := L + 3;
END;    (* WHILE *)
```

Again, the FOR statement takes care of initializing the control variable and incrementing it (by 3 in this example). Notice that the loop control variable need not ever equal the final value; the FOR loop is exited when the control variable *exceeds* the final value. In this problem the values taken by L are 9, 12, . . . 195, 198. The next value would be 201, but since this number exceeds the final value of 200, the loop is exited.

The loop control variable of a FOR loop must be declared, but it is not restricted to INTEGER and CARDINAL. For example, we can use characters, as in

```
FOR Ch := 'A' TO 'F' DO
  Write( Ch ); Write( ' ' );
END;    (* FOR *)
```

This FOR statement will execute the body of the loop 6 times and print the first 6 uppercase letters separated by spaces.

However, a loop control variable cannot be of type REAL. Later we will see that REAL values on different computers do not have unique predecessors nor unique successors. The FOR statement automatically increments or decrements the loop control variable by using the successor or predecessor of its value, and therefore cannot deal with values of type REAL.

A Programming Example with a Loop and an Arithmetic Expression

Before going on to the last iterative statement, let's discuss arithmetic expressions in more detail. For practice we'll try to solve a fairly realistic numeric problem with a Modula-2 program.

Currently in the United States temperatures are given in degrees Fahrenheit. Since the metric system is becoming increasingly important, though, these figures may one day be given in degrees Celsius only. To help us become familiar with this temperature scale, we need a table for converting from Fahrenheit to Celsius.

For our example, we will restrict ourselves to temperatures ranging from -30 degrees Fahrenheit to $+120$ degrees Fahrenheit. We want to print a table giving the Celsius equivalent for each Fahrenheit temperature value. With these assumptions in mind, we could develop a first pseudocode version as follows:

> Temperature
>   Set Fahrenheit to -30
>   Loop
>   Convert Fahrenheit to Celsius
>   Print Fahrenheit, Celsius
>   Increment Fahrenheit by 1
>   Exit if Fahrenheit $>$ 120
>   End Loop
> End Temperature

The only significant problem in this version is the step that performs the actual conversion of a Fahrenheit temperature to Celsius. We know that 32 degrees Fahrenheit is equivalent to 0 degrees Celsius and that 212 degrees Fahrenheit is equivalent to 100 degrees Celsius. In order to convert Fahrenheit temperatures to Celsius temperatures, we must reduce the Fahrenheit value by 32 and multiply the result by $100/(212 - 32)$ or $5/9$. Using this formula, we can produce a refined pseudocode version.

> Temperature
>   Set Fahrenheit to -30
>   Loop
>   Set Celsius to 5(Fahrenheit $-$ 32)/9
>   Print Fahrenheit, Celsius
>   Increment Fahrenheit by 1
>   Exit if Fahrenheit $>$ 120
>   End Loop
> End Temperature

We will use REAL values in order to obtain results with decimal fractions. You may be tempted to use a FOR loop since Fahrenheit is incremented by 1 and used to control the exit condition; however, since we will use a REAL variable for Fahrenheit, we cannot use a FOR loop with Fahrenheit as the loop control variable. Our Modula-2 program using LOOP for iteration is

```
(1)     MODULE Temperature;
(2)     (* Computation and printing of a conversion table for
(3)         Fahrenheit and Celsius temperatures.
(4)                 P. Gabrini         January 1988 *)

(5)     FROM RealInOut IMPORT FWriteReal;
(6)     FROM InOut IMPORT WriteString, WriteLn;
```

```
(7)     CONST Low = -30.0;
(8)           High = 120.0;
(9)     VAR Fahrenheit, Celsius: REAL;

(10)    BEGIN
(11)       WriteString( "Fahrenheit    Celsius" );
(12)       Fahrenheit := Low;
(13)       LOOP
(14)          Celsius := 5.0 * (Fahrenheit - 32.0) / 9.0;
(15)          WriteLn;
(16)          FWriteReal( Fahrenheit, 10, 2 );
(17)          FWriteReal( Celsius, 12, 2 );
(18)          Fahrenheit := Fahrenheit + 1.0;
(19)          IF Fahrenheit > High THEN
(20)             EXIT;
(21)          END;  (* IF *)
(22)       END;  (* LOOP *)
(23)    END Temperature.
```

Let's briefly review this short program. The overall structure follows directly from our pseudocode. Within the loop, line 14 is an assignment statement of the converted value to the variable Celsius. To compute the converted value, we use an *arithmetic expression*. In fact, whenever there is some numeric computation to do, we will use such an expression. To construct an arithmetic expression, we use variables, constants, arithmetic operators, function calls, and parentheses. In this particular case we have to translate into Modula-2 the algebraic formula

$$\frac{5(\text{Fahrenheit} - 32)}{9}$$

The characters in a single line of a program must all be on the same level. In other words, we cannot use subscripts, superscripts, or divisions that have the numerators and denominators on different levels. Therefore, we have to use a one-dimensional way of representing our arithmetic expressions. In Modula-2 our formula becomes

$$5.0 * (\text{Fahrenheit} - 32.0) / 9.0$$

Notice that we use * for multiplication, / for real division, and parentheses for grouping elements. Since we are dealing with numbers of type REAL, the constants must be of that type and have a fractional part (even if it is zero).

In Modula-2 and most other programming languages the arithmetic operations are normally performed from left to right. Multiplication and division, however, have a higher *precedence* than addition and subtraction and are done first. The use of parentheses makes it possible to change the order of the operations. In our case the expression 5.0 * Fahrenheit − 32.0 / 9.0 would not have worked since Fahrenheit would have been multiplied by 5.0 and then 32.0 divided by 9.0 would have been subtracted. The parentheses ensure that the subtraction is done before the multiplication and division.

The remainder of the program is straightforward. The testing of this program is quite simple: we only have to compile it and run it. Since there is no input data, we do not have to generate test data; we just have to examine the output data and check its accuracy with known values. The output will look something like

```
Fahrenheit    Celsius
 -30.00       -34.44
 -29.00       -33.89
 -28.00       -33.33
 -27.00       -32.78
 -26.00       -32.22
     .            .
     .            .
     .            .
```

The exact form of the displayed numbers is very dependent on the implementation of Modula-2, so your output may differ in its format from that displayed here. We have shown a format where real numbers can be printed in decimal notation, using the nonstandard output procedure FWriteReal. The standard output procedure for REAL values is WriteReal; however, your WriteReal routine might print in scientific notation, and your table might have entries like $-3.00000E1$. Consult Appendix E or your system documentation to find out how your system handles the printing of real numbers.

The REPEAT Statement

In the temperature conversion example we used the LOOP statement for repetition of a given set of statements. Notice that in this case the test for an exit condition is situated at the end of the loop. Like the WHILE circumstance, this situation happens quite often. As in the previous case, Modula-2 has another method of repetition—the *REPEAT statement*. The syntax of the REPEAT statement is

```
REPEAT
   statement;
   statement;
      .
      .
      .
UNTIL condition;
```

The exit condition is tested after the statements have been executed (they will therefore be executed at least once, which may not be the case for the WHILE statement). If the exit condition is false, the loop is repeated; if it is true, the loop is terminated. Figure 4.3 illustrates the REPEAT statement with a flow chart.

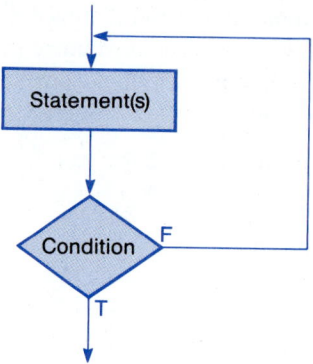

Figure 4.3
REPEAT Statement

We can use this new statement to revise the temperature conversion program. Note that this program is shorter than the version using LOOP.

```
MODULE Temperature;
(* Computation and printing of a conversion table for
   Fahrenheit and Celsius temperatures.
       P. Gabrini         January 1988 *)

FROM RealInOut IMPORT FWriteReal;
FROM InOut IMPORT WriteString, WriteLn;
CONST Low = -30.0;
      High = 120.0;
VAR Fahrenheit, Celsius: REAL;

BEGIN
  WriteString( "   Fahrenheit    Celsius" );
  Fahrenheit := Low;
  REPEAT
    Celsius := 5.0 * (Fahrenheit - 32.0) / 9.0;
    WriteLn;
    FWriteReal( Fahrenheit, 10, 2 );
    FWriteReal( Celsius, 12, 2 );
    Fahrenheit := Fahrenheit + 1.0;
  UNTIL Fahrenheit > High;
END Temperature.
```

A Comparative Summary of LOOP, WHILE, FOR, and REPEAT

In this section we have learned about four looping constructs: LOOP, WHILE, and REPEAT for indefinite iteration, and FOR for definite iteration. We can easily recognize situations where FOR is appropriate since it is well suited for definite iteration. The choice between the three alternatives for indefinite iteration, however, is not as simple.

As a final part of this discussion of iteration we'll do the same problem three ways, using these three kinds of indefinite iteration. This demonstration will serve to summarize our repetition statements and illustrate situations in which the LOOP statement gives a much more natural formulation than WHILE or REPEAT. The example will be a simple interactive program to display equilateral triangles whose size is specified by the user. For our comparison, we are interested only in the repetition of prompting the user, reading the input value, and calling a procedure DrawTriangle. We will assume DrawTriangle requires a single cardinal parameter that determines the size. This procedure might draw a graphical triangle or a triangle of asterisks, depending on the graphics capabilities of your computer system. The version of the statements in the main program using a LOOP statement is

```
LOOP
  WriteString( "Enter the size of the triangle or zero to stop: " );
  ReadCard( Size ); WriteLn;
  IF Size = 0 THEN
    EXIT;
  END; (* IF *);
  DrawTriangle( Size );
END; (* LOOP *)
```

Using a WHILE statement, we arrive at the program segment

```
WriteString( "Enter the size of the triangle or zero to stop: " );
ReadCard( Size ); WriteLn;
WHILE Size # 0 DO
  DrawTriangle( Size );
  WriteString( "Enter the size of the triangle or zero to stop: " );
  ReadCard( Size ); WriteLn;
END; (* WHILE *)
```

Notice that three of the statements before the body of the WHILE loop are repeated at the bottom of the loop, making this version a bit more redundant than the previous version. However, the body of the loop is somewhat simpler from a flow-of-control standpoint.

Using a REPEAT statement produces the program segment

```
REPEAT
  WriteString( "Enter the size of the triangle or zero to stop: " );
  ReadCard( Size ); WriteLn;
  IF Size # 0 THEN
    DrawTriangle( Size );
  END; (* IF *)
UNTIL Size = 0;
```

This version has no redundant statements, but the body of the loop is a bit more complex, and there is a redundant test on the value of Size.

TABLE 4.1 Iterative Statements

	Number of Exit Tests	Location of Test(s)	Nature of Test(s)
WHILE	one	at beginning	exit when condition is false
REPEAT	one	at end	exit when condition is true
LOOP	as many as desired	anywhere in body	exit when condition is true
FOR	one	at beginning	exit when control variable exceeds the final value

The three versions just shown illustrate the differences in the LOOP, WHILE, and REPEAT statements. The LOOP statement is the most general and subsumes the other two, but in many instances the simpler WHILE and REPEAT forms will be quite natural. Details of the differences among the three statements can be identified by considering three basic characteristics of loops:

1. number of exit tests
2. location of the test or tests in the loop
3. nature of test or tests (that is, exit on true or on false)

The characteristics of each statement are given in Table 4.1. We assume that exits from a LOOP statement are controlled by an IF statement, as shown in our examples. For completeness, we have also included the FOR statement; however, as we've made clear, the choice of using the FOR statement is based on whether the problem is one of definite iteration.

Notice that the location of exit tests determines the minimum number of iterations that may occur when a loop is executed. If the test is at the end (REPEAT), the body of the loop is executed at least once. If the test is at the beginning (WHILE, FOR), the body of the loop may not be executed even once. This characteristic is an essential difference between the WHILE and REPEAT statements. We cannot make a general comment about the minimum number of iterations of a LOOP statement, since exit tests can occur anywhere within the loop body.

4.2 Simple Selection

As we said in Chapter 1, selection is the choice between alternatives. Earlier in this chapter we used the *IF statement* in a simple way to control the execution of an EXIT in the body of a LOOP. Now we will discuss the IF in a more general way. A simplified form of the syntax of the IF statement is

```
IF condition THEN
   statements
[ELSE
   statements]
END;
```

SEC. 4.2 Simple Selection

where IF, THEN, ELSE, and END are reserved words, and the square brackets indicate that the ELSE part is optional. An IF with the ELSE part omitted is called a one-branch IF statement since the selection is either to execute a sequence of statements or to skip them. An IF with an ELSE part is called a two-branch IF because the selection is between two possible sequences of statements. We'll look at each of these types of IF statements in turn.

One-Branch IF Statement

Let's return to our temperature conversion program. Maintenance of that program might involve its modification to produce more compact output. We will print three pairs of values on the same line so that the complete output of the program can be displayed on one screen or page. To distinguish the values, we put an F after each Fahrenheit temperature and a C after each Celsius temperature. The desired output is shown here.

```
Fahrenheit-Celsius conversion table

-30.00F    -34.44C    -29.00F    -33.89C    -28.00F    -33.33C
-27.00F    -32.78C    -26.00F    -32.22C    -25.00F    -31.67C
   .          .          .          .          .          .
   .          .          .          .          .          .
   .          .          .          .          .          .
```

An easy way of obtaining this compact form would be to use a variable as a counter, enabling us to print three pairs of values on each line. The counter will have to start at zero and be incremented each time we compute a new value. After printing a pair of values, we should check if the counter has reached three. If it has, we should end the current line and reset the counter to zero. In order to do that, we will use a simple form of the If pseudocode statement introduced in Chapter 1. Our pseudocode solution then becomes

> Temperature
>   Set Fahrenheit to -30
>   Set Counter to 0
>   Repeat
>   Set Celsius to 5(Fahrenheit $-$ 32) / 9
>   Print Fahrenheit, Celsius
>   Increment Counter by 1
>   If Counter $=$ 3 then
>   Advance to next line
>   Set Counter to 0
>   End if
>   Increment Fahrenheit by 1
>   Until Fahrenheit $>$ 120
> End Temperature

TABLE 4.2 Math Notation and Modula-2 Notation

Math Notation	Modula-2 Notation
=	=
≠	#
<	<
≤	<=
>	>
≥	>=

Notice the way the simple If statement operates: if the condition is true, the instructions between the If and corresponding End are executed; otherwise, they are just skipped. This statement will be translated into a simple Modula-2 IF statement whose syntax is

```
IF condition THEN
   statement;
   statement;
      .
      .
      .
END;
```

The statements following THEN will be executed only when the condition is true; otherwise, they will be skipped. For now, all our conditions will be simple comparisons, but the notation for the comparisons is somewhat different from the usual mathematical notation (see Table 4.2). In later chapters we will explain how to formulate more complex conditions.

Figure 4.4 illustrates this simple IF statement with a flow chart.

Translating our pseudocode into Modula-2, we have

```
(1)    MODULE Temperature;
(2)    (* Computation and printing of a conversion table for
(3)        Fahrenheit and Celsius temperatures.
(4)            P. Gabrini            January 1988 *)
```

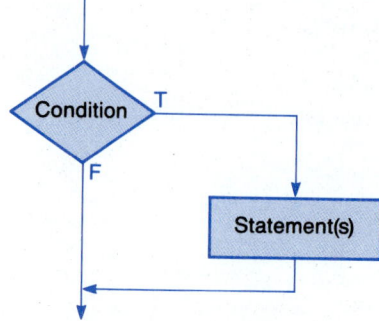

Figure 4.4
One-Branch IF Statement

Simple Selection

```
(5)     FROM InOut IMPORT WriteString, WriteLn;
(6)     FROM RealInOut IMPORT FWriteReal;

(7)     CONST Low = -30.0;
(8)           High = 120.0;
(9)           Title = "Fahrenheit-Celsius conversion table";

(10)    VAR Fahrenheit, Celsius: REAL;
(11)        Counter: CARDINAL;

(12)    BEGIN
(13)       WriteString(Title); WriteLn; WriteLn;
(14)       Counter := 0;
(15)       Fahrenheit := Low;
(16)       REPEAT
(17)          Celsius := 5.0 * (Fahrenheit - 32.0) / 9.0;
(18)          FWriteReal(Fahrenheit, 8, 2); WriteString("F ");
(19)          FWriteReal(Celsius, 8, 2); WriteString("C    ");
(20)          Counter := Counter + 1;
(21)          IF Counter = 3 THEN
(22)             WriteLn;
(23)             Counter := 0;
(24)          END;   (* IF *)
(25)          Fahrenheit := Fahrenheit + 1.0;
(26)       UNTIL Fahrenheit > High;
(27)       WriteLn;
(28)    END Temperature.
```

This new version of our program is similar to the previous one, but let's consider the differences. Line 9 defines a new constant Title, which is a character string. Line 11 declares a new variable, which we named Counter, whose type is CARDINAL. Line 13 prints a title for our output, using the character string constant previously defined. Line 14 gives a zero initial value to Counter. Line 18 outputs the value of Fahrenheit in eight columns with two decimals, followed by two characters, F and a space. Line 19 outputs the value of Celsius in eight columns with two decimals, followed by five characters, the letter C, and four spaces so that the next pair does not begin too close to this pair. Line 20 increments the value of Counter by one. Lines 21 through 24 constitute a one-branch IF statement in which the value of Counter is tested. If it equals three, the condition is true and lines 22 and 23 are executed; line 22 terminates the current line of output; and line 23 resets Counter to zero. If the value of Counter is not three, the condition on line 21 is false and we skip to line 25, the next statement after the end of the IF statement. We have also added line 27, which terminates the last line of the table.

Two-Branch IF Statement

The two-branch IF statement may be viewed as a more general form of the one-branch IF; it selects one of two groups of statements for execution rather than controlling the execution of only one group of statements. Suppose we want to perform a division operation where we have no prior assurance that the divisor is nonzero (this is often the case when the divisor is the result of a calculation). Attempting to perform a division by zero on the computer will produce a run time error—that is, the program will be terminated and an error message will be displayed. To avoid this problem, we will use a two-branch IF statement. In pseudocode we have

> If Divisor = 0 then
>   print warning message
> Else
>   print result of division
> End if

When we translate this pseudocode into a Modula-2 program, we will use a two-branch IF statement whose syntax is

```
IF condition THEN
   statement-sequence-1
ELSE
   statement-sequence-2
END;
```

When the condition is true, statement-sequence-1 is executed and statement-sequence-2 is skipped. When the condition is false, statement-sequence-1 is skipped and statement-sequence-2 is executed. Figure 4.5 illustrates this kind of IF statement.

Using the two-branch IF statement, we arrive at the following code:

```
IF Divisor = 0 THEN
   WriteString( "The divisor was zero." );
ELSE
   WriteString( "The quotient is " );
   WriteReal( Dividend / Divisor, 8 );
END;  (* IF *)
```

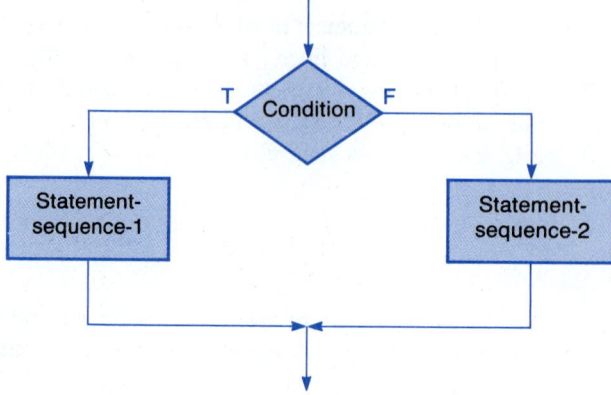

Figure 4.5
A Two-Branch IF Statement

The two preceding sections have described how simple Modula-2 iterative and selection control structures solve simple problems. When these control structures are combined, however, they can solve problems of greater complexity. In the next section we'll explore some of the possibilities of these combinations.

4.3 Using and Debugging Nested Control Structures

In some of the examples offered thus far we've seen that a LOOP statement may contain an IF statement. That is, control structures may be enclosed within other control structures. Such combinations are called *nested control structures*.

The following section looks at three examples of nesting: nested IFs, IFs nested within a loop, and nested loops. We also describe debugging methods because, with increased complexity, comes a greater potential for error.

Nested IFs

Suppose you want to write a procedure that prints "solid", "liquid", or "gas" depending on the melting point and boiling point of a particular substance. In addition to these limits, you would also need to know the current temperature. The pseudocode solution is very simple:

```
PrintState
    If temperature < melting point then
        Print "solid"
    Else
        If temperature > boiling point then
            Print "gas"
        Else
            Print "liquid"
        End if
    End if
End PrintState
```

Notice that we are choosing between three alternatives. If the first alternative (solid) is not true, we must still choose between the remaining alternatives (liquid or gas). The following Modula-2 procedure uses value parameters for argument transmission.

```
PROCEDURE PrintState( MP, BP, Temp: REAL );
(* Print solid, liquid or gas based on the value of Temp in
   relation to the melting point, MP, and boiling point, BP. *)

BEGIN
  IF Temp < MP THEN
    WriteString( "solid" );
```

```
    ELSE
      IF Temp > BP THEN
        WriteString( "gas" );
      ELSE
        WriteString( "liquid" );
      END;    (* IF *)
    END;    (* IF *)
END PrintState;
```

In the next chapter we will study other techniques for selection that will allow us to choose between multiple alternatives.

Nesting IFs within a Loop

Although we have already seen several examples of an IF statement used for exiting a loop, we will consider one more example here. Consider a program segment that calculates the total pay for a worker based on the number of hours worked each day. The worker should receive overtime (one and a half times the normal pay rate) for all time exceeding eight hours a day. The program will read data interactively until a negative value is entered to signal the end of data input. The program should then print the total hours worked and the total pay. The pseudocode solution would be as follows:

> Calculate Pay
>   Set Pay to zero
>   Set Total Hours to zero
>   Loop
>   Read Hours Worked
>   If Hours Worked is negative then
>   Exit
>   End if
>   Add Hours Worked to the Total Hours
>   If Hours Worked is greater than eight then
>   Add 8.0 * Pay Rate + 1.5 * (Hours Worked − 8.0) * Pay Rate
>   to Pay
>   Else
>   Add Hours Worked * Pay Rate to Pay
>   End if
>   End loop
>   Print "total hours worked: ", Total Hours
>   Print "pay earned: ", Pay
> End Calculate Pay

Notice that two If statements, which are not nested, are contained within the loop. The first If controls the exit condition, while the second If controls the pay calculation depending on the number of hours worked each day. The student is encouraged to write this program segment in Modula-2.

Nested Loops

Loops contained within another loop are known as *nested loops*. Nested loops are important in problems dealing with several variables or in problems dealing with arrays, which are discussed in Chapter 9. We start our examination of nested loops by tracing some given program segments. Consider the loops

```
FOR i := 1 TO m DO
   FOR j := 1 TO n DO
      Write( '.' );
   END;   (* FOR *)
END;   (* FOR *)
```

How many dots will be printed? The inner loop prints n dots each time it completes execution. The outer loop executes exactly m times, each time causing the inner loop to execute n times, and thus printing n dots. Therefore, a total of mn dots will be printed. A more challenging question is, how many dots are printed before each Write statement in the inner loop? The outer loop has been completed exactly $i - 1$ times, so the number of dots due to completion of the outer loop is $n(i - 1)$. The inner loop will have executed exactly $j - 1$ times for the current iteration of the outer loop, so the total number of dots printed so far will be $n(i - 1) + j - 1$. We will add this fact as a comment in our program listing.

```
FOR i := 1 TO m DO
   FOR j := 1 TO n DO
      (*   n(i - 1) + j - 1 dots have been printed   *)
      Write( '.' );
   END;   (* FOR *)
END;   (* FOR *)
```

The comment on the third line is an assertion about the number of dots that have been printed whenever execution reaches the point in the program where the assertion is located. Such an assertion, often called a *loop invariant*, is very useful because it precisely describes the action of the loop or nested loops in which it appears.

Let's look at a slightly more difficult example of nested loops and see if we can find the loop invariant.

```
FOR i := 1 TO m DO
   FOR j := 1 TO i DO
      (* loop invariant goes here *)
      Write( '.' );
   END;   (* FOR *)
END;   (* FOR *)
```

In this case the number of iterations for the inner loop is dependent on the value of i from the outer loop. The first time the inner loop completes execution it prints one dot, the second time two dots, and so forth. By the time the ith iteration is ready to begin, the number of dots printed due to the outer loop is

$$1 + 2 + \cdots + i - 1 = (i - 1)\,i\,/\,2$$

using the result stated in Chapter 1. If the inner loop is starting the jth iteration, then it has printed j − 1 dots for the current iteration of the outer loop. Therefore the loop invariant is

(*   (i − 1) i / 2 + j − 1   dots have been printed   *)

A Procedure with Nested Control Structures

Suppose we want to write a procedure that will print out a multiplication table from 0 to a specified Size. For example, if Size is 5, the procedure will print

X	0	1	2	3	4	5
0	0	0	0	0	0	0
1	0	1	2	3	4	5
2	0	2	4	6	8	10
3	0	3	6	9	12	15
4	0	4	8	12	16	20
5	0	5	10	15	20	25

Due to space limitation on a page, we will not allow Size to exceed 12. Our initial pseudocode is quite simple:

> MultiplicationTable
>   If Size > 12 then
>   Print "Table too large"
>   Else
>   Print the multiplication table
>   End if
> End MultiplicationTable

Now we must figure out how to print the multiplication table itself. We see that the top row and line of dashes must be done separately. The entries in the top row depend on the size of the table, so we will use a For loop to print these values.

SEC. 4.3   *Using and Debugging Nested Control Structures*   99

> MultiplicationTable
>   If Size > 12 then
>   Print "Table too large"
>   Else
>   Print " X |"
>   For Count from 0 to Size do
>   Print Count
>   End for
>   Print line of dashes
>   Print the body of the table
>   End if
> End MultiplicationTable

The body of the table is a sequence of rows to be printed. Multiplication involves a left-hand operand times a right-hand operand, such as 2 * 3. We will assume the left-hand operand, 2 in this example, is the vertical index to the table (row number) and the right-hand operand, 3 in this example, is the horizontal index to the table (column number). We have already printed the right-hand operand index. Each row of the table body includes the left-hand operand, a vertical bar, and a sequence of products.

The next refinement of our pseudocode solution is

> MultiplicationTable
>   If Size > 12 then
>   Print "Table too large"
>   Else
>   Print " X |"
>   For Count from 0 to Size do
>   Print Count
>   End for
>   Print line of dashes
>   For LeftOperand from 0 to Size do
>   Print LeftOperand and vertical bar
>   Print sequence of products
>   End for
>   End if
> End MultiplicationTable

To complete our algorithm, we must specify how the sequence of products is printed. Suppose that our table is of Size 5 and we wish to print the products associated with the left-hand operand of 3. This sequence of products is

$$3 * 0 \quad 3 * 1 \quad 3 * 2 \quad 3 * 3 \quad 3 * 4 \quad 3 * 5$$

We can express this sequence as the left-hand operand times the right-hand operand, where we let the right-hand operand range from 0 to Size. As seen in our final pseudocode version, this expression is easily done with a nested For loop.

> MultiplicationTable
>   If Size > 12 then
>   Print "Table too large"
>   Else
>   Print " X |"
>   For Count from 0 to Size do
>   Print Count
>   End for
>   Print line of dashes
>   For LeftOperand from 0 to Size do
>   Print LeftOperand and vertical bar
>   For RightOperand from 0 to Size do
>   Print LeftOperand * RightOperand
>   End for
>   End for
>   End if
> End MultiplicationTable

Our algorithm is fairly complete. The only item left unspecified is how to print the line of dashes. Since the length of this line depends on the size of the table, we will use another For loop to print the appropriate number of dashes, as shown in the following Modula-2 solution:

```
PROCEDURE MultiplicationTable (Size: CARDINAL);
(* Print multiplication table of specified size *)
VAR Count, LeftOperand, RightOperand: CARDINAL;

BEGIN
  IF Size > 12 THEN
    WriteString("Table too large to print."); WriteLn;
  ELSE
    WriteString("  X   |");
    FOR Count := 0 TO Size DO
      WriteCard(Count, 5);
    END; (* FOR *)
    WriteLn; WriteString("------");
    FOR Count := 0 TO Size DO
      WriteString("-----");
    END; (* FOR *)
    WriteLn;
```

```
          FOR LeftOperand := 0 TO Size DO
            WriteCard(LeftOperand, 4); WriteString("  |");
            FOR RightOperand := 0 TO Size DO
              WriteCard(LeftOperand * RightOperand, 5);
            END;    (* FOR *)
            WriteLn;
          END;    (* FOR *)
          WriteLn; WriteLn;
        END;    (* IF *)
      END MultiplicationTable;
```

When we examine this procedure, we see that it was easy to develop in a stepwise fashion, but the resultant structure is fairly complex. The basic control structures are

```
          IF condition THEN
             statements
          ELSE
             FOR statement
             FOR statement
             FOR statement
                FOR statement
```

In this procedure the control structures are nested three levels deep. If a procedure becomes much more complex, the programmer should consider further decomposition by using nested procedures.

Debugging Nested Control Structures

The design of nested control structures must be done carefully. But even with such care, once an algorithm is designed and implemented, it sometimes does not work as the programmer intended. In this section we will first discuss how such "bugs" can be avoided, and then how they can be detected and corrected if they do occur.

The primary way to avoid bugs is by meticulous design, using a variety of techniques to assist in the design process. Stepwise refinement using pseudocode is a useful technique. Developing a loop invariant along with the statements in a loop is another, and we will illustrate this technique in greater detail in later chapters. In Chapter 6 you will learn two techniques—decision trees and decision tables—for designing complex IF statements, possibly involving nesting.

After careful design, algorithms should be "desk checked," using sample data to ensure that the results are correct. Data should include typical values, limiting cases, and abnormal values. If an algorithm's control structure becomes too complex, it should be modularized into simpler pieces. In this way, each piece can be checked individually before being integrated into the complete algorithm.

In spite of a programmer's best effort to avoid bugs, they often do show up once the initial implementation is completed and testing has begun. The first step in debugging is to try to isolate the error to a small segment of code. The test case that gave rise to the error can be "desk checked" on the suspect program segment; this review will often indicate the source of the error. If the design was sound but the code did not faithfully implement the design, the error can often be corrected by rewriting the code. If the design was unsound, you will have to "go back to the drawing board" and redesign a portion of the program. If your program has good modular structure, the portion that must be redesigned will probably be small.

To isolate an error, you may want to insert write statements to indicate the flow of program execution. If this technique does not reveal the problem, these write statements can be modified to print out the values of variables. It is particularly helpful to print out those variables involved in conditions that occur in IF statements or loops. You will often find that the desired alternative was not selected or that a loop executes fewer times than expected or more times than expected. Debugging is a talent that you will develop with experience, but debugging will always be much easier if a program has been well designed.

SUMMARY

Often our problem solution calls for us to do repetitive tasks or to choose between alternative courses of action. The statements that enable us to change the order of program execution are called control structures. The two main classes of control structures in languages like Modula-2 are iteration and selection.

The basic iterative statement is the LOOP, which causes a group of statements to be executed repetitively. The syntax of a LOOP statement is

```
LOOP
   statements;
END;
```

The EXIT statement causes the loop to terminate. An IF statement usually controls the execution of the EXIT statement.

The WHILE statement is a shorter way of writing loops where the test for iteration is at the beginning. The WHILE syntax is

```
WHILE condition DO
   statements;
END;
```

The FOR control structure is commonly used if the number of iterations is known when the loop is entered. The syntax is

```
FOR identifier := expression TO expression [BY constant expression] DO
   statements;
END;
```

The FOR loop automatically initializes, increments, and tests the loop control variable. The test is done at the beginning of the loop.

When the test for an exit condition is at the end of the loop, the iterative control structure REPEAT may be used. The syntax for a REPEAT statement is

```
            REPEAT
              statements;
            UNTIL condition;
```

The REPEAT statement is exited when the condition is true.

Selection is the choice between alternatives. It is implemented with the IF statement. Its syntax is

```
            IF condition THEN
              statement-sequence-1
            [ELSE
              statement-sequence-2]
            END;
```

If the condition is true, then statement-sequence-1 is executed; otherwise, statement-sequence-2 is executed, if the ELSE part is present.

Nested control structures are control structures enclosed within other control structures. They may include nested IFs, IFs nested within a loop, and nested loops. Such structures must be carefully designed, using stepwise refinement, loop invariants, and desk-checking to avoid bugs in the final program.

As we have stated previously, skill with these aspects of Modula-2 comes with using them, so experiment with them as much as you can.

EXERCISES

1. How many line segments are drawn by the Mystery program?
2. Draw flow charts for the three versions of the loop to display triangles in the section entitled "A Comparative Summary of LOOP, WHILE, FOR, and REPEAT."
3. Write the statements that will read two numerical values and print them in ascending order.

4. Modify the statements in Exercise 3 so that the statements read in pairs of integers and print out each pair in ascending order. Indicate the end of data by a pair of zeroes.

5. Write an IF statement to assign to Largest the greatest value of A, B, or C.

6. Rewrite the following sequence of statements using the ELSE option:

```
IF D >= 62 THEN WriteString( "Possible") END (*IF*);
IF D < 20 THEN WriteString( "Too young" ) END (*IF*);
IF (20 <= D) AND (D < 62) THEN WriteString( "Not possible yet" ) END (*IF*);
```

7. What is printed by the following program segment:

```
Z := 83;
WHILE Z > 10 DO
   Z := Z - 9;
END;   (* WHILE *)
WriteCard( Z, 5 );
```

8. Rewrite the program segment in Exercise 7 using a FOR loop.

9. Write the statements necessary to count the number of occurrences of the letter *e* in a line of text entered by the user.

10. Modify the statements in Exercise 9 to allow the user to specify the character to be counted.

11. Write the statements that will print all odd integers between 0 and 50.

12. Modify the temperature conversion program so that it will convert Celsius temperatures to Fahrenheit temperatures.

13. How many dots will be printed by

```
FOR i := 0 TO 5 DO
   FOR j := 1 TO 8 DO
      FOR k := 2 TO 4 DO
         { loop invariant goes here }
         Write( '.' );
      END; (* FOR *)
   END; (* FOR *)
END; (* FOR *)
```

Find the loop invariant for these nested loops.

14. How many dots will be printed by

```
FOR i := 1 TO 2 DO
   FOR j := 2 TO 5 DO
      FOR k := i TO j DO
         { loop invariant goes here }
         Write( '.' );
      END; (* FOR *)
   END; (* FOR *)
END; (* FOR *)
```

Find the loop invariant for these nested loops.

PROGRAMMING PROBLEMS

15. Use the pseudocode solution in Chapter 1 to write a procedure ProcessLine to count the number of words in a line of text. Write an interactive test program for this procedure. Your program should prompt the user for data, process this data, and then display the results.

16. Make the Mystery program into a procedure with two parameters—one for the turning angle and one for the increment added to L. Embed the procedure in an interactive program that allows you to enter the angle and the increment as input.

17. Write a function that is passed two integer parameters, Min and Max, and returns the sum of all integers between (and including) Min and Max. If Max is less than Min, the functions should return zero. Also write an interactive program to test this function.

18. Write a Modula-2 program to read in integers, count the number of positive values and the number of negative values, and stop and print the counts when a zero value is read.

19. Write a Modula-2 program to find and print the smallest positive integer whose square is greater than 10,000.

20. Write and test a procedure to draw a polygon approximation to a circle, using polygon side lengths specified by the user.

21. Write and test a procedure to draw an approximation of a circle whose radius is specified by the user.

22. Write an interactive program where the user specifies the amount of sale and the amount paid and where the program returns the change received. To keep it simple, assume the change is always less than $1.00. The program should print the number of quarters, dimes, nickels, and pennies received. Amounts should be entered as integers for the number of cents. For example, 186 would represent $1.86.

23. Since multiplication is commutative, we can construct an abbreviated multiplication table of the form

0	1	2	3	4	5	X
0	0	0	0	0	0	0
	1	2	3	4	5	1
		4	6	8	10	2
			9	12	15	3
				16	20	4
					25	5

Write a procedure that will print a multiplication table in this form for a size ≤ 12. Also write a test program to make sure your procedure works correctly.

5 Recursion and Multiple Selection

To iterate is human, to recurse divine. L. PETER DEUTCH

In this chapter you will:

- learn about recursion, a powerful problem-solving technique
- practice with several examples to see how recursive algorithms can be translated into Modula-2 programs
- be introduced to two control structures, called ELSIF and CASE, that allow selections between several alternatives

In earlier chapters, when we've described general approaches to problem solving, we've referred several times to the "divide and conquer" strategy. According to this method, if we can divide the original problem into various subproblems, then we can use solutions to the subproblems to solve the original problem. Sometimes, however, the subproblems that we must solve are actually just simpler versions of the original problem. When this situation arises, we can use a special case of the divide and conquer strategy, called recursion, to implement a simple, elegant solution. This chapter explains how recursion works. We look at three examples of recursive algorithms and also a recursive solution to a well-known puzzle.

In the latter half of the chapter, we discuss more control structures for selection between alternatives. As we've seen, the IF statement enables us to choose between two alternatives, but on some occasions a problem calls for us to select between *more* than two alternatives. Chapter 4 demonstrated how a nested IF could accomplish this task. Here we'll learn about two other techniques: the ELSIF option for the IF statement and the CASE statement. These techniques are sometimes useful for expressing recursive algorithms.

5.1 Recursion

The problem-solving technique of reducing a problem to several simpler subproblems has a special case that occurs fairly often. If the subproblems are just smaller versions of the original problem, the problem can be solved by a method known as *recursion*. This technique allows us to concentrate on the problem at hand—without having to consider a number of diverse special cases, or details not directly related to the problem being solved. Solving a problem by recursion involves working on reduced versions of the same problem and leads to elegant solutions.

Since recursion is based on solving the original problem by solving smaller versions of the same problem, we must eventually reach a smallest version, called the *base case*, that can be solved directly. In general, we can express this recursive approach in pseudocode as follows:

> If the problem is a base case then
>   solve the base case directly
> Else
>   solve the general case using solution(s) of simpler case(s)
> End if

This strategy will be illustrated in the following examples. In later chapters we will use recursive algorithms to solve more complex problems.

EXAMPLE 1 *A Recursive Numerical Algorithm*

Consider the problem of finding the factorial of a nonnegative integer. A common mathematical definition of factorial is

$$0! = 1$$
$$n! = n(n - 1)! \text{ for } n > 0$$

or in functional notation

$$f(0) = 1$$
$$f(n) = n f(n - 1) \text{ for } n > 0$$

So, for cardinals greater than zero, the problem of computing the factorial is reduced to the problem of finding the factorial of a smaller number and then doing a multiplication. Since 0! is defined as 1, this problem reduction process is guaranteed to stop. Recursive definitions should *always* include a base case; otherwise, they would not represent a finite process and, consequently, could not be classified as algorithms.

A Modula-2 procedure to compute factorials can be implemented directly from the functional definition just given.

```
PROCEDURE Factorial( K: CARDINAL ): CARDINAL;
(* Recursive computation of K! *)
BEGIN
  IF K = 0 THEN
    RETURN 1;
  ELSE
    RETURN K * Factorial( K - 1 );
  END;    (* IF *)
END Factorial;
```

Notice that Factorial calls itself. This is perfectly acceptable; such procedures are said to be recursive, and the calls are said to be recursive calls. However, a recursive procedure should also have a base case to prevent an infinite sequence of recursive calls. The base case for Factorial is for K = 0.

This example illustrates the ease of translating a recursive mathematical definition into a program in a language that supports recursion. Since computing a factorial involves only a sequence of multiplications, the factorial procedure could also be coded using a simple loop. However, many problems cannot be solved conveniently by iterative methods. These problems usually require the solution of more than one subproblem that is a smaller version of the original problem.

EXAMPLE 2 A Recursive String Algorithm

As another illustration of simple recursion, let's look at a nonnumerical example. We wish to write a procedure that will reverse the characters in a string. For example, the procedure would transform the string "recursion" into the string "noisrucer." Let us first develop a slightly simpler algorithm to print the characters in a string in reverse order. If the string is empty, we do nothing; this is our base case. Otherwise, we print the last character and then print the remaining characters of the string in reverse order. In pseudocode our algorithm is

```
Print In Reverse
   If Length( S ) = 0 then
      { do nothing }
   Else
      Print the last character of S
      Print In Reverse the remaining characters of S
   End if
End Print In Reverse
```

Recursion

Since we do nothing for the base case, we can write our algorithm in a slightly simpler form:

> Print In Reverse
>   If Length(S) > 0 then
>   Print the last character of S
>   Print In Reverse the remaining characters of S
>   End if
> End Print In Reverse

We will use the procedure Delete from the Strings module to form the string consisting of "the remaining characters of S." The following recursive procedure implements this pseudocode algorithm:

```
PROCEDURE PrintInReverse ( S: STRING );
BEGIN
  IF Length( S ) > 0 THEN
    Write( FetchChar( S, Length( S ) - 1) );
    Delete( S, Length( S ) - 1, 1 );
    PrintInReverse( S );
  END;   (* IF *)
END PrintInReverse;
```

The Write statement after THEN prints the last character of S by utilizing the function FetchChar. Write is a procedure in the module InOut. FetchChar is a function in the Strings module that returns a specific character of a string given as the first argument to the function. The second argument of FetchChar gives the position of the character to be returned.

This solution to the simpler problem of printing a string in reverse order suggests a strategy that we can use to solve our original problem of reversing a string. First, observe that if the string is empty or has only one character, there is nothing to be done. That is the base case. But in general, the string will have more than one character. Then we notice that if all the characters but the last could be reversed, we could simply put the last character in front and we would be done.

Consider the following simple example:

given	"abcd"		
split off last character	"abc"	"d"	
reverse the initial string	"cba"	"d"	(* recursive step *)
put last character in front	"d"	"cba"	
and concatenate	"dcba"		

This is a classical example of recursion, since we have reduced the problem to a smaller version of the original problem (reverse the initial part of the original string). We use pseudocode to formalize a recursive definition of reversing a string, S, as follows:

> Reverse String
>   If Length(S) > 1 then
>   Split S into its initial string and last character
>   Reverse the initial string
>   Concatenate last character to beginning of initial string
>   End if
> End Reverse String

The following procedure is based on this pseudocode:

```
PROCEDURE Reverse( VAR S: STRING );
(* Reverse the characters in S *)
VAR Head, Tail: STRING;
BEGIN
  IF Length( S ) > 1 THEN
    (* Assign initial string to Head *)
    Copy( S, 0, Length( S ) - 1, Head );
    (* Assign last character to Tail *)
    Copy( S, Length( S ) - 1, 1, Tail );
    Reverse( Head );
    Concat( Tail, Head, S );
  END; (* IF *)
END Reverse;
```

Consistent with the recursive pseudocode, the base case for this recursive procedure is when the length of the string parameter is less than or equal to one. In that case the procedure does nothing and simply returns the string unchanged. In the general case the string is split into the Head (the string minus the last character) and the Tail (the last character). Head is reversed by a recursive call to Reverse. Then Tail is concatenated with the reversed Head to return the result by means of the VAR parameter S.

EXAMPLE 3 *Another Recursive Numerical Algorithm*

Suppose you are asked to write a numerical algorithm to find a number raised to a cardinal power. For instance, 2 raised to the fifth power is 32, 3 raised to the third power is 27, and so forth. We will not allow negative powers. If we want to raise a number (call it Base) to a specified power (call it Exponent), then an obvious way to solve this problem iteratively is to use a For loop, as indicated in the pseudocode

```
Set Result to 1
For Count from 1 to Exponent
    Set Result to Result times Base
End for
```

The number of multiplications required by this iterative solution is the value of Exponent. Using recursion, we can easily find a more efficient algorithm. We might first observe that

$$\text{Base}^{\text{Exponent}} = \text{Base}^{(\text{Exponent} - 1)} * \text{Base}$$

and the simplest case is

$$\text{Base}^0 = 1$$

Such a recursive definition can easily be translated into a recursive algorithm:

```
Power ( Base, Exponent )
    If Exponent = 0 then
        Return 1
    Else
        Return Power( Base, Exponent − 1 ) * Base
    End if
End Power
```

This recursive algorithm will work as intended, but it is not very efficient since it will end up performing the same number of multiplications as our iterative solution. One reason is that the subproblem is almost as large as the original problem. We should try to find a solution where the subproblems are much smaller than the original problem.

Let's examine our problem again using some specific data. Suppose we want to find 2 raised to the eighth power. Our initial recursive algorithm solved this problem as

$$2^8 = 2^7 * 2$$

We could create smaller subproblems using the approach

$$2^8 = 2^4 * 2^4$$

For an odd exponent, we would modify this approach slightly:

$$2^9 = 2^4 * 2^4 * 2$$

When we apply this method, our pseudocode algorithm becomes

```
Power( Base, Exponent )
  If Exponent = 0 then
    Return 1
  Else
    Set PartialResult to Power( Base, Exponent div 2 )
    If Exponent is odd then
      Return PartialResult * PartialResult * Base
    Else
      Return PartialResult * PartialResult
    End if
  End if
End Power
```

The Modula-2 code follows directly.

```
PROCEDURE Power( Base, Exponent: CARDINAL ) : CARDINAL;
VAR PartialResult: CARDINAL;
BEGIN (* Power *)
  IF Exponent = 0 THEN
    RETURN 1
  ELSE
    PartialResult := Power( Base, Exponent DIV 2 );
    IF ODD( Exponent ) THEN
      RETURN PartialResult * PartialResult * Base;
    ELSE
      RETURN PartialResult * PartialResult;
    END; (* IF *)
  END; (* IF *)
END Power;
```

Efficiency of Recursive Algorithms

Let's compare our two approaches to raising a base to a given power. Consider raising 2 to the 35th power. Our initial recursive algorithm would require 35 recursive calls and hence 35 multiplications. How many calls and multiplications are required for the second version of our algorithm? Table 5.1 shows these values.

TABLE 5.1 Calls and Multiplications Using the Second Recursive Algorithm for Power

Base	Exponent	Number of Calls	Number of Multiplications
2	35	1	2
2	17	1	2
2	8	1	1
2	4	1	1
2	2	1	1
2	1	1	2

As you can see, our second approach requires only six recursive calls and nine multiplications—a significant improvement! In general, to find a number raised to the Nth power, we will need log N recursive calls, where log is the base 2 logarithm. It obviously pays to make the subproblems as small as possible.

With efficiency in mind, let's reconsider the string reversal algorithm. You may have noted that the algorithm required one recursive call for each character in the string. This approach can be simplified significantly by dividing the subproblems into approximately equal size. The solution is left for the student as Programming Problem 24 at the end of this chapter.

EXAMPLE 4 The Towers of Hanoi—A Recursive Puzzle

So far our examples of recursive algorithms have required only one recursive call. Many algorithms require more than one recursive call, and we'll now discuss such an algorithm.

The Towers of Hanoi is an interesting puzzle. Imagine three towers (or pegs) and a set of disks of increasing size that can be slid onto the pegs. The initial puzzle position for three disks is shown in Figure 5.1. The goal of the puzzle is to move all the disks from the peg labeled A to the peg labeled C. Sounds simple enough, but you must accomplish this goal within two constraints: you may move only one disk at a time, and you can never place a larger disk on top of a smaller disk.

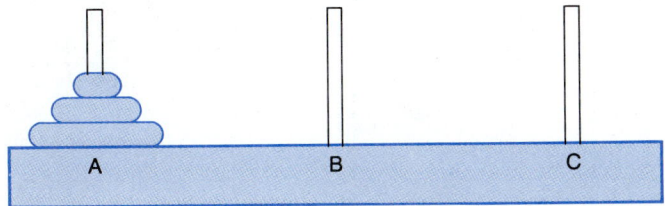

Figure 5.1
Towers of Hanoi: Starting Position

We can solve the three-disk problem if we make the recursive assumption that we know the solution to the two-disk problem. First, we use the recursive step to move the two smallest disks from peg A to peg B (see Figure 5.2). Next we move the largest disk from peg A to peg C (see Figure 5.3). We then use recursion again to move the two smallest disks from peg B to peg C (see Figure 5.4).

Our base case is when there is just one disk to move; we solve this by moving this single disk from the starting peg to the destination peg. Our recursive algorithm can be expressed as

> Hanoi (N, Start, Intermediate, Destination)
>   If N = 1 then
>   move the disk from the Start to the Destination
>   Else
>   move the N − 1 smallest disks from the Start to the Intermediate
>   move the largest disk from the Start to the Destination
>   move the N − 1 smallest disks from the Intermediate to the Destination
>   End If
> End Hanoi

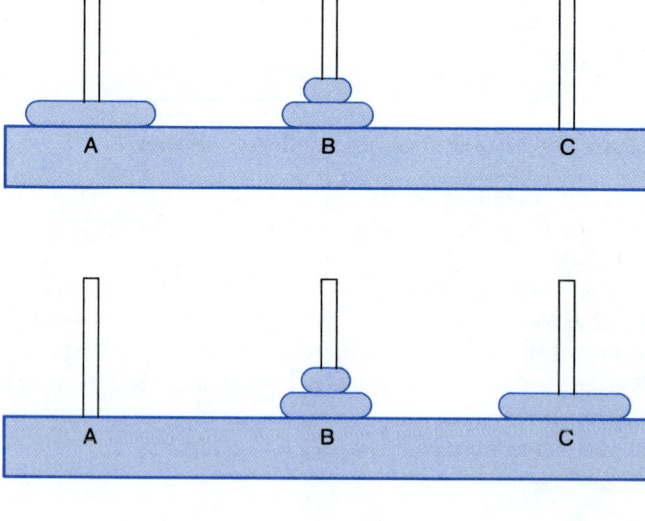

Figure 5.2
Towers of Hanoi:
Step 1

Figure 5.3
Towers of Hanoi:
Step 2

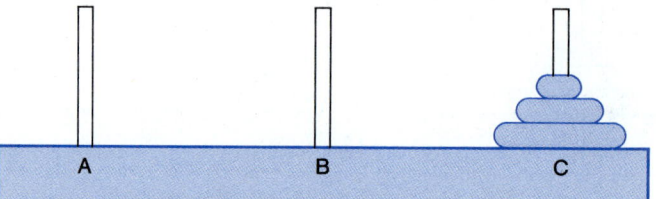

Figure 5.4
Towers of Hanoi:
Step 3

The first and third instructions in the Else part are the recursive calls. To develop a meaningful output, we will have to develop a suitable notation for moves. If the disks are labeled by size from 1 (for the smallest) to n (for the largest), and if the pegs are indicated by the characters "A," "B," and "C," then we would solve the three-disk problem by the procedure call

```
Hanoi( 3, 'A', 'B', 'C' )
```

To show an actual move, we will print out the word *move*, the number of the disk being moved, the word *from*, the character representing the starting peg, the word *to*, and the character representing the destination peg. Our refined algorithm is

```
Hanoi ( N, Start, Intermediate, Destination )
    If N = 1 then
        Print "move ", N, " from ", Start, " to ", Destination
    Else
        Hanoi ( N − 1, Start, Destination, Intermediate )
        Print "move ", N, " from ", Start, " to ", Destination
        Hanoi ( N − 1, Intermediate, Start, Destination )
    End If
End Hanoi
```

The sequence of moves printed for Hanoi (3, 'A', 'B', 'C') would be

```
move 1 from A to C
move 2 from A to B
move 1 from C to B
move 3 from A to C
move 1 from B to A
move 2 from B to C
move 1 from A to C
```

The Modula-2 implementation of Hanoi is left as Programming Problem 21 at the end of this chapter.

How many moves does it take to solve the puzzle for N disks? Let's view our sequence of moves in a treelike structure. We start with the move of the largest disk and then put the moves that precede it to the left and the moves that follow it to the right. We apply this same strategy to each of these groups of moves until we reach the moves for the smallest disk. Figure 5.5 shows the moves for three disks.

Notice that the largest disk is moved once, the next to largest disk twice, and the third from largest disk (the smallest disk in this case) four times. The total number of moves is

$$1 + 2 + 4 = 7$$

Figure 5.5

Moves for the Solution of the Towers of Hanoi Puzzle for Three Disks

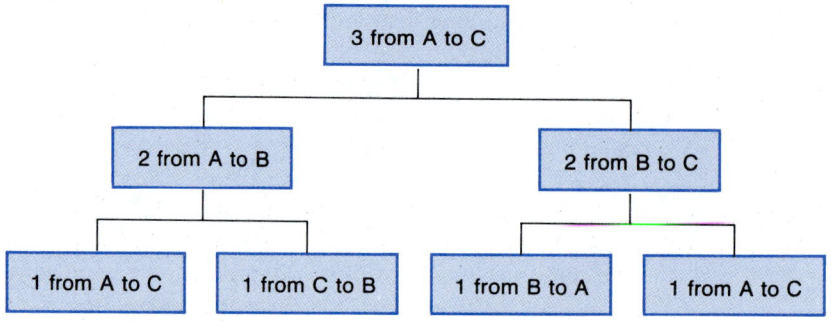

For the N disk problem, the sum of moves will be

$$2^0 + 2^1 + 2^2 + \cdots + 2^{N-1}$$

It can be shown that

$$2^0 + 2^1 + 2^2 + \cdots + 2^{N-1} = 2^N - 1$$

After you have learned about mathematical induction in the next section, you will be able to prove this yourself!

According to a legend, priests in a temple somewhere in the world are solving the Towers of Hanoi problem with a stack of 64 disks. Once they have completed the transfer, the universe is supposed to end! If the priests work very quickly, moving one disk every second, calculate how long, in years, the universe will last. Some modern priests became bored with this activity and decided to use a computer to generate the solution more quickly. Assuming the computer can make a move in one millionth of a second (one microsecond), calculate how long the universe will last.

Mathematical Induction and Recursion

Now that we've seen how recursion works in several examples, let's look at a way of verifying the correctness of a recursive solution. In Chapter 1 we gave the formula for the sum of integers from 1 to N

$$0 + 1 + 2 + 3 + \cdots + N = N(N+1)/2$$

Testing for a few small values of N may convince you that the formula appears to be correct, but we need a way to prove it true for all values of N. Here we will use *mathematical induction*. This method is a way of demonstrating the validity of a formula by proving it holds for the integer 0 and that if it holds for all integers preceding a given integer, it must hold for the next integer.

We first verify that the formula is correct for the simplest case, $N = 0$.

$$0(0+1)/2 = 0 \text{ as expected.}$$

We then assume the formula is correct for all values from 0 to N and show that it is true for $N + 1$.

In particular, for this problem we assume

$$0 + 1 + 2 + 3 + \cdots + N = N(N+1)/2$$

and we must show

$$0 + 1 + 2 + 3 + \cdots + N + (N+1) = (N+1)(N+2)/2$$

Starting with the left-hand side, we first substitute for the sum of the first N terms, using our assumption, to obtain

$$0 + 1 + 2 + 3 + \cdots + N + (N+1) = N(N+1)/2 + (N+1)$$

We write the last term with a denominator of 2 to get

$$= N(N+1)/2 + 2(N+1)/2$$

and we factor out $(N+1)/2$ to get the desired result

$$= ((N+1)/2)(N+2) = (N+1)(N+2)/2$$

We can now use mathematical induction to conclude that the formula is true for all N.

Let us state the principle of mathematical induction more precisely: Let P be a predicate on the cardinal numbers. If we can show that (i) P is true for 0, and (ii) P is true for $n+1$, given that it is true for 0 through n, then P is true for all cardinal numbers.

Perhaps you can now see the similarity between mathematical induction and recursion. Part (i) is similar to the base case for recursion, and part (ii) is similar to the recursive call that solves a problem of size n in terms of problems of smaller size. Based on this similarity, when you code a recursive solution, you can ensure its correctness by:

1. making sure the base case is done correctly
2. making sure the general case is done correctly, assuming that recursive calls generate correct results

This chapter's introduction to recursion has described the basic principles of the method. In Chapter 7, we'll learn more about the way recursive procedures work, and in Chapters 12, 13, and 15 we'll use recursion to develop some very useful algorithms.

The rest of this chapter examines several techniques for selecting between multiple alternatives. Near the end of the chapter we'll see how these techniques may make recursive algorithms more efficient.

5.2 Multiple Selection

In Chapter 4 we saw that the IF statement can be used to select between two alternatives. Sometimes, though, we must select between more than two alternatives. In this section we'll describe two control structures designed for this very need: (1) IF statements with ELSIF parts, and (2) CASE statements. We'll try a programming problem to see how they work, and we'll learn how to choose between the two methods when solving a problem.

IF Statements with ELSIF Parts

As mentioned in Chapter 4, IF statements can be nested as deeply as desired. In some cases, however, nested IFs can be difficult to comprehend, and we should use an option of the IF statement called ELSIF. Let's follow a fairly substantial example to see how the application of nested IFs creates the need for a simpler alternative structure.

For the example, we will develop a program to simulate the popular children's toy, Etch-a-Sketch, which permits a child to draw simple rectilinear figures by turning two knobs attached to a mechanical screen. Turning the first knob in one direction causes an upward line to be drawn, and turning the same knob in the other direction gives a downward line. Turning the second knob yields lines to the left and right. The screen can be cleared by turning over and shaking the toy.

To simulate the operation of the toy, we first choose appropriate characters to represent the possible lines: up, down, left, or right. Then we cause a short line to be drawn in the appropriate direction whenever a key corresponding to one of these characters is pressed. We will need to embed this process in a loop, so that the user can draw as many lines as desired. Pseudocode based on these ideas is as follows:

> Loop
>   read a character
>   if the character is U draw a line up
>   if the character is D draw a line down
>   if the character is L draw a line left
>   if the character is R draw a line right
> End loop

Reflecting on the pseudocode, we observe that we have no way to terminate the simulation. Therefore we add one more option, Q for quit:

> Loop
>   read a character
>   if the character is Q exit the loop
>   if the character is U draw a line up
>   if the character is D draw a line down
>   if the character is L draw a line left
>   if the character is R draw a line right
> End loop

If the TurtleGraphics module is available, you can easily draw the lines; if you do not have TurtleGraphics, you can write characters as described in Programming Problem 15 at the end of the chapter. In this instance we will assume TurtleGraphics is available.

Multiple Selection

Using one variable of type character and a sequence of one-branch IF statements, we can base the first version of our program on the pseudocode as follows:

```
MODULE Sketch;
(* A simulation of Etch-a-Sketch assuming that the
     direction of the Turtle is initially to the right.
          J. M. Adams      January 1988     *)

FROM InOut IMPORT Read;
FROM TurtleGraphics IMPORT TurtleStop, Move, Turn;

CONST SizeOfMove = 10;
VAR Ch: CHAR;

BEGIN
  LOOP
    (* Turtle points to the right *)
    Read(Ch);
    IF Ch = 'Q' THEN
      EXIT;
    END;  (* IF *)
    IF Ch = 'U' THEN
      Turn(90); Move(SizeOfMove); Turn(-90);
    END;  (* IF *)
    IF Ch = 'D' THEN
      Turn(-90); Move(SizeOfMove); Turn(90);
    END;  (* IF *)
    IF Ch = 'L' THEN
      Turn(180); Move(SizeOfMove); Turn(-180);
    END;  (* IF *)
    IF Ch = 'R' THEN
      Move(SizeOfMove);
    END;  (* IF *)
  END;  (* LOOP *)
  TurtleStop;        (* Hold screen *)
END Sketch.
```

We have made the assumption that the initial direction of the turtle is to the right, and we maintain that direction as a loop invariant. For an input of "R," we simply move forward. For any other direction, we must turn the turtle in the appropriate direction, move, then turn the turtle back to the initial direction (pointing right). The program uses one character variable; five character literals, such as "R," and the procedure Read to read a single character. More discussion on the character data type will be given in Chapter 9.

The program is not really complete, because it gives no method of clearing the screen, it gives no message on erroneous input, and it gives no instructions to the user when the program begins. You will be asked to remedy these deficiencies in Programming Problem 14 at the end of this chapter.

Another more subtle deficiency of this program is the fact that it is somewhat inefficient. Each of the five IF statements is executed on every iteration of the loop, even though the ones following the first "successful" IF may be ignored. To remedy this inefficiency we can nest each IF statement within the ELSE part of the preceding IF statement, so that it will be executed only if the preceding conditions are all false. This nesting is done in the following statement:

```
IF Ch = 'Q' THEN
   EXIT;
ELSE
   IF Ch = 'U' THEN
      Turn( 90 ); Move( SizeOfMove ); Turn( -90 );
   ELSE
      IF Ch = 'D' THEN
         Turn( -90 ); Move( SizeOfMove ); Turn( 90 );
      ELSE
         IF Ch = 'L' THEN
            Turn( 180 ); Move( SizeOfMove ); Turn( -180 );
         ELSE
            IF Ch = 'R' THEN
               Move( SizeOfMove );
            ELSE
               WriteString( "The character you just typed has no meaning!" );
            END; (* IF *)
         END; (* IF *)
      END; (* IF *)
   END; (* IF *)
END; (* IF *);
```

Notice that this is really just one long IF statement containing other IF statements nested within it. However, it gives the same results as our previous sequence of five IF statements. We have also added input data validation, which causes the display of a message in the case where the input character does not correspond to a command. This addition was easily accomplished by using the ELSE part of the most deeply nested IF, since reaching that part can only happen if the character is not Q, U, D, L, or R.

Although the nested IF version is more efficient, it looks a bit woolly; the usual indentation conventions quickly drive the statement far to the right, and the ENDs tend to proliferate like rabbits. For this reason Modula-2 has an abbreviation for IF statements with nesting only in the ELSE parts. The abbreviated form uses a new reserved word, ELSIF, as shown here.

```
IF Ch = 'Q' THEN
   EXIT;
ELSIF Ch = 'U' THEN
   Turn( 90 ); Move( SizeOfMove ); Turn( -90 );
```

```
              ELSIF Ch = 'D' THEN
                 Turn( -90 ); Move( SizeOfMove ); Turn( 90 );
              ELSIF Ch = 'L' THEN
                 Turn( 180 ); Move( SizeOfMove ); Turn( -180 );
              ELSIF Ch = 'R' THEN
                 Move( SizeOfMove );
              ELSE
                 WriteString( "The character you just typed has no meaning!" );
              END (* IF *);
```

Because each ELSIF is really a part of the whole IF statement, we chose not to indent them. As you can see, this form is much more understandable and attractive than the previous version.

By now we have discussed all the different options possible in IF statements. We can, therefore, give the complete syntax of the IF statement:

```
              IF condition THEN statements
              { ELSIF Boolean expression THEN statements }
              [ELSE statements]
              END
```

where IF, THEN, ELSE, ELSIF, and END are reserved words. The braces around the second line are used to indicate that you can have zero or more occurrences of ELSIF-THEN parts. The brackets indicate that a single occurrence of the third line may be included but is optional. Check that our examples in this section are syntactically correct according to this definition.

The CASE Statement

The second control structure for choosing among several alternatives is the CASE statement. To introduce the CASE statement, we will present yet another convenient way to implement the selection process that formed the body of the loop of the Sketch program developed in the previous section. The following CASE statement is equivalent to the nested IF statement given for the Sketch program.

```
LOOP
   CASE Ch OF
      'Q'  : EXIT|
      'U'  : Turn( 90 ); Move( SizeOfMove ); Turn( -90 );|
      'D'  : Turn( -90 ); Move( SizeOfMove ); Turn( 90 );|
      'L'  : Turn( 180 ); Move( SizeOfMove ); Turn( -180 );|
      'R'  : Move( SizeOfMove );
      ELSE WriteString( "The character you just typed has no meaning!" );
   END; (* CASE *);
END; (* LOOP *)
```

We call Ch the *selector*, because its value is tested against each of the character constants before the colons. If it equals one of these constants, the statements between the colon and the next vertical bar or the ELSE are executed. Each line in the preceding CASE statement represents a different case, and the character constants preceding the colons are called *case labels*. Notice that cases are separated by a vertical bar and that there is no vertical bar after the last case. If there is an ELSE clause, it covers all remaining cases. It is also possible to specify no action in the ELSE part.

The CASE statement just shown is even shorter and more readable than our previous statement, which used the ELSIF feature. However, the CASE statement applies only to situations in which each alternative is associated with certain fixed values that cause it to be selected. Many times we must have more flexibility in the selection of the action to be taken, and then the use of IF statements is necessary. The example in the next section is of this nature.

The syntax of the CASE statement is

```
CASE expression OF
   list of case labels : statements|
   list of case labels : statements|
               .
               .
               .
   list of case labels : statements
   [ELSE statements]
END
```

where CASE, OF, ELSE, END, the colons, and the vertical bars are all reserved "words." The ellipses indicate that you may have as many cases as desired, but the last case *must not* be terminated with a vertical bar. The brackets indicate that the ELSE part is optional. If it is used, the statements following ELSE are executed only when none of the preceding case labels matches the value of the selector (the expression on the first line). In our example we used that option to display a message on erroneous input. If the ELSE part is not used and no case labels match the selector, an error may occur during execution; it is a good idea to include this part, therefore, even if no action is specified (ELSE followed immediately by END).

In our example we had only one case label before each colon, rather than a list of case labels separated by commas. If a list is used, when the value of the expression matches any case label in the list, the statements between the colon and the next vertical bar are executed. Case labels must be constants and must be compatible with the type of the selector on the first line. Also, no constant may appear in more than one list. The type of the selector may be any basic type (except REAL), an enumeration type, or a subrange type. The latter two types will be discussed in Chapters 6 and 9.

We can improve our example markedly by accepting lowercase as well as uppercase letters. Since users often make mistakes when typing input, we want to protect them from this kind of error whenever possible. Our improved solution becomes

Multiple Selection

```
CASE Ch OF
   'q', 'Q'  : EXIT|
   'u', 'U'  : Turn( 90 );  Move( SizeOfMove );  Turn( -90 );|
   'd', 'D'  : Turn( -90 ); Move( SizeOfMove );  Turn( 90 );|
   'l', 'L'  : Turn( 180 ); Move( SizeOfMove );  Turn( -180 );|
   'r', 'R'  : Move( SizeOfMove );
   ELSE WriteString( "The character you just typed has no meaning!" );
END; (* CASE *);
```

This is an example of a "command-driven" or "menu-driven" program. Programs that rely heavily on user interaction can often be implemented by presenting a menu of choices and acting according to the user input. In subsequent chapters we will have many occasions to use the CASE statement, and we will discuss more complex forms of the statement as they are needed.

A Programming Example of the CASE Statement

To appreciate how the CASE statement works in practice, let's take a look at an extended example. Our goal here is to design and program a utility procedure called Tomorrow. Given a date in the form of three variables— Month, Day, and Year—Tomorrow will change the values of the variables to those of the next day. For example, if the variables have the values 12, 31, and 87, Tomorrow will change them to 1, 1, and 88. We will assume that the three parameters have already been checked to make sure that they represent a valid date; this assumption means we do not have to include the check in our procedure. The algorithm for the years 1901 to 1999 is fairly straightforward. We must first find the number of days in the given month and then use this number to determine tomorrow's date. In other words, we have divided our problem into two subproblems, as shown in the structure chart in Figure 5.6.

This structure chart is formalized in our first pseudocode solution:

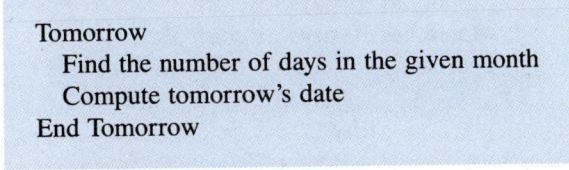

```
Tomorrow
    Find the number of days in the given month
    Compute tomorrow's date
End Tomorrow
```

Figure 5.6
Structure Chart for Tomorrow Problem

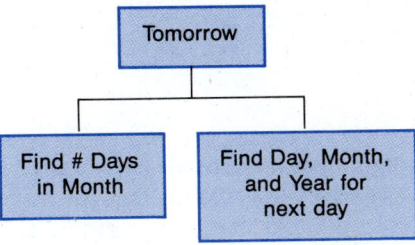

When computing tomorrow's date, we have to check if we are at the end of the month. If we are not at the end of the month, we simply increment the Day by 1; otherwise, we increment Month and reset Day to 1. We must also check for the end of the year. A more detailed pseudocode solution, introducing variables to represent the key quantities, is

```
Tomorrow( Month, Day, Year )
    If Day < Max Days in the Month then
        Increment Day
    Else
        Reset Day to 1
        If Month < 12 then
            Increment Month
        Else
            Reset Month to 1
            Increment Year
        End if
    End if
End Tomorrow
```

At this point we are left with the problem of finding the maximum number of days for Month. We can do this by considering cases, as shown in the following pseudocode version. Notice that we have added an informal case statement to our pseudocode.

```
MaxDays ( Month, Year )
    Case Month of
        Month has 31 days : Return 31
        Month has 30 days : Return 30
        February : If Year is a leap year then
                       Return 29
                   Else
                       Return 28
                   End if
    End case
End MaxDays
```

These pseudocode algorithms are an adequate basis for coding two Modula-2 procedures, Tomorrow and MaxDays. Notice that we have nested MaxDays inside Tomorrow.

SEC. 5.2 *Multiple Selection*

```
PROCEDURE Tomorrow(VAR Month, Day, Year: CARDINAL);
(* Computes tomorrow's date from today's date *)

  PROCEDURE MaxDays(Month, Year: CARDINAL) : CARDINAL;
  (* Given the number of the month, 1 through 12, this procedure
     returns the number of days in the month.  Leap year
     calculations are based on the year being divisible by
     four. *)

  BEGIN
    CASE Month OF
      1, 3, 5, 7, 8, 10, 12 : RETURN 31 |
      4, 6, 9, 11           : RETURN 30 |
      2 :     IF Year MOD 4 = 0 THEN
                 RETURN 29
              ELSE
                 RETURN 28 (* Thanks to Augustus Caesar *)
              END; (* IF *)
    END; (* CASE *);
  END MaxDays;

BEGIN
  IF Day < MaxDays(Month, Year) THEN
    Day := Day + 1
  ELSE
    Day := 1;
    IF Month < 12 THEN
      Month := Month + 1
    ELSE
      Month := 1;
      Year := Year + 1
    END; (* IF *)
  END; (* IF *)
END Tomorrow;
```

These procedures may not work after 1999 because years that are multiples of 100 are not leap years, except every 400 years, and the status of year 2000 has not yet been decided (it may or may not be a leap year).

Improvement of Recursion's Efficiency with Multiple Selection

Having seen how methods of multiple selection operate, we can use them to our advantage in recursive procedures. Recursive procedures are not limited to a single base case, and for reasons of efficiency, it may be best to have several base cases. Consider our power function. The base case used previously was for an exponent of 0; however, exponents of 1 and 2 are easily solved directly without using recursion. A rewritten power function using multiple base cases is as follows:

```
PROCEDURE Power( Base, Exponent: CARDINAL ) : CARDINAL;
VAR PartialResult: CARDINAL;
BEGIN (* Power *)
  IF Exponent = 0 THEN
    RETURN 1;
  ELSIF Exponent = 1 THEN
    RETURN Base;
  ELSIF Exponent = 2 THEN
    RETURN Base * Base;
  ELSIF ODD( Exponent ) THEN
    PartialResult := Power( Base, Exponent DIV 2 );
    RETURN PartialResult * PartialResult * Base;
  ELSE
    PartialResult := Power( Base, Exponent DIV 2 );
    RETURN PartialResult * PartialResult;
  END; (* IF *)
END Power;
```

Often multiple selection can solve several base cases and thus cut down on the number of recursive calls necessary to solve a particular problem.

A Comparison of Methods for Multiple Selection

Unfortunately, no easy formula exists to tell you which form of multiple selection is best for a given problem. The following guidelines, however, may help you choose the most appropriate method.

If nested IFs occur in both the THEN and the ELSE part of an IF, as in the following program structure, there may be no way to use an ELSIF construct.

```
IF condition 1 THEN
  IF condition 2 THEN
    task for 1 and 2 true
  ELSE
    task for 1 true and 2 false
  END;   (* IF *)
ELSE
  IF condition 3 THEN
    task for 1 false and 3 true
  ELSE
    task for 1 false and 3 false
  END;   (* IF *)
END;   (* IF *)
```

Multiple Selection

However, if nesting occurs only in the ELSE part, as in

```
IF condition 1 THEN
   task 1
ELSE
   IF condition 2 THEN
      task 2
   ELSE
      IF condition 3 THEN
         task 3
      ELSE
            .
            .
            .
      END;    (* IF *)
   END;    (* IF *)
END;    (* IF *)
```

then the ELSIF construct may be used, as follows:

```
IF condition 1 THEN
   task 1
ELSIF condition 2 THEN
   task 2
ELSIF condition 3 THEN
   task 3
      .
      .
      .
END;    (* IF *)
```

If the conditions are a test for equality of the same expression resulting in a discrete value (or list of values), the CASE statement may be most appropriate.

```
CASE expr OF
value 1 : task 1 |
value 2 : task 2 |
value 3 : task 3 |
      .
      .
      .
END;    (* CASE *)
```

Menu-driven programs with the input of a single integer or character to indicate the choice selected are prime candidates for the CASE statement. If menus become too long, then multiple levels of menus might be considered. However, if there are too many conditions to be considered or no simple selector expression, then the ELSIF approach is best. Consider the power function with multiple base cases. At first glance the CASE statement may seem appropriate since exponent values of 0, 1, and 2 are each base cases. However, the denotations of odd exponents (3, 5, 7, 9, 11, . . .) and all even exponents (4, 6, 8, 10, 12, . . .) are not finite, so the ELSIF construct is more appropriate for this problem.

SUMMARY

One of the best ways of solving a problem is to divide it into its parts and solve these parts. The solutions to the parts will eventually lead to a solution to the original problem. On some occasions, however, the subproblems are actually just simpler versions of the original problem. When that happens, we can use a method called recursion to reach the solution. Recursion is a method that involves solving reduced versions of the original problem. The smallest version of the problem called the base case, must be solved directly. By using recursion and making our subproblems as balanced in size as possible, we can create more efficient algorithms, leading to effective Modula-2 programs.

When we need to choose between two alternatives, we can use a simple IF statement. In those cases where we have to select between *more* than two alternatives, however, we can use two other control structures: IF statements with ELSIF parts and CASE statements. As we've seen in Chapter 4, the nested IF structure can choose between more than two alternatives, but that structure may become overly complicated. Modula-2 offers a more comprehensible, attractive solution called the ELSIF, an option of the IF statement.

The CASE statement is even shorter than the ELSIF structure, but it applies only to situations in which each alternative is associated with certain fixed values that cause it to be selected. When the selection of actions is more complex, nested IFs or the ELSIF structure must be used. If the nesting occurs only in the ELSE part, the ELSIF form can be used. CASE statements are best for menu-driven programs with the input of a single integer or character to indicate the choice selected.

When there are several base cases in a recursive procedure, one of the control structures capable of multiple selection can help make the recursion more efficient.

EXERCISES

1. In mathematics the successor function adds one to a natural number; the corresponding Modula-2 function is INC. Addition can be defined by applying the successor function recursively. Develop a pseudocode algorithm for adding two numbers by using recursion.

2. Multiplication can be defined by calling an addition function recursively. Develop this pseudocode algorithm.

3. Write an algorithm to compute a factorial using iteration.

4. The Fibonacci numbers are defined by the mathematical relationship

$$f(0) = f(1) = 1$$
$$f(n) = f(n-1) + f(n-2) \text{ for } n > 1$$

Write a recursive algorithm that calculates the *n*th Fibonacci number.

5. Develop an iterative version of your Fibonacci algorithm.

6. Euclid's algorithm, given as an exercise in Chapter 1, can be stated:

    Divide the larger of two positive integers by the smaller one. Then divide the divisor by the remainder. Continue this process of dividing the last divisor by the last remainder until the division is exact. The final divisor is the greatest common divisor of the original two positive integers.

    Develop a recursive algorithm to implement Euclid's algorithm.

7. Given the algorithm

    Mystery (X)
      If X is less than 10 then
        Print the character corresponding to the value of X
      Else
        Mystery (X div 10)
        Print the character corresponding to the remainder of X div 10
      End if
    End Mystery

    describe in simple English (that any sixth-grader could understand) what Mystery does.

8. Write a pseudocode function that is passed a number and returns the sum of the digits in the number. Write both a recursive and an iterative version.

9. Develop an iterative version of the algorithm given in the section entitled "A Recursive String Algorithm" to reverse a string.

10. Develop a recursive pseudocode definition for reversing a string, Str, by splitting off the first character rather than the last and reversing the tail rather than the head.

11. Show by induction that the sum of the first *N* even integers is

    $$N^2 + N$$

12. Show by induction that

    $$1^2 + 2^2 + 3^2 + \cdots + N^2 = N(N+1)(2N+1)/6$$

PROGRAMMING PROBLEMS

13. Write a program that will first read in four integer values, and then compare them and print the largest of the four.

14. Complete the implementation of the Sketch program, using the TurtleGraphics module, if available. The program will provide instructions to the user when it is initiated and will include a command to clear the screen. The program will also prevent movements that would leave the screen (you may use the TurtleGraphics procedure WhereAmI).

15. If your system does not support TurtleGraphics, implement Sketch using the graphics package you have or develop a character-oriented Sketch program. If you use characters, your program may be limited to drawing vertical lines in the down direction only.

16. Write an interactive program that will read in integer values between 1 and 52, and will then display the corresponding playing card. A playing card will be represented by an integer

between 1 and 52 in the following manner: values 1 through 13 are spades, 14 through 26 are hearts, 27 through 39 are diamonds, and 40 through 52 are clubs. Within a given suit the first number corresponds to the ace, the second number to the two, and so on. The thirteenth number corresponds to the king. For example, if the program reads value 24, it should display "Jack of hearts"; if it reads value 30, it should display "4 of diamonds."

17. Extend the Tomorrow procedure to include a check for the validity of the date represented by the parameters, and to make it work for years beyond 1999, assuming the year 2000 will not be a leap year.

18. Write an interactive program to compute the water tax due at the end of a month by the citizens of the community. The rate is defined to be $2 per 100 gallons if total consumption is less than a 1,000 gallons, $3 per 100 gallons if total consumption is less than 3,000 gallons, $4 per 100 gallons if total consumption is less than 5,000 gallons, $5 per 100 gallons if total consumption is less than 7,500 gallons, $6 per 100 gallons if total consumption is less than 10,000 gallons, and $7 for consumptions greater than 10,000 gallons. The program should read in a citizen's name followed by the amount of water used during the month, and it should display the citizen's name and the corresponding amount due.

19. Write a program that will read a collection of data relative to hourly paid workers, and that will compute and display each worker's gross pay. For each worker, the program is given the name and a maximum of seven time cards, each with the identification of the day, the number of hours worked, the hourly rate, and an indication of whether the work was done during daytime or not. The pay rate used will be the hourly rate if the work was done on a weekday and during daytime. The hourly rate will be multiplied by 1.25 if the work was done on a weekend during daytime, by 1.35 if the work was done during the week and not during daytime, or by 1.5 if the work was done on a weekend and not during daytime.

20. Write a program that judges the old game of paper-rock-scissors; the program takes as input pairs of letters (P, R, S or p, r, s) and outputs the appropriate message.

```
"scissors cut paper" for (P, S), (P, s), (p, S), (p, s)
                         (S, P), (s, P), (S, p), or (s, p)
"paper covers rock" for (P, R), (P, r), (p, R), (p, r)
                         (R, P), (r, P), (R, p), (r, p)
"rock breaks scissors" for (R, S), (R, s), (r, S), (r, s)
                            (S, R), (s, R), (S, r), (s, r)
```

21. Implement the Towers of Hanoi algorithm in Modula-2. Write an interactive test program to test your procedure.

22. Improve the efficiency of your Towers of Hanoi algorithm by considering the move of two disks to be a base case.

23. Write a Modula-2 program that prints out the sequence of moves for the Towers of Hanoi pictorially. Limit your values of n to very small values. The first few "pictures" for the three-disk problem might look like

```
start
             X
            XXX
           XXXXX
```

```
move 1
                    XXX
                    XXXXX              X

move 2
                    XXXXX       X            XXX

move 3
                                              X
                    XXXXX                    XXX
```

and so forth.

24. Rewrite the string reversal procedure so that it uses two subproblems of approximately equal size. Write an interactive test program to verify that your procedure works correctly.

25. Develop a recursive function procedure that returns a specified binomial coefficient. The recursive definition of the binomial coefficients is as follows. (You may be more familiar with it as the basis for Pascal's triangle.)

$$c(n, 0) = 1$$
$$c(n, k) = 1 \text{ if } n = k$$
$$c(n, k) = c(n - 1, k) + c(n - 1, k - 1) \text{ if } n > k$$

Be sure to test your procedure adequately. If your system allows it, time $c(n, k)$ for the following pairs of values: (2, 1), (4, 2), (6, 3), (8, 4), (20, 10).

26. Develop an interactive recursive function procedure that returns a specified Sterling number. The recursive definition of a Sterling number is as follows:

$$s(n, 0) = 0 \text{ if } n > 0$$
$$s(n, k) = 1 \text{ if } n = k$$
$$s(n + 1, k) = s(n, k - 1) - n * s(n, k) \text{ if } 0 < k < n$$

6 Data Types

In this chapter, you will:

- learn more about the following built-in data types: CARDINAL, INTEGER, REAL, and BOOLEAN
- learn about subranges for discrete data types
- be introduced to records, a structured data type with components
- use records to build an abstract data type for points in the plane
- learn how to compile an abstract data type in a separate library module

Before using Modula-2 to solve larger problems, we will need additional information about the basic Modula-2 data types. You'll recall that in Table 2.1 we outlined the numeric types CARDINAL, INTEGER, and REAL and the nonnumeric types BOOLEAN, CHAR, and STRING. This chapter explores the numeric and BOOLEAN types in greater detail. For each of them we describe the operations that can be performed on data objects, and we explain how expressions of each type are evaluated. The CHAR and STRING data types will be discussed in greater detail in Chapter 9.

In addition to using the built-in types, you may need to define new types for your particular application. The simplest data types to address this need are subrange types. In this context we can also talk about records, a structured data type that allows you to combine components of any type into a single structure. As an illustration of how to define a new type, we will define a data type for points in a plane. Finally, we will introduce separate compilation of modules so that the point data type can be made into a library module.

6.1 A Conceptual View of Data Types

Before beginning to give the details of each basic data type, let's define data type more formally. All data in a computer are ultimately represented as sequences of the binary digits 0 and 1, or *bits* as they are usually called. However, we do most of our manipulations of data without ever being aware that bit sequence representations are being used in the machine. In other words we can be completely ignorant of the representation and still do computations using the data; indeed we have been doing precisely this with numbers, characters, and strings in our programs so far. Even though the data representation is hidden from us, we can still use the data effectively. This idea is sometimes called *information hiding,* which will be discussed at greater length in Chapter 7.

If the representation of data values belonging to a certain type is not essential for using objects (or operands) of that type, what is essential? We need to know

- the *values* that operands of that type can take
- a precise definition of the *operations* allowed on the operands
- how the operands and operations can be combined to form expressions

In summary, we will consider a data type to be characterized by the allowable values, the operations we can perform on operands of the type, and the ways that we can combine operations and operands to form expressions. We will first concentrate on discussing the operations and expressions of each of the standard numeric types (CARDINAL, INTEGER, and REAL), and the logical type, BOOLEAN.

6.2 Numeric Data Types

Operations, Expressions, and Standard Procedures

In previous chapters we used operands and operations of numeric data types to form arithmetic expressions, which were part of assignment statements. Recall that when an assignment statement such as

```
Sum := Sum + Number
```

is executed, the operations in the expression on the right-hand side are performed to produce a value, which is then stored in the variable to the left of the assignment operator. The result of evaluating the expression must usually be of the same type as that of the variable on the left. A few exceptions to this rule exist; for example, a value of type CARDINAL can be assigned to a variable of type INTEGER.

The permissible operations for the numeric data types are addition, subtraction, multiplication, and division. For the first three operations the same symbols are used for all three numeric types (CARDINAL, INTEGER, REAL), but division is denoted differently for REAL. Specifically, the operators allowed in an arithmetic expression are

+	addition (binary) or positive (unary)
−	subtraction (binary) or negative (unary)
*	multiplication
/	division (for REAL values)
DIV	integer division (no fractional part)
MOD	modulo (remainder from integer division)

The operators + and − may have one or two operands. They are called *unary operators* when they have one operand and *binary operators* when they have two operands. For example, in the expression

$$-A + B$$

the minus is a unary operator and the plus is a binary operator. All the operators in the earlier list, except plus and minus, are always binary.

Both operands of a binary operator must be of the same type, and the result will also be of this type. The binary operators +, −, and * apply to operands that are of type INTEGER, CARDINAL, or REAL. The unary operator − applies to INTEGER and REAL but not to CARDINAL. The division (/) operator applies only to REAL operands and gives a REAL result. The operators DIV and MOD apply only to CARDINAL and in some implementations INTEGER operands, giving results of the same type. Both operands of DIV and MOD must be of the same type. We summarize the application of these operations in Table 6.1.

Most Modula-2 implementations allow the DIV and MOD operations on INTEGER values, but the results are not uniform among the implementations. Therefore, we will restrict our attention to CARDINAL values. For cardinals X and Y, X DIV Y and X MOD Y are quotient and remainder, respectively, as defined by

dividend = quotient * divisor + remainder where 0 <= remainder < divisor

or, using variables and DIV and MOD,

X = (X DIV Y) * Y + (X MOD Y) and 0 <= (X MOD Y) < Y

TABLE 6.1 Operations Allowed for Numeric Data Types

Operation	CARDINAL	INTEGER	REAL
+ (binary)	yes	yes	yes
+ (unary)	yes	yes	yes
− (binary)	yes	yes	yes
− (unary)	no	yes	yes
*	yes	yes	yes
/	no	no	yes
DIV	yes	yes	no
MOD	yes	yes	no

Numeric Data Types

Most of our previous examples of arithmetic expressions were relatively simple, and the results of evaluating the expressions fairly obvious. Because we will need increasingly more complex expressions, we must specify very carefully the order in which operations are performed to obtain the value of an expression. When an arithmetic expression (without parentheses grouping any operations) is evaluated, the order of evaluation is:

1. function calls
2. the operations $*$, $/$, DIV, and MOD
3. the operations binary $+$ and binary $-$

As a result we say that function calls have the highest precedence, and binary $+$ and $-$ the lowest. Operations on any one level—say, all the operations on line 2 above—have equal precedence and are evaluated in left-to-right order. For example, the value of 6 DIV 3 $*$ 2 is 4.

Parentheses may be used in arithmetic expressions to express specific associations of operators and operands. The unary operators $+$ and $-$ can appear only at the start of an expression or immediately following a left parenthesis. Thus, expressions such as

$$-2 * -3$$
$$42.7 / -8.0$$

will result in syntax errors. They can be legally written as

$$-2 * (-3)$$
$$42.7 / (-8.0)$$

If we have the declarations

```
VAR  A, B, C, D : INTEGER;
     I, J       : CARDINAL;
     X, Y, Z    : REAL;
```

and if we have the values initially assigned to these variables

A	B	C	D	I	J	X	Y	Z
-10	3	5	2	6	10	12.5	10.0	2.5

the expressions in Table 6.2 are valid and produce the given results.

TABLE 6.2 Evaluation of Arithmetic Expressions

Expression	Result
I + J	16
$-$A + B	13
C DIV D	2
C MOD D	1
A + D $-$ B $*$ C	-23
3 $*$ (B + (C DIV 3) + 4 $*$ D)	36
Y / Z	4.0
Z $*$ X / Y	3.125

TABLE 6.3 Type Conversion Functions

Function	Type of Argument	Type of Result
INTEGER(c)	CARDINAL	INTEGER
CARDINAL(i)	INTEGER	CARDINAL
FLOAT(c)	CARDINAL	REAL
TRUNC(r)	positive REAL	CARDINAL

Although the operands of an arithmetic operator must be of the same type, we can mix values of different types in the same arithmetic expression by explicitly using *type conversion functions* (sometimes also called type transfer functions). Type conversion functions are supplied in each implementation of Modula-2 and do not have to be imported from another module. The type conversion functions INTEGER and CARDINAL use the same reserved word as the corresponding types while the type conversion functions FLOAT and TRUNC are so-called standard function procedures, which we'll explain shortly (see Table 6.3). Some implementations may provide different or additional conversion functions.

Note that TRUNC returns a result of type CARDINAL, so the REAL argument must be positive. Thus, TRUNC should be used after testing the sign of the real value to be truncated so that negative values can be dealt with properly. Also the CARDINAL conversion function might give strange results if its argument is negative.

With the declarations and initial values given previously, we obtain the results shown in Table 6.4.

Because the basic operations on numeric data types are limited, Modula-2 also has several predefined *standard procedures* that perform other useful operations. We have already seen two of them: TRUNC and FLOAT. Standard function procedures can be considered built in to the Modula-2 system, and there is no need to import them. Some of these procedures are called *generic,* because they can be used on arguments of different types or even on a varying number of arguments. Also, some of the procedures involve objects that we have not yet discussed. Two additional Modula-2 standard function procedures are

ABS(x)   a function that returns the absolute value of x (result type is the same as argument type)

ODD(x)   a Boolean function that returns TRUE if x MOD 2 # 0, and FALSE otherwise

We have already used ODD in our recursive power function in Chapter 5. All the standard procedures are given in Appendix D, and we will discuss them as they are needed.

TABLE 6.4 Evaluation of Expressions Containing Type Conversion Functions

Expression	Result
CARDINAL(B) + J	13
A * B DIV INTEGER(I)	−5
J + TRUNC(X)	22
FLOAT(I) * X / Z	30.0

There also exist several mathematical functions in the standard mathematics module (MathLib0, or a variation of this name, depending on your implementation; see Appendices E and F). These functions have to be imported in order to be used.

sqrt(x)	square root of a real argument
exp(x)	exponential function of a real argument
ln(x)	natural logarithm of a real argument
sin(x)	sine function of a real argument in radians
cos(x)	cosine function of a real argument in radians
arctan(x)	arctangent function of a real argument
real(x)	conversion from integer argument to real value
entier(x)	conversion from real argument to integer value

A Programming Example

To illustrate the use of arithmetic expressions, let's design a program that will compute and print a table of windchill factors for a set of temperatures and wind velocities.

The windchill factor, which is well known by those living in colder climates, is a measure of the relative degree of cold that somebody will experience outdoors. It is normally expressed as a temperature. For instance, if the outdoor temperature is 0 degrees F, and there is a 25 mph wind, then the windchill factor is -40 degrees F. That figure implies that a person going outdoors will experience a cold equivalent to -40 degrees F with no wind. This measure is based on the fact that the body is a source of heat and that, as the wind increases, the body will lose heat faster.

The computation of the windchill factor can be very complex: we could consider the heat loss from the wind as well as the warming effect of the sun rays and the amount of heat generated when a person moves around. Here, though, we'll use a simple method—considering only the heat loss from the body caused by the wind. The following formula gives the windchill factor from the temperature in degrees Fahrenheit and wind velocity in miles per hour (for velocities $>= 10$ mph):

$$WCF = 91.4 - (91.4 - Temp)(0.288 \sqrt{Wind} + 0.45 - 0.019 \, Wind)$$

We will let the temperature vary from -40 degrees F to $+30$ degrees F by steps of 10 degrees F. For each value of the temperature, we will let the wind velocity vary from 10 mph to 30 mph by steps of 5 mph. These limits will be declared as constants, and the constants, rather than the actual numerical values, will be used in the program statements. In this way, changes in the limits can be made by changing only the constant declarations, which greatly facilitates program maintenance.

The following program is relatively short. It uses two *nested loops* very much like our multiplication table procedure in Chapter 4. The structure is so similar we omit giving pseudocode here; however, in this case we nest REPEAT loops instead of FOR loops as in the multiplication table. The inner loop computes and prints values of the windchill factor for different values of the wind velocity (one line of the table). The outer loop controls the values of the temperature (number of lines of the table). Notice that the conversion function TRUNC allows the value of a real numeric expression to be printed in the heading as a whole number.

```
MODULE WindChill;
(* This program computes and prints a table of windchill
   factors for a set of temperatures and wind velocities.  The
   factor is computed by applying the following formula, which
   does not take into account the warming effect of the sun
   or the heat generated by activity.
   WCF = 91.4 - (91.4 - Temp)(0.288 SQRT(Wind) + 0.450 - 0.019Wind)
   This equation considers only the heat loss from the body caused
   by the wind and is valid for wind speeds >= 10mph.
                                    Philippe Gabrini    January 1988

   Reference:  Siple and Passel, "Measurements Of Any Atmosphere
               Cooling In Sub-freezing Temperatures" Proc. Am.
               Philosophical Society, Vol 89, p177-199, 1945 *)
FROM InOut IMPORT WriteString, WriteLn, WriteCard;
FROM RealInOut IMPORT FWriteReal;
FROM MathLib0 IMPORT sqrt;

CONST LowTemp  = -40.0;
      HighTemp = 30.0;
      LowWind  = 10.0;
      WindStep = 5.0;
      HighWind = LowWind + 4.0 * WindStep;
      TempStep = 10.0;

VAR WindChillFactor, Temperature, WindVelocity: REAL;

BEGIN
  WriteString( "   WindChill Factors" );
  WriteLn;
  WriteString( "                                        Wind Velocity" );
  WriteLn;
  WriteString( "  Temperature(F)" );
  WriteCard( TRUNC( LowWind + 0.5 ), 10 );
  WriteCard( TRUNC( LowWind + WindStep + 0.5 ), 10 );
  WriteCard( TRUNC( LowWind + 2.0 * WindStep + 0.5 ), 10 );
  WriteCard( TRUNC( LowWind + 3.0 * WindStep + 0.5 ), 10 );
  WriteCard( TRUNC( LowWind + 4.0 * WindStep + 0.5 ), 10 );
  WriteLn;
  WriteString( "                 _____" );
  WriteLn;
  WriteString( "                         |" );
  WriteLn;
  Temperature := LowTemp;
```

```
    REPEAT
      WindVelocity := LowWind;
      FWriteReal( Temperature, 10, 2 );
      WriteString( "        |" );
      REPEAT
        WindChillFactor := 91.4 - (91.4 - Temperature)
            * ( 0.288 * sqrt( WindVelocity ) +
            0.45 - 0.019 * WindVelocity );
        FWriteReal( WindChillFactor, 10, 2 );
        WindVelocity := WindVelocity + WindStep;
      UNTIL WindVelocity > HighWind;
      WriteLn;
      Temperature := Temperature + TempStep;
    UNTIL Temperature > HighTemp;
END WindChill.
```

The execution of this program produces the following output.

Windchill Factors

			Wind Velocity		
Temperature(F)	10	15	20	25	30
−40.00	−62.43	−76.84	−87.03	−94.53	−100.10
−30.00	−50.72	−64.04	−73.45	−80.38	−85.53
−20.00	−39.02	−51.23	−59.87	−66.23	−70.95
−10.00	−27.31	−38.43	−46.29	−52.08	−56.38
0.00	−15.60	−25.63	−32.71	−37.93	−41.81
10.00	−3.89	−12.82	−19.13	−23.78	−27.23
20.00	7.80	−0.02	−5.55	−9.63	−12.66
30.00	19.51	12.78	8.02	4.51	1.91

As noted in previous programs, the exact format for output of real numbers will depend on your implementation of Modula-2. We have shown a decimal printout.

6.3 BOOLEAN Data Type

Thus far we've been discussing numeric data types. In this chapter we'll also look at one nonnumeric data type—BOOLEAN. BOOLEAN is a simple but very useful type, named for the logician George Boole. Expressions of this type are often called *logical expressions,* because the only permissible values are TRUE and FALSE.

Even though we did not identify them as such, we have already used Boolean expressions in statements such as IF, WHILE, and REPEAT. We called them conditions, which could be either true or false. BOOLEAN is a basic type of Modula-2, and TRUE and FALSE are the Boolean values. Since these are the only two possible Boolean values, the representation of a value can be done with a single bit—for example, with 0 representing FALSE and 1 representing TRUE. However, as we observed earlier, the representation is not as important as the operations we can perform on Boolean values and the way these operations can be used to form Boolean expressions.

The following sections discuss the BOOLEAN data type. We'll see how Boolean expressions are formed and how Boolean operators differ from those of other data types. We'll define mathematical Boolean operators by truth tables and explain the process of evaluating Boolean expressions in Modula-2. Finally, we'll look at the use of decision trees and decision tables to test the equivalence of Boolean expressions.

Boolean Variables, Operations, and Expressions

A Boolean variable is declared in the same way other variables are declared. For instance

```
VAR Flag, X: BOOLEAN;
```

A Boolean expression is used to express conditions, such as

```
N < Number
StudentCount # 0
Counter = 3
Fahrenheit > High
```

which we have already seen. With our previous declaration, we can assign the values of Boolean expressions to Boolean variables, as in

```
Flag := Counter = 3;
X := StudentCount # 0;
```

These assignment statements may look rather odd at first; in fact you may want to use extra parentheses for readability, as in

```
Flag := ( Counter = 3 );
```

More formally, a Boolean expression consists of operands, operators, function calls, and parentheses, just like arithmetic expressions. However, the operators are quite different. We can use *relational operators* such as those shown in Table 6.5. The operands of these relational operators must be of the same type. Thus, in the first example A and B must both be of the same type; in the second example C must be of type CHAR; and so forth. In the spirit of our definition of data types the operations

TABLE 6.5 **Relational Operators**

Symbol	Meaning	Example
=	equal	A = B
#	not equal	C # 'Q'
<	less than	Last < Limit
<=	less than or equal	Time <= 2200
>	greater than	Tax > 1250
>=	greater than or equal	Small >= Max

supported depend on the data type. In general, simple data types support all six forms of relational operators. However, structured data types, such as records, which are introduced later in this chapter, may support only the equal and not equal relational operators. Whatever relational operators are supported for a particular type, the result of a relational operation is always of type BOOLEAN.

Simple expressions involving relational operators are called *relations;* they can be combined to compose more complex Boolean expressions, using the following three *Boolean operators:*

NOT	(unary) negation
AND	logical function and
OR	logical function or

The Boolean operators *must* have Boolean operands, and they are derived from the corresponding mathematical relations defined by the *truth tables* shown in Tables 6.6 to 6.8, where A and B represent the operands. (For reasons that we will discuss in the next section, the Modula-2 definition of Boolean operators does not correspond exactly to the mathematical definition.) Each line of a truth table gives the values for the operands and a corresponding value for the expression. So, the first line of Table 6.6 tells us that if A has the value TRUE and B has the value TRUE, then the value of the expression A or B is TRUE.

Notice that each truth table has a line for each different combination of possible values for the operands. Thus Tables 6.6 and 6.7 have four lines, because there are

TABLE 6.6 Truth Table for "or"

A	B	A or B
TRUE	TRUE	TRUE
TRUE	FALSE	TRUE
FALSE	TRUE	TRUE
FALSE	FALSE	FALSE

TABLE 6.7 Truth Table for "and"

A	B	A and B
TRUE	TRUE	TRUE
TRUE	FALSE	FALSE
FALSE	TRUE	FALSE
FALSE	FALSE	FALSE

TABLE 6.8 Truth Table for "not"

A	not A
TRUE	FALSE
FALSE	TRUE

TABLE 6.9	Evaluation of Boolean Expressions	
	Expression	*Result*
	(A < B) AND (B < C)	TRUE
	(Month = 2) AND (Day = 29)	FALSE
	(Month = 2) AND (Day = 28) AND (Year = 1984)	TRUE
	(Answer = 'Y') OR (Code = 'N')	TRUE
	(Answer = 'N') OR (Code = 'Z') OR (A = 2)	FALSE
	(X = A) OR ((CountDown = 0) AND (X = 0))	TRUE
	NOT(Answer = 'N') AND (Code = 'Y')	FALSE
	(Year MOD 400 = 0) OR ((Year MOD 4 = 0) AND (Year MOD 100 # 0))	TRUE
	(Answer = 'N') OR Done	FALSE
	Flag AND NOT Done	TRUE

two possible values for A, two possible values for B, and, therefore, 2 × 2 combinations of truth values for the two operands.

The operator NOT is a unary operator, since it has only one operand, and it has higher precedence than AND, which in turn has higher precedence than OR. Parentheses may be used to override this operator precedence, and many programmers choose to parenthesize Boolean expressions completely rather than remember the precedence hierarchy.

A few examples of the values of Boolean expressions may be helpful at this point. If the following variables have the indicated values, then the subsequent Boolean expressions give the results shown in Table 6.9.

A	B	C	Month	Day	X	CountDown	Answer	Code	Year	Flag	Done
5	8	10	2	28	0	0	'Y'	'N'	1984	TRUE	FALSE

Evaluation of Boolean Expressions

The precedence of arithmetic, Boolean, and relational operators from highest to lowest is as follows:

NOT
* / DIV MOD AND
+ − OR
= # < <= > >=

The unary operator NOT is applied first; then the multiplication, division, and logical AND operators are applied; next the addition, subtraction, and logical OR operators are applied; and last the relational operators are applied. Operations of equal precedence are done in left-to-right order.

Notice that an expression like

$$X = 12 \text{ AND } B < 100$$

is syntactically incorrect. Because AND has higher precedence than the relational operators, evaluation would begin with

$$12 \text{ AND } B$$

which is incorrect since 12 and B are not of type BOOLEAN. Such an error can be easily corrected by using parentheses

$$(X = 12) \text{ AND } (B < 100)$$

This example explains why we used parentheses in our previous examples of Boolean expressions.

Boolean expressions may involve Boolean functions—that is, functions that return a Boolean result. An example is the standard function called ODD, which takes an integer or cardinal argument and returns TRUE if the argument is odd and FALSE if the argument is even.

When a Boolean expression is evaluated in Modula-2, the evaluation stops as soon as the final result is known. We call this left-to-right (or short circuit) evaluation, and this makes logical operators in Modula-2 slightly different from the same operators defined in mathematics. As a result, some parts of a Boolean expression might not be evaluated, if it is not necessary. For example, consider a Boolean expression with two operands. Depending on the value of the first operand, the second operand might not be evaluated. This is important in particular cases, such as the following:

```
IF ( Employees # 0 ) AND ( Bonus DIV Employees > Trifle ) THEN
    WriteString( "There will be a bonus!" );
END (* IF *);
```

Since a division by zero is not possible, the evaluation of the second operand would result in an error if Employees had value zero. Because of the way Boolean expressions are evaluated, however, this will not happen. If the first condition of an AND expression is FALSE, the entire expression must be FALSE. Therefore the second condition need not be evaluated.

In general, expressions of the form "A AND B" are evaluated according to the following rule:

> If A is FALSE, the result is FALSE;
> otherwise the result is the value of B.

Likewise, expressions of the form "A OR B" are evaluated in the following manner:

> If A is TRUE, then the result is TRUE;
> otherwise the result is the value of B.

Both these rules can be extended to expressions involving more than one operator by considering the second operand, B, to itself be an AND or an OR expression. For example, given A AND B AND C AND D, the first false value, going from left to right, stops evaluation and returns FALSE. If A, B, and C are all true, then the final result is the value of D.

We may have two Boolean expressions that always produce the same value. Such expressions are said to be equivalent. For example, expressions of the following two forms are equivalent:

> NOT A OR NOT B
> NOT(A AND B)

TABLE 6.10 Comparison of Two Truth Tables

A	B	(NOT A)	OR	(NOT B)	NOT	(A AND B)
T	T	F	F	F	F	T
T	F	F	T	T	T	F
F	T	T	T	F	T	F
F	F	T	T	T	T	F

This equivalence can be shown by constructing a truth table for each expression (see Table 6.10). Here we have abbreviated TRUE as T and FALSE as F. The truth value of each parenthesized subexpression is shown under the subexpression, and the truth value of an entire expression is shown under the last operand that is applied: OR for the first expression and NOT for the second. Because the values for the two expressions are the same for each line of the table, the expressions are equivalent. We denote this equivalence as follows:

$$(\text{NOT } A) \text{ OR } (\text{NOT } B) \equiv \text{NOT}(A \text{ AND } B)$$

This particular equivalence is one of DeMorgan's Laws, named for the logician Augustus DeMorgan. We have proved this law by showing the equivalence using truth tables. The other equivalence called DeMorgan's Law is

$$(\text{NOT } A) \text{ AND } (\text{NOT } B) \equiv \text{NOT}(A \text{ OR } B)$$

You will be asked to prove this law in Exercise 9 at the end of this chapter.

It is useful to have a method for checking the equivalence of Boolean expressions, because one form may be simpler than the other, and using simpler forms will make programs more comprehensible. To show that two expressions are *not* equivalent, we need to find only a single line of the truth table where they have different values. The

TABLE 6.11 More Compact Truth Tables

(NOT	A)	OR	(NOT	B)		NOT	(A	AND	B)
F	T	F	F	T		F	T	T	T
F	T	T	T	F		T	T	F	F
T	F	T	F	T		T	F	F	T
T	F	T	T	F		T	F	F	F

TABLE 6.12 A Simple Truth Table

(A	OR	B)	AND	C
T	T	T	T	T
T	T	T	F	F
T	T	F	T	T
T	T	F	F	F
F	T	T	T	T
F	T	T	F	F
F	F	F	F	T
F	F	F	F	F

truth tables for testing equivalence can be made even more compact by eliminating the columns for the operands and showing the truth values for the operands beneath each occurrence of the operand in the expression. Thus Table 6.11 is a more compact form of Table 6.10.

Truth tables can be constructed for expressions involving more operators and operands by including enough lines in the table to cover all possible combinations of truth values for the operands. For example the expression (A OR B) AND C has three operands, so its truth table has $2 \times 2 \times 2$ lines (see Table 6.12). In general, if an expression has n distinct operands, its truth tables will have 2^n rows.

Complex Boolean Expressions, Nested IF Statements, Decision Tables, and Decision Trees

A selection of alternative actions can often be done in several different ways, using simple IF statements with complex Boolean expressions or nested IF statements with simpler Boolean expressions. In this section we will study such formulations and the analysis of these formulations by means of decision tables and decision trees. A simple IF with a Boolean expression can be equivalent to a nested IF, as seen by the following example. If we assume that Credits is a variable of type CARDINAL, and that GPA a variable of type REAL, then the following two statements are equivalent:

```
IF ( Credits > 12 ) AND ( GPA > 3.5 ) THEN
   WriteString( "Congratulations, you made the Dean's list." );
END; (* IF *);

IF ( Credits > 12 ) THEN
   IF ( GPA > 3.5 ) THEN
      WriteString( "Congratulations, you made the Dean's list." );
   END; (* inner IF *)
END; (* outer IF *);
```

If you don't see that these statements are equivalent, use the definition of AND and trace through flow charts for the two statements.

On the other hand, the following two statements are not equivalent:

```
IF ( Credits > 12 ) AND ( GPA > 3.5 ) THEN
   WriteString( "Congratulations, you made the Dean's list." );
ELSE
   WriteString( "Sorry, better luck next semester." );
END; (* IF *);

IF ( Credits > 12 ) THEN
   IF ( GPA > 3.5 ) THEN
      WriteString( "Congratulations, you made the Dean's list." );
   ELSE
      WriteString( "Sorry, better luck next semester." );
   END; (* IF *)
END; (* IF *);
```

To verify this lack of equivalence, check the result of each statement for a student taking less than 12 credits.

Furthermore, we can make a more general observation. If A and B represent Boolean expressions, and S1 and S2 represent statements, then any two IF-THEN-ELSE statements of the following two forms are not equivalent:

```
IF A AND B THEN
   S1
ELSE
   S2
END; (* IF *);

IF A THEN
   IF B THEN
      S1
   ELSE
      S2
   END; (* IF *)
END; (* IF *);
```

Again, you can use flow charts for the two forms and the definition of AND to help you see this lack of equivalence. Using them, you can construct a *decision tree* for each form, as shown in Figures 6.1 and 6.2.

A decision tree is a graphical representation of selection statements. The tree in Figure 6.1 shows that S2 is done when A is FALSE, while the tree in Figure 6.2 shows that no action is taken when A is FALSE since there is no branch for that case. Notice that the nodes of a decision tree are elementary conditions (such as A, B), the branches correspond to the truth values of these conditions, and the leaves of the tree are actions to be taken.

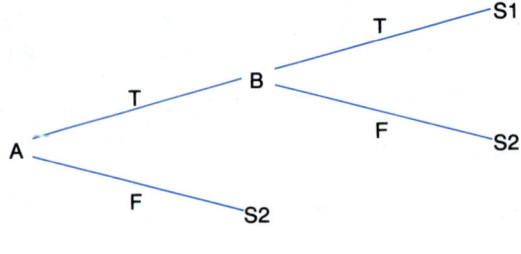

Figure 6.1
Decision Tree for the First Form

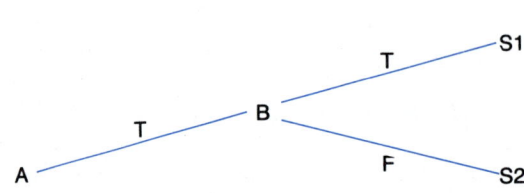

Figure 6.2
Decision Tree for the Second Form

TABLE 6.13 Decision Table for Second Form

A	B	S1	S2	No Action
TRUE	TRUE	X		
TRUE	FALSE		X	
FALSE	TRUE			X
FALSE	FALSE			X

We can also construct *decision tables* to illustrate IF statements. For example, the decision table for the following IF statement (the second form) is shown in Table 6.13. The letter X indicates what action, if any, is performed.

```
IF A THEN
   IF B THEN
      S1
   ELSE
      S2
   END;  (*IF*)
END;  (*IF*)
```

The decision table for the first form

```
IF A AND B THEN
   S1
ELSE
   S2
END;  (*IF*)
```

will be different than the second, and comparing the two tables will show under what conditions the actions of the two forms are different.

To construct a decision table for a nested IF statement, list all the the elementary conditions (such as A, B) in Boolean expressions following IFs and all the actions following THEN and ELSE parts of IFs. Then for each possible combination of truth values for the conditions, put an X under any action that is taken. If there are *n* Boolean expressions, the number of possible combinations is 2 raised to the *n* power.

Decision trees or decision tables can be constructed for entire programs, although the results may be very large. Decision trees and tables are sometimes useful for analyzing complex programs; they can also be helpful in analyzing a complex problem prior to coding. In fact, there are even programs, similar to compilers, that accept decision tables as input and produce programs that perform the actions specified by the tables. Decision trees and tables are also helpful in designing test programs when you want to ensure that every path through the program has been tested.

While decision tables are somewhat similar to truth tables, they are really used at different levels. Truth tables are used to analyze Boolean expressions, while decision tables are used to analyze an entire statement or even a group of statements.

6.4 Subrange Types

The numeric and Boolean data types discussed to this point are built into the language. Situations may arise, though, when we need to create our own data types. In Modula-2 it is possible to define new types to supplement the built-in types. The syntax of a type declaration is

```
TYPE type-name = type-definition;
     type-name = type-definition;
                    .
                    .
                    .
```

where the type name is an identifier used to refer to this new type and the type description specifies the allowed values.

The simplest kind of type that can be defined by a programmer is a *subrange type*. To declare a subrange type, we select two values from a *base type*, which is any scalar type, except REAL. The subrange comprises these two values plus all the values of the base type that fall between them. For example,

```
TYPE GradeValue = [0..100];
     Caps = ['A'..'Z'];
```

The base type of GradeValue is type CARDINAL, and the base type of Caps is type CHAR. All operators of the base type are applicable to variables of the subrange type.

In general, the syntax of a subrange type is

```
TYPE type-name = [constant-expression..constant-expression];
```

where the first constant-expression must not be a successor of the second one.

Subrange types improve the documentation of a program. For a given application we can specify more precisely the values taken by some variables. The limits of the value range may be directly related to the application. Subrange types also take advantage of *automatic range checking* during execution: when assigning a value to a variable, the system checks to see if that value is within the specified range. If it is not within the range, a run time error is generated. It is usually better to have a run time error that indicates a problem than to continue to process erroneous values.

When operations are performed on operands of subrange types, the types need not match exactly. They must only be *compatible*. A type T1 is compatible with a type T2 if

1. T1 is declared by TYPE T1 = T2, or
2. T1 is declared as a subrange of T2, or
3. T1 and T2 are both declared as subranges of the same base type

For instance, type GradeValue just shown is compatible with type CARDINAL. Furthermore, we say a variable is *assignment compatible* with an expression if one of the following conditions is satisfied:

1. their types are compatible
2. both are of type INTEGER or CARDINAL

Therefore if Position is of type INTEGER and Rank of type CARDINAL, the statement

```
Position := Rank;
```

is admissible. Strictly speaking, the statement

```
Rank := Position;
```

is admissible but might cause an error at run time if the value of Position is negative. Unfortunately, some implementations of Modula-2 do not do the run time check and simply assign an erroneous value.

A numeric subrange type is considered a subrange from INTEGER if the lower limit is negative; otherwise, it is a subrange from CARDINAL. Programmers can change this default type assignment if they explicitly specify the desired base type, as in

```
TYPE GradeValue = INTEGER[0..100];
```

Subrange types can also be specified directly in the variable declaration part of a program, and then they are anonymous (unnamed), as in

```
VAR Code: [0..127];
```

There is a very good reason for giving a name to a new type: in the formal parameter list of a procedure, it is invalid to use an anonymous type declaration. The types used in the formal parameter list must have been defined with a TYPE declaration or be standard types. For example

```
PROCEDURE LetterGrade( Grade: [0..100] ): CHAR;
```

is invalid, while

```
PROCEDURE LetterGrade( Grade: GradeValue): CHAR;
```

is valid.

6.5 Records

In our programming so far we have primarily used scalar types. In practice, many problems require the use of structured data types that represent collections or sequences of data values. Structured types can be decomposed into simpler components while a simple type is atomic and cannot be decomposed further.

A *record* is a structured data type with a fixed number of components. Each component is accessed by a name. The syntax for the declaration of a record type is

```
RECORD
   field-identifier list: type;
   field-identifier list: type;
      .
      .
      .
END;
```

where each field-identifier list is a list of names of components of the record. The individual components of a record are called *fields* and have names chosen by the programmer. Each field also has a declared type.

For example, a department store might want to group all the information on a customer in records defined by the type declaration

```
TYPE Client = RECORD
                 Number: CARDINAL;
                 Name, Address: STRING;
                 Balance: INTEGER;
              END;
```

Number, Name, Address, and Balance are fields of the record type Client; Number is of type CARDINAL; Name and Address are strings; and Balance is an INTEGER.

If we now declare a variable by

```
VAR Customer: Client;
```

then the value of Customer, a variable of type Client, is a group of four values: a cardinal value, two string values, and an integer value. Each of these four values is called a component value of the record; in our example, two of our components, the strings, are structured values, which can be further decomposed into character components.

To access the individual components of a record, we use field names. The component is referenced by the record variable name followed by a period and then the field name of the component. For example, the component variable identified by field Name of record Customer is written as Customer.Name (this is sometimes called a *qualified identifier*). The fields of a record can be used as regular variables, as in

```
ReadCard( Customer.Number );
Customer.Balance := Customer.Balance + 12500;
Customer.Name := InputString;
```

Notice that Customer.Balance is of type INTEGER, rather than REAL, to avoid representing fractions of cents. Thus, the actual balance is really 1/100 of the value of Customer.Balance. This is a common technique for handling monetary values, and the factor 1/100 is called a *scale factor*. The scale factor must be applied during output so that the correct value will be printed.

A component of a record can be of any type; in particular it can even be another record. This flexibility makes the record structure very useful. For instance, we could have declared Client type as follows:

```
TYPE Date = RECORD
              Month: [1..12];
              Day: [1..31];
              Year: [1930..2030];
            END;
     Sale = RECORD
              When: Date;
              Amount: INTEGER;
            END;
     PostalAddress = RECORD
                       StNumber: CARDINAL;
                       Street, City, State: STRING;
                       Zip: STRING;
                     END;
     Client = RECORD
                Number: CARDINAL;
                Name: STRING;
                Address: PostalAddress;
                Balance: INTEGER;
                Transaction: Sale;
              END;
```

A record of type Client would have five components—some components being themselves records and, as such, having other components as illustrated in Figure 6.3.

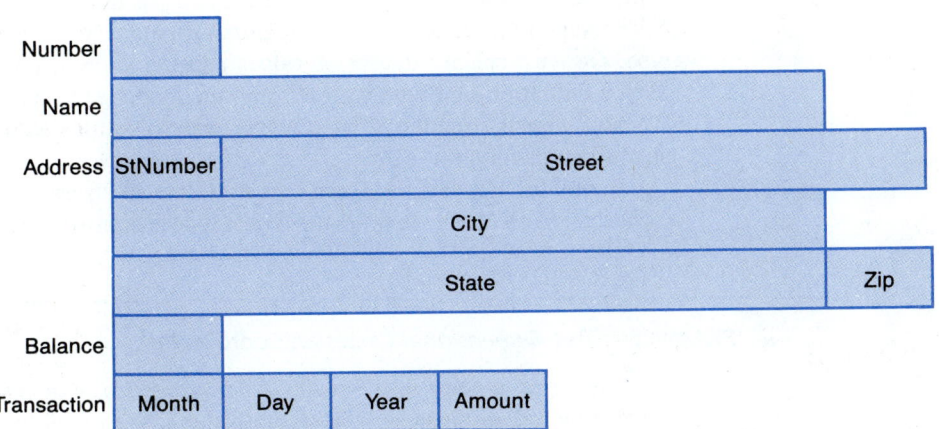

Figure 6.3
Organization of a Record of Type Client

If we declare variables of type Client, as follows,

```
VAR X, Y: Client;
```

then we could give customer X a value in the following way:

```
X.Number := 43227;
X.Name := "Don Segundo";
X.Address.StNumber := 343;
X.Address.Street := "Sombra Street";
X.Address.City := "San Andres";
X.Address.State := "New Mexico";
X.Address.Zip := "88008";
X.Balance := 12500;
X.Transaction.When.Month := 11;
X.Transaction.When.Day := 23;
X.Transaction.When.Year := 1987;
X.Transaction.Amount := 4850;
```

Instead of using assignments, we could have read input data directly into each field.

The value of X is a composite value, which can be assigned to a variable of the same type as in

```
Y := X;
```

This causes the values in all the fields of Y to be assigned the corresponding values in the fields of X.

6.6 An Introduction to Abstract Data Types and External Modules

At the beginning of this chapter we said that a data type includes an allowed set of values and operations on those values. Often we must construct data types that may not be supported directly in a programming language. When defining this new data type, we must specify the set of values and the allowed operations on these values. Such a definition of a type not built into the language is called an *abstract data type*. We have already used the STRING type, which, with its associated operations, forms an abstract data type.

In this section you will learn how to define an abstract data type for points in the Cartesian plane. We'll see how such a data type is defined in Modula-2 using an external module.

EXAMPLE: *Two-Dimensional Cartesian Coordinates*

We can define a point in the plane as an ordered pair of real values where the first value is the x coordinate and the second value is the y coordinate. We write an ordered

Figure 6.4
Operations of Addition and Reflection

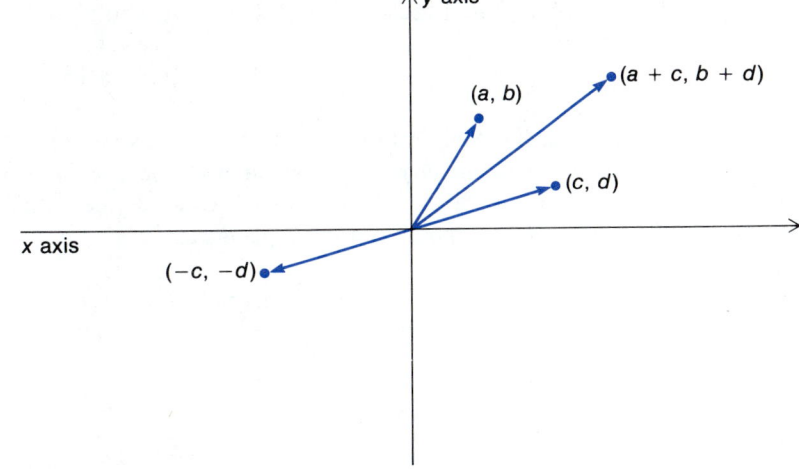

pair as (a, b). The distance from a point, (a, b), to the origin is

$$\sqrt{a^2 + b^2}$$

We can add two points by adding the coordinates

$$(a, b) + (c, d) = (a + c, b + d)$$

We can visualize this addition as adding two vectors (see Figure 6.4). We can define subtraction in an analogous way:

$$(a, b) - (c, d) = (a - c, b - d)$$

The operations of multiplication and division are left as Programming Problem 18. Our final operation involves reflection of a point through the origin, as shown in Figure 6.4. Reflection is accomplished by changing the sign of both coordinates. Graphically, reflection produces a point symmetrical to the original point with respect to the origin. Note that subtraction can be viewed as the addition of the first ordered pair and the reflection of the second ordered pair.

Points in the plane can also be viewed as complex numbers. Instead of (a, b), the notation is $a + bi$, where a is called the real part and b is called the imaginary part.

Defining the Point Data Type

Since there is no built-in data type to represent points in the plane, we must define our own data type. It cannot be a simple type, like a subrange, since points have two components—an x coordinate and a y coordinate. A record is a natural structure for defining points:

```
TYPE   Point = RECORD
                  X, Y : REAL;
               END;
```

To declare variables of type Point, we would need a declaration such as

    VAR P1, P2: Point;

This declaration defines the set of values as an ordered pair of real numbers, but it does not define any of the operations. The operation of finding the distance to the origin results in a real number, so we can define a function that returns the distance when passed a point as a value parameter.

```
PROCEDURE DistanceToOrigin( P : Point ) : REAL;
(* returns the distance of the point P from the origin  *)
BEGIN
   RETURN sqrt( P.X * P.X + P.Y * P.Y );
END DistanceToOrigin;
```

This function follows directly from the definition of distance as the square root of the sum of the *x* coordinate squared and the *y* coordinate squared.

The addition of two points results in a point. Since points are not a simple type, we cannot use a Modula-2 function to return the result value. Therefore, we will use a VAR parameter to return the result, as in the following procedure:

```
PROCEDURE AddPoints( P1, P2: Point; VAR Result: Point );
(* adds points P1 and P2 and returns answer as Result *)
BEGIN
   Result.X := P1.X + P2.X;
   Result.Y := P1.Y + P2.Y;
END AddPoints;
```

The remaining operations are defined in the following section.

Defining a Module

We could define our operations on points as part of a program that uses points, but this approach means that every program that needs to use points would have to redefine the type Point and the allowed operations. Obviously, such repetition would be quite wasteful of both program space and programmer time. Fortunately, in Modula-2 we can define a separately compiled program, called an *external module,* that can make this abstract data type available for all users. We will study modules in more detail in Chapter 11; this section is intended only as a first introduction.

An external module has two parts: the definition part, which says what objects are available for other programs (or modules) to use; and the implementation part, where operations (in the form of procedures) are fully defined. We are already familiar with the definition modules for InOut, Strings, and TurtleGraphics (see Appendices E and F). Strings is a good example of an abstract data type: it included a single type declaration, STRING, and many operations that could be performed on that type. Our definition module for points will follow this same format.

```
DEFINITION MODULE Points;

TYPE   Point = RECORD
                 X, Y : REAL;
               END;

PROCEDURE DistanceToOrigin( P : Point ) : REAL;
(* returns the distance of the point P from the origin *)

PROCEDURE AddPoints( P1, P2: Point; VAR Result: Point );
(* adds the points P1 and P2 and returns the answer as Result *)

PROCEDURE SubtractPoints( P1, P2: Point; VAR Result: Point );
(* subtracts point P2 from P1 and returns the answer as Result *)

PROCEDURE ReflectOrigin( VAR P: Point );
(* reflects the point P through the origin *)

END Points.
```

Definition modules must contain the full declaration of all constants, types, and variables that are made available for import by other programs or modules. The declaration of procedures is limited to procedure headings only. Specifically, these headings include the keyword PROCEDURE, the procedure name, the parameter list (if any), and—for functions—the type of value returned. It is good programming style to include comments following each procedure heading. These comments explain what the procedures do for prospective users.

The implementation part of an external module must fully define the procedures declared in the definition part. The implementation module for Points is as follows:

```
IMPLEMENTATION MODULE Points;
FROM MathLib0 IMPORT sqrt;

PROCEDURE DistanceToOrigin(P : Point) : REAL;
(* returns the distance of the point P from the origin  *)
BEGIN
   RETURN sqrt(P.X * P.X + P.Y * P.Y);
END DistanceToOrigin;

PROCEDURE AddPoints(P1, P2: Point; VAR Result: Point);
(* adds the points P1 and P2 and returns answer as Result *)
BEGIN
   Result.X := P1.X + P2.X;
   Result.Y := P1.Y + P2.Y;
END AddPoints;
```

```
PROCEDURE SubtractPoints (P1, P2: Point; VAR Result: Point);
(* subtract point P2 from P1 and return answer as Result *)
BEGIN
   Result.X := P1.X - P2.X;
   Result.Y := P1.Y - P2.Y;
END SubtractPoints;

PROCEDURE ReflectOrigin (VAR P: Point);
(* reflects the point P through the origin *)
BEGIN
   P.X := -P.X;
   P.Y := -P.Y;
END ReflectOrigin;

END Points.
```

A definition module must be compiled before the corresponding implementation module. The definition module should also be compiled before any program or module that imports objects from that module. Finally, the user should not try to execute a program unless all program components have been compiled.

Using the Points Module

Once the points module has been compiled, other programs can import objects from that module. In this section we will develop two short procedures that will use points and operations on points.

The first procedure will be a function to test if one point is closer to the origin than another point. If the two points are P1 and P2, then P1 is closer than P2 when the distance from the origin to P1 is less than the distance from the origin to P2. Our corresponding Modula-2 procedure follows directly from this definition. We assume that Point and DistanceToOrigin have been imported from Points by our program.

```
PROCEDURE CloserThan( P1, P2: Point ) : BOOLEAN;
BEGIN
   RETURN DistanceToOrigin( P1 ) < DistanceToOrigin( P2 );
END CloserThan;
```

Suppose that we want to find the distance between two points. If P1 has coordinates (a, b) and P2 has coordinates (c, d), then by applying the Pythagorean theorem, we see that this distance is

$$\sqrt{(a - c)^2 + (b - d)^2}$$

This is equivalent to the distance from the origin of P1 − P2, so our distance function is quite simple:

```
        PROCEDURE DistanceBetween( P1, P2: Point ) : REAL;
        VAR Temp: Point;
        BEGIN
           SubtractPoints( P1, P2, Temp );
           RETURN DistanceToOrigin( Temp );
        END DistanceBetween;
```

Again, we assume that the necessary objects have been imported from Points.

As indicated by the name, Modula-2, the concept of module is very important to this language. Niklaus Wirth, the designer of the earlier language, Pascal, also designed Modula-2. But standard Pascal does not include any notion of module or separate compilation. Thus the module is one of the most important features that makes Modula-2 a more advanced programming language than Pascal. We will continue our study of modules throughout the remainder of this text.

SUMMARY

The basic data types in Modula-2 are the numeric types CARDINAL, INTEGER, and REAL, and the nonnumeric types BOOLEAN and CHAR. Each data type is characterized by the values allowed, the operations that can be performed on the operands, and the ways operations and operands can be combined to form expressions.

For the numeric data types the permissible operations are addition, subtraction, multiplication, and division. Unary operators have one operand, while binary operators have two operands. We must carefully specify the order in which operations are performed to determine the value of an expresssion.

The operands of an arithmetic operator must be of the same type, but if the need arises, we can also mix types by using type conversion functions. Modula-2 has a number of built-in standard functions that can act as type conversion functions and perform other useful operations.

BOOLEAN, another basic Modula-2 type, has only two permissible values—TRUE and FALSE. Simple Boolean expressions are constructed with relational operators such as equal, less than, less than or equal to, and so on. These simple expressions can be combined to form more complex expressions with the three Boolean operators: NOT, AND, and OR. These operators are defined in mathematics by truth tables.

Boolean expressions in Modula-2 are evaluated according to the precedence of relational and Boolean operators. These expressions differ from mathematical expressions in that evaluation occurs from left to right, and once the final result is known, the evaluation stops. In some cases two Boolean expressions will always produce the same value; this equivalence can be shown with truth tables.

A simple IF with a complex Boolean expression may sometimes be equivalent to a nested IF. To test the equivalence of IF statements you can form decision tables or decision trees, which show when an action is or is not taken.

To supplement the built-in Modula-2 data types, we may need to define new types such as subrange or record types. A subrange type is a restriction of the range of values of a base type. A record type is a structured data type that can have a fixed number of components of various types.

To define an abstract data type, we must specify its values and the allowed operations. We can implement an abstract data type using external modules that are separately compiled.

EXERCISES

1. Write an IF statement that could serve as the definition of the standard procedure ABS.

2. Write the Modula-2 expressions corresponding to the following mathematical expressions:

$$x + \frac{y}{a+b} + z \qquad \frac{5x^2}{4y} + z$$

3. Given the indicated variables and their values, evaluate the following expressions.

A	B	C	X	Y	Z
18	4	2	12.5	2.0	3.14

   A * B − C DIV 2
   X * Y / Z + 3.0
   (B + C) * 3
   A DIV 2 − 4
   B + A MOD 5 − 1
   (A + B + C) DIV 4
   A # B
   X = Y * Z
   'A' < 'J'
   X * Z / Y <= 19.7

4. Knowing that one liter is equivalent to 0.264 gallons, and given the number of liters of gas needed to cover a distance in miles, write the statements that will compute and print the corresponding number of miles per gallon.

5. Given the indicated variables and their values, evaluate the following Boolean expressions.

A	B	C	D
TRUE	FALSE	FALSE	TRUE

   A AND D OR A AND B
   NOT (C AND D AND A)
   NOT (A AND D) OR (C OR D)
   (A OR B) AND NOT (C OR D)

6. Write the Boolean expression corresponding to the condition

$$x < y < z$$

7. Give a statement to set Eligible to TRUE if Grade is greater than 80, Age is greater than or equal to 18, Height is greater than or equal to MinimumHeight, and Weight is greater than MinimumWeight.

8. Give a general rule for the evaluation of expressions of each of the following forms:

$$A \text{ AND } B \text{ AND } C$$
$$A \text{ OR } B \text{ OR } C$$
$$A \text{ AND } B \text{ OR } C$$
$$A \text{ OR } B \text{ AND } C$$

9. Prove DeMorgan's Law

$$(\text{NOT } A) \text{ AND } (\text{NOT } B) \equiv \text{NOT}(A \text{ OR } B)$$

10. Prove that

$$A \text{ AND } B \text{ OR } C \not\equiv (A \text{ OR } B) \text{ AND } C$$

by constructing a truth table for A AND B OR C and observing where it differs from the truth table given in the section entitled "Evaluation of Boolean Expressions" for

$$(A \text{ OR } B) \text{ AND } C$$

11. Show that IF statements of the following two forms are equivalent

```
IF A AND B THEN
   S
END;  (* IF *);

IF A THEN
   IF B THEN
      S
   END;  (* IF *)
END;  (* IF *);
```

12. Construct a decision table for

```
IF A AND B THEN
   S1
ELSE
   S2
END;  (* IF *)
```

and compare it with the decision table given in the section in this chapter entitled "Evaluation of Boolean Expressions" for

```
IF A THEN
   IF B THEN
      S1
   ELSE
      S2
   END;  (* IF *)
END;  (* IF *);
```

Identify the conditions under which the two forms of the IF-THEN-ELSE differ.

13. Make the two statements given in Exercise 12 equivalent by relocating the END of the second statement.

PROGRAMMING PROBLEMS

14. Write and test a function TruncReal, which accepts a REAL argument and returns an INTEGER result that represents the integer part of the argument. Hint: use TRUNC within an IF statement to handle positive and negative numbers differently.

15. Define and test a function, RoundReal, defined by

    $$\text{RoundReal}(x) = \text{TRUNC}(x + 0.5) \quad \text{if } x >= 0$$
    $$\text{RoundReal}(x) = -\text{TRUNC}(-x + 0.5) \quad \text{if } x < 0$$

    Using this definition of RoundReal, prove that for any x

    $$\text{RoundReal}(-x) = -\text{RoundReal}(x)$$

16. Write and test a Boolean function XOR that will correspond to the "exclusive or" logical function: this function of two arguments is true if only one of the arguments is true.

17. Enter and compile the definition and implementation modules for points. Implement a program to test this module thoroughly.

18. Add the following operations to your points module:

    (a, b) times (c, d) is $(ac - bd, ad + bc)$

    (a, b) divided by (c, d) is $(\,(ac + bd)/\text{denom}, (bc - ad)/\text{denom})$
    where denom $= c * c + d * d$

    Division is not defined when the divisor is the point $(0, 0)$.

19. Define an abstract data type for a student's course record. Assume the following components:

    four programs worth 100 points each

    two midterm exams worth 175 points each

    one final worth 250 points

    Implement the following operations:

    Reset all values to zero

    Assign any specified data value

    Fetch any specified data value

    Compute total points

    Assign grade based on   90–100%   A
                                        80–89.9%   B
                                        70–79.9%   C
                                        60–69.9%   D
                                        below 60%   F

7 Program Structure

In this chapter you will:

- learn about the block structure of Modula-2
- investigate the rules for the scope of identifiers
- learn more about nested procedures
- learn more about how recursion works
- learn more about information hiding

The preceding chapters have introduced you to the following components of Modula-2 programs:

expressions, which may be part of statements such as the assignment statement
statements, which may be grouped to form procedures
procedures, which are basic components of programs
modules, which are collections of objects that may be used by programs

Figure 7.1 illustrates the hierarchy between these components.

Large programs are usually composed of relatively small procedures, and some procedures will, in turn, be composed of procedures declared (or nested) within them. Moreover, large programs usually import objects from external modules for use within the program. In other words, large programs normally have a great deal of structure.

In this chapter we explain the structure of large Modula-2 programs. We begin by defining a program's environment, and the local environments of procedures. We then explain what we mean by a block and a block-structured language. With this background we discuss Modula-2 program structure, rules of scope, nested procedures, and recursive procedures. To illustrate these structural concepts, we look at several examples of nested and recursive procedures. Finally the last section states the information hiding principle and shows how to apply it to obtain good program structures.

Figure 7.1
Program Structure
Hierarchy

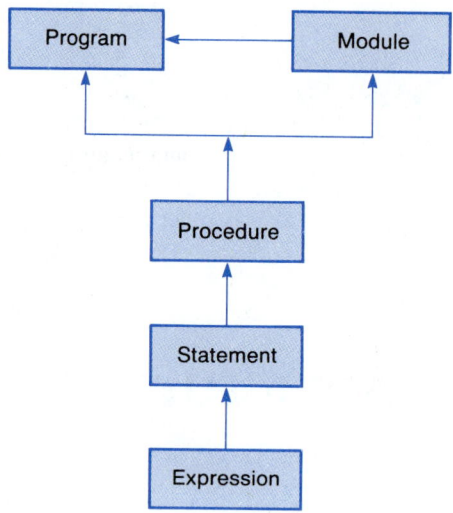

7.1 The Structure of Modula-2 Programs

Procedures and external modules are the structural components of Modula-2 programs. The identifiers that can be accessed in these components may be different from those accessible within the main program. The identifiers that may be accessed by a program or a program component constitute the program's or the component's environment. The environment of a main program or an external module is determined precisely by the declarations and import lists in the main program or external module respectively. However, a procedure can access some identifiers declared outside the procedure, without importing them, as well as identifiers declared within the procedure. As a result we refer to the identifiers declared within a procedure as the *local environment* of the procedure. In the following sections we will discuss the local environments of procedures as well as the identifiers that are accessible outside the local environment. In our discussion we'll be introduced to the block structure of Modula-2 and the three basic rules of scope.

Local Environments of Procedures

Chapters 1 and 4 introduced procedure invocation as one method to control the flow of statement execution in a program. A procedure call transfers program control from the location of the call to the first executable statement in the procedure. After the last statement in a procedure has been executed, control is transferred back to the statement following the procedure call. However, since procedures also have a declaration section, procedure invocation is much more than a simple transfer of control; it is also the invocation of a new local environment in which program execution takes place.

You may have noticed that in Modula-2 the format of procedures is very similar to the format of program modules; each may have declarations and executable statements. We will refer to any such combination of declarations and executable statements as a *block*, and we say that Modula-2 is a *block-structured language*. Predecessors of Modula-2 (ALGOL 60, ALGOL W, and Pascal) were also block structured. This kind of programming language offered the possibility of local environments, determined by local declarations of constants, types, variables, and procedures.

The local environment of a procedure contains all objects declared between the procedure name and the BEGIN statement. In other words, it includes any formal parameters, constants, types, variables, and other procedures declared locally. Consider the following program skeleton:

```
MODULE Environ;
CONST M = 4;
VAR A, B, C: CARDINAL;

  PROCEDURE Proc1( X: CARDINAL );
  CONST T = 45;
  VAR Y: CARDINAL;
  BEGIN
     (* statements *)
  END Proc1;

BEGIN  (* Environ *)
   (* statements *)
   Proc1( 5 );    (* procedure call *)
   (* statements *)
END Environ.
```

Statements in the main program may refer to identifiers in the main program (or global) environment, which contains five objects: the constant M; variable names A, B, and C; and the procedure name Proc1. When Proc1 is called and control is transferred to Proc1, a local environment for Proc1 is established with three objects: the parameter X, the constant T, and the variable Y. From within Proc1 we also have access to the global environment, so a total of eight objects are accessible:

- two constants: T and M
- one parameter: X
- four variables: Y, A, B, and C
- one procedure: Proc1

This access is illustrated in Figure 7.2

The dashed lines around the body of Proc1 represent a one-way window: Proc1 can look out and see objects in the enclosing environment, but the enclosing environment cannot look inside Proc1.

When the end of Proc1 is encountered, control is transferred back to the statement following the procedure call, and the local environment declared by Proc1 disappears.

Although this concept of local environment may at first appear simple, it actually holds a number of more complicated subtleties. What happens if the same identifier name is declared in more than one location? We will investigate this question in the next section on the rules of scope. What happens when procedures are nested—one

Figure 7.2
Blocks of Program Environ

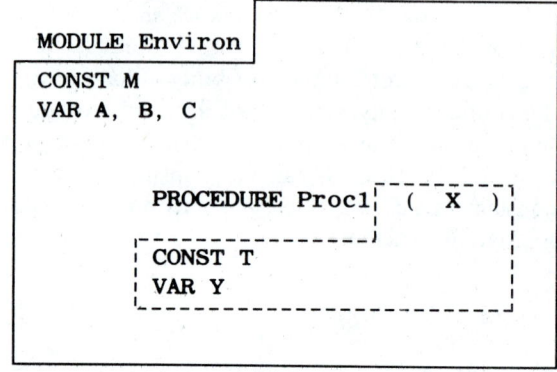

declared within another? What happens to local environments when a procedure calls itself? We will investigate these situations in later sections of this chapter.

Rules of Scope

We introduced rules of scope informally in Chapter 3. Recall that an identifier is the name associated with an object. The scope of an identifier refers to those parts of the program where the identifier is visible such that the associated object is accessible. Let us express these rules more precisely here:

Rule 1 The scope of an identifier is

(a) the block in which the identifier is declared or imported; and

(b) any procedures nested within that block, unless another declaration of the same identifier appears in the nested procedures (this exception will be discussed in detail shortly).

Rule 2 An identifier may be referred to only within its scope. These rules apply to all identifiers, whether they are procedure names, formal parameters, variables, constants, or types.

It is good programming style to declare an object so that its scope is as local as possible. That way the associated object will not be available, and thus subject to change or misuse in parts of the program that should not have access to it. This style of programming is based on the information hiding principle, which we mentioned briefly in Chapter 6 and which we'll discuss in detail at the end of this chapter and stress throughout the book.

Let's look at an example of scope—a simple program, Scope1, with multiply-declared identifiers. Try to predict what this program will print before you read the explanation that follows the program.

```
MODULE Scope1;
FROM InOut IMPORT WriteInt, WriteLn;

VAR X,Y: INTEGER;
```

```
PROCEDURE Print(M, N: INTEGER);
BEGIN
  WriteInt(M, 5);
  WriteInt(N, 5);
  WriteLn;
END Print;

PROCEDURE First;
VAR X: INTEGER;
BEGIN
  X := 7;
  Y := Y + 6;
  Print(X, Y);
END First;

PROCEDURE Second;
VAR X, Y: INTEGER;
BEGIN
  X := 2;
  Y := X + 3;
  Print(X, Y);
END Second;

BEGIN  (* Scope1 *)
  X := 1;
  Y := 2;
  Print(X, Y);
  First;
  Print(X, Y);
  Second;
  Print(X, Y);
END Scope1.
```

Scope1 will print the following:

1	2
7	8
1	8
2	5
1	8

If you correctly predicted this output, you probably used a rule similar to our third scoping rule.

Rule 3 When an identifier is referenced, the most local declaration is used.

The "most local declaration" means that you look in the local procedure first; if you don't find the identifier, you look in the enclosing procedure. This process continues outward toward the main program until you find the first occurrence of the identifier declaration. At the level of the main program, import lists as well as declarations must be searched for the identifier. If the identifier has not been declared or imported, the program will not compile (the compiler should print an "identifier not declared" message).

To emphasize the effect of the scoping rules on Scope1, we have reproduced the program in Figure 7.3 with blocks drawn around the procedures and comments added

Figure 7.3
Scope1 Block Structure

```
MODULE Scope1;

  FROM InOut IMPORT WriteInt, WriteLn;

  VAR X, Y: INTEGER;

  PROCEDURE Print(M, N: INTEGER);
  BEGIN
    WriteInt(M, 5);          (* M in Print *)
    WriteInt(N, 5);          (* N in Print *)
    WriteLn;
  END Print;

  PROCEDURE First;
    VAR X: INTEGER;
  BEGIN
    X := 7;                  (* X in First *)
    Y := Y + 6;              (* global Y *)
    Print(X, Y);             (* X in First, global Y *)
  END First;

  PROCEDURE Second;
    VAR X, Y: INTEGER;
  BEGIN
    X := 2;                  (* X in Second *)
    Y := X + 3;              (* Y in Second *)
    Print(X, Y);             (* X in Second, Y in Second *)
  END Second;

BEGIN   (* Scope1 *)
  X := 1;                    (* global X *)
  Y := 2;                    (* global Y *)
  Print(X, Y);               (* global Print, global X, global Y *)
  First;                     (* global First *)
  Print(X, Y);               (* global Print, global X, global Y *)
  Second;                    (* global Second *)
  Print(X, Y);               (* global Print, global X, global Y *)
END Scope1.
```

to clarify the identifier referenced. This diagram suggests why Modula-2 is called a block-structured language. Note that the main program can reference only global identifiers: those declared or imported in the main program. Global identifiers are visible throughout the program and its procedures, unless there is a more local declaration of the same name. As mentioned before, the blocks around the procedures can be thought of as one-way windows; the procedures can see out to access nonlocal identifiers, but the main program (or enclosing procedure, when applicable) cannot see inside to access local identifiers.

In the case of a multiply-declared identifier, the more global declarations are masked (or hidden) by the most local declaration. For example, in PROCEDURE First, the global variable X is masked by the local declaration of X within the environment of First. So the value associated with X within First may be different from the value associated with the global X.

The masking of more global variables by local variables can be helpful, because it usually avoids difficulties due to inadvertent choices of the same identifier at two places in the program. For example, if I is used as the control variable of a FOR loop in the main program and also in another FOR loop within a procedure, the conflict does not usually create a problem. The potential ambiguity is resolved by Rule 3. Naturally, if you mask a more global variable, which must be used within a nested procedure, you create a problem. However, precisely because such variables are needed, this conflict seldom occurs; when it does, the problem is usually easy to detect and correct.

Scoping and Parameter Passing

Scoping determines what objects are accessible in various components of the program, while parameter passing defines what objects are explicitly passed to and from a procedure. The methods look similar but are fundamentally different, so we will discuss their interaction. First, let's review our two parameter-passing techniques from Chapter 3: value and variable parameters.

> *Value parameter:* A value is received from the procedure call and assigned to the formal parameter. Any change to this parameter is purely local and will not change any values external to the procedure.
>
> *Variable parameter:* Since variable parameters may be used to pass information in *and* out of a procedure, any changes to the value of a variable parameter also change the value of the variable used as the actual parameter.

Since value parameters act like local variables, the rules of scope are the same as for local variables. In fact, Scope1 used value parameters in the Print procedure. Often a procedure must have access to variables not normally visible to that procedure. The best way to provide such access is by using variable parameters. Consider the program Scope2, shown in Figure 7.4.

The Swap procedure switches two integer values; Swap is declared globally so that it can be called from anywhere in the program. However, the variables to be swapped

Figure 7.4
Extension of Scope by VAR Parameters

```
MODULE Scope2;

FROM InOut IMPORT WriteInt, WriteLn;

PROCEDURE Swap (VAR M, N: INTEGER);
  VAR T: INTEGER;
  BEGIN
    T := M;
    M := N;
    N := T;
  END Swap;

PROCEDURE One;
  VAR W, X: INTEGER;

  PROCEDURE Two;
    VAR Y, Z: INTEGER;
    BEGIN
      Y := 3; Z := 4;
      WriteInt(Y, 5); WriteInt(Z, 5); WriteLn;
      Swap(Y, Z);
      WriteInt(Y, 5); WriteInt(Z, 5); WriteLn;
    END Two;

  BEGIN (* One *)
    W := 1; X := 2;
    WriteInt(W, 5); WriteInt(X, 5); WriteLn;
    Swap(W, X);
    WriteInt(W, 5); WriteInt(X, 5); WriteLn;
    Two;
  END One;

BEGIN (* Scope2 *)
  One;
END Scope2.
```

may not be accessible to Swap using the rules of scope. We can overcome this problem by having the parameters declared as variable parameters. Scope2 will print

```
1    2
2    1
3    4
4    3
```

Note that the calling procedure explicitly granted access to its local variables by passing them as variable parameters to the called procedure. If such permission is not granted, an external procedure cannot access these local variables (see Exercise 1 at the end of the chapter).

7.2 Nested Procedures

Thus far we have seen examples of one procedure nested within another. In this section we will investigate a procedure that contains two locally declared procedures. These nested procedures are available to the enclosing procedure but not the main program. Then we will look at a more complex example of procedure nesting and invocation. Here we will analyze the flow of control and the visibility of identifiers as the program executes.

EXAMPLE 1 *Nesting with Locally Declared Procedures*

In Chapter 3, we wrote a procedure that would print a box of asterisks around a one-line title; in this section we will write a procedure to print a box around a three-line title. Each of the lines will be centered in the box, as follows:

```
***********************
*   PROCEDURE TitleBox *
*       B. Kurtz      *
*     January 1988    *
***********************
```

The longest of the three lines, together with a parameter specifying the number of blanks to be placed on each side (padding blanks), will determine the width of the box. We may pad the longest line with zero blanks, as indicated by the following example. However, we may not be able to center each line exactly. In that case, we can append the extra blank at the right, as seen here for the words "Long" and "Longer":

```
********
* Long  *
*Longer *
*Longest*
********
```

Three lines will be required, but it is permissible for any of them to be empty. The following title box has only one nonempty title line.

```
***********************
*                     *
*   A One Line Title  *
*                     *
***********************
```

Figure 7.5
Structure Chart for Multiple Line Title Box

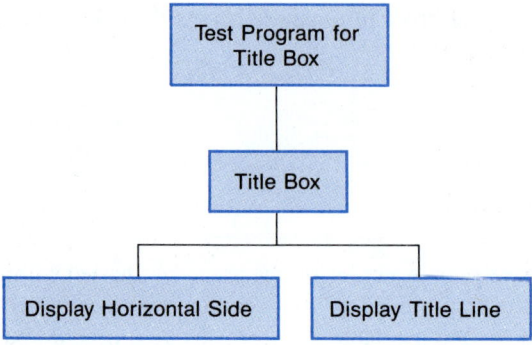

The task, TitleBox, can be decomposed into two subtasks: displaying the horizontal side at the top and bottom, and displaying each title line. We will also need a test program for this procedure. Figure 7.5 gives a structure chart for this problem.

Notice that a structure chart does not show the order in which subprograms are called or the number of times they are called. To do this, we must refine our solution to pseudocode. We will pass four values to TitleBox: the three lines to be printed and the number of blanks to pad on each side of the longest line. If MaxLength is the length of the longest title line, then the width of the box is the length of the longest line plus two asterisk characters plus twice the number of blanks to be added. The corresponding pseudocode is as follows:

```
TitleBox ( Line1, Line2, Line3, NumBlanks )
    Find MaxLength of the three input lines
    Display Horizontal Side ( MaxLength + 2 + 2 * NumBlanks )
    Display Title Line ( Line1, MaxLength, NumBlanks )
    Display Title Line ( Line2, MaxLength, NumBlanks )
    Display Title Line ( Line3, MaxLength, NumBlanks )
    Display Horizontal Side ( MaxLength + 2 + 2 * NumBlanks )
End TitleBox
```

The pseudocode for displaying the horizontal side is very simple:

```
Display Horizontal Side ( Width )
    Form a string of "Width" asterisks
    Print this string
End Display Horizontal Side
```

Printing the title line is more complex than in our previous program because, when there are three lines, the shorter lines must be padded with extra blanks. The following pseudocode indicates how this is done:

> Display Title Line (Line, MaxLength, NumBlanks)
>   Calculate the number of extra blanks
>   Increase NumBlanks by half of the extra blanks
>   Form a string of NumBlanks spaces
>   Print '*', string of NumBlanks spaces, Line, string of NumBlanks spaces
>   If extra blanks is odd then
>   Print a space
>   End if
>   Print '*'
> End Display Title Line

The only problem occurs when the number of extra blanks is odd. Since we cannot split a blank in half, we will put the extra blank in the spaces following the title line. We accomplish this with an If instruction, as shown in the preceding pseudocode. Our program code, shown next, follows directly from the pseudocode. The test program should produce the three patterns illustrated previously.

```
MODULE CheckTitleBox;
(* Tests the procedure TitleBox which displays a three-
   line title like
     **********************
     *   PROCEDURE TitleBox   *
     *        B. Kurtz        *
     *      January 1988      *
     **********************
                                                          *)

FROM InOut IMPORT Write, WriteString, WriteLn;
FROM Strings IMPORT STRING, Copy, Length;

PROCEDURE TitleBox(Line1, Line2, Line3: STRING;
                   NumBlanks: CARDINAL);
(* Display a three-line title within a box of asterisks  *)

VAR MaxLength: CARDINAL;

  PROCEDURE DisplayHorizontalSide(Width: CARDINAL);
  (* display a string of asterisks of specified width *)

  CONST
    Asterisks =
      "*******************************************";
  VAR HorizontalSide: STRING;
```

```
    BEGIN
      Copy(Asterisks, 0, Width, HorizontalSide);
      WriteString(HorizontalSide); WriteLn;
    END DisplayHorizontalSide;

    PROCEDURE DisplayTitleLine(Line: STRING;
                               Width, NumBlanks: CARDINAL);
    (* display a title line padded by blanks and asterisks at
       each end *)

    CONST Blanks = "                         ";
    VAR BlankString: STRING;
        ExtraBlanks: CARDINAL;

    BEGIN
      ExtraBlanks := Width - Length(Line);
      NumBlanks := NumBlanks + ExtraBlanks DIV 2;
      Copy(Blanks, 0, NumBlanks, BlankString);
      Write('*'); WriteString(BlankString);
      WriteString(Line);   WriteString(BlankString);
      IF ODD(ExtraBlanks) THEN
        Write(' ');
      END;   (* IF *)
      Write('*'); WriteLn;
    END DisplayTitleLine;

BEGIN   (* TitleBox *)
  MaxLength := Length(Line1);
  IF Length(Line2) > MaxLength THEN
    MaxLength := Length(Line2);
  END;   (* IF *)
  IF Length(Line3) > MaxLength THEN
    MaxLength := Length(Line3);
  END;   (* IF *)
  DisplayHorizontalSide(MaxLength + 2 + 2 * NumBlanks);
  DisplayTitleLine(Line1, MaxLength, NumBlanks);
  DisplayTitleLine(Line2, MaxLength, NumBlanks);
  DisplayTitleLine(Line3, MaxLength, NumBlanks);
  DisplayHorizontalSide(MaxLength + 2 + 2 * NumBlanks);
END TitleBox;

BEGIN   (* CheckTitleBox *)
  TitleBox("PROCEDURE TitleBox",
           "B. Kurtz",
           "January 1988", 2);
  WriteLn; WriteLn;
  TitleBox("Long",
           "Longer",
           "Longest", 0);
  WriteLn; WriteLn;
  TitleBox("", "A One Line Title", "", 3);
END CheckTitleBox.
```

SEC. 7.2 Nested Procedures

Our program has introduced two procedures declared within another procedure. The scope of the procedures DisplayHorizontalSide and DisplayTitleLine is the procedure TitleBox. It is desirable to indent nested procedures, as done in the preceding example, so that their scope can be easily seen.

The rules of scope apply at any level of nesting. The constant Asterisks and the variable HorizontalSide are local to the procedure DisplayHorizontalSide; this means that they are not accessible from the procedure DrawTitleLine, TitleBox, or the main program. Similarly, the identifiers Blanks, BlankString, and ExtraBlanks are local to the procedure DisplayTitleLine.

EXAMPLE 2 *Flow of Control and Nested Procedures*

Nesting of procedures is a way of structuring the program, but program structure does not necessarily reflect the flow of control at execution time. To illustrate this difference, let's consider a more complex example of nested procedures.

We will study flow of control in a program, called Nest1, containing nested procedures (see Figure 7.6). In this program the procedures print messages to indicate the path of program execution. Each procedure is passed a parameter named Level, which determines the number of dots printed before the message. When one procedure calls another procedure, Level is increased by one. The main program starts off with Level equal to zero. Before reading on, try to determine what will be printed by Nest1.

Figure 7.6
Nesting of Procedures

```
MODULE Nest1;

  FROM InOut IMPORT WriteString, WriteLn;
  FROM Strings IMPORT STRING, Copy;

  VAR Level: INTEGER;

  PROCEDURE WriteMsg(Level: INTEGER; Message: STRING);
    CONST AllDots = "........................";
    VAR Dots: STRING;
    BEGIN
      Copy(AllDots, 0, Level, Dots);
      WriteString(Dots);
      WriteString(Message);
      WriteLn;
    END WriteMsg;

  PROCEDURE Proc1(Level: INTEGER);
    BEGIN
      WriteMsg(Level, "Inside of Proc1");
    END Proc1;
```

Figure 7.6
continued

```
        PROCEDURE Proc2(Level: INTEGER);

        BEGIN
          WriteMsg(Level, "Entering Proc2");
          Proc1(Level + 1);
          WriteMsg(Level, "Leaving Proc2");
        END Proc2;

        PROCEDURE Proc3(Level: INTEGER);

            PROCEDURE Proc4(Level: INTEGER);

            BEGIN
              WriteMsg(Level, "Inside of Proc4");
            END Proc4;

        BEGIN   (* Proc3 *)
          WriteMsg(Level, "Entering Proc3");
          Proc4(Level + 1);
          WriteMsg(Level, "Midway in Proc3");
          Proc2(Level + 1);
          WriteMsg(Level, "Leaving Proc3");
        END Proc3;

        BEGIN   (* Nest1 *)
          Level := 0;
          WriteMsg(Level, "Starting program Nest1");
          Proc2(Level + 1);
          WriteMsg(Level, "Midway in Nest1");
          Proc3(Level + 1);
          WriteMsg(Level, "Ending program Nest1");
        END Nest1.
```

Nest1 will print

```
Starting program Nest1
.Entering Proc2
..Inside of Proc1
.Leaving Proc2
Midway in Nest1
.Entering Proc3
..Inside of Proc4
.Midway in Proc3
..Entering Proc2
...Inside of Proc1
..Leaving Proc2
.Leaving Proc3
Ending program Nest1
```

The dots indicate the level of the procedure calls. No dot indicates the main program or level 0; one dot indicates a procedure called from the main program; two dots indicate a procedure called from a procedure that is called from the main program; and so forth. Notice that the same procedure might have a different number of dots printed depending on where it is called. For example, the first call to Proc2 has one dot, but the second call has two dots. Similarly, Proc1 has two dots the first time and three dots the second time. Thus the level of procedure calls does not have to match the nesting of the procedures within the program, as illustrated by the blocks drawn in Figure 7.6.

The level of procedure calls is determined *dynamically* at run time while the nesting depth is determined *statically* by the structure of the program declarations and can be seen by examining the program listing. When designing a programming language, the designer must decide whether the scope of identifiers is to be determined by the static structure of the program at compile time or by the dynamic order of execution at run time. Almost all block-structured languages, including Modula-2, determine the scope of identifiers statically.

We have given a fairly detailed treatment of nested procedures, because you need to know how they are treated in a block-structured language. However, nesting to a depth of over three is uncommon and usually not desirable, since programs with such depth of structure are difficult to comprehend and maintain.

7.3 Recursive Procedures

As we saw in Chapter 5, recursive problem-solving methods can be directly implemented by procedures that call themselves (recursive procedures). We will now investigate how recursion works in computers. Although it may not be obvious at first, a recursive procedure is a special case of nesting. With recursion, we do not explicitly nest one procedure within another; rather, we need only have the procedure call itself with a simpler argument.

EXAMPLE 1 *Execution of Recursive Calls*

To understand how recursion is accomplished by the computer, we will study the way that recursive calls are executed in two examples. For our first example, we will use a variation of the simple recursive factorial program from Chapter 5, with the addition of a procedure, Trace, to help us follow the recursive calls:

```
MODULE FactTrace;
(* Program to trace the calls of a recursive factorial
   procedure. *)
```

```
FROM InOut IMPORT Write, WriteLn, WriteString, ReadInt,
                 WriteInt;

VAR N, Temp: INTEGER;

PROCEDURE Trace( Entering: BOOLEAN; M: INTEGER );
(* Display a message indicating whether procedure Factorial is
   being entered or exited with argument M.  Message is
   preceded by dots indicating the depth of the recursion.
   Global N is used to determine the depth, N - M. *)

VAR I: INTEGER;

BEGIN
  IF Entering THEN
    FOR I := 1 TO N - M DO Write( '.' ) END; (* FOR *)
    WriteString( "entering Factorial(" ); WriteInt( M, 1 );
    Write( ')' ); WriteLn;
  ELSE
    FOR I := 1 TO N - M DO Write( '.' ) END; (* FOR *)
    WriteString( "leaving Factorial(" ); WriteInt( M, 4 );
    WriteString( "), and returning" );
  END (* IF *)
END Trace;

PROCEDURE Factorial( K: INTEGER ): INTEGER;
(* Recursive computation of K! with tracing of recursive
   calls. *)

VAR Result: INTEGER;
CONST Entering = TRUE;
      Leaving = FALSE;

BEGIN
  Trace( Entering, K );
  IF K = 0 THEN
    Trace( Leaving, K );
    WriteInt( 1, 5 ); WriteLn;
    RETURN 1;
  ELSE
    Result := K * Factorial( K - 1 );
    Trace( Leaving, K );
    WriteInt( Result, 5 ); WriteLn;
    RETURN Result;
  END;   (* IF *)
END Factorial;

BEGIN (* Main *)
  LOOP
    WriteString( "Enter a non-negative integer: " );
    ReadInt( N );   WriteLn; WriteLn;
```

SEC. 7.3 Recursive Procedures

```
      IF N >= 0 THEN
         EXIT
      ELSE
         WriteString( "Your entry was not a non-negative integer." );
         WriteLn;
      END (* IF *);
   END (* LOOP *);
   Temp := Factorial( N );
   WriteLn; WriteLn;
   WriteString( "Factorial of " ); WriteInt( N, 2 );
   WriteString( " is" );
   WriteInt( Temp, 4 );
   WriteLn;
END FactTrace.
```

The output of this program provides us with a trace of the recursive calls. A sample run is as follows:

```
Enter a non-negative integer: 3

   entering Factorial(3)
  .entering Factorial(2)
  ..entering Factorial(1)
  ...entering Factorial(0)
  ...leaving Factorial(0), and returning    1
  ..leaving Factorial(1), and returning    1
  .leaving Factorial(2), and returning    2
   leaving Factorial(3), and returning    6

Factorial of  3 is    6
```

This output illustrates the fact that a recursive call must be completely done before continuing with the statement after the call. Thus the procedure call Factorial(3) in the main program gives rise to a pattern of recursive calls just illustrated. During execution the depth of the recursion is indicated by dots, much like the printout from the program in Figure 7.6. Each dot represents the fact that a recursive call of the procedure Factorial has not been completed. When a recursive call is completed, the correct result is passed to the previous level. The value returned by each call when the procedure is exited is also displayed.

A procedure call not only transfers control but also establishes a new local environment for program execution. We are depending on the establishment of a new local environment for recursion to work properly. The first call to Factorial establishes a local environment where K is 3. The recursive call, Factorial(K − 1), establishes a new local environment where its local identifier K has a value of 2. Notice that the identifier names in this local environment *are exactly the same* as the names in the previous local environment. Therefore, recalling our third scoping rule, we use the most local identifiers. Since this is a new environment, the values for the parameters or local variables can be different from the previous local environment. In fact, the value of at least one parameter must be different since we are doing a recursive call on

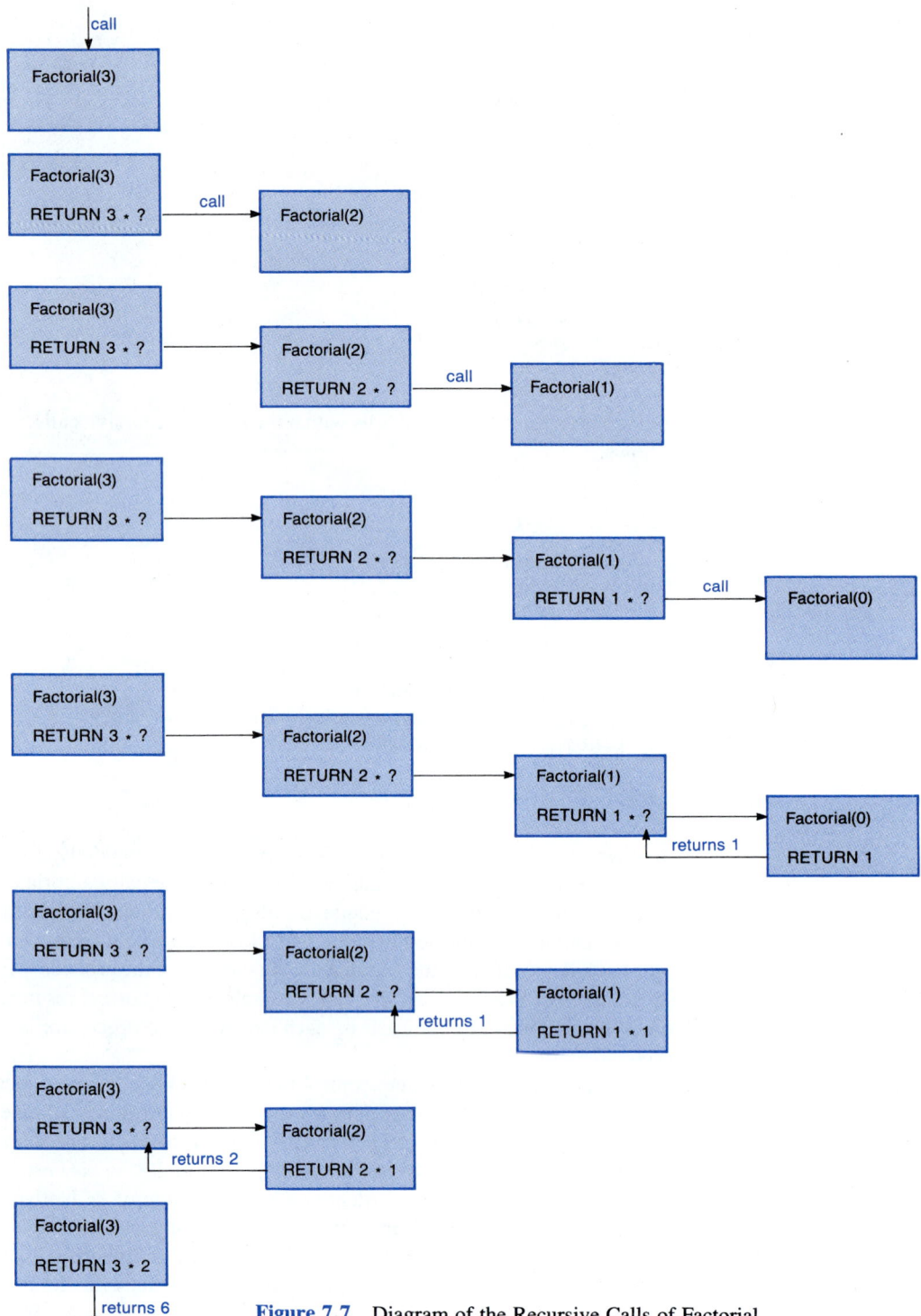

Figure 7.7 Diagram of the Recursive Calls of Factorial

SEC. 7.3   *Recursive Procedures*   **179**

a reduced form of the original problem. In this example the value of K has been reduced from 3 to 2. The recursive calls continue until Factorial is called with K equal to zero. This call of Factorial corresponds to the base case and is completed immediately by returning the value 1.

It is important to understand that all previous calls to Factorial are still awaiting completion. Once the call to Factorial(0) returns the value 1, control is transferred back to Factorial(1). It is completed by returning K * Factorial(0) = 1 * 1 = 1. Now we are back inside Factorial(2), which is completed by returning K * Factorial(1) = 2 * 1 = 2. Finally, we are back inside Factorial(3), which is now completed by returning K * Factorial(2) = 3 * 2 = 6. The entire process is illustrated in Figure 7.7.

EXAMPLE 2   A Recursive Graphical Algorithm

Our second example to help us understand how recursion is done on computers will be a recursive graphical algorithm. Since the algorithm involves two recursive calls, the pattern of execution of recursive calls is more complex than the one for Factorial.

We will develop the algorithm to draw any sequence of figures, called fractals, shown in Figure 7.8. These figures involve a pattern that has a recursive nature since the simpler figures are embedded in the more complex figures. Before going on, see if you can determine the recursive pattern.

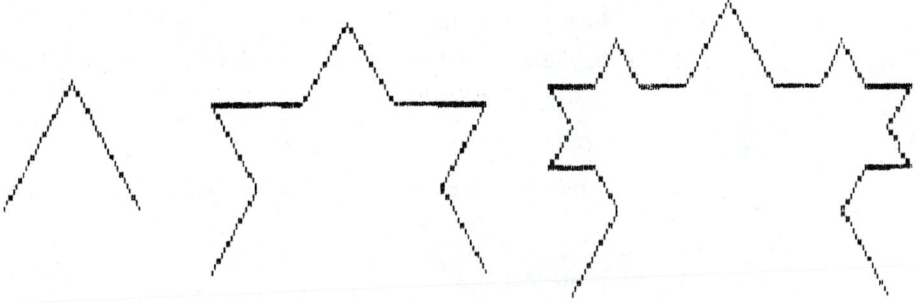

Figure 7.8
Fractals

Notice that drawing the second figure can be described as follows:

turn 60 degrees

draw a short line

draw the first figure at half the size of the second figure

draw a short line

turn −120 degrees

draw a short line

draw the first figure at half the size of the second figure

draw a short line

turn 60 degrees

Similarly, drawing the third figure can be described as follows:

turn 60 degrees

draw a short line

draw the second figure at half the size of the third figure

draw a short line

turn −120 degrees

draw a short line

draw the second figure at half the size of the third figure

draw a short line

turn 60 degrees

Apparently we can always draw one of these figures if we can draw the preceding simpler figure—but this is just recursion!

The general recursive pattern for the nth figure can be described as follows:

turn 60 degrees

draw a short line

draw the $(n - 1)$st figure at half the size of the nth figure

draw a short line

turn −120 degrees

draw a short line

draw the $(n - 1)$st figure at half the size of the nth figure

draw a short line

turn 60 degrees

A recursive pseudocode procedure based on this pattern is as follows:

```
Fractal( K )
  turn( 60 );
  move( 3 * Power( 2, K ) )    { Power returns 2 to the Kth power }
  If K > 1 Then
    Fractal( K − 1 )
  End if
  move( 3 * Power( 2, K ) )
  turn( −120 )
  move( 3 * Power( 2, K ) )
  If K > 1 Then
    Fractal( K − 1 )
  End If
  move( 3 * Power( 2, K ) )
  Turn( 60 )                   { return Turtle to its original orientation }
End Fractal
```

Notice that the distance of each move depends on the parameter K in order for the figures to have the correct relative sizes. For example, the distance is 3 * 2 = 6 when K is 1; 3 * 2 * 2 = 12 when K is 2; 3 * 2 * 2 * 2 = 24 when K is 3; and so on. We have chosen those values so that the first figure drawn (which corresponds to the highest value of K) is drawn at twice the size of the second, the second at twice the size of the third, and so on. In other words, each recursive call will draw a figure half the size of the preceding one.

The following interactive Modula-2 program contains a Fractal procedure based on the pseudocode and a nested procedure to do the computation of the power of 2 needed for Fractal. It also contains a Trace procedure to follow the execution of the recursive calls at the user's option. The input has been limited to no more than 3, because the tracing messages for larger values will not fit on the screen.

```
MODULE DrawFractal;
(* Program to draw a designated fractal between 1 and 3.
                         J. M. Adams January 1988 *)

FROM InOut IMPORT Read, ReadCard,
                  Write, WriteCard, WriteLn, WriteString;
FROM Strings IMPORT STRING;
FROM TurtleGraphics IMPORT Move, Turn, MoveTo, TurtleStop,
                           PenColor, PenMode;

VAR N: CARDINAL;
    C: CHAR;
    Debug: BOOLEAN;

PROCEDURE Trace(Message: STRING; M: CARDINAL);
(* Display Message, which indicates a place (entering, midway,
   or leaving) in the execution of the call of the procedure
   Fractal(M).  Message is preceded by dots indicating the
   depth of the recursion.  Global N is used to determine the
   depth, N - M.  After displaying Message, the procedure halts
   until a key is pressed.                   *)

VAR I: CARDINAL;
    Pause: CHAR;
BEGIN
  FOR I := 1 TO N - M DO Write('.') END;  (* FOR *)
  WriteString(Message); WriteString("Fractal(");
  WriteCard(M, 1); Write(')');
  Read(Pause); WriteLn;
END Trace;

PROCEDURE Fractal(K: CARDINAL);
(* Recursive drawing of the Kth fractal. *)
```

```
PROCEDURE Power(M, K: CARDINAL): CARDINAL;
(* Returns M to the Kth power. *)
VAR I, Result: CARDINAL;
BEGIN
  Result := 1;
  FOR I := 1 TO K DO
    (* Result = M to the (I - 1)st power. *)
    Result := Result * M;
  END; (* FOR *)
  RETURN Result;
END Power;



BEGIN (* Fractal *)
  IF Debug THEN Trace("entering ", K) END; (* IF *)
  Turn(60);
  Move(3 * Power(2, K));
  IF  K > 1 THEN
    Fractal(K - 1);
  END;   (* IF *)
  Move(3 * Power(2, K));
  IF Debug THEN Trace("midway in", K) END; (* IF *)
  Turn(-120);
  Move(3 * Power(2, K));
  IF K > 1 THEN
    Fractal(K - 1);
  END;   (* IF *)
  Move(3 * Power(2, K));
  Turn(60); (* return Turtle to its original orientation *)
  IF Debug THEN Trace( "leaving ", K ) END; (* IF *)
END Fractal;



BEGIN (* DrawFractal *)
  WriteString("Enter y for tracing and n otherwise: ");
  Read(C); WriteLn;
  Debug := (C = 'y') OR (C = 'Y');
  WriteString("Enter an integer between 1 and 3: ");
  ReadCard(N); WriteLn; WriteLn;
  IF (1 <= N) AND (N <= 3) THEN
    Fractal(N);
  ELSE
    WriteString("Your entry was not between 1 and 3.");
    WriteLn;
  END; (* IF *)
  TurtleStop;         (* Hold screen *)
END DrawFractal.
```

The output, with tracing selected and an input value of 3, is

```
Enter y for tracing and n otherwise: y
Enter an integer between 1 and 3: 3
```

```
entering Fractal(3)
.entering Fractal(2)
..entering Fractal(1)
..midway in Fractal(1)
..leaving Fractal(1)
.midway in Fractal(2)
..entering Fractal(1)
..midway in Fractal(1)
..leaving Fractal(1)
.leaving Fractal(2)
midway in Fractal(3)
.entering Fractal(2)
..entering Fractal(1)
..midway in Fractal(1)
..leaving Fractal(1)
.midway in Fractal(2)
..entering Fractal(1)
..midway in Fractal(1)
..leaving Fractal(1)
.leaving Fractal(2)
leaving Fractal(3)
```

Correlate each tracing message with a point in Figure 7.8. For example, the message "entering Fractal(3)" corresponds to the lower left-hand point in Figure 7.8 because the message was written when the Turtle was at that point. Making this correlation will give you a good understanding of how recursion is being done by the computer.

The procedure Fractal is not easily implemented using iteration, because two recursive calls are inside the procedure. In Chapters 13 and 15 we will study additional algorithms involving two recursive calls that have a flow of control very similar to the pattern shown here.

At this point you should not only recognize that recursion is a powerful problem-solving technique but also have a good idea of the operations being performed when a recursive procedure is executed.

One of the main objectives in programming is to design programs that are as clear and easily modifiable as possible. In the last section we'll look at a principle that underlies the writing of such programs.

7.4 The Principle of Information Hiding Applied to Program Structure

In Chapter 6 we alluded to information hiding as a valuable programming technique. We said that we can often use data effectively in programs even though the data representations are hidden from us. In fact this hiding actually adds an element of clarity to the design. Therefore, according to the information hiding principle,

> Modules should be designed so that: (1) The user has all of the information needed to use the module correctly, and nothing more. (2) The implementor has all the information needed to implement the module correctly, and nothing more.*

The word *module* in this definition is general and refers to any encapsulating structure, including procedures.

This section will explore how the information hiding principle applies to program design. We'll begin with a design approach that breaks down a problem into components reflecting the structure of a solution, where each component is provided no more information than it needs to solve its part of the problem.

Problem Decomposition as a Key to Design

Many ways exist to solve a particular problem on a computer. All programs that solve the problem must give correct results, but some program solutions are better than others. Some characteristics of good program solutions are clarity, ease of modification, and efficiency. The first two characteristics are related to program structure. Experience in software development has shown that a program whose structure closely reflects the structure of the problem itself is less likely to have subtle, undetected errors and more likely to be easier to understand and to modify.

The development of program structure starts at the design stage of problem solving, where we use a technique of "divide and conquer" to decompose our problem into smaller subproblems. This approach gives us a high-level solution, which can be depicted

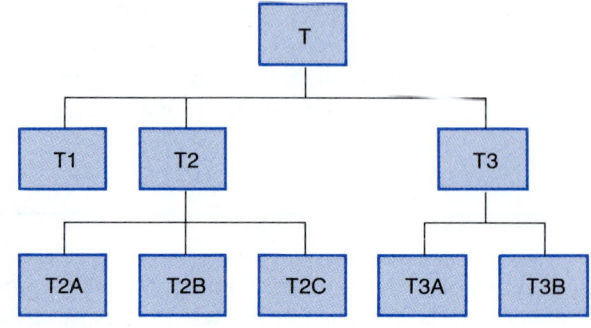

Figure 7.9
A Representative Structure Chart

---

* Bruce J. MacLennan, *Principles of Programming Languages* (New York: Holt, Rinehart and Winston, 1983), p. 84.

by a structure chart. Figure 7.9 illustrates a task, T, which is decomposed into three subtasks—T1, T2, and T3. Some of these subtasks are decomposed further.

One possible program solution would be to write each subtask as a global procedure, as follows:

```
MODULE T;

PROCEDURE T1;
    :
    :
END T1;

PROCEDURE T2;
    :
    :
END T2;

PROCEDURE T3;
    :
    :
END T3;

PROCEDURE T2A;
    :
    :
END T2A;

PROCEDURE T2B;
    :
    :
END T2B;

PROCEDURE T2C;
    :
    :
END T2C;

PROCEDURE T3A;
    :
    :
END T3A;

PROCEDURE T3B;
    :
    :
END T3B;

BEGIN (* T *)
    T1;
    T2;
    T3;
END T;
```

This "flat" program structure does not closely reflect the structure of the problem as depicted in Figure 7.9. The main program has access to tasks T2A, T2B, T2C, T3A, and T3B, although the structure chart does not indicate a need for such access. To design a more appropriate solution, we can use nested procedures as shown in the following program. This solution is better than the preceding one since T2A, T2B, and T2C can be accessed only from T2, and T3A and T3B can be accessed only from T3.

```
MODULE T;

PROCEDURE T1;
    :
END T1;

PROCEDURE T2;

    PROCEDURE T2A;
        :
    END T2A;

    PROCEDURE T2B;
        :
    END T2B;

    PROCEDURE T2C;
        :
    END T2C;

BEGIN (* T2 *)
    :
END T2;

PROCEDURE T3;

    PROCEDURE T3A;
        :
    END T3A;

    PROCEDURE T3B;
        :
    END T3B;
```

SEC. 7.4   *The Principle of Information Hiding Applied to Program Structure*   **187**

```
              BEGIN  (* T3 *)
                 ⋮
              END T3;

              BEGIN  (* T *)
                 T1;
                 T2;
                 T3;
              END T;
```

Access to Nonlocal Identifiers

We can use the rules of scope to help us apply the information hiding principle, although we will see that they are not always sufficient. The rules of scope apply to all identifiers, not just procedures. In the previous example, therefore, procedures T2A, T2B, and T2C have access to the formal parameters, constants, variables, and types declared in T2, as well as global identifiers. In situations like this you may be tempted to use nonlocal variables rather than parameters. Avoid such a temptation! As we said in Chapter 3, a side effect occurs when a procedure changes the value of a nonlocal variable. Such side effects cause programming bugs that are among the most difficult to find and correct. Thus, whenever feasible, use parameters rather than nonlocal variables.

Consider the procedure DisplayTitleLine in the module CheckTitleBox earlier in this chapter. The nonlocal variables MaxLength and NumBlanks are visible from within DisplayTitleLine. Rather than access these nonlocal variables directly, though, we chose to pass them as parameters.

However, occasions do arise when this guideline is not really feasible. For example, the Trace procedures used in the modules FactTrace and DrawFractal earlier in this chapter need access to the global variable N, and avoiding the use of this global variable by using another parameter would be extremely awkward.

Shared Components and Information Hiding

Unfortunately, nested procedures alone are not sufficient for the information hiding needed in some common program decompositions. Suppose that the subtasks T2A, T2B, T2C, T3A, and T3B must use some procedures that are of general utility to all of these subtasks, shown as U1, U2, and U3 in Figure 7.10.

Utility procedure U1 is called by both T2A and T2B, U2 is called by T2C, and U3 is called by T3A and T3B. There is no way to nest a single copy of these utility procedures within the calling tasks and still maintain the appropriate visibility. For example, using nesting, you could at best make U1 and U2 subtasks of T2 so that they could be accessed by T2A, T2B, and T2C. But this approach would violate the information hiding principle since T2C would have access to U1; T2A and T2B would have access to U2; and U1 and U2 would have access to each other. The problem definition

Figure 7.10
Revised Structure
Chart

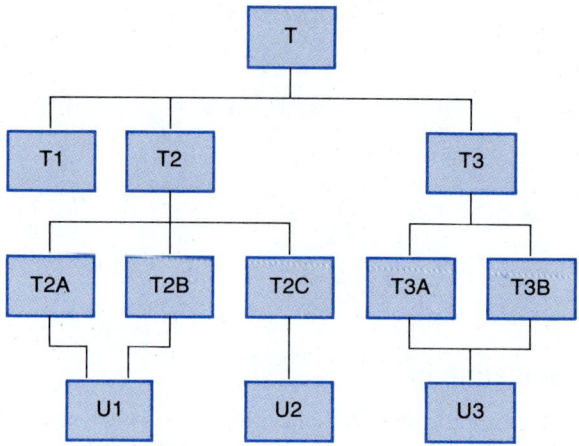

does not warrant such access. This information hiding problem can be solved by using local modules, which we will discuss in Chapter 11.

We have already seen that external modules are a powerful information hiding tool, since objects that the user does not need can be declared in the implementation module, while objects that are needed are declared in the definition module. We did this in the Points module in Chapter 6. We will make increasing use of external modules in subsequent chapters, and they will be discussed in detail in Chapter 11.

SUMMARY

Large Modula-2 programs normally have a great deal of structure. The environment of a main program is determined by the declarations and import lists in the main program. Identifiers declared within a procedure are the local environment of the procedure. A sequence of declarations followed by a sequence of executable statements is referred to as a block. Modula-2 is known as a block-structured language.

The three rules of scope are (1) the scope of an identifier is the block in which the identifier is declared and any procedures nested within that block, (2) an identifier may be referred to only within its scope, and (3) when an identifier is referenced, the most local declaration is used.

Procedures may be nested so that they are available to the enclosing procedure but not the main program, and the nesting depth is determined statically by the textual structure of the program declarations. Nesting to a depth over three is not usually desirable.

Recursion may be considered a special case of nesting in the sense that a procedure can call itself. A recursive call must be completely done before continuing with the statement after the call. Each call to a recursive procedure establishes a new local environment where parameters and variables have the same names but can have different values from the previous environment.

The information hiding principle states that the user of a module should have only the information needed to use a module correctly and the implementor have only enough information to implement the module correctly. To apply this principle we should make sure that the structure of programs reflects the structure of the problem being solved, and that components of the program are provided with only the information they need. Nested procedures can be used for information hiding but are not sufficient in all cases. External modules and local modules, discussed in Chapter 11, will provide additional capability for information hiding.

EXERCISES

1. Consider the program Scope2 in Figure 7.4. What will be the output if we change the parameters of Swap as follows:
    (a) Make M a value parameter and leave N as a variable parameter.
    (b) Leave M as a variable parameter and make N a value parameter.
    (c) Make both M and N value parameters.
2. What will be printed by the program

```
MODULE Scope3;
FROM InOut IMPORT WriteInt, WriteLn;

VAR I, J, K: INTEGER;

PROCEDURE First;
VAR J: INTEGER;
BEGIN
   J := 2;
   K := K + 2;
END First;

PROCEDURE Second;
VAR I: INTEGER;
BEGIN
   I := 2;
   First;
   J := I + J;
   WriteInt(I, 5); WriteInt(J, 5);
   WriteInt(K, 5); WriteLn;
END Second;

PROCEDURE Third;
VAR I, K: INTEGER;
BEGIN
   J := 3;
   K := 1;
   First;
   Second;
END Third;

BEGIN  (* Scope3 *)
   I := 1; J := 1; K := 1;
   Second;
   Third;
END Scope3.
```

3. Carefully trace the following program to find out what will be printed. This is a difficult example; in order to obtain the correct answers, you must remember that the scope of identifiers is determined by the static structure of the program, not the order of procedure calls.

```
MODULE Scope4;
FROM InOut IMPORT WriteInt, WriteLn;

VAR A, B, C: INTEGER;

PROCEDURE One;
BEGIN
  A := A + 2;
  B := B + 3;
  WriteInt(A, 5); WriteInt(B, 5);
  WriteInt(C, 5); WriteLn;
END One;


PROCEDURE Two;
VAR A: INTEGER;
BEGIN
  C := 4;
  A := 5;
  One;
  B := A + C;
  WriteInt(A, 5); WriteInt(B, 5);
  WriteInt(C, 5); WriteLn;
END Two;


PROCEDURE Three;
VAR A, C: INTEGER;

  PROCEDURE One;
  VAR C: INTEGER;
  BEGIN
    A := B + 1;
    C := A + B;
    WriteInt(A, 5); WriteInt(B, 5);
    WriteInt(C, 5); WriteLn;
  END One;

BEGIN   (* Three *)
  B := 3;
  C := 1;
  One;
  Two;
END Three;
```

```
BEGIN (* Scope4 *)
   A := 1;
   B := 2;
   C := 3;
   Three;
END Scope4.
```

4. Indicate the scope of each object declared in program Scope1.
5. Indicate what objects are accessible to procedure Two in the Scope2 program of Figure 7.4.
6. Indicate the scope of each object declared in the program CheckTitleBox.
7. Alter the program CheckTitleBox to allow the user to specify the number of blanks of padding to be used at each end of the title boxes.
8. Rewrite the Factorial function so that it uses iteration instead of recursion.
9. Indicate what modification should be done so that each recursive call to the Fractal procedure draws a figure one-third the size of the preceding call.
10. Indicate why the second program outline in the section "Problem Decomposition as a Key to Design" does not strictly adhere to the information hiding principle.

PROGRAMMING PROBLEMS

11. If you had difficulty implementing the Fibonacci number, Sterling number, or binomial coefficient exercises at the end of Chapter 5, try these problems again now that you have a better understanding of recursion.

12. Design and write an interactive program to compute Ackermann's function for designated arguments. Ackermann's function is defined for pairs of nonnegative integers by

$$f(0, y) = y + 1 \text{ for } y > 0$$
$$f(x, 0) = f(x - 1, 1) \text{ for } x > 0$$
$$f(x, y) = f(x - 1, f(x, y - 1)) \text{ for } x > 0 \text{ and } y > 0$$

Test the program, but be sure to start with small values for the arguments, and observe the time taken for execution.

13. Design and write an interactive Modula-2 program to draw a binary tree with one to six levels. Binary trees with one, two, and three levels are as follows:

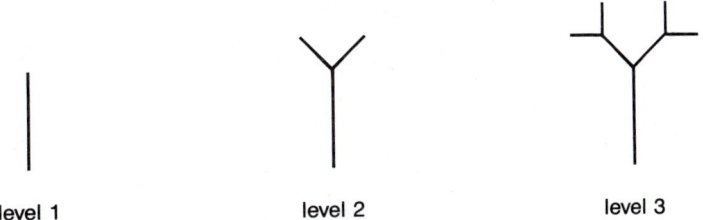

level 1   level 2   level 3

*14. Design and write an interactive Modula-2 program to draw the Dragon curves of any order between 1 and 15. The Dragon curves of order one, two, three, and four are as follows:

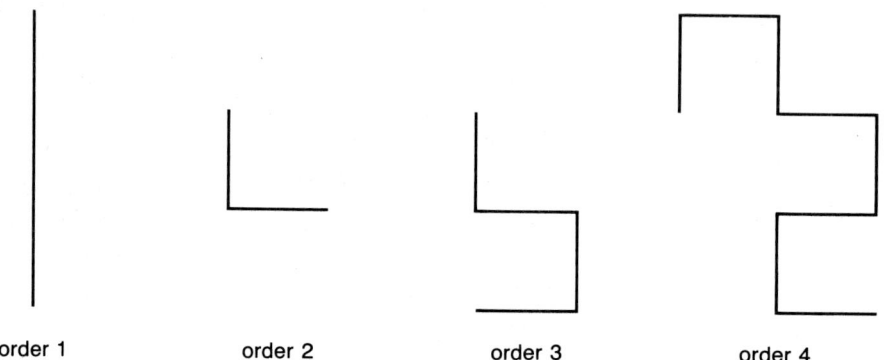

*15. Design and write an interactive Modula-2 program to draw the Hilbert curves of any order between one and five. The Hilbert curves of order one, two, and three are as follows:

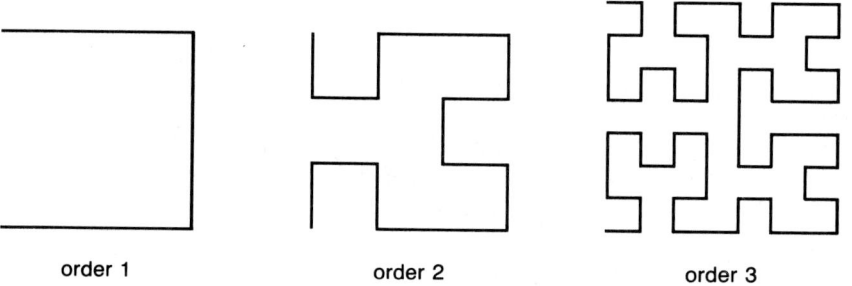

*16. Design and write an interactive Modula-2 program to draw the Kei figures illustrated here for orders one, two, three, and four.

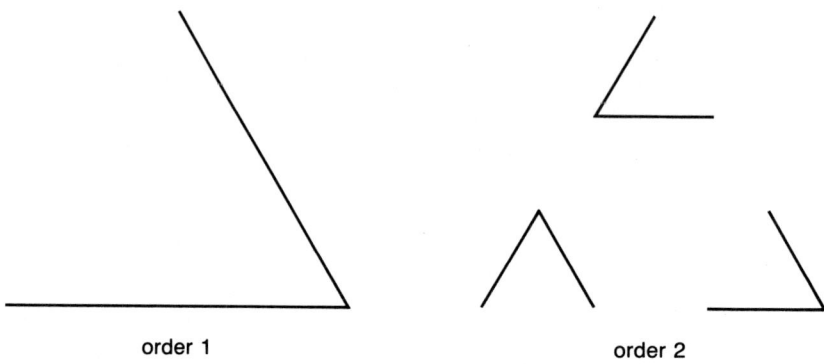

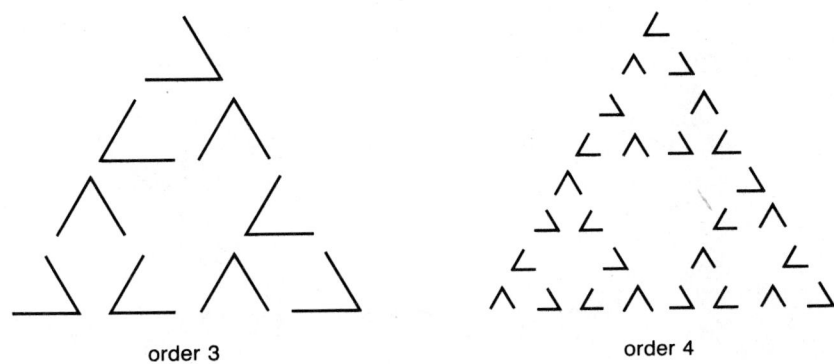

order 3   order 4

8 Problem Solving and Program Development

In this chapter, you will:

- learn more about the problem-solving method introduced in Chapter 1
- see a complete example of the use of this method to develop a program that uses the features of Modula-2 discussed so far

As you learn more features of Modula-2, you will be able to solve more complex problems. Consequently, you must also be much more careful about designing a solution. *The biggest mistake you can make is to rush into coding a program before you have carefully thought out a solution.* The problems so far have been relatively simple. For very small programs, if you coded an ill-advised solution, you could just simply discard the solution and start over since no great amount of effort had been involved. This ease of revision will be less true as you attempt to solve more complex problems. You must learn to resist the almost overwhelming urge to rush to the computer and start coding.

The problem-solving method described in Chapter 1 will help you to take a thoughtful, logical approach to program development. This chapter, therefore, will review the method in detail and give you a complete example of its usage. In Chapter 1 our goal was to use this method to write clear algorithms. Here, though, we'll explore the application of this method specifically to the design and implementation of complete programs. With what we've learned in the intervening chapters about Modula-2 structure, we'll be able to see how this method helps us to organize program development.

The first half of the chapter will go through the six steps, one by one, explaining each step's tasks and describing the product that you should expect at the end of the step. In the chapter's second half we'll practice with a programming problem. We'll follow our progress with structure charts and modular design charts and then show the actual program. At the end you'll be expected to add enhancements to the program as part of the problems.

8.1 The Problem-Solving Method Revisited

The problem-solving method described briefly in Chapter 1 had the following six steps:

1. Define the problem.
2. Design a solution.
3. Refine the solution.
4. Develop a testing strategy.
5. Code and test the program.
6. Complete the documentation.

We will discuss each of these steps in detail in the following sections.

Define the Problem

There is no substitute for understanding the problem. If the definition of a problem is vague or ambiguous, we cannot develop a solution without running into difficulties. Obscure parts must be made precise and ambiguities must be resolved. We can make such changes as we develop the solution, but the development will be much smoother and quicker if we make the problem definition as exact as possible before starting the development.

If the problem is one that you have originated, then you must get your own thoughts in good order so that the definition can be made clear. If the problem was originated by someone else, then you must study the specification to identify parts that are unclear or poorly worded and thoroughly discuss all these trouble spots, in order to come up with a mutually satisfactory and precise definition.

The result of this step is a precise problem specification, including a careful description of the input to be provided and the output that is expected.

Design a Solution

In this step we develop a description of a solution structure by using the powerful problem-solving technique of "divide and conquer." This technique requires us to analyze the problem and decompose it into its major subproblems (the solutions to these subproblems will be the major components of our final solution). Then we break down the subproblems themselves into their major subproblems and continue this decomposition until we have subproblems whose solutions seem fairly obvious. Since a structure chart can be used to depict the decomposition, this entire step is sometimes called structural design.

To illustrate the decomposition process, let's take a simple example. Imagine we have a robot that will try to execute the commands it is given. Now suppose that it is the beginning of April, and we have to prepare our income tax return. It would be very nice if we could solve this problem by giving our robot the command

Prepare my income tax return!

Unfortunately, present robots are not capable of executing that command, and our robot replies: "Please provide more detail." After a little thought, we try the commands

>Gather all papers needed to prepare my income tax return.
>Fill out form 1040.

Our willing but limited robot is still not able to execute the commands, so we decompose the first command into

>Select relevant receipts from file named Bills.
>Get salary information from file named Salary Data.

and continue the decomposition until our robot successfully executes the commands, or we give up and do the job ourselves.

What we have been doing is defining all the tasks that will have to be done in order to accomplish the main task. This method, called *top-down design,* leads to the outline of a solution, which can be illustrated by the structure chart shown in Figure 8.1.

As another example of top-down design, consider the development of a simple payroll program. Like many simple problems, the "top-level" structure could consist of three components: input, processing, and output. This arrangement is illustrated by the structure chart in Figure 8.2.

This design might then be refined by subdividing each of the three second-level components into their major components, as illustrated by the refined structure chart in Figure 8.3.

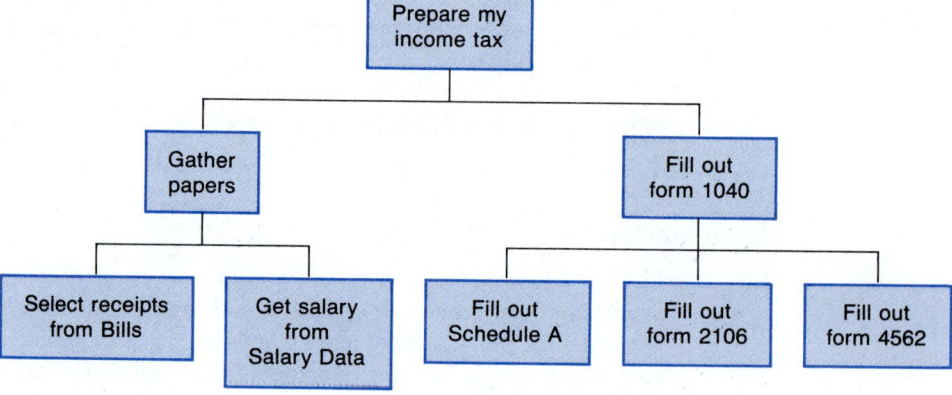

Figure 8.1
Example of a Structure Chart

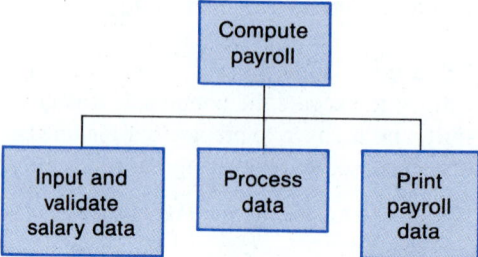

Figure 8.2
Structure Chart for Payroll Program

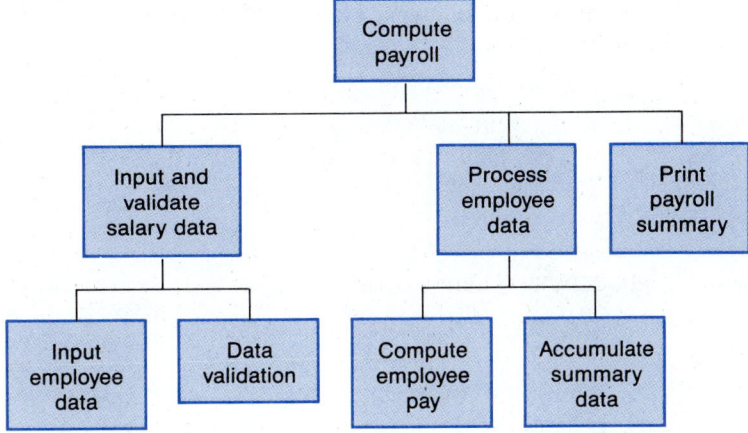

Figure 8.3
Refined Structure Chart for Payroll Program

In effect, a structure chart is a skeleton of the final program structure, where the solutions to the subproblems will be the components that fill out this skeleton. Because there will be some communication between these components, we must develop not only specifications for input and output but also general specifications, called *interfaces,* for the data transmitted between components.

Since there are usually several ways to decompose a problem into subproblems, it is wise to consider various alternatives for doing the decomposition, and consider the relative advantages and disadvantages of each alternative. At first it may be hard to judge the advantages and disadvantages, but your judgment will improve with experience.

In addition to decomposing the problem into subproblems to determine an appropriate structure for the program, you should also try to identify groups of related operations that could be used throughout the program to make implementation easier. If several operations deal with a certain kind of data structure, you may want to include them in a separate module as part of an abstract data type. For example, a program that deals with points in the Cartesian plane could use a module that defines a data type for points, and operations, such as the distance between two points. The example in the next section will develop such a module.

The result of the design step should include documents that describe design decisions, structure charts, and modular design charts (illustrated in Section 8.2 and discussed in detail in Chapter 11). The detailed example in the next section will show you how this documentation is developed.

Refine the Solution

Starting with a skeletal solution developed in the previous step, we refine the solution by adding more detail, which is why this step is also called "detailed design." We use pseudocode to develop the algorithms that provide solutions to the subproblems. For the simple examples we have seen so far, the pseudocode has looked remarkably similar to actual program code, often being in a one-to-one correspondence. As our programs become larger and our knowledge of programming more extensive, our pseudocode will become more abstract—one pseudocode instruction may represent several programming language statements or even entire procedures.

Consider the following example of the development of part of a simple payroll program:

pseudocode

> Accumulate Summary Data
>   Update all payroll totals
> End Accumulate Summary Data

implementation

```
PROCEDURE AccumulateSummaryData( GrossPay, NetPay, FederalTax,
                                 StateTax, SSTax: INTEGER;
                                 VAR GrossTotal, FederalTotal,
                                     StateTotal, SSTotal,
                                     NetTotal: INTEGER );
(* Update all payroll totals *)
BEGIN
  FederalTotal := FederalTotal + FederalTax;
  StateTotal := StateTotal + StateTax;
  SSTotal := SSTotal + SSTax;
  GrossTotal := GrossTotal + GrossPay;
  NetTotal := NetTotal + NetPay;
END AccumulateSummaryData;
```

Notice that part of the pseudocode is made into a comment, which forms a preface for the procedure. This is a good documentation style, since it indicates the function of the actual code.

The pseudocode presented in this book is *language independent:* it can be translated into virtually any programming language. It is particularly well suited for translating into languages such as Modula-2, ALGOL 60, PL/1, Pascal, C, and Ada because its control structures are consistent with those languages.

The major products of the refinement step are the pseudocode algorithms. We will also produce definition modules in this step when external modules are needed in the development.

Develop a Testing Strategy

We must test a program to give us confidence that it gives correct results before we put the program into regular use. It is important to develop a plan for testing *before* we do the actual coding, because developing the test cases may cause us to recognize errors in the design. Correcting these errors at this stage will be *much* easier than correcting erroneous programs. In effect, developing the testing strategy tests the design steps, and the testing strategy itself is subsequently used to test the implementation of the design.

Another advantage of developing a testing strategy before coding is that we are usually much more objective before the coding is done. If we develop a testing strategy after coding, we may end up testing what was actually implemented rather than what was desired.

When developing a testing strategy for smaller programs, we can usually just specify the input data and the corresponding expected results for a wide variety of test cases. Remember, it is very important to test "boundary" or "extreme" cases. For example, test cases for a payroll program should include negative hours worked to ensure that the program produces an appropriate error message.

For large programs, however, we need a plan for doing the testing along with the coding. We may choose a top-down approach, a bottom-up approach, or a combination of both approaches. *Top-down testing* means to start by coding and testing the main program first and then the subprograms. In terms of a structure chart we start developing the program component at the top of the chart and then work down—thus the name "top-down." We will often have to design program *stubs* (incomplete program segments) for the lower-level components during the initial stages of development. These stubs may simply print a message, or they may supply artificial data. For example, the structure chart given in Figure 8.2 shows that the main program component, Compute Payroll, will have three major subcomponents: Input and Validate Salary Data, Process Employee Data, and Print Payroll Summary. We could start a top-down development by coding the main program and these three major procedures, but the procedures at the lower level could merely be stubs. For example, a stub for the DataValidation procedure might be

```
PROCEDURE DataValidation( Hours, Rate, CARDINAL;
                          Name: STRING; VAR ValidData: BOOLEAN );
(* A stub *)
BEGIN
   ValidData := TRUE;
   WriteString( "DataValidation" ); WriteLn;
END DataValidation;
```

An indication that the data are valid is given without any checking at all, and a message is printed to indicate that the procedure has been called. This procedure would later be replaced by a procedure that actually does the desired checking, but meanwhile the program can be run to make sure that

1. procedures are called in the right order
2. interfaces between procedures are correct (that is, the actual parameter lists in the calls match the formal parameter lists in the declaration)

Bottom-up development means that we code and test the components at the bottom of the structure chart first and then integrate these tested components into the next higher level, working our way up the structure chart. Since these bottom-level components usually cannot function as stand-alone programs, we must write *driver* programs to test the components. Driver programs call the procedures that constitute the components.

For the sake of illustration, assume that we have just developed a function procedure to compute the square root of nonnegative real values. Also, assume that we have determined that the function is faster than the sqrt function in the MathLib0 library module, and so we want to use it in a program where execution speed is very important. We should write a small testing program to check the function before we incorporate it into the larger program. If our procedure is named SqRt, an interactive driver program might include the program segment

```
LOOP
  WriteString( "Enter an argument for the square root function: " );
  ReadReal( X ); WriteLn;
  WriteString( "The result of SqRt is: " );
  WriteReal( SqRt( X ), 15 );
  WriteString( " and the result of sqrt is: " );
  WriteReal( sqrt( X ), 15 ); WriteLn; WriteLn;
END; (* LOOP *)
```

This segment would allow you to test a variety of arguments and compare the results to the results given by the function from the standard library. You could even write a more sophisticated testing program, which generated test arguments, compared the results, and provided a message when the results did not agree to some desired accuracy. Essentially, the square root test program (driver) would be a part of a much larger process of testing the large program.

Often both bottom-up and top-down approaches are taken. Utility routines that appear throughout a program might be coded and tested independently using a bottom-up approach. Then development will switch to a top-down approach with stubs being used for major program components. As development continues down the structure chart, the programmers will have confidence that the utility routines can be integrated smoothly since they have been tested independently.

The major product of this step is an outline of the testing strategy, specific input with corresponding output for test cases, and, when appropriate, pseudocode for stubs and drivers.

Program Coding, Programming Style, and Testing

In this step we use our refined pseudocode algorithms and our testing strategy to code and test the actual computer program. For large programs, we do this coding little by little, coding the various components with the necessary stubs and drivers, so that we can test the program components systematically. It is not uncommon to encounter difficulties in coding, due to errors in design or peculiarities of the programming language, which prevent a certain aspect of the design from being implemented. If this happens, we must return to the design step and consider alternative design strategies. This step is completed when all coding has been done and all test data have been successfully processed.

The final program should adhere to generally accepted guidelines for good *programming style*.

Some Programming Style Guidelines

1. Write well-structured programs—composed of procedures of reasonable size, not large monolithic blocks of code.
2. Make the flow of control as straightforward as possible.
3. Avoid coding "tricks" that make the program difficult to understand.
4. Make the program readable by choosing meaningful identifiers, inserting blank lines to separate components, and indenting statements to indicate the flow of control that will be followed at run time.
5. Include meaningful comments, which explain the program. The main program should have an extensive preface, which includes a brief statement of the problem, appropriate references to external documents, name of the original programmer or team, date of the original implementation, and a change log. The *change log* should have an entry for each significant alteration of the program, including the date of the change, the name of the person who made the change, and a brief description of the change. Each procedure should have a small preface describing its function. Difficult sections of code should contain explanatory comments.

The sample program in Section 8.2 provides a demonstration of these guidelines.

If a program has been well structured during the design steps and the design has been faithfully coded using good programming style, program testing should not be inordinately difficult. However some semantic errors nearly always occur, and the debugging necessary to find and correct the errors can be demanding. The following debugging guidelines may help to make this process less onerous.

Some Debugging Guidelines

1. Make sure the expected results for your test cases really are correct. In other words, make sure the result given by the program is really an error before expending the effort to find it.
2. Do a mental trace with the input data to see if you can locate the error quickly.
3. Try to isolate the error to a small segment of the program by using debugging aids that may be available or by inserting write statements at key points in the program. For example, if you suspect that a certain procedure may be the source of the error, insert write statements at the beginning of the procedure to print arguments passed to the procedure and at the end of the procedure to print the results computed by the procedure.
4. If your efforts to isolate the error fail, create and test a simplified version of the program. This version should not contain segments of code inessential to the computation of the test case under consideration. Naturally, since this approach requires careful thought and sometimes considerable effort, it is usually only a last resort.

The results of this coding and testing step are a readable program and information on the testing that has been performed. The program itself is called *internal documentation,* whereas the testing information is part of the *external documentation* (all documentation other than the program listing).

Complete the Documentation

The palest ink is better than the best memory.   A CHINESE PROVERB

If a program is to be used by others, it must be documented. A naive user must have instructions for running the program; someone wishing to alter the program must have information about design decisions, implementation, and testing. Documentation is necessary even for the original programmer, who may be asked to change the program long after initial development. It is surprising how quickly design decisions and their rationale can be forgotten.

Program documentation begins in the first step of program development and continues throughout the lifetime of the program. Documentation of various forms is produced at each step of the program development process.

1. *Define the Problem*—the problem specification, including a general description of the input and output
2. *Design a Solution*—textual description of the design, structure charts, and modular design charts (introduced in the next section and fully discussed in Chapter 11)
3. *Refine the Solution*—data specifications, pseudocode, and definition modules
4. *Develop a Testing Strategy*—outline of testing strategy, test data and expected results, and pseudocode for drivers and stubs
5. *Code and Test the Program*—the program code (internal documentation), test data, and results

All relevant documentation should be collected into a comprehensible form. Items not deemed relevant, such as pseudocode, may be discarded. This documentation should be kept current throughout the software's lifetime. In addition to the documentation generated during development, we may need additional user documentation. The user should be provided with enough information to make full use of the program and its functions but should not be burdened with implementation details. A preliminary version of user documentation may be developed during problem definition and then refined after coding and testing have been done.

Program maintenance needs special emphasis from a documentation standpoint. Maintenance refers to all activities occurring after the program first becomes operational. Programs often have lifetimes exceeding the lifetime of the hardware, and the cost of maintaining programs over this lifetime will usually exceed the total development costs. Program maintenance includes

- locating and fixing previously undetected program bugs
- modifying the program, often to improve performance or to adapt to a new hardware or software environment
- adding new features and capability to the program
- keeping the documentation current

Maintenance documentation may include many of the results of the program development steps: design documents, the program code, and information about testing. An important aspect of maintenance is to reflect any program changes in the documentation. External documentation should be updated, and a change log should be kept in the program preface. The change log should contain the name of the programmer who made the change, the date of the change, and a brief description of the change.

Summary of the Problem-Solving Method

We will often refer to the first four steps of the method as design, and the last two steps as implementation. With the simple programs we have developed so far, it is often difficult to see the differences between design and implementation or to appreciate the need for design. When you are designing a program, you are producing *abstractions*, which are precursors of programs. These abstractions contain the essential elements of the design, without implementation details. They are at a higher level than a particular programming language and are usually produced on paper (some computer-based design tools can automate part of this process). When you are implementing, you are producing an actual physical realization of a software system. Implementation involves translating abstractions into operational and tested programs on a particular computer, operating within a particular software environment.

When developing algorithms in pseudocode, you might have felt it was simpler to code directly in Modula-2. This may be true for the simple programs we have been doing so far, but, as your programs become larger and more complex, you will find design to be an indispensable step in software development. Studies have shown that the earlier flaws in a problem solution are detected, the less expensive they are to correct. These expenses can be "orders of magnitude" different. You will find this true of the longer exercises later in the text, where inadequate or sloppy design will result in great difficulty in the implementation phase. In fact, if you are having a difficult time with implementation, it is often wise to reconsider your design.

In the following section we'll describe a typical programming problem and see how the problem-solving method can be used to reach a solution in a logical fashion.

8.2 Application of the Problem-Solving Method

As part of a system to recognize geometric objects, we are asked to develop a program that will read in the *x* and *y* coordinates of three points, and that will determine if those points represent the vertices of a "recognizable" triangle. Although the program will not be very large, it will illustrate our problem-solving method.

Design

Although we have described the problem, the description does not constitute a complete, precise definition. We must give details about how the coordinates will be entered, how the results will be given, and what constitutes a recognizable triangle.

Define the Problem To define the problem, we say that we must write a program with interactive input to read the Cartesian coordinates of three points, which are the vertices of a triangle. Further, we have to verify that the *x* coordinates are in the range $-340 <= x <= 340$ and the *y* coordinates are in the range $-238 <= y <= 238$. If the points are valid, we must determine if the triangle is "recognizable," where a triangle is considered "recognizable" if it satisfies the following conditions:

1. every side is greater than 10
2. the area is greater than 50
3. one side is horizontal

As output, we can simply indicate whether the triangle was "recognizable."

Design a Solution We use the divide-and-conquer strategy to decompose the problem into subproblems. A reasonable decomposition is shown as a structure chart in Figure 8.4.

In this structure chart the left-to-right order indicates a probable order of execution, although this sequence is not always possible because of unseen loops and condition testing.

The subproblem "Data Input/Validation" is relatively easy, but we should be a little more precise about the nature of the input data. We will specify that the coordinates must be reals.

The subproblem "Output Results" is also straightforward; an appropriate message is displayed.

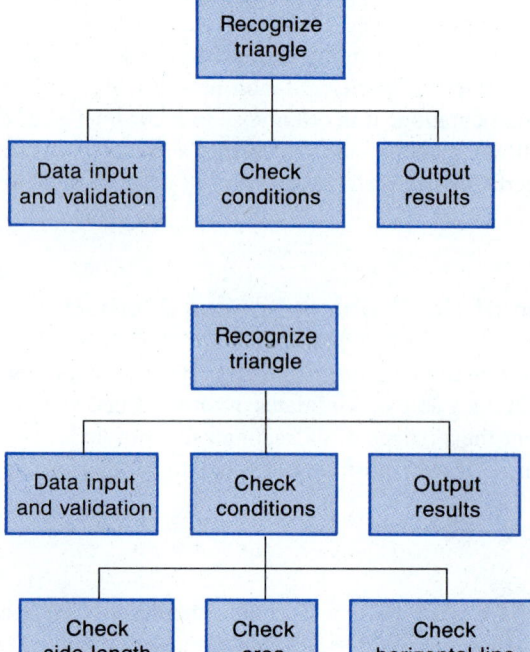

Figure 8.4
Initial Structure Chart for Triangle Recognition

Figure 8.5
Complete Structure Chart for Triangle Recognition

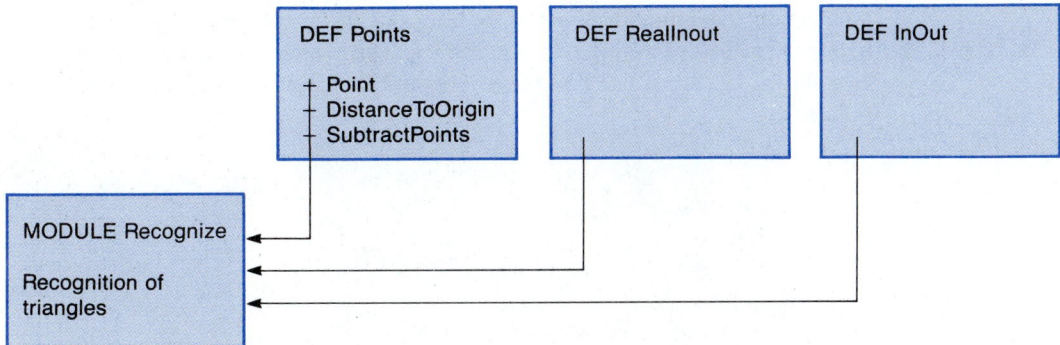

Figure 8.6 Initial Modular Design Chart for Triangle Recognition

The subproblem "Check Conditions" in Figure 8.4 has a natural decomposition into three subproblems corresponding to the three conditions given in the problem definition. This leads to the structure chart shown in Figure 8.5.

Because the choice of data structures for a problem usually has a substantial impact on the design of a solution, we should think carefully about a structure for the points that constitute the data in this problem.

The points are represented by Cartesian coordinates, which are pairs of real numbers. So, we can use the data type Point declared in the Points module developed in Chapter 6. We will plan on importing the type Point along with any procedures that might be useful. In particular, in Chapter 6, we used the procedures DistanceToOrigin and SubtractPoints to determine the distance between two points, and this would be useful in checking the side lengths.

We can also anticipate the need for procedures to do input and output of numbers and strings, so we will need to import objects from the InOut and RealInOut modules.

Our planned use of modules is documented in Figure 8.6, which is called a *modular design chart*.* The chart shows the various interconnections between the program and the definition (DEF) modules we intend to use for this solution, but it is not complete because we don't know exactly which procedures we will need from InOut and RealInOut. We will be able to complete the chart after we refine the solution in the next step.

Refine the Solution We refine the solution designed in the previous step by developing pseudocode for each of the parts of the structure chart. We use pseudocode versions of the imported procedures for these refinements.

The Data Input/Validation component must read three data points and verify that the values of the *x* and *y* coordinates of each point are within the specified ranges. We could read in the values for all three of the data points and then do the validity check for all values, but this approach would not be desirable from the user's standpoint. If one or more of the values were invalid, we would have to ask the user to enter the values again or ask that all the values be reentered. It would be much better to detect

---

* The modular design chart was developed and first presented by Sincovec and Wiener in *Software Engineering with Modula-2 and Ada* (Wiley, 1984).

an invalid value immediately after the value had been entered and request that the value be reentered before asking for other values. The pseudocode based on this approach is as follows, where we use Point1, Point2, and Point3 as the variable names of our data points.

```
InputPoint( I )
    Loop
        Prompt for x coordinate of PointI
        Read PointI.X
        Exit if -340 <= PointI.X <= 340
        Write error message
    End Loop
    Loop
        Prompt for y coordinate of PointI
        Read PointI.Y
        Exit if -238 <= PointI.Y <= 238
        Write error message
    End Loop
End InputPoint

DataInputValidation
    InputPoint( 1 )
    InputPoint( 2 )
    InputPoint( 3 )
End Data InputValidation
```

Checking the side-length condition is easy, using procedures from module Points to compute the distances between points. The pseudocode is

```
Distance( PointI, PointJ ): Real
    SubtractPoints( PointI, PointJ, Difference )
    Return DistanceToOrigin( Difference )
End Distance

CheckSideLength( Point1, Point2, Point3 ): Boolean
    Return ( Distance( Point1, Point2 ) > 10 ) and
           ( Distance( Point1, Point3 ) > 10 ) and
           ( Distance( Point2, Point3 ) > 10 )
End CheckSideLength
```

The area check is a bit more complicated but still not difficult if we use Heron's formula for the area of a triangle:

$$\text{Area} = \sqrt{s*(s-a)*(s-b)*(s-c)}$$

where *a*, *b*, and *c* are the lengths of the sides of the triangle, and

$$s = (a + b + c) / 2$$

The pseudocode based on this formula is

> CheckArea(Point1, Point2, Point3): Boolean
> { Area check based on Heron's formula for the area }
>   Set A to distance between Point1 and Point2
>   Set B to distance between Point1 and Point3
>   Set C to distance between Point2 and Point3
>   Set S to (A + B + C) / 2.0
>   Set Area to $\sqrt{S * (S - A) * (S - B) * (S - C)}$
>   Return Area > 50.0
> End CheckArea

The square root function is needed for this pseudocode, so we will have to import sqrt from the MathLib0 module and add it to our modular design chart as documentation.

The pseudocode for the horizontal line check is done by checking the *y* coordinates of the points as follows:

> CheckHorizLine(Point1, Point2, Point3): Boolean
>   Return (Point1.Y = Point2.Y) or
>   (Point1.Y = Point3.Y) or
>   (Point2.Y = Point3.Y)
> End CheckHorizLine

Pseudocode for the output component has not been developed, since this task is quite straightforward. The main program simply calls the major components, so we also choose not to develop it in pseudocode.

The pseudocode in this section appears very similar to an actual program, particularly since it is shown in typewritten form. In actual practice, pseudocode is often written by hand and may be less formal, as the pseudocode for CheckArea indicates.

> Check Area (Point 1, Point 2, Point 3): Boolean
> {Area check based on Heron's formula}
>   Set A to Distance (Point 1, Point 2)
>   Set B to Distance (Point 1, Point 3)
>   Set C to Distance (Point 2, Point 3)
>   Set S to $\frac{A+B+C}{2}$
>   Set Area to $\sqrt{S(S-A)(S-B)(S-C)}$
>   Return Area > 50
> End Check Area

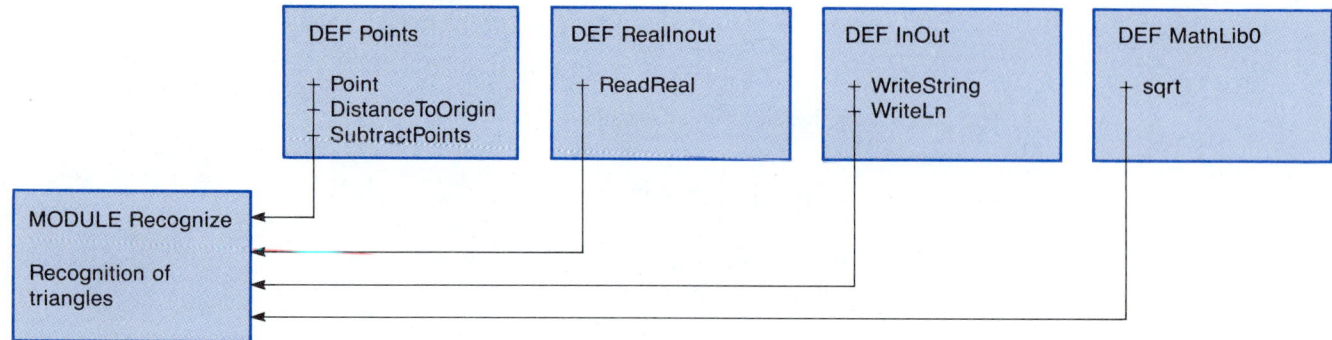

Figure 8.7 Complete Modular Design Chart for Triangle Recognition

From the pseudocode, we can determine which procedures we will need to import from library modules, and thus complete the modular design chart we started earlier in Figure 8.6. The complete chart is shown in Figure 8.7.

The lines showing the interconnections are called the *software bus;* they indicate the importation of objects (constants, types, variables, procedures) into the various modules. Of course, the lines must originate at the appropriate definition module; however, the lines are determined by specific IMPORT lists, not by what is available to import. A more complex problem would lead to a greater number of modules, including many user-defined modules. We will discuss the design and implementation of user-defined modules in detail in Chapter 11.

Develop a Testing Strategy Before we start translating our algorithm into Modula-2, we must plan our program testing. Experience has shown that when testing is not well planned, it takes an enormous amount of time. Furthermore, when testing is planned early, it can lead to modifications of the solution by uncovering forgotten cases or unexpected combinations of data. Such modifications are much easier to make before implementation, since no actual programming has been done. Therefore the testing strategy should be defined before implementation begins and should lead to the definition of a set of test data that is as comprehensive as feasible. A testing strategy ought to be such that every part of the program will be executed at least once. Even when this precaution has been taken, subtle errors may remain. Such bugs may show up later when the program is in regular use, and then they must be corrected by the programmer responsible for maintenance. This possibility is the basis for a well-known saying in programming:

> Testing can show the presence of bugs
> but it cannot guarantee their absence.

For our triangle recognition program, we should test invalid coordinate values (the following cases 1–2) to test our code for input data validation, valid values (cases 3–5) that do not satisfy the recognition conditions, and valid values (case 6) that do satisfy the conditions.

TABLE 8.1 **Test Data**

Point1		Point2		Point3		Expected Result
X	Y	X	Y	X	Y	
−341						error message
−340	−239					error message
−340	−238	−341				error message
−340	−238	−340	−239			error message
−340	−238	−340	−238	−341		error message
−340	−238	−340	−238	−341	−239	error message
−340	−238	−340	−238	−341	−238	not recognizable
341						error message
340	239					error message
340	238	341				error message
340	238	340	239			error message
340	238	340	238	341		error message
340	238	340	238	341	239	error message
340	238	340	238	341	238	not recognizable
0	0	0	9	15	0	not recognizable
0	0	15	9	15	0	not recognizable
0	0	0	15	9	0	not recognizable
0	0	10	1	20	0	not recognizable
0	0	0	20	10	10	not recognizable
0	0	0	20	20	0	recognizable
−10	−10	0	10	10	−10	recognizable

1. x coordinates less than −340 and greater than 340 for each of the three points
2. y coordinates less than −238 and greater than 238 for each of the three points
3. valid points with one side length less than or equal to 10 but satisfying the other conditions
4. valid points with area less than or equal to 50 but satisfying the other conditions
5. valid points with no horizontal line but satisfying the other conditions
6. valid points satisfying all three conditions

It is particularly important to test values on the boundaries of the validity checks and recognition conditions, since semantic errors frequently occur at such boundary values. With this in mind, we define the test data in Table 8.1. The first two groups of test data are checks on input data validation, and each group may be done as a unit. For example, the first value, −341, will cause an error message and the prompt for input will be redisplayed. Then −340 can be entered and subsequently −239, which will cause an error message, and so on.

This set of test cases is the minimum we would recommend; more would be desirable, including, for example, points that cause more than one of the recognition conditions to fail. Even if we tested just this minimal set of test cases, we would find input completely by hand tedious; therefore, we would like to have the program accept data manually or by input redirection. You will be asked to do this in Programming Problem 9 at the end of the chapter.

Implementation

Once the design phase is completed, we can concentrate on implementing the solution we have developed. Here we actually code and test our program and continue documenting our work as we've been doing.

Code and Test the Program   From the pseudocode solution previously defined, we develop the following program:

```
MODULE RecTriangle;
(* A program to read in the coordinates of three points,
   validate that the coordinates are within an acceptable
   range, and determine if the triangle determined by the
   points satisfies the following conditions:
      1. all sides are longer than 10,
      2. the area is greater than 50, and
      3. one side is horizontal.
                           J. M. Adams, January 1988 *)

FROM Points IMPORT Point, DistanceToOrigin, SubtractPoints;
FROM RealInOut IMPORT ReadReal;
FROM InOut IMPORT WriteCard, WriteString, WriteLn;
FROM MathLib0 IMPORT sqrt;


PROCEDURE DataInputValidation( VAR Point1, Point2,
                                   Point3: Point );
(* Input and validate the x and y coordinates of the three
   points. *)

   PROCEDURE InputPoint( VAR P: Point; I: CARDINAL );
   (* Read x coordinate of point I and repeat until input is in
      the range -340 to 340, and read Y coordinate of point I
      and repeat until input is in the range -238 to 238. *)
   BEGIN
     LOOP
       WriteString( "Enter x coordinate of Point" );
       WriteCard( I, 5 );
       WriteString( " from -340 through 340: " );
       ReadReal( P.X ); WriteLn;
       IF ( -340.0 <= P.X ) AND ( P.X <= 340.0 ) THEN
         EXIT;
       END; (*IF*)
       WriteString( " Value not in range, try again. " );
       WriteLn;
     END; (*LOOP*)
```

```
      LOOP
        WriteString( "Enter y coordinate of Point" );
        WriteCard( I, 5 );
        WriteString( " from -238 through 238: " );
        ReadReal( P.Y ); WriteLn;
        IF ( -238.0 <= P.Y ) AND ( P.Y <= 238.0 ) THEN
          EXIT;
        END; (*IF*)
        WriteString( " Value not in range, try again. " );
        WriteLn;
      END; (*LOOP*)
    END InputPoint;

BEGIN (*DataInputValidation*)
  InputPoint( Point1, 1 );
  InputPoint( Point2, 2 );
  InputPoint( Point3, 3 );
END DataInputValidation;


PROCEDURE Distance( PointI, PointJ: Point ): REAL;
(* Return the distance between the two points. *)
VAR Difference: Point;
BEGIN
  SubtractPoints( PointI, PointJ, Difference );
  RETURN DistanceToOrigin( Difference );
END Distance;


PROCEDURE CheckSideLength( Point1, Point2,
                           Point3: Point ): BOOLEAN;
(* Check that side lengths are all greater than 10. *)
BEGIN
  RETURN ( Distance( Point1, Point2 ) > 10.0 ) AND
         ( Distance( Point1, Point3 ) > 10.0 ) AND
         ( Distance( Point2, Point3 ) > 10.0 );
END CheckSideLength;


PROCEDURE CheckArea( Point1, Point2, Point3: Point ): BOOLEAN;
(* Compute area based on Heron's formula, and check that the
   area is greater than 50. *)

VAR A, B, C, S, Area: REAL;
BEGIN
  A := Distance( Point1, Point2 );
  B := Distance( Point1, Point3 );
  C := Distance( Point2, Point3 );
  S := (A + B + C) / 2.0;
  Area := sqrt( S * (S - A) * (S - B) * (S - C) );
  RETURN Area > 50.0;
END CheckArea;
```

```
PROCEDURE CheckHorizLine( Point1, Point2,
                         Point3: Point ): BOOLEAN;
(* Check that one of the sides is horizontal. *)
BEGIN
  RETURN ( Point1.Y = Point2.Y ) OR
         ( Point1.Y = Point3.Y ) OR
         ( Point2.Y = Point3.Y );
END CheckHorizLine;


VAR Point1, Point2, Point3: Point;

BEGIN (* RecTriangle *)
  DataInputValidation( Point1, Point2, Point3 );
  IF CheckSideLength( Point1, Point2, Point3 ) AND
     CheckHorizLine( Point1, Point2, Point3 ) AND
     CheckArea( Point1, Point2, Point3 )
  THEN
    WriteString( "recognizable" );
  ELSE
    WriteString( "not recognizable" );
  END; (*IF*)
  WriteLn;
END RecTriangle.
```

Notice the formatting that has been done to make the program readable. We have used blank lines to set off the procedures that form the program's major structural components. Indentation has been used to emphasize the flow of control aspects of the program: the bodies of procedures, the statements to be repeated inside a loop, and the alternatives in selection statements.

Also, notice the comments that are an important part of the program's internal documentation. The preface at the beginning of the program gives its objectives, its author, and the date of its completion. The prefaces of the procedures give brief statements of their function, and their names have been chosen to suggest functionality as well. Some names, such as CheckHorizLine, have been abbreviated but remain intelligible. Variable names have been chosen to suggest the variable's contents.

We have used several functions in the program. Each function produces only one result and has no side effects (that is, they do not change any nonlocal value nor do input or output). Adhering to this stylistic guideline can be beneficial in debugging large programs, since it helps us isolate the parts of the program that we feel may contain the error. For example, if we suspect that the value of a variable is being altered inadvertently, we can concentrate on examining procedures that are not functions since they may have a side effect causing the undesired alteration.

The program structure does not exactly correspond to the structure shown in our structure chart in Figure 8.5. The procedure Distance has been added as a low-level component. It is used by the functions CheckSideLength and CheckArea, so it cannot be nested within the functions. As a result, the main program and other procedures may call Distance, which is really not warranted. From the standpoint of the information hiding principle, this aspect is undesirable. A solution to this kind of dilemma will be provided in Chapter 11, when we discuss local modules.

Another deviation from our structure chart is that CheckConditions has disappeared, being replaced by an IF statement in the main program. Also, the function InputPoint has been added as a low-level component nested within DataInputValidation. These deviations do not represent essential structural design changes, but the structure charts for the final documentation should be updated to reflect the final program structure.

We should also note that our program is rather inefficient, because the side lengths are computed twice. This redundancy could be avoided by computing the side lengths in the main program and passing them to the CheckSideLength and CheckArea functions instead of the points. You'll be asked to make this change in Programming Problem 10 at the end of the chapter.

Once the program has been written, we compile it. We might have to correct a few syntactical errors before being able to run the program. This revision is normal since we may mistype or be careless in other ways. We then execute the program using the previously defined test data and compare the results we obtain with the expected results. If we run into trouble (program execution stops before the end of the data, wrong results turn up, or various runtime errors arise) we will have to find and correct the errors (debugging). The first thing to do is simply to trace the execution mentally to see if the error can be found quickly. If you are unsuccessful, you can pursue the trace more carefully or add debugging statements at appropriate points in the program. One simple way of doing this is to add statements of the form

```
IF Debug THEN
   WriteString(. . . a message . . .);
   Write . . .(. . . a variable . . .); WriteLn;
      .
      .
      .
END; (* IF *)
```

where Debug is a global Boolean constant and the write statements are appropriate for the types of the variables we wish to print. The write statements will be executed only when Debug is TRUE; therefore, if we declare Debug by "CONST Debug = TRUE", then the write statements will be executed when the program is run. When we are finished with our testing, we can replace the constant declaration with "CONST Debug = FALSE", and then the write statements will be ignored when the program is run. Thus when we are not debugging, the program runs as designed. But when Debug is TRUE, the debugging statements will produce a series of messages that enable us to trace program execution. Using this technique, we can easily switch back and forth between a normal mode of execution and a debugging mode by simply changing a single constant and recompiling our program.

As a simple example, assume that the first statement in function CheckArea in program RecTriangle had been incorrectly entered as

```
A := Distance( Point2, Point2 );
```

When we carefully examine the results of the test cases, we should observe that the results are erroneous. If we fail to notice the error in our quick mental trace, we could put the following statement at the end of the function after importing WriteReal:

```
IF Debug THEN
   WriteString( "A = " );  WriteReal( A, 15 );  WriteLn;
   WriteString( "B = " );  WriteReal( B, 15 );  WriteLn;
   WriteString( "C = " );  WriteReal( C, 15 );  WriteLn;
   WriteString( "Area = " );  WriteReal( Area, 15 );  WriteLn;
END;  (* IF *)
```

After we have run the altered program, we could check the results against hand-computed results, probably revealing the error.

> The use of debugging statements allows us to see precisely what the program *is* doing, rather than what we *think* it is doing.

The technique of using debugging statements is so effective that many programmers include them in their programs at the very beginning—in anticipation of their need in testing.

Many language implementations are supplied with special debugging packages that can simplify the process of tracing or observing intermediate results. If such a package is available, spend some time learning to use it effectively.

Finding errors is very much like detective work—looking for clues and traces. We have to use our reasoning and deductive power to find the culprits (erroneous statements, incorrect declarations, and so on). We may have to add debugging statements at different places in the program and delete other debugging statements as we narrow the search for errors.

For relatively simple programs, such as this example, the coding and testing process just described is usually adequate. When dealing with larger programs, though, we must use a structured approach to coding and testing. Next we will illustrate how a top-down approach might have been done on our example. Referring back to the structure chart of our solution (Figure 8.5), we could begin our development at the top level; such an approach makes it possible to make sure the overall logic design is correct and that the interfaces between procedures work.

In the present case we would write the main program with stubs for DataInputValidation, CheckSideLength, CheckArea, and CheckHorizLine. For example, the stub for DataInputValidation could be

```
PROCEDURE DataInputValidation( VAR Point1, Point2, Point3: Point );
BEGIN
   Point1.X := 0.0;  Point1.Y := 0.0;
   Point2.X := 0.0;  Point2.Y := 0.0;
```

```
     Point3.X := 0.0; Point3.Y := 0.0;
   WriteString( "DataInputValidation called" ); WriteLn;
END DataInputValidation;
```

Stubs may have to supply values for VAR parameters, as we see with the stub for DataInputValidation.

After the program runs correctly with the stubs, the next step is to replace one of the stubs—DataInputValidation, for instance—by the actual procedure and test it; then the other stubs are replaced one by one by the actual procedures and tested. Although this testing process may not be required for a small program like RecTriangle, this example illustrates the top-down testing method.

As already mentioned, another testing method is the bottom-up testing method, whereby the lowest level procedures are tested first. This approach of testing a procedure separately is very useful for critical components where an error would have significant (and disastrous) effects on other components, and also in programming teams where each component is implemented by a different team member. We can also combine top-down and bottom-up methods: critical procedures are tested first, then a top-down approach is used. For example, we could first test function Distance using a driver, before proceeding with top-down testing.

Note that all the testing methods require extra work, such as creating stubs or creating drivers. Those extra programs must also be written and tested. In large projects, the team of programmers assigned to testing may be separate from the development team. This division of responsibilities helps maintain an objective attitude, since the testing team does not have the protective attitude to the program that the development team might have.

Complete the Documentation The level of documentation may vary widely depending on how extensively the program is used. At the very least, the final version of the source code should be documented, as described in this section. Additional external documentation, such as discussion of the design, structure charts, and modular design charts might be maintained so that it is clear why certain design decisions were made and what alternatives were considered.

When we wrote the program, we started our internal documentation. As we have previously stated, the internal documentation includes comments, meaningful identifier names, and program formatting to make the code as self-documenting as possible.

Comments should help others understand what your program does but should not belabor the obvious, as with

```
     FederalTotal := 0;          (* Initialize to zero *)
```

Such comments would clutter the program and eventually render it less clear and legible.

Comments should always be used to construct explanatory prefaces for programs and procedures. They should also help clarify declarations if the identifier names are not sufficient. Finally, they should explain code that is not obvious.

We should emphasize once more the importance of program formatting. An unformatted program would be like a book without paragraph or chapter breaks; it might work, but it certainly would not be easy to read. Extra blank spaces and lines make it possible to see at a glance the main structure of the program, and indentation helps to trace the flow of control that will be followed when the program is executed.

Your code will be much clearer if you choose your identifier names carefully.

```
GrossPay := Hours * Rate;
```

is certainly clearer than

```
C := A * B;
```

The following procedure is definitely not self-documenting code. It is functionally correct but difficult to read and understand.

```
PROCEDURE Ch(P1,P2,P3:Point):BOOLEAN;
VAR A,B,C,S,Ar:REAL;
BEGIN
A:=D(P1,P2);B:=D(P1,P3);C:=D(P2,P3);
S:=(A+B+C)/2.0;Ar:= sqrt(S*(S-A)*(S-B)*(S-C));
RETURN Ar > 50.0;
END Ch;
```

This procedure is the equivalent of our function CheckArea shown in the complete program. Comparing the two procedures shows how important the choice of identifier names and program formatting are.

In general, the use of constants makes code more readable and also much easier to modify. For example, the following declarations could be made in program RecTriangle:

```
CONST MinX = -340.0; MaxX = 340.0;
      MinY = -238.0; MaxY = 238.0;
```

and all occurrences of the numerical values replaced by the corresponding constant identifier. Then, if the constants were to be changed, we would have to modify only the constant declarations and not have to inspect all our statements to find and modify occurrences of the actual values. In this example, because the use of constants complicates the prompts for input values, constants were not used.

The external program documentation is, of course, external to the program code. It usually includes the problem definition, the design documents, a description of testing performed, a history of the program's development and its different versions, and possibly a user's manual. In our example we still have to produce a user's manual that will describe to a naive user how to use the program. The manual for our program is relatively simple.

RecTriangle USER'S MANUAL

RecTriangle is a program to read in the coordinates of three points, validate that the coordinates are within an acceptable range, and determine if the triangle determined by the points satisfies the following conditions:

1. all sides are longer than 10
2. the area is greater than 50
3. one side is horizontal

If the conditions are met, the message "recognizable" is displayed; otherwise, the message "not recognizable" is displayed.

Input is interactive; if an input value is not within the allowable range, an error message is displayed, and the user is prompted to enter another value. The allowable ranges are

x coordinates from -340 through 340

y coordinates from -238 through 238

To run the program, insert the Geometry diskette and run the program RecTriangle. You will be prompted to enter the input data.

Maintenance

Maintenance is not part of the original design and implementation process; it includes all activities after the program becomes operational. These activities include fixing bugs, modifying existing code to improve performance or transfer to a new environment, enhancing capability, and updating documentation. In our case studies in the following chapters, we will illustrate maintenance by assigning exercises that involve program enhancements. For example, our program in this chapter could be enhanced by accepting input data from files by redirection.

SUMMARY

As we begin to consider more complex problems, we must be especially careful to design a solution before we begin implementing a program. An effective problem-solving method for design and implementation is:

Design Define the problem.

Design a solution (structural design).

Refine the solution (detailed design).

Develop a testing strategy.

Implementation Code and test the program.

Complete the documentation.

In the first design step we try to state the problem as unambiguously as possible, and we produce a precise problem specification. During structural design we decompose the problem into its subproblems and determine the structure of a solution. This process typically follows a top-down strategy and can be depicted by a structure chart. Refining the solution involves using the skeletal solution from the previous step to write an algorithmic solution in pseudocode. It is important to design a testing strategy before implementation begins because errors in design should be corrected before coding. We may approach testing in a top-down or bottom-up fashion, or use a combination of the two methods.

A number of guidelines should be followed during the coding phase to ensure a clear and modifiable program. Programs ought to be composed of reasonably sized procedures, and the flow of control should be straightforward. Formatting can help to make the program more readable if blank lines are used to separate components and indentation indicates the flow of control. Comments explaining the program should be written at the start of the program and each procedure and in difficult sections of code.

After we have finished entering the program, we compile it. At this point we may have to correct a few syntactical errors before actually being able to run the program. Then we run the program and compare our results with the results determined in the development of our testing strategy. If we run into errors, the first step of debugging is to trace the program execution mentally. Another method is to add debugging statements. Some language implementations come with debugging packages that are helpful. Structured testing for complex problems uses the top-down and/or the bottom-up approach.

Documentation is necessary for users of the program and even for the original programmer, who may not recall the reasons for earlier design decisions. Documentation begins at the first stage of development and continues throughout the program's lifetime. Program maintenance includes all the error corrections, program modifications, and additions after the program has become operational. During maintenance external documentation must be updated as necessary and a change log should be kept in the program preface.

Adapt the style used in this chapter's example to meet your own needs, and use it to develop the larger programs that will subsequently be assigned. When developing larger programs, you should also design in such a way as to facilitate maintenance. Although the programs you do for the exercises may not be changed after they are completed, other programs that you develop later outside class will undoubtedly need to be maintained. Even more importantly, you must practice clarity in design and documentation, which are critically important traits of any good scientific work.

EXERCISES

1. Modify the RecTriangle program to use constants for the limits of the input values. This alteration will involve changing the input prompts.
2. Draw a structure chart for the following problem:

    Process a collection of checking account transactions (deposits and withdrawals). For each account, the program reads the old balance and a series of transactions in order to compute and print the new balance.

3. Do the design for the following problem:

   Given an inventory of cases for four types of soft drinks—Kid Cola, Eight Up, Quench, and Spring—process weekly transactions (sales and purchases) to produce an updated inventory. The input data items will be four values giving the initial inventories (number of cases on hand) for the four brands at the beginning of the week, followed by a sequence of transactions (brand, amount purchased or sold). The final transaction consists of a zero amount. Your program should produce the inventory at the end of the week.

4. Begin a learning log recording your experiences while at the computer. This log should include new features you learn about an editor, compilation errors and how you corrected them, and programming errors, particularly if they reflected a misunderstanding of Modula-2. A sample entry is as follows:

Date	Nature of Entry	Description
6-17-88	Compiler Error	Compiler would not compile the statement: $$CONST\ InvPi = 1.0/3.14159;$$ evidently a restriction of this compiler, since constant expressions are permitted in Modula-2.

5. Draw a structure chart for the following problem: Do a stylistic analysis of a text by computing the percentage of each vowel in the text (as a percent of all letters) and comparing the computed percentages with input percentages characteristic of a particular author.

PROGRAMMING PROBLEMS

6. Electron Inc. sells three types of display terminals

   Screenview 1001   for $250
   Screenview 2001   for $325
   Screenview 3001   for $450

   The company gives a 10 percent discount to customers whose order totals more than $10,000. The input data on each order are: customer number, product type (S1001, S2001, S3001), and number of units purchased. Design and implement a program that will read all orders and then print for each customer the customer number, the gross dollar amount of orders, the discount (it may be 0.00), and the net amount.

7. In order to promote sales, Electron Inc. is setting up a new discount plan, known as step pricing. The first five units of a particular model are at full price (regardless of the total size of the order), the next ten units have a 10 percent reduction, and any units beyond the fifteenth have a 20 percent reduction. Here is a chart for our three models:

	1–5 Units	6–15 Units	16 or More Units
S1001	250.00	225.00	200.00
S2001	325.00	292.50	260.00
S3001	450.00	405.00	360.00

Note that the count of units is for each particular model and that the price reductions are not retroactive to units already purchased. Revise the solution of Problem 6 to implement these changes.

8. If your system has graphics capability, add a procedure to the RecTriangle program to display "recognizable" triangles.

9. Alter the RecTriangle program to offer the user the option of input redirection, so that test cases could be put in files to be read or entered from the keyboard.

10. Alter the RecTriangle program to correct the inefficiency of computing the side lengths twice, described in the discussion of RecTriangle in Section 8.2.

11. Design and implement a program with interactive input, which will read in the x and y coordinates of two points, and determine the slope of the line connecting the points and the quadrants in which the points lie. To resolve ambiguities in determining the quadrants, assume that the first quadrant contains the positive x and y axes, the second contains the negative x axis, the third contains the negative y axis, and the fourth contains no points on the axes.

12. Design and implement a program with interactive input to read in the coefficients of a quadratic equation and determine the roots of the equation.

9 Characters, Strings, and Arrays

In this chapter you will:

- learn about the representation of the CHAR data type and its effect on character operations
- understand how to define and use your own enumeration types
- learn more about the STRING data type
- see how to define and use ARRAY data types
- practice using array data types in a case study

In Chapter 2 we introduced six basic types: INTEGER, CARDINAL, REAL, BOOLEAN, CHAR, and STRING. We examined the first four in greater detail in Chapter 6, emphasizing operations allowed on these types. Here we will describe operations permitted on the CHAR data type. As we will see, the same operations are defined on all Modula-2 implementations, but the results of these operations depend on the particular character representation used by the operating system and the hardware. Our discussion will introduce the ASCII character set.

We first saw user-defined data types such as subranges and records in Chapter 6. We expand on this concept by introducing enumeration data types—types based on the explicit enumeration (or listing) of all possible values.

We will also learn more about the STRING data type, which can be viewed conceptually as a sequence of characters. To practice with strings, we'll do two brief examples. This discussion is a natural introduction to the ARRAY data type, which allows us to represent sequences of any data object. In fact arrays are a very important data type, because we can use them to design more general data structures and programs. We'll look at one-dimensional arrays, multidimensional arrays, and open array parameters.

The final third of the chapter includes an extended case study that uses the new data type declarations and applies the problem-solving methodology that was discussed in detail in Chapter 8.

9.1 Character Data Type

As we have seen in earlier chapters, a variable declared to be of type CHAR can take as a value a single character, which can be read, compared, modified, or printed. Characters are different from the other basic types in that they have no primitive operations, except the relation operators. All manipulations must be done by procedures, and many of the manipulations depend on the internal representation of characters. Thus we must give more information about the representation of values of type CHAR than we have given for values of other types.

Character Representation

Characters are special objects that can be read and recognized by humans. They are used to print results and to represent input data in a form readable by humans. Because computers handle only sequences of bits, all information in the computer has to be represented as binary numbers. Thus characters must be coded numerically in order for us to be able to enter them into the computer and manipulate them. The numerical character codes constitute what is called a *character set*. Character sets can vary between computers; one of the most widely used is ASCII (American Standard Code for Information Interchange). The complete ASCII character set appears in Appendix A; the numeric codes there are shown in both decimal (base 10) and octal (base 8). The decimal and octal forms are equivalent; in this text, though, we will primarily use the decimal form. However, in certain situations the alternative octal form is useful, as we will see later in this section.

The 128 characters of the ASCII character set are represented by decimal numerical codes from 0 to 127. These character codes determine the order of the characters within the character set. The ASCII codes are grouped as follows:

0–31	control characters (nonprinting)
32–47	punctuation, other symbols
48–57	numerals 0...9
58–64	punctuation, other symbols
65–90	uppercase letters, A...Z
91–96	punctuation, other symbols
97–122	lowercase letters, a...z
123–126	punctuation, other symbols
127	control character (nonprinting)

Control characters (0–31 and 127) perform special functions, such as line feed (LF), cursor return (CR), bell (BEL), backspace (BS), horizontal tab (HT), and so on. Note that the numerals, the uppercase letters, and the lowercase letters are each grouped in consecutive positions with the natural ordering. This is not true of all character sets. For example, the character set used on large IBM computers is not grouped in this way.

Character constants can be represented in Modula-2 by surrounding the character with single or double quotes; we will normally use single quotes. Examples are: 'A', '3', and '$'. We cannot use this form for nonprinting characters, since we have no symbol to put between the quotes. However, we can represent these characters by using a special notation that we will discuss later in the section.

Character Operations

Several built-in functions are available for processing character data. For example, the standard function, ORD, returns the decimal code of a character within the character set. Thus, using ASCII, ORD('2') returns 50, and ORD('C') returns 67. The ORD function operates on character values, such as the character constants discussed in the preceding paragraph, character variables, or any expression, including function calls, that results in a character value. The standard function CHR converts a cardinal denoting a decimal code into the corresponding character. For instance, using ASCII, CHR(50) returns '2', and CHR(67) returns 'C'. The function CHR can be used to specify nonprintable control characters. For example, the statement

```
Write( CHR( 7 ) )
```

will cause a bell to ring, because CHR(7) denotes the control character BEL in the ASCII character set.

As you can see, ORD and CHR are inverses of each other

$$\text{decimal code} \quad \underset{\text{ORD}}{\overset{\text{CHR}}{\rightleftarrows}} \quad \text{character}$$
$$\text{CARDINAL} \qquad\qquad\qquad \text{CHAR}$$

or

$$\text{CHR}(\text{ORD}(Ch)) = Ch$$
$$\text{ORD}(\text{CHR}(N)) = N$$

We can use the six relational operations (=, #, <, <=, >, >=) on characters, but other operations are dependent on standard functions, such as ORD and CHR. For example, to assign a character variable Ch a value five positions beyond its current value, we would write

```
Ch := CHR( ORD( Ch ) + 5 )
```

Before doing this, we should make sure that we will not go beyond the last code in the character set. Later in this section we will see an alternative way to advance a character value by a fixed number of positions.

Characters are different from the other elementary types; even though they are coded numerically, they *cannot* be mixed with values of numeric types. Suppose we want to convert a single-digit integer, 0 to 9, to the corresponding character '0' to '9'. Assuming N contains the integer value, we have

$$Ch := CHR(ORD('0') + N);$$

This method would work with any character set where the characters '0' to '9' are contiguous and in the natural order.

As just noted, characters can be compared by the six relational operators. The result of a comparison depends on the order of the character set. For ASCII

    'A' < 'C'   is TRUE
    '5' = CHR(50)   is FALSE
    CHR(ORD('0')+5) # '5'   is FALSE

Two other useful standard procedures are increment, INC, and decrement, DEC. To advance a character variable value to the next value, we write INC(Ch). A second parameter can be added to specify a larger increment: INC(Ch, 5) would advance the value of Ch by five character positions. The decrement procedure works similarly to backup a character variable value; for example, DEC(Ch, 3) backs up the value of Ch by three character positions.

INC and DEC can have integer or cardinal parameters, and can be used, instead of assignment statements, to increment and decrement integer values. For example, if N is of type INTEGER, INC(N) is equivalent to N := N + 1. DEC and INC can also have parameters of enumeration types, which will be discussed in the next section.

A Program Example

Let's write a program that will generate part of the decimal ASCII table given in Appendix A. Since control characters cause special functions to be performed when written, we will want to generate only the printable characters between space and right brace (}). Since we want to print the characters sequentially, a For loop is appropriate. Here is a pseudocode solution:

> PrintTable
>   For character from space to '}'
>   Print code of character, spaces, the character
>   Advance to the next line
>   End for
> End PrintTable

Here is our actual implementation:

```
MODULE PrintTable;
(* Print a table of ASCII characters between ' ' and '}'
                        B. L. Kurtz    January 1988 *)

FROM InOut IMPORT Write, WriteCard, WriteString, WriteLn;

VAR Ch: CHAR;

BEGIN   (* PrintTable *)
  FOR Ch := ' ' TO '}' DO
    WriteCard( ORD( Ch ), 5 );
    WriteString( "      " );
    Write( Ch ); WriteLn;
  END;    (* FOR *)
END PrintTable.
```

Note the use of procedure Write that displays a value of type CHAR, which is a single character.

Some keyboards allow the user to type any ASCII character; however, most will allow only printable characters to be typed. Two common techniques exist for assigning nonprintable values to characters. One way is to use the CHR function, as we discussed previously. A disadvantage of this approach is that it cannot be used for declared constants, because function calls are not allowed in constant expressions. For example, the decimal code for form feed, which advances the paper to the next page, is 12, but the following declaration of a constant would not compile:

```
CONST FormFeed = CHR( 12 );   (* INVALID CONSTANT DECLARATION! *)
```

The second technique is to use numeric constants equal to the desired character code. However, this must be done with care. Consider the declaration

```
            CONST FormFeed = 12;
```

This would compile but would probably cause trouble later in the program, because the compiler will consider FormFeed to be of type CARDINAL rather than CHAR, as intended.

We can define such character constants by using the character code, written in octal (base 8), followed by a "C". From the table of octal codes given in Appendix A, we find that the octal code for a form feed is 14. Thus a correct declaration is

```
            CONST FormFeed = 14C;
```

The "C" indicates that a value of type CHAR is being declared.

This discussion of character types has introduced the ASCII character set and some of the basic functions for processing character data. In the case study in Section 9.5, we'll see how character types are used in a text processing program.

9.2 Enumeration Data Types

To solve some problems we need to define our own data types. Indeed in certain situations we may want to create a type that allows us specifically to identify all allowed values. These types are known as *enumeration data types*. Let's quickly review our discussion of user-defined types and then take a look at enumeration data types.

Simple and Structured Data Types

As you'll recall from Chapter 6, you can define your own types by using the TYPE declaration

```
TYPE type-name = type-description;
     type-name = type-description;
             .
             .
             .
```

In Chapter 6, you also learned how to declare subranges and records. Subranges are *simple types,* and records are *structured types*. The basic standard types that we have already used (INTEGER, CARDINAL, REAL, BOOLEAN, and CHAR) are simple types. Their values are said to be atomic, because they are not decomposable. On the other hand, structured types have components and can be decomposed. STRING and RECORD are examples of structured types, because we can access the individual components that make up a value of these types.

 The basic standard types are also called *scalar types*—that is, the values are distinct and can be ordered. With the exception of the REAL data type, each value of a scalar data type has a unique predecessor and a unique successor. Mathematically, real numbers on the number line have no unique predecessor or successor. Computers can represent real numbers only to a precision that is dependent on the particular computer being used. Since there are only a finite number of REAL values for a particular computer, these values will have predecessors and successors. However, since this precision will vary between computers, we say in general that REAL values have no unique predecessor and successor. We will study the representation of REAL values in more detail in Chapter 14.

Examples of Enumeration Types

Enumeration types are defined by a list of identifiers denoting values of the type. For instance, the standard type BOOLEAN is an enumeration type, which can be considered as having been specified by the declaration

```
TYPE BOOLEAN = ( FALSE, TRUE );
```

9.2 Enumeration Data Types

For new enumeration types, the type description is a list of identifiers between parentheses, separated by commas. The identifiers in the list are chosen by the programmer and may not be used for any other purpose. For example,

```
TYPE Transport = ( Airplane, Boat, Truck, Train );
     Gender    = ( Masculine, Feminine, Neuter );
     Currency  = ( Dollar, Yen, Pound, Franc, Mark );
```

The identifiers in a type's enumeration list may be used as values in the program, and they denote the *only* values belonging to that type. Such a declaration also defines an order for the values. With the preceding declarations, the order of values would be

```
Airplane < Boat < Truck < Train
Masculine < Feminine < Neuter
Dollar < Yen < Pound < Franc < Mark
```

We can use the procedures DEC and INC with enumeration types. For example, if MeansOfTravel is a variable of type Transport with value Boat, then INC(MeansOfTravel) gives MeansOfTravel the value Truck. Likewise, if Money is a variable of type Currency with value Franc, then DEC(Money) gives Money the value Pound. DEC(Dollar), however, would be erroneous, since Dollar is the first value of type Currency. Such errors are called *range errors,* because they specify values that would be outside the range of allowable values of the type.

The standard function ORD returns the rank (starting from zero) of a value in its type. For example,

```
ORD( Airplane ) = 0
ORD( Franc )    = 3
ORD( TRUE )     = 1
```

Conversely, the standard function VAL, given a type and the rank of a value of that type, returns the value. For example,

```
VAL( Transport, 0 ) = Airplane
VAL( Currency, 3 )  = Franc
VAL( BOOLEAN, 1 )   = TRUE
```

A value that appears in a type's enumeration list cannot appear in another enumeration list, because it would create an ambiguity. For instance, the following declaration is invalid:

```
TYPE Credit = ( Terrible, Average, Good, Excellent );
     Grades = ( Perfect, Average, Mediocre );
```

because the value Average would belong to two different types.

Values of enumeration types cannot be read or printed directly; they must be decoded explicitly by the program, as in

```
WriteString( "Give first letter of currency name ( D, Y, P, F, M )" );
Read( Ch );
CASE Ch OF
   'D':   Money := Dollar|
   'Y':   Money := Yen   |
   'P':   Money := Pound |
   'F':   Money := Franc |
   'M':   Money := Mark
   ELSE WriteString( "Not an available choice" )
END;
```

where Money was declared to be of type Currency.

We can declare subranges of enumeration types, such as

```
TYPE SlowTransport = [Boat..Train];
```

The base type of SlowTransport is type Transport, defined earlier. All operators of the base type are applicable to variables of the subrange type.

In this section we have concentrated on the definition of enumeration types and operations on these types. Enumeration types are valuable because they help to make a program understandable for humans. In older programming languages, the programmer would have to use numeric codes—such as 0 for airplane, 1 for boat, 2 for truck, and 3 for train—to represent conceptual values. Someone reading the program would always have to keep in mind the conversion between the numerical values and the conceptual values. With enumeration types, the programmer can express programs in terms closer to the problem being solved without having to devise a sequence of numerical equivalents for conceptual values. When appropriate, we will use enumeration types in our problem solutions throughout the remainder of the text.

9.3 String Data Type

As we mentioned in Chapter 2, STRING is not a standard Modula-2 data type but is available from a library module in most implementations. The Strings module is an abstract data type that includes the type STRING and allows operations on strings. We have already used Copy, Concat, Length, and Pos in previous examples throughout earlier chapters (to review them see the library module Strings in Appendix F). Now we will introduce two additional procedures—FetchChar and AssignChar—that allow us to access the character components of a string.

Access to Characters in a String

If Str is a STRING variable, we can use the function FetchChar from module Strings to access a specified character from the string value of Str. FetchChar takes a string as its first parameter and a cardinal as its second parameter; it returns the character in the string that is at the position indicated by the cardinal. Since character positions are numbered from zero, FetchChar(Str, 0) will return the first character of the string Str, FetchChar(Str, 1) will return the second character, and so on. The cardinal argument is often called an index. An index is used to identify an element in an ordered group of elements. If the index is greater than or equal to the length of the string, FetchChar returns the null character (the character whose decimal code is zero). We should emphasize that FetchChar returns a result of type character, *not* of type string! Type CHAR is supposed to be compatible with strings of length 1, but some implementations may give a type incompatibility error if you try to mix them.

AssignChar is the inverse of FetchChar: it can be used to replace a character in a string. The first parameter of AssignChar is the character to place in the string specified by the second parameter. The third parameter is the index of the character to be replaced (an invalid index results in no change in the string). For instance,

```
AssignChar( 'Z', Str, 2 )
```

will assign the value 'Z' to the character at index 2 of the string Str. Note that the second actual parameter must be a variable, because a value will be assigned to it.

Two Programming Examples

Let's consider two examples that deal with strings and characters, and make use of FetchChar and AssignChar.

EXAMPLE 1 *Encryption Procedure*

To illustrate the manipulation of characters within a string, we will develop a procedure that will "encrypt" a string of digits into another string of digits. For example, suppose a stereo store manager wants to mark the wholesale price for each item as part of its shelf tag. This knowledge would help the salesperson negotiate a final price with the customer. The manager decides the wholesale price should be encrypted in such a way that customers will not suspect the meaning of the number, yet an employee can easily translate the number back to the wholesale price. Our encrypting scheme will be based on advancing each digit from '0' to '8' by one position, and setting digit '9' back to '0'. Here are some examples of how our scheme will work:

Unencrypted	*Encrypted*
'03995'	'14006'
'0099'	'1100'
'012345'	'123456'

We want to write a Modula-2 procedure that will do the encryption on a parameter that consists of a string of characters that are all digits. Let's write the procedure in pseudocode:

> Encrypt
>   For each character in the string
>   If the character is a '9' then
>   reset it to '0'
>   Else
>   advance it to the next character position
>   End If
>   End For
> End Encrypt

We can use FetchChar and AssignChar to access and replace individual characters in a string. We also need to use the INC procedure to advance the character value. We can now write our Modula-2 procedure:

```
PROCEDURE Encrypt( VAR Str: STRING );
(* A simple encryption, which advances each digit 0 through 8
   within Str to the next value, and changes any 9 digit to 0.
   Str should contain only digits. *)

VAR CharPos: CARDINAL;
    Ch: CHAR;
BEGIN
  FOR CharPos := 0 TO Length( Str ) - 1 DO
    Ch := FetchChar( Str, CharPos );        (* get character *)
    IF Ch = '9' THEN
      AssignChar( '0', Str, CharPos );
    ELSE
      INC( Ch );                             (* increment it *)
      AssignChar( Ch, Str, CharPos );        (* put it back *)
    END;    (* IF *)
  END;    (* FOR *)
END Encrypt;
```

In this example we manipulated the characters '0' through '9' in a string. In the next example we will manipulate alphabetic characters.

EXAMPLE 2 *Conversion of a String to Lowercase*

As another example of character manipulation within a string, we will develop an algorithm to convert uppercase letters to lowercase letters, and we will apply it to an entire character string.

The alphabet contains two sequences of letters: 'A' to 'Z' and 'a' to 'z'. In some computer applications, the case of the character (either uppercase or lowercase) does not make any difference. In such applications, it is simpler to convert all letters to one case. In fact, Modula-2 provides a built-in function, CAP(ch), that will convert a lowercase letter to uppercase. Since there is no built-in function to uncapitalize, let's design one. We will then use this function to convert all uppercase letters to lowercase letters in a string. All other characters, including the lowercase letters, should remain unchanged. First, let's sketch the pseudocode for the entire procedure:

> LowerCase
>   For each character in the string
>   If the character is an uppercase letter then
>   convert it to a lowercase letter
>   End If
>   End For
> End LowerCase

We still must specify how we can determine if a character is an uppercase letter and, if so, how to uncapitalize it.

Assuming the character set is organized so that all uppercase letters are sequential from 'A' to 'Z', we must test whether the current character, say Ch, is greater than or equal to 'A' and is less than or equal to 'Z'. To do that, we will use the Boolean expression

```
( 'A' <= Ch ) AND ( Ch <= 'Z' )
```

Now we must specify how the conversion is to take place. Assuming that both the uppercase letters and the lowercase letters are sequential, we can "line them up."

| uppercase | A | B | C | D | E | F | ... | X | Y | Z |
| lowercase | a | b | c | d | e | f | ... | x | y | z |

Notice that the distance of an uppercase letter from the beginning uppercase letter, 'A', would be the same as the distance of the corresponding lowercase letter from the beginning lowercase letter, 'a'. For example, there is a distance of five characters between 'A' and 'F' and between 'a' and 'f'. We will use this fact to make the conversion. Assume the variable Ch contains the letter to be "uncapitalized." The number of letters from 'A' to Ch is ORD(Ch) − ORD('A'). If we use the INC function to add this displacement to 'a', we will have the desired lowercase letter.

Our LowerCase procedure can now be written:

```
PROCEDURE LowerCase( Ch: CHAR ): CHAR;
(* If Ch is an uppercase letter return the corresponding
   lowercase letter, otherwise return Ch unaltered. *)

VAR Temp: CHAR;
```

```
BEGIN
  IF ( 'A' <= Ch ) AND ( Ch <= 'Z' ) THEN
    Temp := 'a';
    INC( Temp, ORD( Ch ) - ORD( 'A' ) );
    RETURN Temp;
  ELSE
    RETURN Ch;
  END; (* IF *)
END LowerCase;
```

This character function will work for any character set, including ASCII, where the uppercase characters are stored consecutively and the lowercase characters are also stored consecutively in the same order.

To uncapitalize a whole string, we can use the following loop:

```
FOR CharPos := 0 TO Length( Str ) - 1 DO
  AssignChar( LowerCase( FetchChar( Str, CharPos ) ), Str, CharPos );
END; (* FOR *)
```

Notice that the body of the loop has only one statement, but this statement contains three procedure calls: a call to FetchChar, the result of which is used in a call to LowerCase, whose result is used in a call to AssignChar.

Strings are used in a great number of applications, and string manipulations are common. We will return to string processing in our case study later in the chapter.

9.4 Arrays

As a sequence of characters, STRING is a specific instance of a very general and useful structured data type—the array. An *array* is a sequence of objects of any data type, including other structured types such as arrays and records.

One-Dimensional Arrays

An array is a sequence of data elements. The ARRAY data type is a structured data type with a fixed number of components of the *same type*, each component being directly accessible by means of an *index*. The declaration of an object of type ARRAY has the following form.

```
VAR name: ARRAY index-type OF component-type;
```

where ARRAY and OF are reserved words, index-type is the type of the index (enumeration or subrange), and component-type is the type of the data elements (components) that form the array. Such arrays are called *one-dimensional arrays* or *vectors*, because they have only one index.

Figure 9.1   Array of Cardinals

An example of an array declaration is

```
VAR ChapterCount, TextCount: ARRAY ['A'..'Z'] OF CARDINAL;
```

In this example the index type is a subrange of type CHAR, and the component type is CARDINAL; the array type itself is anonymous, since it is not given a name. We could declare those two arrays in a different way, using a type declaration, as

```
TYPE Occurrences = ARRAY ['A'..'Z'] OF CARDINAL;
```

and

```
VAR ChapterCount, TextCount: Occurrences;
```

Generally, assigning a name to a type is preferred since it allows the use of the type in a wider variety of situations, such as parameter passing.

Each element of an array can be accessed directly by using an index. Figure 9.1 represents the ChapterCount array, which has 26 elements, with the indices shown above each element. Accessing an element of an array is easily done by using the name of the array followed by the index value in square brackets. Such a specification is sometimes called an *indexed variable*. If Letter is of type ['A'..'Z'] and has value 'C', the following are examples of indexed variables.

```
ChapterCount[Letter]     the third element of ChapterCount
TextCount['J']           the tenth element of TextCount
```

An index may be any expression that is type compatible with the index type; if Ch is of type ['A'..'Z'], the following are examples of indexed variables:

```
ChapterCount[CAP( Ch )]
TextCount[CHR( ORD( Ch ) + 5 )]
```

Values can be given to arrays by reading or assigning values to the individual elements, as shown here for ChapterCount:

```
FOR Letter := 'A' TO 'Z' DO
  ChapterCount[Letter] := 0;
END (* FOR *);
```

This loop assigns zero to each element of the array ChapterCount.

It is also possible to assign entire arrays as in

$$\text{TextCount} := \text{ChapterCount};$$

which assigns all 26 elements of ChapterCount to the corresponding elements of TextCount. Assignments of this nature can be done only between arrays of *precisely the same type*. For example, such assignments would not even be permitted if ChapterCount and TextCount were declared as follows:

```
VAR ChapterCount: ARRAY ['A'..'Z'] OF CARDINAL;
    TextCount:    ARRAY ['A'..'Z'] OF CARDINAL;
```

because the compiler considers the two types to be distinct even though they have the same structure. Thus variables of array types are assignment compatible only if they are declared to be of the same named type, as in

```
VAR ChapterCount, TextCount: Occurrences;
```

or are declared anonymously at the same time, as in

```
VAR ChapterCount, TextCount: ARRAY ['A'..'Z'] OF CARDINAL;
```

We will illustrate several different one-dimensional arrays by means of the following declarations:

```
TYPE Tenant = (Single, Couple, Family, WithPet);

VAR Building: ARRAY [1..65] OF Tenant;
    Stats   : ARRAY Tenant OF REAL;
    Grades  : ARRAY [1..MaxStudent] OF [0..100];
    Phrase  : ARRAY [1..30] OF CHAR;
```

Figure 9.2
Representation of Arrays

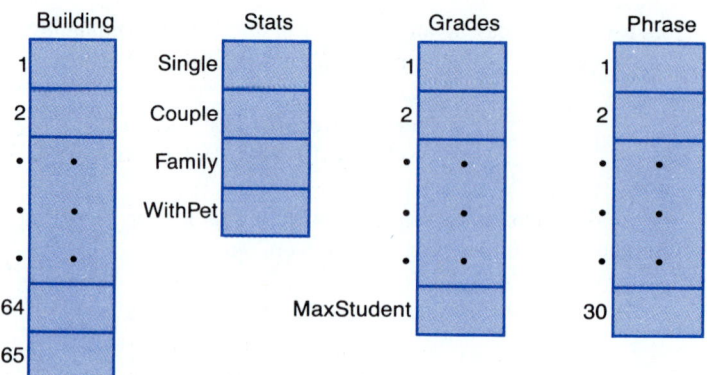

Building is an array of 65 elements, each of which can take one of 4 values: Single, Couple, Family, or WithPet. Stats is an array of 4 elements, each of which has a real value. Grades is an array of MaxStudent elements, each of which has a value greater than or equal to zero and less than or equal to 100. Phrase is an array of 30 characters. These arrays are illustrated in Figure 9.2, where the component types are, from left to right, Tenant, REAL, [0..100], and CHAR.

If Apartment has the value 52, Student has the value 11, Back has the value 12, and Groups has the value Couple, the following indexed variables correspond to the elements indicated:

Grades[Student]	11th element of array
Building[Apartment]	52nd element of array
Phrase[20−Back]	8th element of array
Stats[Groups]	2nd element of array

Let's consider three short examples that illustrate how one-dimensional arrays are used in computations. These examples are so brief that we will omit the pseudocode solution.

EXAMPLE 1 *Computing a Grade Average*

If we had 10 grades to average to determine a final grade, we might use the declarations

```
CONST MaxIndex = 10;
TYPE GradeRange = [1..MaxIndex];
     GradeArray: ARRAY GradeRange OF REAL;
VAR Grades: GradeArray;
    GradeSum, FinalGrade: REAL;
    Index: GradeRange;
```

Using the following program segment, we could read and store the 10 grades, and then compute the final grade:

```
GradeSum := 0.0;
FOR Index := 1 TO MaxIndex DO
   (* GradeSum = Grades[1] + · · · + Grades[Index - 1]  *)
   WriteString( "Enter grade " ); WriteCard( Index, 3 ); WriteString( ":" );
   ReadReal( Grades[Index] ); WriteLn;
   GradeSum := GradeSum + Grades[Index];
END; (* FOR *)
(* GradeSum = Grades[1] + · · · + Grades[MaxIndex]   *)
FinalGrade := GradeSum / FLOAT( MaxIndex );
```

Subsequently we could display all the grades as part of a grade report.

EXAMPLE 2 *Computing the Number of Rainy Days*

Suppose each day we record whether it has rained that day. At the end of the week we want to count the number of rainy days in the week. To solve the problem, we will use the declarations

```
TYPE Day = ( Sunday, Monday, Tuesday, Wednesday, Thursday, Friday, Saturday );
     RainyWeek = ARRAY Day OF BOOLEAN;

VAR Today: Day;
    Rainy: RainyWeek;
    RainyDays: [0..7];
```

Then the following program segment can be used to inspect the Boolean array and count the rainy days.

```
(* Computation of number of rainy days in a week *)
RainyDays := 0;
FOR Today := Sunday TO Saturday DO
  IF Rainy[Today] THEN
    INC( RainyDays );
  END; (* IF *)
END; (* FOR *)
(* RainyDays = number of TRUE values in Rainy[Sunday] . . .
   Rainy[Saturday]   *)
WriteString( "Number of rainy days: " );
WriteCard( RainyDays, 5 ); WriteLn;
```

EXAMPLE 3 *Computing Lengths Between Points*

Suppose we have a one-dimensional array whose values represent the *x* and *y* coordinates for each of 100 points, and we wish to compute the lengths of the lines between consecutive points in the array. The following declarations will be appropriate:

```
CONST NumPoints = 100;
TYPE Point = RECORD
               X, Y : REAL;
             END;
     PointIndex = [1..NumPoints];
VAR Points: ARRAY PointIndex OF Point;
    LineLength: ARRAY [1..NumPoints - 1 OF REAL;
    DeltaX, DeltaY: REAL;
    Index: PointIndex;
```

Notice that we have declared Points to be an array of records, where each record contains a *x* value and a *y* value. The following program segment would perform the desired computations:

```
FOR Index := 1 TO 99 DO
   DeltaX := Points[Index].X - Points[Index + 1].X;
   DeltaY := Points[Index].Y - Points[Index + 1].Y;
   LineLength[Index] := sqrt( DeltaX * DeltaX + DeltaY * DeltaY );
END; (* FOR *)
```

Here we have combined the access mechanism to array components (indexing) with the access mechanism to records (the dot followed by a field name) to fetch the desired information. This approach is summarized in stepwise fashion as follows:

```
Points              is an entire array
Points[Index]       is an array component, a record in this example
Points[Index].X     is a field of that record, a real value
```

In all three examples the FOR statement was the easiest loop structure for processing array elements sequentially.

The STRING Data Type as an Array

In the previous chapters we have actually been using an array data type, STRING, without emphasizing the fact. The data type STRING is usually implemented as an array of characters, often with the declaration

```
TYPE STRING = ARRAY [0..79] OF CHAR;
```

In this declaration the index type is a subrange of CARDINAL, and the component type is CHAR.

Using indexed variables gives us another way to refer to components of strings—in addition to the procedures FetchChar and AssignChar. If Str is declared to be of type STRING, we could use the references

```
Str[0]                  (* first element of Str *)
Str[Length( Str ) - 1]  (* last element of Str *)
```

These references are, however, dependent on the representation of STRING values as arrays, whereas FetchChar and AssignChar are not. It is recommended that you always use the specialized procedures provided to access components of an abstract data type. Accessing string components directly using the array notation can lead to disastrous results if some representation other than arrays has been used for strings. We will elaborate on this point in Chapter 15.

Thus far we've considered examples of arrays that have just one index. All problems, though, will not be so straightforward. For some programs, we'll need to use more complex structures. In the next section, therefore, we'll look at multidimensional arrays.

Multidimensional Arrays

As we have seen, components of arrays can be of any type. In particular, these components can themselves be arrays. For example,

```
VAR Table: ARRAY [1..5] OF ARRAY [0..Max] OF CARDINAL;
```

Here Table is called a *two-dimensional array* or a *matrix*. It can be visualized as a two-dimension figure shown in Figure 9.3, assuming the value of Max to be 9. As shown in this figure, Table has five rows, indexed 1..5, and ten columns, indexed 0..9.

To access components of such an array, we will need two indices—the first to identify what component array we want, and the second to indicate the element we are looking for in that component. This element can be denoted by

```
Table[I][J]
```

which refers to the Jth element of Table[I], where Table[I] is itself an array of one dimension.

There is an abbreviated way of defining multidimensional arrays; the declaration for Table shown at the start of this section could have been written

```
VAR Table: ARRAY [1..5],[0..Max] OF CARDINAL;
```

With either definition, the access to an element can be written

```
Table[I, J]
```

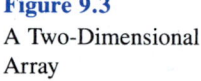

Figure 9.3
A Two-Dimensional Array

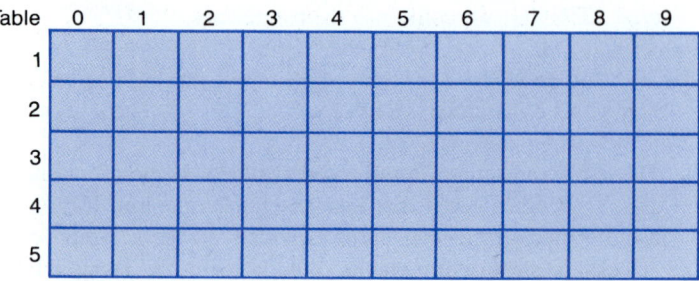

SEC. 9.4 Arrays

Suppose we want to extend our previous example to the computation of rainy days for a year (52 weeks). We can use an array of 52 elements, each element comprising data for a week, in the form of an array of seven BOOLEAN elements (RainyWeek). We can now replace our declaration of Rainy by

```
TYPE Day = ( Sunday, Monday, Tuesday, Wednesday, Thursday, Friday, Saturday );
     RainyWeek = ARRAY Day OF BOOLEAN;
     RainyYear = ARRAY [1..52] OF RainyWeek;

VAR Rainy: RainyYear;
```

or by

```
TYPE Day = ( Sunday, Monday, Tuesday, Wednesday, Thursday, Friday, Saturday );
     RainyYear = ARRAY [1..52], Day OF BOOLEAN;

VAR Rainy: RainyYear;
```

Rainy is now a two-dimensional array with $52 \times 7 = 364$ elements. In order to count the number of rainy days in a year, our program segment must also be modified as follows

```
RainyDays := 0;
FOR Week := 1 TO 52 DO
  FOR Today := Sunday TO Saturday DO
    IF Rainy[Week, Today] THEN
      INC( RainyDays );
    END; (* IF *)
  END; (* FOR *)
END; (* FOR *)
```

The addition of still another dimension is easily done; our example can be extended to the 10 years of a decade by modifying our declarations in the following manner:

```
TYPE Day = ( Sunday, Monday, Tuesday, Wednesday, Thursday, Friday, Saturday );
     RainyWeek = ARRAY Day OF BOOLEAN;
     RainyYear = ARRAY [1..52] OF RainyWeek;
     RainyDecade = ARRAY [1981..1990] OF RainyYear;

VAR Rainy: RainyDecade;
```

or by

```
TYPE Day = ( Sunday, Monday, Tuesday, Wednesday, Thursday, Friday, Saturday );
     RainyDecade = ARRAY [1981..1990], [1..52], Day OF BOOLEAN;

VAR Rainy: RainyDecade;
```

Rainy now has 10 × 52 × 7 = 3640 elements, and our program segment to count the number of rainy days in a decade is

```
RainyDays := 0;
FOR Year := 1981 TO 1990 DO
  FOR Week := 1 TO 52 DO
    FOR Today := Sunday TO Saturday DO
      IF Rainy[Year, Week, Today] THEN
        INC( RainyDays );
      END; (* IF *)
    END; (* FOR *)
  END; (* FOR *)
END; (* FOR *)
```

The number of dimensions of an array can be greater than three, but applications using such arrays are rare. To get an idea of a multidimensional array, consider a library to be a huge collection of characters. Each character can then be uniquely located by eight indices:

1. a floor number
2. an aisle identifier
3. a bookcase number
4. a shelf number
5. a book position on the shelf
6. a page number
7. a line number
8. a character number within the line

In this section we have illustrated arrays that have array components. We can also declare data structures that combine arrays and records, such as an array of records, as we saw in Example 3. Such structures are extremely useful and will be discussed extensively in Chapters 12 and 13, when we study algorithms for searching and sorting.

Open Array Parameters

The rules we have used for arrays so far would be overly restrictive for parameters that are arrays. For example, we could not have general procedures that deal with arrays of varying lengths, such as strings whose lengths may vary. This restriction is overcome in Modula-2 by a feature called open arrays. Before defining this feature, though, let's briefly review and elaborate upon the rules regarding parameters.

As we have previously mentioned, the types used in the formal parameter list of a procedure must be standard types or must have been defined with a TYPE declaration. For instance, if we transform our original rain statistics program segment into a procedure, we could have the procedure heading

```
PROCEDURE RainStats( Rainy: RainyWeek ): CARDINAL;
```

In this case the named type RainyWeek is essential and could not be replaced in the parameter list by ARRAY Day OF BOOLEAN.

Furthermore, when a formal parameter is a structured type, the corresponding actual parameter, used when the procedure is called, must be of the same named type. That is, the names *of the types* of the actual and formal parameters *must* be the same, even though the actual and formal parameter names may, and often are, different.

This requirement of strict correspondence between types of an actual and a formal parameter could be very onerous for arrays. For example, it might mean we would have to have different string procedures for strings of different lengths. As you know, this restriction is not the case, since, for example, Length will accept as an argument any valid string. To accomplish this, we use an open array parameter. The heading for Length is

```
PROCEDURE Length( STR : ARRAY OF CHAR ): CARDINAL;
```

and ARRAY OF CHAR is called an open array, the name being motivated by the fact that no range is specified for the index. In general, an *open array* must be one dimensional and is specified in the formal parameter list by the keywords ARRAY OF followed by the element type.

In open arrays the index type of the actual parameter is unknown and can be of different types for different calls. Whatever the index type of an actual parameter, a correspondence is established between that type and the subrange of cardinals $0..(n-1)$, where n is the number of elements specified by the actual index type. Thus, within the procedure, the lower limit of the index can be taken to be zero, and the upper limit, $n-1$, is given by a call to the standard function HIGH, which takes the open array as its parameter.

The following is an example of the use of open arrays to code a procedure to compute the average of the values stored in an array of cardinals.

```
PROCEDURE Average( Numbers: ARRAY OF CARDINAL ): REAL;
(* Computation of the average of an array of numbers *)
VAR Sum, Index: CARDINAL;
BEGIN
  Sum := 0;
  FOR Index := 0 TO HIGH( Numbers ) DO
    (* Sum = Numbers[0] + · · · + Numbers[Index - 1]    *)
    Sum := Sum + Numbers[Index];
  END;    (* FOR *)
  (* Sum = Numbers[0] + · · · + Numbers[HIGH( Numbers )]    *)
  RETURN FLOAT( Sum ) / FLOAT( HIGH( Numbers ) + 1 );
END Average;
```

Here the calls to HIGH are used to determine the length of the actual parameter. Note also that HIGH returns the highest cardinal index, which is one less than the number of elements in the actual array. This procedure can be used to compute the average of arrays of cardinals of different sizes, such as those declared by

```
VAR ShortVector:  ARRAY[1..10] OF CARDINAL;
    LongVector:   ARRAY[1..50] OF CARDINAL;
    MediumVector: ARRAY[-10..20] OF CARDINAL;
    Alphabet: ARRAY['A'..'Z'] OF CARDINAL;
    Days: ARRAY[Sunday..Saturday] OF CARDINAL;
    Avg1, Avg2, Avg3, Avg4, Avg5: REAL;
```

by means of the calls

```
Avg1 := Average( ShortVector );
Avg2 := Average( LongVector );
Avg3 := Average( MediumVector );
Avg4 := Average( Alphabet );
Avg5 := Average( Days );
```

For some problems, such as searching for a particular array element, an index value needs to be returned by a procedure using an open array parameter. This index must be a CARDINAL since the procedure has no access to the index of the actual parameter. In the program segment calling the procedure, the VAL function can be used to recover the corresponding value for the index of the actual parameter.

Arrays are particularly useful structures in Modula-2 because they enable us to manipulate sequences of any kind of data. For many problems, multidimensional arrays help us organize large amounts of data for systematic processing. Another powerful structure is combining arrays and records; we will study these structures in more detail in Chapters 12 and 13.

9.5 Case Study: Stylistic Analysis of Text

To get a better idea of the practical use of characters, strings, and arrays, let's see how they work together as part of a programming solution. Rather than looking at another of the short, focused examples that we've used so far, though, we'll explore a programming problem from start to finish, using our six-step problem-solving methodology.

An intriguing computer application in recent years has been the stylistic analysis of text. For example, computer-based stylistic analysis has been used to help resolve questions of disputed authorship by comparing stylistic characteristics of the text in question with the same stylistic characteristics of passages of known authorship. In most cases this sort of computer-based stylistic analysis is a complex process. For our case study, though, we will simplify the process so that it involves only counting the occurrences of words (or letters) in several texts, and computing the percentage of occurrences of those words (or letters). This percentage is the result of the division of the number of occurrences of a word (or a letter) by the total number of words (or letters) in the text. We figure the percentage for several texts and then compare the computed percentages. If they are very close, we say the texts have the same style and very probably the same author. If not, their styles differ, and they were probably written by different authors.

One of the more significant such applications involved the Federalist Papers, a series of essays that were precursors of the United States Constitution. Scholars knew that the series was written by Alexander Hamilton, James Madison, and John Jay, but they did not know the authorship of each essay. The goal of the analysis, therefore, was to try to determine which essay was written by which of the three men. With computer-based analysis, they were able to make a determination with a high degree of confidence.

As mentioned earlier, a full-blown stylistic analysis program would be a bit much for us right now, but we can develop a very simplistic program to give us the flavor of this application. We will develop a program to read in a text and some percentages already computed for some author. The program will then do a stylistic analysis based on the percentages of occurrences of each letter computed for the text and the percentages read. The analysis will involve only computing a measure of the differences between the two sets of percentages.

Design

Define the Problem We will assume that the text comes as a sequence of lines of punctuation marks and uppercase and lowercase letters. The program will read the text and count the letters as they are read. No distinction will be made between uppercase and lowercase letters; there will be only one counter for each alphabetic character, which will be incremented each time a letter (uppercase or lowercase) is encountered. Once the text has been read, the program will compute the percentages of occurrences of each letter in the text. The program will then display a histogram that will have a line of output for each alphabetic character considered. This line will give the number of occurrences of the character in the text followed by asterisks as a graphical representation of that number. We will also be given as input the percentages of occurrences of letters characteristic of some author. Then our stylistic analysis of "closeness" will be based on a simple measure: the square root of the sum of the squares of the difference between the given percentages and the computed percentages. More formally,

$$\sqrt{\sum_{L=A}^{Z} (\text{TextPct}_L - \text{AuthorPct}_L)^2}$$

Our output will terminate with the display of the measure of closeness.

A small value indicates that the text is close to the style of the author according to this measure. For example, a closeness measure of zero means the percentages were the same, so that the text is exactly the style of the author according to this simplistic stylistic measure. On the other hand a closeness measure of 10 means that there is a substantial difference between the two styles.

Design a Solution In problems involving more than one input or output data stream, we start the analysis by describing how the data flows through the system.

Figure 9.4
Data Flow Diagram for Stylistic Analysis

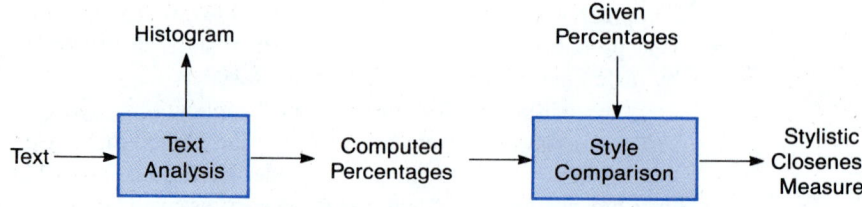

This description is sometimes accomplished with a diagram showing the input and data streams and thereby indicating what the principal components of our system might be. Figure 9.4 gives a data flow diagram for our stylistic analysis system.

The input format will be defined as a stream of characters where line divisions will not be considered. We will assume that the input will be read from the keyboard, although it would be more common to read from a file that had previously been prepared. Input from such a file will be discussed in Chapter 10.

The histogram will consist of 26 lines, each in the format

C 240 **

In this format C stands for any letter, 240 represents the number of occurrences of that letter, and the asterisks provide a graphical representation of the number of occurrences. The maximum number of asterisks will be 60, so an asterisk may stand for more than one occurrence. For example, if a letter count was 240 and we used 60 asterisks to represent the count, each asterisk would represent four occurrences of the letter.

The analysis of the text data seems reasonably straightforward. We read the text a character at a time; as we do so, we keep a count of the total number of letters and a count of the number of occurrences of each letter. We will assume that the text ends with a special character—in this case a percent sign. When we reach the end, we can display the histogram, compute the percentages, and compare the styles. The style comparison involves reading the percentages for a given author, computing the stylistic "closeness" measure, and printing the result.

A structure chart for this solution is shown in Figure 9.5.

Figure 9.5
Stylistic Analysis Structure Chart

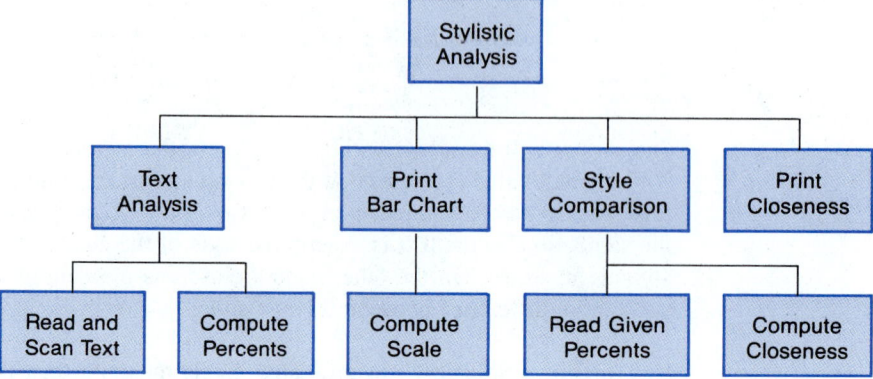

Case Study: Stylistic Analysis of Text

Refine the Solution The critical algorithms, described briefly at the beginning of the design, are developed here in pseudocode. We chose the following names for the variables needed in the pseudocode:

> Frequency : a 26-element array of integers for letter occurrences
> LetterCount: total number of letters in the text
> Percentages: a 26-element array of reals for letter percentages
> Closeness : "closeness" measure, a real

The pseudocode refining the solution outlined in our structure chart is

> StylisticAnalysis
>   TextAnalysis(Percentages, Frequency)
>   BarChart(Frequency)
>   StyleComparison(Percentages, Closeness)
>   Print Closeness
> End StylisticAnalysis
>
> StyleComparison(Percentages, Closeness)
>   Read Given Percents
>   Compute Closeness
> End StyleComparison
>
> TextAnalysis(Percentages, Frequency)
>   Read and Scan Text(Frequency, LetterCount)
>   Compute Percentages
> End TextAnalysis
>
> ReadandScanText(Frequency, LetterCount)
>   Initialize counters
>   Loop
>   Read next character
>   Exit if end of text
>   Update letter counts
>   End Loop
> End ReadandScanText
>
> BarScale(Frequency)
>   Find maximum value of Frequency
>   Set Scale to 1
>   If maximum > line length then
>   Set Scale to line length / maximum
>   End If
> End BarScale

> BarChart(Frequency)
>   Set Scale to BarScale(Frequency)
>   For each letter
>   Print Letter, Frequency of letter
>   If Frequency of letter # 0 then
>   Set Star to Scale * Frequency of letter
>   Print Star asterisks
>   End If
>   New line
>   End For
> End BarChart

In BarChart we use a scaling constant to determine the number of asterisks to print. If the constant has a value of one, an asterisk is printed for each occurrence of a letter. But if the text is long, many letters might have a number of occurrences greater than the line length. As a result, we have included a special function, BarScale, to compute the scaling factor, so that the line length is never exceeded.

We have included parameters in the algorithms to show the data flow, or interface, between them. Thus, for example, TextAnalysis produces the percentages and these are supplied to StyleComparison to compute Closeness.

Since we can see how to implement each step of the pseudocode, we will proceed with the development.

Develop a Testing Strategy The testing strategy will make sure we cover the following cases for text data:

1. short text that makes an easy case to check
2. text with occurrences of all letters and with characters that should not be counted
3. no text
4. letter never used (no asterisks printed)
5. letter used once (one asterisk printed)
6. letter used too many times to fit on a line (to verify that an asterisk will be used to represent more than one occurrence of the letter)

Our text test data are as follows:

Text test data 1:

```
ABCDEFGHIJKLMNOPQRSTUVWXY
%
```

Text test data 2:

```
Any technical revolution has, in the past, caused an intensive
reorganization of the economy and of society.  It can be at the same
```

time the occasion of a crisis and the way out of it. This was the case with the invention of the steam engine, railroads and electricity.

The "computer revolution" will have broader consequences. It is not the only technological innovation of the last few years, but it constitutes the common factor which allows and accelerates all the others. Because of the way in which it changes the processing and conservation of information, it will modify the nervous system of organizations and of the entire society.

Until recently, computing was expensive, not efficient, esoteric, and because of that, limited to a restricted number of organizations: elitist, it remained the monopoly of the powerful. Now mass computing will emerge, feeding society, as does electricity. Two progresses are the causes of this transformation. There were only large computers. Now there are quantities of small and powerful machines, which are not expensive. They are no more isolated, but interconnected through networks.
%

Text test data 3: (no text)

%

Text test data 4 (part of a speech from *Macbeth*, act 3, scene 5):

>Have I not reason, beldams as you are,
>Saucy and overbold? How did you dare
>To trade and traffic with Macbeth
>In riddles and affairs of death,
>And I, the mistress of your charms,
>The close contriver of all harms,
>Was never called to bear my part,
>Or show the glory of our art?
>And, which is worse, all you have done
>Hath been but for a wayward son,
>Spiteful and wrathful, who, as others do,
>Loves for his own ends, not for you.
>But make amends now. Get you gone,
>And at the pit of Acheron
>Meet me i' the morning. Thither he
>Will come to know his destiny.
>Your vessels and your spells provide,
>Your charms and everything beside.
>I am for the air, this night I'll spend
>Unto a dismal and a fatal end.
>Great business must be wrought ere noon.
>Upon the corner of the moon
>There hangs a vaporous drop profound.
>I'll catch it ere it come to ground,

```
            And that distilled by magic sleights
            Shall raise such artificial sprites
            As by the strength of their illusion
            Shall draw him on to his confusion.
            He shall spurn fate, scorn death and bear
            His hopes 'bove wisdom, grace, and fear.
            And you all know security
            Is mortal's chiefest enemy.
            Hark! I am called. My little spirit, see,
            Sits in a foggy cloud and stays for me.
            %
```

In addition to our text test data, we need test data for percentages. Our strategy for given percentages will cover

1. percentages that make an easy case to check
2. "typical" percentages
3. negative percentages
4. percentages greater than 100

Our percent test data for given percentages of letters *A* through *Z* are

Percent test data 1:
4.0 repeated 25 times and 0.0

Percent test data 2 (from *Hamlet*):
7.27 1.46 2.08 3.91 11.67 2.24 1.70 6.31 6.18 0.12 0.91 4.41 3.17
6.20 9.18 1.54 0.10 5.67 6.61 9.10 3.61 1.10 2.55 0.07 2.79 0.05

Percent test data 3:
Negative percentages

Percent test data 4:
Percentages greater than 100

We will use percent test data 1 with text test data 1 for our first test case, which should be easy to check. We will use percent test data 2 (the "typical" test data) with all the text test data. The erroneous percent test data 3 and 4 will be used only with text test data 3 (the null text), since we do not expect meaningful output when the erroneous percent test data are used. The expected results from the seven test data combinations are as follows. We give only the histogram for test case 3, because this case illustrates points 4, 5, and 6 of the text data-testing strategy: letter *J* never appears (no asterisk), letter *K* appears only once, and letter *E* appears 119 times and sets the scaling factor.

Test case 1 (percent test data 1—text test data 1):

```
            The closeness measure is      0.00
```

Test case 2 (percent test data 2—text test data 1):

```
            The closeness measure is     15.48
```

Test case 3 (percent test data 2—text test data 2):

```
Letter frequency bar chart

A     66  *********************************
B      7  ***
C     45  *********************
D     19  *********
E    119  *********************************************************
F     25  ************
G     14  *******
H     42  ********************
I     76  **************************************
J      0
K      1  *
L     33  ****************
M     23  ***********
N     74  *************************************
O     83  *****************************************
P     12  ******
Q      2  *
R     49  ************************
S     60  ******************************
T     97  ************************************************
U     22  **********
V     10  *****
W     20  *********
X      2  *
Y     17  ********
Z      3  *
```

The closeness measure is   5.57

Test case 4 (percent test data 2—text test data 3):

The closeness measure is   25.28

Test case 5 (percent test data 3—text test data 3):

error message and prompt to enter input again

Test case 6 (percent test data 4—text test data 3):

error message and prompt to enter input again

Test case 7 (percent test data 2—text test data 4):

The closeness measure is   3.93

Thus far in the design phase we've gotten the problem clearly in mind, created a solution that could be outlined in a structure chart, written an algorithm in pseudocode, and defined some test data along with the expected results.

Implementation

Code and Test the Program From the preceding pseudocode definition, we derive the following program.

```
MODULE StylisticAnalysis;
(* This program reads a text, then computes the percentage of
   occurrences of each letter, displays a histogram showing the
   number of occurrences of each letter, reads percentages of
   occurrences of each letter that are characteristic of some
   author, compares author's percentages with computed
   percentages by computing sum of squares of differences, and
   displays the result as a measure of stylistic closeness.
              J. M. Adams    December 1987

                     CHANGE LOG
   Date              Programmer          Change

   January 1988      P. Gabrini          Added histogram handling
                                         procedures BarChart,
                                         BarScale                  *)

FROM InOut      IMPORT Read, Write, WriteCard, WriteString,
                       WriteLn;
FROM RealInOut  IMPORT ReadReal, WriteReal;
FROM MathLib0   IMPORT sqrt;

TYPE Alphabet = ['A'..'Z'];
     Occurrences = ARRAY Alphabet OF CARDINAL;
     PercentTable = ARRAY Alphabet OF REAL;

PROCEDURE TextAnalysis(VAR Percent: PercentTable;
                       VAR Count: Occurrences);
(* Compute percentages of each letter in input text *)

  PROCEDURE ReadScanText(VAR Counters: Occurrences;
                         VAR Letters: CARDINAL);
  (* Read input text and count all letters. *)

  CONST StopChar = '%';
  VAR NextChar: CHAR;

  BEGIN
    FOR NextChar := 'A' TO 'Z' DO
      Counters[NextChar] := 0;
    END; (* FOR *)
    Letters := 0;
    WriteString("Enter input text terminated by %");
    WriteLn;
```

```
        LOOP
          Read(NextChar);
          Write(NextChar);
          IF NextChar = StopChar THEN EXIT END;
          NextChar := CAP(NextChar);
          IF ('A' <= NextChar) AND (NextChar <= 'Z') THEN
            INC(Letters);
            INC(Counters[NextChar]);
          END; (* IF *)
        END; (* LOOP *)
      END ReadScanText;

      VAR LetterCount: CARDINAL;
          Letter: Alphabet;

      BEGIN (* TextAnalysis *)
        ReadScanText(Count, LetterCount);
        IF LetterCount # 0 THEN
          FOR Letter := 'A' TO 'Z' DO
            Percent[Letter] := FLOAT(Count[Letter]) /
                          FLOAT(LetterCount) * 100.0;
          END; (* FOR *)
        ELSE
          FOR Letter := 'A' TO 'Z' DO
            Percent[Letter] := 0.0;
          END; (* FOR *)
        END; (* IF *)
      END TextAnalysis;

      PROCEDURE StyleComparison(TextPercentages: PercentTable;
                           VAR Closeness: REAL);
      (* Read percentages characteristic of some author and compute
         "closeness" measure. *)

      VAR AuthorPercent, SumOfSquares: REAL;
          Letter: Alphabet;

        PROCEDURE sqr(Number: REAL): REAL;
        (* Compute square of real argument *)
        BEGIN
          RETURN Number * Number
        END sqr;

        PROCEDURE ReadPcts(VAR Percentage: REAL; Letter: Alphabet);
        (* Read a real value between 0 and 100. *)
        BEGIN
          LOOP
            WriteString("Enter percentage for ");
            Write(Letter); Write(' ');
```

```
        ReadReal(Percentage);
        WriteLn;
        IF (0.0 <= Percentage) AND (Percentage <= 100.0) THEN
          EXIT;
        ELSE
          WriteString("   Percentages must be between 0 and 100.");
          WriteLn;
        END;  (* IF *)
      END;  (* LOOP *)
    END ReadPcts;

  BEGIN  (* StyleComparison *)
    WriteString("Enter percentages characteristic of author.");
    WriteLn;
    SumOfSquares := 0.0;
    FOR Letter := 'A' TO 'Z' DO
      ReadPcts(AuthorPercent, Letter);
      SumOfSquares := SumOfSquares +
                      sqr(TextPercentages[Letter] - AuthorPercent);
    END;  (* FOR *)
    Closeness := sqrt(SumOfSquares);
  END StyleComparison;

  PROCEDURE BarChart(Counters: Occurrences);
  (* Display of a bar chart from an array of values *)

    PROCEDURE BarScale(Counters: Occurrences): REAL;
    (* Determination of the scale to be used for bar chart *)

    CONST LineLength = 60.0;
    VAR Scale: REAL;
        Letter: Alphabet;
        Max: CARDINAL;
    BEGIN
      Max := 0;
      FOR Letter := 'A' TO 'Z' DO
        IF Counters[Letter] > Max THEN
          Max := Counters[Letter];
        END;  (* IF *)
      END;  (* FOR *)
      Scale := 1.0;
      IF FLOAT(Max) > LineLength THEN
        Scale := LineLength / FLOAT(Max);
      END;  (* IF *)
      RETURN Scale;
    END BarScale;

  CONST Stars =
  "************************************************************";
```

```
    VAR Letter: Alphabet;
        Freq: CARDINAL;
        NumStars: INTEGER;
        Scale: REAL;

    BEGIN (* BarChart *)
      Scale := BarScale(Counters);
      WriteString("     Letter frequency bar chart");
      WriteLn; WriteLn;
      FOR Letter := 'A' TO 'Z' DO
        Freq := Counters[Letter];
        Write(Letter); WriteCard(Freq, 5); Write(' ');
        NumStars := TRUNC(Scale * FLOAT(Freq));
        WHILE NumStars > 0 DO
          Write('*');
          DEC(NumStars);
        END; (*WHILE*)
        WriteLn;
      END; (* FOR *)
    END BarChart;

    VAR Frequency: Occurrences;
        Percentages: PercentTable;
        Closeness: REAL;

    BEGIN (* StylisticAnalysis *)
      TextAnalysis(Percentages, Frequency);
      BarChart(Frequency);
      StyleComparison(Percentages, Closeness);
      WriteLn; WriteString("The closeness measure is ");
      WriteReal(Closeness, 10); WriteLn;
    END StylisticAnalysis.
```

Our program structure here is consistent with our design structure. We observed in Chapter 4 that it is a good idea to declare a variable local to a procedure if it is used only by that procedure. Similarly, one procedure should be declared, or nested, within another procedure whenever the inner procedure is used only within the outer procedure. For this reason ReadScanText is nested within TextAnalysis, and sqr is nested within StyleComparison.

In procedure ReadScanText the counters are initialized; then each input character is converted to uppercase (CAP standard function), and for each letter, the corresponding counter is incremented.

In procedure TextAnalysis the percentage of occurrences is computed for each letter by simply dividing its number of occurrences by the total number of letters.

Procedure ReadPcts is a simple input procedure reading and validating one real value. Its loop is exited only when a value between 0 and 100 has been read.

In procedure StyleComparison author percentages are read for each letter. As they are read, the differences between them and the text percentages are computed; these differences are used in the computation of the sum of the squares of the differences. The closeness measure is then computed.

In procedure BarScale, a loop determines the maximum value of all the counters. This maximum is then tested. If it is less than the line length, a scaling factor of one is used; otherwise, the scaling factor is less than one and such that the maximum value will completely fill a line.

In procedure BarChart all the counters are examined; for each one a frequency count is printed with the corresponding letter. If the counter is not zero, the scaling factor is used to compute the number of asterisks to print. This is done simply by multiplying the count value by the scaling factor. A loop displays the desired number of asterisks, one by one.

The program was tested on the seven test cases developed in the previous step and gave the expected results.

Complete the Documentation The documentation should certainly include a careful statement of the problem definition developed in the first step and the data flow diagram and structure chart in Figures 9.4 and 9.5. The pseudocode solution might also be included, but it is optional because the program is fairly short and reasonably self-documenting. The test cases and their output should be part of the documentation. One additional item, a user's manual, will complete the documentation.

USER'S MANUAL

The StylisticAnalysis program reads in a text and computes the percentage of occurrences of each letter. It then prints a histogram of the occurrences of the various letters in the text, reads percentages of occurrences of letters characteristic of some author, and computes a measure of closeness of style, which is the square root of the sum of the squares of the differences of the percentages. This measure is the final output of the program.

Execute the program by loading the disk labeled STYLE, and typing the program name: StylisticAnalysis. Input of your input text and the author's percentages is from the keyboard; output will be on the screen. No validation of the input text is done, but only letters are counted. The author's percentages are checked to make sure each one is between 0 and 100. The input text should end with a percent sign.

Maintenance

Our program can be improved in several ways. One improvement would be to make it possible to enter the text in a data file and have the program accept input either from the terminal or from the data file by input redirection as discussed in Chapter 2. This improvement is going to be necessary if we want to use the program extensively. A second improvement would be to count all special characters. Such special characters might include the following:

",,"

","

"."

"?"

Still another improvement would be to do more validation of the input data. You can try to implement these improvements in Exercises 4, 8, and 9 at the end of the chapter.

SUMMARY

A variable declared to be of a character data type can take as a value a single character that can be read, compared, modified, or printed. Characters are coded numerically and these numerical codes constitute a character set, the most common being ASCII. Among the built-in functions for processing character data are ORD, which returns the decimal code of a character, and CHR, which converts a cardinal denoting a decimal code into the corresponding character. The procedures INC and DEC advance a character value and decrement a character value, respectively.

Enumeration types are defined by a list of identifiers denoting values of the type. The identifiers are chosen by the programmer and are used to make the program more readable. Enumeration values can be compared using relational operators. The built-in procedures ORD, VAL, INC, and DEC can also be applied to enumerated variables.

The Strings module is an abstract data type that includes the type STRING and allows operations on strings. Strings are structured data types; the functions FetchChar and AssignChar allow us to access and change the characters in a string.

Arrays are sequences of objects of any data type, including other structured types such as arrays and records. An array with only one index is known as a one-dimensional array. To access an element in an array we use the name of the array followed by the index value in square brackets.

When the components of an array are themselves arrays, the structure is known as a multidimensional array. Multidimensional arrays are useful for organizing large amounts of data for systematic processing.

Open arrays provide flexibility in the size of a one-dimensional array when they are passed as parameters to procedures. This facility makes it possible to have a single procedure process many different array types providing that the element type is the same.

You should now have a good understanding of the difference between simple and structured data types, basic data types, and an introduction to the building of complex data types by the user.

EXERCISES

1. Define a data type for all the members of your family, and create a subrange of those values.
2. Indicate whether the following declaration is valid. If not, suggest a valid declaration.

```
TYPE Employees=( Programmer, Analyst, Accountant, Janitor, Typist );
     Professionals=( Lawyer, Analyst, Physician, Executive );
```

3. Define a procedure that will capitalize all lowercase letters in a string passed as a variable parameter.
4. The StylisticAnalysis program used two array types—Occurrences and PercentTable—each indexed by Alphabet. These types could be combined into a single array of records, indexed by Alphabet, where each record contains a CARDINAL field for the occurrence count and a REAL field for the percentages. Discuss the pros and cons for making such a change.
5. If you are familiar with conversion between bases, define a procedure that accepts a decimal number and returns the equivalent octal number. Modify the PrintTable program in the text to add extra columns for the octal position of each character. Label your columns carefully.
6. Chris, an inquisitive computer science student, claimed that the THEN part of the IF statement in the function LowerCase could be written as a single RETURN statement

    ```
    RETURN CHR( ORD( 'a' ) + ORD( 'A' ) - ORD( Ch ) )
    ```

    Chris pointed out that this approach also eliminated the need for a local variable. Implement both approaches and write an interactive test program to see if both procedures produce the same result.
7. Can the RETURN statement given in the previous exercise replace the entire IF statement in function LowerCase? Explain your answer.
8. Indicate how to modify the StylisticAnalysis program so that spaces are treated like all other letters.
9. Define a program segment to do additional validation of input percentages in the StyleComparison procedure of program StylisticAnalysis. Make sure the sum is no more than 100.
10. Design a procedure that is passed an open array of points and returns the maximum distance from the origin for all of the points.
11. Modify your procedure in Exercise 10 so that the point that is furthest from the origin is returned.

PROGRAMMING PROBLEMS

12. Write a program that will read in a year in Roman numerals and convert and print it using Arabic numerals.
13. Write a main program to allow repeated testing with interactive input of the Encrypt procedure in the text.
14. Write and test a procedure Decrypt that is the inverse of Encrypt.
15. Alter the Encrypt procedure given in the text and the Decrypt procedure written for Problem 14 to shift by a number of positions specified by a parameter.

16. Choose one of the approaches given in Exercise 7, and complete the coding of the procedure LowerCase in Modula-2. Write an interactive program that will test your LowerCase procedure.

17. Write a program that takes as input an old-fashioned phone number (which includes letters) and produces as output the modern phone number, consisting only of digits.

$$
\begin{array}{rcl}
A\ B\ C & \longrightarrow & 2 \\
D\ E\ F & \longrightarrow & 3 \\
G\ H\ I & \longrightarrow & 4 \\
J\ K\ L & \longrightarrow & 5 \\
M\ N\ O & \longrightarrow & 6 \\
P\ R\ S & \longrightarrow & 7 \\
T\ U\ V & \longrightarrow & 8 \\
W\ X\ Y & \longrightarrow & 9
\end{array}
$$

For instance:

$$
\begin{array}{rcl}
AL3\text{-}2247 & \longrightarrow & 253\text{-}2247 \\
EV2\text{-}3336 & \longrightarrow & 383\text{-}3336 \\
OR1\text{-}4457 & \longrightarrow & 671\text{-}4457
\end{array}
$$

18. Write a procedure that—given today's date (three integers) and a person's birthdate (three integers)—returns that person's age in years and months.

19. Implement and test the procedure suggested in Exercise 11.

20. Define a Triangle data type that is an array of three points, each point being a record. Modify the program in Chapter 8 that recognizes triangles to use this new data type.

10 Input and Output Revisited

In this chapter you will:

- learn details of the input and output operations you have been using in previous chapters
- review redirection: changing the standard input and output devices to accept input from files and direct output to files
- learn about the library module Terminal
- be introduced to a simple library module for performing basic input and output to secondary storage (file operations)
- learn more about graphical screen-oriented output

Ever since introducing our first programming example, we have been using input and output (I/O) operations to read data and print results. The purpose of input and output is to transfer data between the computer memory and input and output devices connected to the computer. Those devices include the terminal (a keyboard for input and a screen for output), printers, plotters, disk drives, tape units, and telecommunication devices.

In the early days of computing, input and output devices were rather limited, and so most early programming languages included input and output statements as part of the language. However, because input and output operations differ from system to system, the designers of one early programming language, ALGOL 60, designed in 1960, did not include any input and output operations in the language definition. Instead, input and output operations were defined with each implementation of the language. Operations handled in this way are said to be implementation dependent, since they differ from one implementation to another. This approach was sensible, because providing very sophisticated input and output capabilities tends to complicate and obscure the language. Unfortunately, ALGOL 60 was not widely used in the United States, and so languages with complex input and output operations became the most commonly used languages. Designers of some more recent programming languages have adopted the ALGOL 60 approach by offering only basic input and output capabilities. This approach simplifies the language but also creates the disadvantage of not providing for a wide range of devices, thus making some applications difficult.

Input and output devices have changed greatly in the past few years. For example, terminals used to be like typewriters. Now most terminals include at least one microprocessor, and there are even terminals that accept simple spoken input and produce spoken output. Obviously, a programming language cannot support input and output operations for all present and future input and output devices. The ALGOL 60 approach looks more appropriate today than it did 25 years ago. The designer of Modula-2, Niklaus Wirth, chose not to include any input and output (I/O) statements in the language but to provide special input and output modules containing I/O procedures. As a matter of fact, another modern programming language, Ada, has followed the same basic approach. The I/O modules are implementation dependent, but each implementation will provide the *same high-level capabilities*. If the basic library modules are not sufficient for a given application, the user can design and implement other input and output modules adapted to a particular application.

10.1 Sequential Input and Output

Most input and output operations are *sequential:* if two items are to be read as input data, the second item cannot be read before the first item has been read. A convenient conceptual model for sequential input and output data is the *stream:* a sequence of data items of the same type (the *stream base type*). The number of items in a stream is called the length of the stream. The length of a stream can be modified only by deleting the whole stream (length becomes zero), or by adding elements at its end (writing).

Most input and output operations involve a *text stream,* where the base type is character. This definition seems identical with the definition of an array; however, the number of elements in a stream is not known prior to reading or writing the entire stream, and this number can vary with time, which is not true for an array.

Some input and output operations involve a *binary stream,* a sequence of binary values (bits). Binary streams are used to transfer information between primary and secondary storage and can be used for values of various types.

Only one element of an input stream is accessible at a given moment. This is the element accessed by what is called the *current position* in the stream. A stream also has a mode: it is either an input stream (which can be read) or an output stream (which will be written). Figure 10.1 illustrates the stream concept.

When an input stream is read, a copy of the value at the current position in the stream is transferred to a variable; the read operation also advances the current position

Figure 10.1
A Stream

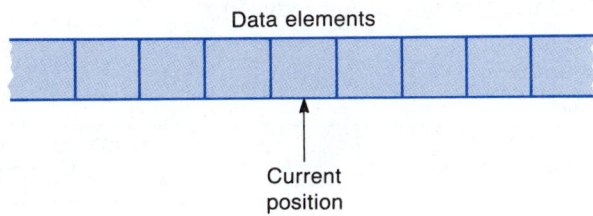

to the next element in the stream. When an output stream is written, a value is copied to the end of the stream.

In Modula-2, even though the input and output operations are not part of the language, they are part of the library modules, such as InOut. The module InOut assumes the existence of two predefined text streams corresponding to a *standard input device* (usually the keyboard) and a *standard output device* (usually the screen). These two streams are actually abstractions of the standard input and output devices, and the library module InOut provides operations on these streams. The operations should perform the same actions, regardless of how they are implemented.

10.2 Legible Input and Output

When we talk about input and output, we must generally make a distinction between legible and illegible input and output. *Legible input and output* is used for communication between the computer and the user, while *illegible input and output* is used between devices and is not intended to be read by humans. Most legible input and output is based on characters—that is, data of type CHAR. However, graphical input and output is also understandable by humans, and its elements are not of type CHAR. For this discussion, we will assume that text streams are used for legible input and output. Legible input is given through keyboards, optical character recognition devices, and so on. Similarly, legible output is displayed on screens, printed on paper, or stored in a file for later access.

All legible data are read or written as a sequence of characters, even though the internal representation in computer memory may not be a sequence of characters. For example, numeric data are not stored as a sequence of characters, as we will see in Chapter 14. Thus input and output operations involve not only the physical transfer of information between input or output devices and main memory but also any transformation of the data to or from their proper representation in memory. This transformation between characters and the internal representation is part of the input and output operations but is hidden from the user. The entire process is depicted in Figure 10.2.

Modula-2 and Ada, another Pascal-based block-structured language, are both strongly typed, particularly in regard to I/O operations. Each operation performs I/O on a single item of a specified type. This is unlike Pascal, where I/O can be performed on an unspecified number of items of a variety of types by a single operation. Although lack of this flexibility in Pascal's descendants may seem inconvenient at first, this strong typing is consistent with the evolution of modern block-structured languages.

All implementations of Modula-2 are expected to have a standard library module named InOut, which includes procedures to perform input and output operations for the common data types. In the following sections we will discuss the objects that can be imported from InOut (see Appendix E).

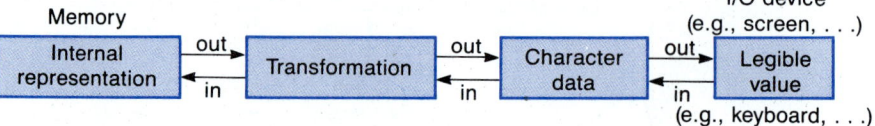

Figure 10.2 Legible Input and Output Operations

Character Data

The standard module InOut provides four procedures to manipulate characters and character strings (arrays of characters).

```
PROCEDURE Read( VAR ch: CHAR );
```

This procedure reads from the input stream a single character, which becomes the value of the parameter ch.

```
PROCEDURE Write( ch: CHAR );
```

This procedure writes a single character supplied as a parameter to the output stream.

```
PROCEDURE ReadString( VAR s: ARRAY OF CHAR );
```

This procedure reads a sequence of characters from the input stream; leading blanks are ignored, and the read operation terminates when a character whose code is less than or equal to 32 (space) is read. Therefore a string read with ReadString cannot contain any embedded blanks. The string becomes the value of the parameter s.

Module InOut also defines global variable termCH of type CHAR, which will contain the character that terminated the string. This variable can be accessed once it has been imported. During input from a terminal, backspacing is allowed to correct errors.

```
PROCEDURE WriteString( s: ARRAY OF CHAR );
```

This procedure writes a sequence of characters to the output stream. The characters written are taken from parameter s, and can include blanks.

Input operations can recognize the end of the input stream; the end is indicated by the variable Done, exported from module InOut. Done is a Boolean variable whose value is set to TRUE after a *successful* input operation, and to FALSE after an *unsuccessful* operation. For example, if we call a Read procedure when the end of the input stream has been reached, Done will be set to FALSE. Typically, the input stream can be read sequentially using a loop that is exited after the first unsuccessful Read statement, as shown in the following example:

```
LOOP
  Read( ch );
  IF NOT Done THEN
    EXIT
  END;
  (*** process the character ***)
         .
         .
         .
END; (* LOOP *)
```

Actually legible input and output are not completely sequential since they are broken into lines. Module InOut exports the constant EOL, which represents the end-of-line character; a line end will be denoted by this single character, which is implementation dependent. Therefore, a line can be read by a loop using the Read procedure and testing for a character equal to EOL.

The parameterless procedure WriteLn terminates the current line on the output stream and starts a new output line. To do that, it simply appends the character EOL to the output stream (thus Write(EOL) is equivalent to WriteLn).

Numeric Data

The standard module InOut provides six procedures for the input and output of numeric data.

```
PROCEDURE ReadCard( VAR c: CARDINAL );
```

This procedure reads characters from the input stream and converts them to a cardinal value, which becomes the value of the parameter c. Leading blanks are ignored; the sequence of characters is an unsigned sequence of digit characters ('0' to '9'). A nondigit character terminates the input operation. The value read is assigned to the parameter c. During terminal input, backspacing is allowed to correct errors.

```
PROCEDURE WriteCard( c, w: CARDINAL );
```

This procedure converts the cardinal value in parameter c into a string of w characters. The string will be padded with leading blanks if necessary (that is, blanks will be added in front of the value so that it fills w characters) and written to the output stream. If the value needs more than w characters, depending on the implementation, the field might be widened to accommodate the value, or an indication given that the value cannot be printed (such as printing asterisks).

```
PROCEDURE ReadInt( VAR i: INTEGER );
```

This procedure reads characters from the input stream and converts them to an integer value. Leading blanks are ignored; the sequence of characters is a sequence of digits, possibly preceded by a + or a − sign. A nondigit character terminates the input. The value read is assigned to the parameter i. During terminal input, backspacing is allowed to correct errors.

```
PROCEDURE WriteInt( i: INTEGER; w: CARDINAL );
```

This procedure converts the integer value in parameter i into a string of w characters, which is then written to the output stream. The string will be padded with leading blanks if necessary. If the value needs more than w characters, depending on the implementation, the field might be widened to accommodate the value, or an indication given that the value cannot be printed.

SEC. 10.2 Legible Input and Output

```
PROCEDURE WriteOct( c, w: CARDINAL );
```

This procedure is similar to procedure WriteCard, but the number printed will be expressed in octal (base 8) notation rather than in decimal notation.

```
PROCEDURE WriteHex( c, w: CARDINAL );
```

This procedure is similar to procedure WriteCard, but the number printed will be expressed in hexadecimal (base 16) notation rather than in decimal notation.

As with character input, the result of input operations can be tested by examining the exported variable Done, as shown in the previous section.

Numeric data of type REAL can be read and written using three standard procedures for real numbers. These procedures should be found in standard module RealInOut (see Appendix E), but in some implementations they may be found in the InOut module. Again the procedures are quite implementation dependent, so you should look carefully at the documentation provided for your system.

```
PROCEDURE ReadReal( VAR r: REAL );
```

This procedure for real numbers reads characters from the input stream and converts them to a real value, which becomes the value of the parameter. Leading blanks are ignored. The number read can be given in two different forms. The first form, called decimal notation, is a sequence of digits possibly followed by a period and another sequence of digits (for instance, 12.34). The second form, called scientific notation, is the first form followed by the letter E, an optional sign, and digits (for example, 0.1234E−12). The letter E indicates an exponent—that is, a power of 10 by which the first part must be multiplied to obtain the actual value.

$$0.1234E-12 = 12.34 \times 10^{-14}$$

Either form may be preceded by a + or − sign. During terminal input, backspacing is allowed to correct errors.

As in module InOut, the variable Done indicates whether the input operation was successful (Done = TRUE) or unsuccessful (Done = FALSE). The module RealInOut exports its own Done variable. If you are using both modules InOut and RealInOut, the compiler will give an error if you attempt to import both Done variables. In such cases the solution is to import the entire module RealInOut (by using IMPORT RealInOut;) and then use the qualified name RealInOut.Done. This approach will be discussed in more detail in Chapter 11.

```
PROCEDURE WriteReal( r: REAL; w: CARDINAL );
```

This procedure for real numbers will convert the real value of parameter r into a string of w characters representing that value. If necessary, leading blanks will be inserted, or, depending on the implementation, the field width might be widened. Generally, the real value will be printed using scientific notation, but some implementations provide additional procedures (like FWriteReal used earlier) to print real values in decimal notation, or add a third parameter to WriteReal to indicate the number of digits to print in the fractional part.

PROCEDURE WriteRealOct(r: REAL; w: CARDINAL);

This procedure for real numbers is similar to the procedure WriteReal but will write the internal representation for r in octal form. The internal representation of real values will be discussed in Chapter 14.

Review of Input and Output Redirection

As discussed in Chapter 2, the library module InOut includes four procedures that make it possible to redefine the input and output streams. By default, the procedures seen thus far use the standard input and output streams, normally corresponding to the user's terminal. Very often, though, we want to redefine the input and output streams, usually to access a file on secondary storage as discussed in the next section. The following procedures give us that capability.

PROCEDURE OpenInput(defext: ARRAY OF CHAR);

This procedure closes (makes unavailable) the standard input stream, requests a file name via the standard input device, and opens (makes available) the stream whose name is given. The form of the name is implementation dependent, and is usually in the form required by the operating system for file names. The parameter defext is used to complete the name given with a default extension (implementation dependent). For instance, with the call: OpenInput("dat"), if the user answers the prompt with a name ending with a period, as in "Grades.", the system will add "dat" to the name to obtain the complete file name "Grades.dat". If the name given does not end with a period, defext is not used. If the procedure is successful, subsequent input will be read from this new input stream; otherwise, input is read from the previous input stream.

PROCEDURE CloseInput;

This parameterless procedure closes the current input stream and subsequent input is taken from the standard input stream.

PROCEDURE OpenOutput(defext: ARRAY OF CHAR);

This procedure is similar to the OpenInput procedure. It closes the standard output stream and opens the stream whose name is supplied by the user. If the procedure is successful, subsequent output will be sent to the new output stream.

PROCEDURE CloseOutput;

This parameterless procedure closes the current output stream and subsequent output is sent to the default output stream.

The success or failure of OpenInput and OpenOutput is indicated by the variable Done. A TRUE value for Done indicates success of the operation, and FALSE indicates failure. Opened streams, other than the standard, *must* be closed before the program terminates. In most implementations we may be able to switch between files without reverting to the standard stream, by simply using two calls to OpenInput (or to OpenOutput) without a call to CloseInput (or to CloseOutput). However, this shortcut may also cause serious problems, since files should be properly closed (by CloseInput or CloseOutput) in order not to lose any information.

10.3 Multiple Input/Output Streams

In the previous section we saw how input/output redirection allows data to be read from an input file or written to an output file. There is still only one input stream and one output stream, but they have been redirected to files. In this section we will learn how to perform terminal I/O while still maintaining redirection of the default I/O streams.

Interaction with the User and Input/Output Redirection

We will assume in this discussion that the default input/output devices are a keyboard and a terminal screen. It is often convenient, during the running of a program, to allow the user to specify interactively desired actions to be taken. This is frequently done in the form of a menu-driven program: the available options are displayed on the terminal screen, and the user inputs a choice on the keyboard. Often, too, the data to be processed are contained in a data file. In this case we require two input streams and possibly two output streams, as shown in Figure 10.3.

As a first attempt at solving this problem, we might try using input/output redirection: whenever interaction is desired with the user, the program returns to the default devices, and whenever file interaction is needed, the program uses redirection to the specified file. However, this approach won't work as desired, because every time we redirect to the files, we begin at the start of the file. Also, this method would require the user to respecify the desired files each time there is redirection. Fortunately, most Modula-2 implementations provide a library module called Terminal that will help us resolve this dilemma.

Figure 10.3
Multiple Input and Output Streams

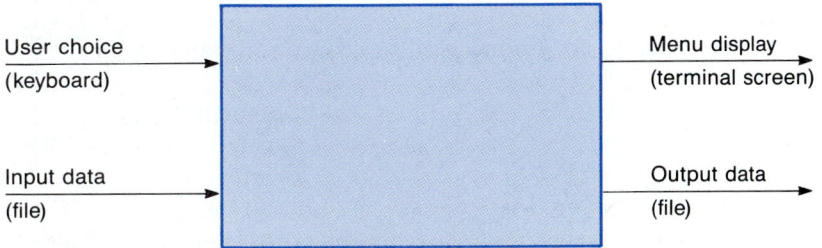

The Library Module Terminal

The operations provided by this module may vary between Modula-2 implementations; for our discussion we will assume the following definition module.

```
DEFINITION MODULE Terminal;

PROCEDURE Read( VAR ch: CHAR );
(* returns the character typed on the keyboard *)

PROCEDURE BusyRead( VAR ch: CHAR );
(* returns 0C if no character was typed *)

PROCEDURE ReadAgain;
(* causes the last character typed to be returned again on the next
   call to Read *)

PROCEDURE Write( ch: CHAR );
(* writes the specified character to the terminal output device *)

PROCEDURE WriteLn;
(* terminates the current line on the terminal output device *)

PROCEDURE WriteString( s: ARRAY OF CHAR );
(* writes the specified string to the terminal output device *)

END Terminal.
```

We have seen all these procedures before, except for BusyRead and ReadAgain. These two procedures are useful when writing programs that periodically check if any user input has occurred.

All input and output are done with the terminal input device and the terminal output device; there is no redirection. This helps us solve our previous dilemma since redirection can be used for file input and output for data while interaction with the user can be done through the procedures in Terminal. We must be careful since many objects exported from Terminal have the same names as objects in InOut. Whenever names are duplicated, it is the programmer's responsibility to tell the compiler which procedure is desired. One approach is to import entire modules, as with

```
IMPORT InOut;
IMPORT Terminal;
```

Objects are distinguished by using qualification, as in

```
InOut.Read( Ch )
```

or

```
Terminal.Read( Ch )
```

Another option is to qualify objects from one module at the time of import and then import the entire other module, as with

```
FROM InOut IMPORT Read, . . . ;
IMPORT Terminal;
```

In this case, Read (without qualification) is assumed to be from InOut.

```
Read( Ch );            (* the Read from InOut *)
```

If the Read from Terminal is desired, it must be qualified.

```
Terminal.Read( Ch )
```

A Programming Example

Suppose you are asked to write a program that will copy one or more files to a specified output file. Since the number of files and their names are not known ahead of time, the program should prompt the user each time a new input file is to be specified. A sample interaction follows; the underlining shows the user input.

```
File Concatenation Program
At the prompt, enter the output file name.
out> file3
At the prompt, enter the input file name.
in> file1
The input file copy is complete.
Do you want to copy another file? (Y/N) Y
At the prompt, enter the input file name.
in> file2
The input file copy is complete.
Do you want to copy another file? (Y/N) N
```

Once this interaction has taken place, file3 will contain the contents of file1 followed by the contents of file2. Since input from the user is not required during the time the input file is open, we can use redirection to switch back and forth between keyboard input and file input. However, since the output file must remain open while the user is prompted for the next input file, output cannot be switched back and forth between screen output and file output. As a result we must use the Terminal module to write data on the screen. This situation is pictured in Figure 10.4, which shows the data flow from the various input devices to the various output devices.

Figure 10.4
Data Flow for File Concatenation Program

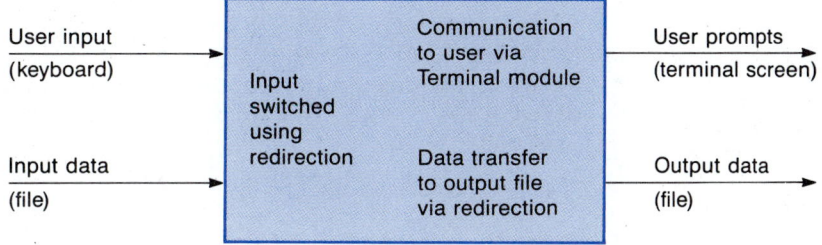

Now that we understand what is expected, we can start our pseudocode development. Our main program will query the user for the output file name and then repeatedly concatenate input files until the user indicates the job is completed. The pseudocode is

> File Concatenation
>   Print message for output file name
>   Open output file using redirection
>   Repeat
>   Copy File
>   Print message on terminal that the copy is complete
>   Print message on terminal asking if there is another file to copy
>   Read response
>   Until response is not yes
>   Close output file
> End File Concatenation

The Copy File program prompts the user for the input file name and performs the copy. We assume the output file is already open.

> Copy File
>   Print prompt on terminal for input file name
>   Open input file using redirection
>   Loop
>   Read a character from the input file
>   Exit if at the end of file
>   Write the character to the output file
>   End loop
>   Close input file
> End Copy File

The prompt for file input name in Copy File and the two messages displayed inside the Repeat loop of the main program should appear on the terminal screen. Since output has been redirected to the output data file, operations from the module Terminal will be used to accomplish this output to the screen. The program follows directly from our pseudocode.

```
MODULE FileConcat;
(* The program copies one or more input files to a single
   output file.  The user provides the names of all files
   involved.
                          B. Kurtz     January 1988    *)
```

```
FROM InOut IMPORT Read, Write, WriteString, WriteLn, Done,
                  OpenInput, CloseInput, OpenOutput,
                  CloseOutput;
IMPORT Terminal;

PROCEDURE CopyFile;
(* Copies contents of specified input file to an output file already
   opened by redirection *)
VAR Ch: CHAR;
BEGIN
  Terminal.WriteString("At the prompt, enter the input file name.");
  Terminal.WriteLn;
  OpenInput("");
  LOOP
    Read(Ch);
    IF NOT Done THEN EXIT END;
    Write(Ch);
  END;   (* LOOP *)
  CloseInput;
END CopyFile;

VAR Response: CHAR;

BEGIN   (* FileConcat *)
  WriteString("File Concatenation Program"); WriteLn;
  WriteString("At the prompt, enter the output file name.");
  WriteLn;
  OpenOutput("");
  REPEAT
    CopyFile;
    Terminal.WriteString("The input file copy is complete.");
    Terminal.WriteLn;
    Terminal.WriteString("Do you want to copy another file? (Y/N) ");
    Read(Response); Terminal.Write(Response);
    Terminal.WriteLn;
  UNTIL (Response # 'y') AND (Response # 'Y');
  CloseOutput;
END FileConcat.
```

As mentioned in the previous section, when a module is imported as a whole, objects in that module must be qualified by the module name. In FileConcat, Terminal is imported whole, so we must use qualification such as Terminal.WriteLn. On the other hand, the objects imported from InOut are specified in the import list. This specification automatically qualifies these objects, so their names can be used directly.

In many instances multiple input or output files must be accessed at the same time. Redirection cannot handle these situations. We will study the FileSystem module in the next section and illustrate its use in the case study in Section 10.6.

10.4 Files

We have already mentioned that some input and output are illegible to a human user. Among such forms are input and output made from and to peripheral devices where information is not written or read by humans. Those devices include secondary storage devices like magnetic tapes and disks, as well as devices controlled in real time by computers (factory machines and sensors, or networks). In these cases illegible data can be of any type—streams of integers, streams of real numbers, and so on. They are all called binary streams, because the values are represented in the raw binary form that they have in computer memory.

The most common usage of binary streams is for storing and retrieving data from secondary storage files: collections of data stored on disks or tapes. Such storage is necessary because the computer's main memory is sometimes not large enough to contain all the data for a problem. In addition, main memory is *volatile:* when the computer is shut off, the data stored in main memory disappear. Secondary storage is nonvolatile and can be used to store data for as long as necessary. Programs can write data to a file and can also read data from a file. The data in files are unchanged as long as a program does not modify them. Once a file has been created by a program, other programs can access data in the file. Files are usually sequential, but they are not necessarily so. However, here we will limit our discussion to sequential files.

The four redirection procedures in Section 10.2 can be used to redirect streams from the standard input and output devices to files. We can also do input and output directly on files without redirection. This method is very useful for storing and retrieving intermediate results, which are not intended for the user but are too large for the main memory. To do file input and output, all implementations of Modula-2 should provide a module giving low-level access to the file system of the operating system. Such a module is obviously implementation dependent and cannot be described in detail here. It will often be named FileSystem, and the standard module InOut will import it, because it is used to implement the redirection procedures. Consult the documentation of your particular implementation to find out what file module is available to you.

In such a module we can expect to find definitions for the following:

- a type FILE on which file procedures will operate
- a procedure to create a new file, given a Modula-2 file variable name and a character string defining the operating system file name
- a procedure to open a file
- a procedure to close a file
- a procedure to delete a file
- a procedure to rename a file
- low-level read and write procedures to transfer basic units of information to and from the files (bytes, words)
- possibly procedures to change the current position of the file, if the operating system supports a file organization other than sequential

As an example of using such a module, we will develop a simple program to copy an existing text file, character by character, into a new file. The algorithm is

> Copy File
>   Open the two files
>   Loop
>   Read a character from source file
>   Exit if end of source file
>   Write character to the destination file
>   End Loop
>   Close both files
> End Copy File

To code this algorithm we will assume the existence of a simplified module FileSystem whose definition module is the following.

```
DEFINITION MODULE FileSystem;

TYPE Response = (done, notdone, notsupported, callerror,
                 unknownmedium, unknownfile, paramerror,
                 toomanyfiles, eom, deviceoff, softparityerror,
                 softprotected, softerror, hardparityerror,
                 hardprotected, timeout, harderror );
     File = RECORD
              id: CARDINAL;
              eof: BOOLEAN;
              res: Response
            END;

PROCEDURE Lookup(VAR F: File; Name: ARRAY OF CHAR;
                 New: BOOLEAN);
(* Open an existing file if New is false, otherwise create a
   new file.  The second parameter is a string comprising the
   operating system's name for the file *)

PROCEDURE ReadChar(VAR F: File; VAR Ch: CHAR);
(* Read a character from file F *)

PROCEDURE ReadWord(VAR F: File; VAR W: WORD);
(* Read a value, which will fit in one word of memory, from
   file F *)

PROCEDURE WriteChar(VAR F: File; Ch: CHAR);
(* Write a character to a file F *)
```

```
PROCEDURE WriteWord(VAR F: File; W: WORD);
(* Write a value, which will fit in one word of memory, to a
   file F *)

PROCEDURE Close(VAR F: File);
(* Close an open file *)

PROCEDURE Reset(VAR F: File);
(* Reset file position pointer to beginning of file *)

PROCEDURE Rename(VAR F:File; Name: ARRAY OF CHAR);
(* Change the name of an open file *)

END FileSystem.
```

Our FileSystem module is in the spirit of an abstract data type: we have defined a type, File, and several operations that can be performed on this type. Users of the module can import this type, declare variables of this type, pass parameters of this type, and perform the operations provided. This module could contain more operations, depending on the operating system used. For instance, it could have an operation to create temporary files, an operation to obtain the length of a file, an operation to delete a file, and so on.

We can now implement our copy file program directly from our pseudocode solution.

```
MODULE CopyFile;
(* Copy a file into a new one.
         P. Gabrini January 1988   *)

FROM FileSystem IMPORT File, Lookup, ReadChar, WriteChar, Close;

VAR F1, F2: File;
    Ch: CHAR;

BEGIN
  Lookup( F1, "TEST.DATA", FALSE );   (* Open existing source file *)
  Lookup( F2, "TEST.NEW", TRUE );     (* Open new destination file *)
  LOOP
    ReadChar( F1, Ch );
    IF F1.eof THEN
      EXIT;
    END; (* IF *)
    WriteChar( F2, Ch );
  END; (* LOOP *)
  Close( F1 ); Close( F2 );
END CopyFile.
```

We have assumed that the file name TEST.NEW is not the name of an existing file. In an actual program, this possibility would be tested after the second Lookup by using implementation-dependent features. We will study a much more elaborate use of the FileSystem module in the case study in Section 10.6.

As we have already mentioned, all input and output are not necessarily sequential. Depending on the implementation, the file system might support direct access files, which allows you to access directly any element of a file, without having to read all the elements of the file that precede it. This method is more efficient because only elements needed are accessed, and the whole file does not have to be read to process a small number of its elements. Direct access files are an implementation-dependent feature, so check your system to see if it supports them.

10.5 Graphical Screen-Oriented Output

Thus far we've assumed that our input and output are always sequences of textual data. Writing text to a screen is essentially sequential, but many screens have graphic capabilities that are not sequential. Screens may also be used to display simultaneously several pictures, each positioned at a different place on the screen. Since graphical applications are varied, we will find it even more difficult than we did with files to define operations that will be general enough to be accepted as standard operations for most applications. Consequently, standards for graphical screen-oriented output modules are emerging, but you can expect to find various forms in different implementations. In several examples, we have done graphical applications based on a specific TurtleGraphics module. Such modules are in common use for teaching but are much simpler than the developing standards.

To use graphics modules, your computer system must have a graphics board, enabling it to send the right signals to your video display terminal. Those of you who do not have such a board have not been able to use the graphical capabilities of your screen, but have had to simulate pictures by character graphics (printing asterisks or other symbols).

A basic subset for general graphics applications should include capabilities to draw lines on the screen; with this capability, you can draw all kinds of figures using lines of different lengths and orientations. If this line-drawing capability is combined with the display of text, the graphics capability will cover many simple applications. Our module TurtleGraphics does just that. Its definition module is given in Appendix F.

We use the screen as a rectangular area whose width and height can be imported. The screen is taken as being a matrix of dots, called *pixels,* for picture elements. Each pixel can be accessed and painted black or white (if we were using color monitors, we could define our module so that we could use any available color).

The TurtleGraphics module has all the basic tools for drawing lines and rectilinear figures. It can also be used to draw more complex figures such as the "spiral galaxy" shown in Figure 4.2. Similarly, we can draw a circle by using the procedures in TurtleGraphics. Since we can draw only lines, we will draw the circle by repeatedly drawing a short line segment and rotating the turtle. This technique actually draws a polygon, but if the number of sides is large enough, the figure will appear to be a circle. The following procedure draws a circle in that way.

```
PROCEDURE DrawCircle;
VAR I: CARDINAL;
BEGIN
  FOR I := 1 TO 36 DO
    Move( 10 );
    Turn( 10 );
  END; (* FOR *)
END DrawCircle;
```

This procedure draws a polygon with 36 sides as an approximation of a circle. Better approximations will result if we draw a polygon with more sides. We can also write more sophisticated algorithms that will take into account the size of the circle in order to decide on the number of sides to be drawn.

In some systems it is possible to store pictures in data files, but this is highly system dependent. In the following case study we solve a problem involving file input and output.

10.6 Case Study: Merging Sorted Files

Files are used in many applications so the study of file operations is an important aspect of computer science. To illustrate the use of files, we will consider the very common operation of merging two sorted files. The items in the files may be of any type that could be ordered; we will take integers for our example.

Design

Since this is a relatively simple problem, the first two steps in our development are easy.

Define the Problem We want a procedure to accept two sorted input files of integers (both in ascending order) and produce an ordered output file composed of all the elements of the first two files.

Design a Solution We will do no validation of the data, so the structure will be quite simple: the merge algorithm and a test that uses the algorithm.

Refine the Solution The real development begins at this step, where we need to develop pseudocode for the merge algorithm. We can base the pseudocode on how we might do this operation manually on two sample files of integers, such as those shown in Figure 10.5.

Figure 10.5
Two Sample Files

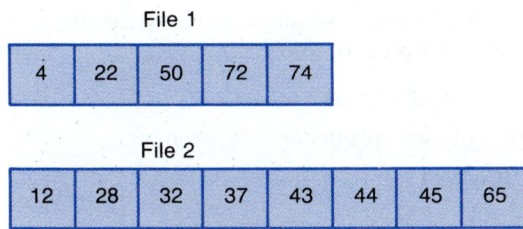

We consider the first numbers of each file (4 and 12) and write the smaller one (4) to the output file. Then we consider the next number from File 1 and the old number of File 2 (22 and 12) and write the smaller (12) to the output file. This sequence gives us a basic pattern of reading, comparing, and writing, which will form the heart of our algorithm. Figure 10.6 illustrates the situation after six steps.

The only remaining problem seems to be how to stop the process. When one of the input files is exhausted (File 2 in our example), we can simply write the remaining elements of the other input file to the output file and halt. However, we must be able to recognize the end of an input file so that this action can be taken. This task is a bit more of a problem than you might think, because different programming languages accomplish it in different ways. The two common ways are

1. You must read an element from the file before you can check for the end of the file. If you are at the end, the element that was read is not meaningful; you can regard it as representing the end of file.
2. You must test for the end of the file before reading an element from the file. Attempting to read before testing will cause an error if the file is empty.

We should always try to avoid such language-dependent issues when designing our algorithms, but we may not always be able to do so. This is one of those cases, because the merge algorithm for reading before testing for end of file is somewhat different from the merge algorithm for testing before reading. As we mentioned in the previous section, our implementation of Modula-2 does reading before testing, so we develop

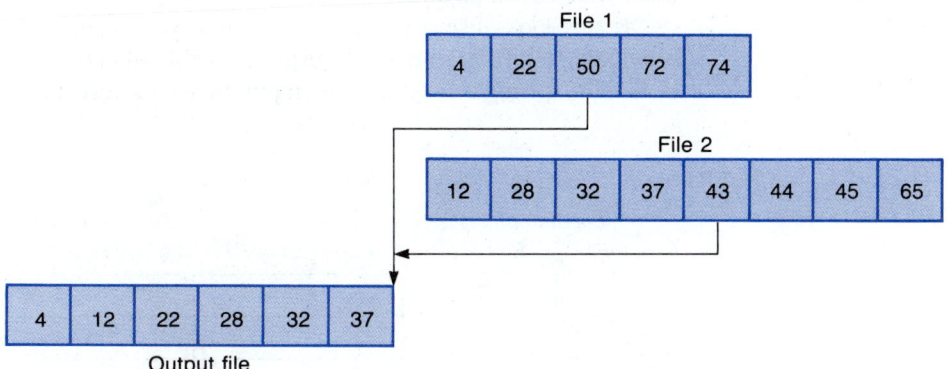

Figure 10.6 Merging Two Sorted Files

our pseudocode accordingly. With this in mind we use the process described informally earlier to write our first pseudocode solution. The names that we use are as follows:

F1, F2: names of input files

I1, I2: names of elements under consideration

F3: name of output file

```
Merge( F1, F2, F3 )
    Read I1 from F1
    Read I2 from F2
    Loop
        If I1 < I2 then
            Write I1 to F3
            Read new I1 from F1   { read before testing }
            If F1 empty then
                Copy rest of F2 to F3
                Exit
            End if
        Else
            Write I2 to F3
            Read new I2 from F2   { read before testing }
            If F2 empty then
                Copy rest of F1 to F3
                Exit
            End if
        End if
    End loop
End Merge
```

We have put some comments in braces, to indicate where the reading-before-testing issue affected our algorithm.

If this looks like a reasonable solution, you should think about our next step: developing a testing strategy. In that step we should consider the possibility that one or both of the input files may be empty. In such a case we would write meaningless

TABLE 10.1 **Decision Table for Merge**

Conditions			Actions		
End of F1	*End of F2*	*Copy rest of F1*	*Copy rest of F2*	*Continue*	*None*
T	T				X
T	F		X		
F	T	X			
F	F			X	

Figure 10.7
Decision Tree for Merge

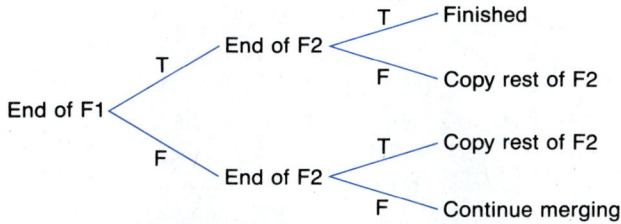

values to the output file! Thus we need to check for empty input files at the beginning of our algorithm and take the appropriate action. At this point we could easily become confused, so we will take time to formalize the desired actions and the conditions that give rise to those actions. We have some convenient tools for this at our disposal: decision tables or decision trees. For practice, we will do both.

The conditions controlling the actions are "end of F1" and "end of F2." The actions are "Copy rest of F1 to F3," "Copy rest of F2 to F3," and "Continue merging both files." We relate the conditions to the actions in the decision table in Table 10.1 and in the decision tree in Figure 10.7. Since both the table and the tree give the same information, use the method that is clearer to you.

As shown by the top branch in the decision tree and the first line in the decision table, no further action is required when we are at the end of both files. Thus we concentrate on the cases where we are not at the end of F1 or not the end of F2 to develop the next version of our algorithm. Using NOT F1.eof and NOT F2.eof as abbreviations for these conditions, we write the following pseudocode. We have used comments in braces to show the conditions that hold at certain key points in the algorithm; that way you can check the algorithm with the decision table or decision tree. As observed in Chapter 4, comments like this are called assertions, and they are very useful in verifying the correctness of algorithms.

```
Merge( F1, F2, F3 )
   Read I1 from F1
   Read I2 from F2
   If NOT F1.eof then
      If NOT F2.eof then    { NOT F1.eof AND NOT F2.eof }
         Merge Both
      Else   { NOT F1.eof AND F2.eof }
         Write I1 to F3
         Copy rest of F1 to F3
      End if
   Else   { F1.eof }
      If NOT F2.eof then    { F1.eof AND NOT F2.eof }
         Write I2 to F3
         Copy rest of F2 to F3
      End if
   End if
End Merge
```

```
Merge Both
   Loop
   { NOT F1.eof AND NOT F2.eof }
      If I1 < I2 then
         Write I1 to F3
         Read I1 from F1
         If F1.eof then    { F1.eof AND NOT F2.eof }
            Write I2 to F3
            Copy rest of F2 to F3
            Exit Loop
         End if
      Else
         Write I2 to F3
         Read new I2 from F2
         If F2.eof then    { NOT F1.eof AND F2.eof }
            Write I1 to F3
            Copy rest of F1 to F3
            Exit Loop
         End if
      End if
   { NOT F1.eof AND NOT F2.eof }
   End loop
End Merge Both
```

Take particular notice of the assertion {NOT F1.eof AND NOT F2.eof} shown at the beginning and end of the loop. We have put it in both places to emphasize the fact that this condition is true at the start of the loop and also at the end of the loop, when we are about to start another iteration (that is, no exit was done). This is another example of asserting a loop invariant.

We have not given any pseudocode for the statements that copy the remaining elements of an input file to the output file, since they are just variations of the copy file procedure given in Section 10.4.

The pseudocode shown here will form the basis for implementing the algorithm, but we should make sure to develop our testing strategy first, in case we have overlooked any other subtle cases.

Develop a Testing Strategy   If we assume that the input files are valid ordered sequences of numbers, the possible cases are

1. F1 and F2 empty
2. F1 empty, F2 nonempty
3. F1 nonempty, F2 empty
4. F1 and F2 nonempty, with

    (a) all numbers of F1 less than all numbers of F2, or
    (b) all numbers of F2 less than all numbers of F1, or
    (c) no particular relation between numbers of F1 and F2

The output in these cases should be

1. F3 empty
2. F3 identical to F2
3. F3 identical to F1
4. F3 contains all the numbers from F1 and F2 in ascending order

Our earlier example, shown in Figure 10.5, can be used for the typical case, 4(c), as follows:

Input Files

F1:   4, 22, 50 72, 74

F2:   12, 28, 32, 37, 43, 44, 45, 65

Output File

F3:   4, 12, 22, 28, 32, 37, 43, 44, 45, 50, 65, 72, 74

Specification of test data for the other cases is left to the reader.

Since we have not overlooked any subtle cases, we can proceed to implementation.

Implementation

Code and Test the Program   When considering our final pseudocode solution, we should observe that the operation of copying the rest of the elements of an input file to the output file occurs in four places. This makes the operation a good candidate for a procedure. The following Modula-2 solution takes advantage of this observation and uses the module FileSystem defined earlier.

```
MODULE MergeTest;
(* Test of the Merge procedure.  TestF1.dat and TestF2.dat
   must be input files that have been previously created.
   TestF3.dat is the output file and is created by the test;
   it should be removed after running the test.
                       J. Mack Adams    January 1988   *)

FROM FileSystem IMPORT File, Response, Lookup, Close,
                      Reset, ReadWord, WriteWord;
FROM InOut IMPORT WriteString, WriteInt, WriteLn;

  PROCEDURE Merge(VAR F1, F2, F3: File);
  (* Merges F1 and F2 into F3.  F1 and F2 should be
     files of integers (binary files) in ascending order. *)

    PROCEDURE CopyRest(VAR F, G: File);
    (* Writes the remaining elements of F to G. *)
    VAR J: INTEGER;
```

```
          BEGIN
            WriteLn;
            LOOP
              ReadWord(F, J);
              IF F.eof THEN
                EXIT
              END;  (* IF *)
              WriteWord(G, J);
            END,  (* LOOP *)
          END CopyRest;

       VAR I1, I2: INTEGER;

       BEGIN (* Merge *)
         ReadWord(F1, I1);
         ReadWord(F2, I2);
         IF NOT F1.eof THEN
           IF NOT F2.eof THEN
             LOOP
                (* NOT F1.eof AND NOT F2.eof *)
                IF I1 < I2 THEN
                  WriteWord(F3, I1);
                  ReadWord(F1, I1);
                  IF F1.eof THEN  (* F1.eof AND NOT F2.eof *)
                    WriteWord(F3, I2);
                    CopyRest(F2, F3);
                    EXIT
                  END;  (* IF *)
                ELSE
                  WriteWord(F3, I2);
                  ReadWord(F2, I2);
                  IF F2.eof THEN  (* NOT F1.eof AND F2.eof *)
                    WriteWord(F3, I1);
                    CopyRest(F1, F3);
                    EXIT
                  END;  (* IF *)
                END;  (* IF *)
                (* NOT F1.eof AND NOT F2.eof *)
             END;  (* LOOP *)
           ELSE  (* NOT F1.eof AND F2.eof *)
             WriteWord(F3, I1);
             CopyRest(F1, F3);
           END;  (* IF *)
         ELSE  (* F1.eof *)
           IF NOT F2.eof THEN  (* F1.eof AND NOT F2.eof *)
             WriteWord(F3, I2);
             CopyRest(F2, F3);
           END;  (* IF *)
         END ;  (* IF *)
       END Merge;
```

```
        VAR F, G, H: File;
            I: INTEGER;

        BEGIN (* MergeTest *)
          Lookup(F, "TestF1.dat", FALSE);
          Lookup(G, "TestF2.dat", FALSE);
          Lookup(H, "TestF3.dat", TRUE);

          Merge(F, G, H);

          Reset(H);
          LOOP
            ReadWord(H, I);
            IF H.eof THEN
              EXIT;
            END; (* IF *)
            WriteInt(I, 6);
          END; (* LOOP *)
          WriteLn;

          Close(F);
          Close(G);
          Close(H);
        END MergeTest.
```

Notice that ReadWord was used to read the elements of the input files and WriteWord was used to write the elements of the output file. This is the only way that we can do input and output for binary files, but because an integer value occupies one word of memory in most computers, we can use these procedures for our integer values.

The program was tested on four test cases corresponding to our testing strategy and gave correct results. The program could be improved by validating the input files (see Programming Problem 7 at the end of the chapter).

Complete the Documentation A variation of this program might be used as a general utility program in a library module, and for this purpose, the program itself would be sufficient documentation.

SUMMARY

Most input and output operations are sequential. That is, if two sequential items are to be read as input, the second item cannot be read until the first has been read. Thus, we commonly picture sequential input and output as a stream. When CHAR is the base type, the structure is known as a text stream. A sequence of binary values that represents data flowing between devices is a binary stream. Legible input and output refer to communication between the computer and the user; illegible input and output are communications that take place between devices and are not intended to be understood by humans.

Modula-2 does not have input and output statements in the language but provides input and output modules that contain I/O procedures. For instance, all Modula-2 implementations should have standard library modules named InOut and RealInOut, which include procedures to perform input and output operations. The standard module InOut has four procedures for character and character string I/O, and six procedures for numeric I/O. The standard module RealInOut has three procedures for real number I/O.

The standard input and output streams in Modula-2 correspond to the keyboard and the terminal. If the user wants to redefine these streams—perhaps to access a file on secondary storage—the library module InOut offers four procedures to accomplish redirection.

Binary streams are commonly used for storing and retrieving data to and from secondary storage files. Such files are necessary because the main memory capacity may be exceeded and because the secondary storage is nonvolatile. All Modula-2 implementations should provide a module, perhaps called FileSystem, for input and output to and from files.

Although most text writing is sequential, computer screens also have nonsequential or graphical capabilities. For graphics applications the user must access a graphics module, such as the TurtleGraphics module.

At this time, you should have a general understanding of input and output operations, and be familiar enough with the operations and implementation-dependent features of your system to use them effectively.

EXERCISES

1. Modula-2 does not provide any standard procedures to read and write Boolean values. Develop two procedures, ReadBoolean and WriteBoolean, which read and write Boolean values. Make sure that procedure ReadBoolean can read a value written by WriteBoolean.

2. Develop a new output procedure, OpenToAppend, which will open a sequential file of characters and position the file pointer so that it will be possible to add information to the file by using WriteChar from our FileSystem module (or an equivalent procedure from your implementation).

3. Design a menu-driven program using the module FileSystem in Section 10.4 that provides the following options:

   - to indicate whether a file is present or not
   - to create an empty file
   - to delete a file
   - to copy from one file to another

   The copy option should warn the user if the specified destination file already exists and should write over this file only if told to do so. A file may be deleted by renaming it with the empty string and then closing it. Try to be efficient in your design, using simpler procedures whenever possible to define more complex procedures.

4. The file copy option in Exercise 3 can be time consuming. Modify your algorithm to print a message "Copying in progress" followed by a dot each time 20 characters are transferred.

PROGRAMMING PROBLEMS

5. Modify the file copying program given in Section 10.4, so that it compiles and executes correctly on your system.

6. Modify the merge program given in Section 10.6, so that it compiles and executes correctly on your particular system.

7. Enhance the merge program given in Section 10.6, so that it validates the input files by checking that they are in ascending order. Try to do this with only one pass through each file.

8. Alter the merge program given in Section 10.6, so that it will merge two alphabetically sorted files of English words into a third file. Assume that words are given one per line with no space characters. Capitalization should not affect the order.

9. Implement and test the program suggested in Exercises 3 and 4.

10. Write a program that will generate a list of all the words used in a text, as well as the number of times each word is used. The end of words will be indicated by spaces or punctuation marks; uppercase and lowercase letters will be considered to be the same letter. The text will be read from a file. The output list should be in alphabetical order and should be displayed on your terminal screen and written into a file.

11. Write a procedure to merge two sorted arrays of integers into a third array, assuming the length of the third array is at least as large as the sum of the lengths of the first two arrays.

12. Write a program that prints "personalized letters." The text of the letter is in an input file and includes symbols <name> and <address>. A second input file contains a list of names and addresses: name on the first line, followed by three lines of address (unused lines can be left blank). The program will read the letter text from the first file; it will then read a name and an address from the second file, insert name and address in the letter, and print the letter. This sequence will be repeated for all the names and addresses in the second file.

13. Write a program that takes as input a nonindented Modula-2 program stored in a file and produces a "pretty print" version of the program in a second file. To simplify the pretty print program, do not indent declarations. You will need a table of reserved words. Follow the pretty printing rules used in the program examples you have seen so far.

14. Write a program that:
    - reads a sequence of employee names and stores them in a query file
    - prints the records from a sorted employee record file (employee name and salary) for those employees whose name appears in the query file

15. Write and test a procedure to draw an approximation to a circle whose radius is specified by the user, and whose number of sides is adjusted to fit this radius value. In other words, small "circles" may need fewer sides, while large "circles" require more sides.

11 Modules

In this chapter you will:

- investigate external modules in more detail
- learn more about separate compilation of modules
- use modular design charts to show the interconnections between modules
- be introduced to local modules, which are contained within other modules

We will start this chapter with a discussion of the problems encountered by computer scientists in developing large programs that are reliable. The problems have been so difficult that many people refer to the difficulties as the software crisis. Computer scientists have been actively investigating principles and techniques to make the development of software easier and the resulting software more reliable. Some of these concepts, such as the information hiding principle, have proven effective and have led to the addition of programming language features to support them. The modules of Modula-2 are such a feature.

  Ever since you started writing Modula-2 programs, you have been using modules. A main program is itself a module, as indicated in its heading, and it usually uses objects from library modules. A main program can also use objects from external modules developed especially for the program. In Chapter 6, in the short introduction to modules, you read about the external module named Points, and you used objects from this module in the RecTriangle program in Chapter 8. In this chapter you will learn more about developing your own external modules. You will have a chance to follow the development of the Strings module as an example of an external module that implements an abstract data type. You will also see how modular design charts help you manage the complexity of the interconnections (interfaces) between modules in large programs. Finally, you will also learn how to use local modules within other modules to accomplish information hiding that would be difficult or impossible with nested procedures. The chapter concludes with a case study involving the design of an external module that could be part of a word processing package.

11.1 Programming Languages and the Software Crisis

The module feature of Modula-2 is a relatively new feature of programming languages, which was designed to address a problem so severe that it is sometimes referred to as the software crisis. This crisis has been created by the difficulties computer scientists have encountered in developing reliable programs for the solution of large problems. We will discuss the history and reasons for this difficulty in this section.

As we have previously observed, computers are digital devices that deal with sequences of bits, binary digits of 1 or 0. At the machine level, both instructions and data are in binary, although, for compactness, numbers are often written in the octal or hexadecimal number bases. Thus machine language programs are in binary, a form that is quite unsuitable for humans. The first stored-program computers were programmed in machine language, and consequently programming was extremely tedious.

The next stage of development, assembly languages, made programming less tiresome by allowing meaningful mnemonics for operation codes and symbolic names for memory locations. Even so, assembly language programs still have a simple correspondence with machine code; as a result, doing large software projects in assembly language is time consuming and error prone.

In high-level programming languages a single statement may correspond to tens or hundreds of machine level instructions. High-level languages allow the programmer to express a program in a manner closer to the problem domain and more remote from the physical machine that will execute the program. The development of high-level languages has permitted programmers to do software projects that are larger than those practical with assembly language. To appreciate the diversity of high-level programming languages, let's review several of the important languages here.

FORTRAN was the first successful high-level language. To this day, it remains one of the most efficient languages for scientific data processing that involves extensive "number crunching." ALGOL 60 was designed in the late 1950s, and its specification appeared in 1960. Although ALGOL 60 did not become a commercial success, many of its features were simple and elegant. Thus, ALGOL 60 has had a strong influence on the design of subsequent languages, including Pascal, Modula-2, and Ada. COBOL, which is still widely used today, was designed in the early 1960s to suit the needs of business data processing. It was the first widely adopted language to support the record data structure. In the late 1960s, designers, trying to combine the features of FORTRAN, ALGOL 60, and COBOL, produced PL/1. Due to its sheer size and complexity, however, PL/1 had only limited acceptance as a major programming language. Pascal was designed in the late 1960s and became available in the early 1970s. The language marked a return to the simplicity and elegance of ALGOL 60, but this time it came in a form that provided programming flexibility, particularly in the design of data structures. Designed as a teaching language, Pascal has been used extensively for this purpose in the late 1970s and 1980s.

Despite all these advances in programming language design, difficulties with large software projects of the late 1960s and early 1970s led to a software crisis. Small software systems were rarely designed; instead they were "hacked" to death. Program code was often poorly documented and very difficult to maintain. Features in early programming languages, such as the GOTO (an unrestricted jump to anywhere in the program), often led to "spaghetti" code with a flow of control that could not even be explained by the programmer. Large software systems often exceeded a hundred thousand lines of code, and, even when there was a concentrated effort to design the solution, the programming languages did not support the necessary features for careful design. Here is just one "horror story" among many to illustrate this software crisis.

FORTRAN uses a DO statement for looping, as shown here (with similar Modula-2 code next to it):

```
      DO 400 I = 1, 100                FOR I = 1 TO 100 DO
         loop body goes here              loop body goes here
  400 CONTINUE                         END; (* FOR *)
```

The designers of FORTRAN made two questionable decisions:

1. All blanks are stripped out before the compilation process begins.
2. If a variable is not declared, the following is assumed:

   - Variables starting with letters between I and N are of type integer.
   - Variables starting with any other letters are of type real.

In place of the DO statement shown earlier, suppose the programmer typed

```
      DO 400 I = 1. 100
```

After the spaces are removed, this line becomes

```
      DO400I=1.100
```

The "variable" DO400I defaults to type real and is assigned the value of 1.100 (the assignment operator in FORTRAN is =). This illustration may seem like a contrived example, but, in fact, an error of this very nature caused the loss of a Venus planetary probe!

By 1970 many research computer scientists were advocating sound software engineering principles, such as information hiding and abstract data types. Unfortunately, the languages of the early 1970s, even standard Pascal, did not support these principles of software engineering. However, two languages that emerged in the late 1970s—Modula-2 and Ada—were designed explicitly to support programming based on sound software engineering principles. Both languages are Pascal based, a tribute to a powerful yet elegantly simple language.

Modula-2 and Ada extend Pascal by providing a higher level of modularity that provides support for information hiding and the design of abstract data types. In Ada this level of modularity is done with a language feature called packages. In Modula-2 it is done with modules, which is also the topic of this chapter. Despite these similarities in design goals, Modula-2 and Ada are very different. Modula-2 is a modest extension of Pascal, intended to provide features necessary for systems programming. Ada used Pascal as a basis, but it has many more extensions, at least doubling or tripling the complexity of the language. After learning Modula-2, you can more easily learn the powerful and complex language Ada.

11.2 Development of External Modules

Learning Modula-2 is partly a matter of appreciating the usefulness of its modularity. As you've seen thus far, the main program is regarded as a module. To save time and effort, you can import objects from library modules. Apart from the main program, though, you can also develop your own modules that can be used by *your program*. These modules, which are really *external modules*, thereby also constitute further library modules that make their contents available to other users. External modules provide another level of abstraction and information hiding. You have actually been using external modules since you started writing Modula-2 programs—such as when you imported objects from the Modula-2 standard modules. Because external modules can be separately compiled, they are also a very convenient tool for developing large programs.

As we saw with module Points in Chapter 6, external modules differ from main program modules in a very important way. Each external module is split into two distinct parts—the definition and implementation sections. Each section is called a module and, oddly enough, taken together they are also called a module. Obviously the term "module" is a bit overworked.

Definition Module

As we explained in Chapters 2 and 6, the definition module contains the declarations of objects to be exported. Appendix E includes some definition modules. The following is a short example of the definition module format:

```
DEFINITION MODULE Figures;
(* A module for drawing simple geometric figures. *)

VAR OffScreen: BOOLEAN;

PROCEDURE Circle( Radius: CARDINAL );
(* Draws a circle with the specified radius.  The current
   position will be the lowest point on the circle.       *)

PROCEDURE Triangle( Size: CARDINAL );
(* Draws an equilateral triangle with each side of the specified
   size.  One side will be horizontal and the current position
   will be the left end of the horizontal side.                 *)

PROCEDURE Rectangle( Height, Width: CARDINAL );
(* Draws a rectangle with vertical sides of size Height and
   horizontal sides of size Width.  The current position will
   be the left end of the base.                              *)

END Figures.
```

Of course, many other objects could be added to and exported from this module, but those shown will be enough for illustrative purposes. In older versions of Modula-2, an export list is required for external modules: it contains the names of objects that are available for import by other modules. In this example the export list would have been

```
EXPORT QUALIFIED OffScreen, Circle, Triangle, Rectangle;
```

and would have immediately followed the module heading. In newer versions of Modula-2, all objects declared in the definition module are automatically exported with qualification. As we mentioned in Chapter 10, qualification is important for importing from different modules objects having the same name. We will say more about this issue when we discuss import lists later in this section.

The objects commonly appearing in a definition module are constants, types, variables, and procedures. Constants, types, and variables are declared as in a main program (we will study an exception to this rule, opaque types, in Chapter 15). Only the heading is given for procedures; the body of the procedure appears in the implementation module. As illustrated in our example, comments should describe *what* the procedure does and what the parameters represent. The comments should *not* describe *how* the task is accomplished, because that is the purpose of the implementation module. Although not demonstrated in our example, the definition module can import items from other definition modules.

The syntax for the definition module is as follows. As usual, braces indicate zero or more occurrences, and square brackets zero or one occurrence of the items they enclose.

```
DEFINITION MODULE identifier;
  { [FROM module-name] IMPORT list-of-identifiers; }
  {declarations}
END identifier.
```

The declarations in a definition module may include constant, type, and variable declarations, as well as procedure headings.

The import list names all objects that must be obtained from other modules. There can be several import lists, and each import list can have two forms. We have used the first form in most of our previous examples: this form includes a FROM part, giving the name of a module where the objects will be found. This form enables us to use the imported objects directly by using the names included in list-of-identifiers, as we have done before. The second form has no FROM part; the names in list-of-identifiers must then be module names, and all the objects in the modules are imported. In that case, to use the objects in the imported modules, we must *qualify* their names by prefixing them with the module name. For example, if we have

```
IMPORT InOut;
```

all the calls to InOut procedures must be prefixed by InOut, as in

```
InOut.WriteString( "Qualified identifier" );
InOut.WriteLn;
InOut.WriteCard( Value, 5 ); InOut.WriteLn;
```

Since, with a FROM part, the object names do not have to be qualified, it is often said that the FROM part qualifies the objects in list-of-identifiers.

In any program the only objects that may be imported must have been declared in some definition module. If an object is imported by a module, it will be visible throughout the importing module. Thus the imported objects are global in the importing module.

Older versions of Modula-2 use an export list, which follows the import lists. Its syntax is:

```
[EXPORT [QUALIFIED] list-of-identifiers;]
```

where list-of-identifiers is a list of all exported objects.

Implementation Module

Only objects that must be made visible to importing modules should be included in the definition module. All other objects should be put in the implementation module, where they will be hidden. The user has access only to the definition module, not to the implementation module, as illustrated in Figure 11.1. The syntax for the implementation module is identical to a main program module, except for the reserved word IMPLEMENTATION, which is added before MODULE to indicate that there is a corresponding definition module. The syntax for an implementation module is the following:

```
IMPLEMENTATION MODULE identifier;
  {[FROM module-name] IMPORT list-of-identifiers}
  {declarations}
  [BEGIN
    {statement}]
  END identifier.
```

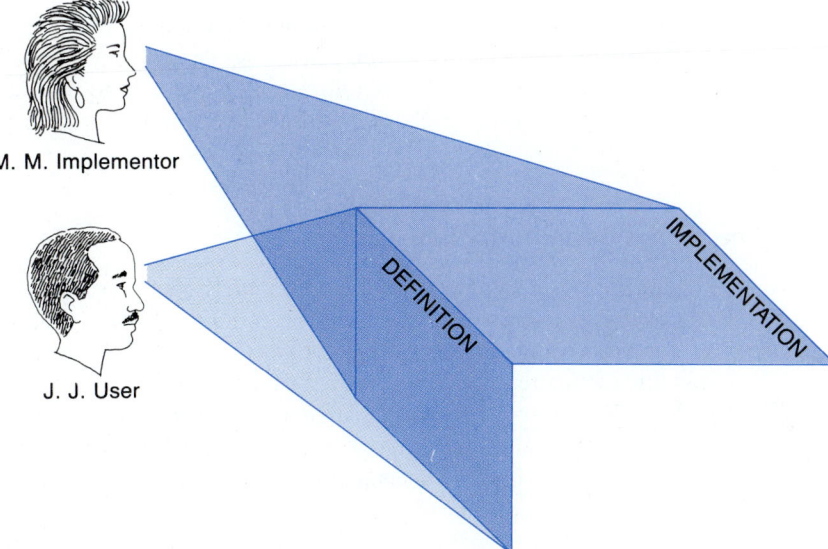

Figure 11.1 User and Implementor Visibility

The BEGIN and the statements between BEGIN and END are optional. If they are present, the statements are executed exactly once when the module is imported. They are useful for initializing variables or executing initialization procedures.

As an example of information hiding, consider the Figures module discussed earlier in this section. The implementation module might have to import many items from the TurtleGraphics module, including the procedures Move, MoveTo, Turn, TurnTo, PenColor, and so on. This importation can be hidden in the implementation module. If any of these imported procedures are changed in the TurtleGraphics definition module, we will have to make corresponding changes and recompile the Figures implementation module. However, we will *not* have to change or recompile the Figures definition module, nor any module that imports and uses objects from Figures, because the declaration of the variable OffScreen and the three procedure headings make no reference to the objects from TurtleGraphics.

This feature is an important advantage of information hiding: it enables us to change parts of a large program without worrying about adverse effects on the rest of the program. It provides software developers with a technique that has been used effectively by designers of hardware and machines in general. For example, automotive engineers can design a better radiator without being concerned about its effect on the transmission.

11.3 Strings: A Sample External Module

With this explanation of external modules, let's see how we would develop an external module in practice. We have introduced and used strings throughout this book, but the presentation has been largely informal. In this section, we will discuss strings more extensively as part of our example. Strings, as we've said before, are not built-in data types in Modula-2. Support for strings is largely dependent on the particular compiler you are using. Some Modula-2 implementations support a strings library module, while others do not. Of course, you can always design your own strings module if one is not supplied. This example, therefore, will show how to do just that. We will examine a user-defined string package and use it to implement a string manipulation algorithm.

The Strings Definition Module

As shown in Figure 11.1, the definition module contains the names of objects made available to users of a module. The Strings module contains a single type (STRING) and procedures for manipulating objects of this type. The Strings definition module in this section represents an abstract data type for strings.

Recall from Chapter 6 that an abstract data type includes the name of the type, the set of legal values for the type, *and* the operations allowed on objects of the type. Users need to have only a conceptual understanding of the values of the type (for example, a string is a sequence of characters); they do not need to know the actual representation of the values. Our Strings definition module does not hide this representation, but in

Chapter 15 we will learn how to hide the representation from the user. The other components of an abstract data type are the allowable operations for the type. These allowable operations essentially characterize the data type. For example, we might have another abstract data type—let us call it Numeral—that is a sequence of characters restricted to '0' through '9'. On the surface this type may appear to be very similar to strings, but, in fact, the operations provided will probably be entirely different. For example,

```
PROCEDURE AddNumeral( Operand1,Operand2: Numeral; VAR Sum: Numeral );
```

would make sense with these numeral strings but would be meaningless for strings in general.

To summarize, an abstract data type includes the name of the type, the set of legal values for objects of that type, and the allowed operations, but it does *not* include the representation.

The complete definition module, including explanatory comments, is as follows. Look it over carefully before proceeding.

```
DEFINITION MODULE Strings;

(* Unless specifically noted otherwise, invalid parameter
   values (e.g. a position that is negative or beyond the
   length of the string) will cause run time errors and the
   program will be aborted.
                            D. Corgan  January 1988 *)

TYPE STRING = ARRAY[0..79] OF CHAR;
(* This type of string is provided for applications where a
   maximum of 80 characters is appropriate.  If the working
   length of the string is less than 80 characters, then the
   string is terminated by a null character (0C).  If the
   procedure Assign is used, the remainder of the string is set
   to null characters (but this is not required for procedures
   to run correctly). *)

PROCEDURE InitString (VAR S: ARRAY OF CHAR);
(* Initializes S to the empty string by filling the entire
   array with null characters *)

PROCEDURE Assign(VAR STR: ARRAY OF CHAR; A: ARRAY OF CHAR);
(* Assigns the sequence of characters in A to the string STR;
   any remaining characters are set to null. *)

PROCEDURE Insert(SRC: ARRAY OF CHAR; VAR DEST: ARRAY OF CHAR;
                 INDEX: CARDINAL);
(* Inserts SRC into DEST before the position INDEX.  The
   remainder of DEST, including the character at INDEX, is
   moved to the right.  If INDEX equals the length of DEST,
   then Insert functions like string concatenation.      *)
```

```
PROCEDURE Delete(VAR SRC: ARRAY OF CHAR; INDEX, COUNT: CARDINAL);
(* Deletes COUNT characters from SRC starting at position
   INDEX.  The remainder of SRC, if any, is moved to
   the left *)

PROCEDURE Concat(STR1, STR2: ARRAY OF CHAR;
                 VAR DEST: ARRAY OF CHAR);
(* Concatenates STR2 to the end of STR1 and returns the result
   in DEST. *)

PROCEDURE Copy(SRC: ARRAY OF CHAR; INDEX, COUNT: CARDINAL;
               VAR DEST: ARRAY OF CHAR);
(* Copies COUNT characters from SRC starting a position INDEX
   into the result DEST. *)

PROCEDURE Pos(PATTERN, SRC: ARRAY OF CHAR) : CARDINAL;
(* If PATTERN is found in SRC, then the INDEX within SRC of the
   first character of the leftmost occurrence is returned.  If
   not found, the length of the SRC is returned. *)

PROCEDURE RPos(PATTERN, SRC: ARRAY OF CHAR) : CARDINAL;
(* If PATTERN is found in SRC, then the INDEX within SRC of the
   first character of the rightmost occurrence is returned.  If
   not found, the length of the SRC is returned. *)

PROCEDURE Length(STR: ARRAY OF CHAR) : CARDINAL;
(* Returns the current length of STR. *)

PROCEDURE FetchChar(STR: ARRAY OF CHAR; I: CARDINAL) : CHAR;
(* Returns the character at index I in string STR.  Strings are
   zero based; that is, the first character is at position 0,
   the second character at position 1, and so forth. *)

PROCEDURE AssignChar(CH: CHAR; VAR STR: ARRAY OF CHAR;
                     I: CARDINAL);
(* Replaces the current character value at position I in STR
   with the value of CH. *)

PROCEDURE StringGreater(STR1, STR2: ARRAY OF CHAR) : BOOLEAN;
(* Returns TRUE if STR1 follows STR2 in lexicographic
   (dictionary) order. *)

PROCEDURE StringEqual(STR1, STR2: ARRAY OF CHAR) : BOOLEAN;
(* Returns TRUE is STR1 is equal to STR2. *)

PROCEDURE ReadLine(VAR STR: ARRAY OF CHAR; ECHO: BOOLEAN);
(* Reads a sequence of characters from the current input device
   and returns them in STR.  If ECHO is TRUE, then the input is
   printed to the current output device.  Input is terminated
   by any ASCII character with ordinal position <= 31, which
```

includes a return. The default input device can be
redirected if the standard module InOut supports
redirection. *)

PROCEDURE WriteLine(STR: ARRAY OF CHAR);
(* Prints the value of STR followed by a return on the current
   output device. *)

PROCEDURE ToChar(STR: ARRAY OF CHAR) : CHAR;
(* If STR is a string with length 1, then STR returns that
   single character as a CHAR. If STR has any other length, a
   run time error occurs. For strings of other lengths,
   FetchChar can be used. *)

PROCEDURE ToString(CH: CHAR; VAR STR: ARRAY OF CHAR);
(* Returns in STR a one-character string with the character
   value of CH. *)

END Strings.

To implement this module using older Modula-2 systems, you will need to add an export list. The following discussion explains the items of the Strings definition module that have not been covered in earlier chapters.

The type STRING is exported so users of the Strings module can declare string variables that can store up to 80 characters. STRING is declared as an array of characters so that it is compatible with string constants in Modula-2. The procedures in the Strings module use open arrays of characters as parameters and can actually work with strings of any length; however, the 80-character string is very common since this size matches the width of most terminal screens. The use of open array parameters has the advantage of making the procedures compatible with Modula-2 string constants. If more or less than 80 characters are required, the programmer simply declares strings of appropriate length, as in

```
         TYPE   String25 = ARRAY [0..24] OF CHAR;

         VAR    Name, Address: String25;
```

Such declarations are fully compatible with the open array parameters required by the string operations.

There are two procedures for assignment: InitString, which makes a string empty (that is, containing no characters), and Assign, which allows a nonempty sequence of characters to be assigned to the target string. Here are some sample applications (assuming Str1, Str2, and Str3 are strings):

```
InitString( Str1 );          (* Str1 is now empty *)
Assign( Str2, "Hello" );     (* Str2 has the value "Hello" *)
Assign( Str3, Str2 );        (* Str3 now also has the value "Hello" *)
```

Notice that the first actual parameter of a call to Assign and the actual parameter of a call to InitString must always be variables. We can see this from the definition module since these parameters are variable parameters. However, the second parameter to Assign is a value parameter; thus as the actual parameter, we can use constants (as in the second line of the preceding example), variables (as in the third line), or any expression that results in a string value.

Two Boolean functions allow comparisons of strings. The strings need not be of the same length since the comparison is lexicographic (that is, in the same order as a dictionary). The case of letters (upper or lower) makes a difference; in ASCII, uppercase letters precede lowercase letters. Here are some examples:

```
StringGreater( "ABC","A" )         returns TRUE
StringEqual( "ABC ","ABCD" )       returns FALSE
StringGreater( "ABC ","ABCD" )     returns FALSE
```

The order of the parameters does not matter for StringEqual; however, it is critical for StringGreater. A StringLess function need not be provided; the programmer can use StringGreater and reverse the actual parameters to have the same effect. By using NOT, we can make other comparisons:

```
NOT( StringEqual( Str1,Str2 ) )       returns TRUE if Str1 and Str2 are
                                         not equal

NOT( StringGreater( Str1,Str2 ) )     returns TRUE if Str1 precedes Str2
                                         or if Str1 equals Str2
```

Several procedures are designed to modify existing strings in particular ways. The Delete procedure removes a specified number of characters from a string, starting at a specified index. Consider the following example:

```
Assign( Str1, "This is the delete example." );
Delete( Str1, 18, 9 );
WriteString( Str1 );        (* "This is the delete" *)
Delete( Str1, Pos( "the ",Str1 ), 4 );
WriteString( Str1 );        (* "This is delete" *)
```

We can also add a string of characters at a specified position by using the Insert function:

```
Assign( Str1, "This is insert" );
Insert( "the ", Str1, 8 );
WriteString( Str1 );      (* "This is the insert" *)
```

Insert puts the string specified by the first parameter before the character specified by the index. Insert also allows for one special case where the specified position equals the length of the string. Notice that the length is one character beyond the last valid character. The effect is to insert the string after the given string, as in

```
Assign( Str1, "Computer science is " );
Insert( "EXCITING!", Str1, Length( Str1 ) );
WriteString( Str1 );    (* "Computer Science is EXCITING!" *)
```

A ReadLine procedure is provided to read a string from the current input device. The standard module InOut does provide a ReadString procedure; however, its input terminates when a space character is typed. Since strings have embedded spaces for many applications, ReadLine will read a sequence of characters, including space characters. The terminating character can be any control character, including a return. The procedure requires a second Boolean parameter, since for some applications, such as entering a password, you may not want to echo the characters typed.

The WriteLine procedure is the same as WriteString from InOut, except that the cursor moves to the start of the next line after the string is written.

We discussed the Pos function in Chapter 1; it searches for the leftmost occurrence of a pattern within a source string. If this pattern is found, the position of the first matching character is returned. For a source string of working length n, the possible values for a match are 0 to $n - 1$, since the last character in the string is at position $n - 1$. If the pattern is not found, n is returned since it is not a valid position in the source string. RPos is a similar routine, except that it searches for the rightmost occurrence of the pattern in the source string.

Finally, we must discuss the relationship between strings and characters. In older implementations of Modula-2, a character and a string that contains a single character are incompatible types. Therefore, the Strings module provides the functions ToChar and ToString to make this conversion. ToChar is a function that accepts a one-character string and returns the corresponding character. ToChar provides additional security since it will result in a run time error if the length of the string is not one. To extract a character from a longer string, you can use the FetchChar function. ToString accepts a character and returns the one-character string with that character.

Using the Strings Module

Having developed the definition module, we show how to use our Strings module in a program. As an example, we'll create a program to count the number of words in a paragraph.

In Section 1.4, we developed an algorithm to count the number of words in a text passage. Here is a slight variation of the pseudocode we developed to count the words in a single line:

> CountWords(Line): Cardinal
>   Set Count to 0
>   Loop
>   Exit If LENGTH Line = 0
>   Set Count to Count + 1
>   Set Blank Position to POS " ", Line
>   If Blank found then
>   DELETE Line, 0, BlankPosition + 1

> Else
>   DELETE Line, 0, LENGTH Line
>   End Loop
>   Return Count
> End CountWords

We now have the tools to code CountWords in Modula-2. Since the exit condition is at the top of the loop, we will use a WHILE loop.

```
PROCEDURE CountWords( Line: STRING ): CARDINAL;
(* Return the number of words in Line, assuming a pair of words
is separated by a single blank.                                 *)

VAR Count, BlankPosition: CARDINAL;
    Blank: STRING;

BEGIN
  Count := 0;
  Blank := ' ';
  WHILE Length( Line ) > 0 DO
    Count := Count + 1;
    BlankPosition := Pos( Blank, Line );
    IF BlankPosition # Length( Line ) THEN
      Delete( Line, 0, BlankPosition + 1 );
    ELSE
      Delete( Line, 0, Length( Line ) );
    END; (* IF *)
  END; (* WHILE *)
  RETURN Count;
END  CountWords;
```

As we said, here we want to write a program to count the number of words in an entire paragraph (the pseudocode was developed in Section 1.4). For simplicity, we assume that lines are read sequentially as the user types them interactively. An empty line will be used to indicate the end of the paragraph. After the paragraph is entered, the word count will be printed. Since this is an interactive program, we will use a LOOP structure with a "middle" exit.

```
MODULE TestCountWords;
  (* This program counts the words in a paragraph that is entered
     interactively.  The entry of an empty line indicates the end
     of the paragraph, at which time the word count is printed.
                    B. L. Kurtz   January 1988    *)

FROM InOut IMPORT WriteString, WriteCard, WriteLn;
FROM Strings IMPORT STRING, Pos, Length, Delete, ReadLine;
```

```
VAR WordCount: CARDINAL;
    Line: STRING;

PROCEDURE CountWords( Line: STRING ): CARDINAL;
VAR Count, BlankPosition: CARDINAL;
    Blank: STRING;
BEGIN
  Count := 0;
  Blank := ' ';
  WHILE Length( Line ) > 0 DO
    Count := Count + 1;
    BlankPosition := Pos( Blank, Line );
    IF BlankPosition # Length( Line ) THEN
      Delete( Line, 0, BlankPosition + 1 );
    ELSE
      Delete( Line, 0, Length( Line ) );
    END;   (* IF *)
  END;   (* WHILE *)
  RETURN Count;
END  CountWords;

BEGIN   (* TestCountWords *)
  WordCount := 0;
  LOOP
    ReadLine( Line, TRUE );
    IF Length( Line ) = 0 THEN
      EXIT
    END;    (* IF *)
    WordCount := WordCount + CountWords( Line );
  END;   (* LOOP *)
  WriteString( "The word count is " );
  WriteCard( WordCount, 3 );   WriteLn;
END TestCountWords.
```

The following is an example of this program's input and output:

> Input   Now is the time
> to count all of the words
> in this paragraph.
>
> Output   The word count is   13

As you can see, our program is relatively simple because it uses the tools contained in the Strings module. In general, you will be able to write much simpler programs if you take advantage of tools in existing modules or develop external modules to provide the needed tools.

The Strings Implementation Module

The remaining part of the Strings module is the implementation module. Here we put all the details that completely define the objects in the module but that are hidden from the user. Recall that the format for implementation modules is

```
IMPLEMENTATION MODULE identifier;
    {import list}
    {declaration}
[BEGIN
    {statement}]
END identifier.
```

All procedures given in the corresponding definition module must be declared. Additional constants, types, variables, and procedures that are only tools for implementation may also be included. These will not be visible outside the module if they are not listed in the definition module.

The implementation module for Strings uses several internal procedures. Since the complete implementation module for Strings is rather large, we will present only a skeletal version containing the declarations of two procedures.

```
IMPLEMENTATION MODULE Strings;
(*
PURPOSE: Provides the support for strings.

IMPLEMENTED BY: David Corgan

DATE: December 1987

NEW MEXICO STATE UNIVERSITY
DEPARTMENT OF COMPUTER SCIENCE

CHANGE LOG:
   Converted to Modula Corp. native code compiler January 1988.
                                          David Corgan     *)
   .
   .
   .

PROCEDURE Length(STR: ARRAY OF CHAR): CARDINAL;
(* Returns the current length of STR. *)
VAR Count, Last: CARDINAL;
BEGIN
  Last := HIGH(STR); (* Last gets the index of the last character *)
  Count := 0;
  WHILE (Count <= Last) (* while not at the end of the string *)
    AND (FetchChar(STR, Count) # 0C) DO (* and null not found *)
      INC(Count);                    (* increment the count *)
  END; (* WHILE *)
  RETURN Count;
END Length;
```

```
              .
              .
      PROCEDURE Copy(SRC: ARRAY OF CHAR; INDEX, COUNT: CARDINAL;
                    VAR DEST: ARRAY OF CHAR);
      (* Copies COUNT characters from SRC starting at position INDEX
         into the result DEST. *)
      BEGIN
        IF ( INDEX + COUNT <= Length( SRC ) )     (* valid substring *)
           AND (COUNT < HIGH(DEST) ) THEN    (* it fits into DEST *)
          Delete (SRC, 0, INDEX);  (* delete preceding characters *)
          Delete (SRC, COUNT, Length(SRC) - COUNT); (* delete following characters *)
          Assign (DEST, SRC);    (* assign result to destination *)
        ELSE
          WriteLine("bad parameters to Copy");
          WriteString("SRC = "); WriteLine(SRC);
          WriteString("INDEX = "); WriteCard(INDEX, 5); WriteLn;
          WriteString("COUNT = "); WriteCard(COUNT, 5); WriteLn;
          WriteString("Size of DEST = "); WriteCard(HIGH(DEST)+1, 5);
          WriteLn;
          HALT;
        END; (* IF *)
      END Copy;
              .
              .
      END Strings.
```

In the declaration of Length, the call to standard function HIGH will return the maximum index of the open array parameter STR. The leftmost null character, represented by 0C here, marks the logical end of the string if it is less than the maximum size. The Length function counts the characters until the last character is reached or until the null character is found. Since it is possible for the string to be empty, the WHILE loop is used to test at the top of the loop before the count is incremented.

It is possible, and usually desirable, to use previously declared procedures, as is done in the declaration of the Copy procedure. In this case Length, Delete, and Assign are used to copy a substring, represented here by S's, from a source string illustrated by

xxxxxxSSSSSSSSSSSSSSxxxxxxxxx

The three procedures are used to accomplish the following sequence of actions:

1. Delete from the source string any characters preceding the desired substring.
2. Delete from the source string any characters following the desired substring.
3. Assign the resultant source string to the destination.

These actions are taken only if the desired substring lies within the current working length of the source string and if the destination string is large enough to receive a copy of the substring. Otherwise, an appropriate error message is generated and the procedure halts.

Notice that it is acceptable to modify the formal parameter SRC within Copy since it is a value parameter and will not result in the actual parameter being changed. Also, we are depending on Delete to do nothing when the number of characters to be deleted is zero.

Another approach to Copy would be to make a character-by-character copy from the desired substring in the source to the destination string. A version of Copy based on this idea could be implemented, tested, and then substituted for the previous version in the implementation module without recompilation of the definition module or any programs using the Strings module. This approach is an example of the great advantage of hiding implementation details.

In this section we have examined a Strings module that is already defined. In the next two sections we will see how we can use several modules as part of the software design process.

11.4 Modular Design Charts

Modular design charts will help us visualize the interconnection of external modules.* Two important concepts relating to this interconnection are *cohesion* and *coupling*. A module contains a collection of identifiers representing constants, variables, types, and procedures that are used to define objects and operations on these objects. Cohesion is a measure of the "single-mindedness" of a module. For example, the Strings module has high cohesion since all procedures are related to operations on open arrays of characters used to represent strings.

Coupling is a measure of the interconnection between modules in a complete software package. The degree of coupling depends on the number of interconnections and the types of interconnections. The sharing of data by passing data parameters to procedures is an example of low coupling. As already mentioned, information hiding enables us to change parts of a program without having to worry about adverse effects on the rest of the program. Another way to say this is that information hiding reduces coupling. Sharing global data or passing Boolean variables that directly affect flow of control are examples of high coupling. High coupling causes changes in one part of a program to ripple to other parts and makes maintenance difficult.

A general principle of good program design is to *maximize cohesion* and *minimize coupling*. The modular design chart is a useful tool for visually showing the cohesiveness of a module and the amount of coupling between modules.

A main program in Modula-2 usually imports items from other modules but cannot export items. A definition module contains items to be exported and may also import from other modules. An implementation module may also import from other modules, and, like the main program, it cannot export items. In accordance with the information hiding principle, only those objects that are needed by the user of the module should

---

* R. Wiener and R. Sincovec, *Software Engineering with Modula-2 and Ada* (New York: John Wiley & Sons, 1984), 130–32.

Figure 11.2
A Sample Modular Design Chart

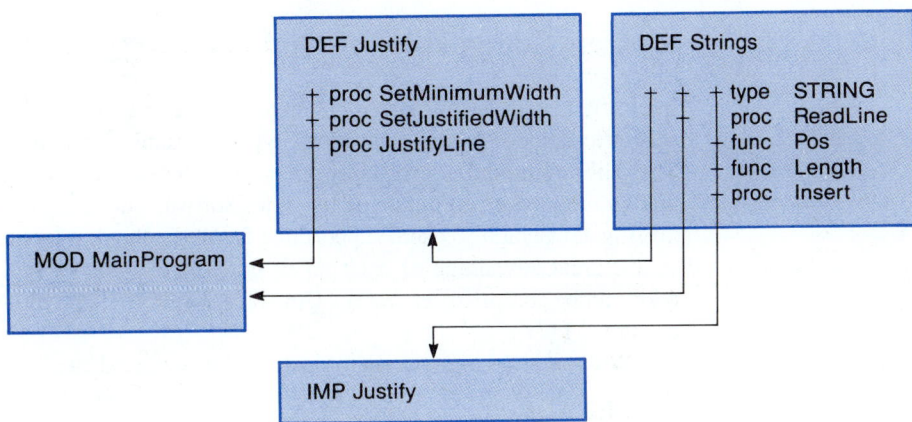

be placed in the definition module; all other objects should be hidden in the implementation module. The interconnections between modules can be shown using a modular design chart (see Figure 11.2).

In this example the programmer is defining and implementing a module called Justify. It exports three procedures: SetMinimumWidth, SetJustifiedWidth, and JustifyLine. The programmer imports all three objects into the main program module, as shown by the line from the DEF Justify box to the MOD MainProgram box. Module Justify manipulates strings, so the definition module imports type STRING, as shown by the line from DEF Strings to DEF Justify. The main program must also import this type along with ReadLine for input. Notice that the line from DEF Strings to MOD MainProgram has a + sign next to every object that is actually imported. Examining the line from DEF Strings to IMP Justify, we see that the implementation module for Justify imports STRING, Pos, Length, and Insert. Since Length and Pos are procedures that return values, we have indicated this by using "func" as short for function.

You may have noted that we did not draw an implementation box for Strings. Since this predefined module comes from a library, we need not be concerned with what DEF Strings and IMP Strings need to import to do their job.

As we said in Chapter 8, the group of lines connecting modules is called a software bus. A software bus that has become too complex indicates that the modules may be too highly coupled. The type of objects also tells us about the degree of coupling. Typically, if a module imports variables, this arrangement represents sharing global data, which may be suspected of high coupling. If many objects declared in a module appear unrelated, there may be a lack of cohesion.

The modular design chart also gives us an indication of information hiding. Notice that DEF Justify imports only the type STRING, probably to be used as a parameter for one of the procedures; however, the implementation module imports other string operations. Typically, the definition module is generally available and, along with documentation, is all that a user needs to know in order to use the module effectively. The implementation details, including what is imported by the implementation module, need be known only by the module developer, *not* by the module user.

We will implement a module Justify in our case study in this chapter. The actual modular design chart for Justify will be bigger since it will be necessary to import additional items from the standard module InOut.

11.5 Separate Compilation of Modules

In our first Modula-2 program in Chapter 2, we saw how import lists were used to gain access to named objects (constants, types, variables, procedures) in library modules. These library modules are simply other programs that have been written by the company that supplies your compiler or by other software developers. In this section we will investigate operating system support that facilitates the development of separate modules.

A great advantage of external modules is that the definition and implementation parts can be compiled separately. Consider the abbreviated modular design chart shown in Figure 11.3.

Without showing specific objects being imported, we see that:

- DEF A and B both export objects.
- Neither DEF B nor IMP B imports any objects.
- DEF A and IMP A import objects from B.
- The main program imports objects from both A and B.

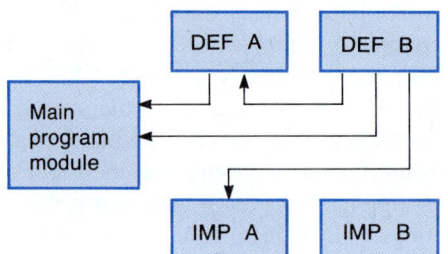

Figure 11.3
An Abbreviated Modular Design Chart

Each box in Figures 11.2 and 11.3 is called a *compilation unit* because it is compiled separately. In order to compile a module that imports objects from another module, the definition part of the exporting module must be compiled first. For our example the definition module for B must be compiled before both the definition and implementation modules of A, and the definition modules for both A and B must be compiled before the main program is compiled. Neither implementation part need be compiled before the main program is compiled. However, you *cannot execute* the main program until the implementation modules have been compiled, because the code for imported procedures does not exist until such compilation has been completed.

An implementation module can be compiled only after: (1) its definition module has been compiled, and (2) the definition modules containing objects it imports have been compiled. The implementation module for B can be compiled after the definition module for B has been compiled. The implementation module for A can be compiled only after the definition module for B and the definition module for A have both been compiled, in that order.

Separate compilation of the definition and implementation modules allows a programmer to change the actual implementation without changing the definition module. This means that all other modules using the objects in the definition module need not be recompiled just because of changes in implementation. However, if a definition module is changed, then every module that uses this definition module must be recompiled. Some operating systems have features that help you keep track of modules by means of version numbers, which are changed whenever the modules are recompiled.

Usually the modular design chart is not a complete specification for a definition module since many details such as constant values, type definitions, and procedure parameter lists are not given. The definition modules actually complete the design indicated by the modular design chart. It is recommended that the definition modules and a skeleton of the main program be completed during program design and compiled to check the consistency of design. This step will reduce the number of problems you will encounter during program coding when the implementation modules are done.

11.6 Local Modules

In Section 11.1 we noted that one of the original motivations behind Modula-2 was the need for information hiding—allowing the user access to only what is necessary. The separate definition and implementation modules support this principle. Another feature of Modula-2 that contributes to information hiding is the use of local modules.

The main program module, or any module for that matter, can also contain internal modules, called *local modules*. Such modules are thereby "nested." But here, in contrast to nested procedures, local modules provide a better mechanism for controlling access to data and procedures from other parts of the same program.

Declaration of Local Modules

Local modules can be declared anywhere that declarations can appear. Thus they can be declared within the main program, within the definition or implementation parts of external modules, or within other local modules. We will limit most of our remarks to nesting within the main program.

The syntax for a local module declaration is

```
MODULE identifier;
  {[FROM module-name] IMPORT list-of-identifiers;}
  [EXPORT [QUALIFIED] list-of-identifiers;]
  {declaration}
[BEGIN
  {statement}]
END identifier;
```

As mentioned before, an import list names all objects to be obtained from other modules. Local modules can import from the enclosing program and, indirectly, from external modules. If the import is from the enclosing program, there is no FROM part, only the reserved word IMPORT followed by a list of objects visible in the enclosing program. If the import is from an external module, the import list can have a FROM part. However, the external module has to be imported by the enclosing program in order to be accessible.

The export list names all items within the local module that may be accessed from the enclosing module or procedure. It is introduced by the reserved word EXPORT. The reserved word QUALIFIED is used only to resolve possible ambiguities, as in the case where two objects exported by two different modules have the same name. If the exported objects are qualified, their name can be prefixed in the importing program by the name of their module, so that no ambiguity exists.

The declarations in a local module may include the declarations of constants, types, variables, and procedures. However, unlike definition modules of external modules, the declarations of procedures must be complete because there is no corresponding implementation module.

Unlike procedures, the local module has a complete barrier around it; only items explicitly named in the import list can be brought in from the outside, and only items explicitly named in the export list can be accessed outside the local module.

The reserved word BEGIN and the statement body are optional in a local module. If present, the statements are typically used to initialize variables. Furthermore, once variables in a local module have been given values, they retain those values until the module or procedure, within which the local module is nested, ceases to exist. So, for example, the variables of a local module nested within the main program retain their values until execution of the main program is completed. Thus, the variables of a local module are unlike the local variables of a procedure, whose values are discarded when the procedure is exited.

Figure 11.4 gives a skeletal local module, which illustrates the two forms of import, as well as export and identifier qualification.

Figure 11.4
Import and Export in a Local Module

```
MODULE MainProgram;

IMPORT InOut; (* entire module *)
FROM RealInOut IMPORT WriteReal;
(* import only one procedure *)

    MODULE Internal;

    FROM InOut IMPORT WriteString;
    IMPORT WriteReal;
    EXPORT Prime;

        PROCEDURE P;
            .
            .
            .
            WriteString( "X = " );
            WriteReal( X );
            .
            .
            .
        END P;
```

```
            PROCEDURE Prime;
                :
            END Prime;

        END Internal;

    BEGIN
        :
        Prime;
        :
        InOut.WriteString( "Message" );
        InOut.WriteLn;
        :
        WriteReal (X, 5 );
        :
    END MainProgram.
```

Since module InOut is imported in the main program, we can import selectively from it in local module Internal. We have imported WriteReal in the main program, and it is available for direct import in the local module. Note that since we have imported the entire InOut module in the main program, we must qualify all its objects when we use them in that main program. The FROM clause automatically qualifies imported objects; this is why WriteString does not have to be qualified in module Internal, and WriteReal does not have to be qualified in the main program. Actually, it would be impossible to qualify WriteReal because the name RealInOut is unknown in the main program (it has not been imported). Note that objects, like Prime, exported by a local module do not have to be imported by the enclosing program or module.

Let's now use local modules to implement the structure chart shown in Figure 11.5, which was first discussed in Chapter 6.

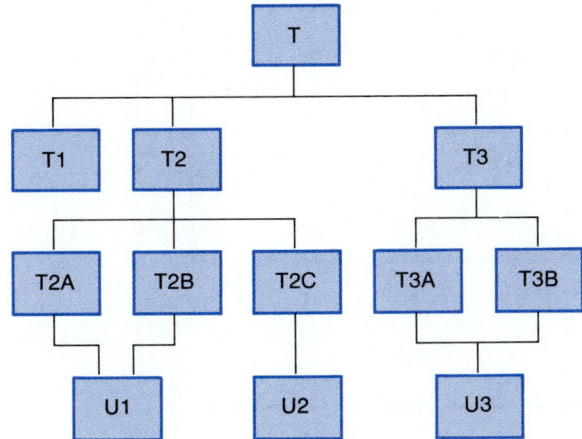

Figure 11.5
Structure Chart with Shared Components

For simplicity, we will restrict our attention to the portion of the chart consisting of T2 and its descendants. An appropriate Modula-2 structure for this portion of the chart is given in Figure 11.6.

Figure 11.6
Information Hiding Using a Local Module

```
PROCEDURE T2;

    MODULE Local1;

    IMPORT (* as necessary *);
    EXPORT T2A, T2B;

        PROCEDURE U1;
            :
            :
        END U1;


        PROCEDURE T2A;
            :
            :
        END T2A;


        PROCEDURE T2B;
            :
            :
        END T2B;

    END Local1;


    PROCEDURE T2C;

        PROCEDURE U2;
            :
            :
        END U2;

    BEGIN (* T2C *)
        :
        :
    END T2C;

BEGIN (* T2 *)
    :
    :
END T2;
```

By using a local module inside of procedure T2 and by nesting U2 inside of T2C, we have accomplished the following:

- T2C does not have access to U1.
- T2A and T2B do not have access to U2.
- U1 and U2 do not have access to each other.

Thus far, we have discussed only access to identifiers that are procedure names. Recall that procedure invocation creates a new local environment with constants, types, and variables, as well as local procedures. What about access to these other items? In module Local1, U1 does *not* have access to the local environments of T2A and T2B (rules of scope). On the other hand, since U2 is nested inside T2C to prevent access to it from anywhere outside of T2C, we have also allowed U2 access to the local environment of T2C. This access must be controlled, as we have seen in Chapter 6, by using only parameters for information transfer to and from a procedure. If we want to make such access impossible, while keeping U2 inaccessible to anyone but T2C, we should not nest U2 inside of T2C but rather create a second local module. In order to do that, we would need to replace the procedure T2C in Figure 11.6 with the local module shown in Figure 11.7.

Figure 11.7
Hiding Procedure U2

```
MODULE Local2;

IMPORT (* as necessary *);
EXPORT T2C;

    PROCEDURE U2;
    .
    .
    .
    END U2;


    PROCEDURE T2C;
    .
    .
    .
    END T2C;

END Local2;
```

Using Local Modules

In what sorts of circumstances would the controlled access afforded by local modules be useful? The following section looks at a situation in which the designer wants to protect certain data from inadvertent change.

To make use of local modules, we must be aware that each local module establishes a *scope of visibility* of identifiers. This scope is like that of procedures in the sense that objects declared within modules are visible only within that scope. There are two exceptions to this description:

1. The scope of visibility of an identifier declared within a local module can be extended outside the module by including it in the module's export list.
2. An identifier visible in the scope surrounding a local module is not visible within a local module, unless it is included in the module's import list.

Thus, if we use import and export statements, we can control the scope of identifiers more tightly in modules than in procedures.

As mentioned previously, the values of variables declared within a local module are more enduring than values of variables local to a procedure. The values of local variables of a procedure disappear on exit from the procedure. But variables of a local module retain their last assigned values as long as the procedure or module containing the local module exists. So, for example, the values of variables of a local module nested in the main program are retained until the main program terminates.

We will use retention of values of local module variables in the following example of a password security system. The names and passwords of users of a computing system will be declared in a local module to protect them from inadvertent changes. Then, even though execution leaves the local module, values of the names and passwords will be retained, so that they are available when execution returns to the local module for validation of a name and password.

The initialization section of our password security module is used to assign values to names and passwords. These values cannot be changed because the names and passwords are not exported. The only item exported from our local module is a Boolean procedure ValidPassword. When passed two string parameters, a name and a password, this procedure will return TRUE only if the name is present and the password is correct for that name. We will use one array to store the allowable names and another array to store the valid passwords.

In addition to hiding the name and password data, our local module will also hide a utility procedure to find the index for a given name. If the name is not present in the name array, the index one past the maximum index for the array is returned. Here is our pseudocode:

```
FindName ( Name ) : Position
   Set Index to 0
   While Index <= MaxIndex and Name does not match NameData[Index] do
      Increment Index
   End while
   Return Index
End FindName
```

FindName does a sequential search through the array NameData until the name is located or until the data are exhausted. We will study searching techniques in more detail in Chapter 12.

Local Modules

Using FindName, we can write the pseudocode for our ValidPassword function directly:

> ValidPassword (Name, Password) : Boolean
>   Set Index to the result of calling FindName (Name)
>   Return (Index <= MaxIndex)   {Name was found}
>   and (Password = PasswordData[Index]) {and the password matches}
> End ValidPassword

Here is the complete code for our local module as well as a test program.

```
MODULE PasswordDemo;
(* Demonstrates a password system where the name and password
   data, along with a utility procedure, are hidden in a local
   module.
                       B. Kurtz     January 1988               *)

FROM InOut IMPORT WriteLn, WriteString;
FROM Strings IMPORT STRING, ReadLine, WriteLine, StringEqual;

MODULE PasswordSystem;
IMPORT STRING, StringEqual;
EXPORT ValidPassword;

CONST MaxIndex = 9;
TYPE DataArray = ARRAY [0..MaxIndex] OF STRING;
     Position = [0..MaxIndex + 1];
VAR NameData, PasswordData: DataArray;

PROCEDURE FindName(Name: ARRAY OF CHAR): Position;
(* If Name is present in NameData, then its index is returned;
   otherwise, MaxIndex + 1 is returned.                         *)
VAR Index: Position;
BEGIN (* FindName *)
  Index:= 0;
  WHILE (Index <= MaxIndex) AND
        NOT StringEqual(Name, NameData[Index]) DO
    INC(Index);
  END;  (* WHILE *)
  RETURN Index;
END FindName;

PROCEDURE ValidPassword  (Name, Password: ARRAY OF CHAR): BOOLEAN;
(* Returns TRUE if the Name is present and the Password
   matches; otherwise, returns FALSE.                    *)
VAR Index: Position;
```

```
BEGIN (* ValidPassword *)
  Index := FindName(Name);
  RETURN (Index <= MaxIndex) AND
         StringEqual(Password, PasswordData[Index]);
END ValidPassword;

BEGIN (* PasswordSystem *)
  NameData[0] := "Bell";    PasswordData[0] := "ringer";
  NameData[1] := "Walker";  PasswordData[1] := "runner";
  NameData[2] := "Curry";   PasswordData[2] := "spicy";
  NameData[3] := "Taylor";  PasswordData[3] := "sewing";
  NameData[4] := "Burn";    PasswordData[4] := "fire";
  NameData[5] := "Cobbler"; PasswordData[5] := "shoes";
  NameData[6] := "Monk";    PasswordData[6] := "recluse";
  NameData[7] := "Villa";   PasswordData[7] := "estate";
  NameData[8] := "Farmer";  PasswordData[8] := "grower";
  NameData[9] := "Holiday"; PasswordData[9] := "vacation";
END PasswordSystem;

VAR Name, Password: STRING;
BEGIN (* PasswordDemo *)
  LOOP
    WriteString("Name: ");
    ReadLine(Name, TRUE);
    IF StringEqual(Name, "") THEN EXIT END;
    WriteString("Password: ");
    ReadLine(Password, FALSE); WriteLn;
    IF ValidPassword(Name, Password) THEN
      WriteLine("valid password");
    ELSE
      WriteLine("invalid, try again");
    END; (* IF *)
  END; (* LOOP *)
END PasswordDemo.
```

The local module PasswordSystem hides the objects

constants: MaxIndex

types: DataArray, Position

variables: NameData, PasswordData

procedures: FindName

Notice that this hiding is only from inadvertent access from outside the local module, and that intentional changes cannot be prevented. For example, the source code for the local module can be examined to determine that the password of "Bell" is "ringer", and this information can be used in the program containing the local module.

Local modules are useful for preventing mistakes; also if the module is small, it saves the steps of additional compilation. If protection from intentional changes is deemed necessary, you can compile the module separately as an external module.

11.7 Case Study: Line Justification

The discussions in this chapter of external modules, modular design charts, and local modules have given us our first concentrated picture of the modularity that gives Modula-2 its name. The case study here will present an opportunity to experiment with these features.

We have been asked to write a program that will input lines of text and print these same lines with both left and right margins justified (that is, aligned vertically). The specifications are such that we do not need to move text from one line to the next; therefore we can simplify the problem to justifying one line at a time. Also, lines shorter than a specified width should not be altered.

As you can see, this problem definition is not precise. Such imprecision will often be the case, however, when dealing with clients, particularly those who are computer "naive." As always, it is tempting to rush to the computer and start coding, but much of the coding may be useless if we do not complete the design process before implementation. We will develop this case study using the methods presented for software design and implementation.

Design

Define the Problem The user may specify two values: the line width after justification and the minimum line width to be justified, or may use default values set at 65 and 50, respectively. Any line that is initially less than the minimum width or greater than the justified width will not be altered. Since most terminal screens are 80 characters wide, we will assume all lines have a length less than or equal to 80. The letters in an input line of text can be classified as blanks (or spaces) and nonblanks (anything other than a space). A typical line is shown in Figure 11.8. This line starts with text; other lines, such as those indented for a paragraph, may start with blanks.

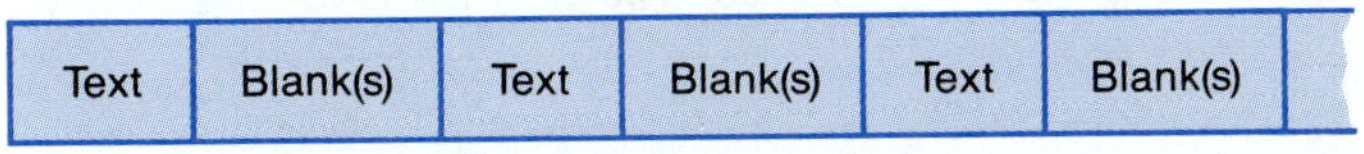

Figure 11.8
Typical Line Format

| Text | Blank(s) | Text | Blank(s) | Text | Blank(s) |

We will assume all characters are the same size and that a character space cannot be split into pieces. This assumption actually differs from the specifications for typeset books in which some characters, such as "i", are narrow and others, such as "w", are wide.

Justification will require increasing the total number of characters to the number specified as justification width. The only characters we want to add are spaces, and these should be added only at existing sequences of blanks. Furthermore, these extra spaces should be spread evenly throughout the line so that the line is aesthetically pleasing. In the rare case where there are no blanks within the line to be justified (yet the line is at least as long as the minimum width), the line should not be altered.

Design a Solution We will want to design a separate module that will carry out the justification process on a given line of text. Using the principle of information hiding, we will control the user's access to internal objects.

Since the user may specify the justified width and the minimum width for justification, we will export two procedures, SetJustifiedWidth and SetMinimumWidth, to allow these values to be set. Justification will be one line at a time; therefore, we will need a procedure, JustifyLine, that receives the unjustified line and returns the justified line. We will assume that this procedure will alter only lines of the appropriate length and containing at least one embedded blank.

The definition and implementation modules for Justify will not make up an independent program. Therefore, we will write a test program that will allow us to use our justification module under a variety of conditions. This test program will be interactive and will require importing procedures from the standard library module InOut.

Although we could write our Justify modules "from scratch," that would be unwise since we have a module, Strings, that will help us perform the string manipulations necessary to convert an unjustified line of text into a justified line. Figure 11.9 shows a preliminary version of our modular design chart.

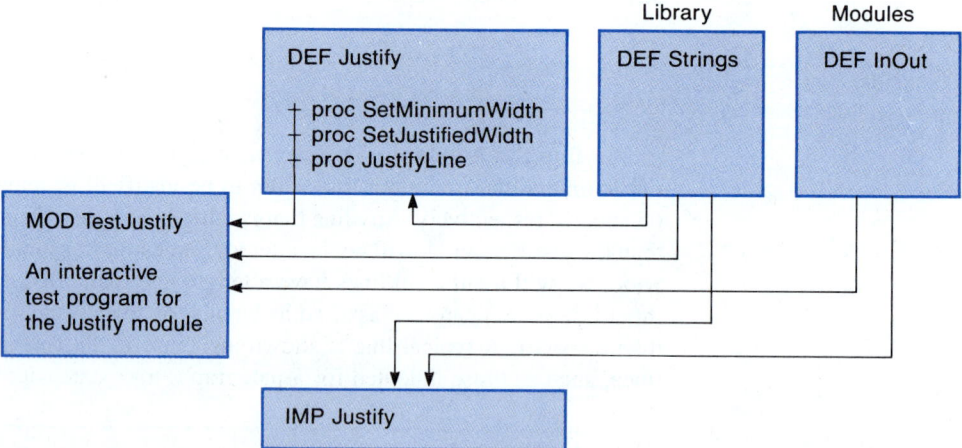

Figure 11.9
Preliminary Modular Design Chart for Justification

This chart is incomplete since we have not specified what items will be imported from Strings and InOut. We will fill in these details during the detailed design phase. However, the following is clear:

- The test program will import from three modules: Justify (three procedures), Strings (at least the type STRING and possibly more), and InOut (whatever is necessary for input and output in the test program).

- The definition module for Justify will import type STRING since the parameter of JustifyLine will be of this type.

- The implementation module for Justify will import type STRING and whatever string procedures are necessary to perform line justification, as well as input and output procedures needed for entering values of justified width and minimum width.

In our modular design chart we have not drawn boxes for the implementation modules for Strings and InOut. We know such modules exist, but we have no need to know what information they must import or how the implementation is accomplished. For library modules, we will show only the definition modules.

The design for Justify Line will be fairly complex. Assuming the line is to be justified, we need to count the number of gaps in the line, calculate the number of spaces to be inserted into each gap, and then do the insertion. The structure chart for this solution is shown in Figure 11.10.

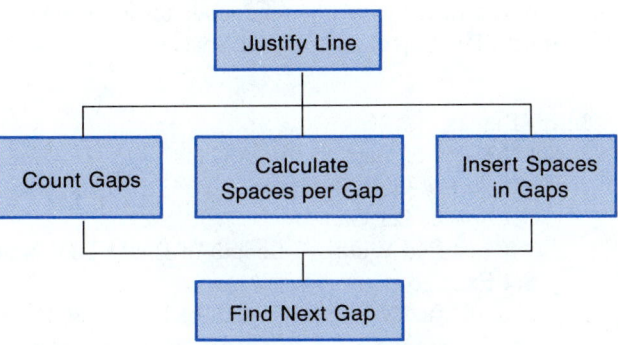

Figure 11.10
Structure Chart for Justify Line

As indicated on the structure chart, we want to have a function that finds the next gap. It will be used by two procedures: one to count gaps and another to insert spaces at each gap.

Refine the Solution The procedures for setting minimum width and justified width will be exported from the Justify definition module. Variables Minimum Width and Justified Width will be set by those procedures. These variables will be hidden from the user in the implementation module.

Justify Line does a check of the length of the line before calling Insert Spaces to do "all of the hard work." A pseudocode version of our solution is

```
Justify Line
    If length of line < Justified Width and
        length of line >= Minimum Width then
        Insert Spaces
    End if
End Justify Line
```

Before we can write the pseudocode for Insert Spaces, we must develop a technique for inserting the spaces throughout the line. Let's consider a specific example:

    The quick brown fox jumped over the lazy dog's back.

This line has 52 characters (assuming it ends at the period) and 9 gaps. If the line is to be justified to 65 characters, we must insert 13 spaces into these 9 gaps. If we insert 1 space at each gap, we have 4 spaces left to distribute. For the first 4 gaps, we will add an extra space. So, for the first 4 gaps, we add 2 spaces; then for the last 5 gaps, we add 1 space, giving a total of 13 spaces. Arithmetically, the necessary formulas are

- The integer quotient of (Justified Width − Length of Line) divided by the number of gaps is the number of spaces to add to every gap.
- The integer remainder of (Justified Width − Length of Line) divided by the number of gaps is the number of gaps that must have one additional space added.

We can now proceed to write pseudocode for inserting blanks, using the temporary variables Spaces Per Gap and String Of Spaces.

```
Insert Blanks
    Set Number of Gaps to Count Gaps
    If Number of Gaps > 0 then
        Set Spaces Per Gap to
            ( Justified Width − Length of Line ) DIV Number of Gaps
        Set Extra to
            ( Justified Width − Length of Line ) MOD Number of Gaps
        Set String Of Spaces to Spaces Per Gap + 1 spaces
        For each gap from 1 to Extra
            Find Next Gap
            Insert String Of Spaces
        End For
        Delete one space from String Of Spaces
        For each gap from Extra + 1 to Number of Gaps
            Find Next Gap
            Insert String Of Spaces
        End For
    End If
End Insert Blanks
```

The following pseudocode is for a procedure to count the total number of gaps:

```
Count Gaps
    Set Count to 0
    Loop
        Exit if Find Next Gap returns end of line indication
        Increment count
```

```
        End Loop
        Return Count
End Count Gaps
```

Finally, we need to develop a procedure to find the next gap. The next gap will be indicated by the first blank character following the next sequence of nonblank characters.

```
Find Next Gap
    Skip all leading blanks starting at current position
    If not at end of line then
        Skip all contiguous nonblank characters
            until space is found or line ends
    End if
    Return Position of space or end of line indication
End Find Next Gap
```

This pseudocode completes the algorithm development for the Justify module. Now we must develop an algorithm for our test program. The user will initially use the default minimum and justified width. The program will give instructions to the user and prompt for line input using a ">" prompt. When input is entered, the program will print the justified line. Input will continue until an empty line is entered to indicate the end of program execution. The same process will be repeated after asking the user to give new values to minimum and justified width. Our pseudocode follows.

```
Test Justify
    Print instructions for user
    Loop {test with default values for widths}
        Read line of text
        Exit if line is empty
        Justify the line
        Print the line
    End Loop
    Set Minimum Width
    Set Justified Width
    Loop {test with new values for widths}
        Read line of text
        Exit if line is empty
        Justify the line
        Print the line
    End Loop
End Test Justify
```

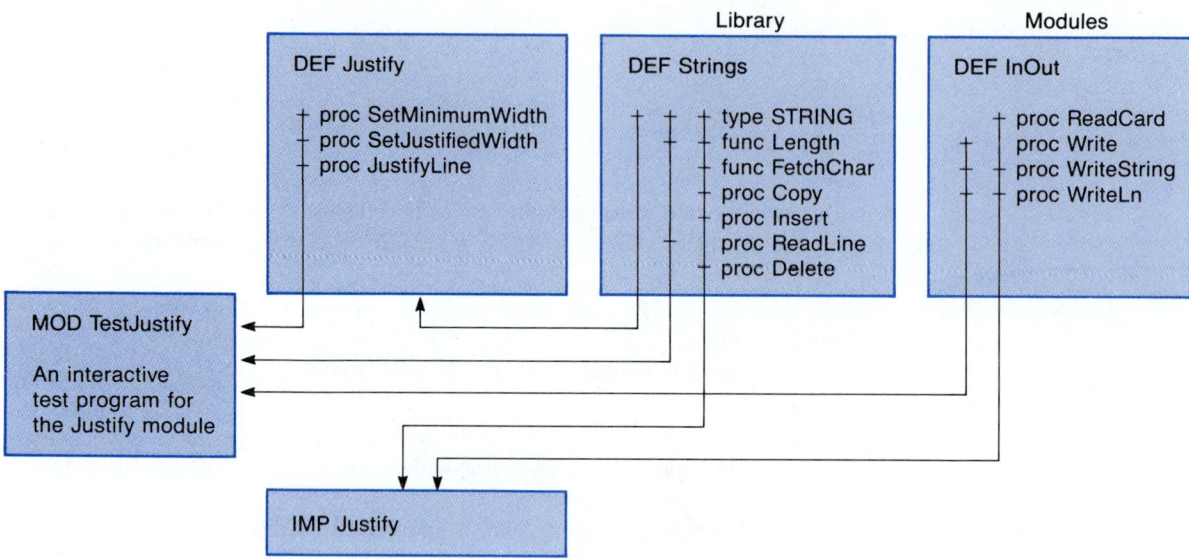

Figure 11.11   Final Modular Design Chart for Justification

We now have enough details to complete our modular design chart. The test program will use InOut. We will need Write to print the ">" prompt, WriteString to print other prompt messages and the instructions to the user, and WriteLn to advance to a new line. The test program will also need to import from the Strings module the STRING type (for variables that hold a line of text), the Length function (to check if the line is empty), and the ReadLine procedure (to input the line).

The definition module for Justify will have to import STRING since the parameter for the JustifyLine procedure will be of this type. The implementation module for Justify will have to import:

- the STRING type
- the Length function to find the original line length
- FetchChar to search a string for blank or nonblank characters
- Copy to form a string of blanks of the appropriate length
- Insert to put the string of blanks into the given line
- Delete to delete the extra space if necessary
- ReadCard and WriteString to input the widths

Figure 11.11 shows our completed modular design chart.

At this point the definition module for Justify can be compiled. The definition module based on our detailed design is as follows:

```
DEFINITION MODULE Justify;
(* Justification of lines of text.
            B. L. Kurtz   January 1988 *)
```

```
FROM Strings IMPORT STRING;
(* Strings are character sequences up to a maximum of 80 characters *)

PROCEDURE SetJustifiedWidth;
(* Set justified width interactively *)

PROCEDURE SetMinimumWidth;
(* Set minimum width interactively *)

PROCEDURE JustifyLine( VAR Line: STRING );
(* If the line is of length >= minimum width and < justified width,
   this procedure inserts spaces into the string to make the length
   match the justified width.  The number of inserted spaces for each
   gap will differ by no more than one space. *)

END Justify.
```

Notice that comments have been added to the procedures to describe what operation they perform; this is very different from describing how the operation is actually accomplished. By choosing type CARDINAL for JustifiedWidth and MinimumWidth, we can be assured that these values are nonnegative.

Now a skeletal version of the main program, including all import lists, can be compiled to check the consistency of the interfaces of the design. If the compilation does not succeed, we know there is a mismatch in the interface between the main program and an external module or between two external modules. If that happens, we should correct the problem before proceeding.

Develop a Testing Strategy Our testing of the module Justify should include the following cases:

- empty text line
- line shorter than the minimum length (line should not be altered)
- line the same length as the minimum length (line should be justified, assuming justified length is greater than minimum length)
- several "typical cases" where line length is greater than minimum width and less than justified width (line should be justified)
- line with no embedded spaces (not altered, regardless of length)
- line the same length as justified width (line is not altered)
- line longer than the justified length (line not altered)
- justified length equal to minimum length (no input will be altered)
- justified length less than minimum length (no input will be altered)
- single nonblank character, followed by spaces, followed by another nonblank character (if line is justified, single characters should be at left and right margins)

Notice that there are no test cases on the validity of input to the test program (such as ensuring all widths are less than or equal to 80). These cases were omitted on purpose since our goal is to test the module Justify, not the test program itself.

The following output shows several of these cases:

```
>The quick brown fox jumped over the lazy dog's back.
The    quick    brown    fox    jumped    over    the    lazy    dog's    back.
>
Enter minimum width to be justified: 1
Enter justified width: 20
>12345678901234567890
12345678901234567890
>This is a test.
This    is    a    test.
>  Leading blanks.
   Leading       blanks.
>Trailing blanks.
Trailing    blanks.
>   Both
    Both
>NoGapsAtAll
NoGapsAtAll
>One Gap
One                 Gap
>Normal sentence?
Normal       sentence?
>123456789 1234567890
123456789 1234567890
>This sentence is longer than the justified width.
This sentence is longer than the justified width.
>Length is greater than 20.
Length is greater than 20.
>
```

Implementation

Code and Test the Program   The implementation module for Justify will include the declaration of the procedures SetJustifiedWidth, SetMinimumWidth, JustifyLine, as well as the procedure InsertSpaces and the procedures CountGaps and FindNextGap used by InsertSpaces.

```
IMPLEMENTATION MODULE Justify;
(* Justification of lines of text.
            B. L. Kurtz   January 1988 *)

FROM Strings IMPORT STRING, FetchChar, Length, Copy, Insert, Delete;
FROM InOut IMPORT WriteString, ReadCard, WriteLn;

VAR JustifiedWidth, (* should only be altered by SetJustifiedWidth *)
    MinimumWidth:  (* should only be altered by SetMinimumWidth *)
              CARDINAL;
```

```
PROCEDURE InsertSpaces(VAR Line: STRING);
(* Insert blanks into Line until it is justified at JustifiedWidth *)

CONST Spaces = "                                                           ";
VAR Count, SpacesPerGap, ExtraBlank, CurrPosition,
    NumberOfGaps: CARDINAL;
    StringOfSpaces: STRING;

  PROCEDURE FindNextGap(Str: STRING; VAR CurrPos: CARDINAL);
  (* After skipping leading spaces, scan through nonblank
     characters until the next space is encountered.  Return
     position of this space in CurrPos.  If no more spaces are
     found, set CurrPos to the length of the string to indicate
     the end of line has been reached. *)

  CONST Space = ' ';
  VAR Len: CARDINAL;

  BEGIN
    Len := Length(Str);
    WHILE (CurrPos < Len) AND (FetchChar(Str, CurrPos) = Space) DO
      INC(CurrPos);
    END; (* WHILE *)
    (* (CurrPos = Len) or (FetchChar(Str, CurrPos) # Space) *)
    IF CurrPos # Len THEN
      WHILE (CurrPos # Len) AND (FetchChar(Str, CurrPos) # Space) DO
        INC(CurrPos);
      END; (* WHILE *)
      (* (CurrPos = Len) or (FetchChar(Str, CurrPos) = Space) *)
    END; (* IF *)
  END FindNextGap;

  PROCEDURE CountGaps(Str: STRING): CARDINAL;
  (* Return the total number of gaps in string Str.  Any leading
     spaces are not counted as a gap, but trailing spaces count
     as a gap *)

  VAR Count, Scan: CARDINAL;

  BEGIN
    Count := 0;
    Scan := 0;
    LOOP
      FindNextGap(Str, Scan);
      IF Scan = Length(Str) THEN
        EXIT;
      ELSE
        INC(Count);
      END; (* IF *)
    END; (* LOOP *)
```

```
      RETURN Count;
   END CountGaps;


BEGIN (* InsertSpaces *)
   NumberOfGaps := CountGaps(Line);
   IF NumberOfGaps > 0 THEN
     CurrPosition := 0;
     SpacesPerGap := (JustifiedWidth - Length(Line)) DIV NumberOfGaps;
     ExtraBlank := (JustifiedWidth - Length(Line)) MOD NumberOfGaps;
     Copy(Spaces, 0, SpacesPerGap + 1, StringOfSpaces);
     FOR Count := 1 TO ExtraBlank DO
       FindNextGap(Line, CurrPosition);
       Insert(StringOfSpaces, Line, CurrPosition);
     END; (* FOR *)
     Delete(StringOfSpaces, 0, 1);
     FOR Count := ExtraBlank + 1 TO NumberOfGaps DO
       FindNextGap(Line, CurrPosition);
       Insert(StringOfSpaces, Line, CurrPosition);
     END; (* FOR *)
   END; (* IF *)
END InsertSpaces;


PROCEDURE JustifyLine(VAR Line: STRING);
(* For lines of length >= minimum width and < justified width,
   spaces are inserted at existing gaps until the line length
   matches the justified width *)

BEGIN
   IF (Length(Line) < JustifiedWidth) AND
      (Length(Line) >= MinimumWidth) THEN
     InsertSpaces(Line);
   END; (* IF *)
END JustifyLine;


PROCEDURE SetJustifiedWidth;
(* Set justified width interactively *)
BEGIN
   WriteString("Enter justified width: ");
   ReadCard(JustifiedWidth); WriteLn;
END SetJustifiedWidth;


PROCEDURE SetMinimumWidth;
(* Set minimum width interactively *)
BEGIN
   WriteString("Enter minimum width: ");
   ReadCard(MinimumWidth); WriteLn;
END SetMinimumWidth;
```

```
BEGIN   (* Set default values *)
  JustifiedWidth := 65;
  MinimumWidth := 50;
END Justify.
```

In the procedure InsertSpaces, notice that a constant string of all spaces is used by the Copy procedure to form the string of spaces to be inserted at each gap. An enclosing IF statement ensures the main body of the procedure will be executed only if there is at least one gap present. We initialize StringOfSpaces to the computed number of spaces to insert in the first ExtraBlank gaps, and the first FOR loop does the insertion in each gap. The Delete statement removes a space from StringOfSpaces, and the second FOR loop inserts the reduced StringOfSpaces in the remaining gaps. The Insert procedure relies on CurrPosition, the variable parameter for FindNextGap, for the correct position to insert the string of blanks. This loop continues until all gaps have spaces inserted. (Note that the insertion of zero spaces is perfectly reasonable in this algorithm.)

Procedure FindNextGap starts at the current position provided as a parameter and skips any leading spaces by using a WHILE loop. Notice that the WHILE loop continues only if *two* conditions are true: the current position is less than the length of the line *and* the character in that position is a space. Thus, the loop will terminate due to one of two conditions: the end of the string was reached, or a nonblank character was encountered. These conditions are documented in an assertional comment at the end of the loop. If the first condition, CurrPos = Len, is true, then no gap was found and no further action is necessary. Otherwise, another WHILE loop is used to scan through the succeeding characters looking for the next space, indicating the start of the next gap, or the end of the string. The termination condition for the the second WHILE loop has also been documented with an assertion at the end of the loop.

Procedure CountGaps is very simple. It repeatedly calls FindNextGap and increments Count, until FindNextGap reaches the end of the string. The value of Count is returned; note that it can be zero.

Procedures JustifyLine, SetJustifiedWidth, and SetMinimumWidth are all self-explanatory. The two instructions of module Justify will be executed when the module is imported and will give initial values to JustifiedWidth and MinimumWidth.

The Justify implementation module uses JustifiedWidth and MinimumWidth as global variables. Procedures SetJustifiedWidth, SetMinimumWidth, JustifyLine, and InsertSpaces access these global variables. This usage seems to violate the information hiding principle. However, the problem of providing the user with default values for JustifiedWidth and MinimumWidth, and also making it possible to modify these values, leads us to this solution. Because this choice is really a delicate matter of style, some observers may disagree with our approach. We find it acceptable, however, for the following reasons:

- Only two specialized procedures, SetJustifiedWidth and SetMinimumWidth, can change the values of the global variables.
- MinimumWidth and JustifiedWidth are actually pseudo-constants—that is, their values are set once for an application and are not supposed to change thereafter.
- The size of the module is very small, so checking for inappropriate modifications of the two variables is easy.

For the sake of completeness, we present the test program here. It should require no further explanation.

```
MODULE TestJustify;
(* Interactive test program for the Justify module.  The user
   enters lines for justification before and after setting the
   minimum width and the justified width. A blank line
   terminates the execution of each part.
                        B. L. Kurtz    January 1988 *)

FROM InOut IMPORT Write, WriteString, WriteLn;
FROM Strings IMPORT STRING, Length, ReadLine;
FROM Justify IMPORT SetMinimumWidth, SetJustifiedWidth,
                    JustifyLine;

CONST Echo = TRUE;
VAR Line: STRING;

PROCEDURE GiveInstructions;
BEGIN
  WriteString("This test program will justify individual lines of ");
  WriteLn;
  WriteString("text. Initially the minimum width to justify is 50, and ");
  WriteLn;
  WriteString("the justified width is 65. Any line shorter than the ");
  WriteLn;
  WriteString("minimum line length, will not be justified. Any line ");
  WriteLn;
  WriteString("initially longer than the justified width will not be ");
  WriteLn;
  WriteString("altered. Testing will be interactive. When you see the ");
  WriteLn;
  WriteString("> prompt, type in the unjustified line. The program will");
  WriteLn;
  WriteString(" print the justified line below the entered line. Entry ");
  WriteLn;
  WriteString("of a blank line will terminate the first part of the ");
  WriteLn;
  WriteString("program. The second part of the program will ask you to ");
  WriteLn;
  WriteString("specify the minimum length and the justified length, and");
  WriteLn;
  WriteString("will then operate as the first part did."); WriteLn;
END GiveInstructions;

BEGIN (* TestJustify *)
  GiveInstructions; WriteLn;
  LOOP   (* Test with default values *)
    WriteLn; Write('>'); ReadLine(Line, Echo);
    IF Length(Line) = 0 THEN EXIT END;
```

```
      JustifyLine(Line);
      WriteString(Line); WriteLn;
   END; (* LOOP *)
   SetMinimumWidth;
   SetJustifiedWidth;
   LOOP   (* Test with new values *)
      WriteLn; Write('>'); ReadLine(Line, Echo);
      IF Length(Line) = 0 THEN EXIT END;
      JustifyLine(Line);
      WriteString(Line); WriteLn;
   END; (* LOOP *)
END TestJustify.
```

Complete the Documentation   In previous chapters we have discussed two types of documentation: user documentation and maintenance documentation. The user documentation for an external module is sometimes called *module documentation*. This documentation is intended for Modula-2 programmers who are considering use of a module developed by somebody else. They need not have any knowledge of the implementation module. As a minimum, though, they should have access to the information in the definition module. But they should not have access to the file containing the definition module, since any changes in the definition module can have disastrous effects. Many Modula-2 implementations keep track of version numbers, and even recompiling the definition module without any changes would require all modules importing from this module to be recompiled! In some cases, a well-commented definition module may provide sufficient module documentation, but often additional information should be provided.

Module documentation should include information on the use of the program and also on the problem-solving method, if that will help the user understand how to apply the program. For example, in this case study, more details should be given about the justification technique itself, as illustrated by the following comment, which should be added as the preface to the definition module.

```
(*  Strings    greater   than    or   equal    to   the
    minimum  width   and   less   than   the justified width
    will   be  increased   to   the   justified width by the
    insertion  of   spaces   into   any   gaps between words
    (or   any   other   sequence   of   nonblank characters).
    An   initial   sequence   of   spaces in the string will
    not   be   counted   as a gap, and no additional spaces
    will   be   added   (so paragraph indentations will not
    be   altered).   Any  trailing spaces in the line will
    be   counted   as   a   gap;  in this case the last non-
    blank   character   will   not   be printed at the right
    margin.   Otherwise,   spaces   are inserted uniformly
    into   the  gaps.   Specifically, the number of spaces
    inserted   into   each   gap will differ by at most one
    space   with   the   larger  insertions being at the left
    of   the   line   and   the   shorter  insertions at the
    right of the line.
```

Assume that the minimum width is 1 and the justified width is 20. In the following examples, strings are shown in quotes so that leading and trailing spaces are obvious.

```
            INPUT                          OUTPUT
"12345678901234567890"          "12345678901234567890"
"This is a test."               "This    is   a   test."
"  Leading blanks."             "  Leading      blanks."
"Trailing blanks.   "           "Trailing   blanks.    "
"   Both   "                    "   Both                "
"NoGapsAtAll"                   "NoGapsAtAll"
"One Gap"                       "One                Gap"
"Length is greater than 20."    "Length is greater than 20."
                                                             *)
```

Note that the test program TestJustify was not designed for the user and, therefore, does not need extensive documentation.

In contrast to module documentation, maintenance documentation is written for the programmer who will be responsible for ensuring program maintenance: removing bugs when they are discovered, improving efficiency, adapting to new systems, and adding enhancements.

Sometimes maintenance is needed because a program produces unexpected results for unusual cases. For example, the Justify module does not consider leading blanks in a line to be a gap and does not attempt to insert additional spaces. In most applications, such as indenting for a paragraph, this would be the desired operation. However, if a string has trailing blanks, these are counted as a gap and will possibly be enlarged by the insertion of more spaces. This result might be unexpected for many users, who would expect trailing blanks to be automatically removed before justification is attempted. If this is the case for most users, a maintenance change would be appropriate.

Maintenance also involves enhancements to a program or module. The Justify module always adds the additional spaces to the gaps on the left side of the line. When many lines are printed sequentially, all with slightly larger gaps on the left side, the appearance of a complete text passage can appear uneven. If the module user could specify whether the extra spaces were to be added from the left side or the right side, an entire passage would look more balanced when this decision was switched on alternate lines.

For the module Justify, the maintenance documentation should include the structure chart, modular design chart, source code, and test results.

SUMMARY

In the 1960s and 1970s program designers, using the high-level programming languages that were then available, were not always able to create large software projects that would be reliable. Features in these languages allowed designers to commit errors that would later lead to software failures. Subsequently, in the late 1970s, languages such as Modula-2 and Ada were developed with features that supported good software engineering principles, such as information hiding and abstract data types.

Modules are one of these features. In Modula-2 the main program is itself a module, and it often imports objects from library modules. In addition the program designer can create external modules that offer another level of abstraction and information hiding. An import list names the objects to be obtained from other modules.

An external module has two parts: a definition module and an implementation module. The definition module contains the declarations of objects to be exported. The objects include constants, types, variables, and procedures. The implementation module contains all the objects that do not need to be visible to importing modules. Hiding such information in implementation modules allows us to make changes in part of a program without worrying about adverse effects on other parts of the program.

Modular design charts help us to visualize the interconnections between modules. Cohesion is a measure of a module's single-mindedness. Coupling, another measure, tells us the degree of interconnection between modules in a software package. For instance, a software bus that has become too complex indicates that the modules may be too highly coupled. Good program design aims to maximize cohesion and minimize coupling.

One important advantage of using external modules is that definition and implementation parts can be compiled separately. This separate compilation allows a programmer to change the actual implementation without changing the definition module.

Main program modules, or any other modules, can contain nested internal modules, called local modules. These structures offer a way to control access to data and procedures from other parts of the same program. Although they are nested like procedures, local modules have barriers around them so that only items explicitly named can be brought in or out. Local modules also retain variable values even when the module has been exited. Local modules are useful for preventing unintentional changes to part of a program.

EXERCISES

1. In the United States, dates are written in the following format:

    March 24, 1987

    In Europe, dates are given in a different form:

    24 March 1987

    Write a procedure to convert dates from the European format to the American format. Assume there is exactly one blank between adjoining fields.

2. How would the implementation module for Justify in Section 11.7 be modified so that trailing blanks are removed? This should be done before the check on line length and before justification.

3. Alter the JustifyLine procedure in Section 11.7 to add a second parameter of type Boolean. A TRUE value would indicate insertion of extra spaces from the left; a FALSE value would indicate insertion from the right.

4. Design a procedure to justify a paragraph of text to some position specified as the right margin. Short lines should be expanded and long lines "wrapped around" to another line.

5. Write a definition module to define the abstract data type Numeral. The values are sequences of character digits, '0' to '9', and the operations are add, subtract, multiply, and (integer) divide.

6. Write the implementation module for the numeral operations add and subtract suggested in Exercise 5.

PROGRAMMING PROBLEMS

7. Implement and test the changes to Justify suggested in Exercises 2 and 3.

8. Implement and test the procedure to justify a paragraph, described in Exercise 4.

9. Implement and test the numeral operations add and subtract suggested in Exercises 5 and 6.

10. Redo the PasswordSystem in Section 11.6 as an external module.

11. Extend the PasswordSystem in Problem 10 to support changing of a password, but only by a valid user with that password.

12. Write a Boolean function to determine if a given vector is ordered.

13. Write a procedure to add a new element to an ordered vector; the procedure should include a nested procedure to search the vector sequentially. Note that the vector can be partially filled, and that insertion could cause overflow of the vector.

14. Write a procedure to produce the median value of an ordered vector of integers. The median value is the middle element if the vector is ordered and has an odd number of elements; it is the arithmetic mean of the two middle elements if the vector has an even number of elements.

15. Combine the procedures from Problems 12, 13, and 14 in a module to implement vectors as a simple abstract data type.

12 Arrays of Records, Searching, and Sets

In this chapter you will:

- learn more about records and arrays of records
- find out about linear searching of unordered data and binary searching of ordered data
- be introduced to informal analysis of complexity of algorithms
- become familiar with sets and set operations

In Chapter 6, we learned about records, a structured data type for storing values of different types. Subsequently, in Chapter 9, we discussed arrays, a structured data type for storing values of the same type, and mentioned how the two data structures could be combined into arrays of records. In this chapter we will take a closer look at and make use of arrays of records and discuss some additional features of the record data structure.

One of the most important uses for the array of records data structure is the representation of sequences of data records containing information about a person or an object. In addition to descriptive information about the person or object, each record contains a field with a value, usually called a key, that uniquely identifies the record. For example, the record for each student in a university registration system might use the student's social security number as a key. This structure makes it possible to locate a student's record by searching for the key. We will examine some elementary algorithms for searching both unordered and ordered arrays of data. Our discussion here will include an informal analysis of the efficiency of these algorithms.

We will also investigate the set data type, which models the concept of sets used in mathematics. The set data type facilitates input data validation. Finally, a case study demonstrates the use of arrays of records, search techniques, and the set data type.

12.1 Arrays of Records

Let's start by reviewing the characteristics of the structured types array and record. An array is a sequence of components of uniform type, and individual components are selected by an index. This selection is done at run time when the index is evaluated. A record is a collection of components that may be of different types. Components of a record are selected by a field name within the record, and so the selection is determined at compile time. These characteristics are summarized in Table 12.1.

Consequently, an array is used when we have a sequence of objects of the same type, whereas a record is used when we have a collection of objects of different types. When we want to represent a sequence of items where each item is a collection of objects of varying types, we use both structures, creating an array of records.

For instance, an array of records would be an appropriate data structure for storing and processing information about a business's customers. The following declaration uses the record structure introduced in Chapter 6 in the declaration of the data type Clients, which is an array of records data structure.

```
CONST MaxClient = 1000;

TYPE Date = RECORD
              Month: [1..12];
              Day: [1..31];
              Year: [1930..2030];
            END;
     Sale = RECORD
              When: Date;
              Amount: INTEGER;
            END;
     PostalAddress = RECORD
                       StNumber: CARDINAL;
                       Street, City, State: STRING;
                       Zip: STRING;
                     END;
     Client = RECORD
                Number: CARDINAL;
                Name: STRING;
                Address: PostalAddress;
                Balance: INTEGER;
                Transaction: Sale;
              END;
     ClientIndex = [1..MaxClient];
     Clients = ARRAY ClientIndex OF Client;

VAR Customers: Clients;
```

SEC. 12.1   Arrays of Records

TABLE 12.1   **Arrays and Records**

	Component Types	Component Selection	Time of Selection
Arrays	Are all identical	By index expression	At run time
Records	May be different	By fixed field name	At compilation time

The variable Customers is of type Clients, and thus is an array of records. A specific record of the Customers array is selected by an index. For example, Customers[8] is the eighth element of Customers and is a record of type Client. To access the Balance component of this customer, we write

$$\text{Customers[8].Balance}$$

Let's write a procedure to update interest charges on our customers' records. At the end of a month this update calls for an immediate increase of some specified percentage for all customers having a positive balance. The procedure can be defined as follows:

```
PROCEDURE InterestCharge( VAR List: Clients; PerCent: INTEGER );
(* Increase all positive balances by a given percentage.
   The percentage should be an integer with a scale factor of 1/1000:
   e.g., 18 would represent 1.8%.
                P. Gabrini    January 1988    *)

VAR I: CARDINAL;
BEGIN
  FOR I := 1 TO MaxClient DO
    IF List[I].Balance > 0 THEN
      List[I].Balance := List[I].Balance +
                 ( List[I].Balance * PerCent ) DIV 1000;
    END; (* IF *)
  END; (* FOR *)
END InterestCharge;
```

This procedure considers the customers in List sequentially and, for each positive balance, updates the balance. Note that the division by 1000 is necessary to adjust for the scale factor of 1/1000 used for percentages. Fractions of cents are lost by this division, and it would be desirable to round before dividing. We will leave this improvement as an exercise. Also note that the assignment statement could be made a bit more efficient by factoring the expression on the right, as follows:

```
List[I].Balance := List[I].Balance * ( 1000 + PerCent ) DIV 1000;
```

12.2 Abbreviation of Field Selectors with the WITH Statement

Since much of this chapter discusses working with records, we might just take note here of a statement that helps us shorten references to the fields of records.

Often it is tedious to write a sequence of field selectors. For example, if X is of type Client as defined in the previous section, we might give values to the various fields as follows:

```
X.Number  := 43227;
X.Name    := "Don Segundo";
X.Address.StNumber := 343;
X.Address.Street := "Sombra Street    ";
X.Address.City := "San Andres   ";
X.Address.State := "New Mexico       ";
X.Address.Zip := "88008";
X.Balance := 12500;
X.Transaction.When.Month := 11;
X.Transaction.When.Day := 23;
X.Transaction.When.Year := 1987;
X.Transaction.Amount := 4850;
```

The WITH statement enables us to abbreviate the notation by specifying the record name only once and then using the field identifiers to select the components. The syntax of the WITH statement has the form

```
WITH record-variable DO
    statements
END;
```

The statements between the DO and END are within the scope of the WITH since the record-variable may apply to identifiers in any of the statements. For instance, we could write

```
WITH X DO
  Number := 43227;
  Name := "Don Segundo";
  Balance := 12500;
END; (* WITH *)
```

in order to assign values to the fields Number, Name, and Balance of a variable X of type Client as defined previously.

WITH statements can also be nested; this is useful when components of a record are records themselves. Statements to assign values to all fields of X can be written as

```
WITH X DO
  WITH Address DO
    WITH Transaction DO
      WITH When DO
        Number := 43227;
        Name   := "Don Segundo";
```

```
                StNumber := 343;
                Street   := "Sombra Street     ";
                City     := "San Andres    ";
                State    := "New Mexico        ";
                Zip      := 88008;
                Balance  := 12500;
                Month    := 11;
                Day      := 23;
                Year     := 1987;
                Amount   := 4850;
              END; (* WITH *)
            END; (* WITH *)
          END; (* WITH *)
       END; (* WITH *)
```

From the declaration of X, the compiler can determine that the first WITH applies to all the assignment statements, the second WITH to the third through the seventh statements, the third WITH to the last four statements, and the fourth WITH to the ninth through the eleventh statements. Compare this form with the previous longer form to see that they are equivalent.

Exercise care when using WITH, especially when using subscripts, because the record-variable between WITH and DO cannot be modified inside the scope of the WITH. For example, if you want to examine all the customer records and count the number of delinquent and paid up customers, you can write

```
         FOR I := 1 TO MaxClient DO
           WITH Customers[I] DO
             IF Balance = 0 THEN
               INC( Paidup );
             ELSE
               INC( Delinquent );
             END; (* IF *)
           END; (* WITH *)
         END; (* FOR *)
```

but this code segment cannot be written with the FOR and WITH statements reversed

```
         WITH Customers[I] DO
           FOR I := 1 TO MaxClient DO
             IF Balance = 0 THEN
               INC( Paidup );
             ELSE
               INC( Delinquent );
             END; (* IF *)
           END; (* FOR *)
         END; (* WITH *)
```

The WITH statement fixes Customer[I] to the record corresponding to the current value of I; changing the value of I later inside the range of the WITH will not change that record, and the loop will deal only with a single record.

12.3 Variant Records

As we have seen, the record type allows us to group several related pieces of data of different types into a single composite object. In some applications, though, we may want to have variations within the components of a composite object but still consider these composite objects to be of the same type. Let's consider an example that illustrates this idea. A company may keep all its information on employees in a personnel file. Typically, employee records contain an identification part (first name, family name), an address, an indication of sex, a social security number, a salary, a family status, and a birthdate. Such a record could be defined as

```
Employee = RECORD
            Identification: RECORD
                              FirstName, Name: STRING;
                            END;
            Address: PostalAddress;
            Sex: ( Male, Female );
            SSN: ARRAY[1..11] OF CHAR;
            Salary: CARDINAL;
            Status: ( Married, Widowed, Divorced, Single );
            Birth: Date;
          END;
```

This organization may not be sufficient for a large company, where some employees are paid hourly, other employees are paid monthly, and a few upper-management personnel are paid annually. Obviously, salary information for these three categories will be different. Likewise, depending on the family status, it might be necessary to keep the spouse's name. To be able to use those variations and keep only one definition for the employee type, we can use records with *variant parts,* or *variant records.* The employee record type can be redefined with two variant parts in the following manner.

```
TYPE Classification = ( Hourly, Monthly, Annually );
     Marital = ( Married, Widowed, Divorced, Single );
     Employee = RECORD
                 Identification: RECORD
                                   FirstName, Name: STRING;
                                 END;
                 Address: PostalAddress;
                 Sex: ( Male, Female );
                 SSN: ARRAY[1..11] OF CHAR;
                 CASE Category: Classification OF
                   Hourly: HourlyRate, OvertimeRate: CARDINAL|
                   Monthly: MonthlySalary: CARDINAL;
                            BonusStatus: BOOLEAN|
                   Annually: AnnualSalary: CARDINAL
                 END;
```

```
            CASE Status: Marital OF
               Married: Spouse: STRING
               ELSE (* empty *)
            END;
         Birth: Date;
      END;
```

A variant record is introduced by a CASE clause followed by the variant parts, which are identified by a given label and include definitions of fields. An ELSE clause can also be used. Although the syntax is similar to a case statement, this is the declaration of a type, rather than the specification of an executable statement. Following the reserved word CASE, there may be an identifier and a type indication; this identifier defines a special field of the record called a *tag field*. The value of this tag field in a given record indicates what variant part is present. Category and Status are the tag fields of the two variant parts in the preceding example. Thus, if we have declared a variable as

```
         VAR E1: Employee;
```

then the designator E1.Spouse is applicable only if E1.Status = Married. For example, we might have the following statement in our program:

```
         IF E1.Status = Married THEN
            WriteString( E1.Spouse );
         END; (* IF *)
```

The tag field can be used to avoid referring to nonexistent fields, resulting in run time errors.

Figure 12.1 illustrates examples of variants of employee records. This figure is for illustrative purposes only; actual space allocation for variant records is implementation dependent.

In Chapter 6, the syntax of the record structure was given as:

```
         RECORD
            field-identifier list: type;
            field-identifier list: type;
                     .
                     .
                     .
         END;
```

Now that we have learned about variant records, we must expand this syntax to:

```
         RECORD
            field-list { ; field-list }
         END;
```

Figure 12.1
Examples of Variant Records

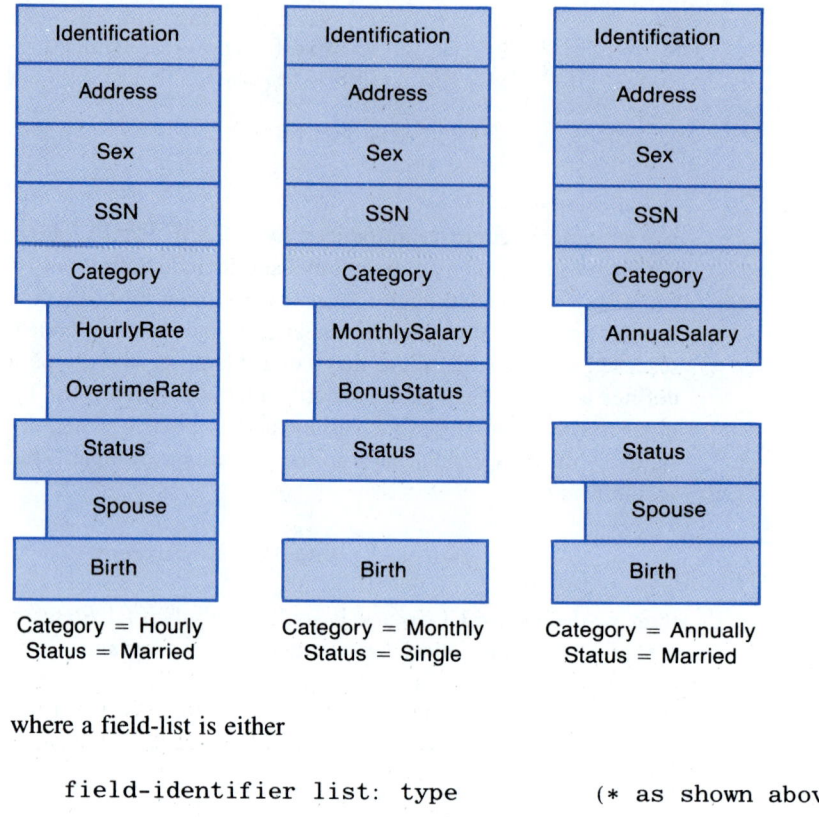

where a field-list is either

```
field-identifier list: type        (* as shown above *)
```

or

```
CASE [tag-field-name] : tag-field-type OF
  variant { | variant }
[ELSE
  field-list { ; field-list }]
END;
```

where the variant is

```
list of case labels : field-list { ; field-list }
```

Our example has illustrated most of the possible varieties for this structure. First we have seen a mixture of fields that are either non-variant (they will be present in all versions of the record) or variant (with the variant being selected by the case label). The field list for the variant can either contain a single item, as with the case label Annually, multiple items of the same type, as with the case label Hourly, or multiple items of different types, as with the case label Monthly. A variant part of a record can also have an optional ELSE part, as illustrated by the variant for Marital. Finally, it should be mentioned that the tag-field-name is optional, although we highly recommend that it always be included as part of the variant record.

12.4 Searching

Arrays are one of the most useful data structures, because they give us a natural way to represent lists of objects. Many applications involve lists of one sort or another, such as lists of names, addresses, books, countries, and so on. One of the most common operations on lists is searching for an object. For example, we might want to search to see if a given book is in the list of library holdings, or search to see if a given item is in an inventory list.

This section first describes a straightforward searching technique that works for either unordered or ordered data. Then the discussion turns to a more efficient algorithm for searching ordered data.

Linear Search

In a *linear search* of unordered data we examine objects sequentially until we either find the desired object or we have looked at all objects and have failed to find the desired object. Our example here develops a simple algorithm, similar to one used in Chapter 11, to search an array of objects for a particular object. We will assume that the objects are records and that each record contains one or more fields, including a key field. During searching the key field is compared to the desired key value. We will also assume each key value is unique so that a search for a specific key either results in finding a single record with that key or not finding any record with that key. This situation is very common in many applications. For example, in a payroll program employees may be assigned a unique employee number because names may not be unique. Our search will proceed iteratively from the smallest to the largest index of the array. At the beginning of each iteration we will know that the object of our search does not lie in the portion of the list examined so far.

```
Linear Search ( SearchKey, Index )
    Set Index to smallest index
    While ( Index # largest index + 1 ) And
          ( Object.Key at position Index # SearchKey ) do
        {SearchKey is not at positions smallest index . . . Index}
        Increment Index
    End While
    {Index = largest index + 1 or Object.Key at position Index = SearchKey}
End LinearSearch
```

The pseudocode includes two comments in braces, which are assertions about what is true at that point in the program. The assertion at the start of the iteration is a loop invariant illustrated in Figure 12.2.

The assertion at the end of the algorithm is sometimes called an output assertion because it documents the final result. The output assertion is illustrated in Figure 12.3.

The coding of this algorithm is very direct and results in a procedure that is passed an open array to be searched and the search key. The procedure returns an index,

Figure 12.2
Illustration of the
Loop Invariant for
Linear Search

Figure 12.3
Illustration of the
Output Assertion for
Linear Search

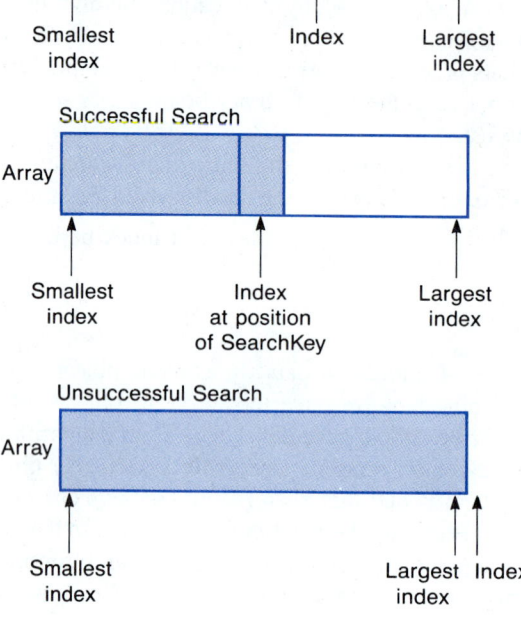

indicating success if it is in the range of array indices and failure if it is equal to the largest open array index + 1.

```
TYPE KeyType = . . .  (* some type that can be tested for equality *)
     Info = RECORD
              Key: KeyType;
              .
              .
              .
           END;
              .
              .
              .

PROCEDURE LinearSearch (Arr: ARRAY OF Info; SearchKey: KeyType;
                        VAR Index: CARDINAL);
(* It is assumed that Info is a record that contains a field
   called Key of type KeyType.  If a record is found with a key
   that matches SearchKey, then Index is set to the open array
   index of that record.  This value can be converted to the
   original index by using the VAL function after the procedure
   call.  Otherwise Index is set to the highest open array
   index plus one.
                B. L. Kurtz          January 1988           *)
```

SEC. 12.4 Searching

```
    VAR Last: CARDINAL;
    BEGIN
      Index := 0;
      Last := HIGH[Arr];
      WHILE (Index # Last + 1) AND (Arr[Index].Key # SearchKey) DO
         (* SearchKey does not equal Arr[0].Key .. Arr[Index].Key *)
        INC(Index);
      END; (* WHILE *)
      (* Index = High(Arr) + 1 or Arr[Index].Key = SearchKey *)
    END LinearSearch;
```

Note that the WHILE loop can increment Index beyond the end of the array Arr, to Last + 1. However, because of the left-to-right evaluation of Boolean expressions, the first subexpression (Index # Last + 1) will evaluate to FALSE and stop the loop, and the second subexpression (Arr[Index].Key # SearchKey) will not be evaluated (its evaluation is unnecessary, the first part of the AND being FALSE), thus avoiding an index out of range error.

Notice also that the index of the open array parameter Arr is returned by the procedure to indicate the position at which the key was found. This is because the index type of the actual array is hidden from the search procedure. The program that calls the procedure can use this cardinal index to determine if the search was successful. If the index is less than the size of the input array, the search was successful and the index of the matching element can be obtained by applying the standard function VAL. LinearSearch is thus very general, because it can search arrays of records where the index type is any subrange or enumeration type, as shown in the following program skeleton:

```
    CONST NumberofDays = 7;

    TYPE Days = ( Monday, Tuesday, Wednesday,
                  Thursday, Friday, Saturday, Sunday );
         Info = RECORD
                  Key: CARDINAL;
                    .
                    .
                    .
                END;
         ArrayOfData = ARRAY Days OF Info;

    VAR  Data: ArrayOfData;
         When: Days;
         Index: CARDINAL;
           .    .
            .  .
             ..

         BEGIN
            .
            .
            .
```

```
LinearSearch( Data, 24, Index );
IF Index < NumberofDays THEN
   When := VAL( Days, Index );
   (* handle successful search *)
ELSE
   (* handle unsuccessful search *)
END; (* IF *)
   .
   .
   .
```

A variation of our linear search could have an additional variable parameter of type BOOLEAN to indicate directly the success or failure of the search. We will leave this variation as an exercise (see Exercise 4).

Because searching is done so frequently, we must be concerned about the efficiency of our methods. We can measure a search method's efficiency by the expected number of comparisons needed to find, or not find, an object in the array. This number is usually a function of the length of the array, which we will denote by n. On the average, using our linear search, we can expect to find an object in the array after searching halfway through the array. In other words, the expected number of comparisons for a successful search is $n/2$, assuming that it is equally likely that a search will be made for any of the elements. Obviously, an unsuccessful search will require n comparisons.

Binary Search

To develop an even more efficient technique for ordered arrays, We can simulate a method we all use quite frequently. When we look up a name in the phone book, we don't make a linear search through all the names until we find the one we want or until we've reached the last name. Because the names are organized in alphabetical order, we can find the desired name much more quickly. Our general strategy is to guess at an approximate location, compare the name there with the one for which we are searching to see if we need to go forward or backward, and then to guess at another location in the appropriate direction. We may use a linear search once we have the location narrowed down to a few names.

A binary search works in a similar way. We choose the middle element of the list and compare the value for which we're searching with that element. If they are equal, we've made a very lucky first guess! Otherwise, if the middle element is greater than the desired value, we look in the first half of the data; if the middle element is less than the desired value, we look in the second half. We then choose the middle element for the half that remains and repeat the process. This method is called a *binary search* because at each step, called a *probe,* we either find the item or can eliminate half the remaining items to be searched. The strategy is illustrated in Figure 12.4.

Let's use some actual data to illustrate this process. Assume we have a phone book with ten entries, illustrated in Figure 12.5.

Figure 12.4
Binary Search
Strategy

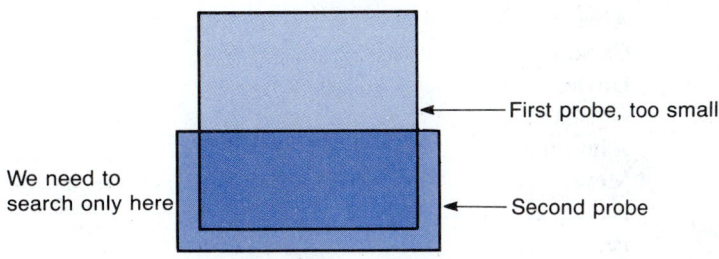

Figure 12.5
A Miniature Phone
Book

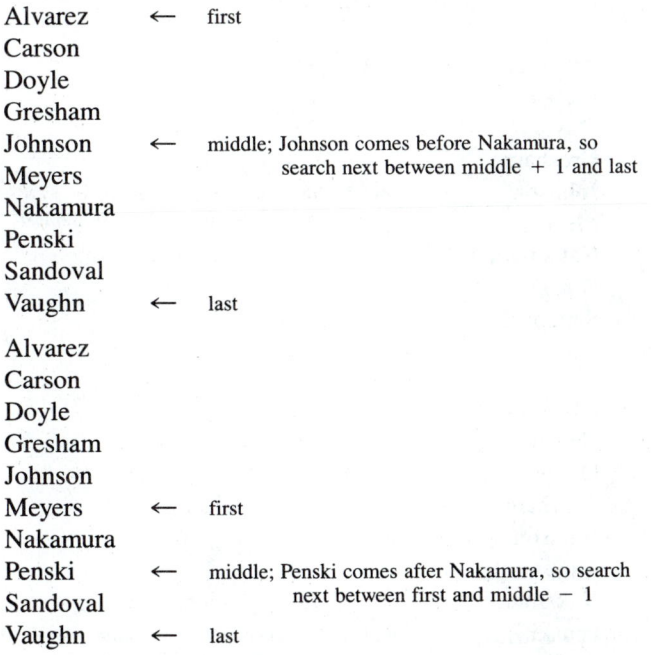

Suppose we are searching for Nakamura. Our indices range from 1 to 10, so we will start by probing the "middle" entry, which is the fifth entry, found by calculating (1 + 10) DIV 2.

```
Alvarez       ← first
Carson
Doyle
Gresham
Johnson       ← middle; Johnson comes before Nakamura, so
Meyers             search next between middle + 1 and last
Nakamura
Penski
Sandoval
Vaughn        ← last

Alvarez
Carson
Doyle
Gresham
Johnson
Meyers        ← first
Nakamura
Penski        ← middle; Penski comes after Nakamura, so search
Sandoval           next between first and middle − 1
Vaughn        ← last
```

Alvarez
Carson
Doyle
Gresham
Johnson
Meyers   ←   first and middle; Meyers comes before Nakamura, so
Nakamura   ←   last   search next between middle + 1 and last
Penski
Sandoval
Vaughn

Alvarez
Carson
Doyle
Gresham
Johnson
Meyers
Nakamura   ←   first, middle, and last; name is located
Penski
Sandoval
Vaughn

This search took four probes to locate Nakamura; the process, therefore, is somewhat more efficient than a linear search, which would have taken seven probes. Let's now search for a name not in the phone book and see how our approach detects this absence. We will look for Smith.

Alvarez   ←   first
Carson
Doyle
Gresham
Johnson   ←   middle; Johnson comes before Smith, so search
Meyers   next between middle + 1 and last
Nakamura
Penski
Sandoval
Vaughn   ←   last

Alvarez
Carson
Doyle
Gresham
Johnson
Meyers   ←   first
Nakamura
Penski   ←   middle; Penski comes before Smith, so search
Sandoval   next between middle + 1 and last
Vaughn   ←   last

Alvarez
Carson
Doyle
Gresham
Johnson
Meyers
Nakamura
Penski
Sandoval   ←   first and middle; Sandoval comes before Smith, so search next between
Vaughn   ←   last   middle + 1 and last

Alvarez
Carson
Doyle
Gresham
Johnson
Meyers
Nakamura
Penski
Sandoval
Vaughn   ←   first, middle, and last; not Smith, so search fails

This time the binary search took four probes before we could decide on failure; a linear search would have taken ten probes. With longer lists, the differences are even more substantial: If we use a binary search, a list of 100 elements would require at most seven probes, and a list of 1,000 elements would require at most ten probes.

Recursive Binary Search Since a binary search performs the *same* operations on smaller and smaller lists of data, it is recursive in nature. Furthermore, the process eventually gets to a base case where no recursion is necessary, because the list of possible values becomes smaller at each step.

For each invocation of the procedure, we will need to have the data, the first and last indices, and the name being sought. The pseudocode version of our binary search algorithm is as follows:

```
BinarySearch ( Data, First, Last, Name, Middle )
    Set Middle to (First + Last) div 2
    If First < Last then
        If Name precedes entry at Middle position then
            {Name not in second half}
            BinarySearch ( Data, First, Middle − 1, Name, Middle )
        Elsif Name comes after entry at Middle position then
            {Name not in first half}
            BinarySearch ( Data, Middle + 1, Last, Name, Middle )
        End if
    End if
End BinarySearch
```

Notice that the recursion can end in one of two ways,

1. Middle is the index of Name, or
2. First $>=$ Last.

As in linear search, the user of the algorithm must examine the element at position Middle to determine if the search succeeded or failed.

The test in the Elsif part of BinarySearch is really unnecessary. If it is omitted, one more iteration is required for each search. However, the test is avoided on each iteration, so there is an overall increase in efficiency.

An Analysis of the Efficiency of Binary Search Since each probe in a binary search eliminates half the data, the search is limited by the number of times we can divide the list in half. For a list of n items this number is about $\log_2 n$. To understand how we arrive at this result, let p be the number of probes for the worst case, such as searching for a value not in the data. A list of the approximate number of items remaining after each probe is as follows:

Probe	1	2	3	$\cdots$	p
Items remaining after probe	$\dfrac{n}{2}$	$\dfrac{n}{4}$	$\dfrac{n}{8}$	$\cdots$	$\dfrac{n}{2^p}$

When we reach an interval with one item remaining, we know we can stop searching. Thus we can say

$$\frac{n}{2^p} = 1 \quad \text{or simply } n = 2^p$$

Taking the log (base 2) of both sides of the equation, we have $\log_2 n = p$, the expected result.

Note that the number of items, n, does not have to be a power of 2: it was not in our example, where we had 10 elements. In such cases, $\log_2 n$ is not an integer, so the number of probes is the smallest integer greater than $\log_2 n$.

The number of probes, $\log_2 n$, is certainly better than the n probes required for an *unsuccessful* linear search. However, remember that a binary search works *only* on ordered data, while a linear search works on any data.

Iterative Binary Searches Using recursion for the binary search illustrates *tail recursion*. This means that the recursive call is the *last* statement to be executed in the procedure. Simple recursion of this form is usually slower than iteration, due to the time taken for the recursive procedure calls. Any algorithm using tail recursion can also easily be formulated iteratively, as the following pseudocode illustrates for binary search:

SEC. 12.4 Searching

```
Binary Search( Data, First, Last, Name, Middle )
    Set Middle to (First + Last) div 2
    While First < Last do
        {If Name is in the table, it must be between indices First and Last}
        If Name precedes entry at Middle position then
            {Name is not in the second half}
            Set Last to Middle − 1
        Elsif Name comes after entry at Middle position then
            {Name is not in the first half}
            Set First to Middle + 1
        Else {Name is at Middle position}
            Set First and Last to Middle
        End If
        Set Middle to (First + Last) div 2
    End While
    {First >= Last or Name is at Middle position}
End Binary Search
```

As usual, comments in braces have been included to indicate assertions about the algorithm. The loop invariant at the top of the loop indicates what is known to be true before each iteration. The loop invariant for this program can be illustrated pictorially as shown in Figure 12.6.

Figure 12.6
Illustration of the Loop Invariant for Binary Search

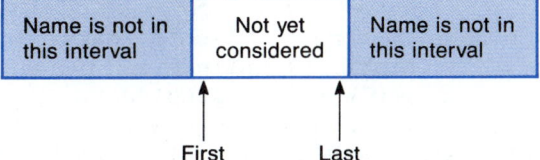

The output assertion at the end of the algorithm indicates what must be true when execution of the algorithm is completed. Note two characteristics of this search:

1. Testing for success or failure of the search must be done outside the algorithm.
2. Since the Middle probe always stays within the bounds of the array, an extra element need not be added (compare with the linear search).

The implementation of this iterative version of binary search is left as an exercise (see Programming Problem 15).

A Library Module Using Linear and Binary Search

Let's create a library module that uses both linear and binary search. Assume that a business has a small database of customer data. The actual data will be stored in an array of records as described by the type Clients given in Section 12.1. Suppose the database is always ordered by customer number, but the customer number is not the index to the array of clients. We must often look up a transaction for a given customer number (ordered data) or a given customer name (unordered data). For simplicity, we will assume that each customer has at most one transaction in the database. The search routines are to be implemented as a separate library module. A skeleton for the definition module is as follows:

```
DEFINITION MODULE SearchForCustomer;

CONST MaxClient = ...

TYPE Date = ...
     Sale = ...
     PostalAddress = ...
     NameType = ...
     Client = ...
     SearchIndex = [1..MaxClient + 1];
     ClientIndex = [1..MaxClient];
     Clients = ARRAY ClientIndex OF Client;

PROCEDURE FindClientNumber(Customers: Clients; Number: CARDINAL;
                           VAR Where: ClientIndex; VAR Found: BOOLEAN);
(* Binary search of Customers for the specified Number.  If located,
   Customers[Where].Number = Number and Found is true; if not
   found, no item in Customers had the specified Number, and
   Where is set to zero and Found to false.            *)

PROCEDURE FindClientName(Customers: Clients; Name: NameType;
                         Start: ClientIndex;
                         VAR Where: SearchIndex;
                         VAR Found: BOOLEAN);
(* Linear search of Customers beginning at start for the
   specified Name.  If located, its Index is returned in Where
   and Found is true; otherwise, Where is set to zero and Found
   to false.                       *)

END SearchForCustomer.
```

If you have an older implementation of Modula-2, you may have to add an export list to the definition module. Since the customer records are ordered by unique customer numbers, the implementation of FindClientNumber can use a binary search strategy. It is the user's responsibility to test for the success or failure of the search by testing the Boolean result of FindClientNumber.

FindClientName allows the user to specify a starting index for the search. Since customer names may not be unique, the first occurrence of a name may not be the desired one. By specifying a starting location beyond the last occurrence of the same name, the search can be continued for the remainder of the database. Completion of the definition and implementation modules is left as an exercise (see Programming Problem 17).

12.5 Sets

Arrays and records are important data types in Modula-2. We have now introduced most of the types in Modula-2. There remain three more types to introduce and discuss: set type, procedure type, and pointer type. We will introduce set type here and the latter two types in Chapters 14 and 15.

As we have already mentioned, simple data types, enumeration types, and subrange types are unstructured types. Their values are atomic, or not decomposable. Structured data types, on the other hand, have components. The set data type is a structured data type, and Modula-2 has one built-in set data type, BITSET. Other set types may be defined by the programmer.

In mathematics a *set* is a collection of objects; the order of the objects is immaterial, and the set size may be infinite. Modula-2 sets are similar, with the restriction that the objects of a set must be of the same type and that the size of sets is finite and implementation dependent.

The *set data type* allows us to perform the usual set operations of union, intersection, and set difference; it also enables us to determine quite easily whether a particular object belongs to a certain set.

SET Types

In Modula-2, a standard set type is predefined and called BITSET; it is predefined as

```
TYPE BITSET = SET OF [0..W - 1];
```

where W is the word length of the computer used—that is, the number of binary digits (bits) in a memory cell (usually 16 or 32). The values belonging to this type are sets of integers between 0 and W − 1. Constants of type BITSET are denoted in the usual mathematical notation, as in

{}	empty set
{2, 4, 6, 8}	a set of type BITSET with four integer elements
{4, 2, 8, 6}	the same set as above (the order of elements is not significant)

You may declare other set types in order to use sets of elements other than integers. However, the elements must be values of an enumeration or subrange base type.

To declare a set data type, we use the reserved words SET OF as in

```
TYPE set type = SET OF base type;
```

Set type is an identifier that you choose to name the type. Base type is a declaration of an enumeration or subrange type or an identifier of such a type that has been previously declared. Values of the set type are all possible sets of elements of the base type. For example, the largest set consists of all the elements of the base type and the smallest set has no members at all. Values of set type are denoted by lists of values from the base type enclosed in braces and preceded by the name of the set type. For example,

$$\texttt{LetterSet\{ 'A', 'E', 'I', 'O', 'U' \}}$$

is a set denoting the vowels, where we assume that a declaration, such as the following, has appeared previously:

$$\texttt{TYPE LetterSet = SET OF ['A'..'Z'];}$$

We can declare variables of set types in the usual way as in

$$\texttt{VAR Indices, LoopIndices, Unknowns: LetterSet;}$$

and assign values to the variables as follows:

$$\texttt{Indices := LetterSet\{ 'I', 'J', 'K', 'M', 'N' \};}$$
$$\texttt{LoopIndices := LetterSet\{ 'I', 'J', 'K' \};}$$

Also, we can define set constants as in

$$\texttt{CONST Vowels = LetterSet\{ 'A', 'E', 'I', 'O', 'U' \};}$$

Operations

Several operators can be used with sets; these operators include set operators and relational operators. When relational operators are used to compare sets, the base type of the sets to be compared must be compatible. The set relational operators are shown in Table 12.2.

In a membership test such as "x IN S", the expression S must be of type SET OF T, where T is the type of x.

TABLE 12.2 **Set Relational Operators**

Symbol	Meaning	Example
=	equality	{2, 4} = {4, 2} is TRUE
#	inequality	{1, 2} # {1, 2} is FALSE
<=	subset	LoopIndices <= Indices is TRUE
<	proper subset	{1, 2} < {1, 2, 3} is TRUE
>=	superset	{1, 2} >= {1, 2} is TRUE
>	proper superset	{1, 2, 3} > {1, 2} is TRUE
IN	set membership	'J' IN Indices is TRUE

TABLE 12.3 Operators for Sets of the Same Type

Symbol	Meaning	Usage	Definition
+	union	S1 + S2	set of elements in either S1 or S2 (or both)
*	intersection	S1 * S2	set of elements common to both
−	set difference	S1 − S2	set of elements that are in S1 but not in S2
/	symmetric difference	S1 / S2	set of elements either in S1 or in S2 but not in both

The operations on sets of the same type are union, intersection, difference and symmetric difference. They are denoted by the operators shown in Table 12.3.

Examples:

$$\{1, 2, 3, 4\} + \{3, 4, 5\} = \{1, 2, 3, 4, 5\} \quad \text{No duplicate values}$$
$$\{1, 2, 3\} * \{2, 4, 6\} = \{2\}$$
$$\{1, 2, 3, 4\} - \{3, 4, 5\} = \{1, 2\}$$
$$\{1, 2, 3, 4\} / \{3, 4, 5\} = \{1, 2, 5\}$$
```
Vowels * LoopIndices = LetterSet{ 'I' }
Indices - LoopIndices = LetterSet{ 'M', 'N' }
```

In addition to these operators, there are two standard procedures to manipulate sets.

```
INCL( S, x )     include element x in set S
EXCL( S, x )     exclude element x from set S
```

S must be a set type variable, and x must be an expression of the base type of S. For example,

```
INCL( Indices, 'L' );
```

would give the value LetterSet{ 'I', 'J', 'K', 'L', 'M', 'N' } to Indices. Likewise,

```
EXCL( LoopIndices, 'K' )
```

would give the value LetterSet{ 'I', 'J' } to LoopIndices.

Applications

In Modula-2, the size of sets is limited to the size of the computer memory word or a small multiple of it, usually 16 or 32. This restriction can create problems. For example, if the set size is limited to 16, the declaration of LetterSet shown in the preceding section would not be allowed, because it would permit sets with as many as 26 elements.

Also, the restriction is dependent on the characteristics of a particular computer and this dependency might create software portability problems—that is, a program might have to be changed when transferred from one computer to another.

You will have to check your implementation to find out what your set size limit is. If it is small, sets may be of limited value. However, even with small sizes, sets can be useful in the validation of input data.

Suppose, for instance, that we read an input character that identifies the processing to be done in an interactive accounting package. If the valid values for that character are 'N' for adding a new account, 'P' for printing an account, 'L' for listing all accounts, 'E' for examining details of an account, and 'F' for terminating execution, then we can check the validity of the choice character using Boolean expressions in the following way:

```
IF ( Choice = 'N' ) OR ( Choice = 'P' ) OR ( Choice = 'L' ) OR
   ( Choice = 'E' )  OR ( Choice = 'F' ) THEN
      (* processing *)
         .
         .
         .
ELSE
  WriteString( "Error in choice field: " );
  Write( Choice ); WriteLn;
END;
```

Using set values, we can shorten the test by using the IN operator once we have defined a set type:

```
TYPE Commands = SET OF ['E'..'P'];
    .
    .
    .
IF Choice IN Commands{ 'N', 'P', 'L', 'E', 'F' } THEN
   (* processing *)
      .
      .
      .
ELSE
  WriteString( "Error in choice field: " );
  Write( Choice ); WriteLn;
END;
```

Likewise, an earlier example to compute tomorrow's date could be rewritten using sets. The first part of the example could be written as

```
IF Month IN { 1, 3, 5, 7, 8, 10, 12 } THEN
   MaxDays := 31
ELSIF Month IN {4, 6, 9, 11} THEN
   MaxDays := 30
```

```
          ELSIF Year MOD 4 = 0 THEN
             MaxDays := 29
          ELSE
             MaxDays := 28
          END;
              .
              .
              .
```

12.6 Case Study: Doña Ana's Restaurant

The data structures and search techniques described in this chapter are especially useful for businesses that want to track data about their clientele. This case study profiles a typical programming solution.

Doña Ana's Restaurant has become popular. To get a better sense of her customers' spending habits at her restaurant, Doña Ana has decided to computerize the data about patron visits. She has asked us to write a program that will accept monthly data about customer visits and compute the average amount spent per visit for each customer. The program should also check if the customer has a preferred day of the week for dining at her restaurant. Finally, Doña Ana would like some summary statistics about all visits.

Design

Define the Problem Doña Ana has given us a good general idea of the information she desires, but we need more detail before beginning the design of the program. In response to our questions, she is able to provide the following additional information.

The input data for each visit includes the customer's name, the day of the week, and the amount spent.

The information desired for each customer is the number of visits, the average expenditure per visit, and the preferred day of the week based on the number of visits on each day of the week for the entire month.

The summary statistics should include average expenditure over all customers and the most popular day of the week, if there is one.

Design a Solution Given this problem definition, we can see that our problem has three subproblems:

1. Read and validate the input data on all visits to the restaurant.
2. Compute and print information about the visits of each customer.
3. Compute and print summary statistics for all visits.

We can also anticipate the need to initialize several numerical values, such as the counts for the visits on each day. With these observations in mind, we develop the structure chart for a solution, as shown in Figure 12.7.

Figure 12.7
Structure Chart for
Doña Ana's Statistics

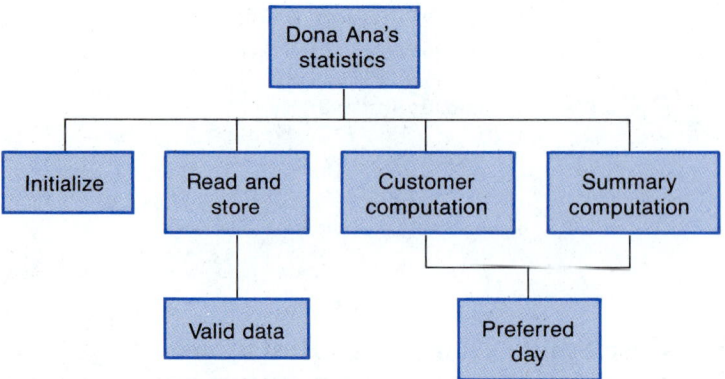

As indicated by the structure chart, we feel that the preferred day computation will be very similar in both the customer and the summary computation, so this component may be shared.

The corresponding modular design chart is very simple. It consists of one module, which imports procedures from standard modules InOut and RealInOut, and from the module Strings. Since it is so simple, we do not need to show it here.

Refine the Solution   To refine our solution, we need more detail about input and output formats. Our input data are provided in a simple format: a 10-character string for the customer's name, an integer for the day of the visit (0 = Monday, 1 = Tuesday, and so on), and a number not exceeding 50,000 for the expenditure of the visit (given in cents, as typical of monetary values). For instance,

         Mary   6   2750

Input will be read from a file specified by using input redirection.

The output format will also be simple; at the top there will be a two-line heading

    Number   Average   Preferred   First Name
    of Visits   Exp.   Day

Then for each customer, the output will include an integer in 5 columns, a cost in 8 columns (with a period separating the dollar amount and the cents amount), a character string in 16 columns (day of week), and a character string in 10 columns for the name, as in

            4   17.55   Tuesday   Mary

The same format will be used for Doña Ana's summary statistics.

In addition to our input and output formats, we will also need to define the data structures to be used in our pseudocode. For each customer we have to keep: a character string for customer name, seven cardinals for counting the visits on each day of the week, and a cardinal value for total expenditure. Because the data are of two types,

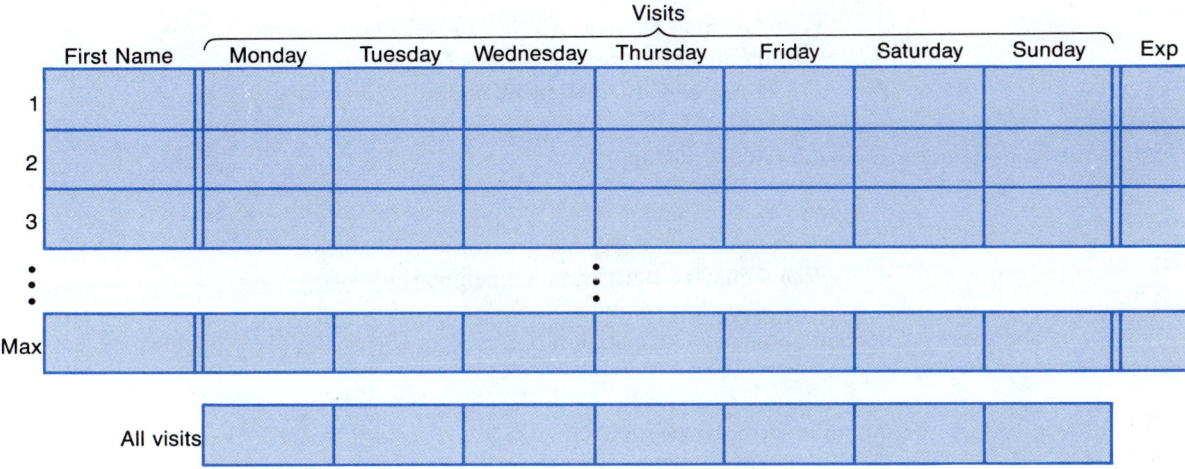

Figure 12.8 Data Structure for Visits

we will use a record for each customer and an array of records for all the information for all the customers. Figure 12.8, illustrates this data structure as well as a vector to store the number of visits to the restaurant for each day.

We will want the array of customer records to be ordered alphabetically by customer name. This ordering can be accomplished by an insertion scheme to maintain an ordered array of records as we enter information. Suppose that data for visits by Mary, Steven, and Kim are entered in that order. Mary's record is put at position 1 and Steven's at position 2, because S follows M alphabetically. Kim's record should precede Mary's, so we must move Steven's record to position 3 and Mary's to position 2 so that Kim's record can be inserted at position 1. If we use this scheme, the records will be ordered by name after all the data have been entered.

We are now ready to develop our first pseudocode solution.

```
Doña Ana
    Initialize
    Read and Store Input Data
    Customer Computation
    Summary Computation
End Doña Ana

Customer Computation
    Print heading
    For each customer do
        For each day of week do
            Accumulate daily visits
            Accumulate total visits
        End For
        Compute Average Expenditure of customer's visits
```

            Update total number of visits and expenditure
            Print number of visits, Average Expenditure,
                Preferred Day, customer's name
        End For
    End Customer Computation

    Summary Computation
        Compute Average Expenditure for all customers
        Print summary statistics: total number of visits,
            Average Expenditure, Preferred Day for visit
    End Summary Computation

    Initialize
        For each day do
            Set accumulated visits to zero
        End For
        For all records in the customer array do
            Set Expenditure to zero
            For each day do
                Set number of visits to zero
            End For
        End For
    End Initialize

    Valid Data
        Set OK to true
        If Not(0 <= Visit <= 6) then
            Set OK to false
        End If
        If Not(0 <= Expense <= 50000) then
            Set OK to false
        End If
        Return OK
    End Valid Data

    Read and Store Input Data
        Set Number of Customers to 0
        Loop
            Read Name
            Exit if no more data
            Read Visit, Expense
            If Valid Data then
                Find customer's position in customer array
                If new customer and still room in customer array then
                    Shift customers appearing next in customer array
                    Insert new customer

```
            Set Number of Customers to Number of Customers + 1
        End If
        If Customer in customer array then
            Update customer's visits with Visit
            Update customer's expenditure with Expense
        Else
            Print "No room left for" Name
        End If
    End If
    End Loop
End Read and Store Input Data

Preferred Day
    Set Previous to none
    Set Prefer to Monday
    For each day from Tuesday to Sunday do
        If number of visits >= visits on Prefer day then
            Set Previous to Prefer
            Set Prefer to new day
        End If
    End For
    If Previous = Prefer then
        Print "no day"
    Else
        Print preferred day
    End If
End Preferred Day
```

The main algorithm corresponds to the structure chart of our design: initialization, reading of input data, computation of statistics for each customer, and computation of statistics for all customers.

The Initialize and Valid Data procedures are self-explanatory. However, the Read and Store algorithm is more complex since we must be careful not to insert a new name in the customer array if it is full. We must also recognize a name that is already in the customer array. To find the name position in the customer array, we will have to use a loop, inspecting the names already in the customer array and finding either where the name already is or where to insert it. If there is no room left, a message is printed and the corresponding data are ignored. Otherwise, if the name is not already in the customer array, it is inserted at the right place. The visit and expenditure data are then updated.

The Customer Computation algorithm accumulates the visits and computes average expenditure by customer, and the Summary Computation computes the average expenditure over all customers. Both algorithms use Preferred Day, which inspects visits in the week and looks for a maximum. If there is a unique maximum, the corresponding day is the preferred day; otherwise, there is no preferred day.

Develop a Testing Strategy To see if our algorithm is prepared to deal with all the possible circumstances, we will want to test the following cases:

1. too many customers
2. a normal number of different customers
3. a customer with only one visit
4. a customer with no preferred day
5. a customer with a preferred day
6. a data set where all customers have a preferred day
7. a data set where all customers have no preferred day

One sample input data set covering cases 2 to 6 is

Mary	6	2750
Steven	3	1825
Kim	2	1530
Mary	1	1210
Karl	1	1050
Cathy	3	1418
Juanita	4	250
Adam	5	030
Louis	3	1218
Alexandra	2	5060
Mary	1	2630
Cathy	2	1415
Juanita	3	1000
Adam	4	1530
Karl	5	500
Steven	6	300
Louis	0	100
Steven	6	1900
Steven	5	1200
Karl	4	1500
Kim	3	950
Cathy	0	1020
Juanita	5	850
Mary	4	430
Louis	3	1230
Steven	1	1155
Cathy	2	1234

The expected results for this input data are

Number of Visits	Average Exp.	Preferred Day	First Name
2	7.80	no day	Adam
1	50.60	Wednesday	Alexandra
4	12.72	Wednesday	Cathy
3	7.00	no day	Juanita
3	10.17	no day	Karl
2	12.40	no day	Kim
3	8.49	Thursday	Louis
4	17.55	Tuesday	Mary
5	12.76	Sunday	Steven
27	13.07	Thursday	all customers

Other sample data sets will be needed for cases 1 and 7. Case 1 can easily be covered by adding 8 lines with 8 new names to the previous data set. Case 7 is easily tested with 7 customers, each on a different day.

The completion of our testing strategy indicates the end of our design and we can now proceed to the implementation phase.

Implementation

Code and Test the Program The following program adheres closely to the pseudocode.

```
MODULE DonaAna;
(* This program computes the statistics for Dona Ana's
   restaurant.  After initializing the arrays, the program
   reads the input data.  Each data line consists of a name, the
   day of the week as a cardinal, the expenditure on the visit
   as a cardinal. Data are accumulated in a general array of
   records.  For each customer, statistics are computed and
   printed: number of visits, average expenditure on visit,
   preferred day for visit if there is one.  Then summary
   statistics for the restaurant are computed and printed:
   total number of visits, average expenditure on visit and
   preferred day for a visit if there is one.
                            Philippe Gabrini   December 1987

                            Change Log

January 1988 J. M. Adams   Moved the code for the customer
                           computation and the summary
                           computation from the main program
                           to separate procedures.           *)
```

```
FROM InOut IMPORT Done, WriteInt, WriteString, WriteLn,
                  ReadString, ReadCard, WriteCard, Write,
                  OpenInput, OpenOutput, CloseInput, CloseOutput;
FROM Strings IMPORT STRING, Assign, StringEqual, StringGreater;

CONST Max = 15;

TYPE Day = ( Monday, Tuesday, Wednesday, Thursday, Friday,
             Saturday, Sunday );
     Week = ARRAY Day OF CARDINAL;
     Customer = RECORD
                   FirstName: STRING;
                   Visits: Week;
                   Exp: CARDINAL;
                END;
     Clients = ARRAY [1..Max] OF Customer;

VAR
   NCustomers,          (* number of different customers *)
   DATotal: CARDINAL;
            (* number of visits to Dona Ana's restaurant *)
   TotExp: CARDINAL;    (* total expenditure on visits *)
   DAVisits: Week;      (* Dona Ana restaurant visits by day *)
   CustomersVisits: Clients; (* array of customer records *)

PROCEDURE Initialize( VAR CustomersVisits: Clients; VAR DAVisits: Week );
VAR WeekDay: Day; J: CARDINAL;
BEGIN
   FOR WeekDay := Monday TO Sunday DO
      DAVisits[WeekDay] := 0;
   END; (* FOR *)
   FOR J := 1 TO Max DO
      WITH CustomersVisits[J] DO
         Exp := 0;
         FOR WeekDay := Monday TO Sunday DO
            Visits[WeekDay] := 0;
         END; (* FOR *)
      END; (* WITH *)
   END; (* FOR *)
END Initialize;

PROCEDURE ReadandStore( VAR NCustomers: CARDINAL;
                       VAR CustomersVisits: Clients );
(* Read all the data relative to Dona Ana's restaurant visits:
         name of customer
         day of visit
         expenditure on visit.
   Validate data, store it in customer array *)
```

SEC. 12.6   Case Study: Doña Ana's Restaurant

```
VAR J, K, Visit: CARDINAL;
    Expense: CARDINAL;
    Name: STRING;
    WeekDay: Day;

PROCEDURE ValidData( Amount, Visit: CARDINAL ): BOOLEAN;
(* Validate visit data: day and expenditure *)
CONST FiveHundred = 50000;
VAR OK: BOOLEAN;
BEGIN
  OK := Visit IN {0..6};
  IF ( Amount < 0 ) OR ( Amount > FiveHundred ) THEN
    OK := FALSE;
  END; (* IF *)
  RETURN OK;
END ValidData;

BEGIN (* ReadandStore *)
(* Read input data, validate it, sort it, and store it. *)
  NCustomers := 0;
  LOOP
    ReadString( Name );
    ReadCard( Visit );
    IF NOT Done THEN
      EXIT;
    END; (* IF *)
    ReadCard( Expense );
    IF ValidData( Expense, Visit ) THEN
      J := 1;
      WHILE ( J <= NCustomers ) AND
          ( StringGreater( Name, CustomersVisits[J].FirstName ) ) DO
        (* name is not in positions 1..J *)
        INC( J );
      END; (* WHILE *)
      IF NOT( StringEqual( Name, CustomersVisits[J].FirstName ) )
          AND ( NCustomers < Max ) THEN
        FOR K := NCustomers TO J BY -1 DO
          CustomersVisits[K + 1] := CustomersVisits[K]
        END; (* FOR *)
        Assign( CustomersVisits[J].FirstName, Name );
        FOR WeekDay := Monday TO Sunday DO
          CustomersVisits[J].Visits[WeekDay] := 0
        END; (* FOR *)
        CustomersVisits[J].Exp := 0;
        INC( NCustomers );
      END; (* IF *)
      IF StringEqual( Name, CustomersVisits[J].FirstName ) THEN
        WeekDay := VAL( Day, Visit ); (* Get visit index and add visit *)
```

```
          INC( CustomersVisits[J].Visits[WeekDay] );
          CustomersVisits[J].Exp := CustomersVisits[J].Exp + Expense;
        ELSE
          WriteString( "No room left for " );
          WriteString( Name ); WriteLn;
        END; (* IF *)
      ELSE
        WriteString( "Invalid day or expense" ); WriteLn;
      END; (* IF *)
   END; (* LOOP *)
END ReadandStore;


PROCEDURE PreferredDay( TheVisit: ARRAY OF CARDINAL );
(* Examine array of cardinal and looks for a single maximum.
   If one then print corresponding day otherwise print "no
   preferred day". *)
VAR K, NPrec, NPref, PrefDay: CARDINAL;
BEGIN
  NPref := TheVisit[0]; (* first index in open array = first day *)
  NPrec := 0;
  PrefDay:=0;
  FOR K := 1 TO 6 DO
    (* NPref >= TheVisit[0]..TheVisit[K - 1] *)
    IF NPref <= TheVisit[K] THEN
      NPrec := NPref;
      NPref := TheVisit[K];
      PrefDay := K;
    END; (* IF *)
  END; (* FOR *)
  IF NPref = NPrec THEN
    WriteString( "     no day      " );
  ELSE
    CASE PrefDay OF
        0: WriteString( "    Monday     " )|
        1: WriteString( "    Tuesday    " )|
        2: WriteString( "    Wednesday  " )|
        3: WriteString( "    Thursday   " )|
        4: WriteString( "    Friday     " )|
        5: WriteString( "    Saturday   " )|
        6: WriteString( "    Sunday     " )
    END; (* CASE *)
  END; (* IF *)
END PreferredDay;


PROCEDURE PrintExpense( Amount: CARDINAL );
(* Print an amount in the usual dollars and cents manner. *)
VAR Cents: CARDINAL;
```

```
  BEGIN
    WriteCard( Amount DIV 100, 5 );
    Write( '.' );
    Cents := Amount MOD 100;
    IF Cents IN {0..9} THEN
      Write( '0' );                        (* print leading zero *)
      WriteCard( Cents, 1 );
    ELSE
      WriteCard( Cents, 2 );
    END;    (* IF *)
  END PrintExpense;


  PROCEDURE CustomerComp( CustomerVisits: Clients; NCustomers: CARDINAL;
                          VAR DATotal, TotExp: CARDINAL; DAVisits: Week );
  (* Computation of statistics for each customer *)
  VAR TotalVisits, J, N, AvExp: CARDINAL;
          WeekDay: Day;
  BEGIN
    WriteString( " Number   Average   Preferred   First Name" );
    WriteLn;
    WriteString( "of Visits  Exp.        Day" ); WriteLn;
    DATotal := 0;
    TotExp := 0;
    FOR J := 1 TO NCustomers DO
      TotalVisits := 0;
      FOR WeekDay := Monday TO Sunday DO  (* accumulate number of visits *)
        N := CustomersVisits[J].Visits[WeekDay];
        DAVisits[WeekDay] := DAVisits[WeekDay] + N;
        TotalVisits := TotalVisits + N;
      END;    (* FOR *)
      AvExp := CustomersVisits[J].Exp DIV TotalVisits;
      DATotal := DATotal + TotalVisits;
      TotExp := TotExp + CustomersVisits[J].Exp;
      WriteInt( TotalVisits, 5 ); PrintExpense( AvExp );
      PreferredDay( CustomersVisits[J].Visits );
      WriteString( CustomersVisits[J].FirstName ); WriteLn;
    END;    (* FOR *)
  END CustomerComp;


  PROCEDURE SummaryComp( TotExp, DATotal: CARDINAL; DAVisits: Week );
  (* Compute and print summary statistics. *)
  VAR AvExp: CARDINAL;
  BEGIN
    AvExp := TotExp DIV DATotal;
    WriteLn; WriteInt( DATotal, 5 ); PrintExpense( AvExp );
    PreferredDay( DAVisits );
    WriteString( "all customers" ); WriteLn;
  END SummaryComp;
```

```
BEGIN (* DonaAna *)
  Initialize( CustomersVisits, DAVisits );

  OpenInput( "" );           (* Ask for input file name. *)
  OpenOutput( "" );          (* Ask for output file name. *)
  ReadandStore( NCustomers, CustomersVisits );

  CustomerComp( CustomersVisits, NCustomers, DATotal, TotExp, DAVisits );

  SummaryComp( TotExp, DATotal, DAVisits );

  CloseInput;
  CloseOutput;
END DonaAna.
```

Procedure Initialize sets the visits and expenditures arrays to zero, so that it is possible to accumulate the input data.

Procedure ReadandStore has a loop with one iteration for input and validation of each line of data. Notice that the set {0..6} is used to validate the input Visit. ReadandStore then locates the position of the customer's name in the ordered customer array, using a linear search because the array is so small. If the array were larger, a binary search could be used for faster searching. At the end of the search, J points to the final position of the input name in the customer array. If the name is not already there and if the array is not full, the name has to be inserted at this position of the array. The elements of the rest of the table are shifted one position up and the new name is inserted in its proper position. The corresponding input data are then accumulated. Notice the use of the standard function VAL to convert the input cardinal to a value of type Day. Standard procedure INC is used to increment the number of visits by one. The input expenditure is added to the total expenditure of the corresponding customer.

Procedure PreferredDay starts by taking the first position in the array as the preferred day; it then loops through the remainder of the array to check if another number of visits is greater than or equal to the current maximum. We keep track of the previous maximum, so that at the end of the loop we can check if the maximum is unique. If the maximum is not unique, we know that at least two days show the same number of visits, so there is no single preferred day. Otherwise, we use the index of the day to print the appropriate day.

Complete the Documentation We first gather together documentation already completed: the problem definition, the structure chart, input and output data formats, the program listing, and test results. Then we complete this documentation by providing a user's manual.

USER'S MANUAL

Doña Ana's statistics program reads in a number of input lines, each line identifying a customer's visit (customer's name, day of visit, expenditure on visit). Some sample data are as follows:

Mary	6	2750
Steven	3	1825
Kim	2	1530
Mary	1	1210
Karl	1	1050
Cari	3	1418

Notice that cardinals are used to denote the day of the week, from 0 for Monday to 6 for Sunday. Cardinals are also used to denote expenses in cents.

Once all the input data have been read, statistics are computed and displayed for each customer and for all customers. The maximum number of different customers is limited to 15.

To execute the program, type "DonaAna". The program will then read the input data. If the day is not indicated by a value in [0..6], or the expense by a value in [0..50000], the message "Invalid day or expense" is printed and the input line is ignored. If the input data are valid, the program will then compute and display the statistical results.

If you get the message "No room left for Customer Name," it means that the program has detected more than 15 different names. In this case the customer array is full and you cannot insert another name, so the data following that name on the input line are ignored. Check for typing mistakes in the name on this input line, since a misspelled name is taken as a new name. For instance, Mary and mary are two distinct names. Misspellings on previous input may also have added extra names, so they should be checked as well.

SUMMARY

An array is a sequence of components of the same type. A record, on the other hand, is a group of components of different types. When we need to represent a sequence of components, where each component is a collection of objects of different types, we combine data structures to form an array of records.

Variant records can group together components, where one (or more) component may be allowed to vary in its type, and yet the composite objects with such variations may be considered to be of the same type.

One of the most common operations performed on lists is a search. Linear searches examine objects of data sequentially until either the desired object is found or all the objects have been searched without success. Linear searches may be done on ordered or unordered data. On ordered data, we can use a binary search, which continually chooses the middle element in the list and matches it against the desired element. The binary search method is by far the more efficient approach, but it may be used only on ordered data.

The set data type includes the operations of union, intersection, set difference, and symmetric difference, and gives us a convenient way of checking the validity of input. The built-in set type in Modula-2 is called BITSET.

EXERCISES

1. Give declarations for data structures suitable for representation of a daily schedule of bus service between 10 cities or towns in your area. It should indicate arrival and departure times and destination for each bus. You may choose reasonable limits for any arrays used.

2. Give declarations for data structures suitable for representing the class schedule at your institution. You may choose reasonable limits for any arrays used.

3. Alter the procedure InterestCharge in Section 12.1 to round the numerator before dividing by 1000.

4. Alter the procedure LinearSearch in Section 12.4 to include a VAR parameter of type BOOLEAN to indicate the success or failure of the search.

5. We could improve our linear search in the unsuccessful cases if we could assume the array was ordered. Assuming that the elements are in increasing order, change the IF statement in the search loop of the LinearSearch procedure to exit the loop if the name has already been passed.

6. With the change suggested in Exercise 5, what is the expected number of comparisons for an unsuccessful search, assuming that searches for all keys not in the array are equally likely.

7. A student noticed that the iterative version of the binary search in this chapter had two copies of the assignment statement for Middle—one before the WHILE loop and one at the bottom of the loop. The following pseudocode is an attempt to simplify the program by having a single assignment statement for Middle at the top of the while loop.

    Binary Search(Data, First, Last, Name, Middle)
       While First < Last do
          {If Name is in table, it must be between indices First and Last}
          Set Middle to (First + Last) div 2
          If Name precedes entry at Middle position then
             {Name not in second half}
             Set Last to Middle − 1
          Elsif Name comes after entry at Middle position then
             {Name not in first half}
             Set First to Middle + 1
          Else {Name is at Middle position}
             Set First and Last to Middle
          End If
       End While
       {First >= Last or Name is at Middle position}
    End Binary Search

    Unfortunately, this approach does not work. Give a specific example of data for which this modified version of binary search fails.

8. It is possible to implement the iterative version of binary search in this chapter with a single assignment statement for Middle provided that the while loop is replaced by a loop statement. Give the pseudocode for this modified version of binary search.

9. Explain why the index range had to go one beyond the array index range for a linear search but not for a binary search.

10. Replace each of the following Boolean expressions by another one using the set operation IN.

    ((Years = 2) OR (Years = 4)) OR
    ((Years = 6) OR (Years = 8) OR (Years = 10))

    ("I" <= Ch) AND (Ch <= "N")

11. Given the Boolean expression

    ((10 <= B) AND (B <= 20)) OR
    ((30 <= B) AND (B <= 40)) OR
    ((52 <= B) AND (B <= 81)) OR
    ((89 <= B) AND (B <= 99))

    write an equivalent expression using a set.

12. Give the declarations necessary for defining a data type, called Bag or Multiset, which is a set with duplicates—that is, a set where a given value can appear several times.

PROGRAMMING PROBLEMS

13. Design and implement a procedure to find the largest and smallest values in an array of integers. Make the procedure as efficient as you can; it is possible to do it in less than $3n/2$ comparisons.

14. Implement and test the recursive binary search algorithm in Section 12.4.

15. Implement and test the iterative binary search algorithm in Section 12.4.

16. Implement and test a variation of the DoñaAna program in Section 12.6, using a larger maximum for the number of customers and also the iterative binary search developed for Problem 15.

17. Complete the definition and implementation modules for searching a small database of customers, described in Section 12.4.

18. Using test data stored in a file, write a test program for the library module constructed in Exercise 17.

19. Write a procedure that, given a value of a set type, counts the elements of a set.

20. Define and implement a module to define and manipulate sets of objects not restricted to the maximum size imposed by your version of Modula-2.

13 Sorting and Analysis of Algorithms

Time is the loan no one can repay. UNKNOWN

In this chapter you will:

- see some simple sorting algorithms
- learn about analyzing algorithms to determine their complexity
- be introduced to an efficient sorting algorithm, called Quicksort

In Chapter 12, we developed simple algorithms for searching and analyzed these algorithms informally. That short discussion provided just a glimpse of a very important area of computer science called analysis of algorithms. The analysis of algorithms is important because it is not enough to have an algorithm to solve a problem; we must also know that the algorithm can be executed in some reasonable amount of time. For example, the algorithm that determines if the game of chess is a forced victory for the white pieces is impractical because the algorithm would require eons to execute on our fastest computers. We must analyze algorithms to determine if they are practical. This chapter will address that issue.

We start off by developing some simple sorting algorithms. Then we introduce the Big-*O* notation as the mathematical basis for analyzing an algorithm to determine its complexity. The word *complexity* here refers to an algorithm's efficiency, rather than its subtlety or intricacy. You may wish to think of an algorithm's complexity as an estimate of its execution time, but the estimate should be independent of any particular computer or programming language. We also develop another sorting routine, Quicksort, which is significantly more efficient than the simple sorting algorithms. The

13.1 Simple Sorting Algorithms

chapter concludes with a case study illustrating the development of a very efficient algorithm for sorting data into three groups. The specific example is sorting physical substances into solids, liquids, and gases for a given temperature.

13.1 Simple Sorting Algorithms

In this section we will develop two simple sorting algorithms and informally analyze their complexity. The algorithms will sort a nonempty array of integers into ascending order. The more usual case of sorting an array of records on some key field is an easy extension of our algorithms.

Selection Sort

When considering how to sort an array, you may first think of using another array of equal size to hold the result. Unfortunately, this approach is not practical if the array is very large since the memory of your computer may not be able to hold both arrays along with the program and the run time system. Since this is a common situation, we will avoid using another array and try to do the sorting "in place." We can easily formulate a recursive solution by reducing our problem to a smaller problem and then use a recursive call for the reduced problem. More specifically, we might

> Find the smallest element of the array
> Swap this element with the first element of the array
> Sort the remaining elements

This certainly looks simple, but we have not been quite careful enough; we have not provided a base case. Such an omission is easily remedied, however, because we know that an array with one element is already sorted and thus serves as the base case. Since we do nothing for the base case, we can refine our algorithm to

> If length of the array > 1 then {general case}
>   Find the smallest element of the array
>   Swap this element with the first element of the array
>   Sort the remaining elements of the array
> End If

Now we've made a good start, and for our next refinement we notice that this algorithm is tail recursive and thus can be easily reformulated iteratively. As we mentioned in Chapter 12, iteration will usually be faster, which is a significant consideration for a common operation such as sorting. If we assume that the array to be sorted is A[0] through A[n], our first iterative formulation is

> SelectionSort
>   For i from 0 to $n - 1$ do
>   Find the smallest element of A[i] through A[n]
>   Swap this element with A[i]
>   {The elements A[0] through A[i] are in their proper positions.}
>   End For
>   {The elements A[0] through A[n] are in their proper positions.}
> End SelectionSort

Notice that if A has one element, $n - 1 = -1$ and no iterations are done. This condition corresponds to the base case of our recursive formulation. If A has more than one element, after the first iteration of the loop the smallest element will be in its proper place; after the second iteration, the two smallest will be in their proper places; and in general, after the ith iteration, the ith smallest elements will be in their proper places. This observation is documented by the assertion at the bottom of the loop. After $n - 1$ iterations the elements A[0] through A[$n - 1$] are in their proper places, and so A[n] must also be in its proper place. Thus all elements are in order, as documented by the assertion at the end of the algorithm.

Adding a few details, we create the refined iterative solution

> SelectionSort
>   For i from 0 to $n - 1$ do
>   Find s, the index of the smallest element of A[i] through A[n]
>   Swap A[s] with A[i]
>   {The elements A[0] through A[i] are in their proper positions.}
>   End For
>   {The elements A[0] through A[n] are in their proper positions.}
> End SelectionSort

The algorithm is called SelectionSort, because in each pass we "select" the correct element to place in the array, working from the lowest to the highest. Its execution is illustrated in Figure 13.1 on an array with five elements.

Figure 13.1 Selection Sort

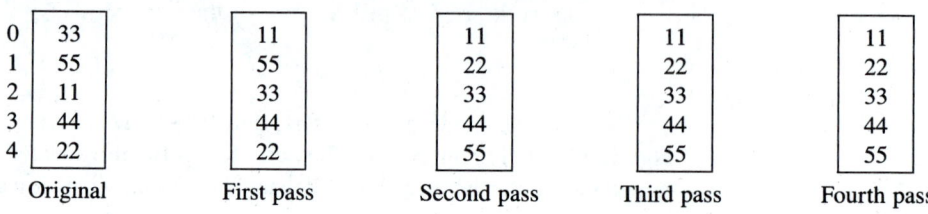

SEC. 13.1 Simple Sorting Algorithms

The first iteration, or pass as it is often called in sorting, looks for the smallest element in the entire array, 11 in this example. When it is found, it is swapped with the A[0] element, 33. The second pass looks for the smallest element in the subarray A[1] through A[4], which is 22 in this case. When found, it is swapped with the A[1] element, 55. In passes 3 and 4, the selected element, A[s], swaps with itself, resulting in no change in the data. The following procedure implements this algorithm.

```
PROCEDURE SelectionSort(VAR A: ARRAY OF INTEGER);
(* Sort array of integers into ascending order.   *)

VAR Temp: INTEGER;
    I, J, N, S: CARDINAL;
BEGIN
  N := HIGH(A);

  FOR I := 0 TO N - 1 DO
    (* Find S, the index of the smallest element of A[I] through A[N] *)
    S := I;
    FOR J := I + 1 TO N DO
      IF A[J] < A[S] THEN
        S := J;
      END; (* IF *)
      (* A[S] is less than or equal A[I]..A[J] *)
    END; (* FOR *)
    (* A[S] is less than or equal A[I]..A[N] *)
    (* Swap A[S] with A[I] *)
    Temp := A[I];
    A[I] := A[S];
    A[S] := Temp;
    (* A[0]..A[I] are in their proper positions. *)
  END; (* FOR *)
  (* A[0]..A[N] are in their proper positions. *)
END SelectionSort;
```

Some additional assertions have been included as documentation for the inner FOR loop, which finds the index of the smallest element of A[I] through A[N]. The assertions before each END; (* FOR *) are our loop invariants.

Complexity analysis considers the number of comparisons between elements being sorted and the number of times elements being sorted are moved. Let's first find the number of comparisons. On the first pass there are n comparisons, assuming $n + 1$ is the length of the array. On the second pass there are $n - 1$ comparisons, on the third $n - 2$, and so on until the last pass where there is a single comparison. Thus there are

$$1 + 2 + \cdots + (n - 1) + n = \sum_{i=1}^{n} i = \frac{n(n + 1)}{2} \text{ comparisons}$$

The number of comparisons is based on the size of the array and does not depend on the ordering of the initial data. Based on this analysis, we can say that the number of comparisons for a selection sort is proportional to *n* squared, where *n* is the number of elements in the array.

There is at most one exchange, comprising three moves, for each pass, so the number of moves is proportional to *n*. Again, the complexity is determined solely by the size of the array and does not depend on the ordering of the initial data. Thus, for a large array (large *n*), the execution time will be determined primarily by the number of comparisons and we say the entire algorithm executes in time proportional to *n* squared.

An Introduction to Proving a Program Correct

In addition to analyzing algorithms to determine their complexity, we must also make sure that we develop correct programs for the algorithms. Here we'll look at part of our SelectionSort and work out a proof of its correctness.

Our comment giving a loop invariant for the outer FOR statement in the SelectionSort has asserted

```
A[0]..A[I] are in their proper positions
```

or a bit more carefully,

```
A[0]..A[I] is ordered   AND   A[I] <= the remaining elements
```

We can express this mathematically as

```
A[J - 1] <= A[J] for J = 1..I   AND   A[I] <= A[K] for K = I + 1..N
```

We can also see that the control variable I starts at 0, is incremented by 1, and on completion of the last iteration, I = N − 1. Substituting this in our loop invariant, we can assert that

```
A[J - 1] <= A[J] for J = 1..N - 1   AND   A[N - 1] <= A[K] for K = N..N
```

holds on completion of the last iteration; or more simply,

```
A[J - 1] <= A[J] for J = 1..N - 1   AND   A[N - 1] <= A[N]
```

or even more simply,

```
A[J - 1] <= A[J] for J = 1..N
```

In other words, all elements of the array are in order.

This "proof" is far from complete. Among other things, we must show:

- The loop invariant for the outer FOR loop is indeed true at the end of every iteration.

Simple Sorting Algorithms

- The inner FOR loop with a nested IF is correct.

A problem very similar to the latter task appears as Exercise 10 at the end of the chapter.

For now, this section has given you the flavor of proving a program correct (also called *program verification*). As you might guess, formal proofs are as difficult as program development itself—in fact, if you are a careful programmer, you should be informally doing the proof as you develop the program. We will investigate another proof of correctness after presenting another sorting algorithm, the insertion sort.

Insertion Sort

Another simple sorting method can be based on a variation of the recursive formulation used in developing the selection sort. In the selection sort we found the smallest element and then did a recursive call to sort the remaining elements. For the insertion sort we reverse the steps; we first sort a subarray consisting of all the elements but the last one, and then insert that element into its proper place. Our recursive version of the insertion sort is

> If length of the array > 1 Then {general case}
>   Sort all the elements but the last one
>   Find the correct position for the last element and insert it there
> End if

As before, for reasons of efficiency, we will reformulate this algorithm to obtain an iterative version. Because this recursive version is not tail recursion (the recursive call is at the beginning rather than the end), the reformulation is slightly more difficult. If we follow the recursive calls all the way down to the deepest level (the base case), we see that no changes to the array are made on the way down. All the changes are made as we back out of all the recursive calls. Thus we can do the same job iteratively by starting with a subarray of the first element only. We insert the second element in its proper position, then insert the third element in its proper position in this two-element subarray, and so forth until we have backed all the way out of recursion. We insert the last element into the sorted array of all elements but the last. This process is illustrated by Figure 13.2.

The first pass considers the first element to be sorted and puts the second element, 55, in its place in the sorted part. Since it is already in its correct position, there is no

Figure 13.2 Insertion Sort

Index	Original	First pass	Second pass	Third pass	Fourth pass
0	33	33	11	11	11
1	55	55	33	33	22
2	11	11	55	44	33
4	44	44	44	55	44
5	22	22	22	22	55

change as a result of the first pass. The second pass places 11 at the start of the part already sorted, moving 33 and 55 to make room. The third pass places 44 in the sorted part, moving 55 to make room. The last pass puts 22 in its position in the sorted part of the array, moving 33, 44, and 55 to make room. This method is the basis for the first iterative pseudocode version of the simple insertion sort for array A[0] through A[n].

> InsertionSort
>   For i from 1 to n do
>   Insert A[i] in its proper place in A[0] through A[i − 1]
>   {A[0] through A[i] are in order}
>   End for
>   {A[0] through A[n] are in order}
> End InsertionSort

Naturally, the insertion will involve finding the proper place as well as doing the insertion itself. Also, the insertion will involve moving some elements to make room for the insertion. Using these ideas, we can refine the algorithm as follows:

> InsertionSort
>   For i from 1 to n do
>   Set j to the proper position within A[0]..A[i − 1] to put A[i]
>   Move A[j + 1] through A[i − 1] to make room for A[i]
>   Insert A[i] at position j
>   {A[0] through A[i] are in order}
>   End for
>   {A[0] through A[n] are in order}
> End InsertionSort

Finding the proper position involves searching from the element at the (i − 1)st position back toward 0 until the proper position is found. Then we have to go back through these elements, starting at the index i − 1, moving them one at a time to the next higher position. Rather than pass through this part of the data twice, we can look ahead and move the data, when appropriate, at the same time. Since we don't know ahead of time when this process will stop, we introduce a loop with an exit test at the top in our final pseudocode algorithm.

> InsertionSort
>   For i from 1 to n do
>   Set temp to A[i]
>   Set j to i
>   Loop
>   {temp <= A[j]..A[i] and A[0]..A[j − 1] are in order
>   and A[j + 1]..A[i] are in order}

SEC. 13.1 Simple Sorting Algorithms

> Exit if (*j* = 0) or (A[*j* − 1] <= temp)
> Move A[*j* − 1] to A[*j*]
> Decrement *j*
> End loop
> Set A[*j*] to temp
> {A[0] through A[*i*] are in order}
> End for
> {A[0] through A[*n*] are in order}
> End InsertionSort

Our procedure follows directly from this pseudocode solution.

```
PROCEDURE InsertionSort(VAR A: ARRAY OF INTEGER);
(* Sort array of integers into ascending order.   *)

VAR I, J, N: CARDINAL;
    Temp: INTEGER;

BEGIN
  N := HIGH(A);
  FOR I := 1 TO N DO
    (* A[0]..A[I - 1] are in order *)
    Temp := A[I]; J := I;
    LOOP
       (* Temp <= A[J]..A[I] and A[0]..A[J] are in order
          and A[J+1]..A[I] are in order              *)
       IF (J = 0) OR (A[J - 1] <= Temp) THEN EXIT; END; (* IF *)
       A[J] := A[J - 1];
       DEC(J);
    END; (* LOOP *)
    (* A[0]..A[J - 1] <= Temp <= A[J + 1]..A[I]
       and the two subarrays are in order *)
    A[J] := Temp;
    (* A[0]..A[I] are in order *)
  END (* FOR *)

  (* A[0]..A[N] are in order *)
END InsertionSort;
```

Since our array parameter, A, is an open array, the FOR loop goes from 1 to the index HIGH(A). Although the exit condition for the inner LOOP is at the top, we have chosen to use the LOOP structure instead of the WHILE loop since it is clearer that our loop assertion holds before the test for loop exit. Notice that the OR condition in the loop exit depends on left-to-right evaluation of Boolean expressions. The loop terminates when J is decremented down to 0. At that time, A[J − 1] would be an illegal array reference. However, J = 0 is already TRUE, so we don't even evaluate the expression A[J − 1] <= Temp.

Unlike the selection sort, the insertion sort has the property that the total number of comparisons will depend on the order of the initial data. To see this, we should consider the best case, the worst case, and the average case. In the best case the data are already sorted, and it will take one comparison for each pass to determine that the element to be inserted is larger than the elements that have already been sorted. The worst case is when the initial data are in reverse order. As the sort progresses, each element to be inserted will be placed at the first position in the array, thus requiring as many comparisons as the selection sort ($n * (n + 1)/2$). For randomly ordered data, we would expect the number of comparisons to be half the worst case, which would still be proportional to n squared.

In the average case the number of moves is also proportional to n squared, whereas only n moves were needed in selection sort. To see this, observe that for $n - 1$ elements, we must find the place to insert the element and then do the insertion. On the average, we will have to search through half the elements to find the position for the insertion and move these elements in order to make room for the insertion. So, on the average, the number of moves will be half of $1 + 2 + \cdots + (n - 1)$, which is proportional to n squared, as claimed. As with the number of comparisons, this value is dependent on the initial ordering of the data. In the best case (the data are already sorted), the element to be inserted will remain in its current position. For the worst case (the data are in reverse order), the number of moves is $n(n - 1)/2$. As stated, the average case will be half this.

Our analyses of searching and sorting algorithms, such as the analysis just described, have been rather informal and have included little mathematical notation. In Section 13.2, we will introduce some useful notation and discuss the topic of analysis of algorithms in a more general way. First, we return to the issue of proving a program correct.

Program Correctness Revisited

With the selection sort, we proved the final result correct provided the loop invariant for the outer loop was correct. With the insertion sort, we will prove the entire program correct, except for the inner loop.

Proving a loop correct typically involves three steps:

1. The loop invariant is correct when first encountered.
2. The loop invariant remains correct for each iteration of the loop.
3. The loop invariant combined with the exit condition can be used to prove the assertion following the loop.

The outer loop invariant states

    A[0]..A[I - 1] are in order

We first must show that this statement is initially true. Since the FOR loop initializes I to 1, A[0]..A[0] contains only one element and is in order. The next step is to show that the loop invariant remains true after the loop is executed. The assertion after the inner LOOP states that

$$A[0]..A[J - 1] <= \text{Temp} <= A[J + 1]..A[I]$$
$$\text{and each of the subarrays are in order}$$

The assignment of Temp to A[J] leads directly to the assertion at the bottom of the loop,

$$A[0]..A[I] \text{ are in order}$$

Then at the top of the FOR loop, I is incremented by 1. Since I is now 1 larger, we can assert only that the elements A[0]..A[I − 1] are in order.

Finally, we must show that the loop invariant combined with the loop exit condition results in the final assertion,

$$A[0]..A[N] \text{ are in order}$$

The FOR loop increments I from 1 to N; after the last iteration, I is incremented to N + 1, and the loop is exited. Combining I = N + 1 with the loop invariant, A[0]..A[I − 1] is in order, leads directly to the final assertion.

13.2 Elementary Analysis of Algorithms

In Chapter 12, we discussed two algorithms for searching, and we have just developed two algorithms for sorting. These algorithms were analyzed informally by calculating the number of comparisons required and, in the case of sorting, the number of moves or exchanges required.

In the selection sort the number of comparisons is proportional to n^2 where n is the number of items being sorted. The number of exchanges is proportional to n. We say that the complexity of the selection sort algorithm is proportional to n^2 because this is the dominant term (as n increases, n^2 grows much more rapidly than n). In this section we will examine complexity more formally and try to understand more deeply the meaning of an algorithm having complexity n^2 or n or other values.

The Big-O Notation

To determine the complexity of an algorithm, we first find an expression that gives us an estimate of the execution time of the algorithm, and then we analyze that expression. The expression for execution time is usually a function of a variable (or variables) that is a measure of the size of the particular task that the algorithm is being asked to perform. For example, the size of a sorting task would be the length, say n, of the sequence to be sorted. When we say that the run time for a sorting algorithm is proportional to n^2, we are expressing a functional relationship between the size of the sorting job and the amount of work required to complete the job. The mathematical notation used to express such relationships is called the *Big-O notation*. To determine the Big-O value for a given expression, we must find the dominant term or terms in the expression. We will illustrate this process with a specific sorting algorithm.

Returning to our selection sort given earlier in the chapter, we found that for $n + 1$ items there would be $n(n + 1)/2$ comparisons. Each pass involves an exchange (even when an item is exchanged with itself) and each exchange takes three moves; so there would be $3n$ moves since the number of passes is n. Thus, an expression giving an estimate for execution time of the algorithm is

$$\frac{n(n + 1)}{2} + 3n$$

The first term represents the number of comparisons and the second term the number of assignments. The actual times for these operations are hardware dependent, and a more detailed run time analysis for a particular computer would have to involve these times. Here, because we are trying to analyze the algorithm in a machine-independent fashion, we will proceed with a mathematical analysis. Let's call the function just shown $g(n)$ and expand it to obtain

$$g(n) = \frac{n^2}{2} + \frac{7n}{2}$$

Table 13.1 gives the values (truncated to integers) of the n^2 and $7n/2$ terms for small values of n. Notice that for very small n, the second term is larger than the first due to the fact that the second is multiplied by 7/2 while the first is divided by 2. However, this relationship does not last long. By the time n is equal to 7, they are equal; and when n is 10, the first is almost double the second. Thus the first term

TABLE 13.1 Growth of Terms of $g(n)$

n	$n^2/2$	$7n/2$
2	2	7
3	4	10
4	8	14
5	12	17
6	18	21
7	24	24
8	32	28
9	40	31
10	50	35
50	1250	175
100	5000	350

dominates the other term, and so we say the complexity of g is proportional to n^2. We express this in Big-O notation by saying

$$g(n) \text{ is } O(n^2)$$

or, less formally, we say that the selection sort is order n^2.

Two points should be noted:

1. A proportionality constant, such as 1/2 in our example, does not affect the complexity of an algorithm.
2. The domination need be true only past a particular value of n, such as 7 in our example.

We can formally define Big-O notation mathematically as follows:

DEFINITION We say that $g(n))$ is $O(f(n))$ if there exist two nonnegative constants C and k such that $|g(n)| <= C|f(n)|$ for all $n > k$.

EXAMPLE 1

For selection sort, we have calculated $g(n) = n^2/2 + 7n/2$. In order to show that $g(n)$ is $O(n^2)$, according to our definition, we take $f(n) = n^2$. Now we must find values of C and k, which cause the inequality $|g(n)| <= C|f(n)|$ for all $n > k$, to be satisfied. Using Table 13.1, we note that $g(7) = 48$, and since $7^2 = 49$, we take $C = 48/49$, and $k = 7$. Actually we can take C to be any value greater than or equal to 48/49, such as 1, and k to be any value greater than or equal to 7, but it is common to give the least possible values if they are not too difficult to find.

EXAMPLE 2

Suppose we want to find the complexity of an algorithm whose execution time can be estimated by the expression $1^2 + 2^2 + 3^2 + \cdots + n^2$. To do our analysis, we first need to find a closed form, eliminating the ellipses (. . .) notation, for this summation. Using induction (Exercise 12, Chapter 5), we can show that

$$1^2 + 2^2 + 3^2 + \cdots + n^2 = \frac{n(n+1)(2n+1)}{6}$$

If we choose C to be 1 and k to be 1, then

$$\left| \frac{n(n+1)(2n+1)}{6} \right| <= |n^3| \text{ for all } n >= 1$$

so we say the complexity is $O(n^3)$. Of course, our original sum of squares is also bounded by n^4 or n^5, and so on; however, we usually want this bound to be as small as possible since this gives us more information about how the growth of the execution time is bounded.

Complexity Classes

The complexity of an algorithm could be expressed by many Big-O classifications. However, there are some commonly occurring classifications, which we will examine in this section. Table 13.2 lists common complexity classes. We refer to the first six classes as polynomial classes, and of course, there are many other polynomial classes such as $O(n^4)$. We have already seen algorithms of logarithmic, linear, and quadratic complexity.

A constant complexity means that the run time is independent of the size of the problem, which is clearly an uncommon situation.

Other complexities, such as the complexity of the binary search, involve the logarithmic function. The following formula converts logarithms from one base to another:

$$\log_a x = \frac{\log_b x}{\log_b a}$$

Since $\log_b a$ is a constant, the choice of the logarithm base does not affect the algorithm complexity. We will write log to indicate base two logarithms.

An exponential complexity involves raising a constant to the nth power.

In order to appreciate how fast each of these functions grow, we will make a table for small values of n. We choose powers of two so that the logarithms result in integer values. The data are presented in tabular form in Table 13.3 and shown graphically in Figure 13.3.

From the rates of growth you can see that the complexity of an algorithm can make a big difference in run time, especially for larger values of n. In particular, notice how the exponential 2^n surges past the polynomials illustrated at about $n = 10$. This growth is often called "explosive." For this reason, algorithms of exponential complexity are

TABLE 13.2 Common Complexity Classes

constant	$O(1)$
logarithmic	$O(\log n)$
linear	$O(n)$
$n \log n$	$O(n \log n)$
quadratic	$O(n^2)$
cubic	$O(n^3)$
exponential	$O(2^n)$, $O(10^n)$, and so on

TABLE 13.3 Values for Various Functions

	$\log n$	n	$n \log n$	n^2	n^3	2^n
$n = 1$	0	1	0	1	1	2
$n = 2$	1	2	2	4	8	4
$n = 4$	2	4	8	16	64	16
$n = 16$	4	16	64	256	4096	65536
$n = 256$	8	256	2048	65536	16777216	1.16×10^{77}
$n = 1024$	10	1024	10240	1048576	1.07×10^9	1.80×10^{308}

Figure 13.3
A Graphical Comparison of Complexities

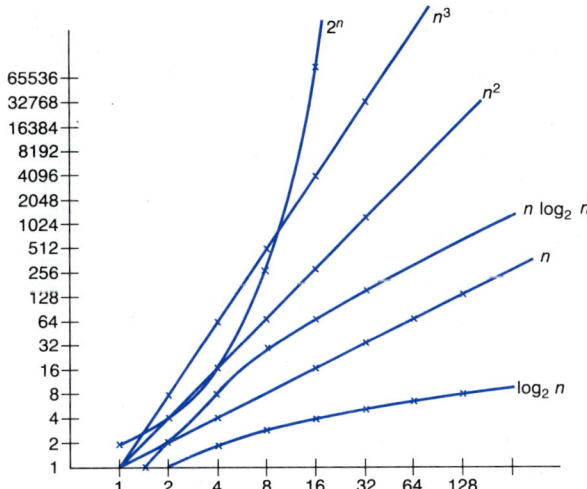

called "intractable," since they would not be practical computing methods for larger problems.

For algorithms with polynomial complexity, we obviously prefer those algorithms with complexity of low order, such as n and $n \log n$, since they will be more efficient for large problems. You have learned two sorting methods, each with complexity of n^2. In the next section you will see a technique with lower complexity, $n \log n$. We would expect a substantial difference in run time for these two classes of algorithms when sorting large arrays.

13.3 Quicksort

A sorting algorithm developed in 1961 by C. A. R. Hoare was promptly named Quicksort because of its excellent performance. Apparently Hoare had the idea for this algorithm several years earlier but was unable to implement it. He subsequently read about recursion in the ALGOL 60 Report, and, a short time later while attending a tutorial session on the "new" programming language ALGOL 60, he again attempted an implementation. This time he used recursion and was successful. The resulting program delighted the instructors of the tutorial and has subsequently delighted generations of computer scientists because of its elegance and efficiency.

Quicksort is a "divide-and-conquer" sorting method: it partitions the array of elements to be sorted into two smaller parts, and then recursively sorts each smaller part. More specifically, an element, call it P, is chosen arbitrarily, and the array is partitioned in such a way that:

- All elements in the left partition are less than or equal to P.
- All the elements in the right partition are greater than or equal to P.

The result of a typical partition is illustrated in Figure 13.4. The element P is usually called a pivot.

Figure 13.4
Result of Partitioning

The result of the partitioning step is illustrated on an example in Figure 13.5, where 45 was chosen as the pivot for the first partition step and 9 and 54 were chosen as pivots for the second partitions. The brackets ("[" and "]") delimit the partitions remaining to be sorted.

Figure 13.5
Examples of Partitioning

Original array	54	63	18	99	45	9	27	72	51
First partitions	[27	9	18	45]	[99	63	54	72	51]
Second partitions	[9]	[27	18	45]	[51	54]	[63	72	99]

After the partition is done, the sorting method is applied recursively to the left and right partitions. The base case for the recursion is a partition with one element, which cannot be further partitioned, as illustrated by [9] in Figure 13.5.

Our pseudocode algorithm is

```
Quicksort
    If there are elements to sort
        Choose a pivot value
        Partition the array based on the pivot value
        Quicksort the left partition
        Quicksort the right partition
    End If
End Quicksort
```

At this point in the development of our previous sorting algorithms, we reformulated the algorithms iteratively. However, iteration would not be easy for Quicksort because it has two recursive calls. This algorithm structure appeared in two earlier problems: the Towers of Hanoi (Chapter 5) and Fractals (Chapter 7). Generally, this form of recursion is more efficient than simple recursion, particularly when the subproblems are of nearly equal size. It is also more difficult to formulate iterative versions of algorithms using this form of recursion, so we will continue to develop our recursive solution.

We need to refine the algorithm by giving more detail for the partitioning step. To do the partitioning, we scan the array from its left end until we find an element greater than or equal to the pivot. We then scan the array from its right end until we find an element smaller than or equal to the pivot.

In Figure 13.6 I has scanned from the left and stopped on an element greater than or equal to the pivot, and J has scanned from the right and stopped on an element less than or equal to the pivot. These two elements are then exchanged. You might wonder why elements equal in value to the pivot can appear in either partition. This is because either I or J or both might encounter a value equal to the pivot in cases where there are multiple occurrences of the pivot value. This process of scanning and exchanging continues until the scans meet. When they meet, all elements to the right of J are greater

Figure 13.6
The Partitioning Process

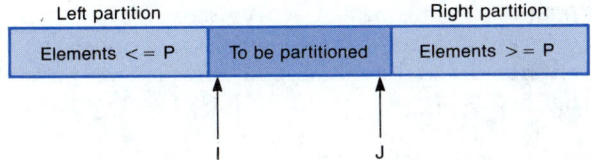

than or equal to the pivot. All elements to the left of I are less than or equal to the pivot, as illustrated in Figures 13.4 and 13.5. Do this procedure manually on the examples given in Figure 13.5 and on other examples until you feel confident of the process.

The pseudocode follows directly from this description.

> Partition
>   Set Pivot to value at index (I + J) div 2
>   Set I to the left index
>   Set J to the right index
>   Repeat
>   Move I to the right until a value >= Pivot is found
>   {A[Left] .. A[I − 1] < Pivot and A[I] >= Pivot}
>   Move J to the left until a value <= Pivot is found
>   {Pivot < A[J + 1] .. A[Right] and A[J] <= Pivot}
>   If I and J have not passed each other
>   Exchange A[I] and A[J]
>   Move I right one position
>   Move J left one position
>   End If
>   Until I and J pass each other
>   {A[Left] .. A[J] <= Pivot and Pivot <= A[I] .. A[Right]}
> End Partition;

Using these pseudocode algorithms, we implement Quicksort as a procedure to sort an array of integers.

```
CONST Max = 1000;

TYPE Vector = ARRAY [1..Max] OF INTEGER;

PROCEDURE QuickSort(VAR A: Vector; Left, Right: CARDINAL);
(* Application of C.A.R. Hoare's Quicksort method to the
   sorting of an array of integers.  A pivot element is chosen
   and the vector is partitioned in such a way that all the
   elements with a value less than or equal to the pivot are in
   the left partition and all the elements with a value greater
   than or equal to the pivot are in the right partition.  The
   process is then applied to each partition. *)

VAR I, J: CARDINAL;
```

```
PROCEDURE Partition(VAR A: Vector; VAR I, J: CARDINAL);
(* The pivot value is the value at index (I + J) DIV 2.  The
   elements of A are swapped until two partitions are formed:
   A[Left]..A[J] <= Pivot   and Pivot <= A[I]..A[Right] *)

VAR Pivot, Temp: INTEGER;
BEGIN
  Pivot := A[(I + J) DIV 2];
  REPEAT
    WHILE A[I] < Pivot DO         (* Scan I to right *)
      INC(I);
    END; (* WHILE *)
    (* A[Left]..A[I-1] < Pivot  and  A[I] >= Pivot *)
    WHILE A[J] > Pivot DO         (* Scan J to left *)
      DEC(J);
    END; (* WHILE *)
    (* Pivot < A[J + 1]..A[Right] and  A[J] <= Pivot *)
    IF I <= J THEN                (* Exchange values *)
      Temp := A[I];
      A[I] := A[J];
      A[J] := Temp;
      INC(I);                     (* and advance scanners *)
      DEC(J);
    END; (* IF *)
  UNTIL I > J;                    (* Partition done *)
  (* A[Left]..A[J] <= Pivot   and Pivot <= A[I]..A[Right] *)
END Partition;

BEGIN
  IF Right > Left THEN
    I := Left;
    J := Right;
    Partition(A, I, J);
    QuickSort(A, Left, J);
    QuickSort(A, I, Right)
  END (* IF *)
  (* A[I - 1] <= A[I] for I = Left + 1..Right *)
END QuickSort;
```

Procedure Quicksort has three parameters: the array to be sorted, A, and the limits of the partition to sort, Left and Right. For each recursive call, the partition to be sorted becomes smaller and smaller. Eventually Left will be greater than or equal to Right, in which case there is nothing to do. In the Partition procedure the pivot value chosen is the value of the middle element, and the REPEAT loop partitions the array by applying the method we presented earlier. The array is scanned from the left and from the right until values are found that must be exchanged or until the scans pass each other. Once the partition of the array is done, Quicksort is called recursively on each of the partitions. Notice that the partitions being sorted by these recursive calls do not overlap. If we had a system with more than one central processor, we could have separate processors sort each partition. This approach, called concurrent processing, has the potential of substantially increasing the execution speed of some algorithms. We will discuss concurrency in greater detail in Chapter 16.

We'll split the analysis of the Quicksort algorithm into finding the complexity of forming the partition and finding the number of passes that need to be made. We first find the complexity of partitioning. Let n be the number of elements to be partitioned. Since every element is compared to the pivot and the pivot might be compared to itself twice, or once, or never, the total number of comparisons is either $n - 1$, n, or $n + 1$. All these values are of complexity $O(n)$. The number of exchanges depends on the ordering of the data. The best case would be an array with the pivot value at the center and all elements less than the pivot to the left and all elements greater than the pivot to the right. No exchanges would be necessary for this array. The worst case is just the opposite (namely, the pivot at the center, larger elements to the left, and smaller elements to the right). This case would require $n/2$ exchanges. Using statistical methods, we can show that the average case will require approximately $n/6$ exchanges. Thus, the average case is approximately n comparisons plus $n/6$ exchanges, and so the complexity of the partition is $O(n)$.

The second part of the analysis is to determine the number of passes to be made. This number depends on the pivot value selected. The best case is when the pivot value is always the median (that is, the value such that half the items are less than this value and half the items are greater than this value). The data are partitioned into two equal halves, so if this process continues, the partition sizes will reach one element in $\log n$ passes, as we saw when we analyzed binary search. The worst selection for the pivot is either the smallest or the largest value in the array. In this case, given an original array of n elements, the partition sizes are 1 and $n - 1$ elements. If this unlucky choice is made again for the remaining $n - 1$ elements, the resulting partitions will be 1 and $n - 2$ elements. If this continues, n passes will be required. Surprisingly, for the average case where we assume the pivot value is random, the number of passes can be shown to be $1.39 \log n$, only slightly worse than the best case.

The overall complexity of the algorithm will be the product of the complexity for the partitioning times the number of passes. We can summarize our results as follows:

best case:	$n \log n$, which is $O(n \log n)$
average case:	$1.39\, n \log n$, which is $O(n \log n)$
worst case:	$n \times n$, which is $O(n^2)$

We need to say a few words about the selection of the pivot. Two obvious choices are the first element of the partition or the last element of the partition. If the data are in totally random order, these choices are as good as any others. However, if the data are already partially sorted, these would be poor choices since they would tend to be extreme values. Therefore the algorithm given in this section selects the pivot at the center of the array. (Note that this selection does not imply the value will be the median value—that is, the middle element of the ordered values.) Another alternative is to find the median of three values—the first, the last, and the central element—and use that as the pivot. In this way we may be more likely to be close to the median for all the data.

Since recursion involves substantial overhead at run time, when partitions become small enough, we can use some other sorting method on the smaller subarrays in order to improve efficiency even further. We can also implement Quicksort using iteration rather than recursion, but it is substantially more complicated.

The approach used in Quicksort can be adapted to provide a useful technique for finding the median for unsorted arrays of data without having to sort the array. The general strategy is to select a pivot and partition the data. Rather than applying the search recursively to both partitions, we only select the partition that will contain the median element (the $(n + 1)$ DIV 2 position). For example, in Figure 13.5 the array has nine elements, so we would expect the median to end up in the fifth position if the array was sorted. After the first partition, we see that the fifth position is in the right partition, so we only have to seek the median in the right partition. We continue selecting the correct partition each time until we reach a partition with one element at the position of the median. That element is the median. This algorithm can be shown to have an average complexity of $O(n)$. A similar approach can be used to find the kth element in the sorted array without having to sort the array.

13.4 Case Study: Sorting into Three Parts

In this section we'll work our way through a problem requiring us to develop an algorithm that is similar to partitioning in Quicksort. We'll follow our usual six-step method and then analyze our algorithm's complexity.

Suppose you work for a chemical company that has a large database containing chemical and physical properties for thousands of substances. Two important properties are the melting point and the boiling point for each substance. You have been asked to write a procedure that for a given temperature will sort this data into three categories: solid, liquid, and gas. The program must be efficient, so your boss has asked you to find a linear time, $O(n)$, algorithm to solve the problem. (You already know that Quicksort can solve the problem in $O(n \log n)$ time.) Your boss has also suggested that you use a small artificial set of data, rather than working on thousands of substances and possibly damaging the database while debugging your algorithm. Once working, the procedure can be adapted to handle the entire database. In addition to writing the sorting routine requested, you will have to have a way of testing the routine. Therefore, you will also write procedures to initialize a small set of data and print this data.

Design

Define the Problem We will assume that the substance data have been read into an array of records, each record containing a substance name, a classification field (to be assigned), the melting point, and the boiling point. The following types will be used:

```
Name: STRING
Classification: ( gas, liquid, solid )
MeltingPoint, BoilingPoint: REAL
```

Figure 13.7
Structure Chart for TriSort and Test Program

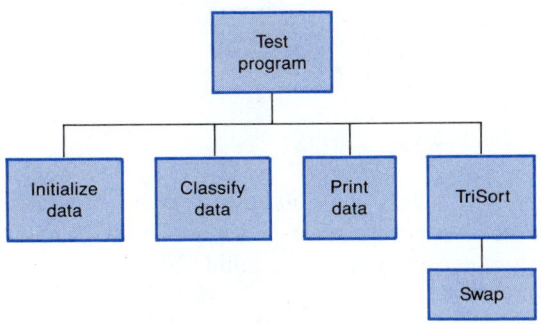

After the sort has been performed, the solids should be grouped at the low end of the array, the liquids in the middle of the array, and the gases at the high end of the array.

The calling program will ensure there is at least one data item, but there is no guarantee that every category will be present in the data being sorted.

Design a Solution To test our program, we will need procedures to initialize data and to print data, both before and after the sort. Before calling the sort routine, we will need a procedure to classify the substances for a given temperature. The sort itself will be based on exchanges, so we will create a swap routine for two records. The complete structure chart is shown in Figure 13.7.

Refine the Solution The hard part of this problem is finding a linear algorithm to perform the sort. This means that the data can be examined only a fixed number of times since the number of comparisons has to be proportional to n. We will try to develop an algorithm where each item is examined only once. In the Quicksort algorithm we saw how in one pass the data can be grouped into two categories: (1) less than or equal to the pivot, and (2) greater than or equal to the pivot. Remember that this grouping is accomplished by moving two indices inward from the ends of the array until the indices meet in the middle. During the partition our array looked like Figure 13.8.

We will try a similar approach to partition the data into three parts by using three indices—let's call them Solid, Liquid, and Gas. Figure 13.9 illustrates this scheme.

The Solid index will start on the left side and move right with only solids to its left. The Liquid and Gas indices will both start on the right and move left, with data arrangements as shown in Figure 13.9. The Liquid index will select the next item to be sorted. Gas will index the item to the left of the partition containing gases. Solid will index the item to the right of the partition containing solids. If the item that is indexed by Liquid is a liquid, then it is in the proper position. That is, no swaps have to be made, and Liquid can move left. If a solid is encountered, it is swapped with the

Figure 13.8
The Partitioning Process in Quicksort

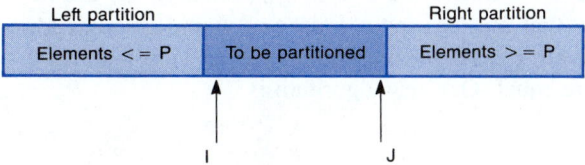

Figure 13.9

Sorting Arrangement and Indices

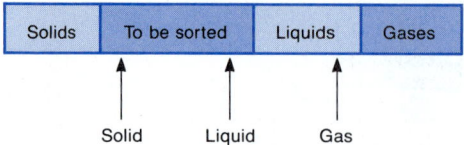

contents at the Solid index, and Solid moves right. If a gas is encountered, then it is swapped with the contents at the Gas index, and both the Gas and Liquid indices move left. This process continues until the Solid index and Liquid index cross, indicating that the sort has been completed.

The data arrangement shown in Figure 13.9 and the accompanying discussion leads to our first attempt at an algorithm for TriSort.

> TriSort
>   Set Solid to 0   {our array will be zero based}
>   Set Liquid and Gas to $n - 1$ {our array has n items}
>   While Liquid $>=$ Solid
>   {Data[0]..Data[Solid $-$ 1] are solids and Data[Liquid $+$ 1]..Data[Gas]
>   are liquids and Data[Gas $+$ 1]..Data[$n - 1$] are gases}
>   Case Data[Liquid]
>   solid: Swap items at Liquid and Solid, and increment Solid
>   liquid: Decrement Liquid
>   gas: Swap items at Liquid and Gas, decrement Liquid and Gas
>   End Case
>   End While
>   {The array is sorted such that Data[0]..Data[Solid $-$ 1] are solids
>   and Data[Liquid $+$ 1]..Data[Gas] are liquids
>   and Data[Gas $+$ 1]..Data [$n - 1$] are gases.
>   Furthermore, Liquid $+$ 1 $=$ Solid, so all elements are sorted.}
> End TriSort

The loop invariant given at the beginning of the While loop simply states what is depicted in Figure 13.9. This algorithm requires only one pass through the data to perform the desired sort; however, the algorithm is not very efficient since it may end up making swaps that are not needed. For example, if the list contains only solids, then solids will be continually swapped with solids until the indices meet. The same thing will happen if the list contains only gases. If there are only liquids, then no swaps will be made. We can improve the efficiency of the algorithm by moving the Solid index to the right until a nonsolid is found and moving the Liquid index to the left until a nonliquid is found. Before swapping the item at the Liquid index and the Gas index, we verify that the Gas index indexes a liquid (that is, at least one liquid has been encountered); otherwise, we would swap an item with itself since the Liquid and Gas indices are equal. Our new algorithm is

Case Study: Sorting into Three Parts

```
TriSort
    Set Solid to 0                          {our array will be zero based}
    Set Liquid and Gas to n − 1             {our array has n items}
    While Liquid >= Solid
        {Data[0]..Data[Solid − 1] are solids and Data[Liquid + 1]..Data[Gas]
         are liquids and Data[Gas + 1]..Data[n − 1] are gases           }
        While Data[Solid] is a solid
            Increment Solid
        End While
        While Data[Liquid] is a liquid
            Decrement Liquid
        End While
        If Solid <= Liquid then             {make sure they didn't cross}
            Case Data[Liquid]
                solid: Swap items at Liquid and Solid, Increment Solid
                gas  : If Data[Gas] is a liquid
                            Swap items at Liquid and Gas
                       End If
                       Decrement Liquid and Gas
            End Case
        End If
    End While
    {The array is sorted such that Data[0]..Data[Solid − 1] are solids
     and Data[Liquid + 1]..Data[Gas] are liquids
     and Data[Gas + 1]..Data [n − 1] are gases.
     Furthermore, Liquid + 1 = Solid, so all elements are sorted.}
End TriSort
```

The Initialize procedure, the Print procedure, and the Swap procedure are straightforward, so we will develop pseudocode only for the main program and the classify procedure.

```
Test TriSort
    Initialize Data
    Read temperature
    Classify
    Print Data
    TriSort
    Print Data
End Test TriSort
```

> Classify
>   For each substance
>   If temperature <= melting point
>   classification is solid
>   Elsif temperature <= boiling point
>   classification is liquid
>   Else
>   classification is gas
>   End if
>   End for
> End Classify

Develop a Testing Strategy Normally we would expect the classification of substances to contain all three categories (solids, liquids, and gases), but this may not always be the case. By changing the temperature, we can check various combinations of data. We should try to include

- a random mixture of solids, liquids, and gases
- a sorted mixture of solids, liquids, and gases
- solids and gases only
- solids and liquids only
- liquids and gases only
- solids only
- liquids only
- gases only

If our algorithm is efficient, there should be no exchanges for the second case and the last three cases. We will assume that the calling program will check that the initial array is not empty.

Specific data values and expected results for several temperatures (in Celsius) are shown in Tables 13.4 and 13.5.

TABLE 13.4 Melting and Boiling Points for Ten Substances

Substance	Melting Point	Boiling Point
ammonia	−77.7	−33.35
bromine	−7.2	58.78
lead	327.502	1740.0
mercury	−38.87	356.58
oxygen	−218.4	−182.962
potassium	63.65	774.0
sodium	97.81	882.9
sulfur dioxide	−72.7	−10.0
sulfuric acid	10.36	338.0
water	0.0	100.0

TABLE 13.5 Substance States at Various Temperatures

At −250 degrees Celsius			At −200 degrees Celsius	
ammonia	solid		ammonia	solid
bromine	solid		bromine	solid
lead	solid		lead	solid
mercury	solid		mercury	solid
oxygen	solid		water	solid
potassium	solid		potassium	solid
sodium	solid		sodium	solid
sulfur dioxide	solid		sulfur dioxide	solid
sulfuric acid	solid		sulfuric acid	solid
water	solid		oxygen	liquid

At −150 degrees Celsius			At −100 degrees Celsius	
ammonia	solid		ammonia	solid
bromine	solid		bromine	solid
lead	solid		lead	solid
mercury	solid		mercury	solid
water	solid		water	solid
potassium	solid		potassium	solid
sodium	solid		sodium	solid
sulfur dioxide	solid		sulfur dioxide	solid
sulfuric acid	solid		sulfuric acid	solid
oxygen	gas		oxygen	gas

At −50 degrees Celsius			At 0 degrees Celsius	
sulfuric acid	solid		sulfuric acid	solid
bromine	solid		sodium	solid
lead	solid		lead	solid
mercury	solid		potassium	solid
water	solid		water	solid
potassium	solid		mercury	liquid
sodium	solid		bromine	liquid
sulfur dioxide	liquid		sulfur dioxide	gas
ammonia	liquid		ammonia	gas
oxygen	gas		oxygen	gas

At 50 degrees Celsius			At 100 degrees Celsius	
potassium	solid		lead	solid
sodium	solid		sodium	liquid
lead	solid		potassium	liquid
sulfuric acid	liquid		sulfuric acid	liquid
water	liquid		water	liquid
mercury	liquid		mercury	liquid
bromine	liquid		bromine	gas
sulfur dioxide	gas		sulfur dioxide	gas
ammonia	gas		ammonia	gas
oxygen	gas		oxygen	gas

TABLE 13.5 **Substance States at Various Temperatures (continued)**

At 150 degrees Celsius		At 400 degrees Celsius	
lead	solid	lead	liquid
sodium	liquid	sodium	liquid
potassium	liquid	potassium	liquid
sulfuric acid	liquid	sulfuric acid	gas
mercury	liquid	mercury	gas
water	gas	water	gas
bromine	gas	bromine	gas
sulfur dioxide	gas	sulfur dioxide	gas
ammonia	gas	ammonia	gas
oxygen	gas	oxygen	gas

At 1,750 degrees Celsius	
lead	gas
sodium	gas
potassium	gas
sulfuric acid	gas
mercury	gas
water	gas
bromine	gas
sulfur dioxide	gas
ammonia	gas
oxygen	gas

Implementation

Code and Test the Program The coding in Modula-2 for the constants, types, and procedures Classify, Swap, and TriSort is as follows. The remainder of the program is left as an exercise (see Programming Problem 16).

```
CONST MaxNumSubstances = 9;
      MaxPlusOne = MaxNumSubstances + 1;

TYPE SubstanceType = (gas, liquid, solid);
     SubstanceData = RECORD
                       Name: STRING;
                       Classification: SubstanceType;
                       MeltingPoint, BoilingPoint: REAL
                     END;   (* RECORD *)
     IndexRange = [-1..MaxPlusOne];

PROCEDURE Classify(VAR Data: ARRAY OF SubstanceData;
                   Temperature: REAL);
VAR Count: CARDINAL;
```

SEC. 13.4 Case Study: Sorting into Three Parts

```
    BEGIN  (* Classify *)
      FOR Count := 0 TO HIGH(Data) DO
        WITH Data[Count] DO
          IF Temperature <= MeltingPoint THEN Classification := solid
          ELSIF Temperature <= BoilingPoint THEN Classification := liquid
          ELSE Classification := gas;
          END; (* IF *)
        END; (* WITH *)
      END; (* FOR *)
    END Classify;

    PROCEDURE Swap(VAR ItemA, ItemB: SubstanceData);
    (* exchanges contents of the two actual parameters *)
    VAR Temp: SubstanceData;
    BEGIN
      Temp := ItemA;
      ItemA := ItemB;
      ItemB := Temp;
    END Swap;

    PROCEDURE TriSort(VAR Data: ARRAY OF SubstanceData);
    VAR Solid, Liquid, Gas: IndexRange;
    BEGIN
      Solid := 1;                    (* solids will have lowest indices *)
      Liquid := HIGH(Data - 1); (* liquids will have midrange indices *)
      Gas := Liquid              (* gases will have highest indices *)
      WHILE Solid <= Liquid DO
         (* Data[1]..Data[Solid - 1] are solid and
            Data[Liquid + 1]..Data[Gas] are liquid and
            Data[Gas + 1]..Data[HIGH(Data - 1)] are gas *)

        WHILE (Solid < INTEGER(HIGH(Data))) AND
              (Data[Solid].Classification = solid) DO
          INC(Solid);              (* advance Solid index past solids *)
        END; (* WHILE *)
        WHILE (Liquid > 0) AND
              (Data[Liquid].Classification = liquid) DO
          DEC(Liquid);     (* move liquids index left past liquids *)
        END; (* WHILE *)
        IF Solid <= Liquid THEN (* make sure the indices didn't cross *)
          CASE Data[Liquid].Classification OF
            solid: Swap(Data[Solid], Data[Liquid]); INC(Solid); |
            gas:   IF Data[Gas].Classification # gas THEN
                     Swap(Data[Liquid], Data[Gas]);
                   END; (* IF *)
                   DEC(Liquid); DEC(Gas);
            ELSE
          END; (* CASE *)
        END; (* IF *)
      END; (* WHILE *)
```

```
         (* Data[1]..Data[Solid - 1] are solid and
            Data[Liquid + 1]..Data[Gas] are liquid and
            Data[Gas + 1]..Data[High(Data - 1)] are gas  and
            Liquid + 1 = Solid                         *)

END TriSort;
```

The loop invariant immediately after the first WHILE in procedure Sort documents the most important aspect of our algorithm. This was illustrated in Figure 13.9; carefully compare the invariant with that figure.

You may have noticed that the code in the procedure Sort varies slightly from the pseudocode algorithm. To understand these changes, we must examine IndexRange which goes from -1 to MaxPlusOne. The valid data in the array is from indices 0 to Max, the values -1 and MaxPlusOne are included for those limiting cases (such as all solids or all gases) where the algorithm causes a search index (Solid, Liquid, or Gas) to go beyond the bounds of valid data. When mapped into the open array index, which is always a cardinal, we have -1 mapping to 0, 0 mapping to 1, . . ., Max mapping to HIGH(Data) $-$ 1, and MaxPlusOne mapping to HIGH(Data). This results in changes such as initializing Solid to 1 and Liquid/Gas to HIGH(Data) $-$ 1. The loop invariants have also been changed accordingly. You should verify that the loop invariant after the first WHILE loop still matches the illustration in Figure 13.7, which does not show the "invalid" index positions.

Complete the Documentation   We do not need a user's manual in this case study, since the final product is the TriSort procedure rather than an entire program. The internal program documentation coupled with design documentation is sufficient for this case study.

Complexity Analysis

Since TriSort works with one pass through the data, we suspect the complexity will be $O(n)$. Clearly we will need to examine every item once and only once. A more difficult question is the number of exchanges. The best case is no exchanges; the data are already sorted properly. During the design phase we modified our algorithm to ensure that we never exchanged two items of the same type. What will be the worst case for the number of exchanges? Suppose the array contains an equal number of extreme elements (solids and gases in our example) and no elements in the middle category. Furthermore, assume the two extremes are completely out of place, as shown in Figure 13.10. We can see that this data would require $n/2$ exchanges. Thus, the overall complexity of this algorithm is $O(n)$, as we originally suspected.

Figure 13.10
Worst Case for TriSort

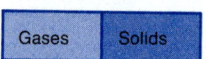

Application to Quicksort

The Quicksort algorithm given in Section 13.3 partitions the initial array into two groups of elements: those less than or equal to the pivot element and those greater than or equal to the pivot element. Using our TriSort routine, we can modify our partitioning in Quicksort to give us three partitions, as shown in Figure 13.11.

Figure 13.11
Quicksort with Three Partitions

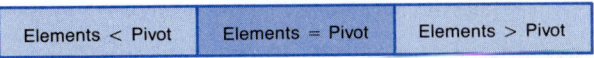

The elements equal to the pivot are already in the correct position, so that this partition need not be sorted. If there are a reasonable number of duplicate pivot elements, the other partitions are smaller and the sort will proceed more quickly. However, if duplicates are rare or nonexistent, the TriSort partitioning would not be worth the extra time needed to maintain three indices and to do more switching since elements smaller than the pivot and equal to the pivot no longer fall into the same partition. We'll leave it as an exercise to modify the Quicksort algorithm to use this partitioning into three parts (see Programming Problem 17).

SUMMARY

Two simple sorting methods are the selection sort and the insertion sort. With the selection sort we find the smallest remaining element, put it in its proper position, and then sort the remaining elements. A recursive insertion sort begins by sorting a subarray consisting of all the elements but the last; then we insert that element into its proper place. The iterative version inserts the element at the ith position into the sorted subarray of elements previous to the ith element.

As we write programs, we should make sure they are correct. This process, called program verification, should be done informally as we develop the program.

Algorithms must be able to be executed in a reasonable amount of time. Whenever we develop algorithms, therefore, we must also analyze their complexity: efficiency in solving the problem. For instance, a complexity analysis of a sorting algorithm would consider the number of comparisons between elements being sorted and the number of times elements being sorted are moved.

The mathematical notation used to express an algorithm's complexity is called Big-O notation. It allows us to classify algorithms according to their complexity. Some commonly occurring classifications are constant, logarithmic, linear, $n \log n$, quadratic, cubic, and exponential. Algorithms of exponential complexity are considered intractable because they are not practical for larger problems.

The simple sorting algorithms selection sort and insertion sort have quadratic complexity, $O(n^2)$. Quicksort is a more efficient sorting algorithm developed in the early 1960s. It partitions the array of elements to be sorted into smaller parts, and then recursively sorts each smaller part. The average complexity of Quicksort is $O(n \log n)$.

EXERCISES

1. Find the complexity classification for the following expressions:

    (a) $3000m + 45000000$

    (b) $(x^3 - 1)/(x - 1)$

    (c) $Y^5 - 3Y^3 + 2^Y$

2. Modify the Quicksort algorithm to sort records based on a key field.

3. Modify the Quicksort program to use the median of the first entry, the last entry, and the central entry as the pivot value.

4. Write a program to find the median, based on the Quicksort program, without sorting all elements.

5. Modify your solution to Exercise 4 to find the kth element in an unsorted array without sorting all elements.

6. Modify the Quicksort program so that the smallest partition is always sorted first. This will ensure the number of suspended recursive calls at any one time never exceeds $\log n$.

7. Do an analysis of the bubble sort described in Problem 12 to determine its complexity.

8. What is the complexity of the improved bubble sort described in Problem 13?

9. What is the complexity of the shaker sort described in Problem 14?

10. The following procedure, similar to the inner FOR loop of the selection sort, returns the index of the smallest element in an array of integers.

```
PROCEDURE Min( A: ARRAY OF INTEGER ): CARDINAL;
(* Find the index of the smallest element of the array A. *)

VAR  N, I, IndexOfSmallest: CARDINAL;

BEGIN
  N := HIGH( A );
  IndexOfSmallest := 0;
  FOR I := 1 TO N DO
      (* Loop Invariant:  ( A[IndexOfSmallest] <= A[0]..A[I - 1] )
                     AND ( I <= N + 1 ) *)
    IF A[I] < A[IndexOfSmallest] THEN
      IndexOfSmallest := I;
    END; (* IF *)
  END; (* FOR *)
  (* Final Assertion: A[IndexOfSmallest] <= A[0]..A[N] *)
  RETURN IndexOfSmallest;
END Max;
```

Prove that

- The loop invariant is initially true.
- The loop invariant remains true for each iteration of the loop.
- The loop invariant combined with the exit condition results in the final assertion.

PROGRAMMING PROBLEMS

11. Implement and test the Quicksort procedure. Add a Boolean constant that, when set to TRUE, causes the array to be printed after the completion of the Partition procedure. Print square brackets to indicate the partition just processed.

12. Write and test a procedure for the bubble sort. The bubble sort makes several passes over the array elements to put them in order. In each pass, pairs of adjacent elements are compared, and if the two elements that constitute the pair are not in order, they are exchanged. The first pass considers all the elements in this pairwise fashion, comparing A[1] with A[2], A[2] with A[3], and so forth. When the pass is completed, the largest element will have "bubbled" to its correct place at the last position of the array. If we consider the last position to be the "top" of the array, we can think of the largest element "bubbling" to the top during the first pass. Also, some localized reordering will have taken place. The second pass considers all the elements but the last one, and when completed, the second-largest value will have bubbled to the next-to-last position of the array. This process is continued until there is only one element left to be considered; that element is then already in its final position.

13. The bubble sort described in Problem 12 can be improved somewhat by stopping the sort after any pass in which no exchanges are made. Implement this improved bubble sort. *Hint:* Use a BOOLEAN variable to indicate whether or not there has been an exchange during a pass.

14. Implement a version of the bubble sort from Problem 12, called the shaker sort, in which consecutive passes are done in alternate directions.

15. It is possible to implement Quicksort iteratively provided you have a means of remembering partitions to be sorted. A partition can be defined by a record that contains the lower and upper bounds. You can save these records in an array. By sorting the smallest partition (see Exercise 6), you can guarantee that an array of size log n is sufficient. Implement this iterative Quicksort algorithm.

16. Complete and test the TriSort program by writing the initialization procedure, print procedure, and main program. Use input and output redirection.

17. Modify the Quicksort program to use partitioning into three parts: elements less than the pivot, elements equal to the pivot, and elements greater than the pivot.

18. Using the TriSort strategy, design a new algorithm, Quadsort, to sort elements into four categories in linear time.

14 Numerical Methods

In this chapter you will

- be introduced to the field of numerical analysis, which involves the development of methods for solution of numerical problems on computers
- learn about the representation of numeric values
- see the development of algorithms for computing approximations
- be introduced to procedure types
- explore the generation of random numbers

This chapter will introduce you to numerical methods, which is an important topic for the application of computers to scientific problems. The first significant applications of computers involved the solution of scientific and engineering problems that required complex or tedious numerical computations. In fact, you may recall that in the Introduction we mentioned that the primary motivation for the development of the first electronic computer, the ENIAC, was the preparation of ballistic tables used to compute the trajectories of projectiles. *Numerical analysis,* the development of numerical methods suitable for digital computers, has become an important area of scientific investigation.

Before discussing some common numerical methods, we must discuss how numbers are represented in the computer. The details of number representation may not be critical for some applications, but the effectiveness of many numerical methods can be critically dependent on the representation used. We'll review the basics of the binary system and see how values of types CARDINAL, INTEGER, and REAL are numerically represented in computer memory. Then we'll explore three numeric applications: series approximations, numerical integration, and use of random numbers. Finally, in the case study we use the method of bisection to find a root of a polynomial equation.

14.1 Computer Arithmetic

Although computers use binary notation, we can discuss computer arithmetic using decimal notation. This notation will be easier for us because we are more used to thinking in decimal than in binary.

A computer memory is typically considered to be a sequence of cells, called *words*, where each memory word can contain a value. The size of a memory word varies from one computer to another. We will assume that we have a decimal computer where each word can contain eight symbols taken from 0, 1, 2, 3, 4, 5, 6, 7, 8, 9, −, or +. For example, a value of type INTEGER would be stored as

With such a computer the largest integer value that can be stored is

The smallest possible negative integer value would be -9999999. Whenever we try to store a value greater than the maximum or less than the minimum, we have what is called *overflow*. When that happens, computers generally display an error message and abort execution of the program.

Values of type REAL are stored in a form similar to scientific notation like

$$12.34E-5$$

Each value will be expressed in two parts: a fractional part (also called the *mantissa*) and an *exponent* part. In order not to waste any space, the fractional part will always start with a nonzero digit. The preceding value will be stored as

$$.1234E-3$$

that is,

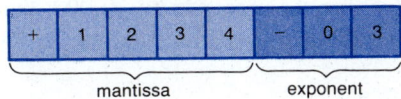

where the machine assumes the decimal point will always precede the mantissa. With this representation the maximum value for real numbers is $0.9999E99$, and the minimum value is $-0.9999E99$. The smallest positive real value will be $0.1000E-99$, and the largest negative value will be $-0.1000E-99$. Trying to store values whose magnitude is larger than the maximum value causes an overflow. In some cases values are close to zero, but their magnitude is smaller than the smallest positive value or larger than the largest negative value. This situation causes an error called *underflow*. Some systems will give an error message in cases of underflow, but most do not. Instead they

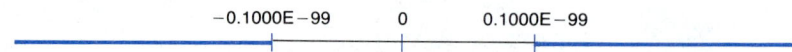

Figure 14.1 Real Value Representation

simply store incorrect values. Figure 14.1 shows the actual real values that could be handled with our decimal representation, where with the exception of zero, values between $-0.1000E-99$ and $0.1000E-99$ could not be represented.

Let's compare integer and real constants. Suppose we have the same value expressed as an integer or as a real, 1234567 and 1234567.0. Using our decimal computer, we will have

This example illustrates the fact that computer arithmetic may be exact for integer values, if they are within the limits of the representation, while real value representations may be an approximation of the actual number.

As another example, the number 1/3 will be represented by $0.3333E+00$. This means that if three instances of this number are added, the result will be $0.9999E+00$, not $0.1000E+01$. If we were to test whether $1/3 + 1/3 + 1/3 = 1$, the result would be false. This is an example of our first "rule of thumb" for real numbers.

1. Do not test real numbers for equality.

When values of type REAL are used, errors will occur because the values stored are only approximate. Doing numerical computations with real values can, therefore, lead to a loss of precision. As an example, let's assume we want a result that can be obtained by adding the results of two previous computations, which are stored as $0.4000E5$ and $0.3000E1$. The computer cannot add two real numbers unless they have the same exponent. Thus, to add these values, the computer must alter one of them so that the exponents are equal; then the mantissas can be added. In this example the second mantissa must be altered so that the exponent becomes 5. This can be done by dividing the mantissa by 10,000; the second number becomes $0.00003E5$. Then the mantissas are added as follows:

$$\begin{array}{r} 0.4000 \\ \underline{0.00003} \\ 0.40003 \end{array}$$

This value is what could be expected; unfortunately, it cannot be stored within the allowed precision. The stored result is then $0.4000E5$, which is the value of our first number, *unchanged*. Thus, with our representation of real numbers, adding these two values would simply give the first value, and the second value would have had no effect whatsoever. As a result some precision is lost. In some numerical applications this loss of precision may be immaterial, but in others it may be disastrous, especially when multiple operations cause the error to build up, or propagate.

When several additions and subtractions are to be done on real values, the order of operations may affect the final result. We recommend using the following two "rules of thumb" for performing additions and subtractions.

2. Try to add real numbers of similar size.
3. Try not to subtract real numbers of similar size.

When operations like multiplication or division are performed, their result usually has more digits than their operands. Very frequently those extra digits cannot be stored and are lost—at the expense of accuracy. For example, consider a multiplication of the following two numbers: 732.0 and 0.220. The result should be 161.04; however, the last digit will be lost in the representation used here, because there is no room to store it. Even if the values of the two operands were accurately represented, the value of their product is not. If this value is used in further computations, it will introduce a slight error, which might propagate and affect the final result. Even if computers actually store more than four significant decimal digits for real values (most store 7), the same problem will still occur, although with more significant digits it will be less severe.

The development of numerical methods that give meaningful results is a challenging and important area that involves considerable knowledge of both mathematics and computer science. In the next few sections we will discuss actual binary number representations and present some numerical methods representative of the field.

An Aside on Fixed Point Numbers

In many applications, such as those involving monetary values, it is important to avoid such peculiarities as those just described. People rather resent check payments that are not exact. To avoid such peculiarities, we may choose to represent some values with fractional parts by using integers together with scale factors. This approach was taken in Chapter 12, where we used integers with a scale factor of 1/100 to represent monetary values. In this way we can handle rounding in a way so that such peculiarities are avoided. Numbers represented in this fashion are called *fixed point numbers,* because they have a decimal point assumed to be at some fixed position from the rightmost position of the actual representation. For monetary values this position would be two decimal places to the left. By contrast, our representation of real numbers is often referred to as *floating point,* which is the origin of the name of the transfer function FLOAT.

14.2 The Binary Number System

Like the usual decimal representation, the binary representation used in most computers is a positional notation, but it uses the base 2 rather than the usual base 10. When we write a number, like 4096, the position of each digit in the number is used to determine the value of the number. In elementary school we learned that each number has a ones digit, a tens digit, a hundreds digit, and so on. So our example of 4096 stands for the sum

$$4 \times 10^3 + 0 \times 10^2 + 9 \times 10^1 + 6 \times 10^0$$

Usually we become so used to this notation that we do not even think about it; the representation has become subconscious. When using a different number base, however, we must bring the notation back to the level of conscious thought. Formally, the position of a digit within a number determines the exponent of the base that multiplies the digit. In the decimal system (base 10), the ones digit is associated with an exponent of 0, the tens digit with an exponent of 1, the hundreds digit with an exponent of 2, and so on—as illustrated by the representation of 4096 just shown.

The basic idea is the same for the binary, base 2, system except that we have only two digits, 0 and 1, and we use powers of 2 rather than powers of 10. For example, the binary number 10010 stands for the sum

$$1 \times 2^4 + 0 \times 2^3 + 0 \times 2^2 + 1 \times 2^1 + 0 \times 2^0$$

or 18 in decimal. Often we write the equivalence between the same number written in two different bases by using subscripts that indicate the bases. For example,

$$10010_2 = 18_{10}$$

It is also possible to convert from a decimal number to the equivalent binary number. Rather than guess at the powers of 2 that must be included, we can use an algorithm based on successive integer division by 2 and the remainders of these divisions. Here is how this algorithm works to find the binary representation of 18:

```
18 div 2 = 9 rem 0  ↑
 9 div 2 = 4 rem 1     Read remainders backward to find
 4 div 2 = 2 rem 0     the equivalent binary number
 2 div 2 = 1 rem 0
 1 div 2 = 0 rem 1     We stop when the quotient becomes 0
```

Binary fractions follow the same principle as decimal fractions. Each digit position corresponds to a negative power of the base. For instance,

$$0.1802 = 1 \times 10^{-1} + 8 \times 10^{-2} + 0 \times 10^{-3} + 2 \times 10^{-4}$$

In binary we use the same notation,

$$0.1011 = 1 \times 2^{-1} + 0 \times 2^{-2} + 1 \times 2^{-3} + 1 \times 2^{-4}$$

Some fractions can be represented by a finite sequence of digits like

$$0.25_{10} = 0.01_2$$

But some fractions might be represented by a finite sequence of digits in one number system but not in the other, such as

$$0.1_{10} = 0.0001100110011\ldots_2$$

Having introduced the mechanics of the binary number system used by computers, we can now move on to look at how the values of types CARDINAL, INTEGER, and REAL are actually represented within the computer.

14.3 Internal Representations of Numeric Values

All values are represented in computer memory by binary digits or bits—that is, a sequence of zeros and ones. The representation of values of type CARDINAL is the most straightforward; we simply represent the nonnegative integers using binary notation. The length of such a representation is longer than the decimal notation, as shown in Table 14.1.

In a machine representation of values of type CARDINAL, a certain number of bits are allocated for the binary representation of each value. Although this varies with implementations, on microcomputers it is common to allocate 16 bits, while on larger machines 32 bits or more may be used. If 16 bits are allocated, the largest possible value is

$$1 \times 2^{15} + 1 \times 2^{14} + 1 \times 2^{13} + 1 \times 2^{12} + \ldots + 1 \times 2^1 + 1 \times 2^0$$

or equivalently,

$$2^{16} - 1 \text{ or in decimal } 65{,}535$$

With 32 bits the largest possible value is

$$2^{32} - 1 \text{ or in decimal } 4{,}294{,}967{,}295$$

TABLE 14.1 Representation of CARDINALs in Decimal and Binary

Decimal	Binary
0	0
1	1
2	10
3	11
4	100
5	101
6	110
7	111
8	1000
9	1001
10	1010
11	1011
12	1100
13	1101
14	1110
15	1111
16	10000
17	10001
18	10010
.	.
.	.
.	.

Thus larger machines may be able to represent many more cardinals than smaller machines. This is not a restriction of the language used; it will be present in any implementation.

The standard procedures MAX and MIN return the actual maximum and minimum values for a given type, but these procedures may not be available on all implementations. If 16 bits are used to represent cardinals, MAX(CARDINAL) will return 65,535.

The representation of values of type INTEGER is complicated by the need to represent the sign of the value. Three common approaches to this representation are sign and magnitude, one's complement, and two's complement. The first two are flawed because they have two representations for the value zero, so we will concentrate on the third. Arithmetic operations are also easier to perform using two's complement.

In the two's complement representation the nonnegative integers are formed in the same way as cardinals, but a negative integer is formed by

1. taking the complement of the corresponding positive integer by changing every 0 to a 1 and every 1 to a 0, and
2. adding 1 to the complement

You can easily remember this procedure as "complement then increment." For example, with 16 bits, -4 is represented by complementing 0000000000000100 to obtain 1111111111111011 and adding 1 to obtain 1111111111111100. With 16 bits, the largest value is 0111111111111111, which is $2^{15} - 1$, and the smallest value is 1000000000000000, which is $-(2^{15})$.

In general, if n bits are used to represent integers, the range of possible values is from $2^{n-1} - 1$ down to $-(2^{n-1})$. On many microcomputers, 16 bits are used to represent integers, so that the maximum integer is $2^{15} - 1$ or 32,767. If this is the case, it is a good idea for Modula-2 implementations to use only 15 bits to represent cardinal values in order that the type CARDINAL is a subrange of the type INTEGER. However, some implementations use 16 bits for both cardinal and integer values. This approach expands the range of cardinal values, but it also creates problems because the larger values of type CARDINAL cannot be converted to type INTEGER.

Arithmetic operations are easy to perform using two's complement, as illustrated by the addition problem

Decimal	16 Bit, Two's Complement
-4	1111111111111100
$\underline{7}$	$\underline{0000000000000111}$
3	0000000000000011

Notice that a carry bit is propagated to the left as the addition is performed; if we had an extra bit of precision, the result would be 10000000000000011. Provided the original operands are of opposite sign (the most significant bits in the two's complement numbers are not the same), we can ignore this carry bit and obtain the correct answer. The issues of a carry bit and an overflow bit (which is set when we have a carry when adding numbers of the same sign) can be complex and are discussed in detail in machine organization/assembly language courses.

Numbers outside the allowable range for type INTEGER may be represented with values of type REAL. Real values are represented in a form with two parts, the mantissa and the exponent, which are expressed in binary. The base is usually a power of 2 (2 or 16 is commonly used). On many computers, 32 bits are used to represent a value of type REAL. As a simple example, 24 bits could be used to represent a signed mantissa, which will be considered to be a fractional part less than 1. Then, 8 bits could be used to represent a signed integral exponent of 2. If we let M denote the mantissa and E the exponent, the value would be

$$M \times 2^E$$

With 8 bits, E could range from -128 to 127, using two's complement. So we could represent positive real values ranging from about 2^{-128} to 2^{127}, which corresponds approximately to 10^{-38} to 10^{38} in decimal. A corresponding range of negative values could also be represented. The actual positioning of bits within this representation does vary; in the following example we assume the mantissa uses the first 24 bits and the exponent the last 8 bits.

Consider the decimal number -0.125,

$$-0.125 = -0.1 \times 2^{-2} \text{ (assuming a base of 2)}$$

so the mantissa is -1 and the exponent is -2. The internal representation is

$$\underline{1\,1\,1\,1\,1\,1\,1\,1\,1\,1\,1\,1\,1\,1\,1\,1\,1\,1\,1\,1\,1\,1\,1\,1} \quad \underline{1\,1\,1\,1\,1\,1\,1\,0}$$

Mantissa $= -1$ Exponent $= -2$

The precision of the values depends on the number of bits used for the mantissa. With this representation, it would be less than 7 decimal digits, because 24 binary digits correspond to between 6 and 7 decimal digits. Since for many numerical methods this precision is inadequate, Modula-2 has a standard type LONGREAL. This type is implemented only on some systems and is usually based on a 64-bit representation, which offers greater precision and possibly an extended range for the exponent.

14.4 Series Approximations

One very common class of numerical techniques involves finding an approximation to a result that would be difficult or impossible to compute exactly. In this section we will discuss such a technique: approximation using a series. We will consider a very simple approximation to the natural logarithm function

$$\ln x = (x - 1) - \frac{(x - 1)^2}{2} + \frac{(x - 1)^3}{3} - \frac{(x - 1)^4}{4} + \cdots$$

This is the power series, or Taylor series, expansion of the natural logarithm function for $0 < x \leq 2$. Since it is an infinite series, we cannot possibly sum all the terms. But we can use the sum of the first few terms as an approximation. Note that the nth term of the sum, which we will call $t(n)$, can be expressed as

$$t(n) = (-1)^{n+1} \times \frac{(x - 1)^n}{n} \text{ for } n = 1, 2, \ldots$$

This formula could be used to compute an approximation with the first ten terms as follows:

> Set Approx to zero
> For n from 1 to 10 do
>   Set Term to $(-1)^{n+1} ((x-1)^n)/n$
>   Set Approx to Approx + Term
> End for

Computing the numerator for each term would be very inefficient, and commonly used functions such as this should be done efficiently. We can improve the efficiency by noting that the numerator for each term, after the first, can easily be computed by multiplying the numerator of the preceding term by $(-1)(x-1)$. Using this multiplier, we can transform the preceding pseudocode (again for 10 terms) to the following:

> Set Approx to $x - 1$
> Set Numerator to $x - 1$
> For n from 2 to 10 do
>   Set Numerator to $(-1)(x-1)$Numerator
>   Set Approx to Approx + Numerator/n
> End for

However, we chose 10 terms only as an example; therefore, we must now address the issue of how many terms will yield an adequate accuracy. All the neglected terms represent the exact error of the approximation, but it can be shown mathematically that for a series of decreasing terms of alternating signs, the error is no greater than the first term that is neglected. Since in general our accuracy requirements will vary depending on the application, we should write a function that uses as many terms as necessary to achieve the desired accuracy. The number of terms will depend on the argument x, so we will use a WHILE loop rather than a FOR loop. Our function, embedded in a testing program, is as follows:

```
MODULE TestLn;
(* Test natural logarithm procedure
                              J. M. Adams    January 1988 *)
FROM InOut IMPORT WriteString, WriteLn;
FROM RealInOut IMPORT ReadReal, WriteReal;
FROM MathLib0 IMPORT ln;

CONST Err = 1.0E-7;

PROCEDURE Ln(X: REAL): REAL;
(* Compute an approximation to the natural logarithm function
   by using the power series approximation *)
VAR Approx, Numerator, Xminus1, N: REAL;
```

```
    BEGIN
      Xminus1 := X - 1.0;
      Numerator := Xminus1;
      Approx := Numerator;
      N := 1.0;
      WHILE ABS(Numerator)/N > Err DO
        N := N + 1.0;
        Numerator := -Numerator * Xminus1;
        Approx := Approx + Numerator / N;
      END; (* WHILE *)
      RETURN Approx;
    END Ln;

    VAR A: REAL;

    BEGIN (* TestLn *)
      LOOP
        WriteString("Enter value (0 < x < 2) or 0 to stop: ");
        ReadReal(A); WriteLn;
        IF A = 0.0 THEN EXIT END;
        IF (A > 0.0) AND (A < 2.0) THEN
          WriteString("Natural logarithm is "); WriteReal(Ln(A), 15);
          WriteLn;
          WriteString("Should have been     "); WriteReal(ln(A), 15);
          WriteLn;
        END; (* IF *)
      END; (* LOOP *)
    END TestLn.
```

Because the terms decrease in size rather slowly and we haven't picked extreme values for A, the results produced by our function Ln are close to the results produced by the standard library function ln. But the standard function probably uses a more sophisticated series approximation that is more efficient than the power series. Series approximations are also used for the trigonometric and exponential functions in the standard library. An error analysis should be done for series approximations to determine the accuracy of the approximation and the loss of precision in the computation, but that is beyond the scope of this text. In Exercises 10, 11, and 12, you will see an example where the loss of precision leads to erroneous results for calculating the exponential function for an extreme value.

An Aside on Polynomial Evaluation

Suppose we need to evaluate the function

$$f(x) = 3x^4 + 5x^3 - 2x^2 + 10x - 7$$

If we do the operations from left to right, we would need to perform 10 multiplicative operations and 4 additive operations. However, if we rewrite this function as

$$f(x) = (((3x + 5)x - 2)x + 10)x - 7$$

then we need only 4 multiplicative operations and 4 additive operations. This is a substantial savings if this function is going to be evaluated many times. This technique is called *Horner's Method*. In general, we can write the polynomial

$$c_n x^n + c_{n-1} x^{n-1} + c_{n-2} x^{n-2} + \cdots + c_1 x + c_0$$

as

$$((\cdots (c_n x + c_{n-1})x + c_{n-2})x + \cdots + c_1)x + c_0$$

14.5 Numerical Integration and Procedure Types

Like series approximation, numerical integration is a useful numerical technique. Many applications require finding the area under a curve. For example, the area under an electrical power curve, showing the kilowatts used over a time period in hours, represents the work done in kilowatt hours, which is the basis for utilization charges. In some cases the area under a curve can be found analytically by integration, using methods from calculus. In other cases, though, this approach may be impossible or impractical, and then we must use numerical integration to find an adequate approximation. We will present a simple technique for numerical integration that can easily be depicted graphically.

Consider the problem of finding the area under the curve $y = f(x)$ between $x = a$ and $x = b$, as shown in Figure 14.2.

A gross approximation is the area of the trapezoid with base $b - a$ and sides $f(a)$ and $f(b)$,

$$(b - a)(f(a) + f(b))/2$$

Obviously this approximation will not be very good for most curves. To improve on this approach, we could subdivide the interval from $x = a$ to $x = b$ into many small intervals, which subdivide the large area into many small strips. Then we could approximate the area of each strip by the area of a small trapezoid, and take the sum of the

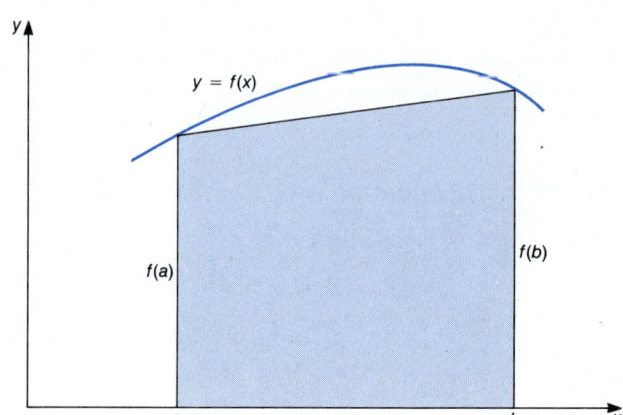

Figure 14.2
Illustration of the Area Under a Curve

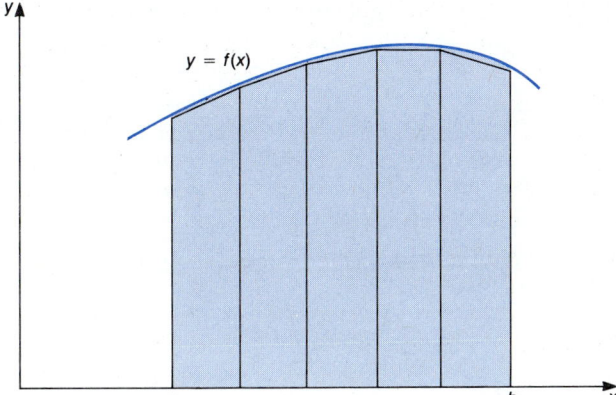

Figure 14.3
Approximation Using Trapezoids

areas of the small trapezoids as our final approximation. This improvement is illustrated in Figure 14.3.

In general, for *n* equal subintervals, we denote the end points of the subintervals by

$$x_i \text{ for } i = 0, \ldots, n$$

and the values of the function at these points by

$$y_i = f(x_i) \text{ for } i = 0, \ldots, n$$

then the areas of the small trapezoids are

$$h(y_i + y_{i+1})/2 \text{ for } i = 0, \ldots, n - 1 \text{ where } h = (b - a)/n$$

The sum of all the areas of these trapezoids is our approximation

$$(h/2)(y_0 + 2y_1 + 2y_2 + \cdots + 2y_{n-1} + y_n)$$

Not surprisingly, this method of numerical integration is called the *trapezoidal rule*.

The number of subdivisions is the critical factor in obtaining the desired mathematical accuracy, just as the number of terms is critical in determining the accuracy for a series approximation. However, precision is lost due to propagation of errors in the computation, and the error due to roundoff can increase as the number of terms increases.

When developing a Modula-2 procedure for numerical integration using the trapezoidal rule, we will need to provide as parameters the end points *a* and *b*, and the number of subdivisions, *n*. However, for the procedure to be very useful it should be general enough to provide answers for more than one function. Thus we need a parameter that will be used to pass a function, *f*, to the procedure. The graph of *f* determines the area we wish to approximate. Using the parameter *f*, we can compute the values

$$y_i = f(a + ih) \text{ for } i = 0, \ldots, n$$

needed for the approximation. To have a parameter whose value is a function, we must have a new type, called a *procedure type* in Modula-2. Specifically, for our application, we need the type declaration

```
TYPE Function = PROCEDURE ( REAL ): REAL;
```

We can use this type to implement the trapezoidal rule as shown in the following program.

```
MODULE TestIntegrate;
(* Test numerical integration by trapezoidal rule procedure
            J. M. Adams    January   1988 *)

FROM InOut IMPORT WriteString, WriteLn;
FROM RealInOut IMPORT WriteReal;
FROM MathLib0 IMPORT exp, sin;

TYPE Function = PROCEDURE(REAL): REAL;

PROCEDURE XSquared(X: REAL): REAL;
(* Test function for Integrate *)
BEGIN
  RETURN X * X;
END XSquared;

PROCEDURE Fx(X: REAL): REAL;
(* Test function for Integrate *)
CONST TwoPi = 6.28318;
BEGIN
  RETURN exp(-X) + sin(TwoPi * X);
END Fx;

PROCEDURE Integrate(f: Function; a,b: REAL; n: CARDINAL): REAL;
(* Compute an approximation to the area under the graph of the
   function f, from x = a to x = b using n subdivisions *)
VAR Sum, h: REAL;
    I: CARDINAL;
BEGIN
  h := (b - a) / FLOAT(n);
  Sum := f(a);
  FOR I := 1 TO n - 1 DO
    Sum := Sum + 2.0 * f(a + FLOAT(I) * h);
  END; (* FOR *)
  Sum := Sum + f(b);
  RETURN (h / 2.0) * Sum;
END Integrate;

BEGIN (* TestIntegrate *)
  WriteString("The area under x squared from x = 1 to x = 3");
  WriteString(" is approximately ");
  WriteReal(Integrate(XSquared, 1.0, 3.0, 10), 15);
  WriteLn; WriteLn;
  WriteString("The area under exp(-x) + sin(2 pi x) from x = 0 to ");
  WriteString("x = 64 is approximately ");
  WriteReal(Integrate(Fx, 0.0, 64.0, 150), 15); WriteLn;
END TestIntegrate.
```

The first result computed by this program is 8.68, whereas the true value is 8-2/3. A better approximation can be obtained by using a larger number of subdivisions than 10, but in practice more sophisticated numerical integration routines are used.

Procedure types are very useful in this kind of application, where a function must be provided as a parameter to a procedure that performs computations involving values of the function. Procedure types are also useful in programs that plot the graphs of functions; Exercise 18 deals with this application. The syntax for declaring a procedure type in Modula-2 is

```
PROCEDURE ( formal type list )
```

or,

```
PROCEDURE ( formal type list ) : type
```

where the syntax of formal type list is

```
[ [VAR] type { "," [VAR] type } ]
```

For example, we can have the following procedure type declarations.

```
TYPE Proc2Card   = PROCEDURE ( CARDINAL, CARDINAL );
     SpecialProc = PROCEDURE ( STRING, VAR GiftSet );
     IntRealFunc = PROCEDURE ( INTEGER ) : REAL;
```

The standard type PROC denotes a parameterless procedure and has been predeclared as

```
PROC = PROCEDURE;
```

so we can also have declarations such as

```
TYPE ProcSansParams = PROC;
```

14.6 Random Numbers

Our final example of numerical methods will be of a nature much different from the preceding ones. In fact we will actually use the loss of precision, which previously plagued us, to our advantage.

In many applications, both numeric and nonnumeric, we want to model some random event—for example, to simulate the motion of elementary particles in a nuclear

Figure 14.4
Path of a "Random" Turtle

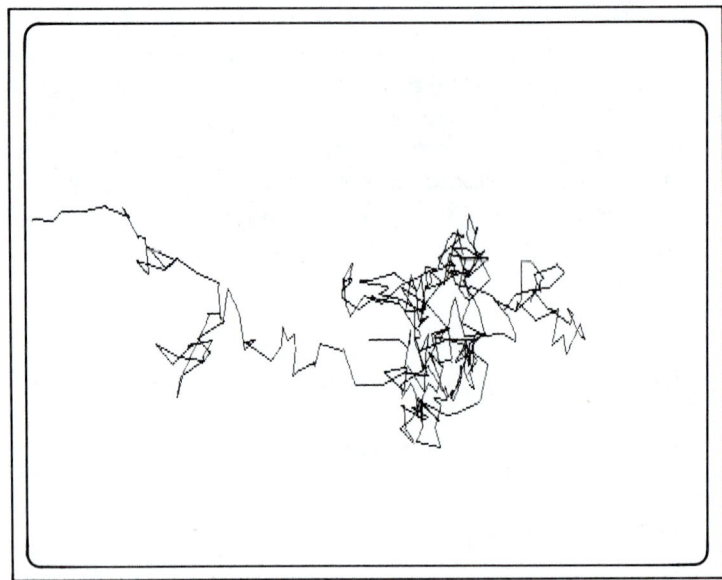

reactor, or to simulate the arrival of vehicles in a study of traffic patterns. To model these random events, we need to be able to generate random numbers. In our examples the random numbers would be used to determine the directions of elementary particles, or the arrival times of vehicles at intersections. We cannot generate truly random numbers with a digital computer, because a computer is a finite device, and thus any sequence of numbers generated by a computer must eventually be repetitive. However, we can program a computer to generate *pseudorandom numbers,* which will give the appearance of being random over a considerable period of time. A function that generates such numbers is used in the following program, which draws the path of a random turtle, shown in Figure 14.4.

```
MODULE RandomWalk;
(* Draws a random path
                            J. M. Adams   January 1988    *)

FROM TurtleGraphics IMPORT TurtleStop, ShowTurtle, MaxXSize,
                           MaxYSize, Move, TurnTo, WhereAmI;
VAR Seed: REAL;
    X, Y, Direction: INTEGER;

PROCEDURE RandomReal(): REAL;
(* Return a pseudorandom real value from 0 up to,
   but not including 1 *)
BEGIN
   Seed := 27.182813 * Seed + 31.415917;
   Seed := Seed - FLOAT(TRUNC(Seed));
   RETURN Seed;
END RandomReal;
```

```
      BEGIN
        ShowTurtle(FALSE);
        Seed := 1.23456789;
        X := 0; Y := 0;
        WHILE (ABS(X) < MaxXSize) AND (ABS(Y) < MaxYSize) DO
          Move(TRUNC(30.0 * RandomReal()));
          TurnTo(TRUNC(361.0 * RandomReal()));
          WhereAmI(X, Y, Direction);
        END; (* WHILE *)
        TurtleStop;
      END RandomWalk.
```

The function RandomReal generates pseudorandom numbers in the interval from 0 up to, but not including, 1. It does this by taking advantage of the loss of precision in representing numbers by a certain fixed number of bits. The function uses an appropriate bit pattern, called a seed, to start the generation and then performs arithmetic operations on the seed to forestall repetition for a long period. The constants in RandomReal have been selected based on testing that demonstrates long periods without repetition. Note that RandomReal is a parameterless function, since it does not need an argument.

Using RandomReal, we generate a random step length of 0 to 30 and a random direction for the turtle's next step. This process is repeated until the turtle finally wanders over the edge of the screen. The procedure WhereAmI returns the position and direction of the turtle, which is used to stop the turtle at the edge. The resulting path, shown in Figure 14.4, appears to be random; however, we know that the pattern must eventually repeat. If we reduce the maximum step length to 5, we can see more of the path before the turtle reaches the edge of the screen. As shown in Figure 14.5, with the reduced step size, the pattern has started repeating itself.

Figure 14.5

A Longer Path for a "Random" Turtle

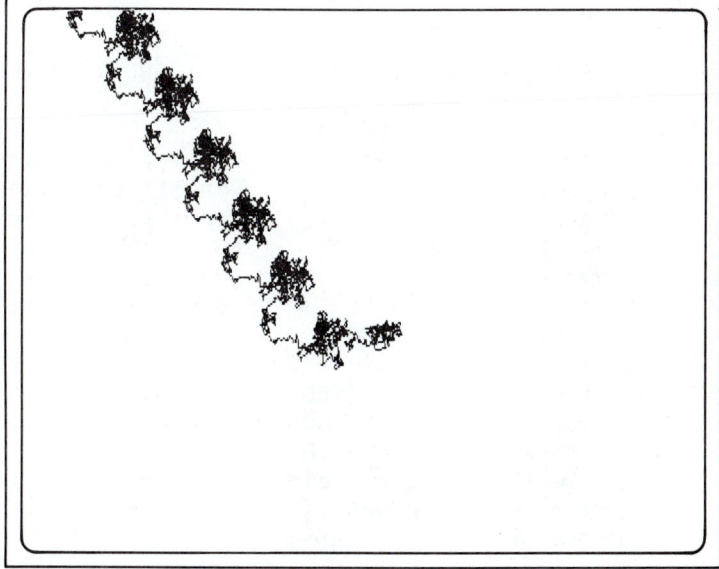

A nonnumeric application of a pseudorandom number generator is shown in the following program, which generates random sentences.

```
MODULE RandomSentences;
(* Test Random by generating random sentences
                              P. Gabrini   January 1988 *)

FROM InOut IMPORT WriteString, WriteLn;
FROM Strings IMPORT STRING;

MODULE PseudoRandom;
  EXPORT Random;

  VAR Seed: REAL;

  PROCEDURE Random(): REAL;
  (* Return pseudorandom value from zero up to
     but not including 1 *)
  BEGIN
    Seed := 27.182813 * Seed + 31.415917;
    Seed := Seed - FLOAT(TRUNC(Seed));
    RETURN Seed;
  END Random;

BEGIN (* PseudoRandom *)
  Seed := 1.23456789;
END PseudoRandom;

CONST N = 3.0;
      Max = 3;

VAR I: CARDINAL;
    Article, Noun, Verb, Adverb: ARRAY [0..Max - 1] OF STRING;

BEGIN (* RandomSentences *)
  Article[0] := "the ";      Verb[0] := "eats ";
  Article[1] := "a ";        Verb[1] := "likes ";
  Article[2] := "our ";      Verb[2] := "sees ";
  Noun[0] := "dog ";         Adverb[0] := "often ";
  Noun[1] := "cat ";         Adverb[1] := "sometimes ";
  Noun[2] := "food ";        Adverb[2] := "well ";
  FOR I := 1 TO 20 DO
    WriteString(Article[TRUNC(N * Random())]);
    WriteString(Noun[TRUNC(N * Random())]);
    WriteString(Verb[TRUNC(N * Random())]);
    IF Random() < 0.5 THEN
      WriteString(Article[TRUNC(N * Random())]);
      WriteString(Noun[TRUNC(N * Random())]);
    END; (* IF *)
```

```
        IF Random() > 0.5 THEN
          WriteString(Adverb[TRUNC(N * Random())]);
        END; (* IF *)
        WriteLn;
      END; (* FOR *)
  END RandomSentences.
```

In this program, Random has been placed in a local module to hide the variable used to store the seed. Notice that the seed retains its current value even when executing code outside the local module. Exercise 19 will ask you to code a library module for pseudorandom number generation. Using Random, we can generate sentences by choosing and writing first an article, then a noun, and then a verb. After that we can randomly add a complement consisting of an article and a noun and possibly end the sentence with an adverb. Our vocabulary here is rather limited but can be readily expanded. The following are some sample sentences generated by the program.

> the dog sees
>
> a cat eats our dog
>
> a cat sees a cat sometimes
>
> our food sees
>
> the dog likes our food sometimes
>
> our food eats our cat well

As you can see, the generation of pseudorandom numbers can be used in a variety of applications.

14.7 Case Study: Finding a Root of an Equation

Thus far in this chapter we've seen several common numerical techniques implemented as Modula-2 programs. Here let's consider a problem in which we must design a program to find the roots of an equation. We will use the method of bisection. Since we are only designing a procedure and want to concentrate on the numerical method, we will simply divide our solution into a design phase and an implementation phase.

Design

If we are given a function $f(x)$, we often want to find values of x that make $f(x)$ equal zero. In other words, we are solving the equation $f(x) = 0$. For example, consider the simple function

$$f(x) = x^2 - 3$$

Figure 14.6 shows a graph for $f(x)$.

Figure 14.6
A Graph of
$f(x) = x^2 - 3$

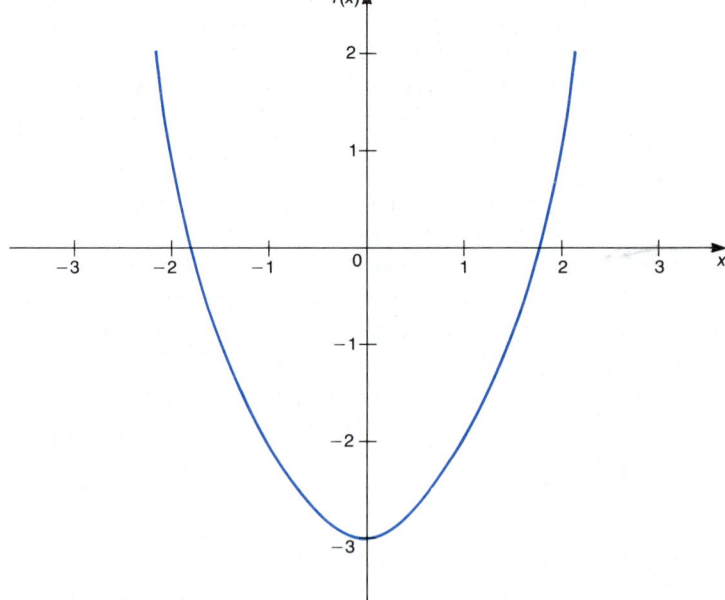

The root or roots of an equation $f(x) = 0$ are those places where the graph crosses the x axis. For the equation in Figure 14.6, there are two roots—at plus and minus the square root of 3. Other equations may have no real roots, such as $f(x) = x^2 + 3$. For our program in this case study, we will assume that the given function does have a root and that we will be given an interval on the x axis within which the root lies.

We will use the method of bisection to locate the given root. Consider $f(x)$ as graphed in Figure 14.6 and suppose that we know a root lies in the interval from $+1$ to $+2$. We will assume a single root in this interval, which means that $f(1)$ and $f(2)$ must have opposite signs. We now find the midpoint of the interval, 1.5, and calculate the value of $f(x)$ at this point. Graphically, our solution thus far looks like Figure 14.7.

Since f(Mid) and f(High) have opposite signs, we know that the root must lie in the interval between Mid and High. Therefore, Mid becomes our new Low value and

Figure 14.7
Bisection of Interval (1, 2)

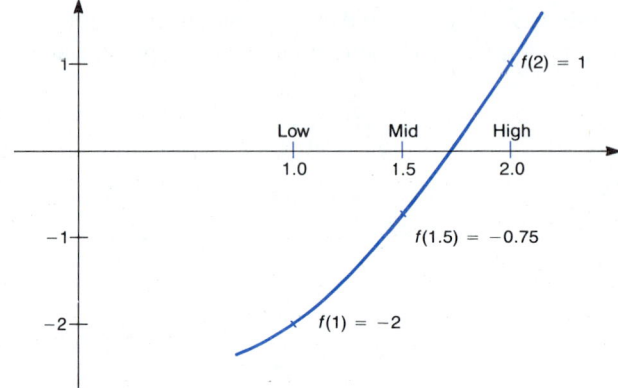

High remains our High value. We repeat this process. The new Mid value is 1.75, and $f(1.75) = 0.0625$. In this case the lower half of the interval from 1.5 to 1.75, which we denote by (1.5, 1.75), must contain the root, so Low remains the same, and the new value of High is assigned the value of Mid. We continue this process until we have narrowed the interval for the root to a prescribed degree of accuracy. Here is the pseudocode algorithm for the method of bisection.

```
Bisection ( f, Low, High ) : real
    If f(Low) and f(High) have the same sign then
        Print a message that bisection won't be attempted
        Return 0.0
    Else
        While High − Low exceeds desired accuracy do
            Set Mid to (Low + High) / 2.0
            If f(Low) and f(Mid) have the same sign then
                Set Low to Mid         {root is in upper half of interval}
            Else
                Set High to Mid        {root is in lower half of interval}
            End if
        End while
        Return (Low + High) / 2.0
    End if
End Bisection
```

Notice that if $f(Low)$ and $f(High)$ have opposite signs, then for a continuous function there is guaranteed to be at least one root in the interval. If $f(Low)$ and $f(High)$ have the same sign, there could be multiple roots in the interval (consider Low = −2 and High = 2 for $f(x) = x * x - 3$), or there might be no roots in the interval (consider Low = 2 and High = 3 for $f(x) = x * x - 3$). In any case, where $f(Low)$ and $f(High)$ have the same sign, our simple approach of bisection will not be attempted.

We have not completely specified how we measure the desired accuracy. Suppose we have an approximate value, a, for an exact value e. We define the *absolute error* to be the difference, $a - e$. In our problem we do not have the exact value, the square root of 3. In fact, it is impossible to represent the square root of 3 exactly on any computer! However, it is convenient to use the size of the interval, High − Low, to represent the maximum possible value for our absolute error.

For very large or very small values of real numbers, absolute error may cause some difficulty. For example, suppose we want a root with an absolute error of less than 0.001 yet the interval for that root is between 1,000,000 and 1,000,001. To be successful, our internal representation must be able to differentiate values such as 1,000,000.555 and 1,000,000.556. This level may exceed the accuracy possible on many computers, and the algorithm for bisection may never terminate. The opposite problem exists for small values. Suppose we know that the root of an equation lies in the interval from 0.0005 and 0.0006. Given this initial interval, our absolute error criterion is already satisfied and the bisection algorithm would simply return the

TABLE 14.2 Roots of Two Simple Functions Using the Bisection Program

Function	Interval	Root
f1	(1, 2)	1.732051
f2	(0.5, 0.75)	0.593176
f1	(2.0, 3.0)	Function values have same sign
f2	(−0.75, 0.75)	Warning: attempt to divide by zero

midpoint, 0.00055, without calculating any function values. To avoid problems such as these, we introduce the notion of *relative error*.

Given an approximate value, a, and an exact value, e, the relative error there is $(a - e)/e$, provided $e \neq 0$. Of course, we do not know the exact value e since that is what we are trying to approximate. However, we can usually obtain a bound for $a - e$ in the numerator and take the value of a instead of e in the denominator to obtain a reasonable approximation to the relative error. In our bisection algorithm we know that a and e lie in the interval (Low, High), so the numerator $a - e$ is no greater than High − Low. Using our best guess so far, (Low + High)/2.0, as the denominator, we can take (High − Low)/((Low + High)/2.0) as a reasonable approximation of the relative error. In the program developed in this section we will use relative error measurement.

We will test our bisection program with two simple functions,

$$f1(x) = x^2 - 3$$
$$f2(x) = e^{-x} + \sin 2\pi x$$

with the expected results shown in Table 14.2.

Implementation

The code for the bisection procedure and the test program follows directly from the pseudocode specification.

```
MODULE Root;
(* Program to test the bisection method of approximating the
   root of an equation.
                                    B. Kurtz   January 1988 *)

FROM RealInOut IMPORT FWriteReal;
FROM InOut IMPORT WriteString, WriteLn;
FROM MathLib0 IMPORT exp, sin;

TYPE Function = PROCEDURE ( REAL ): REAL;

PROCEDURE F1(X: REAL): REAL;
(* Test function for bisection *)
BEGIN
   RETURN X * X - 3.0;
END F1;
```

SEC. 14.7   Case Study: Finding a Root of an Equation

```
PROCEDURE F2(X: REAL): REAL;
(* Test function for bisection *)
CONST TwoPi = 6.28318;
BEGIN
  RETURN exp(-X) + sin(TwoPi * X);
END F2;

PROCEDURE SameSign(R1, R2: REAL) : BOOLEAN;
(* Returns TRUE only when R1 and R2 have the same sign.  *)
BEGIN
  RETURN ((R1 < 0.0) AND (R2 < 0.0)) OR ((R1 > 0.0) AND (R2 > 0.0));
END SameSign;

PROCEDURE AlmostEqualRelative (Low, High,
                               DecimalPercentError: REAL) : BOOLEAN;
(* Returns TRUE when the relative error between Low and High is
   less than the specified decimal percentage.             *)
VAR Mid: REAL;
BEGIN
  Mid := (Low + High)/2.0;
  IF Mid # 0.0 THEN
    RETURN ABS((High - Low)/Mid) < DecimalPercentError;
  ELSE
    WriteLn;
    WriteString("Warning: attempt to divide by zero in relative error.");
    WriteLn;
    RETURN TRUE;
  END; (* IF *)
END AlmostEqualRelative;

PROCEDURE Bisection(f: Function; Low, High: REAL) : REAL;
(* If f(Low) and f(High) have opposite signs, then there is
   some value, call it root, in the interval (Low, High) such
   that f(root) = 0.  This function uses the method of
   bisection to return an approximate value for root.  This
   procedure uses relative error measure.         *)

CONST RelativeDifference = 0.00001;
VAR Mid, FuncLow, FuncMid, FuncHigh: REAL;

BEGIN
  FuncLow := f(Low);
  FuncHigh := f(High);
  IF SameSign(FuncLow, FuncHigh) THEN
    WriteLn;
    WriteString("Function values at given boundaries have the same sign.");
    WriteLn;
    WriteString("Bisection not attempted and 0.0 is returned."); WriteLn;
    RETURN 0.0;
```

```
      ELSE
        WHILE NOT
            AlmostEqualRelative(Low, High, RelativeDifference) DO
          Mid := (Low + High)/2.0;
          FuncMid := f(Mid);
          IF SameSign(FuncLow, FuncMid) THEN
            Low := Mid;             (* root between Mid and High *)
          ELSE
            High := Mid;            (* root between Low and Mid *)
          END; (* IF *)
        END; (* WHILE *)
        RETURN (High + Low)/2.0;
    END; (* IF *)
END Bisection;

BEGIN (* Root *)
    WriteString("In the interval 1.0 to 2.0, the function f(x) = x * x - 3");
    WriteLn; WriteString("has a root at x = ");
    FWriteReal(Bisection(F1, 1.0, 2.0), 10,6); WriteLn; WriteLn;
    WriteString("In the interval 0.5 to 0.75, the function F2");
    WriteLn; WriteString("has a root at x = ");
    FWriteReal(Bisection(F2, 0.5, 0.75), 10,6);
    WriteLn; WriteLn;
    WriteString("In the interval 2.0 to 3.0, the function f(x) = x * x - 3");
    WriteLn; WriteString("has a root at x = ");
    FWriteReal(Bisection(F1, 2.0, 3.0), 10,6); WriteLn; WriteLn;
    WriteString("In the interval -0.75 to 0.75, the function F2");
    WriteLn; WriteString("has a root at x = ");
    FWriteReal(Bisection(F2, -0.75, 0.75), 10,6); WriteLn;
END Root.
```

The output generated by this program is

```
In the interval 1.0 to 2.0, the function f(x) = x * x - 3
has a root at x =   1.732048

In the interval 0.5 to 0.75, the function F2
has a root at x =   0.593176

In the interval 2.0 to 3.0, the function f(x) = x * x - 3
has a root at x =
Function values at given boundaries have the same sign.
Bisection not attempted and 0.0 is returned.
    0.000000

In the interval -0.75 to 0.75, the function F2
has a root at x =
Warning: attempt to divide by zero in relative error.
    0.000000
```

This output matched our expected results.

SUMMARY

Some of the most important uses of computers involve solutions to problems requiring complex numerical computations. One aspect of programming with Modula-2 or any other language, therefore, is learning to adapt numerical techniques for the computer. Modern numerical analysis is concerned with the development of numerical methods for digital computers.

To perform computer arithmetic, we must understand how computers represent and store numeric values and what level of precision can be assured. Within the computer, values of type CARDINAL are represented in binary notation. Values of type INTEGER are slightly more complicated because the sign of the value must be represented. The two's complement method offers the easiest way to store integer values. Values of type REAL are represented in a form with a mantissa and an exponent.

We can design Modula-2 programs to compute results based on common numerical techniques. In this chapter we examined techniques to find a series approximation, perform numerical integration using the trapezoidal rule, generate pseudorandom numbers, and find a root of an equation using bisection. We also learned about the declaration and use of procedure types.

This chapter on numerical methods should give you some insight into how such methods are developed and used. If you study numerical analysis in a more advanced course, you will investigate numerical methods in much greater detail. Even without going into numerical analysis, the actual representation of numbers on a given machine is an important topic in subsequent courses involving computer organization.

You are now aware that the actual representation of numbers on a given machine has a direct influence on numerical applications. Subsequent work at a level closer to the machine will give you a better understanding of the inner working of a computer and also better examples of the various binary representations that were introduced here.

EXERCISES

1. Find the decimal numbers corresponding to the binary numbers 1001001, 11100000, and 1111111111. How could the fact that 1111111111 + 1 = 10000000000 help you calculate the latter value quickly?

2. Find the binary numbers corresponding to the decimal numbers 123, 1001, and 8191.

3. On a decimal machine, what is the least number of digits that would have to be in the mantissa of the representation of real values to avoid losing precision when performing the following additions:
   (a) 0.4 + 0.0007
   (b) 0.4 + 0.000007

4. Using two's complement, what is the largest possible integer value that could be represented with 32 bits? What is the smallest possible value?

5. Write the two's complement representations and their decimal equivalents for all the possible integers using 3 bits. How can you easily tell the negative values from the nonnegative values?

6. If 16 bits are used to represent both values of type CARDINAL and of type INTEGER, what values of type CARDINAL cannot be converted to type INTEGER?

7. Using 16 bits and two's complement representation, add -4 and -3.

8. Write a function to compute the function sine x, for an angle in radians, using the series

$$\text{sine } x = x - \frac{x^3}{3!} + \frac{x^5}{5!} - \frac{x^7}{7!} + \frac{x^9}{9!} - \cdots$$

9. Write a function to compute the function arctan x, for $x > 1$, using the series:

$$\arctan x = \frac{\pi}{2} - \frac{1}{x} + \frac{1}{3x^3} - \frac{1}{5x^5} + \cdots$$

10. The expansion for the exponential function is

$$e^x = 1 + x + \frac{x^2}{2!} + \frac{x^3}{3!} + \frac{x^4}{4!} + \frac{x^5}{5!} + \cdots$$

Assuming a decimal precision of five digits and $x = 0.5$, use a calculator to find each term of the series until the terms become 0. Sum these terms and compare the sum to the actual value (approx. 1.64872127).

11. Repeat Exercise 10 using $x = -4$. It will take many more terms before they start approaching 0. Remember to use only five-digit accuracy on each term. Compare your final result with the actual value of 0.01831564 (approx.). How do you account for this error?

12. Repeat Exercise 11 but use $x = 4$. You need not recalculate the values since this simply makes the sign of all terms positive. Then use the fact that

$$e^{-4} = \frac{1}{e^4}$$

to find the exponential of -4. Is your result any better than that found in Exercise 11?

13. If you have learned about Newton's method in your calculus classes, use it to find the roots of $x^2 - 3$. Does it approximate the roots more quickly than using bisection?

PROGRAMMING PROBLEMS

14. Write a program that displays a table comparing the values of the natural logarithm function produced by the procedure given in this chapter and the function in MathLib0.

15. Implement the functions in Exercises 8 and 9 in your own external math library module. Write a test program to compare the results for your functions with those in MathLib0.

16. Develop an external module for integration using the trapizoidal method presented in Section 14.5.

17. Develop a second method for numerical integration based on approximations using small rectangles rather than small trapezoids. Use a parameter to indicate the choice of the height of the rectangle based on the following options:

    use f(left) where left is the left-hand boundary of the interval

    use f(right) where right is the right-hand boundary of the interval

    use $(f(\text{left}) + f(\text{right}))/2.0$

    use f(Mid) where Mid is (left + right)/2.0

Compare the results of these methods with those of the trapezoidal rule for the sine function on the interval 0 to $\pi/2$, and the square root function on the interval 0.5 to 4.

18. Develop a procedure that will plot points on the graph of a function provided as an input parameter. The starting point, increment, and number of points should also be provided as parameters. If you have graphics capabilities, implement and test this procedure using the functions e^{-x}, $\sin 2\pi x$, and $e^{-x} + \sin 2\pi x$.

19. Implement and test your own library module for random number generation with functions RandomCard and RandomReal as well as a procedure AssignSeed.

20. Develop a procedure that, when called, will display a "word" of random length between 1 and 10 and consisting of randomly selected lowercase letters. Implement and test this procedure.

21. Implement and test a procedure that, when called, will display a four-letter "word" whose letters are chosen according to the probabilities:

a, e, h, i, n, o, r, s, t	0.6
d, f, l, m, u, w, y	0.3
b, c, g, k, p, v	0.1

15 Abstract Data Types and Dynamic Data Structures

In this chapter you will:

- be introduced to opaque types as a technique for information hiding
- learn about pointers in Modula-2, and how they are used to implement dynamic data structures and opaque types

In this chapter we will introduce topics that will be covered in more detail in subsequent computer science courses. We will start by presenting opaque types, which make it possible to implement complete information hiding in external modules. Then we will discuss pointers, which are used to form dynamic data structures appropriate for many applications and which are used to implement opaque types. The chapter ends with a brief look at two useful dynamic data structures, linked lists and binary trees.

15.1 Abstract Data Types

In Chapter 11 we discussed the abstract data type for strings. We saw that the Strings definition module included the type STRING declaration

```
TYPE STRING = ARRAY[0..79] OF CHAR;
```

and string procedures such as

```
PROCEDURE InitString( STR: ARRAY OF CHAR );

PROCEDURE Length( STR: ARRAY OF CHAR ): CARDINAL;

PROCEDURE FetchChar( S: ARRAY OF CHAR; I: CARDINAL ): CHAR;

PROCEDURE AssignChar( CH: CHAR; VAR S: ARRAY OF CHAR; I: CARDINAL );
```

Abstract Data Types

An abstract data type should include the name of the type and the permissible operations on values of the type but not the actual representation of values of the type. Including the actual representation, such as ARRAY [0..79] OF CHAR for type STRING, is inconsistent with our notion of hiding the representation of an abstract data type. In the next section we will discuss this inconsistency, and in a subsequent section we will show how to hide the representation.

Strings

For our discussion we will briefly review the representation of strings used in the Strings module discussed in Chapter 11. The representation is ARRAY [0..79] OF CHAR, and so a value of type STRING can have a length from 0 to 80, depending on the value of the string. We will call the length of the string its *current length* to distinguish it from the maximum length of 80. As we saw in the implementation of the Length function, the length of a string is determined by the position of the first null character in the string. If no null is found, then 80, the last index plus 1, is returned.

The representation of strings as arrays has the advantage of being compatible with the definition of string constants, or literals, in Modula-2. For example, using an array representation makes it possible to pass a string literal, such as "this is a literal", as a value parameter to procedures in the Strings module. However, the fact that the representation of strings as arrays is not hidden can lead to severe problems when accessing characters within a string.

The FetchChar and AssignChar procedures in the Strings definition module are provided for access to individual characters within a string. As mentioned in Chapter 9, knowing that arrays are used to represent strings, you might be tempted to write

    `Str1[7]`   in place of   `FetchChar( Str1, 7 )`

or

    `Str1[5] := 'A'`   in place of   `AssignChar( 'A', Str1, 5 )`

If the indexed array element is within the current length of the string, these approaches would be equivalent. However, in other cases, there may be some undesirable outcomes. Consider the actual representation for "SHORT STRING" shown in Figure 15.1. The current length of this string is 12. If the character at position 16 is requested using FetchChar, then a null character is returned regardless of the actual value stored at that position. By directly indexing this position, Str[16], we have no guarantee that a null will be returned and thus no way of knowing that the character retrieved in this way is a valid character in the string. If it is not and if we have not

Figure 15.1
String Representation

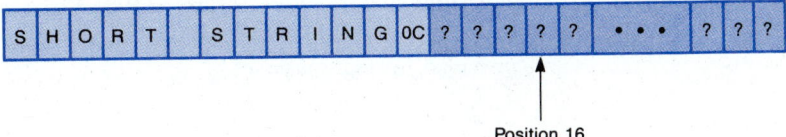

checked the current length of the string ourselves, the results of our processing will be erroneous.

The AssignChar procedure does not alter the string if the specified index is beyond the current length of the string (as in Figure 15.1). When we directly index the array, we have no such guarantee. If an indexed assignment is made beyond the first null character, the logical value of the string will not be altered. But if the assignment is made at the position of the leftmost null character, position 12 in the string in Figure 15.1, then the string will be altered in a very unpredictable way.

By making the representation of a string "public," as is done in our Strings definition module by declaring type STRING as ARRAY [0..79] OF CHAR, we have no way to prevent access to individual components. In general, if the representation of a structured type is given as part of the type declaration in the definition module, access to the components of this type cannot be prevented. Often such access is unintentional, but in other cases it may be malicious, as when somebody tries to "crash the system." In either case the results are usually undesirable.

By using a direct access, such as Str1[5], to a string representation, the programmer makes the program dependent on the specific representation. If that representation is changed, then the program using the strings module may no longer function properly (and will probably no longer even compile). However, if FetchChar and AssignChar were used, then these procedures would be revised for the new structure and the user program would still compile and run correctly. Controlled access to an object with unknown structure is in accordance with the information hiding principle. This not only gives protection from indiscriminate access but also allows the underlying representation to be changed without requiring changes in user programs. In the next section we will learn how to hide the actual representation of an object by using an opaque type.

Opaque Types

Modula-2 allows the representation of a type to be left unspecified in the definition module. We will call such types *opaque types*. This lack of specification provides complete information hiding by preventing direct access to values of opaque types.

An opaque type is achieved by declaring *only* the name of the type in the definition module. If we are going to design a Strings module with information hiding—let's call it NewStrings—our type declaration in the definition module will be

```
TYPE STRING;
```

In this declaration there is absolutely no information about the representation of values. As a result, any program that imports the type STRING from NewStrings and declares variables of this type is prevented from directly accessing values of the variable, except by procedures provided for that purpose.

Declarations without representations are allowed in Modula-2, because the complete syntax for a type declaration in a definition module is

```
TYPE { identifier [= type representation]; }
```

If the type representation is specified, the type is said to be *transparent;* if the type representation is not specified, the type is *opaque*. For opaque types, the complete type representation *must* appear in the *corresponding* implementation module. Since the user cannot see or access the implementation module, the representation is hidden. Even if the type representation is known, the compiler should forbid its direct use outside the implementation module. Thus, direct access to values of an opaque type is prevented.

We now return to the development of our NewStrings definition module. In addition to declaring the opaque type STRING, we will have procedure headings for all the procedures needed to manipulate values of our new type of string. These procedures will include all the procedures used in our old Strings module. However, the string parameters in the headings of these procedures must be declared as STRING, rather than the representation-dependent ARRAY OF CHAR specification used in our old Strings module. For example, we will have

```
PROCEDURE InitString( STR: STRING );

PROCEDURE Length( STR: STRING ): CARDINAL;

PROCEDURE FetchChar( S: STRING; I: CARDINAL ): CHAR;

PROCEDURE AssignChar( CH: CHAR; VAR S: STRING; I: CARDINAL );
```

One procedure, however, must be handled differently. Our Assign procedure will now be limited to assigning a string literal (string constant) to a string variable, because string constants are arrays of characters, not of our new opaque type STRING.

```
PROCEDURE Assign( VAR STR: STRING; A: ARRAY OF CHAR );
(* Assigns the string constant in A to the string STR *)
```

With this restriction of Assign, we need another procedure to assign the value of one string variable to another string variable. We will call this procedure Duplicate.

```
PROCEDURE Duplicate( S: STRING; VAR R: STRING );
(* Makes R to be a copy of S *)
```

Our new procedures may be used in the same way we used the procedures in our old Strings module, with one exception. We will now be required to call InitString before using a string variable. The reason for this requirement is related to the actual representation that will appear in the implementation module, which we discuss in subsequent sections. Because of this representation issue, we must also have one entirely new procedure to dispose of strings.

```
PROCEDURE Dispose( VAR S: STRING );
(* Sets a previously initialized string to the empty string *)
```

As a result of the new representation, all strings should be disposed before the end of the block where the string variables are declared. This is now an explicit responsibility of the programmer.

With the NewStrings module, access to string values is completely controlled. Such controlled access should be the *only* access possible to values of any opaque type. Therefore, users' programs cannot be written in a way that makes them dependent on a specific representation. As a result, implementation modules can be replaced with improved versions without adversely affecting users' programs. By using an opaque type, we can completely hide the representation of a data type and thereby achieve the declaration of a truly abstract data type.

The implementation of our NewStrings module depends on the actual representation chosen for strings, and we need to know about pointers for this representation. We will give more details on the implementation module once we have introduced pointers in the following section.

15.2 Dynamic Data Structures and Pointers

All the data types we have seen so far, structured or not, have a common characteristic: their size and form do not change during program execution. The structured types include a number of components, but that number must be known at compilation time. The number of fields of a record is known at declaration time, and so is the number of elements of an array. Even variant records have a maximum size based on the maximum possible variant. The data types we have used until now are called *static data types*, since the values of the types have a maximum size that can be determined at compilation time.

In a number of applications—text processing and artificial intelligence, for example—we cannot know in advance how many data elements we will need or even the structure of the data. Consequently, we have to have *dynamic data structures*, which can grow or shrink as the program executes, and whose size and shape may change. Dynamic data structures are sometimes called linked data structures, because they are collections of elements containing links (or pointers) to other elements.

Dynamic structures are created on demand during program execution. Since the size of dynamic structures is not known before the execution of the statements using them, the storage space needed for the structures cannot be determined at compilation time. Unlike static structures, dynamic structures cannot be directly referenced by using a variable name. They can only be indirectly referenced through special static variables, called *pointer variables*, or *pointers*, which we'll explain in the upcoming section on dynamic structures.

Static Structures

As we said in Chapter 14, computer memories are typically considered to be arrays of memory cells, or words. The most common word sizes for microcomputers and minicomputers are 16 bits and 32 bits. Just as each element in an array has an index, each word in memory has an associated address, as shown in Figure 15.2.

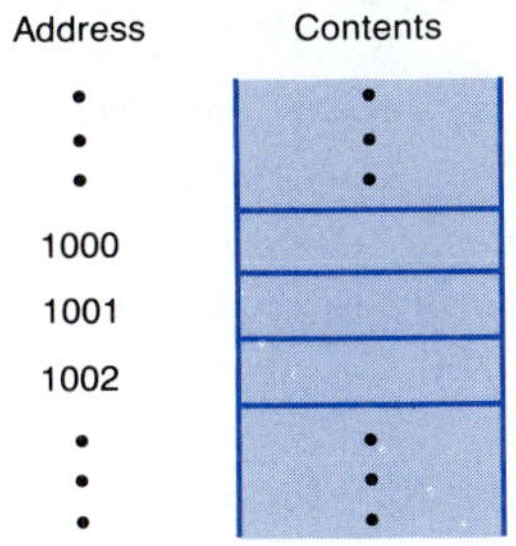

Figure 15.2
Computer Memory Organization

When a variable is declared within a program block, storage space is allocated for that variable, but the contents of the storage space are unknown. The amount of memory allocated is dependent on the type of the variable. Within the scope of this variable, its name is associated with the memory allocated. At run time, a value may be assigned to all or part of this allocated space either by an assignment statement or by a read statement.

Consider the declaration

```
TYPE DataType = ARRAY [1..100] OF INTEGER;
VAR Data1, Data2: DataType;
```

If a single word can accommodate a value of type INTEGER, the compiler determines that one hundred contiguous words are to be allocated and the address of the first word is associated with the identifier Data1. The values are undefined until run time, but the amount of space to hold these values has been determined. In a similar manner, another hundred words are to be allocated for Data2. If during execution the elements of Data2 have been assigned values, then the assignment Data1 := Data2 would assign values to all one hundred words of Data1, while the assignment Data1[4] := 3 would assign a value to only one word of the allocated memory.

Data1 and Data2 are called *static variables,* meaning that a fixed amount of space is allocated for their values. During execution, when the block in which Data1 and Data2 are declared is entered, space is automatically allocated for these variables. This space is returned to the system upon leaving the block.

Dynamic Structures

Modula-2 offers another alternative for memory allocation: dynamic allocation where space for objects is allocated and released under programmer control. This means that the programmer must specifically request memory allocation (the system does not allocate space automatically), and the programmer is responsible for returning the space to the system (otherwise it is unavailable for future use). Since objects whose space is allocated dynamically do not exist at compile time, they cannot be referenced by using variable names directly. To reference these dynamic objects, we use pointer variables. A pointer variable is a static variable which contains the address of the object it references. Pointer variables are declared as having a special type introduced by the reserved words "POINTER TO". For instance,

$$\text{VAR} \quad \text{A, B: POINTER TO INTEGER;}$$
$$\text{C: POINTER TO CHAR;}$$

declare three variables of two different types—pointer to integer and pointer to character. Such a declaration is for static variables, so the compiler must ensure that enough space will be allocated to store an address for each pointer variable declared and that the names of the variables are associated with these memory locations, as shown in Figure 15.3.

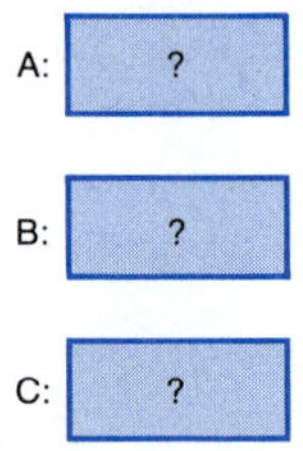

Figure 15.3
Memory After Pointer Declaration

After the declaration the contents of these pointer variables are uninitialized, like any other declared variable. Even though the pointer variables have been allocated space, the objects they will point to have not been allocated space. The allocation of space must be done on demand at run time, and space can be deallocated on demand at run time as it is no longer needed.

In Modula-2, the dynamic allocation of space is implementation dependent and is usually done by a call to the procedure ALLOCATE, imported from module Storage. Some implementations may provide the simpler procedure called NEW, whose use requires the import of ALLOCATE.

At the time a call to ALLOCATE is executed, the run time system must allocate memory space for the object pointed to by the pointer variable. The amount of space to be allocated for the object is implementation dependent. However, it can be deter-

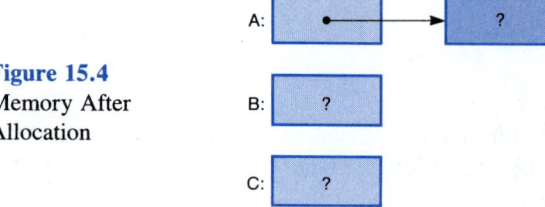

Figure 15.4
Memory After Allocation

mined by using the standard function SIZE, which returns the amount of space needed for the type given as a parameter. For example, with the preceding declarations, the statement ALLOCATE(A, SIZE(INTEGER)) allocates space to store an integer and puts the (starting) address of that space in A. Figure 15.4 shows A pointing to the space allocated for an integer value; notice that the integer value has not yet been initialized. Variables B and C remain uninitialized.

The newly created object is sometimes called a *dynamic variable*. Dynamic variables are created at run time by calls to ALLOCATE, hence the name dynamic. Since a dynamic variable has no declared name, we use the pointer variable name followed by the *dereference sign,* which is an up arrow or caret character (^). For example, to make an assignment to the integer pointed to by A, we write:

$$A\verb|^| := 3;$$

A^ is called the *referent* of A and can be considered to be the name of the dynamic variable pointed to by the static variable A. After the assignment, this dynamic variable has the value 3. So we read this assignment as: the referent of A is assigned 3. Figure 15.5 shows the result of this assignment as well as similar statements for the referent of B and the referent of C.

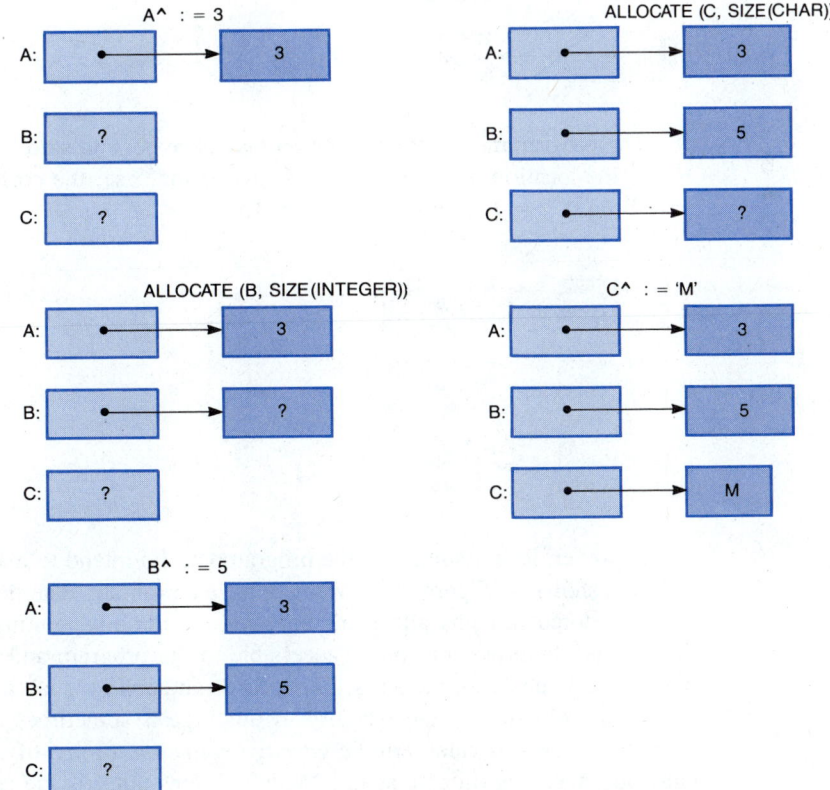

Figure 15.5 Manipulating Pointer Variables

Before continuing this example, we must emphasize two points:

- Reference to a pointer variable directly, such as A, refers to the *address* stored in that pointer variable.
- A dereferenced pointer variable, such as A^, specifies the *object pointed to,* an integer in this case. This dereference has meaning only *after* a call to ALLOCATE has been executed.

As with other variables, it is possible to assign values to pointer variables. We have seen that calls to ALLOCATE do just that. We can use the assignment statement to assign one pointer variable to another pointer variable of the same type (that is, which points to the same type of object), or to assign the pointer constant NIL. NIL is a special pointer value in Modula-2, indicating a pointer that points nowhere. Figure 15.6 shows the result of the assignment A := B. It would not be possible to assign the value of C to A; although both are pointers, they do not point to objects of the same type.

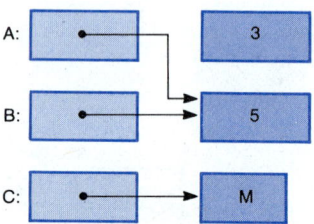

Figure 15.6
Pointer Assignment

The programmer's actual intention may have been to store the value pointed to by B into the location pointed to by A. If that is the case, the correct assignment would have been A^ := B^, leading to Figure 15.7.

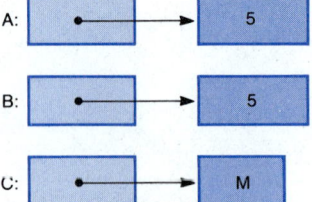

Figure 15.7
Referent Assignment

However, let's assume that the programmer did intend to make the pointer assignment, as shown in Figure 15.6. We now have a problem. The memory location where the 3 is stored remains allocated, but there is nothing pointing to it. This memory location is, therefore, no longer accessible to the program and has been wasted. For pointers to large data structures, like records and arrays, such a situation can become a serious problem. Wasted memory of this type is sometimes called "garbage," and some languages provide periodic *garbage collection* to identify such space automatically and make it available again. Modula-2 does not provide automatic garbage collection but provides an implementation-dependent procedure called DEALLOCATE, from module Storage, for deallocating memory space associated with pointer variables. When a dynamic variable like A^ is no longer needed, the statement DEALLOCATE(A, SIZE(INTEGER)) frees the memory space associated with it. Given the situation in Figure 15.5, if the statement sequence

```
DEALLOCATE ( A, SIZE ( INTEGER ) );
A : = B;
```

had been executed, the results would be as shown in Figure 15.8. The memory used to store the integer 3 that A had pointed to has been returned to the system for possible future use.

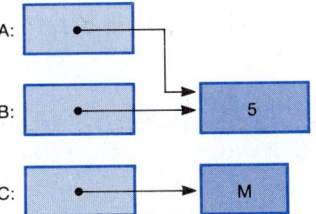

Figure 15.8
Deallocation and Pointer Assignment

Starting with the situation shown in Figure 15.8, assume that the following statements are executed:

```
WriteInt ( B^, 7 );
A^ : = 2;
WriteInt ( B^, 7 );
```

Before reading the following explanation, try to predict what will be printed by this program segment.

If you predicted that the program would print 5 and 5, you are only half right. The first WriteInt does print 5, but the second WriteInt prints 2. The value of B^ was changed between the print statements. Examining Figure 15.8, we see that A and B point to the same object. If we change the value stored in that object by an assignment to A^, the value of B^ also changes. This situation is called *aliasing:* two dynamic variables (in this case A^ and B^) are associated with the *same* memory location. Note that even if A^ and B^ are aliases, it does not follow that A and B are aliases. Since aliases are easily created, intentionally or unintentionally, we must exercise great care when using pointer variables.

In this section we have discussed how dynamic data structures are possible using pointer variables and dynamic variables that are referents of pointer variables. However, we have presented only examples of very simple structures that had just one dynamic variable that could be created with ALLOCATE and disposed with DEALLOCATE. In the next section we will see how to create dynamic data structures that can grow to any desired size, subject to the limitations of memory. These dynamic structures may be composed of many dynamic variables (using many pointers). The variables will be created as the structure grows and will be disposed as it contracts. First, though, we return to the implementation of opaque data types using pointers.

Opaque Strings Implementation

When we introduced opaque types earlier in this chapter, we mentioned that opaque types were implemented with pointers. Now that we have had an introduction to pointers, we can complete our discussion on the NewStrings implementation module. We will still use an array of characters to represent a string, but the type STRING declaration will be completed in the implementation module by

```
TYPE STRING = POINTER TO ARRAY[0..79] OF CHAR;
```

Therefore, if an object X is declared to be of type STRING in that module, X^ is the associated array of 80 characters and in the implementation module we can access the individual characters by: X^[0], X^[1], and so on. However, the user will not be able to access directly the individual characters in a string. For example, if a user program contains

```
FROM NewStrings IMPORT STRING;
VAR S1: STRING;
```

then S1^[0] should result in a compilation error. Such a reference will be valid only within the NewStrings implementation module, as in the declaration of the FetchChar function.

```
PROCEDURE FetchChar ( S: STRING; I: CARDINAL ): CHAR;
(* Returns character at index I in string S,
   or 0C if out of range *)
BEGIN
  IF (I < Length( S )) THEN
    RETURN S^[I];
  ELSE
    RETURN 0C;
  END; (* IF *)
END FetchChar;
```

Note that when we need access to the array itself, we use the pointer by writing S^. Also note that to call procedures that expect a parameter of type STRING, we do *not* use the dereferenced pointer; rather we pass the string directly.

Since strings are actually pointers, InitString simply assigns NIL as the pointer value. If the Assign procedure detects a NIL string, it will call ALLOCATE to create the array of characters. Suppose we have two string variables, S1 and S2, that have been initialized. The statement sequence

```
Assign( S1, "Have a nice day." );
Duplicate( S1, S2 );
```

results in S1 and S2 both having the value "Have a nice day.", but they are separate copies of the same string value. On the other hand, the statement sequence

```
Assign( S1, "Have a nice day." );
S2 := S1;
```

results in S1 and S2 accessing the same string structure with a value "Have a nice day." In this case the structures accessed by S1 and S2 are aliases.

In the implementation module, DEALLOCATE will be used in defining Dispose to return allocated memory to the system. The pointer variable itself may disappear on block exit, but, as we saw earlier in this section, the structure pointed at is not automatically removed. Rather, the programmer should remove the dynamic structure if a dispose procedure is provided.

We must exercise care when opaque types are passed as actual parameters, even if the formal parameter is a value parameter. The actual opaque parameter, which is an address, is protected from changes. However, the opaque structure, which is pointed to by the address, might be changed. Consider the example

```
PROCEDURE ConcatAll( Str1, Str2, Str3: STRING; VAR Str4: STRING );
BEGIN
  Concat( Str1, Str2, Str1 );
  Concat( Str1, Str3, Str4 );
END ConcatAll;
```

In this procedure the string associated with Str1 will be permanently changed, even though this was probably not the programmer's intent. Try to rewrite this procedure so that the strings associated with Str1, Str2, and Str3 are not changed.

The Dispose procedure from the Strings implementation module, shown in Section 11.3, also would not work as intended if the type STRING were opaque. See if you can spot the problem and modify Dispose to remedy it.

One of the major disadvantages of the array structure for representing strings is its fixed size. Although we have hidden this structure by having a pointer to an array, the string itself is still limited to a maximum of 80 characters. In an application involving strings we often want to have strings as large as necessary for that particular application. We can have them if we use dynamic structures called linked lists.

Linked Lists

Used carefully, pointers can enable us to create dynamic data structures. Because of the pointers, such structures use more space than static structures, but they are also more easily altered. Substantial changes can be made by merely changing a few pointers, whereas a similar change in a static structure might involve moving many data items. Even a simple dynamic structure such as a linked list offers such an advantage.

Figure 15.9 is an example of a common structure, called a linear linked list. The data in this structure happen to be integers, but they could be any type we wished. As we already mentioned, such a data structure is called dynamic because it can change size during program execution. It is beyond the scope of this introductory book to study these structures in detail. However, we will look at the construction of the very simple

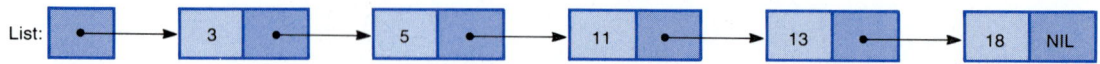

Figure 15.9 A Linear Linked List of Integers

linear linked list of characters shown in Figure 15.10. The letters 'H' and 'I' represent characters; NIL is the Modula-2 pointer constant that does not point to anything. It is used to indicate the end of a linked structure (in our case the end of a list).

Figure 15.10
A Linear Linked List of Characters

Our first task is to design the appropriate data types. CharList is obviously a pointer; but what does it point to? Examining the diagram, we see that the next item has two components, a character and a pointer. Since these are of different types, we will have to use a record structure for the declaration. Obviously the pointer CharList and the pointer in the record itself point to values with the same two-part structure. When used in a list, such a record structure is often called a *node*. Using this information, we make the declarations

```
TYPE NodePtr = POINTER TO Node;
     Node    = RECORD
                 Ch:   CHAR;
                 Link: NodePtr;
               END;
VAR  CharList: NodePtr;
```

These declarations are circular; NodePtr depends on the definition of Node, and Node depends on the definition of NodePtr. As a result, such structures are called *recursive data structures*. Figure 15.11 illustrates the step-by-step development of the desired data structure.

Notice the combined use of the caret, ^, to dereference pointer variables, and the dot, as the field selector for a record structure. At each stage we must keep in mind the type of data structure involved.

variable	type
CharList	POINTER TO Node
CharList^	Node
CharList^.Ch	CHAR
CharList^.Link	POINTER TO Node
CharList^.Link^	Node
CharList^.Link^.Ch	CHAR
CharList^.Link^.Link	POINTER TO Node

If we had to manipulate all dynamic data structures by starting at the beginning of the structure and specifying the list of pointers and fields to access the desired element,

Figure 15.11
Constructing a Linear Linked List

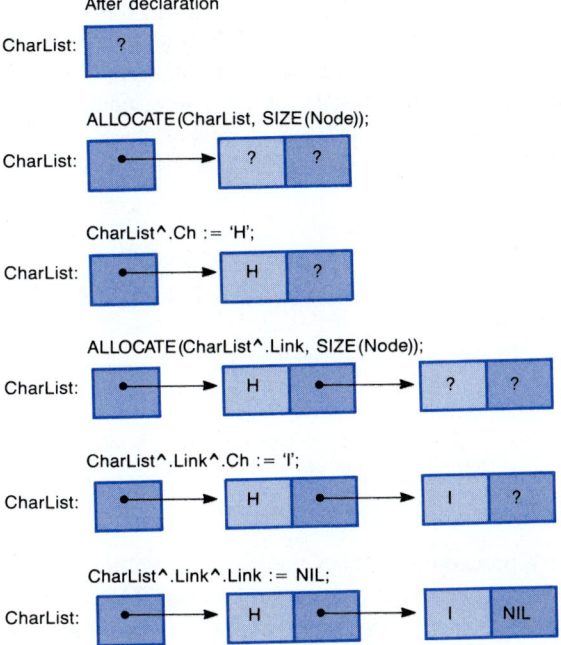

such structures would be of limited use. A more manageable approach is to use temporary pointers to point to locations in the structure that are currently being considered. Using that approach, we can program the building of a linear linked list in a more general way in order to create a list of as many characters as necessary. The following program segment illustrates this approach.

```
VAR CharList, LastNode, NewNode: NodePtr;
    Character: CHAR;


        Read( Character );                          (* First character *)
        IF Done THEN
           ALLOCATE( CharList, SIZE( Node ) );      (* First node *)
           CharList^.Ch := Character;               (* Store character *)
           CharList^.Link := NIL;                   (* End of list *)
           LastNode := CharList;                    (* Points to only node *)
           LOOP
              Read( Character );
              IF NOT Done THEN EXIT END;
              ALLOCATE( NewNode, SIZE( Node ) );    (* New node *)
              NewNode^.Ch := Character;             (* Store character *)
              NewNode^.Link := NIL;                 (* New end of list *)
              LastNode^.Link := NewNode;            (* Link last node to new node *)
              LastNode := NewNode;                  (* New last node *)
           END; (* LOOP *)
        END; (* IF *)
```

Note that the first element is treated as a special case, since we want to have the CharList pointer point to it. We then use two temporary pointers repeatedly to create new elements, referenced by NewNode, and link them to the end of the list, indicated by LastNode. If the characters 'H' and 'I' were input, the execution of this program segment would result in the structure at the bottom of Figure 15.10.

We can develop other procedures, such as a procedure to count the number of elements in a list:

```
PROCEDURE Count( L: NodePtr ): CARDINAL;
(* Count the number of elements in L *)
BEGIN
  IF L = NIL THEN
    RETURN 0;
  ELSE
    RETURN 1 + Count( L^.Link );
  END; (* IF *)
END Count;
```

This recursive procedure matches the recursive nature of a linked list structure. Since the procedure involves tail recursion, in Exercise 4 you'll be asked to write an iterative version. When we study more complex recursive data structures, such as trees in the next section, we will find it easy to develop recursive algorithms but difficult to implement comparable iterative algorithms.

We could use linear lists to implement dynamic character strings that would no longer be limited to 80 characters. Without modifying our NewStrings definition module, we could redefine the corresponding implementation module, starting with the STRING type,

```
TYPE STRING = POINTER TO Node;
```

All the procedures and functions would then have to be redefined. For example, redefinition of the Length function would be very similar to the procedure Count shown earlier.

The linear linked list representation of strings requires more space to represent strings, but it is very easy to change strings. For example, two strings can be concatenated by changing the pointer at the end of the first string, rather than moving characters in the second string. This flexibility of manipulation is characteristic of more complex dynamic data structures as well. We will briefly discuss one such structure.

Binary Trees

Using pointers, we can create dynamic structures that are much more complex than linear lists. One common structure is the *binary tree*. Figure 15.12 illustrates the idea of a binary tree, where each element, or node, may have one or two successors (or descendants) instead of one for a linear list.

Dynamic Data Structures and Pointers

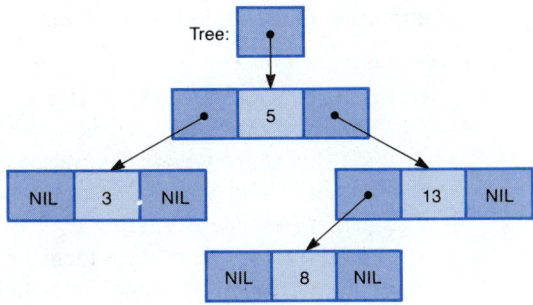

Figure 15.12 A Binary Tree

Binary trees are used for a large number of applications. Figure 15.12 illustrates a binary search tree created in such a way that its elements are ordered. For any node, all the elements in the left subtree are less than the node value, whereas all the elements in the right subtree are greater than the node value. The declarations for such a structure are

```
TYPE NodePtr = POINTER TO Node;
     Node    =    RECORD
                    Info: INTEGER;
                    Left, Right: NodePtr;
                  END;
VAR  Tree: NodePtr;
```

We could create the tree in Figure 15.12 by the statements

```
ALLOCATE( Tree, SIZE( Node ) );
Tree^.Info := 5;
ALLOCATE( Tree^.Left, SIZE( Node ) );
Tree^.Left^.Info := 3;
Tree^.Left^.Left := NIL;
Tree^.Left^.Right := NIL;
ALLOCATE( Tree^.Right, SIZE( Node ) );
Tree^.Right^.Info := 13;
Tree^.Right^.Right := NIL;
ALLOCATE( Tree^.Right^.Left, SIZE( Node ) );
Tree^.Right^.Left^.Info := 8;
Tree^.Right^.Left^.Left := NIL;
Tree^.Right^.Left^.Right := NIL;
```

Obviously, such an approach would not be very practical for larger trees. Therefore, we will develop an algorithm to insert a node with a specified value at its proper place in the binary search tree, or, if the node is already present, report that the insertion is a duplicate. Our pseudocode solution is

```
InsertElement( Value, VAR Tree );
    If Tree = nil then                              {create a new node}
        Allocate new node for Tree
        Set Info to Value
        Set Left and Right to NIL
    Elsif Value < Tree^.Info then                   {insert in left subtree}
        InsertElement( Value, Tree^.Left )
    Elsif Value > Tree^.Info then                   {insert in right subtree}
        InsertElement( Value, Tree^.Right )
    Else {Value = Tree^.Info , a duplicate entry}
        Print duplicate message
    End if
End InsertElement
```

The procedure InsertElement seems simple enough: if the tree is empty, it creates a new node; otherwise, it does a recursive call on the left or right subtree depending on the value to be inserted. There are two base cases. In one base case, the node is already present and a message is printed. In the other base case, when a place has been reached in the tree where an insertion is to be made, the value of parameter Tree is NIL, and a node is allocated to insert a new node. Since Tree is a variable parameter, the call to ALLOCATE connects this new node to the remainder of the tree at the appropriate position. For example, suppose we start with the tree in Figure 15.12 and want to add an element with value 1. The execution of InsertElement is traced as follows, where the indentation indicates the level of recursion:

```
InsertElement ( 1, Tree )
    Tree # NIL
    InsertElement ( 1, Tree^.Left )
        Tree^.Left # NIL
        InsertElement ( 1, Tree^.Left^.Left )
            Tree^.Left^.Left = NIL
            Allocate Tree^.Left^.Left {creates a node and connects it}
            Store value and two NIL pointers
            Return
        Return
    Return
```

We assume that the type of the Info field is ElementType, for which there exists a procedure WriteElement. With the previous definition of Node, ElementType would be INTEGER and WriteElement would be replaced by WriteInt.

SEC. 15.2   Dynamic Data Structures and Pointers

The Modula-2 code follows directly from our pseudocode.

```
PROCEDURE InsertElement( Value: ElementType; VAR Tree: NodePtr );
(* Insert element Value in Tree *)
BEGIN
   IF Tree=NIL THEN                         (* Create new node *)
      ALLOCATE( Tree, SIZE( Node ) );
      WITH Tree^ DO
         Info := Value;
         Left := NIL;
         Right := NIL;
      END; (* WITH *)
   ELSIF Value < Tree^.Info THEN            (* Insert into left subtree *)
      InsertElement( Value, Tree^.Left );
   ELSIF Value > Tree^.Info THEN            (* Insert into right subtree *)
      InsertElement( Value, Tree^.Right );
   ELSE
      WriteString( "Duplicate element: " );
      WriteElement( Value ); WriteLn;
   END; (* IF *)
END InsertElement;
```

Other useful operations on trees are searching for a particular value in a tree and traversal of a tree. Searching a balanced binary search tree with n nodes has complexity $O(\log n)$. A tree traversal is an operation that makes sure every node of a tree is visited once. We can illustrate such a traversal with the following short procedure, which, given a search tree like the one in Figure 15.12, will print its elements in order.

```
PROCEDURE InOrder ( Tree: NodePtr );
(* Print tree elements in order *)
BEGIN
   IF Tree # NIL THEN
      InOrder( Tree^.Left );
      WriteInt( Tree^.Info, 5 ); WriteLn;
      InOrder( Tree^.Right );
   END; (* IF *)
END InOrder;
```

This recursive procedure will visit every node in the tree, starting with the leftmost element, and ending with the rightmost element. Given the tree from Figure 15.12, the procedure would print: 3, 5, 8, 13. It is not difficult to devise other ways of traversing a tree, just by changing the order of the instructions in procedure InOrder.

Other common operations for trees include creating an empty tree, making a copy of a tree, and deleting a node from a tree. Deletion of a node is somewhat more difficult than the other operations, and you may wish to reflect on how it might be done.

If you continue on in the study of computer science, you will investigate dynamic data structures extensively in data structures courses.

SUMMARY

Abstract data types should include the name of the type and the permissible operations on values of the type but not the actual representation of values. Including the representation would violate the information hiding principle. One way to hide the actual representation is to use opaque types. These types declare only the name of the type in the definition module, thereby preventing indiscriminate access to values. The complete type declaration must appear in the corresponding implementation module.

Static data types have a maximum size that can be determined at compile time. Similarly, static variables have a fixed amount of space allocated for their values. In some cases, however, we must use dynamic data structures, which can grow or shrink as the program executes. Dynamic variables are created on demand during program execution. They cannot be directly referenced by using a variable name but must be referenced indirectly through special variables called pointers. The objects pointed to by pointer variables are called dynamic variables, which are created at run time by calls to the procedure ALLOCATE. A situation, called aliasing, occurs when two pointer variables point to the same memory location.

Dynamic structures, such as linear linked lists, enable us to design data structures in which substantial changes can be easily made. An even more complex dynamic structure is the binary tree. These structures have nodes with two successors, unlike the linear list, whose nodes have just one. Such dynamic structures are so important that they are discussed extensively in subsequent computer science courses dealing with data structures.

EXERCISES

1. Given the declarations and program segment,

    ```
    VAR CH1, CH2, CH3: POINTER TO CHAR
            .
            .
            .
    ALLOCATE( CH1, SIZE( CHAR ) );
    CH1^ := 'A';
    ALLOCATE( CH2, SIZE( CHAR ) );
    CH2^ := 'B';
    ALLOCATE( CH3, SIZE( CHAR ) );
    CH1 := CH2;
    CH3 := CH1;
    Write( CH1^ );
    Write( CH2^ );
    Write( CH3^ );
            .
            .
            .
    ```

    what will be printed by executing the program segment?

2. Here is a picture of a data structure consisting of a linked list of linked lists.

CharList: → [•|•] → [•|NIL]
              ↓   ↓
            [H|•]   [N|•]
              ↓   ↓
            [A|•]   [O|•]
              ↓   ↓
            [C|•]   [T|NIL]
              ↓
            [K|NIL]

Give the appropriate declarations for this structure and then the sequence of statements that would construct the structure with the indicated values.

3. Trace the function Count on the linear list of Figure 15.9.

4. Write an iterative version of the Count function in Section 15.2.

5. Trace the InsertElement procedure in Section 15.2 with the binary tree of Figure 15.12 in order to insert an element with value 12.

6. Write a procedure to print a binary search tree in descending order.

7. A linear list of single characters is a space-inefficient method for implementing dynamic strings. Give the type declarations for a more space-efficient structure that could hold up to 80 characters at each node in a linked structure.

PROGRAMMING PROBLEMS

8. Develop a Modula-2 program that will read 13 cards representing a bridge hand in the order in which they might be dealt. Do a simple evaluation of the hand, and display the hand and the point count. The input should be in the form of the rank of the card, followed by a single blank, followed by the suit. Put one card per line as illustrated here:

    2 heart

    K spade

    10 diamond

    J club

    A club

    Q heart

    .
    .
    .

The point count evaluation is based on the following:

Aces   : 4 each
Kings   : 3 each
Queens : 2 each
Jacks   : 1 each
void (no cards in a suit)   : 3 each
singleton (one card in a suit)   : 2 each
doubleton (two cards in a suit)   : 1 each

The output should be ordered by suit and within suit by rank, as illustrated here:

Spades   A J 10 8 5 4
Hearts   Q 3 2
Diamonds 10 7
Clubs   9 2

Point count = 9

9. Extend the program written for Problem 8 to provide a Bridge module containing the following items that can be exported.
   (a) an opaque type Hand
   (b) a procedure named Enter, which will allow the user to enter four bridge hands in the format used for Problem 8 and which validates the input
   (c) a procedure named Evaluate, which will do a point count evaluation as described in Problem 8
   (d) a procedure named Display, which will display four hands as illustrated below

Write a test program for the module that uses input redirection. Also prepare at least four test data files.

The display should take the following form:

```
                          North
                Spades    A J 10 8 5
                Hearts    Q 3 2
                Diamonds  10 7
                Clubs     10 9 2
                Point count = 8

      West                                              East
Spades    K 3                                  Spades    9 7
Hearts    A 10 9 4                             Hearts    J 8 7 6
Diamonds  Q 6                                  Diamonds  9 4
Clubs     Q 8 7 6 4                            Clubs     A K J 5 3
Point count = 13                               Point count = 11

                          South
                Spades    Q 6 4 2
                Hearts    K 5
                Diamonds  A K J 8 5 3 2
                Clubs
                Point count = 17
```

Programming Problems

10. Add to the Bridge module done for Problem 9 a procedure named Deal, which will simulate a random deal of four hands. Write a test program for Deal.

11. Write and implement the necessary procedures to create a NewStrings implementation module based on linked lists.

12. Using your type declarations in Exercise 7 for a dynamic string structure with up to 80 characters per node, write a length function assuming that all nodes, except possibly the last, are completely full.

13. Modify the length procedure in Problem 12 to work with strings, where any of the nodes may be partially filled.

14. Write an insert procedure for dynamic strings with up to 80 characters per node.

15. Build a simple strings module starting with Problems 13 and 14 and then implement a test program to check your procedures.

16 Concurrency

In this chapter you will:

> learn about concurrent processing of computations that have little interaction
>
> be introduced to the problems of coordinating the interaction between concurrent processes

The term *concurrent processing* here refers to algorithms that involve several relatively independent computations that could be done simultaneously with little interaction; such computations will be known as *processes*. Most implementations of Modula-2 include a library module that offers some support for concurrent processing. In this chapter we will use one such module to do some simple examples of concurrent processing. We will also discuss the problems that arise when processes have greater interaction than these simple examples.

16.1 Concurrent Processing and Multiprocessing

The importance of concurrent processing is based on the possibility of concurrent execution of processes that are relatively independent of one another. As mentioned in our discussion of Quicksort in Chapter 12, concurrent execution may be faster than strictly sequential execution, depending on the nature of the computing system in use. The most common possibilities are:

1. Execution is done on a *multiprocessing system* with several *identical* processors that can execute instructions simultaneously. The processes that constitute the computation may be executed on separate processors. In this case the execution is genuinely concurrent, and the computation may be much faster than sequential execution on a single processor.

2. Execution is done on a computer with only one processing unit. Execution is

switched back and forth among the processes, giving the appearance of simultaneous execution but naturally at a slower rate. In this case the processing is called *quasi-concurrent processing* or *multitasking*. Even though computation time may be no less than strictly sequential operation, the formulation of the computation in this way may be more natural than a strictly sequential formulation. The examples in Section 16.2 will illustrate this.

3. Several different processing units are used to execute different processes. Many computers have only a single processing unit for the main computation but have specialized processing units to perform input and output. In such systems the time for input and output of data can be overlapped with the time for processing the data.

As you can see, "concurrent execution" is a phrase that is used in several ways in computer science.

Most modern programming languages have features that support concurrency, and some, such as Ada, have sophisticated high-level facilities. Although Modula-2 is designed primarily for computers with a single processing unit, some basic facilities for concurrent processing are usually provided in a library module. In the next section we will discuss these facilities by working out two simple examples of concurrency.

16.2 Concurrency in Modula-2

In many versions of Modula-2, support for concurrent processing is provided by a library module called Processes. The definition module for Processes is as follows.

```
DEFINITION MODULE Processes;

TYPE SIGNAL;   (* to provide interaction between processes by *)
               (* using the procedures SEND and WAIT          *)

PROCEDURE StartProcess( P: PROC; varSize, codeSize: CARDINAL );
(* Starts a concurrent process with procedure P, providing P with a
   work space for variables of size varSize and code space of size
   codeSize. PROC is a standard type defined as PROC = PROCEDURE *)

PROCEDURE SEND( VAR s: SIGNAL );
(* send a signal that a process waiting on s may be resumed *)

PROCEDURE WAIT( VAR s: SIGNAL );
(* wait on s until another process sends a signal to s *)

PROCEDURE AWAITED( s: SIGNAL ): BOOLEAN;
(* TRUE if a process is waiting for s and FALSE otherwise *)

PROCEDURE INIT( VAR s: SIGNAL );
(* compulsory initialization of a signal *)

END Processes.
```

The Processes module makes use of Modula-2 low-level facilities from the standard module SYSTEM (see Appendix E). It is beyond the scope of this book to show the actual implementation of Processes; however, the following examples will illustrate use of this module.

EXAMPLE 1   *Independently Moving Particles*

In this example we want to observe the movement of two particles—call them A and B—moving at different speeds in two different rectangular areas of a screen. The particles are independent of each other, so we will represent them with independent processes, which could be executed concurrently. Our first pseudocode solution is

```
AParticleProcess
    Set initial position of particle A
    Set increment for each move of particle A
    Loop
        Move particle A
    End Loop
End AParticleProcess

BParticleProcess
    Set initial position of particle B
    Set increment for each move of particle B
    Loop
        Move particle B
    End Loop
End BParticleProcess

IndependentParticles
    Start AParticleProcess
    Start BParticleProcess
End IndependentParticles
```

The main program IndependentParticles starts the processes, which then move the particles until the program is stopped by some external means. The processes representing each particle could be executed by two different processors in a multiprocessing system, but our machine has only one central processor, so the processes must share the processor. In some languages, such as Ada, this sharing may be performed automatically. However, in Modula-2, we must explicitly program the sharing of the processor. We accomplish this by using two signals called AParticleSignal and BParticleSignal. After each move of particle A, the process for A will perform a WAIT on AParticleSignal, and similarly after each move of particle B, the process for particle B will perform a WAIT on BParticleSignal. Also, we will have the main program alternately perform a SEND of these signals to keep the particles moving. Using signals and refining MoveParticle into a separate procedure, we obtain a more detailed pseudocode solution,

```
MoveParticle
    Erase particle
    Compute new position of particle
    If new position is at edge of rectangular space then
        change move increment to cause a bounce
    Display particle at new position
End MoveParticle

AParticleProcess
    Set initial position of particle
    Set increment for each move of particle
    Loop
        MoveParticle
        WAIT AParticleSignal
    End Loop
End AParticleProcess

BParticleProcess
    Set initial position of particle
    Set increment for each move of particle
    Loop
        MoveParticle
        WAIT BParticleSignal
    End Loop
End BParticleProcess

IndependentParticles
    Start AParticleProcess
    Start BParticleProcess
    Loop
        SEND AParticleSignal
        SEND BParticleSignal
    End Loop
End IndependentParticles
```

This solution actually involves three processes: the main program and the processes for the two particles. Quasi-concurrent execution on a system with a single central processing unit starts with the main program IndependentParticles, which immediately initiates and relinquishes control to AParticleProcess. After the first move of particle A, AParticleProcess performs a WAIT on AParticleSignal, which causes the main program to resume control at the second statement in the loop. This statement initiates and relinquishes control to BParticleProcess. After the first move of the B particle,

BParticleProcess performs a WAIT on BParticleSignal, which causes the main program to resume control and go to the beginning of the loop. The first statement of the loop sends AParticleSignal, which causes AParticleProcess to resume execution. Hereafter, control switches back and forth between the three processes in the manner illustrated in Figure 16.1.

Figure 16.1
Interaction Between Three Processes

Further refinements depend on the method by which we will do the display. Unfortunately, we have only one screen on our machine, so we will use the left half of the screen to show the movement of one particle—say, the slow one—and the right half for the fast particle. To do the actual display we will use another library module available with our implementation of Modula-2. The module, called Graphics, treats the screen as a rectangular area with coordinates as shown in Figure 16.2.

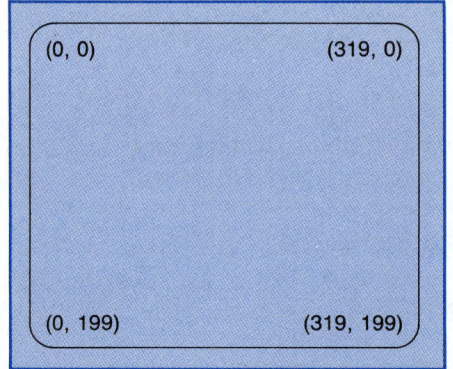

Figure 16.2
Coordinates of Screen for Graphics Module

Graphics is a large module, but the only items we need are

```
TYPE MODE = ( replace, invert, paint, erase );

PROCEDURE SetMode( displaymode: CARDINAL );
(* Sets the mode of the IBM graphics display *)

PROCEDURE DisplayChar( chr: CHAR; x, y: INTEGER;
                      color: COLOR; mode: MODE );
(* Displays chr at position (x,y) in specified color and mode *)
```

In fact we need to use these types and procedures in only a very limited way. At the beginning of our program we will use SetMode(5) to prepare the screen for graphical display. The parameter 5 indicates that the size of the screen as is illustrated in Figure 16.2. We will use DisplayChar to erase and display a character representing a particle. The parameter color will always be 1 in our calls of DisplayChar, indicating that the character will be drawn in white on a black-and-white screen.

Now we can implement the program using the modules Graphics and Processes, as follows:

```
MODULE IndependentParticles;
(* Program to display the motion of two particles, a slow
   particle in the left half of the screen (0 <= x <= 154),
   and a fast one in the right half (165 <= x <= 319). This
   program is designed to run on an IBM PC with a graphics card
   using the one-pass Modula Corporation compiler.
                            J. M. Adams, January 1988  *)

FROM Graphics IMPORT MODE, SetMode, DisplayChar;
FROM Processes IMPORT SIGNAL, StartProcess, SEND, WAIT, Init;

TYPE OrderedPair = RECORD
                     X, Y: INTEGER;
                   END;

VAR A, B, DeltaA, DeltaB : OrderedPair;
    AParticleSignal, BParticleSignal: SIGNAL;

PROCEDURE MoveParticle( VAR P, Delta: OrderedPair;
                            leftedge, rightedge: INTEGER );
CONST YMin = 0; YMax = 199;
BEGIN
  DisplayChar( 'O', P.X, P.Y, 1, erase );  (* erase at old position *)
  INC( P.X, Delta.X );
  INC( P.Y, Delta.Y );                     (* new position *)
  IF ( P.X <= leftedge ) OR ( P.X >= rightedge ) THEN
    (* bounce at left or right edge of screen *)
    Delta.X := -(Delta.X);
  END; (* IF *)
  IF ( P.Y <= YMin ) OR ( P.Y >= YMax ) THEN
    (* bounce at top or bottom of screen *)
    Delta.Y := -(Delta.Y);
  END; (* IF *)
  DisplayChar( 'O', P.X, P.Y, 1, replace );  (* draw at new position *)
END MoveParticle;

PROCEDURE AParticleProcess;
CONST SmallDelta = 4;
      AInitialX = 0; AInitialY = 60;
BEGIN
  A.X := AInitialX;
  A.Y := AInitialY;                  (* initial position *)
  DeltaA.X := SmallDelta;
  DeltaA.Y := SmallDelta;
```

```
      LOOP
        MoveParticle( A, DeltaA, 0, 154 );
        WAIT( AParticleSignal )        (* let other process run *)
      END;    (* LOOP *)
    END AParticleProcess;

    PROCEDURE BParticleProcess;
    CONST BigDelta = 8;
          BInitialX = 165; BInitialY = 60;
    BEGIN
      B.X := BInitialX;
      B.Y := BInitialY;                (* initial position *)
      DeltaB.X := BigDelta;
      DeltaB.Y := BigDelta;
      LOOP
        MoveParticle( B, DeltaB, 165, 319 );
        WAIT( BParticleSignal )        (* let other process run *)
      END;    (* LOOP *)
    END BParticleProcess;

    BEGIN (* Main *)
      SetMode( 5 );                    (* set screen to graphics mode *)
      Init( AParticleSignal );
      Init( BParticleSignal );
      StartProcess( AParticleProcess, 200, 400 );
      StartProcess( BParticleProcess, 200, 400 );
      LOOP
        SEND( AParticleSignal );
        SEND( BParticleSignal );
      END; (* LOOP *)
    END IndependentParticles.
```

As mentioned previously, this program will run until interrupted by some external means. Since such an arrangement is not very satisfactory, we could alter the main program to terminate execution when a key is pressed. This enhancement is easily done using the module Terminal. We will leave this as an exercise (see Programming Problem 5). As part of this enhancement, you should return the screen to the text mode using the command SetMode(2) just before terminating execution. The parameter 2 indicates the normal text mode of 25 lines of 80 characters on the IBM PC.

This example is a rather straightforward application of quasi-concurrency, since the processes have no interaction beyond that required to share the single processing unit. In our next example the processes have a little interaction.

EXAMPLE 2 *Colliding Particles*

In this example we will display two particles moving in the same space at the same speed. There will be some interaction between the particles when they collide. How-

SEC. 16.2 *Concurrency in Modula-2* 449

ever, this interaction is easy to handle. We merely need to check for a collision immediately after a particle has been moved and take appropriate action if there is a collision. The appropriate action is merely to swap the increments of the two particles, since particle A will bounce precisely in the direction that particle B was traveling and vice versa. Our pseudocode for the processes becomes

> AParticleProcess
>   Set initial position of particle A
>   Set increment for each move of particle A
>   Loop
>   Move particle A
>   CheckCollision
>   WAIT AParticleSignal
>   End Loop
> End AParticleProcess
>
> BParticleProcess
>   Set initial position of particle B
>   Set increment for each move of particle B
>   Loop
>   Move particle B
>   CheckCollision
>   WAIT BParticleSignal
>   End Loop
> End BParticleProcess
>
> IndependentParticles
>   Start AParticleProcess
>   Start BParticleProcess
>   Loop
>   SEND AParticleSignal
>   SEND BParticleSignal
>   End Loop
> End IndependentParticles

The pseudocode for MoveParticle is the same as our previous example, and the pseudocode for CheckCollision is very straightforward.

> CheckCollision
>   If positions of particles overlap then
>   swap the increments of the particles
> End CheckCollision

If CheckCollision is to be implemented as a procedure, it must have access to the positions and increments of both particles; therefore, the variables representing these entities can no longer be local to the processes. However, making them global violates the information hiding principle. We steadfastly adhere to our principles by using a library module for the processes and the procedures MoveParticle and CheckCollision, as follows:

```
DEFINITION MODULE LocalParticles;
(* Module to display the motion of two particles moving at the
   same speed.  The particles bounce away from each other when
   collisions are detected.  The program is designed to run on
   an IBM PC with a graphics board, using the Modula
   Corporation version of Modula-2.
                             J. M. Adams, January 1988      *)

FROM Processes IMPORT SIGNAL;

VAR AParticleSignal, BParticleSignal: SIGNAL;

PROCEDURE AParticleProcess;
PROCEDURE BParticleProcess;

END LocalParticles.

IMPLEMENTATION MODULE LocalParticles;
(* Module to display the motion of two particles moving at the
   same speed.  The particles bounce away from each other when
   collisions are detected.  The program is designed to run on
   an IBM PC with a graphics board, using the Modula
   Corporation version of Modula-2.
                             J. M. Adams, January 1988      *)

FROM Graphics IMPORT MODE, DisplayChar;
FROM Processes IMPORT WAIT;

CONST Delta = 6;

TYPE OrderedPair = RECORD
                     X, Y: INTEGER;
                   END;

VAR A, B, DeltaA, DeltaB : OrderedPair;

PROCEDURE MoveParticle( C: CHAR; VAR P, Delta: OrderedPair );
CONST XMin = 0; XMax = 319;
      YMin = 0; YMax = 199;
BEGIN
  DisplayChar( C, P.X, P.Y, 1, erase );  (* erase at old position *)
  INC( P.X, Delta.X );
  INC( P.Y, Delta.Y );                   (* new position *)
```

```
      IF ( P.X <= XMin ) OR ( P.X >= XMax ) THEN
      (* bounce at left or right edge of screen *)
        Delta.X := -(Delta.X);
      END; (* IF *)
      IF ( P.Y <= YMin ) OR ( P.Y >= YMax ) THEN
      (* bounce at top or bottom of screen *)
        Delta.Y := -(Delta.Y);
      END; (* IF *)
      DisplayChar( C, P.X, P.Y, 1, replace ); (* draw at new position *)
    END MoveParticle;

    PROCEDURE Swap( VAR X, Y: INTEGER );
    VAR Temp: INTEGER;
    BEGIN
      Temp := X; X := Y; Y := Temp;
    END Swap;

    PROCEDURE CheckCollision;
    CONST CloseDistance = 10;
    BEGIN
      IF   ( ABS( A.X - B.X ) < CloseDistance ) AND
                      ( ABS( A.Y - B.Y ) < CloseDistance )   THEN
        (* particles collide, so swap deltaX and deltaY values *)
        Swap(DeltaA.X, DeltaB.X);
        Swap(DeltaA.Y, DeltaB.Y);
      END; (* IF *)
    END CheckCollision;

    PROCEDURE AParticleProcess;
    CONST AInitialX = 0; AInitialY = 60;
    BEGIN
      A.X := AInitialX;
      A.Y := AInitialY;                    (* initial position *)
      DeltaA.X := Delta;
      DeltaA.Y := Delta;
      LOOP
        MoveParticle( 'o', A, DeltaA );
        CheckCollision;
        WAIT( AParticleSignal )           (* let other process run *)
      END;   (* LOOP *)
    END AParticleProcess;

    PROCEDURE BParticleProcess;
    CONST BInitialX = 165; BInitialY = 60;
    BEGIN
      B.X := BInitialX;
      B.Y := BInitialY;                    (* initial position *)
      DeltaB.X := Delta;
      DeltaB.Y := Delta;
      LOOP
        MoveParticle( '*', B, DeltaB );
```

```
            CheckCollision;
            WAIT( BParticleSignal )         (* let other process run *)
        END;    (* LOOP *)
    END BParticleProcess;

END LocalParticles.
```

Our test program is very simple.

```
MODULE Collide;
(* Program to display the motion of two particles moving at the same
   speed.  The particles bounce away from each other when collisions
   are detected.  The program is designed to run on an IBM PC with a
   graphics board, using the Modula Corporation version of Modula-2.
                    J. M. Adams, January 1988           *)

FROM Graphics IMPORT SetMode;
FROM Processes IMPORT StartProcess, SEND, Init;
FROM LocalParticles IMPORT AParticleSignal, BParticleSignal,
                           AParticleProcess, BParticleProcess;

BEGIN
    SetMode( 5 );                           (* set screen to graphics mode *)
    Init( AParticleSignal );
    Init( BParticleSignal );
    StartProcess( AParticleProcess, 200, 400 );
    StartProcess( BParticleProcess, 200, 400 );
    LOOP
        SEND( AParticleSignal );
        SEND( BParticleSignal );
    END; (* LOOP *)
END Collide.
```

The processes in this example still have very little interaction. Often processes that form part of the solution to a problem have more interaction. For example, one process may send data to another process, and the second process may have to wait until the data are provided before it can accomplish some parts of the computation for which it is responsible. We will describe a typical problem in the next section.

16.3 The Producer-Consumer Problem

If processes have greater interaction than our previous examples, their execution must be synchronized more carefully, and they must be protected from each other's activities. To give you a better idea of how some of these problems are handled, we will discuss one simple but common problem: synchronization between a process that produces data and a process that uses, or consumes, the data. This is often called the *producer-consumer problem*.

Since the producer may be producing data at a rate different from that at which the consumer uses it, the transfer of data between the two processes must be synchronized. Similar problems occur in physical systems such as production and consumption of oil. In such systems, storage tanks and valves are used to solve the problem. Storage tanks temporarily hold excess amounts, and valves control the flow to and from the tanks. We will use analogous means: an area in memory, called a *buffer*, for temporary storage of data, and an abstract data type, called a *semaphore*, for controlling the flow of data from the producer to the buffer and from the buffer to the consumer.

Let's start off with an easy solution of this problem, based on two simplifying assumptions. We will assume that we have an infinitely large buffer. We will also assume that transfers of data into and out of the buffer are not done simultaneously.

If we use an array as the data structure for our buffer, we need indices to control the flow of data into and out of the buffer, as illustrated in Figure 16.3.

Figure 16.3
Use of a Buffer

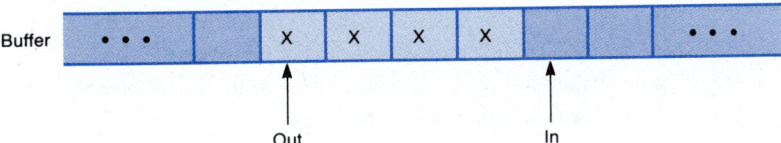

The producer adds items at the In pointer, as indicated by the pseudocode

```
Producer
    Loop
        Produce new item
        Append new item at Buffer[In]
        Increment In
    End Loop
End Producer
```

The consumer removes items at the location of the Out index. Removal is possible only if there is at least one item in the buffer. If the buffer is empty, the consumer must wait until an item is added. The buffer is not empty whenever In > Out, so we can write the following pseudocode for the consumer.

```
Consumer
    Loop
        Wait until In > Out
        Take item at Buffer[Out]
        Increment Out
        Consume Item
    End Loop
End Consumer
```

Let NumItems = In − Out; then NumItems represents the number of items in the buffer. NumItems is initially zero and can increase or decrease arbitrarily except that it can never go below zero. Also, when NumItems equals zero, the consumer task will be suspended until NumItems becomes positive.

We now introduce a new abstract data type, called a semaphore, that is a more powerful synchronizing device than the SIGNAL used in our previous examples. Semaphores will aid us in removing our simplifying assumptions. A semaphore—call it S—is an integer that can have only nonnegative values. Furthermore, the only permissible operations on a semaphore are Wait(S) and Signal(S), which are defined as follows:

- Wait(S): If S > 0, then decrement S; otherwise, the process calling Wait(S) is suspended.
- Signal(S): If some process has been suspended by a previous Wait(S) on the semaphore S, then resume this process; otherwise increment S.

Apart from initialization, no other operation, not even inspecting the value of a semaphore, is allowed. Wait and Signal are atomic operations; once one of them is initiated, it cannot be interrupted before it is completed. If more than one process has been suspended by a Wait on a particular semaphore, the definition of Signal does not specify which process will be resumed.

Now we return to the producer-consumer problem and implement it with semaphores. Suppose that NumItems is a semaphore representing the number of items in the buffer and is initialized to 0. Our pseudocode becomes

```
Producer
    Loop
        Produce
        Append
        Signal( NumItems )
    End Loop
End Producer

Consumer
    Loop
        Wait( NumItems )
        Take
        Consume
    End Loop
End Consumer
```

The operations Produce, Append, Take, and Consume are abbreviations for the operations in our previous version. Remember that one of our simplifying assumptions was that an Append and a Take did not occur simultaneously. If we cannot make this assumption, we need a mechanism to delay one of them until the other is finished. This situation is very common, since the memory of most computers cannot be accessed simultaneously by two processes. Preventing such simultaneous access is called *mutual exclusion*. Semaphores provide the mechanism we need to implement mutual exclusion. In particular, we will introduce another semaphore, called Buffer, that will be initialized to 1. When a process needs to access the buffer by either Append or Take, it will first wait on Buffer to make sure the buffer is not in use (in other words, wait until Buffer is nonzero). Suppose Buffer is 1, indicating the buffer is not in use, then Wait(Buffer) sets Buffer to 0 and allows the calling process to access the buffer. If Buffer is 0, any other process executing a Wait on Buffer is blocked from accessing the buffer until Buffer becomes 1 again. After accessing the buffer, the process releases it by calling Signal(Buffer), which increments Buffer. These ideas are incorporated in the revised pseudocode.

```
Producer
    Loop
        Produce
        Wait( Buffer )
        Append
        Signal( Buffer )
        Signal( NumItems )
    End Loop
End Producer

Consumer
    Loop
        Wait( NumItems )
        Wait( Buffer )
        Take
        Signal( Buffer )
        Consume
    End Loop
End Consumer
```

With only one producer and one consumer, the semaphore Buffer will only have values of 0 and 1; as a result it is called a *binary semaphore*. The order of the Wait calls in the consumer process is very important. Suppose that the consumer does the Wait(Buffer) before the Wait(NumItems). If both processes are started up at the same time, the consumer will probably be ready to consume immediately even if the producer has not put anything in the buffer. Since the buffer is initially available, the consumer calling Wait(Buffer) will reserve the buffer for the consumer task until it is released by a Signal(Buffer). But the next action is a Wait(NumItems); since the buffer is empty, the consumer task is suspended until something is put into the buffer. But the producer task is blocked from putting anything into the buffer since Buffer was set to 0 by the Wait(Buffer) in the consumer! Since neither task can proceed, we have reached a state called *deadlock,* or the *deadly embrace*. You should convince yourself that the ordering of the Wait calls given earlier will not result in deadlock. This seemingly minor error of switching the order of two Wait calls, resulting in a complete suspension of all activities, illustrates one of the difficulties in multiprocessing.

We have one final problem to solve: we cannot assume an infinite amount of memory for the buffer. Let's assume the buffer size is specified by a constant, SizeOfBuffer. If the producer generates items fast enough, the buffer may become full. In this case the producer will have to be suspended until the consumer takes an item from the buffer. Of course, once an item is removed, there will be a space for the producer to add an item, so the producer task should be resumed every time the consuming task removes an item. This synchronization is accomplished by introducing yet another semaphore, Space, representing the number of empty spaces in the buffer. Space will be initialized to SizeOfBuffer, but if it should ever reach 0, the producer will have to be suspended. Our final version of the pseudocode program follows. The main program, BoundedBuffer, is also included to indicate the initial semaphore values. You should trace through this program with limiting conditions (buffer empty, buffer full) to verify that there is no deadlock in these cases.

```
BoundedBuffer
    Set Buffer to 1
    Set NumItems to 0
    Set Space to SizeOfBuffer
    Start Producer and Consumer
End BoundedBuffer

Producer
    Loop
        Produce
        Wait( Space )
        Wait( Buffer )
        Append
        Signal( Buffer )
        Signal( NumItems )
    End Loop
End Producer

Consumer
    Loop
        Wait( NumItems )
        Wait( Buffer )
        Take
        Signal( Buffer )
        Signal( Space )
        Consume
    End Loop
End Consumer
```

SUMMARY

Concurrent processing involves processes consisting of several relatively independent computations that can be executed simultaneously with little interaction. Such concurrent execution may be faster than strictly sequential execution.

There are three situations where concurrent processing commonly occurs. The first is a multiprocessing system, which has a number of identical processors executing instructions simultaneously. The second case, called quasi-concurrent processing or multitasking, takes place when one processing unit executes several processes by switching back and forth among the processes to give the appearance of simultaneous execution. The third instance involves computers with several processing units for input and output so that the time for I/O can be overlapped with the time for processing the data.

In Modula-2 the basic facilities for concurrent processing are provided in a library module, usually called Processes. This module contains procedures for controlling the interaction between processes. When processes have a significant amount of interaction, their execution must be synchronized. One common situation, known as the producer-consumer problem, is the synchronization between a process that produces data and a process that uses the data. In some cases the producer may be producing data faster than the consumer uses it, or the consumer may be consuming data faster than the producer produces it. An area in memory called a buffer can be used for temporary data storage, and an abstract data type called a semaphore can be used for controlling the data flow. The prevention of simultaneous access to computer memory is called mutual exclusion.

Concurrency provides the potential for increased speed of processing using systems with more than one processor, which can execute processes in a truly concurrent fashion. This potential is one of the primary reasons that the topic of concurrency is of such great importance in the fields of computer architecture and operating systems.

EXERCISES

1. Draw a modular design chart for the IndependentParticles program in Section 16.2.
2. Draw a modular design chart for the the Collide program in Section 16.2.
3. Design new procedures for MoveParticle and CheckCollision used in the Collide program in Section 16.2. The new procedures should cause a particle to slow down when it bounces off the boundary of the rectangular space and cause both particles to slow down when a collision occurs. The particles should eventually stop.

PROGRAMMING PROBLEMS

4. If your implementation of Modula-2 has the appropriate library modules, implement a new version of the Collide program using the MoveParticle and CheckCollision procedures designed for Exercise 3.

5. If your implementation of Modula-2 has the appropriate library modules, implement the enhancement to the IndependentParticles program described at the end of Example 1 in Section 16.2.

6. If your implementation of Modula-2 has the appropriate library modules, implement a new version of the Collide program given in Section 16.2 that will display the movement of three particles. Each particle should be represented on the screen by a different character and the program should stop or start a particle when the character on the keyboard that represents the particle is pressed.

17 An Overview of Selected Topics in Computer Science

In this chapter you will:

- follow the development of computer architecture
- see the evolution of operating systems
- be introduced to the issues of programming language design
- explore a number of topics in the field of artificial intelligence

Now that you have had a thorough introduction to problem solving and programming, you will want to explore the major areas of computer science in more detail. This chapter contains a short introduction to some of the most important topics. We will try to give you a feeling for these areas and, in doing so, a better understanding of the field of computer science.

We'll see how computer architecture and operating systems have developed over the years to improve efficiency and ease of use. The section on programming languages describes the historical development of the high-level programming languages and discusses the formal definitions of language syntax and semantics. Finally we take a brief look at several topics in artificial intelligence research.

17.1 Computer Architecture and Operating Systems

Traditionally the field of computer architecture has been concerned with the organization of computer hardware, sometimes with little regard for the computations to be performed. However, hardware by itself cannot be used easily. We need collections of programs, called software, to facilitate the use of the hardware. If we consider the software to be in layers covering the underlying machine, the layer closest to the hardware would be the operating system. Programs in the next layer, such as editors and compilers, would use operations provided by the operating system. In essence, these software layers transform the hardware into a machine with which we can communicate more naturally. Since the most basic layer of software is the operating system, the areas of computer architecture and operating systems are very closely related. In the following sections we will discuss the evolution of computer architecture, the evolution of operating systems, and then a topic currently of great importance to both fields—multiprocessing.

Evolution of Computer Architecture

As mentioned in the Introduction, the first large electronic computer, the ENIAC, was not "programmed" in the sense that we use that word today. The computer had to be wired for each specific computation; programming, therefore, involved physically modifying the computer. This made programming a very tedious process.

The idea of having a program stored in memory along with data was developed in the late 1940s by John von Neumann, and also by J. Presper Eckert and John Mauchly. This innovation permitted programming to be done much more easily, without dealing directly with the hardware, and thus was a critical architectural development. Single-processor stored program computers are often called *von Neumann machines,* and the stored program concept is still very basic for much of contemporary computer architecture.

In the Introduction we gave a description of a simple von Neumann machine as a system made of five basic units. Figure 17.1 gives a slightly more detailed version but still with the five basic units.

1. *Memory unit:* stores *both* instructions and data.
2. *Arithmetic-logic unit:* performs arithmetic and logical operations.
3. *Control unit:* interprets instructions and directs the other units to perform the actions indicated by the instructions.

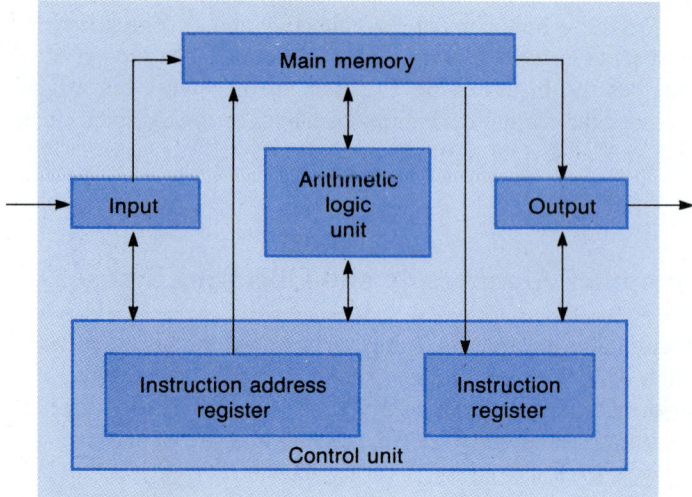

Figure 17.1
Simple Von Neumann Machine

4. *Input unit:* transmits data and instructions from external devices to main memory.
5. *Output unit:* transmits results from main memory to external devices.

The control unit together with the arithmetic-logic unit are often called the *central processing unit* (CPU).

The *instruction execution cycle* in such a machine is defined in the following way.

1. The control unit fetches from memory the next instruction at the location specified by the instruction address register and stores it in the instruction register.
2. The instruction address register is incremented.
3. The control unit decodes the fetched instruction to determine what action is to be performed.
4. If the decoded instruction has operands, they are fetched from memory. The instruction is then executed. Some instructions may store a result in memory. If the instruction causes a branch from the sequential execution of instructions, the instruction address register will be changed.
5. Return to step 1.

The CPUs of first-generation von Neumann machines (from about 1949 to 1958) were constructed with vacuum tubes, and the architectural advances of that period included input/output processors, interrupt capability, and microprogramming. The following discussion briefly describes these features.

The operation of early computers was simple and sequential, since everything was controlled by the CPU. This arrangement left the CPU idle most of the time while it waited for input or output operations to be completed. The input and output operations were mechanical and thus much slower than the electronic operation of the CPU. For better CPU utilization, developers made input and output operations independent of the CPU by using small specialized *input/output processors,* sometimes called *channels,* to control I/O operations. This way the CPU could operate at very high speed, while I/O operations were performed concurrently at much slower speeds. However, as we have seen in Chapter 16, concurrent processing requires some synchronization of the concurrent processes. Synchronization was achieved by providing the computers with interrupt capabilities to signal the CPU that an I/O task had been completed.

The concept of an interrupt is simple. In our daily life, interruptions, such as telephone calls, occur and make us suspend what we are doing to "process" the interruption before resuming the suspended task. In general, in an interrupt-driven system, a slow task generates an interrupt signal when it has finished. When a fast task detects this interrupt signal, the fast task suspends its current operation to accept the results of the slow task. After accepting the results and perhaps starting a new slow task, the fast task continues the interrupted operation.

Another early significant development in computer architecture addressed the problem of resolving the conflicting goals of programmers and computer designers. When programming in assembly language, programmers want to have available powerful machine-language instructions. But hardware designers want to build simple machines to make them more reliable. Microprogramming helped to resolve this conflict. The concept was introduced in 1953 by Maurice Wilkes, but it took some time for the technology to improve and allow cost-effective implementation. The execution of a machine-language instruction can be broken down into a sequence of elementary steps called microinstructions. Execution of a machine-language instruction then involves execution of the corresponding sequence of microinstructions, and a special unit controls the execution of the microinstructions. Since machine-language instructions can share sequences of microinstructions, this way of implementing machine instructions is economical. Microprogramming makes it practical to design a series of computers of varying capabilities yet with compatible machine languages. A working program can then be more easily moved from one computer in the series to another; this desirable feature is known as *portability*. Microprogramming can also be used by a company to build a machine that operates like another machine, perhaps an earlier model or a competitor's machine. This is called *emulation*.

Second-generation machines (from about 1958 to 1964) were constructed with transistors, which made possible faster, more reliable, and more powerful computers. Architectural innovations of that period included virtual memory and multiprocessors.

Programmers often develop software that will not fit into main memory. *Virtual memory* gives programmers the illusion that memory is not limited by the physical size of the computer's main memory. For a program to execute, it need not be entirely resident in memory. For instance, the first half of the program might first be loaded into memory, and execution started. When a reference is made to a part of the program not in memory, that part is loaded, replacing parts not in use anymore. Swapping parts of a program in and out in this fashion can be quite complicated, unless the computer has special features for *memory management*. Such features began to be provided in second-generation computers.

During the second generation, hardware designers began to include within a single computer, not just one powerful processor and several specialized I/O processors, but multiple processors each as powerful as a CPU. Such *multiprocessors* could cooperate to solve larger problems more quickly. The problems of effectively using such multiprocessing systems are great, but the potential benefits are even greater. As discussed in Chapter 16, the possibility of true concurrent execution of processes can provide significant overall increases in processing speed.

Subsequent to the second generation of computers, the advent of large-scale integrated circuits (LSI) and then very large-scale integrated circuits (VLSI) has made it possible to reduce the size of computer circuitry drastically. We can now put an entire CPU on a single silicon chip; such a CPU is called a *microprocessor*. This capability makes it possible to design multiprocessing systems with large numbers of powerful processors, thus making concurrent processing, or what is sometimes called *parallel processing*, possible on a large scale.

Evolution of Operating Systems

An operating system is a coherent system of programs that makes the hardware easier to use; it acts as an interface between the computer user and the computer hardware. Indeed an operating system is essentially a manager of hardware and software resources. The two most important goals of an operating system are convenience for the user and efficiency of operation of the computer system.

Early computers had very little software to assist the user. In particular, there were neither operating systems nor compilers. The high cost of those computers, however, soon prompted designers to create the first operating systems in an attempt to use computer time more efficiently. From then on, operating systems and computer architecture have influenced each other: operating systems were developed to facilitate the use of hardware, then hardware was designed to facilitate operating system functions, and so on.

When using the early computers without operating systems or compilers, users had to program in machine language. Running programs involved having complete control over the computer. After reserving time for using the computer, the programmer ran programs from the computer console after loading them into memory. If necessary, the programmer could stop program execution from the console, examine the contents of memory, modify memory if necessary and restart the program. If things went wrong, the period of time reserved was probably not sufficient; on the other hand, if things went well and the programmer was finished early, the computer would be idle until the next programmer arrived.

The scenario just described may not seem very unusual if you use microcomputers in a laboratory, but your microcomputers are relatively inexpensive whereas early computers cost hundreds of thousands of dollars. Thus, idle time on early computers was very uneconomical. It was particularly expensive when jobs required a long setup time: loading punched cards into card readers, mounting magnetic tapes on tape drives, and so on.

In the 1950s, simple operating systems were developed in order to maximize the use of computer time. Programs, or jobs, as they were called, were grouped in *batches* in order to reduce setup time; professional computer operators were hired, and programmers no longer were permitted to operate the computer. At the end of each job, control was returned to the operating system, which cleaned up the previous job and set up the next job. This mode of operation is called *batch processing*.

Although batch processing with automatic job sequencing improved the usage efficiency of computers, the CPU was still idle much of the time. This was due to the difference of speed between the CPU and input and output devices, such as card readers and line printers. These devices were about a thousand times slower than the CPU; thus jobs that involved reading stacks of cards and printing scores of lines would result in the CPU being idle most of the time.

In the 1960s, a number of new concepts emerged. To improve *throughput* (work processed per time unit), developers created operating systems to give the appearance of concurrent execution of many programs. The execution could really be only quasi-concurrent, as explained in Chapter 16, since the computers of that time had only one CPU. This quasi-concurrent execution of programs was called *multiprogramming*. Multiprogramming attempted to increase CPU usage by always having something for the CPU to execute. The operating system would select a program and start its execution on the CPU. If the program had to wait for something, like completion of an input or output operation, the operating system switched to another program and started its execution on the CPU, while the input/output operation of the first program was being completed on an input/output processor. When the second program had to wait, the operating system could switch back to the first program—if its input/output operation had been completed—or to a third program. As long as there was some program to execute, the CPU would not be idle. Scheduling and synchronizing the execution of these programs were challenging problems, and these problems were the forerunners of the current problems of scheduling and synchronizing the execution of processes by multiprocessor systems.

By the 1970s, commercial *timesharing* systems had become available. Such systems applied multiprogramming techniques to provide interactive use of computers at a reasonable cost. Those with timesharing systems could communicate directly with the computer on computer terminals. Users were able to type in requests to the system, and the requests would be processed and responses returned in a matter of seconds. Such systems have eliminated the long delays typical of batch systems. Many people can share a computer, because typically each individual's action or command tends to be short and requires only a short CPU time. The system, with its multiprogramming capabilities, switches rapidly from one person to the next, so that users are given the impression that each of them controls the computer. If you work in a laboratory with terminals to a minicomputer or a larger "mainframe" computer, you are working in this type of environment.

Operating systems to handle multiprocessing were developed after multiprogramming systems. Initially they dealt with independent computer systems communicating with each other (*computer networks*), and later they also dealt with single systems containing multiple processors. As mentioned in Chapter 16, the problems in developing operating systems for multiprocessors are of considerable difficulty. For example, there are usually more processes to be done than there are processors to do them. Thus processors must be scheduled to perform the processes, and this scheduling should be done in an effective manner by attempting to maximize throughput, minimize overhead, give preference to processes holding key resources, enforce priorities, make sure that no process is postponed indefinitely, balance resource usage, and so on. Since these goals conflict, process scheduling is a complex problem for operating systems. Another complex problem is process synchronization. Because there are usually many active processes at a given time, their execution must be synchronized and they must be protected from each other's activities. The producer-consumer problem discussed in Chapter 16 was an example of the difficulties involved in process synchronization.

Present computers are often networked with other computers. Personal computers can operate independently or can be connected by communication lines to other computers so that they act as terminals. Larger computers operate independently and communicate through the communication lines of the network. The advantages of such networks are that resources available at one site can be used by another site, computations can be performed faster if done on several computers, reliability is enhanced because when one computer breaks down the others continue working, communication between different sites is possible (electronic mail), and so on. Thus computer power is brought to the place where it is needed, instead of the user having to bring the data to a centralized computer. Such *distributed systems* are complex systems of computers and communication devices; the problems of synchronization and communication here are, therefore, even more challenging than those faced by operating systems for a single computer with multiple processors.

We'll summarize our discussion of the evolution of operating systems by saying that we view modern operating systems primarily as resource managers. The primary resource they manage is hardware: processors, storages, input and output, and communication devices. Operating systems are collections of programs that make the hardware more convenient to use and that increase usage efficiency. They are usually written in assembly language, or an appropriate high-level language, or a combination of the two. Due to their low-level facilities, Modula-2, C, and Ada are three appropriate languages for implementing operating systems. Sometimes portions of operating systems are implemented in *firmware*. Firmware consists of fast machine code programs, sometimes permanently stored in ROM (Read Only Memory) so that they will execute very rapidly.

Modern operating systems must be able to monitor program execution by loading programs into physical memory, starting execution, detecting errors, and taking appropriate action. They must provide means to perform input and output operations since user programs generally cannot execute input and output operations directly. Operating systems must also maintain usage statistics to keep track of what resources users have been using, generate bills for computer usage, and measure system performance. Finally they must also provide systems to create, delete, and manipulate files on secondary storage devices. If the file system has a directory structure, some other tools must be available to manipulate file directories. Compilers, assemblers, loaders, and various utility programs are not really part of operating systems but are available through them.

Over the years, operating systems have become more user oriented, and the ultimate goal is embodied by the *virtual machine* concept. Users are normally interested not in the physical machine but in its virtual characteristics—the powers it seems to possess. For example, virtual memory may make a computer appear to have an extremely large memory when in fact it is small. In an ideal situation users would seem to have machines perfectly suited for their applications—that is, appropriate virtual machines. Operating systems and high-level programming languages attempt to provide such virtual machines.

17.2 Programming Languages

In a certain respect, programming languages have been the key to effective use of computers. As the level of programming languages has become closer to that of problems we wish to solve, we have been able to express solutions much more naturally. Thus we have been able to move from forms of expressions oriented toward machines to forms of expression more natural for human problem solvers. This development, in turn, has made possible the implementation of larger and more reliable programs, and has fostered an increasingly more fruitful interaction between humans and computers. As a simple example, the LOOP and IF control structures used in Modula-2 had to be formulated at a lower level with GOTO instructions in earlier languages. Such formulations were clumsy and error prone.

In this section we will trace the development of programming languages, and then we will discuss some aspects of programming language definition.

Evolution of Programming Languages

The first digital computers were programmed in machine language at the level of binary representation of commands and addresses. Naturally, such a process was very laborious and error prone. The first software tools were libraries of subprograms that enabled programmers to take advantage of other programmers' efforts. These libraries were the early forerunners of our Modula-2 library modules but could hardly be considered languages.

The first true language development came in the form of *assembly languages*, which permitted programmers to use mnemonic operation codes and symbolic addresses, rather than the numbers required by machine language. Although the development of assembly languages was a small step, it was an important one; an instruction such as "ADD TAX" was certainly much more comprehensible than something like "30 1007". Of course, assembly language instructions had to be translated into machine code before they could be executed. The translating programs, called *assemblers,* were the forerunners of compilers.

The 1950s saw considerable work on the development of higher-level languages and compilers for these languages. The first high-level programming language to be widely used was FORTRAN, developed in the mid-1950s by a group of IBM scientists headed by John Backus. FORTRAN, which stands for FORmula TRANslation, was developed primarily for scientific applications, and over the years the language has been extended and improved. However, it is quite difficult to add new features to a language while maintaining compatibility with older versions of the language. As a result, current versions of FORTRAN do not support modern programming principles as well as some newer languages.

In 1957, an international group of scientists produced a report describing a language called the International Algebraic Language. Subsequently, the language became known as ALGOL 60, which stands for ALGOrithmic Language, 1960. ALGOL 60 was used extensively in Europe, but its usage in the United States was primarily limited to universities.

ALGOL 60, which was the first block-structured language, had control structures much like those we have studied. It has had a profound impact on programming language design, particularly on a line of newer languages, which includes Pascal, C, Modula-2, and Ada. One very significant feature of the definition of ALGOL 60 is that its syntax was precisely defined using a technique called *Backus-Naur Form,* or BNF. Variations of BNF are now commonly used to define the syntax of programming languages (see Appendix B).

In 1959, the U.S. government sponsored the development of COBOL, or COmmon Business Oriented Language. COBOL has been widely used for business data processing, and probably has been used more than any other programming language. One particularly important feature of COBOL is its data division, which was the forerunner of the current emphasis on data types in newer languages.

Development of a very different language, called LISP (from LISt Processing) was begun in 1959 by a group at MIT directed by John McCarthy. A simple, elegant language, LISP can be precisely and succinctly described because its origin was as a formal mathematical language. LISP has one powerful but simple data structure, called a list. Programs as well as data are represented by lists, so that LISP programs can construct and then execute other LISP programs. This is an important feature for writing programs that "learn." LISP has been used extensively in artificial intelligence applications and seems to gain in popularity as the years pass.

Subsequently, many programming languages have been developed, ranging from large and complex general-purpose languages, such as ALGOL 68 and PL/1, to relatively simple but powerful languages, such as Pascal and C. In general, the simpler languages have been more successful, since the complexity of the larger languages has impeded rather than eased the process of developing programs.

One very important new language is Ada, named for Lord Byron's daughter Ada, Countess of Lovelace, who worked with Charles Babbage on the design of the Analytical Engine. She is sometimes called the world's first programmer. The development of the Ada programming language was sponsored by the U.S. government in an attempt to provide a language that will make software development easier and less costly. The initial design of Ada was fairly simple, but subsequently many features have been added. Ada will be an important language, but it is too early to tell if its complexity will be a barrier to straightforward and effective program development.

During the past ten years a very different style of programming, called *logic programming*, has become increasingly popular. Logic programming seems very effective for certain applications, such as artifical intelligence, and the Japanese have made logic programming an important part of their research in artificial intelligence.

The best-known logic programming language is Prolog. Statements in Prolog have the nature of a relatively simple form of expression in mathematical logic and contain very little specification of flow of control. Thus a Prolog program has the nature of a specification of what is desired rather than a specification of the actions to be performed to achieve a desired result. For many problems, one can develop a Prolog program that is very similar to the problem specification and hence less prone to errors of misinterpretation of the specifications than solutions in more standard languages. Unfortunately, execution of Prolog programs is sometimes very inefficient and thus not very practical. We are still in the early stages of developing languages for logic programming and of learning the appropriate styles to use in designing logic programs. If we are able to achieve adequate efficiency and develop effective languages and styles, logic programming could be a very attractive method of solving many problems.

Another trend in the evolution of programming languages is the emergence of *object-oriented* languages. Smalltalk is one well-known example of an object-oriented language. The predominant paradigm of Smalltalk is the simulation of objects that communicate by sending and receiving messages. This paradigm has been applied to other programming languages, including Scheme, a dialect of LISP and C++, a dialect of C.

Formal Definition of Programming Language Syntax

Throughout this book we have specified the syntax of Modula-2 in a very informal way using English language descriptions and very little notation. As mentioned in the previous section, the syntax of programming languages can be precisely defined using a method called Backus-Naur Form, or BNF. BNF is a formal method with a very specific notation. For example, the specification of the octal digits in a variant of BNF used for Modula-2 in Appendix B is

```
OctalDigit = "0" | "1" | "2" | "3" | "4" | "5" | "6" | "7"
```

The item being defined is denoted by a descriptive name at the beginning of the definition. It is followed by " = ", which stands for "is defined by." The symbols in quotes stand for themselves, and the symbol "|" stands for "or". Thus this definition would be read as: an octal digit is defined to be a 0 or a 1 or a 2 or a 3 or a 4 or a 5 or a 6 or a 7. We can then define a digit as

```
Digit = OctalDigit | "8" | "9"
```

Recursive definitions are used to define more complex syntactic entities, such as Ident (for identifier),

```
Ident = Letter | Ident Letter | Ident Digit
```

where Letter has been defined in a manner similar to Digit. This definition would be read as: an identifier is a letter, or an identifier followed by a letter, or an identifier followed by a digit. The base of this recursive definition is the first possibility, and the other two possibilities are obviously recursive. In simple cases such as this, a recursive specification can be replaced by specifications with an iterative nature using some additional notation, as we have done in Appendix B.

A formal definition of the syntax of a programming language is very important for the development of a compiler for the language. Such a definition specifies the syntactically valid programs, and the first thing that a compiler must do is establish whether a program is syntactically valid before translating the program into machine language. In fact, there are programs that will accept a formal definition of syntax in BNF form as input and produce the part of the compiler (called a parser) that checks for syntactic validity. In other words, part of the process of writing a compiler can be automated by using formal methods like BNF.

A BNF specification of the syntax of a programming language is not a *complete* specification of syntax, because we cannot represent the syntax of parts of the program that depend on other parts of the program. For example, an identifier used in an assignment statement in Modula-2 must be declared elsewhere in the program. In this sense Modula-2 is context sensitive, and BNF cannot specify these context-sensitive aspects of a programming language.

Formal Definition of Programming Language Semantics

You might very well ask if the entire process of compiler writing can be automated. Unfortunately, this is not currently practical. Extensions of BNF can be used to specify the context-sensitive parts of a programming language, but we still have no truly effective means for the formal specification of the semantics of a programming language. Usually the semantics of a programming language are defined in an informal manner similar to the descriptions of the meanings of Modula-2 statements that we have given.

Researchers in programming languages have shown that it is possible to give formal semantic specifications, but current specification techniques are so complex that they do not provide a practical basis for automating the entire process of writing a compiler.

To give you a feeling for the techniques for formally specifying semantics, we will briefly describe one method, called *axiomatic semantics*. In this method a rule is given for each kind of statement in the language; the rule must define *exactly* what the result will be of executing the statement. More precisely, if a machine is in a given state (that is, with certain values for variables), then the rule must specify what state the machine will be in after the statement is executed. The states can be specified by assertions such as those used in previous chapters.

For example, the rule for the assignment statement must allow us to conclude that after executing the assignment statement X := Y, the value of X is the same value that Y had before the statement was executed. Assuming Y has previously been given a value of 1024, we could write

```
(* Y = 1024 *)
X := Y;
(* Y = 1024 and X = 1024 *)
```

as a formal statement of the result of executing the assignment statement. The state of the machine before the statement is executed is described by the assertion preceding the statement, and the state of the machine after executing the statement is described by the assertion following the statement.

Formal statements of the rules of axiomatic semantics would be a bit advanced for this text, but we will illustrate the use of assertions and our intuitive notions of semantics to construct a "correctness proof" in the next section.

Program Verification: An Example

In this section we will use assertions to give an informal, but complete, *proof of correctness*. We will develop a proof for a procedure that finds the index of the largest element of an array of integers. The procedure is shown here with assertions as comments. Each assertion should be true when execution reaches the point in the program at which the assertion is given. The assertion labeled "Final Assertion" expresses what the procedure is supposed to achieve, so we must convince ourselves that this assertion really holds at the end of the procedure. We will use the other assertions, and particularly the one labeled "Loop Invariant," to make a convincing argument.

```
PROCEDURE Max( A: ARRAY OF INTEGER ): CARDINAL;
(* Find the index of the largest element of the array A. *)

VAR   N, I, J: CARDINAL;
```

```
BEGIN
   N := HIGH( A );
   (* 0 <= N *)
   I := 0;
   (* 0 <= N and I = 0 *)
   J := 0;
   (* 0 <= N and I = 0  and J = 0 *)
   LOOP
      (* Loop Invariant:  ( A[J] >= A[0]..A[I] ) AND ( I <= N ) *)
      IF I = N THEN
         EXIT
      END; (* IF *)
      IF A[J] < A[I + 1] THEN
         J := I + 1;
      END; (* IF *)
      I := I + 1;
   END; (* LOOP *)
   (* Final Assertion: A[J] >= A[0]..A[N] *)
   RETURN J;
END Max;
```

It is quite reasonable that the first three assertions will be true when execution reaches the point at which they occur, but the truth of the loop invariant may not be so clear. We show the position of the loop invariant in the flow chart, given in Figure 17.2.

We must now convince ourselves that the loop invariant is true every time execution reaches the top of the loop. To do this, we must prove that

- the loop invariant is true after executing the initial statements
- the loop invariant remains true after executing the loop

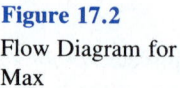

Figure 17.2
Flow Diagram for Max

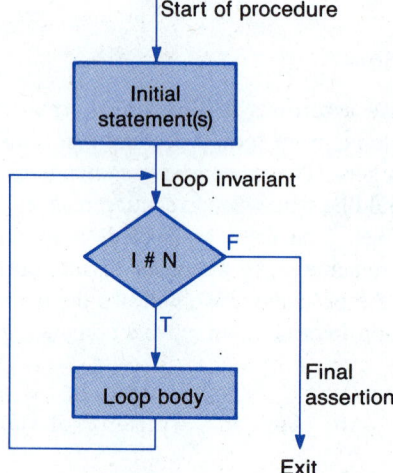

For the first of these two proofs, we use the third assertion, which holds after the initial statements are executed. This assertion tells us that I and J are both 0 at the beginning of the loop. Rewriting the loop assertion with these values of I and J gives us

$$(\ A[0]\ >=\ A[0]\ )\ \text{AND}\ (\ 0\ <=\ N\ )$$

The first part is obviously true, and from the first term of the third assertion we know that $0 <= N$.

We must now show that the loop invariant remains true after the loop has been executed, assuming it was true before the loop was executed. The condition for exiting the loop is $I = N$, so the condition for continuing the loop is $I \# N$. Thus the following assertion is true immediately before the second IF statement:

$$(*\ (\ A[J]\ >=\ A[0]..A[I]\ )\ \text{AND}\ (\ I < N\ )\ *)$$

Now we must demonstrate that the second IF statement in the loop body has the desired effect, as indicated by

```
(*  ( A[J] >= A[0]..A[I] ) AND ( I < N ) *)
IF A[J] < A[I + 1] THEN
    J := I + 1;
END; (* IF *)
(*  ( A[J] >= A[0]..A[I + 1] ) AND ( I < N ) *)
```

This seems reasonable from our intuitive understanding of the IF statement, but we must say it very carefully to avoid any hidden pitfalls. The second part, $I < N$, of the loop invariant is certainly true after the IF statement, since neither I nor N is changed within the statement. Thus we can restrict our attention to the first part of the loop invariant. If the condition, $A[J] < A[I + 1]$, governing the IF statement, is true, then, using the first part of the loop assertion, we can infer that $A[0]..A[I] < A[I + 1]$. So, if we assign $I + 1$ to J, the first part of the assertion following the IF will be true. On the other hand, if $A[J] >= A[I + 1]$, we need do nothing to make the first part of the assertion true. Thus the IF statement has the desired effect.

Now we need to show

```
(*  ( A[J] >= A[0]..A[I + 1] ) AND ( I < N ) *)
I := I + 1;
(*  ( A[J] >= A[0]..A[I] ) AND ( I <= N) *)
```

but this seems perfectly reasonable from our intuitive understanding of the assignment statement, so we have shown that the loop invariant holds at the bottom of the loop, and hence the top of the loop as well.

Finally, all that remains is to show that the final assertion follows from the loop invariant when the loop terminates, as illustrated in Figure 17.2. Since the loop terminates when $I = N$, we can substitute N for I in our loop invariant, and the first part of the loop invariant becomes our final assertion!

The most substantive part of our correctness argument was the two-step proof that (1) the loop invariant was true initially, and (2) the loop invariant remained true after executing the loop, assuming it was true before executing the loop. As noted in Chapter 13, this may be viewed as a proof by mathematical induction.

Our example of a proof of correctness was lengthy despite the fact that it was not done very formally. As you can see, program verification is not trivial. Software has been developed to help with the verification process, but proofs using the software are not fully automated. For example, theorem-proving programs are available, but humans often need to supply the key assertions to be proved. In any event, it is desirable to include key assertions as comments whether the program is going to be formally verified or not, since all programs should be informally verified as well as thoroughly tested.

17.3 Artificial Intelligence

The field of artificial intelligence (AI) is almost as old as computer science itself; however, it has been popularized in the media only recently. The discipline is perhaps the most misunderstood field in computer science due, in part, to a lack of consensus about what is "intelligent behavior." In 1950, the English mathematician Alan Turing wrote an influential paper in which he proposed a test for intelligent behavior (since called the *Turing test*). A simple form of the Turing test would be as follows. Suppose you are communicating via a terminal with a person and with a computer, but each claims to be a person. If you could not decide which is the person and which is the computer (above the level of chance), then we could say that the computer is exhibiting intelligent behavior.

What a layperson may consider intelligent, such as solving a differential equation for an engineering problem, may not be considered intelligent behavior by a computer scientist. Perhaps a better name for artificial intelligence systems is *knowledge-based systems* to indicate that the computer is processing complex knowledge representations rather than simple numeric or character data more commonly associated with traditional data processing. The knowledge representation might be based on sensor input, such as a TV camera, natural language input, plans of action to control robot output, and so on. Not every knowledge-based system has to involve humanlike senses; many commonly use traditional terminal input and output. We will discuss some of the areas of artificial intelligence research and then illustrate, by example, some techniques used in artificial intelligence programming.

Selected Areas of Artificial Intelligence Research

Vision A vision system typically accepts TV-like input and attempts to understand the image at a conceptual level as humans do so naturally. A television set or computer terminal would not be considered a vision system because, although they display visual images, they have no "understanding" of those images. One of the most difficult jobs in image analysis is object recognition. The object might be in two dimensions, such as handwriting on a page, or in three dimensions, such as items moving past an inspection station on a conveyor belt. These systems require tremendous processing resources due to the vast amount of data and the need for rapid analysis.

To get some understanding of the data flow rate, let's consider some specific values. Suppose our vision system will provide a sequence of frames, each with a resolution of 1,000 by 1,000 pixels; that is, a frame will be made up of a square with 1,000 dots on each side, giving a total of 1,000,000 dots. Human vision has higher resolution than this, although the degree of resolution is not uniform throughout the field of view. Each dot or pixel can have one of 256 color values, again less than the number of colors a human can detect. Finally, we will assume our camera produces 30 frames a second (a typical rate for TV cameras). So in one second the system is receiving 30 frames, each with 1,000,000 dots where each dot can have 256 possible color values! This is a data transfer rate of 240,000,000 bits per second. Obviously we will need a very powerful computer and sophisticated algorithms to process such a vast flow of data. Object recognition is a complex process; it includes low-level processing, such as detection of edges and contiguous regions, and higher-level processing, such as determining the boundaries of objects and developing descriptions of surfaces and shapes.

Robotics Many of the robot systems you see in auto factories really aren't "intelligent." A moving assembly line exactly positions a car body at a known location for the preprogrammed robot arm to carry out some action, such as spot welding. This robot does not have to respond to a variety of input stimuli. On the other hand, consider a robot that is doing quality control for sheet metal parts moving down a conveyor belt. This robot will require a vision system to inspect the parts, an algorithm to decide if they pass quality control standards, and a robot arm to pick up and remove defective parts. Since the parts may be sitting on the conveyor belt in various orientations and since the parts are moving, the robot hand must have sophisticated planning strategies to end up in the proper position to remove a defective part from the moving conveyor belt and drop it into the discard bin.

Language Understanding One of the early problems investigated in language understanding involved using computers to do language translation. However, even after millions of dollars had been spent for research during the 1950s and 1960s, the translations were still so poor that they required post editing by humans, which ended up costing more than if humans had done the original translation. One of the central problems is word sense disambiguation. Consider the following sentences:*

John took a plane.

John took an aspirin.

John took Mary.

John took a beating.

John took the job.

---

* Roger Schank and Christopher Riesbeck, *Inside Computer Understanding* (Hillsdale, N.J.: Lawrence Erlbaum Assoc., 1981), 21.

John took the match.

John took the food.

John took the picture.

John took my advice.

Despite the similarity in structure and the use of the same verb, these sentences clearly involve different meanings for the verb. As a mental exercise, try to express the meaning for each of these sentences by using a different verb in each sentence.

Language understanding involves syntax (the grammatical structure of the sentence), semantics (the meaning of the sentence), and pragmatics (the intent of the sentence based on commonsense knowledge). For example, "Can you pass the salt?" can be syntactically parsed as shown in Figure 17.3.

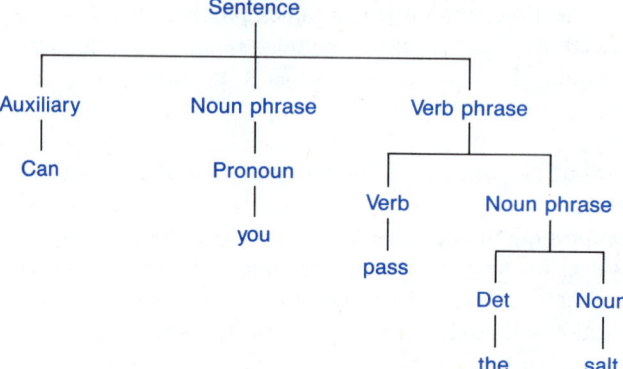

Figure 17.3
Parsing of a Sentence

From a strict semantic standpoint, this sentence is a question that should be answered yes or no, but pragmatically it is a request for an action to be carried out with no verbal answer required. (Try answering this question "yes" without passing the salt and see how startled, confused, or even angry the other person becomes.)

Language understanding and machine translation are still active areas of research. Most working natural language systems handle only a subset of a language, such as query systems for a database.

help make information in databases accessible to nontechnical users. An expert system is another tool for processing a knowledge database. The expert system goes beyond just retrieving data; it attempts to reason about the data. Some of the most successful expert systems have dealt with medical diagnosis, spectograph analysis, natural resource exploration, computer configuration, and so on. Recently many commercial expert systems have been developed. Expert systems are typically rule-based systems about some problem domain and include inference techniques that can deal with uncertainty. These systems are often programmed in LISP or Prolog. Building an expert system usually involves an AI researcher interviewing one or more people who are recognized experts in the field being modeled. The subjects are asked to explain their expertise in solving typical problems. The subject matter expert and the AI researcher then try to define a set of rules that would encompass the problem-solving techniques being used and develop a program based on these rules.

Reasoning The basic mechanism for reasoning in a knowledge-based system is inference. How this "inference engine" works and what constitutes its formal mathematical basis are not uniformly agreed upon and, in fact, are still evolving. In the early 1970s, procedural approaches to inference generation were quite popular. The procedural approach is an imperative style, in which actions are specified in a manner similar to the specification of statements in a language like Modula-2.

The current trend in AI is toward declarative systems based on logic or logic programming. Given a set of premises (or rules or axioms as they are sometimes called), the rules of logic can be used to derive all consequences of those premises. Assuming that the premises are correct, the consequences will also be correct. Such reasoning is called monotonic since the set of premises and consequences can only grow larger. In other words, there is no way to withdraw a premise or conclusion.

When dealing with human problems, you often have to reason with uncertainty. In other words, you may draw a conclusion that proves to be incorrect and then you have to retract it. For example, if you know that John Brown is the son of Mary Brown, you would assume Mary Brown is John's biological parent. However, Mary may be John's stepmother, or John may have been adopted. If you were dealing with family medical history, you would want to know that Mary and John were not related biologically. In this case you would have to retract your original hypothesis. Monotonic reasoning cannot deal well with uncertainty of this nature.

A Sample Problem: The Eight Puzzle

Many people associate artificial intelligence with solving puzzles or playing games. Much of the early work on playing checkers or chess has been useful in the development of search strategies that can be applied to more practical problems. In this section we will illustrate these search strategies using a simple puzzle—the eight puzzle.

Description The eight puzzle is a simplified version of a small hand puzzle played by children. In the children's puzzle, 15 interlocking tiles are arranged in a 4-by-4 format. Since one position for a tile is left blank, the other tiles can be moved around the board. Each tile has a number or letter. The goal is to arrange the tiles in a particular pattern. Our eight puzzle is similar but has been simplified: we assume a 3-by-3 board with 8 tiles numbered 1 through 8. Figure 17.4 illustrates a possible starting position, or state, and the target pattern, called the goal state.

The following set of moves is one sequence of moves that will transform the initial state into the goal state.

```
  1 3        1  .3       1 2 3      1 2 3      1 2 3
  4 2 6      4 2 6       4   6      4 5 6      4 5 6
  7 5 8      7 5 8       7 5 8      7   8      7 8
```

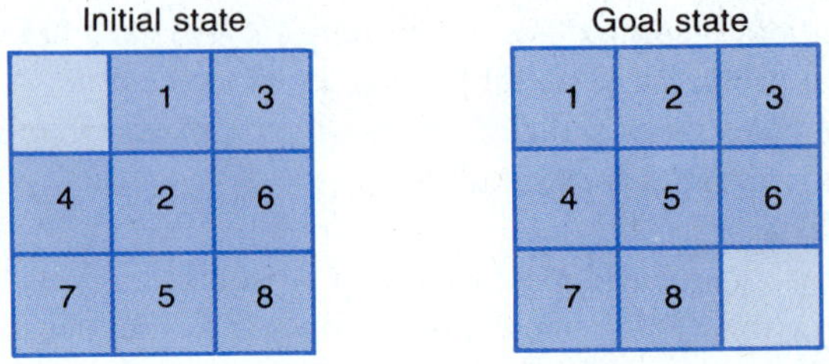

Figure 17.4
A Sample Initial State and Goal State

Initial state

	1	3
4	2	6
7	5	8

Goal state

1	2	3
4	5	6
7	8	

This sequence happens to be an optimal solution requiring only four moves to reach the goal state; there are longer sequences of moves that will eventually reach the same goal state. This puzzle is also prone to cycling—that is, coming back to a state you encountered previously. Any program searching for a solution will have to recognize such cycling or it may never find a solution.

Representation Our representation of a particular state will depend on the programming language used. In Modula-2, a 3-by-3 array is a natural representation.

```
TYPE Tile = [0..8];      (* 0 will represent the blank position *)
     Board = ARRAY[1..3],[1..3] of Tile;
```

However, since LISP is a common language for AI programming, we will choose to represent the puzzle state as a list, which is the basic data structure in LISP. Two reasonable list representations for the initial state shown in Figure 17.4 are

```
((0 1 3) (4 2 6) (7 5 8))   (* a list of three lists, each sublist is a
                                row ordered from top to bottom *)
(0 1 3 4 2 6 7 5 8)         (* a single list of tiles starting from the top left
                                across rows until the bottom right is reached *)
```

Since the blank moves both horizontally and vertically, the latter representation will be a bit easier to manipulate since there is only one list to worry about. For this representation, the goal state is

```
(1 2 3 4 5 6 7 8 0)
```

Search Tree We now return to the problem of finding a sequence of moves from an initial state to the goal state. Given a puzzle state, we can easily generate all possible states that result from moving a single tile. For simplicity, we will talk about moving the blank position although we know this is accomplished by moving another tile into the blank position. If the blank is in one of the corners, then there are two possible moves, one horizontal and one vertical. If the blank is in a middle position along an edge, there are three possible moves: to one of the two corners or into the center square. If the blank tile is in the center, there are four possible moves: up, down, left, right. If we consider each possible move from an initial state, and then each possible move from these resulting states, and so on, we would end up constructing a search tree.

Artificial Intelligence

With the initial state shown in Figure 17.4, the blank can move into two different positions so two new states are possible. Each of these two states will generate other states, and so on, as shown in Figure 17.5. This figure is called the *search tree* for the given initial state. A complete search tree would include all possible states and their interconnections by means of moves. Note that we stopped expanding the tree after the fourth move, because we reached the goal state, but all other puzzle states can still be expanded.

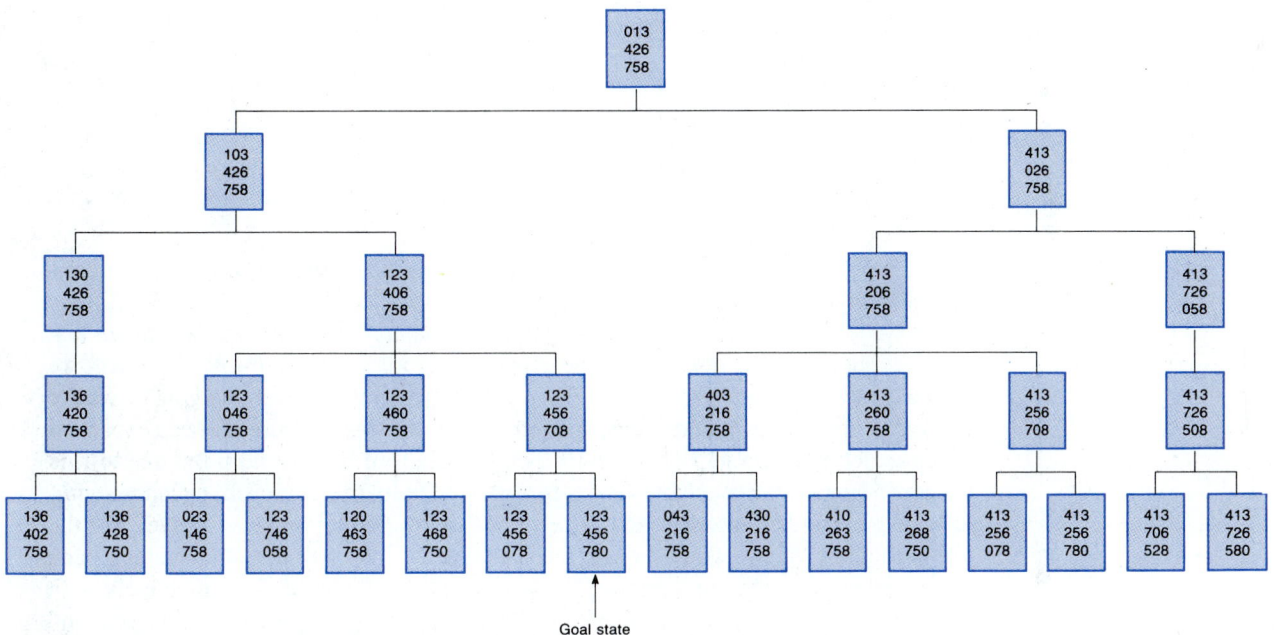

Figure 17.5 A Sample Search Tree

The number of states grows rapidly. This growth happens even though this search tree has already been simplified by not allowing the previous move to be repeated. For example, if you move the blank from the upper left corner to the right (as shown in the leftmost state on the second level), you are not allowed to move it back into the upper left corner on the next move. This prohibition does not prevent cycling since repeated states can result after a longer sequence of moves; however, it does help cut down the size of our search tree.

Search Strategy We want to explore the search tree in a systematic manner so that we reach the goal state. The computer will not have the complete tree as shown in Figure 17.5, rather it must build the tree by expanding states one at a time. We expand our initial configuration to generate a tree one level deep with two unexpanded

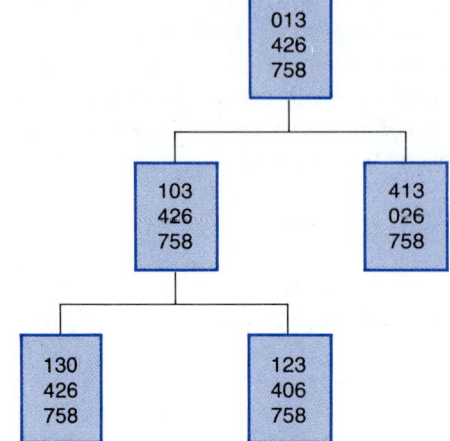

Figure 17.6
The Search Tree After Two Expansions

states. Let's assume the state on the left side is expanded next. The resulting tree is shown in Figure 17.6.

If we want to search the tree in a systematic manner, we must have a strategy that precisely identifies the next state to be expanded. If we use a *depth-first* approach, we keep expanding the leftmost state (1 3 0 4 2 6 7 5 8) until we reach the goal or we are blocked. For this puzzle, a repeated state (that is, a state that has already been expanded in the search tree) would be a block. When blocked, we backtrack up the tree to find the next leftmost state available for expansion. An alternative approach, called *breadth-first*, is to expand all the states at one level before proceeding to the next level. For the tree in Figure 17.6, we would expand the state (4 1 3 0 2 6 7 5 8) next. Neither approach is very good at solving this puzzle, because they are not able to deal effectively with the "combinatorial explosion" of possible states. For this reason, both depth-first and breadth-first searches are called *blind searches*.

Use of Heuristics To improve on the blind search strategies just described, we might try to measure the "goodness" of each state and choose the one that appears most promising. This strategy might be called heuristic or "rule of thumb"; it does not guarantee success, but it is certainly an improvement over a blind search. The heart of this heuristic approach to searching is the development of a *heuristic evaluation function* to help measure the "goodness" of a state. For this problem, one approach is to measure how far each tile is out of place and then find the total for all tiles. The distance out of place will be measured by the number of moves (horizontal and vertical) to put the tile into place if no other tiles were in the way. In our initial state shown in Figure 17.6, the value would be 4, since the tiles 1, 2, 5, and 8 are each one move out of place. Let's now use this evaluation function to guide our search. Our strategy is to expand the state with the lowest value; if two states have the same value, we will choose the leftmost one for expansion. If a state has already been expanded earlier in the tree, we will assign an evaluation value of infinity to avoid further expansion. The resultant

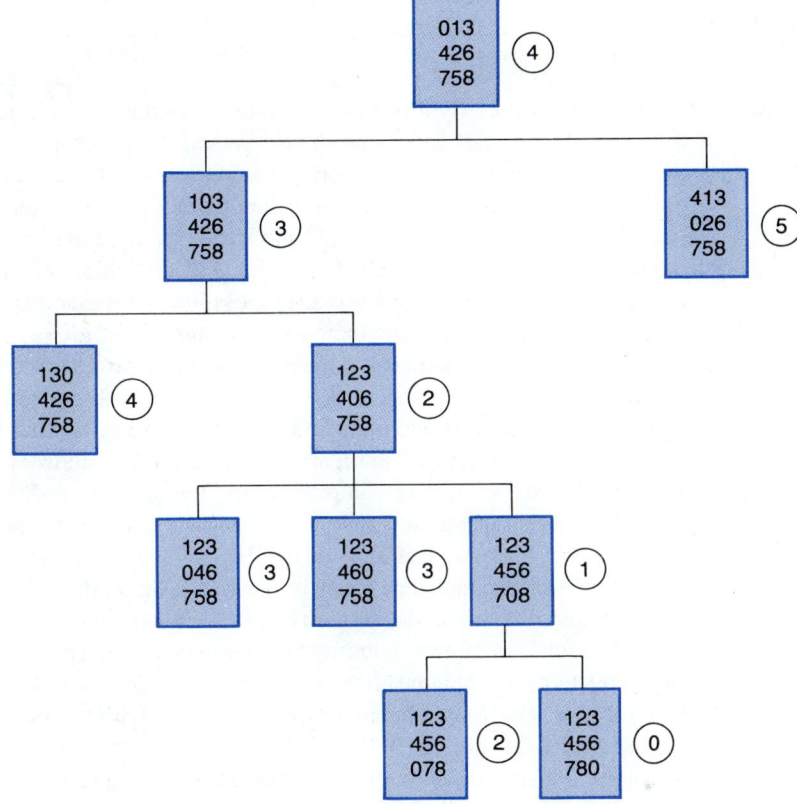

Figure 17.7
Search Tree Using an Evaluation Function

search tree is shown in Figure 17.7; the value of each state is shown in a circle next to the state.

With this particular initial state, our evaluation function worked well and led us directly to the goal. With other initial states, such as (1 3 5 4 2 0 7 8 6), states that are not on the path to the correct solution may be expanded. Despite an occasional miscue, we can think of an evaluation function as a heuristic to help guide the program toward a solution. It may not be ideal, but it will probably be an improvement over a blind search. In this way, we can say the program made "intelligent" choices.

Artificial intelligence is a fascinating area of computer science research. In spite of the optimistic predictions in the popular media, progress is bound to be slow due to the enormity of the task. When we attempt to program a computer to emulate common human behavior, such as use of vision or language, we become aware of how brilliantly humans are adapted to these tasks and how poorly any computer program performs the same task. While computers do well at playing games and solving puzzles, we have barely begun to scratch the surface with vision, natural language understanding, real-world knowledge representations, and learning. Artificial intelligence will remain one of the most challenging fields of computer science research for many years to come.

SUMMARY

The first advance in computer architecture came with the idea of having a program stored in memory. Architectural innovations during the first generation of computers in the 1950s included input/output processors, the interrupt capability, and microprogramming. The second generation of machines, which were constructed with transistors, witnessed the development of virtual memory and multiprocessors. In subsequent generations, integrated circuits (LSI and VLSI) have led to significant advances, including the creation of an entire CPU on a single silicon chip, called a microprocessor. The inexpensive microprocessor has made it possible to design computer systems with many CPUs cooperating to execute the currently running program.

An operating system is a coherent system of programs that makes the hardware easier to use. It acts as a manager of hardware and software resources. New designs in operating systems have facilitated the use of hardware, and hardware innovations have contributed to the ease of implementing operating systems. In the 1950s, operating systems helped to improve computer usage by allowing programs to be processed in batches. Multiprogramming was developed in the 1960s to increase CPU utilization. Timesharing systems, available in the 1970s, allowed many users to share a single computer. A major challenge today is to develop software systems for parallel machines that contain tens, hundreds, or thousands of CPUs.

The evolution of programming languages has been a progression toward languages that allow human problem solvers to express solutions naturally in terms of the problem being solved. High-level languages, which began with the language FORTRAN, have included ALGOL 60, COBOL, LISP, C, PL/1, Pascal, Modula-2, Ada, Prolog, and Smalltalk. An important feature of some of these languages has been the use of Backus-Naur Form, or BNF, to define the language syntax precisely. A formal defintion of a programming language's syntax specifies syntactically valid programs. Thus far there is no generally accepted way to define the semantics of a programming language formally, so it is usually defined informally.

Artificial intelligence systems are knowledge-based systems in the sense that with them the computer is processing complex knowledge representations rather than simple numeric or character data. Among the areas of AI research are vision systems, robotics, language understanding, and expert systems.

This brief survey of some of the fields of computer science has given you an idea of what you will find in other computer science courses. Keep in mind, however, that this survey is incomplete and offers only a glimpse of what lies ahead. Now that you have a thorough knowledge of a programming language, you need to use it to gain programming experience. Programming is certainly not all there is to computer science, but it is an important step in solving problems using computers. As you progress in computer science, programming should become second nature to you. You will learn other programming languages, but the basic concepts that you have discovered here will still apply. Your learning experience in computer science is now on its way and should continue throughout your career in this ever-changing field.

He who rides the tiger can never dismount. — **CHINESE PROVERB**

APPENDIX A

Decimal and Octal Representation for the ASCII Character Set

Decimal Code	Octal Code	Character	Decimal Code	Octal Code	Character	Decimal Code	Octal Code	Character	Decimal Code	Octal Code	Character
0	0	NUL	32	40	SP	64	100	@	96	140	`
1	1	SOH	33	41	!	65	101	A	97	141	a
2	2	STX	34	42	"	66	102	B	98	142	b
3	3	ETX	35	43	#	67	103	C	99	143	c
4	4	EOT	36	44	$	68	104	D	100	144	d
5	5	ENQ	37	45	%	69	105	E	101	145	e
6	6	ACK	38	46	&	70	106	F	102	146	f
7	7	BEL	39	47	'	71	107	G	103	147	g
8	10	BT	40	50	(	72	110	H	104	150	h
9	11	HT	41	51	)	73	111	I	105	151	i
10	12	LF	42	52	*	74	112	J	106	152	j
11	13	VT	43	53	+	75	113	K	107	153	k
12	14	FF	44	54	,	76	114	L	108	154	l
13	15	CR	45	55	−	77	115	M	109	155	m
14	16	SO	46	56	.	78	116	N	110	156	n
15	17	SI	47	57	/	79	117	O	111	157	o
16	20	DLE	48	60	0	80	120	P	112	160	p
17	21	DC1	49	61	1	81	121	Q	113	161	q
18	22	DC2	50	62	2	82	122	R	114	162	r
19	23	DC3	51	63	3	83	123	S	115	163	s
20	24	DC4	52	64	4	84	124	T	116	164	t
21	25	NAK	53	65	5	85	125	U	117	165	u
22	26	SYN	54	66	6	86	126	V	118	166	v
23	27	ETB	55	67	7	87	127	W	119	167	w
24	30	CAN	56	70	8	88	130	X	120	170	x
25	31	EM	57	71	9	89	131	Y	121	171	y
26	32	SUB	58	72	:	90	132	Z	122	172	z
27	33	ESC	59	73	;	91	133	[	123	173	{
28	34	FS	60	74	<	92	134	\	124	174	|
29	35	GS	61	75	=	93	135	]	125	175	}
30	36	RS	62	76	>	94	136	^	126	176	~
31	37	US	63	77	?	95	137	_	127	177	DEL

APPENDIX B
Modula-2 Syntax (Using EBNF)

To describe the syntax of a given language, one must use a language. It is possible to use the given language to describe its own syntax, just as you can describe the syntax of the English language in English. The language used to describe syntax is often called a meta-language. In order to describe the syntax of Modula-2, we will use a meta-language known as EBNF (Extended Backus Naur Form).

The EBNF meta-language uses meta-symbols =, |, [,], {, }, ", ', parentheses, and the period. The equal sign and the period are used for the definition of terms, as in

$$T = X Y.$$

where T is defined to be the concatenation of X and Y.

The vertical bar indicates a choice between alternatives, as in

$$T = X \mid Y.$$

which defines T as either X or Y.

The square brackets indicate an optional part, as in

$$T = X [Y].$$

which defines T as either X or XY.

The braces indicate any number of repetitions of their contents (including none), as in

$$T = X \{Y\}.$$

which defines T as X, XY, XYY, XYYY, and so forth.

Parentheses are used to group terms as in

$$T = X (Y \mid Z).$$

which defines T as XY or XZ.

In the following definition of the syntax of Modula-2, quotation marks (single or double) are used to indicate symbols which should be used as they appear. These are called *terminal symbols*. Terminal symbols include reserved words, which are written in uppercase letters and are used without any modification. A list of reserved words for Modula-2 follows.

AND	ELSIF	LOOP	REPEAT
ARRAY	END	MOD	RETURN
BEGIN	EXIT	MODULE	SET
BY	EXPORT	NOT	THEN
CASE	FOR	OF	TO
CONST	FROM	OR	TYPE
DEFINITION	IF	POINTER	UNTIL
DIV	IMPLEMENTATION	PROCEDURE	VAR
DO	IMPORT	QUALIFIED	WHILE
ELSE	IN	RECORD	WITH

Reserved words will appear directly in the syntax definition without being enclosed in quotation marks. The complete syntax definition of Modula-2 follows.

Appendix B

1. Compilation Units

1.1   CompilationUnit = DefinitionModule |
       [IMPLEMENTATION] ProgramModule.

1.2   DefinitionModule = DEFINITION MODULE Ident ";" {Import}
       {Definition} END Ident ".".

1.3   ProgramModule =
       MODULE Ident [Priority] ";" {Import} Block Ident ".".

2. Declarations

2.1   Definition = CONST {ConstantDeclaration ";"} |
       TYPE {Ident ["=" Type] ";"} |
       VAR {VariableDeclaration ";"} |
       ProcedureHeading ";".

2.2   Block = {Declaration} [BEGIN StatementSequence] END.

2.3   Declaration = CONST {ConstantDeclaration ";"} |
       TYPE {TypeDeclaration ";"} |
       VAR {VariableDeclaration ";"} |
       ProcedureDeclaration ";" | ModuleDeclaration ";".

2.4   ConstantDeclaration = Ident "=" ConstExpression.

2.5   TypeDeclaration = Ident "=" Type.

2.6   VariableDeclaration = IdentList ":" Type.

2.7   ProcedureDeclaration = ProcedureHeading ";" Block Ident.

2.8   ProcedureHeading = PROCEDURE Ident [FormalParameters].

2.9   FormalParameters =
       "(" [FPSection {";" FPSection}] ")" [":" Qualident].

2.10   FPSection = [VAR] IdentList ":" FormalType.

2.11   ModuleDeclaration =
       MODULE Ident [Priority] ";" {Import} [Export] Block Ident.

2.12   Priority = "[" ConstExpression "]".

2.13   Import = [FROM Ident] IMPORT IdentList ";".

2.14   Export = EXPORT [QUALIFIED] IdentList ";".

3. Types

3.1   Type = SimpleType | ArrayType | RecordType | SetType |
       PointerType | ProcedureType.

3.2 SimpleType = Qualident | Enumeration | SubrangeType.

3.3 Enumeration = "(" IdentList ")".

3.4 SubrangeType = [Qualident]
     "[" ConstExpression ".." ConstExpression "]".

3.5 ArrayType = ARRAY SimpleType {"," SimpleType} OF Type.

3.6 RecordType = RECORD FieldListSequence END.

3.7 FieldListSequence = FieldList {";" FieldList}.

3.8 FieldList = [IdentList ":" Type |
     CASE [Ident] ":" Qualident OF Variant {"|" Variant}
     [ELSE FieldListSequence] END].

3.9 Variant = [CaseLabelList ":" FieldListSequence].

3.10 SetType = SET OF SimpleType.

3.11 PointerType = POINTER TO Type.

3.12 ProcedureType = PROCEDURE [FormalTypeList].

3.13 FormalTypeList = "(" [[VAR] FormalType
     {"," [VAR] FormalType}] ")" [":" Qualident].

3.14 FormalType = [ARRAY OF] Qualident.

4. Statements

4.1 StatementSequence = Statement {";" Statement}.

4.2 Statement = [Assignment | ProcedureCall |
     IfStatement | CaseStatement | WhileStatement |
     RepeatStatement | LoopStatement | ForStatement |
     WithStatement | EXIT | RETURN [Expression]].

4.3 Assignment = Designator ":=" Expression.

4.4 ProcedureCall = Designator [ActualParameters].

4.5 IfStatement = IF Expression THEN StatementSequence
     {ELSIF Expression THEN StatementSequence}
     [ELSE StatementSequence] END.

4.6 CaseStatement = CASE Expression OF Case {"|" Case}
     [ELSE StatementSequence] END.

4.7 Case = [CaseLabelList ":" StatementSequence].

4.8 CaseLabelList = CaseLabels {"," CaseLabels}.

4.9 CaseLabels = ConstExpression [".." ConstExpression].

4.10 LoopStatement = LOOP StatementSequence END.

4.11 WhileStatement = WHILE Expression DO StatementSequence END.

4.12 RepeatStatement = REPEAT StatementSequence UNTIL Expression.

4.13 ForStatement = FOR Ident ":=" Expression TO Expression
     [BY ConstExpression] DO StatementSequence END.

4.14 WithStatement = WITH Designator DO StatementSequence END.

5. Expressions

5.1. ExpList = Expression {"," Expression}.

5.2 ConstExpression = Expression.

5.3 Expression = SimpleExpression [Relation SimpleExpression].

5.4 SimpleExpression = ["+" | "-"] Term {AddOperator Term}.

5.5 Term = Factor {MulOperator Factor}.

5.6. Factor = Number | String | Set |
     Designator [ActualParameters] |
     "(" Expression ")" | NOT Factor.

5.7 Relation = "=" | "#" | "<" | "<=" | ">" | ">=" | IN.

5.8 AddOperator = "+" | "-" | OR.

5.9 MulOperator = "*" | "/" | DIV | MOD | AND.

5.10 Set = [Qualident] "{" [Element {"," Element}] "}".

5.11 Element = Expression [".." Expression].

5.12 Designator = Qualident {"." Ident | "[" ExpList "]" | "^"}.

5.13 ActualParameters = "(" [ExpList] ")".

6. Names and Literals

6.1 IdentList = Ident {"," Ident}.

6.2 Qualident = Ident {"." Ident}.

6.3 Ident = Letter {Letter | Digit}.

6.4 Number = Integer | Real.

6.5 Integer = Digit {Digit} |
    OctalDigit {OctalDigit} ("B" | "C") |
    Digit {HexDigit} "H".

```
6.6   Real = Digit {Digit} "." {Digit} [ScaleFactor].
6.7   ScaleFactor = "E" ["+" | "-"] Digit {Digit}.
6.8   HexDigit = Digit | "A" | "B" | "C" | "D" | "E" | "F".
6.9   Digit = OctalDigit | "8" | "9".
6.10  OctalDigit = "0" | "1" | "2" | "3" | "4" | "5" | "6" | "7".
6.11  String = "'" {Character} "'" | '"' {Character} '"'.
```

Cross References

"	6.11
#	5.7
'	6.11
(	2.9, 3.3, 3.13, 5.6, 5.13
)	2.9, 3.3, 3.13, 5.6, 5.13
*	5.9
+	5.4, 5.8, 6.7
,	3.5, 3.13, 4.8, 5.1, 5.10, 6.1
-	5.4, 5.8, 6.7
/	5.9
:	2.6, 2.9, 2.10, 3.8, 3.9, 3.13, 4.7
:=	4.3, 4.13
;	1.2, 1.3, 2.1, 2.3, 2.7, 2.9, 2.13, 2.14, 3.7, 4.1
<	5.7
<=	5.7
=	2.1, 2.4, 2.5, 5.7
>	5.7
>=	5.7
[	2.12, 3.4, 5.12
]	2.12, 3.4, 5.12
^	5.12
{	5.10
|	3.8, 4.6
}	5.10

ActualParameters (5.13) 4.4, 5.6
AddOperator (5.8) 5.4
AND 5.9
ARRAY 3.5, 3.14
ArrayType (3.5) 3.1
Assignment (4.3) 4.2
BEGIN 2.2
Block (2.2) 1.3, 2.7, 2.11
BY 4.13
CASE 3.8, 4.6
Case (4.7) 4.6

CaseLabelList (4.8) 3.9, 4.7
CaseLabels (4.9) 4.8
CaseStatement (4.6) 4.2
Character 6.11
CompilationUnit (1.1)
CONST 2.1, 2.3
ConstantDeclaration (2.4) 2.1, 2.3
ConstExpression (5.2) 2.4, 2.12, 3.4, 4.9, 4.13
Declaration (2.3) 2.2
Definition (2.1) 1.2
DEFINITION 1.2
DefinitionModule (1.2) 1.1
Designator (5.12) 4.3, 4.4, 4.14, 5.6
Digit (6.9) 6.3, 6.5, 6.6, 6.7, 6.8
DIV 5.9
DO 4.11, 4.13, 4.14
Element (5.11) 5.10
ELSE 3.8, 4.5, 4.6
ELSIF 4.5
END 1.2, 2.2, 3.6, 3.8, 4.5, 4.6, 4.10, 4.11, 4.13, 4.14
Enumeration (3.3) 3.2
EXIT 4.2
ExpList (5.1) 5.12, 5.13
Export (2.14) 2.11
EXPORT 2.14
Expression (5.3) 4.2, 4.3, 4.5, 4.6, 4.11, 4.12, 4.13, 5.1, 5.2, 5.6, 5.11
Factor (5.6) 5.5, 5.6
FieldList (3.8) 3.7
FieldListSequence (3.7) 3.6, 3.8, 3.9
FOR 4.13
FormalParameters (2.9) 2.8
FormalType (3.14) 2.10, 3.13
FormalTypeList (3.13) 3.12
ForStatement (4.13) 4.2
FPSection (2.10) 2.9
FROM 2.13
HexDigit (6.8) 6.5
Ident (6.3) 1.2, 1.3, 2.1, 2.4, 2.5, 2.7, 2.8, 2.11, 2.13, 3.8, 4.13, 5.12, 6.1, 6.2
IdentList (6.1) 2.6, 2.10, 2.13, 2.14, 3.3, 3.8
IF 4.5
IfStatement (4.5) 4.2
IMPLEMENTATION 1.1
Import (2.13) 1.2, 1.3, 2.11
IMPORT 2.13
IN 5.7
Integer (6.5) 6.4
Letter 6.3
LOOP 4.10
LoopStatement (4.10) 4.2
MOD 5.9

MODULE 1.2, 1.3, 2.11
ModuleDeclaration (2.11) 2.3
MulOperator (5.9) 5.5
Number (6.4) 5.6
NOT 5.6
OctalDigit (6.10) 6.5, 6.9
OF 3.5, 3.8, 3.10, 3.14, 4.6
OR 5.8
POINTER 3.11
PointerType (3.11) 3.1
Priority (2.12) 1.3, 2.11
PROCEDURE 2.8, 3.12
ProcedureCall (4.4) 4.2
ProcedureDeclaration (2.7) 2.3
ProcedureHeading (2.8) 2.1, 2.7
ProcedureType (3.12) 3.1
ProgramModule (1.3) 1.1
Qualident (6.2) 2.9, 3.2, 3.4, 3.8, 3.13, 3.14, 5.10, 5.12
QUALIFIED 2.14
Real (6.6) 6.4
RECORD 3.6
RecordType (3.6) 3.1
Relation (5.7) 5.3
REPEAT 4.12
RepeatStatement (4.12) 4.2
RETURN 4.2
ScaleFactor (6.7) 6.6
Set (5.10) 5.6
SET 3.10
SetType (3.10) 3.1
SimpleExpression (5.4) 5.3
SimpleType (3.2) 3.1, 3.5, 3.10
Statement (4.2) 4.1
StatementSequence (4.1) 2.2, 4.5, 4.6, 4.7, 4.10, 4.11, 4.12, 4.13, 4.14
String (6.11) 5.6
SubrangeType (3.4) 3.2
Term (5.5) 5.4
THEN 4.5
TO 3.11, 4.13
Type (3.1) 2.1, 2.5, 2.6, 3.5, 3.8, 3.11
TYPE 2.1, 2.3
TypeDeclaration (2.5) 2.3
UNTIL 4.12
VAR 2.1, 2.3, 2.10, 3.13
VariableDeclaration (2.6) 2.1, 2.3
Variant (3.9) 3.8
WHILE 4.11
WhileStatement (4.11) 4.2
WITH 4.14
WithStatement (4.14) 4.2

APPENDIX C
Modula-2 Syntax Diagrams

1. Compilation Units

1.1 CompilationUnit

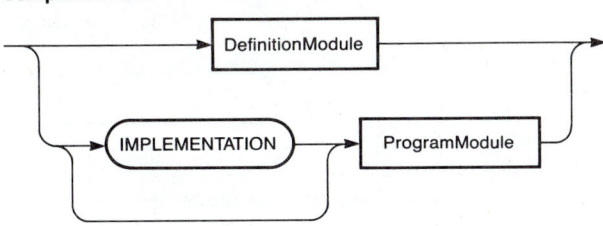

1.2 DefinitionModule

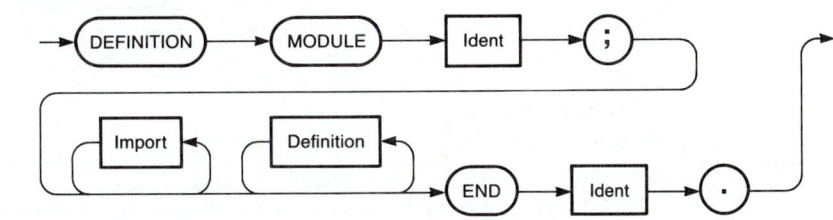

1.3 ProgramModule

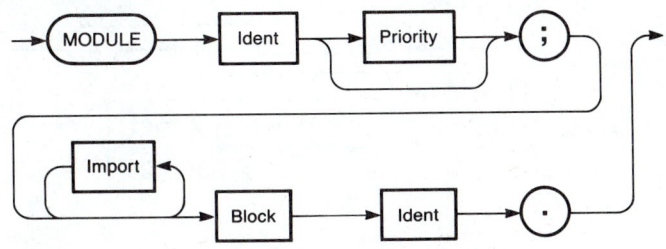

2. Declarations

2.1 Definition

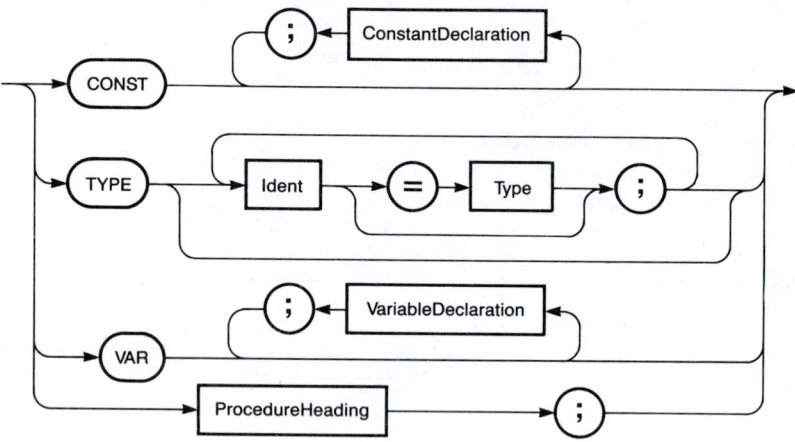

2.2 Block

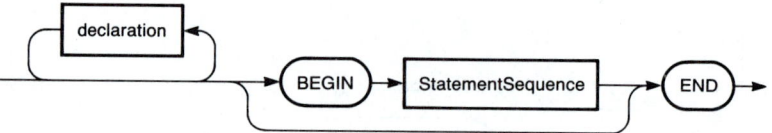

2.3 Declaration

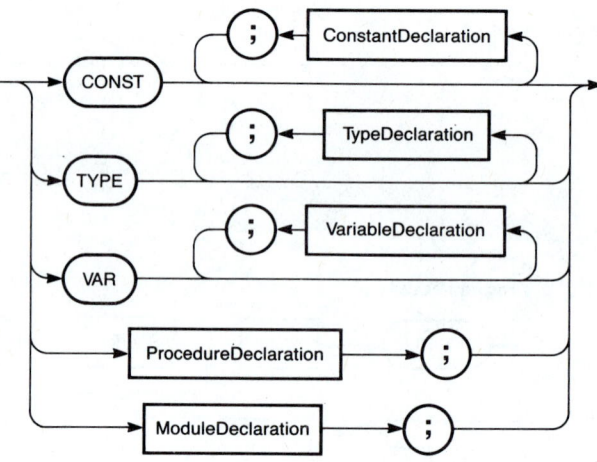

2.4 ConstantDeclaration

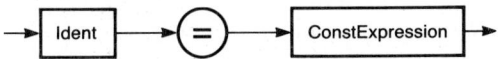

2.5 TypeDeclaration

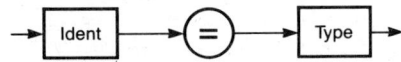

2.6 VariableDeclaration

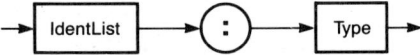

2.7 ProcedureDeclaration

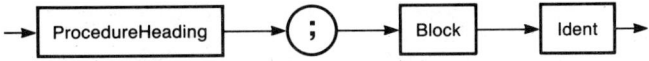

2.8 ProcedureHeading

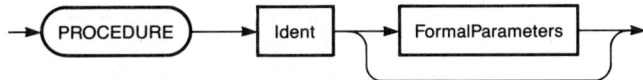

2.9 FormalParameters

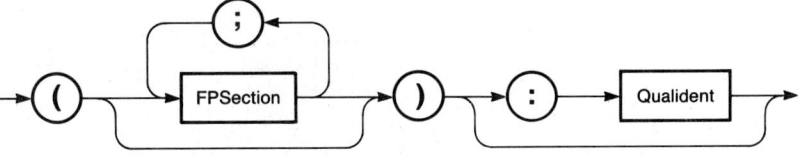

2.10 FPSection

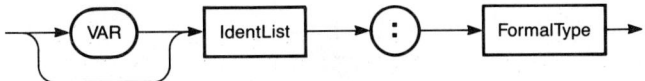

2.11 ModuleDeclaration

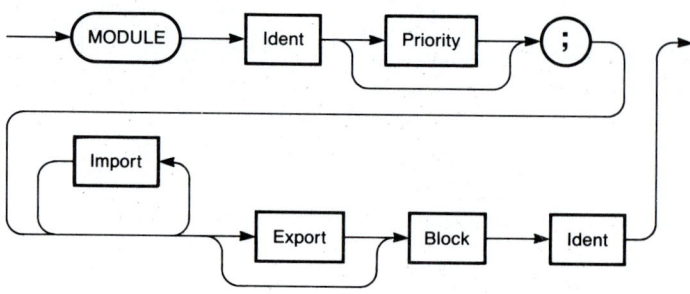

2.12 Priority

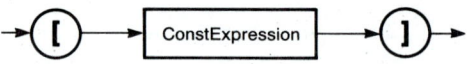

2.13 Import

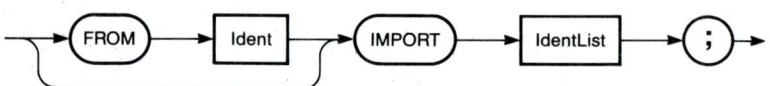

2.14 Export

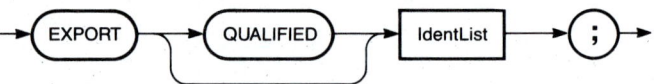

3. Types

3.1 Type

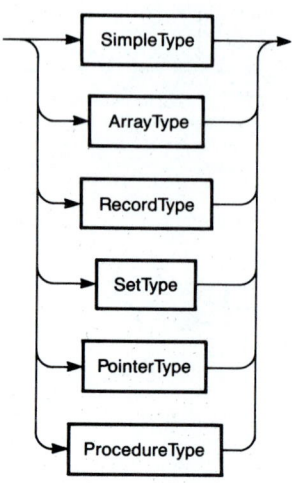

3.2 SimpleType

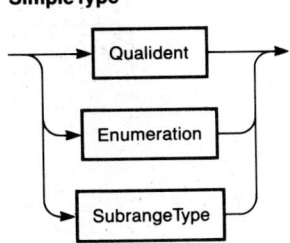

3.3 Enumeration

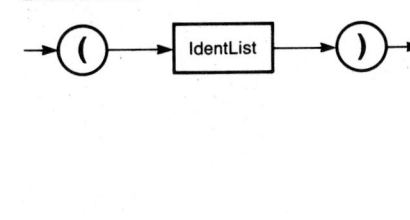

3.4 SubrangeType

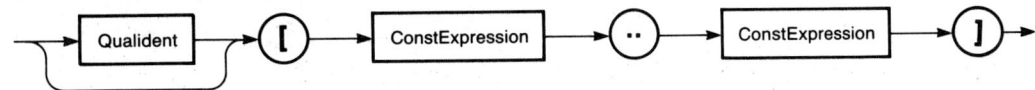

3.5 ArrayType

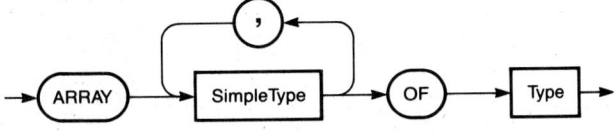

3.6 RecordType

3.7 FieldListSequence

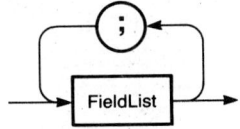

3.8 FieldList

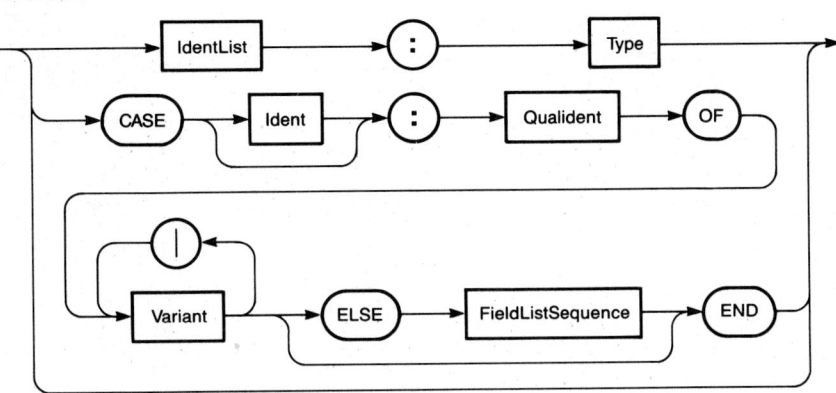

3.9   Variant

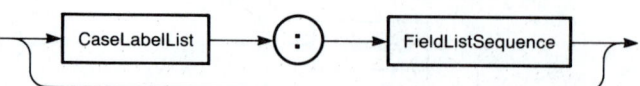

3.10   SetType

3.11   PointerType

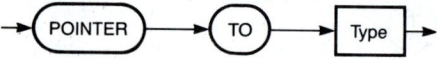

3.12   ProcedureType

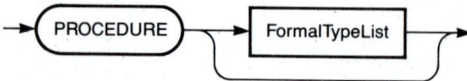

3.13   FormalTypeList

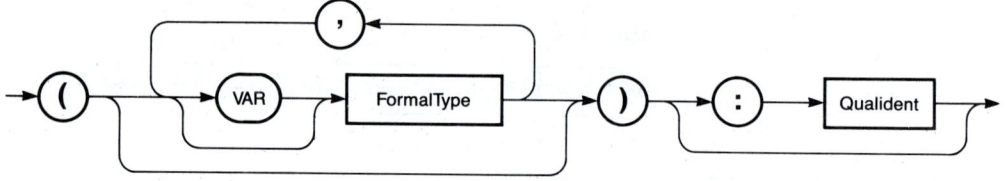

3.14   FormalType

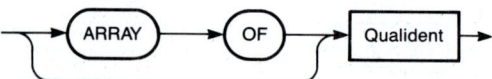

4. Statements

4.1   StatementSequence

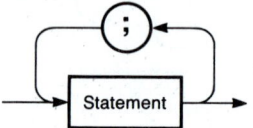

Appendix C

4.2 Statement

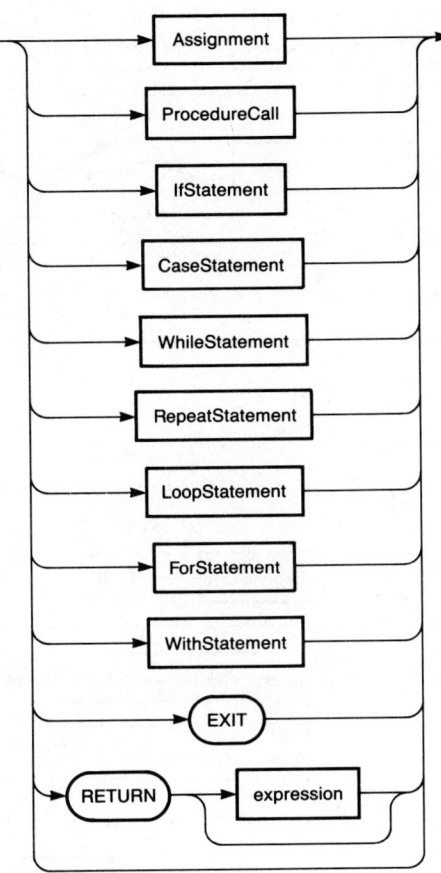

4.3 Assignment

4.4 ProcedureCall

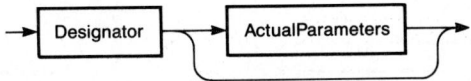

4.5   IfStatement

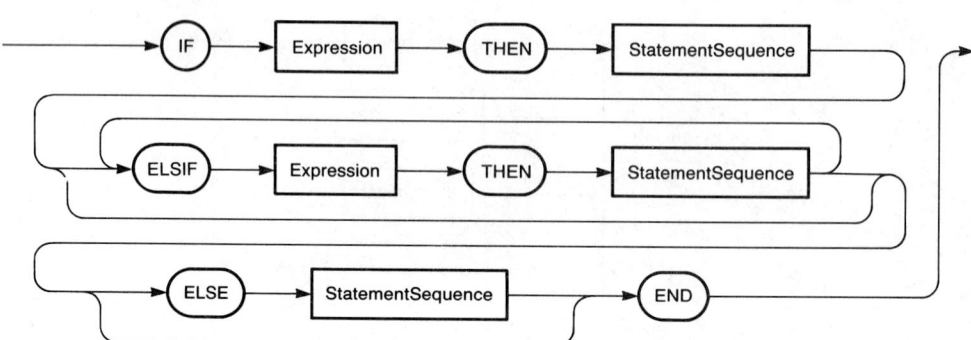

4.6   CaseStatement

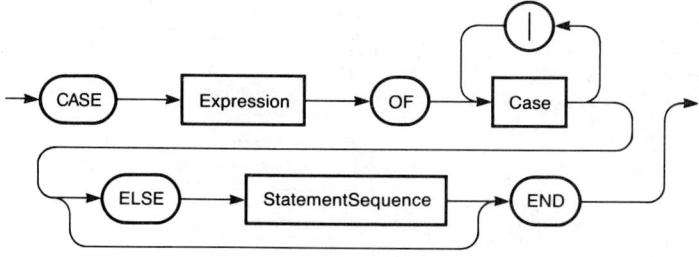

4.7   Case

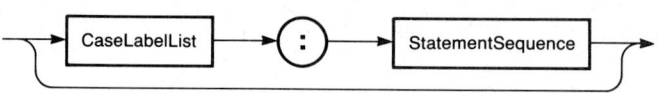

4.8   CaseLabelList

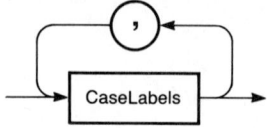

4.9   CaseLabels

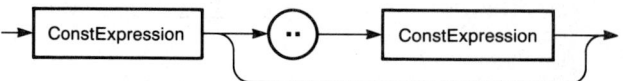

Appendix C

4.10 LoopStatement

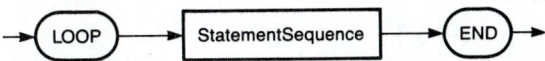

4.11 WhileStatement

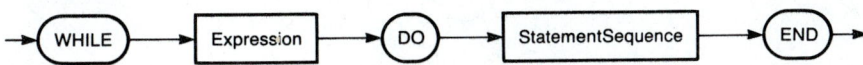

4.12 RepeatStatement

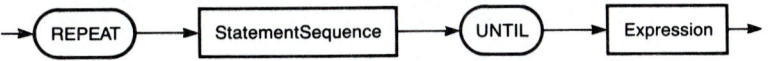

4.13 ForStatement

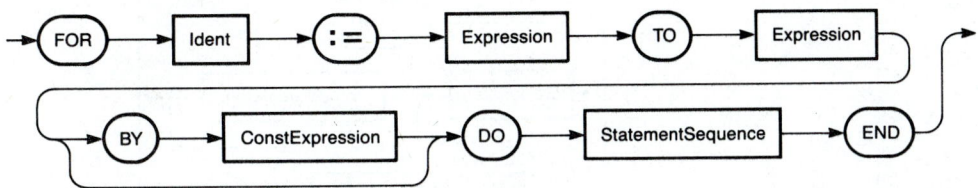

4.14 WithStatement

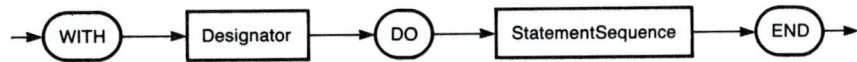

5. Expressions

5.1 ExpList   **5.2 ConstExpression**

5.3 Expression

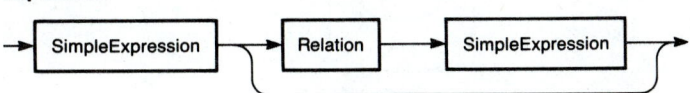

5.4 **SimpleExpression**

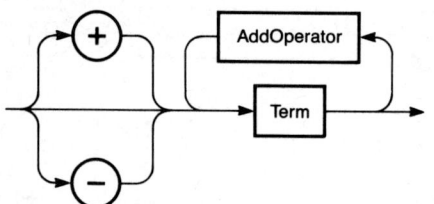

5.5 **Term**

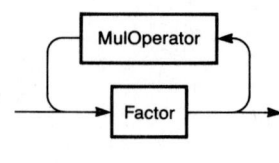

5.6 **Factor**

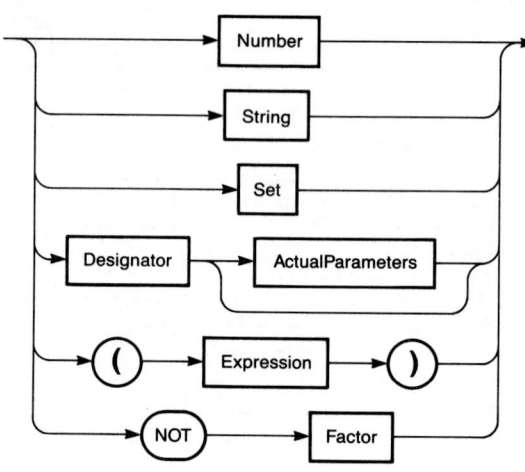

5.7 **Relation**

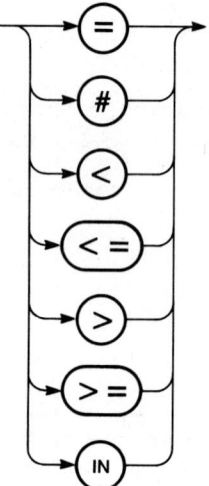

5.8 AddOperator / 5.9 MulOperator

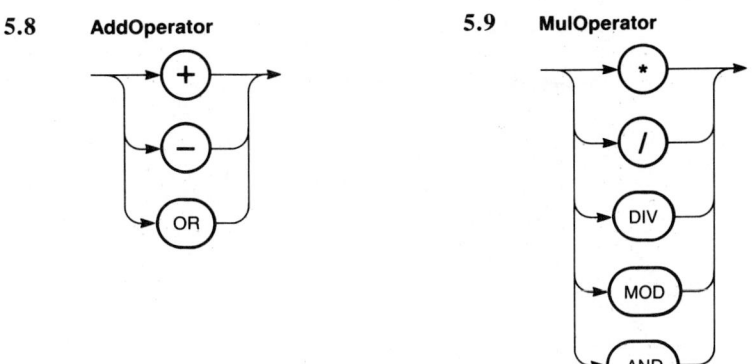

5.10 Set

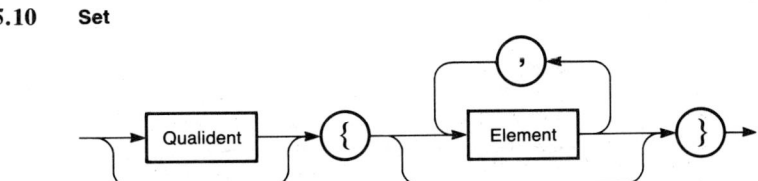

5.11 Element

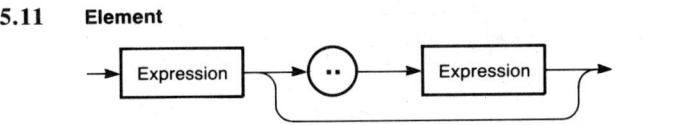

5.12 Designator

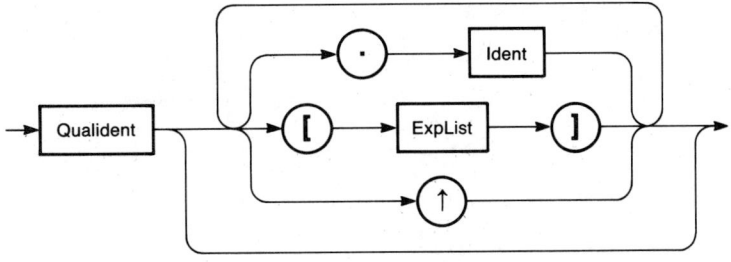

5.13 ActualParameters

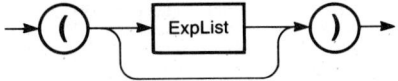

6. Names and Literals

6.1 IdentList

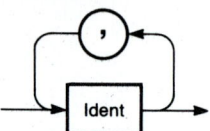

6.2 Qualident

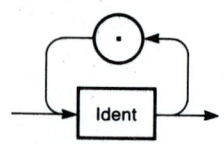

6.3 Ident

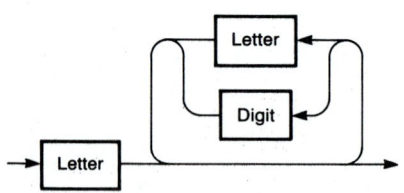

6.4 Number

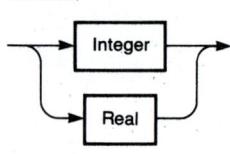

6.5 Integer

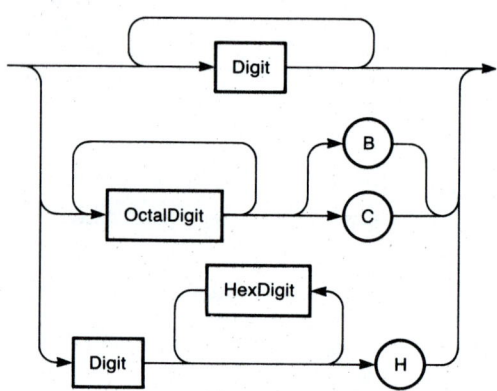

6.6 Real

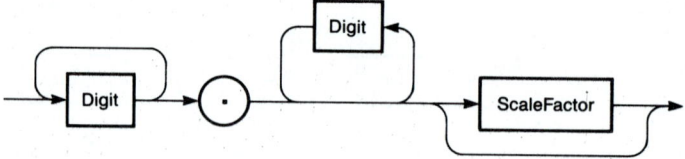

6.7 ScaleFactor

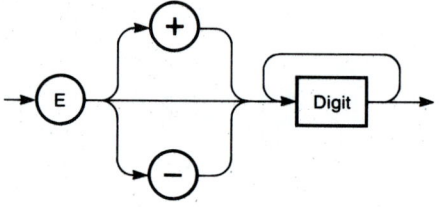

Appendix C

6.8 HexDigit

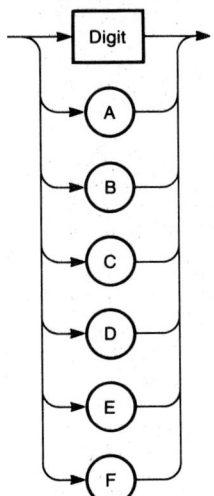

6.9 Digit

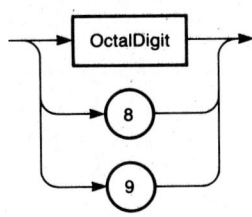

6.10 OctalDigit

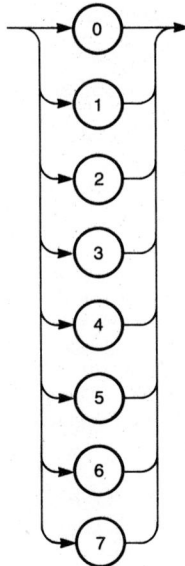

6.11 String

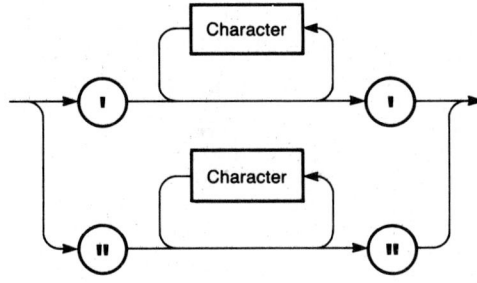

APPENDIX D
Standard Procedures and Functions

ABS(x)	Absolute value function: x is numeric; result type = argument type.
CAP(ch)	Capitalization function: returns the capital letter corresponding to ch, or ch if already a capital letter.
CHR(x)	Character transfer function: returns the character with ordinal number x.
DEC(x) DEC(x,n)	Decrement procedure for scalar values other than REAL: the cardinal value of the decrement equals 1 or n.
EXCL(s,i)	Exclude procedure: s is a set, i is an element with the base type of the set. Removes i from s, if present.
FLOAT(x)	Real conversion function: x is a CARDINAL; returns the equivalent value of type REAL.
HALT	Terminate program execution.
HIGH(a)	High index function: returns upper bound of index of array a; lower bound is assumed to be zero.
INC(x) INC(x,n)	Increment procedure for scalar value other than REAL: the cardinal value of the increment equals 1 or n.
INCL(s,i)	Include procedure: s is a set, i is an element of the base type of the set.
MAX(T)	Maximum value of type T.
MIN(T)	Minimum value of type T.
ODD(x)	Odd function for integer or cardinal: returns x MOD 2 # 0.
ORD(x)	Ordinal function: returns position (of type CARDINAL) of x in the values defined by type T. T is any enumeration type, CHAR, INTEGER, or CARDINAL, and x is of type T.
SIZE(T)	Size of variable T (if T is a variable) or of a variable of type T (if T is a type).
TRUNC(x)	Truncation function: returns non-negative real number x truncated to its integral part (of type CARDINAL).
VAL(T,x)	Value transfer function: returns the value with ordinal number x and with type T. T is any enumeration type, CHAR, INTEGER, or CARDINAL. VAL(T,ORD(x)) = x if x is of type T.

APPENDIX E
Standard Modules

```
DEFINITION MODULE InOut;

(* Module InOut provides high level input and output (I/O)
   procedures. Procedures for reading and writing characters,
   strings, cardinals, and integers are provided. Procedures
   for real number I/O are available in module RealInOut.
   Although I/O is normally done using the keyboard and screen,
   there are facilities (OpenInput and OpenOutput) for
   redirecting the I/O to files. If you want to use the screen
   and files at the same time, module Terminal provides I/O
   procedures that are not redirected. *)

FROM SYSTEM IMPORT WORD;
FROM FileSystem IMPORT File;

CONST
    EOL = 36C;
    (* EOL is the character used to mark the end of a line. *)

VAR
    Done : BOOLEAN;
        (* This 'flag' is used by OpenInput, OpenOutput and some of
           the input procedures. See the appropriate procedure
           descriptions for detailed information. *)

    termCH : CHAR;
        (* termCH is set by ReadString, and possibly by other input
           procedures, to the character that the user typed to
           terminate the input. Any character less than or equal to
           a blank will terminate input for the procedures
           ReadString, ReadInt, and ReadCard. *)

PROCEDURE OpenInput( DefaultExtension : ARRAY OF CHAR );
(* At runtime OpenInput prompts the user for the name of an
   input file. OpenInput then opens the input file and causes
   all input procedures in InOut to read from this file. Only
   one input file may be used at a time. If the user enters a
   period at the end of the input file name, the string
   DefaultExtension is concatenated to the end of the input
   file name. If the file cannot be opened then Done is set to
   FALSE, otherwise Done is set to TRUE. *)

PROCEDURE OpenOutput( DefaultExtension : ARRAY OF CHAR );
(* At runtime OpenOutput prompts the user for the name of an
   output file. OpenOutput then opens the output file and
```

causes all output procedures in InOut to write to this file. Only one output file may be used at a time. If the user enters a period at the end of the output file name, the string DefaultExtension is concatenated to the end of the output file name. If the file cannot be opened then Done is set to FALSE, otherwise Done is set to TRUE. See CloseOutput for more information. *)

PROCEDURE CloseInput;
(* CloseInput closes the file opened by OpenInput and causes the input procedures to read directly from the keyboard. If no file is open, CloseInput has no effect. *)

PROCEDURE CloseOutput;
(* CloseOutput closes the file opened by OpenOutput and causes the output procedures to write directly to the screen. If no file is open, CloseOutput has no effect. If an output file is not closed before the program terminates, some of the data in the file may be lost. ALWAYS close output files. *)

PROCEDURE Read(VAR CH : CHAR);
(* Read inputs a single character and returns as soon as a single character is received. Done will be set to TRUE if a character is read, and to FALSE if an error occurs or if the end of the file is reached. *)

PROCEDURE ReadString(VAR S : ARRAY OF CHAR);
(* ReadString inputs a character string. Input is terminated by any character less than or equal to a blank (see termCH). Leading blanks--blanks at the front of the string--are ignored. If the number of characters read exceeds the length of the string, any characters beyond the end of the string are discarded. A NUL character (0C) or the end of the array is used to mark the end of the string. *)

PROCEDURE ReadInt(VAR X : INTEGER);
(* ReadInt inputs a string representing an INTEGER value and converts the string to INTEGER format.

$$integer = ['+'|'-'] \text{Digit} \{\text{Digit}\}$$

Leading blanks and trailing non-digit characters are ignored. Input is terminated by any character less than or equal to a blank (see termCH). Done is set to TRUE if a number is successfully read, FALSE if the input is invalid. *)

PROCEDURE ReadCard(VAR X : CARDINAL);
(* ReadCard inputs a string representing a CARDINAL value and converts the string to CARDINAL format.

$$\text{cardinal} = \text{Digit} \{\text{Digit}\}$$

Leading blanks and trailing non-digit characters are ignored. Input is terminated by any character less than or equal to a blank (see termCH). Done is set to TRUE if a number is successfully read, FALSE if the input is invalid. *)

PROCEDURE Write(CH : CHAR);
(* Write outputs a single character. *)

PROCEDURE WriteLn;
(* WriteLn outputs an EOL character and is equivalent to Write(EOL). *)

PROCEDURE WriteString(S : ARRAY OF CHAR);
(* WriteString outputs a string of characters until a NUL character (0C) or the end of the array is encountered. *)

(* NOTE: The following output procedures convert numbers to string representations. If the length of the string is shorter than the FieldLength, then blank spaces are added to the front of the string. The output will always be at least FieldLength characters long. If the number requires more than FieldLength characters, the number is output using as many characters as necessary. *)

PROCEDURE WriteInt(X : INTEGER; FieldLength : CARDINAL);
(* WriteInt outputs an INTEGER in decimal notation. See the preceding NOTE for a description of FieldLength. *)

PROCEDURE WriteCard(X, FieldLength : CARDINAL);
(* WriteCard outputs a CARDINAL in decimal notation. See the preceding NOTE for a description of FieldLength. *)

PROCEDURE WriteOct(X, FieldLength : CARDINAL);
(* WriteOct outputs a CARDINAL in octal notation. See the preceding NOTE for a description of FieldLength. *)

PROCEDURE WriteHex(X, FieldLength : CARDINAL);
(* WriteHex outputs a CARDINAL in hexadecimal notation. See the preceding NOTE for a description of FieldLength. *)

END InOut.

DEFINITION MODULE RealInOut;
(* Module RealInOut is an extension of Module InOut that provides input and output for REAL numbers. RealInOut will be redirected when InOut is redirected using OpenInput and OpenOutput.

The output procedures convert REAL values to string
representations. If the string's length is less than the
FieldLength then blank spaces are added to the front of the
string. A REAL number will always take up at least
FieldLength spaces of output. *)

VAR
    Done : BOOLEAN;
    (* ReadReal will set Done to TRUE if a REAL number was
       successfully read, FALSE if the input was not a valid
       REAL number. *)

PROCEDURE ReadReal(VAR X : REAL);
(* ReadReal reads a REAL number. The number may be in either
   decimal format or scientific notation.

            ['+'|'-']Digit{Digit} ['. 'Digit{Digit}]
                  ['E'['+'|'-']Digit{Digit}]

   If the characters read do not represent a REAL value, Done
   is set to FALSE. If a REAL number is read, Done is set to
   TRUE. *)

PROCEDURE WriteReal(X : REAL; FieldLength : CARDINAL);
(* WriteReal outputs a REAL value. If the FieldLength is too
   small, least significant digits are dropped (with rounding)
   until either the number will fit in the FieldLength or one
   decimal digit is left. If the number will not fit in the
   FieldLength even with only one decimal digit, the number
   will overrun the FieldLength. *)

PROCEDURE WriteRealOct(X : REAL);
(* WriteRealOct outputs a REAL value using the internal octal
   representation with exponent and mantissa. *)

END RealInOut.

DEFINITION MODULE MathLib0;
(* Module MathLib0 provides procedures that perform a number of
   mathematical functions and REAL/INTEGER conversions. If a
   procedure in MathLib0 cannot produce a correct answer, the
   program is halted and an error message printed on the
   screen. *)

PROCEDURE real(X : INTEGER) : REAL;
(* real returns the REAL equivalent of the INTEGER
   parameter. *)

PROCEDURE entier(X : REAL) : INTEGER;
(* entier returns the INTEGER equivalent of the REAL parameter.

Appendix E

If the REAL value is too large to fit in an INTEGER, an
error message will be printed and the program halted. *)

PROCEDURE sqrt(X : REAL) : REAL;
(* sqrt returns the square root of X. X must be greater than or
equal to 0.0. *)

PROCEDURE ln(X : REAL) : REAL;
(* ln returns the natural logarithm of X. X must be greater
than 0.0. *)

PROCEDURE exp(X : REAL) : REAL;
(* exp returns the exponential of X. *)

PROCEDURE sin(X : REAL) : REAL;
(* sin returns the sine of X (X is an angle in radians). *)

PROCEDURE cos(X : REAL) : REAL;
(* cos returns the cosine of X (X is an angle in radians). *)

PROCEDURE arctan(X : REAL) : REAL;
(* arctan returns the arctangent of X expressed in radians. *)

END MathLib0.

DEFINITION MODULE Terminal;

(* Module Terminal provides basic input/output procedures for
the console or terminal. *)

PROCEDURE Read(VAR CH : CHAR);
(* Read inputs a single character and returns as soon as a
single character is received. The character is not
displayed. *)

PROCEDURE BusyRead(VAR CH : CHAR);
(* BusyRead works like Read. However, if no character is
available to read, BusyRead will set CH to 0C and return
immediately. *)

PROCEDURE ReadAgain;
(* ReadAgain will cause Read to return the same character Read
returned at its last invocation. *)

PROCEDURE Write(CH : CHAR);
(* Write outputs a single character to the screen. *)

PROCEDURE WriteLn;
(* WriteLn outputs an EOL character and is equivalent to
Write(EOL). *)

```
PROCEDURE WriteString( S : ARRAY OF CHAR );
(* WriteString outputs characters from a string until a NUL
   character (0C) or the end of the array is encountered. *)

END Terminal.
```

```
DEFINITION MODULE Storage;

(* Module Storage provides support for dynamic allocation and
   deallocation of memory. *)

FROM SYSTEM IMPORT ADDRESS;

PROCEDURE ALLOCATE( VAR A : ADDRESS; Size : CARDINAL );
(* ALLOCATE reserves Size storage units of memory and returns
   in A the address of the memory reserved. If there is not
   enough memory to reserve the space, the program is
   terminated and an error message is displayed. *)

PROCEDURE DEALLOCATE( VAR A : ADDRESS; Size : CARDINAL );
(* DEALLOCATE frees Size storage units of memory starting at
   the address in A. If there are not Size storage units
   reserved at A, then the program is terminated and an error
   message displayed. *)

PROCEDURE Available( Size : CARDINAL ) : BOOLEAN;
(* Available will return TRUE if there is enough memory
   available to reserve Size storage units, FALSE if there is
   not enough memory. *)

END Storage.
```

```
DEFINITION MODULE SYSTEM;

(* Module SYSTEM is a pseudo-module. Even though these types
   and procedures must be imported, they are implemented as
   part of the compiler. These types and procedures are highly
   system-dependent and may vary for each implementation of
   Modula-2. *)

TYPE

    WORD,
    (* WORD is a generic type which is assignment compatible
       with all data types that require one word of memory. The
       size of a word will vary on different computers. *)

    ADDRESS;
    (* ADDRESS is a generic type which is defined as POINTER TO
       WORD. *)
```

Appendix E

```
PROCEDURE ADR( X : ANYTYPE ) : ADDRESS;
(* ADR returns the address of the variable X which may be of
   any type. *)

PROCEDURE TSIZE( ANYTYPE ) : CARDINAL;
(* TSIZE returns the size of a data type. The parameter is a
   type name or a variable name. The number returned may be in
   bytes or in words depending on the individual system. *)

PROCEDURE NEWPROCESS( P : PROC; A : ADDRESS; Size : CARDINAL;
                      VAR New : ADDRESS );
(* P is the parameterless procedure which constitutes the new
   process. A is the origin of a workspace where local
   variables of the process and other information will be
   stored. Size is the size of the workspace in storage units.
   New is assigned the starting address of the new process. *)

PROCEDURE TRANSFER( VAR Source, Dest : ADDRESS );
(* Suspend the Source process and resume the Dest process at
   its current point of suspension. *)

(* This module may contain further facilities depending on the
   individual implementation. *)

END SYSTEM.
```

APPENDIX F
Nonstandard Modules

DEFINITION MODULE Strings;

(* Module Strings provides a number of procedures for
   manipulating strings of characters. A string is an array of
   characters. If a string does not fill an array completely,
   the end of the string must be marked by a NUL character
   (0C). A NUL character is not needed if the string fills the
   array.

   Strings are indexed starting at 0. The first character in
   the string can be accessed using FetchChar(Str, 0). The
   length of the string is one greater than the index of the
   last character in the string, so FetchChar(Str, Length
   (Str) - 1) accesses the last character.

   The procedures in this module attempt to catch as many
   errors as possible. When an error is detected, the program
   is halted by using the Modula-2 command HALT, and an error
   message is printed on the screen. The error message will
   include the name of the procedure in Strings and a list of
   the parameters that were passed to the procedure. *)

TYPE STRING = ARRAY[0..79] OF CHAR;
(* Type STRING is provided for applications where a maximum of
   80 characters is appropriate. *)

PROCEDURE InitString(VAR S : ARRAY OF CHAR);
(* InitString initializes a string to the empty string. *)

PROCEDURE Assign(VAR STR : ARRAY OF CHAR; A : ARRAY OF CHAR);
(* Assign copies string A into string STR. If string A will not
   fit in STR, the program is halted. *)

PROCEDURE Insert(SRC : ARRAY OF CHAR; VAR DEST : ARRAY OF CHAR;
                  INDEX : CARDINAL);
(* Insert the string SRC into the string DEST at INDEX. The
   characters in DEST after INDEX are moved to the right to
   make room for the new characters. If INDEX is one beyond the
   end of DEST, SRC is concatenated to the end of DEST. If
   INDEX is greater than the length of DEST or the new string
   is too large for DEST, the program is halted. *)

PROCEDURE Delete(VAR SRC : ARRAY OF CHAR;
                  INDEX, COUNT : CARDINAL);
(* Delete COUNT characters from the string SRC starting at
   INDEX. The remainder of the string, if any, is moved to the

left to fill the empty space. If INDEX is beyond the end of
the string or there are not COUNT characters available to
delete, the program is halted. *)

```
PROCEDURE Concat( STR1, STR2 : ARRAY OF CHAR;
                  VAR DEST : ARRAY OF CHAR );
```
(* Concatenate the string STR2 to the end of the string STR1
and return the result in DEST. If the new string will not
fit in DEST, the program is halted. *)

```
PROCEDURE Copy( SRC : ARRAY OF CHAR; INDEX, COUNT : CARDINAL;
                VAR DEST : ARRAY OF CHAR );
```
(* Copy COUNT characters from the string SRC starting at INDEX
and return the result in DEST. The program will be halted if
INDEX is beyond the length of SRC, there are not COUNT
characters to be copied, or the substring will not fit in
DEST. *)

```
PROCEDURE Pos( PATTERN, SRC : ARRAY OF CHAR ) : CARDINAL;
```
(* Pos finds the leftmost occurrence of the substring PATTERN
in the string SRC. If PATTERN is found in SRC, then the
index of the PATTERN (first character) in SRC is returned.
If PATTERN is not found in SRC, then the length of SRC is
returned. *)

```
PROCEDURE RPos( PATTERN, SRC : ARRAY OF CHAR ) : CARDINAL;
```
(* RPos finds the rightmost occurrence of the substring PATTERN
in the string SRC. If PATTERN is found in SRC, then the
index of the PATTERN (first character) in SRC is returned.
If PATTERN is not found in SRC, then the length of SRC is
returned. *)

```
PROCEDURE Length( STR : ARRAY OF CHAR ) : CARDINAL;
```
(* Length returns the number of characters in the string
STR. *)

```
PROCEDURE FetchChar( S : ARRAY OF CHAR; I : CARDINAL ) : CHAR;
```
(* FetchChar returns the character at index I in the string S.
If I is beyond the end of the string, the program is
halted. *)

```
PROCEDURE AssignChar( CH : CHAR; VAR S : ARRAY OF CHAR;
                      I : CARDINAL );
```
(* AssignChar replaces the character at index I in the string S
with the value of CH. If I is beyond the end of the string,
the program is halted. *)

```
PROCEDURE StringGreater( ST1, ST2 : ARRAY OF CHAR ) : BOOLEAN;
```
(* StringGreater performs a lexicographical (alphabetical)
comparison and returns TRUE if ST1 is greater than (after)
ST2. *)

```
PROCEDURE StringEqual( ST1, ST2 : ARRAY OF CHAR ) : BOOLEAN;
(* StringEqual compares ST1 and ST2 and returns TRUE if the two
   strings are identical. *)

PROCEDURE ReadLine( VAR STR : ARRAY OF CHAR; ECHO : BOOLEAN );
(* ReadLine inputs a character string. Input is terminated by
   any character less than or equal to the ASCII character 31,
   such as return or escape. If the number of characters read
   exceeds the length of the string, any characters beyond the
   end of the string are discarded. A NUL character (0C) or the
   end of the array is used to mark the end of the string. If
   ECHO is set to TRUE, then the input is echoed to the current
   output device. If it is set to FALSE, the string is not
   echoed. ReadLine is different from ReadString (in module
   InOut) in that ReadLine can read blank spaces. ReadLine does
   use Read and Write from InOut so that ReadLine is redirected
   when InOut is redirected. *)

PROCEDURE WriteLine( S : ARRAY OF CHAR );
(* WriteLine outputs characters from a string until a NUL
   character (0C) or the end of the array is encountered. An
   EOL character is automatically output after the string. *)

PROCEDURE ToChar( STR : ARRAY OF CHAR ) : CHAR;
(* If STR is a string with length 1, then ToChar returns that
   single character as a CHAR. If STR has any other length, the
   program is halted. For strings of other lengths, FetchChar
   can be used. *)

PROCEDURE ToString( CH : CHAR; VAR STR : ARRAY OF CHAR );
(* ToString returns a string STR of length one. The character
   CH is the one character put in STR. *)

END Strings.
```

```
DEFINITION MODULE TurtleGraphics;

(* Module TurtleGraphics provides simple graphics procedures
   for drawing lines on the screen. Lines are drawn by moving a
   'turtle' around on the screen. An arrow appears on the
   screen to show where the turtle is and in which direction it
   is going. The screen can be considered as graph paper with
   the origin (0, 0) at the center of the screen. The x axis is
   horizontal with positive to the right. The y axis is
   vertical with positive to the top. The turtle starts out at
   the center of the screen facing toward the right edge of the
   screen. *)

CONST MaxXSize = 340;
      MaxYSize = 238;
(* The center of the screen is location (0, 0). +MaxXSize is
```

Appendix F

the x coordinate of the right edge of the screen; -MaxXSize
is the x coordinate of the left edge of the screen;
+MaxYSize is the y coordinate of the top edge of the screen;
and -MaxYSize is the y coordinate of the bottom edge of the
screen. *)

TYPE PenMode = (Black, White, Invert, None);
(* See procedure PenColor for a description of this type. *)

PROCEDURE TurtleStop;
(* TurtleStop will display the message "Type any key to
   continue:" at the bottom of the screen and will wait for the
   user to press a key. This can be used to pause a program so
   that the screen may be viewed before changes are
   displayed. *)

PROCEDURE ShowTurtle(TorF : BOOLEAN);
(* Normally an arrow is shown on the screen indicating the
   turtle's location and direction. ShowTurtle can be used to
   remove the arrow so that it does not appear on the screen.
   If TorF is FALSE the turtle will not be displayed after that
   point. The default value is TRUE. *)

PROCEDURE PenColor(Pen : PenMode);
(* PenColor changes the type of line that is drawn when the
   turtle is moved. Possibilities are PenColor(Black),
   PenColor(White), PenColor(Invert), PenColor(None). PenMode
   must be imported in order to use PenColor. Black will erase
   existing lines as it draws; White will draw white lines on
   the screen; Invert changes white lines to black and black
   lines to white lines. None draws no line at all. *)

PROCEDURE Move(Distance : INTEGER);
(* Move the turtle Distance using the current pencolor. The
   turtle is moved forward (backward if Distance is negative)
   in the current direction. A line is drawn with the current
   pencolor from the old point to the new point. *)

PROCEDURE MoveTo(X, Y : INTEGER);
(* MoveTo moves the turtle to the location (X, Y). A line is
   drawn (using the current pencolor) from the old point to the
   new point. *)

PROCEDURE Turn(Degrees : INTEGER);
(* Turn the turtle Degrees degrees. If Degrees is positive the
   turtle is turned counterclockwise; if Degrees is negative
   the turtle is turned clockwise. *)

PROCEDURE TurnTo(Degrees : INTEGER);
(* TurnTo turns the turtle to the angle Degrees. The turtle
   points to the right when it is at angle 0. *)

```
PROCEDURE ClearScreen;
(* ClearScreen clears the entire screen, sets the cursor and
   turtle locations to ( 0, 0), and turns the turtle to angle
   0. *)

PROCEDURE WhereAmI( VAR X, Y, A : INTEGER );
(* WhereAmI returns the location (X, Y) and direction (A) of
   the turtle. A is in degrees. *)

PROCEDURE OffScreen() : BOOLEAN;
(* OffScreen returns TRUE if the turtle is off the screen,
   FALSE otherwise. *)

PROCEDURE PutCursor( XLoc, YLoc : CARDINAL );
(* PutCursor puts the text cursor at location (XLoc, YLoc).
   This is the point where characters will appear when read and
   write routines are used. For the text screen the location
   (0, 0) is the top left-hand corner of the screen, with
   positive x values to the right and positive y values
   down. *)

PROCEDURE PrintScreen( FileName : ARRAY OF CHAR );
(* PrintScreen writes a bitmap copy of the screen to the file
   FileName. The file created has the same format as the
   character set files. *)

END TurtleGraphics.
```

```
DEFINITION MODULE FileSystem;

(* This module FileSystem is one possible implementation of
   file input/output. The term 'file position pointer' is used
   in several places below. This refers to the position of the
   next piece of data that will be read or written in the file.
   Each read and write procedure advances the file position
   pointer past the data that was read or written. *)

FROM SYSTEM IMPORT WORD;

TYPE Response = ( done, notdone, notsupported, callerror,
                  unknownmedium, unknownfile, paramerror,
                  toomanyfiles, eom, deviceoff, softparityerror,
                  softprotected, softerror, hardparityerror,
                  hardprotected, timeout, harderror )
    (* These response values are used to return error flags for
       file operations. The exact values and meanings may vary
       on different computers. *)
```

```
File = RECORD
        id : CARDINAL; (* This field is system dependent
                          and should not be used by the
                          programmer. *)
        eof : BOOLEAN; (* eof is set to TRUE when the file
                          position pointer is moved past
                          the end of the file. *)
        res : Response;(* res is used to return errors. *)
      END;
```

PROCEDURE Close(VAR F : File);
(* Close a file that has been opened by Lookup. After Close has
   been called, the file must be reopened by Lookup before it
   can be accessed again. If the file has been changed (written
   to) since it was opened, it MUST be closed before the
   program terminates. If the file is not closed, some data may
   not be saved on the disk. *)

PROCEDURE Lookup(VAR F : File; filename : ARRAY OF CHAR;
                  New : BOOLEAN)
(* Lookup opens a file for reading and writing. The filename is
   the operating system's name for the file. If New is FALSE
   the file must already exist. If New is TRUE the file will be
   created. *)

PROCEDURE Rename(VAR F : File; filename : ARRAY OF CHAR);
(* Change the name of the file to filename. The file must
   already be open for Rename to work. *)

PROCEDURE ReadChar(VAR F : File; VAR CH : CHAR);
(* ReadChar reads a single character from the file F. The file
   must already be open for ReadChar to work. If the file
   position pointer is past the end of the file, F.eof will be
   set to TRUE. *)

PROCEDURE ReadWord(VAR F : File; VAR W : WORD);
(* ReadWord reads a word from the file F. The type WORD is a
   generic type and its actual representation is system
   dependent. If the file position pointer is past the end of
   the file, F.eof will be set to TRUE. *)

PROCEDURE Reset(VAR F : File);
(* Reset sets the file position pointer to the beginning of the
   file. If F.eof is TRUE it will be reset to FALSE. *)

PROCEDURE WriteChar(VAR F : File; CH : CHAR);
(* WriteChar writes a single character to the file. The file
   must already be open for WriteChar to work. If the file

position pointer is past the end of the file, the character
will be added to the end of the file. *)

PROCEDURE WriteWord(VAR F : File; W : WORD);
(* WriteWord writes a word to the file F. The type WORD is a
generic type and its actual representation is system
dependent. If the file position pointer is past the end of
the file, the word will be added to the end of the file. *)

END FileSystem.

DEFINITION MODULE Processes;

(* Module Processes provides support for concurrent execution
of processes and for communication between processes. *)

TYPE SIGNAL;
(* SIGNAL is an opaque type used to provide communication
between different processes. *)

PROCEDURE StartProcess(P : PROC; N : CARDINAL);
(* StartProcess starts a concurrent process P. N storage units
of memory are reserved for P to use. PROC is the standard
type of parameterless procedures. *)

PROCEDURE SEND(VAR S : SIGNAL);
(* SEND resumes one process that is waiting for the signal
S. *)

PROCEDURE WAIT(VAR S : SIGNAL);
(* WAIT will suspend execution until the signal S is sent by
another process. *)

PROCEDURE Awaited(S : SIGNAL) : BOOLEAN;
(* Awaited returns TRUE if there is a process waiting for the
signal S, FALSE if there is no process waiting. *)

PROCEDURE Init(VAR S : SIGNAL);
(* A signal MUST be initiated with Init before the signal can
be used. *)

END Processes.

Modula Corporation Implementation (IBM PC)

Module InOut includes two more variables "in" and "out" of type File, and two more procedures:

PROCEDURE ReadWrd(VAR w : WORD);
(* Low-level input of one word of data from a disk file. *)

```
PROCEDURE WriteWrd( w : WORD );
(* Low-level output of one word of data to a disk file. *)
```

Module RealInOut includes two more procedures:

```
PROCEDURE FWriteReal( x : REAL; FieldLength : CARDINAL );
(* Write a real value in decimal notation. If there is
    insufficient space in FieldLength, then fill the field with
    asterisks. *)

PROCEDURE GWriteReal( x : REAL; FieldLength : CARDINAL );
(* Do FWriteReal if FieldLength sufficient, otherwise do
    WriteReal. *)
```

Module MathLib0 does not exist. It is replaced by module MathLib1 which includes all the MathLib0 procedures as well as a number of extra elements.

```
VAR Done : BOOLEAN;
        (* True if last function returned valid data. *)
        ShowErr : BOOLEAN;
        (* If set to FALSE by user, function's error messages are
            not displayed on screen. Done still reports success or
            failure of a function. *)


PROCEDURE log( x : REAL ) : REAL;
(* Returns common logarithm of x. *)

PROCEDURE TenToX( x : REAL ) : REAL;
(* Returns ten to the x power. *)

PROCEDURE tan( x : REAL ) : REAL;
(* Returns tangent of x. *)

PROCEDURE atan( x : REAL ) : REAL;
(* Returns ArcTangent of x, same as arctan in MathLib0. *)

PROCEDURE asin( x : REAL ) : REAL;
(* Returns ArcSine of x. *)

PROCEDURE acos( x : REAL ) : REAL;
(* Returns ArcCosine of x. *)

PROCEDURE sinh( x : REAL ) : REAL;
(* Returns hyperbolic sine of x. *)

PROCEDURE cosh( x : REAL ) : REAL;
(* Returns hyperbolic cosine of x. *)

PROCEDURE tanh( x : REAL ) : REAL;
(* Returns hyperbolic tangent of x. *)
```

```
PROCEDURE power( x, y : REAL ) : REAL;
(* Returns x to the y power. *)

PROCEDURE ipower( x : REAL; y : INTEGER ) : REAL;
(* Returns x to the integer y power. *)

PROCEDURE Magnitude( x : REAL ) : INTEGER;
(* Returns value equivalent to entier( log( x ) ), the order of
   magnitude of x. *)
```

There also exists a module FileSystem with a record type File that offers file handling procedures. A complete Graphics module allows you to draw circles and lines and to fill polygonal areas. Sets are limited to 16 elements.

Logitech Implementation (IBM PC)

The Logitech implementation offers a Strings module for handling strings of characters, but does not offer a Graphics module. The regular standard modules are present, and module SYSTEM includes several additions:

>a type BYTE
>procedures GETREG and SETREG to access machine registers
>procedure DOSCALL to give the programmer access to all DOS calls

In addition the system offers two important tools for debugging: a high-level post-mortem debugger, and a high-level runtime debugger. The latter makes it possible to execute the program step by step and to set up breakpoints where values of variables may be displayed or modified.

MacMETH and MetCom Implementations (Apple Macintosh)

As indicated by its name, this implementation comes from the ETH in Zurich, the birthplace of Modula-2. The implementation is a fast one-pass compiler which forbids forward references (except for pointer types), and therefore provides a FORWARD statement to indicate that a procedure will be declared later as in:

```
PROCEDURE P( parameter list ); FORWARD;
```

The system automatically provides module keys to keep track of the compiled versions and force a recompilation of an implementation module if the corresponding definition module has been changed.

The system offers extra standard types LONGINT, LONGCARD, and LONGREAL as well as the standard procedures FLOATD and TRUNCD which apply to LONGREALs. Standard module InOut exports two variables, "in" and "out," of type File and two procedures ReadWrd and WriteWrd (see Modula Corporation implementation). Module RealInOut exports ReadReal and WriteReal; module LongRealInOut exports ReadLongReal and WriteLongReal. Module MathLib exports the usual mathematical functions, but the names have been capitalized: Sqrt, Exp, Ln, Sin, Cos, ArcTan, Real, Entier. There is also a LongMathLib module with LongSqrt, LongExp, and the like. A FileSystem module, a Terminal module, and other modules like CursorMouse, Windows, GraphicWindows are also available.

Sets are limited to 16 elements. It is possible to access the Macintosh toolbox. The system comprises an editor and an excellent interactive symbolic debugger.

Appendix F **A39**

VAX UNIX Implementation (DEC WRL Version)

This implementation of Modula-2 does not include standard modules InOut and RealInOut (although those modules and a module FileSystem have been developed and are available from New Mexico State University Computer Science Department). Module "io" provides access to i/o operations similar to C's "scanf" and "printf." Module "strings" exports three procedures Compare, Assign, and Append which make it possible to manipulate arrays of characters.

Standard module Storage exports type ADDRESS and procedures ALLOCATE and DEALLOCATE (but procedures New and Dispose are available and do not require the import of ALLOCATE and DEALLOCATE). Module "memory" completes module Storage. Module "math" includes the following functions:

```
PROCEDURE sin( x : REAL ) : REAL;
PROCEDURE cos( x : REAL ) : REAL;
PROCEDURE atan( x : REAL ) : REAL;
PROCEDURE atan2( x, y : REAL ) : REAL;
PROCEDURE exp( x : REAL ) : REAL;
PROCEDURE sqrt( x : REAL ) : REAL;
PROCEDURE log( x : REAL ) : REAL;
PROCEDURE ldexp( x : REAL; exp : INTEGER ) : REAL;
```

It also includes the same functions whose name is prefixed by "long" for parameters and results of type LONGREAL.

Beside the regular objects exported by standard module SYSTEM, module "system" exports constants BYTESPERWORD, BITSPERWORD, MOSTSIGBIT, LEASTSIGBIT, MAXINT, MAXUNSIGNED, and MAXCARD. It also exports types Byte, Process, and procedures Size, ByteSize, ByteTSize, and CPUTime. In addition module "bitoperations" performs bit manipulation operations. Module "parameters" accesses command line parameters and module "unix" provides some UNIX system calls.

Waterloo Modula-2 (VM/SP CMS)

Waterloo Modula-2 implements Modula-2 as described in Wirth's "Programming in Modula-2," third edition. Structured return values are allowed for function procedures. BITSET can have 32 elements, and sets have a maximum of 256 elements.

Standard modules InOut, RealInOut, MathLib0 (which exports constants pi, e, and ln10), and SYSTEM are defined. In addition a Strings module is defined as follows:

```
DEFINITION MODULE Strings;

CONST
    StrLen = 80;
    EOS = 0C;

TYPE
    String = ARRAY [0..StrLen-1] OF CHAR;
```

```
PROCEDURE Assign( source : ARRAY OF CHAR;
                  VAR dest : ARRAY OF CHAR );
(* Copy source into dest. Append EOS if source is shorter than
   dest. No checks are done to validate source string for unde-
   fined values. *)

PROCEDURE CompareStr( s1, s2 : ARRAY OF CHAR ) : INTEGER;
(* Compare s1 against s2.
        Return:   -1  if s1 < s2
                   0  if s1 = s2
                  +1  if s1 > s2   *)

PROCEDURE Concat( s1, s2 : ARRAY OF CHAR;
                  VAR result : ARRAY OF CHAR );
(* Place s1 into result, followed by s2. *)

PROCEDURE Copy( str : ARRAY OF CHAR; index : CARDINAL;
                len : CARDINAL; VAR result : ARRAY OF CHAR );
(* Copy up to len characters from str starting at str[index]. *)

PROCEDURE Delete( VAR str : ARRAY OF CHAR; index : CARDINAL;
                  len : CARDINAL );
(* Delete up to len characters from str starting at str[index]. *)

PROCEDURE Insert( substr : ARRAY OF CHAR; VAR str : ARRAY OF
                  CHAR; index : CARDINAL );
(* Insert substr into str starting at str[index.] If index >
   Length( str ), then blanks are padded between str and
   substr. *)

PROCEDURE Length( str : ARRAY OF CHAR ) : CARDINAL;
(* Determine the number of characters in string str. *)

PROCEDURE Pos( substr, str : ARRAY OF CHAR ) : CARDINAL;
(* Determine if substr is located in str. If it is, return the
   index of the first character, otherwise return HIGH( str )
   + 1. *)

END Strings.
```

A number of library modules are available, including Files, FInOut, FRealInOut, Storage, StreamFiles, and Terminal.

FTL Implementation (IBM PC)

FTL Modula-2 offers a complete programming environment. The system comprises an editor (much like WordStar), and makes it possible to go back and forth between edition and compilation easily. The compiler is a one-pass compiler, that provides a FORWARD statement (see Mac-

METH). The first 32 characters of identifiers are significant. BITSET has 16 elements, while sets may have up to 1024 elements.

Module InOut offers extra procedures ReadLine, SkipEOL, SwitchInStream, SwitchOutStream, PopInStream, and PopOutStream. Module RealInOut offers two extra procedures WriteRealFixed and atoi (to raise a real to an integer power). Module MathLib0 is replaced by module Maths, which exports functions SIN, COS, TAN, LN, EXP, SQRT, ARCTAN, ARCTAN2, ENTIER, and constants PI, OneOnPI, and e. The system also offers a Strings module exporting the String type, and procedures Pos, Insert, Concat, Length, Assign, StoS, Delete, Copy, Replace, PosLast and AddPath.

Modules Files and Streams are available for file processing. Modules Storage, Terminal, and Processes are also available, as well as a great number of nonstandard modules which make it possible to interact with the environment and MS/DOS (MSDOS, Conversions, Command, GetFiles, Sort, CallProg, and so forth).

Besides the integrated compiler and editor, the system offers a library manager, that is particularly useful in obtaining the source of all definition modules. Module SYSTEM defines a new type BYTE and defines the type ADDRESS, compatible with all POINTER types, as POINTER TO BYTE.

$$R;\ T\ =\ 0.01/0.05\ 09:02:15$$

Answers to Selected Exercises

Chapter 1

2. (b) Omelet
    If there are no more eggs then
        go to a restaurant
    Else
        break all eggs in a bowl
        put pan on stove
        put chunk of butter in pan
        put heat on
        beat the eggs
        pour beaten eggs in pan
        cook on moderate heat until omelet done
        salt, pepper and serve
End Omelet

3. Paint Job
   Get size of area
   Multiply result by 2
   Divide area by 300
   Round result to next greater integer value
   Print rounded result
End Paint Job

4. Euclid
   Get integers A and B
   While A # B do
     If A > B then
        Set A to remainder of A divided by B
     Else
        Set B to remainder of B divided by A
     End if
   End while
   Print A
End Euclid

9. Equilateral Triangle
   Read Side
   Move Side
   Turn 120
   Move Side
   Turn 120
   Move Side
   Turn 120
End Equilateral Triangle

10.

Instruction	N	Sum	Number	Condition
1	0	—	—	—
2	0	0	—	—
3	0	0	1	—
4	0	0	1	true
7		print "The sum is 0"		
8		stop		

11.

Inst.	WordCount	Line	Length Line	Blank Position	Condition
1	0	" "	0	—	true
stop					
1	0	"Hello"	5	—	false
2	1	"Hello"	5	—	—
3	1	"Hello"	5	5	—
4	1	"Hello"	5	5	false
6	1	" "	0	5	—
1	1	" "	0	5	true
stop					

12. Read and Print
    Set N to 0
    Loop
      Read Value
      Exit if Value is zero
      Set N to N + 1
      Print Value
    End loop
    Print "Number of values: " N
  End Read and Print

13. Series
    Set N to 3
    Loop
      Print N
      Set N to N + 3
      Exit if N = 102
    End loop
  End Series

14. Pair numbers 1 and 100, 2 and 99,..., 50 and 51. This gives 50 pairs whose value is 101. The sum is therefore $50 \times 101 = 5050$.

16. Compute Tax
    Set Taxable to 0
    Set Non Taxable to 0
    Set Total to 0
    Loop
      Read Price, Kind

Answers to Selected Exercises

```
        Exit if Kind = F
        If Kind = T then
           Set Taxable to Taxable + Price
        Else
           Set Non Taxable to Non Taxable + Price
        End if
     End loop
     Set Tax to 0.0525 * Taxable
     Set Total to Taxable + Non Taxable + Tax
     Print "Taxable" Taxable "No tax" Non Taxable
        "Tax" Tax "Total" Total
  End Compute Tax
```

17. Dates
```
     Read M1, D1, Y1, M2, D2, Y2
     Set Answer to false
     If Y1 < Y2 then
        Set Answer to true
     Else
        If Y1 = Y2 then
           If M1 < M2 then
              Set Answer to true
           Else
              If M1 = M2 then
                 If J1 < J2 then
                    Set Answer to true
                 End if
              End if
           End if
        End if
     End if
     Print "First date is: "
     If Answer then
        Print M1, D1, Y1
     Else
        Print M2, D2, Y2
     End if
  End Dates
```

18. Equals
```
     Read A, B, C
     If A = B + C then
        Print "A=B+C" A
     Else
        If B = A + C then
           Print "B=A+C" B
        Else
           If C = A + B then
              Print "C=A+B" C
           Else
              Print "No solution"
```

                End if
              End if
            End if
          End Equals

19. Running Speed
      Loop
        Read Minutes, Seconds
        Exit if Minutes = 0
        Set Time to Minutes * 60 + Seconds
        Set Speed to 1500 / Time
        Print Minutes, Seconds, Speed
      End loop
    End Running Speed

20. Manhattan
      Set Year to 1626
      Set Capital to 24.0
      Loop
        Set Interest to Capital * 0.006
        Set Capital to Capital + Interest
        Set Year to Year + 1
        Exit if Year = 1986
      End loop
      Print Capital
    End Manhattan

21. Gas Range
      Set Size to 15
      Loop
        Set Mpg to 15
        Print "Consumption for tank size:", Size
        Loop
          Set Range to Size * Mpg
          Print Mpg, Range
          Set Mpg to Mpg + 5
          Exit if Mpg = 40
        End loop
        Set Size to Size + 5
        Exit if Size = 45
      End loop
    End Gas Range

Chapter 2

1. Y, Invoice, Employee52, ValidData, C2H5OH

2. ```
   CONST YardsPerMile = 1760;
         LitersPerGallon = 3.785;
         RadiansToDegrees = 180.0 / 3.14159;
   ```
   ```

Answers to Selected Exercises

3. VAR StudyYear: CARDINAL;
       GPA: REAL;
       StudentStatus: CHAR;

4. WriteString("Computer Science");
   WriteString(" is good for your health!");

6. Impossible to assign a value to an expression.
   Constant declaration should use an equal sign, not :=.

7. The results are: 128
       32
       2 numbers printed

8. VAR ... Sum, Difference: INTEGER;
       .
       .
       .
       Sum := I + J;
       Difference := I - J;
       WriteString("The sum is ");
       WriteInt(Sum, 6); WriteLn;
       WriteString("The difference is ");
       WriteInt(Difference, 6); WriteLn;
       .
       .
       .

9. Replace the four Turn statements by Turn(-90).

10. Replace the call to procedure Concat by: Concat(S2, S1, BigS).

15. MODULE Square;
    FROM InOut IMPORT WriteString, WriteLn;
    BEGIN
       WriteString("*****"); WriteLn;
       WriteString("*   *"); WriteLn;
       WriteString("*   *"); WriteLn;
       WriteString("*   *"); WriteLn;
       WriteString("*****"); WriteLn;
    END Square.

Chapter 3

1. PROCEDURE DrawTriangle(Size: CARDINAL);
   CONST Asterisks =
      "***";
   VAR Middle, Height: STRING;
   BEGIN
      Copy(Asterisks, 0, Size DIV 2, Middle);

```
        Copy( Asterisks, 0, Size, Height );
        WriteString( "*" ); WriteLn;
        WriteString( Middle ); WriteLn;
        WriteString( Height ); WriteLn;
        WriteString( Middle ); WriteLn;
        WriteString( "*" ); WriteLn;
    END DrawTriangle;
```

2. ```
    MODULE SailingFlags;
    FROM InOut IMPORT WriteString, WriteLn;
    FROM Strings IMPORT STRING, Copy;
    (* Procedure DrawTriangle goes here *)
    BEGIN
        DrawTriangle( 4 );
        DrawTriangle( 12 );
        DrawTriangle( 8 );
    END SailingFlags.
   ```

3. Change comment and ConversionFactor = 180.0 / pi; in ConvertAngle.

9. ```
    MODULE YardsMeters;
    FROM RealInOut IMPORT ReadReal, WriteReal;
    FROM InOut IMPORT WriteString, WriteLn;
    VAR Measure: REAL;

    PROCEDURE Convert( Yards: REAL ): REAL;
      BEGIN
        RETURN Yards * 0.914;
      END Convert;

    BEGIN
      WriteString( "Enter a measure in yards " );
      ReadReal( Measure ); WriteLn;
      WriteString( "Measure in meters is: " );
      WriteReal( Convert( Measure ), 10 ); WriteLn;
    END YardsMeters.
   ```

10. ```
    PROCEDURE Decompose( Expression: STRING;
                         VAR Term1, Term2: STRING );
    VAR PlusPos: CARDINAL;
    BEGIN
      PlusPos := Pos( "+", Expression );
      Copy( Expression, 0, PlusPos, Term1 );
      Copy( Expression, PlusPos + 1, Length( Expression ) -
            PlusPos - 1, Term2 );
    END Decompose;
    ```
    ```

Chapter 4

1. The same number as the number of move statements executed, that is 64.

2.

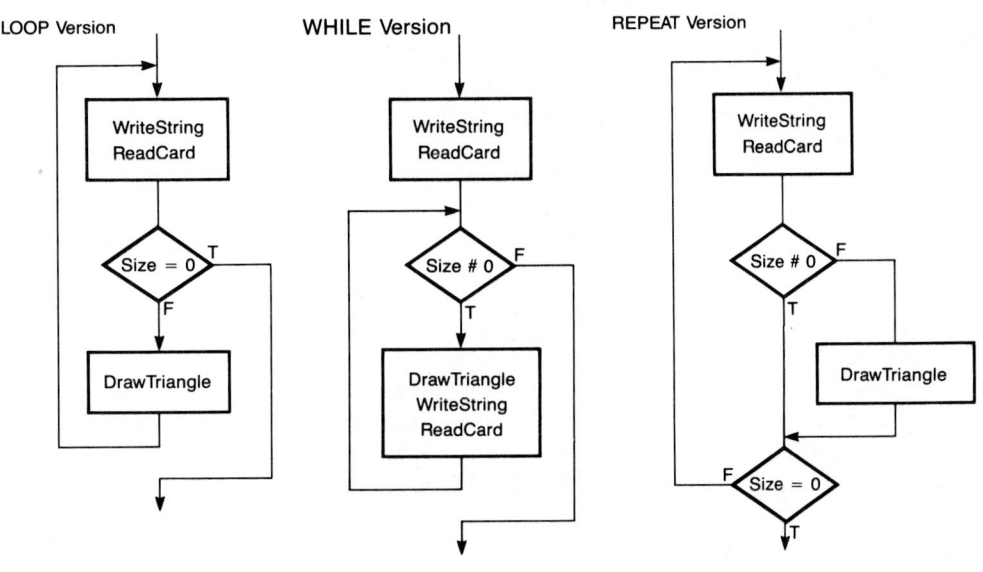

3.  ```
    MODULE Order;
    FROM InOut IMPORT WriteString, WriteLn, ReadCard,
                      WriteCard;
    VAR A, B: CARDINAL;
    BEGIN
      WriteString( "Enter 2 integer values: " );
      ReadCard( A ); ReadCard( B ); WriteLn;
      WriteString( "Here are the 2 values, ordered: " ); WriteLn;
      IF A < B THEN
        WriteCard( A, 5 ); WriteLn;
        WriteCard( B, 5 ); WriteLn;
      ELSE
        WriteCard( B, 5 ); WriteLn;
        WriteCard( A, 5 ); WriteLn;
      END; (* IF *)
    END Order.
    ```

4. Add:
    ```
    LOOP
      WriteString ...
      ReadCard ...
      IF ( A = 0 ) AND ( B = 0 ) THEN EXIT END;
      WriteString ...
      IF ...
    END; (* LOOP *)
    ```
    ```

5.  ```
    IF A > B THEN
       IF A > C THEN
          Largest := A;
       ELSE
          Largest := C;
       END; (* IF *)
    ELSE
       IF B > C THEN
          Largest := B;
       ELSE
          Largest := C;
       END; (* IF *)
    END; (* IF *)
    ```

6.  ```
    IF D < 20 THEN
       WriteString( "Too young" );
    ELSE IF D < 62 THEN
            WriteString( "Not possible yet" );
         ELSE IF D >= 62 THEN
                 WriteString( "Possible" );
              END; (* IF *)
         END; (* IF *)
    END; (* IF *)
    ```

7. 2

8.  ```
    FOR Z := 83 TO 1 BY -9 DO
       WriteCard( Z, 5 );
    END; (* FOR *)
    ```

11. ```
    MODULE Odds;
    FROM InOut IMPORT WriteCard, WriteLn;
    VAR I: CARDINAL;
    BEGIN
       FOR I := 1 TO 49 BY 2 DO
          WriteCard( I, 5 ); WriteLn;
       END; (* FOR *)
    END Odds.
    ```

12. Replace Celsius by Fahrenheit and Fahrenheit by Celsius, except in the conversion statement which becomes:
    ```
    Fahrenheit := 9.0 * Celsius / 5.0 + 32.0;
    ```
    Modify table title and comments as well.

13. 144 dots
    (* i * 24 + 3 * (j - 1) + (k - 2) dots have been printed *)

14. 24 dots
    (* (i - 1) * 14 + (j - i) * (j - i + 1) / 2 + (k - i) dots printed *)

Answers to Selected Exercises

16.
```
PROCEDURE Mystery( Inc, Angle: CARDINAL );
VAR L: CARDINAL;
BEGIN
  L := 9;
  WHILE L < 160 DO
    Move( L );
    Turn( Angle );
    L := L + Inc;
  END; (* WHILE *)
END Mystery;
```

18.
```
MODULE ReadAndCount;
FROM InOut IMPORT ReadInt, WriteCard, WriteString, WriteLn;
VAR Pos, Neg: CARDINAL;
    Value: INTEGER;
BEGIN
  Pos := 0; Neg := 0;
  LOOP
    ReadInt( Value );
    IF Value = 0 THEN EXIT END;
    IF Value < 0 THEN
      INC( Neg );
    ELSE
      INC( Pos );
    END; (* IF *)
  END; (* LOOP *)
  WriteString( "Number of positive values" );
  WriteCard( Pos, 5 ); WriteLn;
  WriteString( "Number of negative values" );
  WriteCard( Neg, 5 ); WriteLn;
END ReadAndCount.
```

19.
```
MODULE SmallInteger;
FROM InOut IMPORT WriteString, WriteInt, WriteLn;
CONST Limit = 10000;
VAR Number, Square: INTEGER;   (* or LONGINT *)
BEGIN
  Number := 1;
  LOOP
    Square := Number * Number;
    IF Square > Limit THEN
      EXIT
    END; (* IF *)
    Number := Number + 1;
  END;
  WriteString( "Smallest integer whose square is > " );
  WriteInt( Limit, 6 ); WriteString( " = " );
  WriteInt( Number, 5 ); WriteLn;
END SmallInteger.
```

Chapter 5

2. Multiplication(A, B)
    If B = 1
      return A
    Else
      return A + Multiplication(A, B − 1)
    End if
  End Multiplication

3. Factorial(N)
    If N > 0
      Set Fact to 1
      For i = 1 to N
        Set Fact to Fact * i
      End for
    End if
    Return Fact
  End Factorial

4. ```
PROCEDURE Fibonacci(N: CARDINAL): CARDINAL;
BEGIN
   IF (N = 0) OR (N = 1) THEN
      RETURN 1;
   ELSE
      RETURN Fibonacci(N - 1) + Fibonacci(N - 2);
   END; (* IF *)
END Fibonacci;
```

5. Fibonacci(N)
    If N = 0 or N = 1
      Set Fibo to 1
    Else
      Set Next To Last to 1
      Set Last to 1
      For i = 2 to N
        Set Fibo to Next To Last + Last
        Set Next To Last to Last
        Set Last to Fibo
      End for
    End if
    Return Fibo
  End Fibonacci

7. Prints number X one digit at a time.

8. Sum Of Digits( N )
    If N < 10
      Return N
    Else
      Return remainder of N div 10 + Sum Of Digits( N div 10 )
    End if
  End Sum Of Digits
```

Answers to Selected Exercises

10. Reverse(S)
      If Length(S) > 1 then
        Copy(S, 0, 1, Head)
        Copy(S, 1, Length(S) − 1, Tail)
        Reverse(Tail)
        Concat(Tail, Head, S)
    End Reverse

11. (a) Base step: the formula holds for $N = 1$.
    $$1 * 1 + 1 = 2 \text{ (first even integer)}$$

    (b) Assume this is true for N, the sum of the first N even numbers is $N * N + N$. The Nth even number is $2 * N$. If we add the next even number $2 * (N + 1)$ we have:
    $$N * N + N + 2 * N + 2 = N * N + 3 * N + 2 =$$
    $$(N + 1) * (N + 1) + N + 1$$

12. (a) Base step: $N = 1$, $1(1 + 1)(1 + 2) / 6 = 1$.
    (b) If true for N, add next number squared:
    $$N * (N + 1) * (2 * N + 1) + (N + 1) * (N + 1)$$
    which is: $(N * (N + 1) * (2 * N + 1) + 6 * (N + 1) * (N + 1)) / 6$
    or: $(N + 1) * (2 * N * N + 7 * N + 6) / 6$
    which is: $(N + 1) * (N + 2) * (2 * N + 3) / 6$
    or: $(N + 1) * (N + 2) * (2 * (N + 1) + 1) / 6$

16.
```
MODULE Cards;
(* Show card values from integers *)
FROM InOut IMPORT WriteString, ReadCard, WriteCard,
                  WriteLn;
CONST CardsInSuit = 13;
VAR CardNumber: CARDINAL;
BEGIN
  LOOP
    WriteString( "Give a card number, 1.. 52, or 0
                  to stop" );
    ReadCard( CardNumber ); WriteLn;
    IF CardNumber = 0 THEN EXIT END;
    IF ( CardNumber <= 52 ) AND ( CardNumber >= 1 ) THEN
      CASE CardNumber MOD CardsInSuit OF
        0     : WriteString( "King of " );|
        1     : WriteString( "Ace    of " );|
        2..10: WriteCard( CardNumber MOD CardsInSuit, 2 );
               WriteString( "    of " );|
        11    : WriteString( "Jack of " );|
        12    : WriteString( "Queen of " )
      END; (* CASE *)
      CASE ( CardNumber - 1 ) DIV CardsInSuit OF
        0: WriteString( "spades" ); WriteLn;   |
        1: WriteString( "hearts" ); WriteLn;   |
        2: WriteString( "diamonds" ); WriteLn; |
        3: WriteString( "clubs" ); WriteLn;
      END; (* CASE *)
```

```
        ELSE
          WriteString( "Value must be between 1 and 52" );
          WriteLn;
        END; (* IF *)
      END; (* LOOP *)
    END Cards.
```

17. Add local declarations:
```
    CONST LowerYear = 1950;
          UpperYear = 1999;
```
Add right after BEGIN:
```
    CASE Month OF
      1,3,5,7,8,10,12: MaxDays := 31;
      4,6,9,11       : MaxDays := 30;
      2              : IF ( ( Year MOD 400 = 0 )
                          AND ( Year # 2000 ) ) OR
                         ( ( Year MOD 4 = 0 )
                          AND ( Year MOD 100 # 0 ) ) THEN
                         MaxDays := 29;
                       ELSE
                         MaxDays := 28;
                       END;
    ELSE
       WriteString( " Month out of range" ); WriteLn;
       MaxDays := 31;
       Month := 0;
    END; (* CASE *)
    IF ( Day < 1 ) OR ( Day > MaxDays ) THEN
      WriteString( "Day out of range" ); WriteLn;
      Day := 0;
    END; (* IF *)
    IF ( Year < LowerYear ) OR ( Year > UpperYear ) THEN
      WriteString( "Year out of range" ); WriteLn;
      Year := 0;
    END; (* IF *)
    IF ( Month = 0 ) OR ( Day = 0 ) OR ( Year = 0 ) THEN
      RETURN
    ELSE
         .
         .
         .
```

25.
```
    PROCEDURE C( N, K: CARDINAL ): CARDINAL;
    BEGIN
      IF K = 0 THEN
        RETURN 1;
      ELSIF N = K THEN
        RETURN 1;
      ELSIF N > K THEN
        RETURN C( N - 1, K ) + C( N - 1, K - 1 );
      ELSE
```

```
            WriteString( 'C( n, k ) is not defined for k > n' );
        END; (* IF *)
    END C;

26. PROCEDURE Sterling( N, K: CARDINAL ): CARDINAL;
    BEGIN
        IF ( N > 0 ) AND ( K = 0 ) THEN
            RETURN 0;
        ELSIF N = K THEN
            RETURN 1;
        ELSIF ( K > 0 ) AND ( K < N ) THEN
            RETURN Sterling( N - 1, K - 1 ) - N *
                    Sterling( N - 1, K );
        END; (* IF *)
    END Sterling;
```

Chapter 6

1.  ```
    IF X >= 0 THEN
        RETURN X;
    ELSE
        RETURN -X;
    END;
    ```

2. X + Y / (A + B) + Z
    5 * X * X / (4 * Y) + Z

3. (a) 71
    (b) 10.96178
    (c) 18
    (d) 5
    (e) 6
    (f) 6
    (g) TRUE
    (h) FALSE
    (i) TRUE
    (j) TRUE

4. MPG := DISTANCE / LITERS / 0.264

5. (a) TRUE
    (b) TRUE
    (c) TRUE
    (d) FALSE

6. (X < Y) AND (Y < Z)

7.  ```
    Eligible := (Grade > 80) AND (Age >= 18)
                AND (Height >= MinimumHeight)
                AND (Weight > MinimumWeight);
    ```

8. Evaluate first subexpression from the left and then use result to evaluate complete expression.

9. (NOT a) AND (NOT b) = NOT (a OR b)

F	T	F	F	T	F	T	T	T
F	T	F	T	F	F	T	T	F
T	F	F	F	T	F	F	T	T
T	F	T	T	F	T	F	F	F

10. a AND b OR c # (a OR b) AND c

T	T	T	T	T	T	T	T	T
T	T	T	T	F	T	T	T	F	F
T	F	F	T	T	T	T	F	T
T	F	F	F	F	T	T	F	F	F
F	F	T	T	T	F	T	T	T
F	F	T	F	F	F	T	T	F	F
F	F	F	T	T	F	F	F	F	T
F	F	F	F	F	F	F	F	F	F

11.

A	B	S	A	B	S
T	T	X	T	T	X
T	F		T	F	
F	T		F	T	
F	F		F	F	

12.

A	B	S1	S2	A	B	S1	S2
T	T	X		T	T	X	
T	F		X	T	F		X
F	T		X	F	T		←
F	F		X	F	F		←

13.
```
IF A THEN
   IF B THEN
      S1;
   ELSE S2;          ←
   END;
ELSE
   S2;
END;
```

14.
```
PROCEDURE TruncReal( X: REAL ): INTEGER;
BEGIN
   IF X >= 0 THEN
      RETURN INTEGER( TRUNC( X ) );
   ELSE
      RETURN -INTEGER( TRUNC( -X ) );
   END;  (* IF *)
END TruncReal;
```

15.
```
PROCEDURE RoundReal( X: REAL ): INTEGER;
   (* rounds a real value to the closest integer value, as in:
```

```
                  5.234    returns   5
                  6.789    returns   7
                 -1.987    returns  -2                                    *)
      BEGIN
         IF X >= 0.0 THEN
            RETURN TruncReal( X + 0.5 );
         ELSE
            RETURN TruncReal( X - 0.5 );
         END;
      END RoundReal;
```

16. ```
    PROCEDURE XOR( A, B: BOOLEAN ): BOOLEAN;
    BEGIN
       RETURN A # B;
    END XOR;
    ```

Chapter 7

1. (a) 1 2   (b) 1 2   (c) 1 2
       1 1   2 2   1 2
       3 4   3 4   3 4
       3 3   4 4   3 4

2. 2 3 3
   2 5 7

3. 4 3 7
   3 6 4
   5 9 4

4. X, Y, Print, First, Second are global.
   M, N are local to Print.
   X is local to First.
   X and Y are local to Second.

5. Swap, One, W, X, Y, Z

6. Global: Write, WriteString, WriteLn, STRING, Copy,
             Length, TitleBox
   Scope TitleBox: DisplayHorizontalLine, MaxLength,
                   DisplayTitleLine, Line1, Line2, Line3,
                   NumBlanks
   Scope DisplayHorizontalLine: Asterisks, HorizontalSide,
                                 Width
   Scope DisplayTitleLine: Blanks, BlankString,
                          ExtraBlanks, Line, Width, NumBlanks

8. ```
   PROCEDURE Factorial( K: INTEGER ): INTEGER;
   (* Iterative computation of factorial K! *)
   VAR Result: INTEGER;
   BEGIN
      Result := 1;
   ```

```
        FOR I := 1 TO K DO
          Result := Result * I;
        END; (* FOR *)
        RETURN Result;
     END Factorial;
```

9. Change the four Move instructions to: Move(3 * Power(3, K));

10. T2A, T2B, and T2C have access to each other and to T1, T2, and T3 when they should not! Likewise T3A and T3B have access to each other and to T1, T2, and T3 when they should not!

12.
```
    PROCEDURE Ackerman( X, Y: CARDINAL ): CARDINAL;
    BEGIN
      IF X = 0 THEN
        RETURN Y + 1;
      ELSIF Y = 0 THEN
        RETURN Ackerman( X - 1, 1 );
      ELSE
        RETURN Ackerman( X - 1, Ackerman( X, Y - 1 ) );
      END; (* IF *)
    END Ackerman;
```

14.
```
    PROCEDURE DragonCurve( Size, Level, Sign: INTEGER );
    (* Drawing of dragon curves for levels 1 to 15 *)
    VAR NewSize: INTEGER;
    BEGIN
      IF Level <= 1 THEN
        Move( Size );
      ELSE
        NewSize := TRUNC( FLOAT( Size ) * 0.707 + 0.5 );
        Turn( 45 * Sign );
        DragonCurve( NewSize, Level - 1, 1 );
        Turn( -90 * Sign );
        DragonCurve( NewSize, Level - 1, -1 );
        Turn( 45 * Sign );
      END; (* IF *)
    END DragonCurve;
```

Chapter 8

1. Add the following declarations and modify procedure InputPoint in the way indicated.
```
    CONST MinX = -340.0;  MaxX = 340.0;
          MinY = -238.0;  MaxY = 238.0;
          .
          .

    PROCEDURE InputPoint( VAR P: Point; I: CARDINAL );
    (*  ....... same comments   .......  *)
    BEGIN
      LOOP
        WriteString( "Enter X coordinate of point " );
        WriteCard( I, 1 ); WriteString( " from " );
```

```
            WriteReal( MinX, 6 ); WriteString( " through " );
            WriteReal( MaxX, 6 ); ReadReal( P.X );
            IF ( MinX <= P.X ) AND ( P.X <= MaxX ) THEN
               EXIT
            END; (* IF *)
         END; (* LOOP *)
         ..... same changes for Y .....
```

2.

```
                    ┌──────────────┐
                    │   Process    │
                    │   accounts   │
                    └──────┬───────┘
          ┌────────────────┼────────────────┐
    ┌─────┴─────┐    ┌─────┴─────┐    ┌─────┴─────┐
    │ Read old  │    │ Process a │    │   Print   │
    │  balance  │    │transaction│    │new balance│
    └───────────┘    └───────────┘    └───────────┘
```

5.

```
                          ┌──────────────┐
                          │  Stylistic   │
                          │   analysis   │
                          └──────┬───────┘
            ┌────────────────────┼────────────────┐
      ┌─────┴─────┐        ┌─────┴─────┐    ┌─────┴─────┐
      │   Text    │        │   Style   │    │   Print   │
      │ analysis  │        │comparison │    │  results  │
      └─────┬─────┘        └─────┬─────┘    └───────────┘
     ┌──────┴──────┐             │
  ┌──┴───┐    ┌────┴────┐   ┌────┴────┐
  │ Read │    │ Compute │   │  Read   │
  │ text │    │percents │   │percents │
  └──────┘    └─────────┘   └─────────┘
```

7. Just modify the statements for the computation of Total and Discount in the following manner:

```
      .
      .
      .
   Discount := 0;
   Total := Total1001 * 250;
   IF Total1001 > 15 THEN
      Discount := 10 * 25 + (Total1001 - 15) * 50;
   ELSIF Total1001 > 5 THEN
      Discount := (Total1001 - 5) * 25;
   END;
      .
      .
      .
```

   Apply the same pattern for Total2001 and Total3001 and accumulate Total and Discount.

9. Add the following to import list and DataInputValidation statements:
      FROM InOut IMPORT .... OpenInput, CloseInput;

```
                    BEGIN (* DataInputValidation *)
                      OpenInput( "data" );
                          .
                          .
                          .
                      CloseInput;
                    END DataInputValidation;
```

10. Add the following declaration:
    ```
    VAR Length1, Length2, Length3: REAL;
    ```
    Modify the main program in the following way:
    ```
                    BEGIN (* Main *)
                      DataInputValidation( Point1, Point2, Point3 );
                      Length1 := Distance( Point1, Point2 );
                      Length2 := Distance( Point1, Point3 );
                      Length3 := Distance( Point2, Point3 );
                      IF CheckSideLength( Length1, Length2, Length3 ) AND
                         CheckHorizLine( Point1, Point2, Point3 )       AND
                         CheckArea( Length1, Length2, Length3 )         THEN
                          .
                          .
                          .
    ```

12. ```
    MODULE QuadraticEquation;
      (* Compute the roots of a given quadratic equation *)
      FROM InOut IMPORT WriteString, WriteLn;
      FROM RealInOut IMPORT ReadReal, WriteReal;
      FROM MathLib0 IMPORT sqrt;

      VAR A, B, C, X1, X2, Real, Imaginary, Discriminant: REAL;

    BEGIN
      WriteString( "Give values of three coefficients: " );
      ReadReal( A ); ReadReal( B ); ReadReal( C ); WriteLn;
      IF ( A = 0 ) THEN
        IF ( B = 0 ) THEN
          WriteString( "Contradiction ") ; WriteReal( C, 6 );
          WriteString( " = 0" ); WriteLn;
        ELSE
          WriteString( "One root: " );
          WriteReal( -C/B, 10 ); WriteLn;
        END; (* IF *)
      ELSE
        Discriminant := B * B - 4.0 * A * C;
        IF ( Discriminant >= 0 ) THEN
          R := sqrt( Discriminant );
          IF ( B = 0 ) THEN
            X1 := R/(2.0 * A);
            X2 := -X1;
    ```
    ```

```
            ELSE
                X1 := -(B + R)/(2.0 * A);
                X2 := C/(A * X1);
            END;  (* IF *)
            WriteString( "Root 1 = " );
            WriteReal( X1, 10 ); WriteLn;
            WriteString( "Root 2 = " );
            WriteReal( X2, 10 ); WriteLn;
        ELSE
            R := sqrt( ABS( Discriminant ) );
            Real := -B/(2.0 * A);
            Imaginary := R/(2.0 * A);
            WriteString( "Complex roots: " );
            WriteReal( Real, 10 );
            WriteString( " +/- " );
            WriteReal( Imaginary, 10 ); WriteLn;
        END;  (* IF *)
    END;  (* IF *)
END QuadraticEquation.
```

Chapter 9

1. ```
   TYPE Family = ( Daddy, Mommy, John, Ann, Michael, Philip );
        Children = [John..Philip];
   ```

2. Not valid, the value Analyst appears in two distinct types.

3. ```
   PROCEDURE Capitalize( VAR Str: STRING );
   VAR CharPos: CARDINAL;
   BEGIN
       FOR CharPos := 0 TO Length( Str ) - 1 DO
           AssignChar( CAP( FetchChar( Str, CharPos ) ), Str,
                       CharPos );
       END;  (* FOR *)
   END Capitalize;
   ```

4. ```
   TYPE Stats = RECORD
                    Occurrence: CARDINAL;
                    PerCent    : REAL
                END;
   VAR StatsTable: ARRAY Alphabet OF Stats;
   ```

   This array of records would be the single array parameter to TextAnalysis, ReadScanText (which will not use the REAL field).

5. ```
   MODULE PrintTable;
   FROM InOut IMPORT Write, WriteCard, WriteString, WriteLn;
   CONST Length = 50;

   PROCEDURE PrintOctal( N, W: CARDINAL );
   VAR Octal: ARRAY [1..Length] OF CHAR;
       I: CARDINAL;
   ```

```
            BEGIN
              FOR I := W TO 1 BY -1 DO
                IF N # 0 THEN
                  Octal[I] := CHR( ORD( '0' ) + N MOD 8 );
                  N := N DIV 8;
                ELSE
                  Octal[I] := ' ';
                END; (* IF *)
              END; (* FOR *)
              FOR I := 1 TO W DO
                Write(Octal[I]);
              END; (* FOR *)
            END PrintOctal;

            VAR Ch: CHAR;
            BEGIN
              FOR Ch := ' ' TO '}' DO
                WriteCard( ORD( Ch ), 3 );
                WriteString( "   " );
                PrintOctal( ORD( Ch ), 3 );
                WriteString( "   " );
                Write( Ch ); WriteLn;
              END; (* FOR *)
            END PrintTable.
```

6. The statement should be: RETURN CHR(ORD('a') + ORD(Ch) - ORD('A'))

7. No, because we cannot apply that transformation to characters other than capital letters; if we do, we will get unexpected results. The IF statement is still needed.

8. Add a special counter for spaces, and a test in ReadScanText to update that counter. Add statements to compute the percentage for spaces in TextAnalysis. Add statements to read space percentage and update SumOfSquares in StyleComparison. Add statements in BarScale to consider spaces. Add statements to print spaces bar in BarChart.

9. Add a counter TotalPerCent in which each percentage read is accumulated. After all percentages have been read, check that counter to see if it is greater than 100, and if so write an appropriate message; otherwise compute the closeness value.

10.
```
       TYPE Complex = RECORD
                        Re, Im: REAL
                      END;
       PROCEDURE Furthest( Points: ARRAY OF Complex ): REAL;
       VAR MaxDistance, Distance: REAL;
           I: CARDINAL;
       BEGIN
         MaxDistance := 0.0;
         FOR I := 0 TO HIGH( Points ) DO
           Distance := sqrt( Points[I].Re * Points[I].Re +
                             Points[I].Im * Points[I].Im );
           IF Distance > MaxDistance THEN
```

```
        MaxDistance := Distance;
      END; (* IF *)
    END; (* FOR *)
    RETURN MaxDistance;
  END Furthest;
```

13.
```
MODULE TestEncrypt;
(* Test of Encrypt procedure *)
FROM InOut IMPORT WriteString, WriteLn, ReadString;
FROM Strings IMPORT STRING;
VAR Code: STRING;
(* Procedure Encrypt goes here *)
BEGIN
  LOOP
    WriteString( "Enter a number to encrypt:" );
    ReadString( Code ); WriteLn;
    IF StringEqual( Code, "" ) THEN EXIT END;
    Encrypt( Code );
    WriteString( "Encoded string is: " );
    WriteString( Code ); WriteLn;
  END; (* LOOP *)
END TestEncrypt.
```

18.
```
PROCEDURE Age( TMonth, TDay, TYear, BMonth, BDay,
               BYear: CARDINAL;
               VAR Years, Months: CARDINAL );
BEGIN
  Years := TYear - BYear;
  IF TMonth < BMonth THEN
    Years := Years - 1;
    Months := 12 - ( BMonth - TMonth );
  ELSE
    Months := TMonth - BMonth;
  END; (* IF *)
END Age;
```

20.
```
TYPE Point = RECORD
               X, Y: REAL
             END;
     Triangle = ARRAY [1..3] OF Point;
```

In procedures CheckSideLength, CheckArea, and CheckHorizLine, replace the parameters by Candidate: Triangle. In the statements of these procedures replace: Point1 by Candidate[1]
          Point2 by Candidate[2]
          Point3 by Candidate[3]

In main program declare Possible: Triangle; then replace Point1 by Possible[1], Point2 by Possible[2], Point3 by Possible[3].

Chapter 10

1.  ```
    PROCEDURE ReadBoolean( VAR X: BOOLEAN );
    (* Reads in a Boolean value X *)
    VAR Ch: CHAR;
    BEGIN
      Read( Ch );
      WHILE Ch = ' ' DO
        Read( Ch );
      END; (* WHILE *)
      X := ( Ch = 'T' ) OR ( Ch = 't' );
      WHILE ( Ch # ' ' ) AND ( Ch # EOL ) DO
        Read( Ch );
      END; (* WHILE *)
    END ReadBoolean;

    PROCEDURE WriteBoolean( X: BOOLEAN; W: CARDINAL );
    (* Prints TRUE or FALSE or T or F based on size W *)
    VAR I: CARDINAL;
    BEGIN
      IF W > 5 THEN
        FOR I := 1 TO W - 5 DO
          Write( ' ' );
        END; (* FOR *)
        IF X THEN
          WriteString( "TRUE" );
        ELSE
          WriteString( "FALSE" );
        END; (* IF *)
      ELSE
        FOR I := 1 TO W - 1 DO
          Write( ' ' );
        END; (* FOR *)
        IF X THEN Write( 'T' )
        ELSE Write( 'F' )
        END; (* IF *)
      END; (* IF *)
    END WriteBoolean;
    ```

2.  ```
    PROCEDURE OpenToAppend( FileName: STRING );
    VAR F: File;
        Ch: CHAR;
    BEGIN
      Lookup( F, FileName, FALSE );
      REPEAT
        ReadChar( F, Ch );
      UNTIL F.eof;
    END OpenToAppend;
    ```

11. ```
    PROCEDURE MergeArrays( Table1, Table2: ARRAY OF INTEGER;
                           VAR Table3: ARRAY OF INTEGER );
    VAR Index1, Index2, Index3: CARDINAL;
    ```
    ```

```
            PROCEDURE CopyRest( Source: ARRAY OF INTEGER;
                                Ind: CARDINAL;
                                VAR Dest: ARRAY OF INTEGER;
                                Index: CARDINAL );
            VAR I: CARDINAL;
            BEGIN
              FOR I := Ind TO HIGH( Source ) DO
                Dest[Index] := Source[I];
                INC( Index );
              END; (* FOR *)
            END CopyRest;

            BEGIN
              Index1 := 0;
              Index2 := 0;
              Index3 := 0;
              IF Index1 <= HIGH( Table1 ) THEN
                IF Index2 <= HIGH( Table2 ) THEN
                  LOOP
                    IF Table1[Index1] < Table2[Index2] THEN
                      Table3[Index3] := Table1[Index1];
                      INC( Index1 ); INC( Index3 );
                      IF Index1 > HIGH( Table1 ) THEN
                        CopyRest( Table2, Index2, Table3, Index3 );
                        EXIT;
                      END; (* IF *)
                    ELSE
                      Table3[Index3] := Table2[Index2];
                      INC( Index2 ); INC( Index3 );
                      IF Index2 > HIGH( Table2 ) THEN
                        CopyRest( Table1, Index1, Table3, Index3 );
                        EXIT;
                      END; (* IF *)
                    END; (* IF *)
                  END; (* LOOP *)
                ELSE
                  CopyRest( Table1, Index1, Table3, Index3 );
                END; (* IF *)
              ELSE
                IF Index2 <= HIGH( Table2 ) THEN
                  CopyRest( Table2, Index2, Table3, Index3 );
                END; (* IF *)
              END; (* IF *)
            END MergeArrays;

         12. MODULE Personalize;
             FROM FileSystem IMPORT Lookup, ReadChar, Close, File,
                                    Response, Reset;
             FROM InOut IMPORT WriteString, WriteLn, EOL, OpenOutput,
                         CloseOutput;
```

```
FROM Strings IMPORT STRING, ReadLine, StringEqual,
                    AssignChar, Assign;

CONST Max = 79;
VAR F1, F2: File;
    LetterFile, AddressFile, Symbol, Name, Ad1,
    Ad2, Ad3: STRING;
    Ch: CHAR;

PROCEDURE ReadString( VAR S: STRING; VAR EndChar: CHAR );
VAR Index: CARDINAL;
BEGIN
  Index := 0;
  LOOP
    ReadChar( F1, EndChar );
    IF ( F1.eof ) OR (EndChar = ' ' )
      OR ( EndChar = EOL ) THEN EXIT END;
    AssignChar( EndChar, S, Index );
    INC( Index );
  END; (* LOOP *)
  AssignChar( 0C, S, Index );
END ReadString;

PROCEDURE ReadLn( VAR Line: STRING );
VAR Index: CARDINAL;
    Ch: CHAR;
BEGIN
  Index := 0;
  LOOP
    ReadChar( F2, Ch );
    IF ( F2.eof ) OR ( Ch = EOL )
      OR (Index > Max ) THEN EXIT END;
    AssignChar( Ch, Line, Index );
    INC( Index );
  END; (* LOOP *)
  IF Index <= Max THEN
    AssignChar( 0C, Line, Index );
  End; (* IF *)
END ReadLn;

PROCEDURE OpenFile( Prompt: STRING;
                    VAR SystemFileName: STRING;
                    VAR FileName: File );
BEGIN
  LOOP
    WriteString( Prompt );
    ReadLine( SystemFileName, TRUE );
    Lookup( FileName, SystemFileName, FALSE );
    IF FileName.res = done THEN
      EXIT;
```

```
              ELSE
                WriteString( "file does not exist, try again" );
                WriteLn;
              END; (* IF *)
            END; (* LOOP *)
          END OpenFile;

        BEGIN (* Personalize *)
          OpenFile( "letter file: ", LetterFile, F1 );
          OpenFile( "address file: ", AddressFile, F2 );
          OpenOutput( "" );
          LOOP
            IF F2.eof THEN EXIT END;
            Name := "                                          ";
            Ad1  := "                                          ";
            Ad2  := "                                          ";
            Ad3  := "                                          ";
            ReadLn( Name );
            IF StringEqual( Name, "" ) THEN EXIT END;
            ReadLn( Ad1 );
            ReadLn( Ad2 );
            ReadLn( Ad3 );
            WHILE NOT F1.eof DO
              Symbol := "                                       ";
              ReadString( Symbol, Ch );
              IF StringEqual( Symbol, "<name>" ) THEN
                Assign( Symbol, Name );
              ELSIF StringEqual( Symbol, "<address>" ) THEN
                WriteString( Ad1 ); WriteLn;
                WriteString( Ad2 ); WriteLn;
                Assign( Symbol, Ad3 );
                Ch := EOL;
              END; (* IF *)
              WriteString( Symbol ); WriteString( ' ' );
              IF Ch = EOL THEN
                WriteLn;
              END; (* IF *)
            END; (* WHILE *)
            WriteLn; WriteLn; WriteLn;
            Close( F1 );
            Lookup( F1, LetterFile, FALSE );
          END; (* LOOP *)
          Close( F1 ); Close( F2 ); CloseOutput;
        END Personalize.
```

Chapter 11

1. MODULE Dates;
   FROM InOut IMPORT WriteString, WriteCard, WriteLn;

```
FROM Strings IMPORT STRING, Pos, Length, Delete,
                    Copy, Concat, InitString, Assign,
                    ReadLine, ToString;

CONST CommaChar = ',';
VAR Line, Comma: STRING;

PROCEDURE SwitchDate( VAR Date: STRING );
(* accepts dates as 4 July 1776, and returns July
   4, 1776 *)
CONST Space = ' ';
VAR Day, Month, Year: STRING;
    BlankPosition: CARDINAL;
    Blank: STRING;

BEGIN
  ToString( Space, Blank );
  BlankPosition := Pos( Blank, Date );
  IF BlankPosition = Length( Date ) THEN
    WriteString( "Error in date format" );
    Delete( Date, 0, Length( Date ) )
  ELSE
    Copy( Date, 0, BlankPosition, Day );
    Delete( Date, 0, BlankPosition + 1 );
    BlankPosition := Pos( Blank, Date );
    IF BlankPosition = Length( Date ) THEN
      WriteString( "Error in date format" );
      Delete( Date, 0, Length( Date ) );
    ELSE
      Copy( Date, 0, BlankPosition + 1, Month );
      Delete( Date, 0, BlankPosition + 1 );
      Assign( Year, Date );
      InitString( Date );
      Concat( Date, Month, Date );
      Concat( Date, Day, Date );
      Concat( Date, ", ", Date );
      Concat( Date, Year, Date );
    END; (* IF *)
  END; (* IF *)
END SwitchDate;

BEGIN (* Dates *)
  ToString( CommaChar, Comma );
  LOOP
    WriteString( "> " );
    ReadLine( Line, TRUE );
    IF Length( Line ) = 0 THEN EXIT END;
    IF Pos( Comma, Line ) = Length( Line ) THEN
      SwitchDate( Line );
```

```
           END;  (* IF *)
           WriteString( Line );
           WriteLn;
        END;  (* LOOP *)
     END Dates.

2. PROCEDURE JustifyLine( VAR Line: STRING );
   VAR I: CARDINAL;
   BEGIN
      I := Length( Line );
      REPEAT
         I := I - 1;
      UNTIL FetchChar( Line, I ) # ' ';
      Delete( Line, I + 1, Length( Line ) - I - 1 );
      IF ( Length( Line ) < JustifiedWidth ) AND
         ( Length( line ) >= MinimumWidth ) THEN
            InsertSpaces( Line );
      END;  (* IF *)
   END JustifyLine;
```

3. Modify InsertSpaces in the following way (FindNextGap and CountGaps are not changed).

```
        PROCEDURE InsertSpaces( VAR Line: STRING; Left: BOOLEAN);
          .
          .
          .
        BEGIN (* InsertSpaces *)
          NumberOfGaps := CountGaps( Line );
          IF NumberOfGaps > 0 THEN
            CurrPosition := 0;
            SpacesPerGap :=
               ( JustifiedWidth - Length( Line ) ) DIV NumberOfGaps;
            ExtraBlank :=
               ( JustifiedWidth - Length( Line ) ) MOD NumberOfGaps;
          IF Left THEN
          Copy( Spaces, 0, SpacesPerGap + 1, StringOfSpaces );
          FOR Count := 1 TO ExtraBlank DO
            FindNextGap( Line, CurrPosition );
            Insert( StringOfSpaces, Line, CurrPosition );
          END; (* FOR *)
          Delete( StringOfSpaces, 0, 1 );
          FOR Count := ExtraBlank + 1 TO NumberOfGaps DO
            FindNextGap( Line, CurrPosition );
            Insert( StringOfSpaces, Line, CurrPosition );
          END; (* FOR *)
          ELSE
            Copy( Spaces, 0, SpacesPerGap, StringOfSpaces );
            FOR Count := 1 TO NumberOfGaps - ExtraBlank DO
              FindNextGap( Line, CurrPosition );
              Insert( StringOfSpaces, Line, CurrPosition );
```

```
            END; (* FOR *)
            Insert( " ", StringOfSpaces, 0 );
            FOR Count :=
              NumberOfGaps - ExtraBlank + 1 TO NumberOfGaps DO
                FindNextGap( Line, CurrPosition );
                Insert( StringOfSpaces, Line, CurrPosition );
            END; (* FOR *)
          END; (* IF *)
        END; (* IF *)
      END InsertSpaces;
```

5.  ```
    DEFINITION MODULE NumeralArithmetic;
      CONST EON = '.'; (* End of Numeral character using ASCII *)
      TYPE Numeral = ARRAY [1..20] OF ['+'..'9'];
      (* In ASCII, we have to include + and -, and will use the
         period whose code follows '-', to indicate the end of a
         numeral. Another character set will require different
         definitions *)
      PROCEDURE Add( X, Y: Numeral; VAR Z: Numeral );
      (* Add two numerals X and Y *)
      PROCEDURE Subtract( X, Y: Numeral: VAR Z: Numeral );
      (* Subtract two numerals Y from X *)
      PROCEDURE Multiply( X, Y: Numeral; VAR Z: Numeral );
      (* Multiply two numerals X and Y *)
      PROCEDURE Divide( X, Y: Numeral; VAR Z: Numeral );
      (* Divide two numerals X by Y *)
    END NumeralArithmetic.
    ```

11. ```
    DEFINITION MODULE PasswordSystem;
    (* Implementation of a system of passwords *)

      PROCEDURE ValidPassword ( Name,
               Password: ARRAY OF CHAR ): BOOLEAN;
      (* Validation of the pair Name and Password.
         Returns TRUE if the Name is present and the
         Password matches; otherwise returns FALSE  *)

      PROCEDURE ChangePassword( Name: ARRAY OF CHAR );
      (* Change password by owner of password *)

    END PasswordSystem.
    ```

12. ```
    PROCEDURE Ordered( V: Vector; N: CARDINAL ): BOOLEAN;
    VAR Order: BOOLEAN;
        I: CARDINAL;
    BEGIN
      Order := TRUE;
      FOR I := 1 TO N - 1 DO
        Order := ( V[I] < V[I + 1] ) AND Order;
      END; (* FOR *)
    ```
    ```

```
            RETURN Order;
         END Ordered;
13.   TYPE Vector = ARRAY [1..Max] OF INTEGER;
      PROCEDURE AddElement( Value: INTEGER; N: CARDINAL;
                            VAR V: Vector );
                            VAR I, J: CARDINAL;

         PROCEDURE Search( V: Vector; N: CARDINAL;
                           Value: INTEGER ): CARDINAL;
                           VAR Found: BOOLEAN;
                               I: CARDINAL;
         BEGIN
           Found := FALSE;
           I := 0;
           WHILE ( I < N ) AND NOT Found DO
             I := I + 1;
             Found := Value < V[I];
           END; (* WHILE *)
           IF Found THEN
             RETURN I;
           ELSE
             RETURN 0;
           END; (* IF *)
         END Search;

      BEGIN
        IF N = Max THEN
          WriteString( "Vector is full" );
          RETURN;
        ELSE
          I := Search( V, N, Value );
          IF I # 0 THEN
            FOR J := N TO I BY -1 DO
              V[J + 1] := V[J];
            END; (* FOR *)
            V[I] := Value;
          ELSE
            V[N + 1] := Value;
          END; (* IF *)
        END; (* IF *)
      END AddElement;

14.   TYPE Vector = ARRAY [1..Max] OF INTEGER;
      PROCEDURE Median( V: Vector; N: CARDINAL ): INTEGER;
      (* Procedure Ordered goes here *)
      BEGIN (* Median *)
        IF Ordered( V, N ) THEN
          IF ODD( N ) THEN
            RETURN V[N DIV 2 + 1]
          ELSE
```

```
                RETURN ( V[N DIV 2] + V[N DIV 2 + 1] ) DIV 2
            END;  (* IF *)
        ELSE
            WriteString( "Vector not ordered" );
            RETURN 0;
        END;  (* IF *)
    END Median;
```

Chapter 12

1.  ```
    TYPE Bus = RECORD
                   Origin, Destination: STRING;
                   DepartureTime, ArrivalTime: CARDINAL;
               END;
         Schedule = ARRAY [1..100] OF Bus;
    ```

2.  ```
    TYPE Course = RECORD
                      Number, Place, Description: STRING;
                      Time: ARRAY[1..3] OF RECORD
                                              Day:  ( Sun,
                                                      Mon,
                                                      Tue,
                                                      Wed,
                                                      Thu,
                                                      Fri,
                                                      Sat );
                                              Hour: CARDINAL;
                                          END;
                  END;
    ```

3. Replace assignment statement in loop by:
    ```
    List[I].Balance := List[I].Balance +
             ( List[I].Balance * PerCent + 500 ) DIV 1000;
    ```

4. Alter procedure heading to:
    ```
    PROCEDURE LinearSearch(Arr: ARRAY OF Info;
                           SearchKey: KeyType;
                           VAR Index: CARDINAL;
                           VAR Success: BOOLEAN);
    ```

    Add after END; (* WHILE *):
    ```
      Success := Index # ( Last + 1 );
    ```

5.  ```
    WHILE ( Index < Last + 1 ) AND
          ( Arr[Index].Key < SearchKey ) DO
            INC( Index );
    END;  (* WHILE *)
    ```

6. $n/2$

7. An array of one element will make the algorithm fail as Middle is not initialized.

8.  ```
    LOOP
        Middle := ( Last + First ) DIV 2;
        IF Last <= First THEN EXIT END;
    ```

```
END;  (* LOOP *)
```

9. In a binary search the procedure reduces the size of the table, so that we never exceed the limits of the table. On the other hand, in a linear search we must be sure to examine sequentially all elements. We increase the index automatically so that it ends up beyond the array's last position.

10. Years IN { 2, 4, 6, 8, 10 }
    Ch IN Letters{ 'I'..'N' }

11. B IN Numbers{ 10..20 } OR
    B IN Numbers{ 30..40 } OR
    B IN Numbers{ 52..81 } OR
    B IN Numbers{ 89..99 }
    Note that you might have to use several sets depending on your implementation.

12. ```
    DEFINITION Module BagType;

        TYPE Bag = RECORD
                    Number: CARDINAL;
                    Set: ARRAY [1..Max] OF CARDINAL;
                  END;
        PROCEDURE Member( X: CARDINAL; Y: Bag ): BOOLEAN;
        PROCEDURE Include( X: CARDINAL; VAR Y: Bag );
        PROCEDURE Exclude( X: CARDINAL; VAR Y: Bag );
        PROCEDURE Union( X,Y: Bag; VAR Z: Bag );
        PROCEDURE Intersection( X, Y: Bag; VAR Z: Bag );
    END BagType;
    ```

15. ```
    PROCEDURE FindPosition( A: Vector;
                            Index, KeyValue: INTEGER;
                            VAR Position: INTEGER );
    (* Binary search of vector A [1..Index] for position where
       to insert KeyValue *)
    VAR Left, Right, Middle: INTEGER;
    BEGIN
      Left := 1;
      Right := Index;
      WHILE Left <= Right DO           (* Compare middle element *)
         Middle := ( Left + Right ) DIV 2;
         IF KeyValue < A[Middle].Key THEN
            Right := Middle - 1         (* Keep lower half *)
         ELSE
            Left := Middle + 1   (* Keep upper half *)
         END
      END;
      Position := Left                  (* Position where to insert *)
    END FindPosition;
    ```

Chapter 13

1. (a) $O(n)$
   (b) $O(n^3)$
   (c) $O(n^5)$

3. Add:
```
PROCEDURE Median( A, B, C: INTEGER ): INTEGER;
BEGIN
  IF A <= B THEN
    IF B <= C THEN
      RETURN B;
    ELSE
      RETURN C;
    END;
  ELSIF A <= C THEN
    RETURN A;
  ELSIF B <= C THEN
    RETURN C;
  ELSE
    RETURN B;
  END;
END Median;
```

Replace the assignment to Pivot by:
```
Pivot :=
  Median( A[Left], A[( Left + Right ) DIV 2], A[Right] );
```

7. In analyzing BubbleSort, we notice that each pass involves a diminishing number of comparisons, from $n - 1$ on the first to 1 on the last, where n is the number of elements in the array. So the procedure does

$$1 + 2 + \ldots + (n - 1) = \frac{(n - 1)n}{2} \text{ comparisons.}$$

For moves, the worst possible case for BubbleSort is when it starts with an array in reverse order; it then takes $n - 1$ swaps for the first pass, $n - 2$ for the second, down to 1 for the last. Thus the number of swaps for the worst case is also

$$\frac{(n - 1)(n - 2)}{2}$$

and the number of moves is three times as many. The average number of moves is half this amount, or

$$\frac{3(n - 1)(n - 2)}{4}$$

Thus the number of comparisons and the number of moves, and hence the execution time, are proportional to n squared.

8. If the array is already sorted, we need only one pass which makes the algorithm $O(n)$, but in the worst case we still have the same number of passes as the straight Bubble Sort, and the algorithm is after all $O(n^2)$.

10. (a) Since IndexOfSmallest = 0 and I = 1 the first part of the assertion becomes: A[0] <= A[0] which is obviously true. The second part of the assertion will always be true since we are using a FOR loop: I < N + 1 inside the loop since the terminating condition is I > N.

   (b) Assume the loop invariant is true before the loop body is executed:
   (A[IndexOfSmallest] <= A[0]..A[I − 1]) AND (I < N + 1).

Let us prove it is true after the loop body is executed. The effect of executing the statement in the loop body is such that:

- if the condition A[I] < A[IndexOfSmallest] is true then the first part of the assertion gives A[I] < A[IndexOfSmallest] <= A[0]..A[I − 1], and the execution of the assignment statement gives IndexOfSmallest = I, therefore A[I] <= A[0]..A[I − 1] and certainly A[I] <= A[0]..A[I] or A[IndexOfSmallest] <= A[0]..A[I]

- if the condition is false, nothing is done and we know that A[I] >= A[IndexOfSmallest], which added to the original assertion gives A[IndexOfSmallest] <= A[0]..A[I]

- the second part of the assertion remains true as neither I nor N is changed

(c) The last time the loop is executed I = N, so at the end of this last execution, according to (b), we have: A[IndexOfSmallest] <= A[0]..A[N] AND I < N + 1

12.
```
    PROCEDURE BubbleSort( VAR A:  ARRAY OF INTEGER );
    (* The array A is sorted into increasing order *)
    VAR I, J: CARDINAL;
        Temp: INTEGER;
    BEGIN
      FOR I := HIGH( A ) TO 1 BY -1 DO
        FOR J := 1 TO I DO
          IF A[J - 1] > A[J] THEN
            Temp := A[J];
            A[J] := A[J - 1];
            A[J - 1] := Temp
          END (* IF *)
        END (* FOR *)
      END (* FOR *)
    END BubbleSort;
```

Chapter 14

1. 73, 224, 1023 = $2^{10} - 1$

2. 1111011, 1111101000, 111111111111

3. (a) 4 digits
   (b) 6 digits

4. $2^{31} - 1$ = 2,147,483,647
   -2^{31} = −2,147,483,648

5. 000   0
   001   1
   010   2
   011   3
   100   −4
   101   −3
   110   −2
   111   −1

6. Values in [32768..65535]

8. ```
PROCEDURE Sine(X: REAL): REAL;
CONST Epsilon = 1.0E-6;
VAR Num, Denom, SineX, N, Term: REAL;

BEGIN
  N := 1.0;
  Denom := 1.0;
  Num := X;
  SineX := X;
  LOOP
    N := N + 2.0;
    Num := -Num * X * X;
    Denom := Denom * N * (N - 1.0);
    Term := Num / Denom;
    IF Term < Epsilon THEN EXIT END;
    SineX := SineX + Term;
  END; (* LOOP *)
  RETURN SineX;
END Sine;
```

9. ```
PROCEDURE ArcTan( X: REAL ): REAL;
CONST Epsilon = 1.0E-6;
      Pi = 3.1415926535;
VAR ArctanX, Num, N, Term: REAL;

BEGIN
  Num := -1.0;
  ArctanX := Pi / 2.0;
  N := 1.0;
  LOOP
    Term := Num / ( N * Power( X, N ) );
    IF ABS( Term ) < Epsilon THEN EXIT END;
    ArctanX := ArctanX + Term;
    N := N + 2.0;
    Num := -Num;
  END; (* LOOP *)
  RETURN ArctanX;
END ArcTan;
```

20. ```
PROCEDURE RandomWord;
VAR N, I: CARDINAL;
BEGIN
  N := 1 + TRUNC(10.0 * Random());
  FOR I := 1 TO N DO
    Write(CHR(ORD('a') + TRUNC(26.0 * Random())));
  END; (* FOR *)
  WriteLn;
END RandomWord;
```

21. ```
PROCEDURE PrintWord;
VAR T: ARRAY [0..80] OF CHAR;
    I: CARDINAL;
```

Answers to Selected Exercises

```
BEGIN
  T[0]:='a';T[1]:='e';T[2]:='h';T[3]:='i';T[4]:='n';
  T[5]:='o';T[6]:='r';T[7]:='s';T[8]:='t';
  T[9]:='d';T[10]:='f';T[11]:='l';T[12]:='m';
  T[13]:='u';T[14]:='w';T[15]:='y';
  T[16]:='b';T[17]:='c';T[18]:='g';T[19]:='k';
  T[20]:='p';T[21]:='v';
  T[22]:='a';T[23]:='e';T[24]:='h';T[25]:='i';T[26]:='n';
  T[27]:='o';T[28]:='r';T[29]:='s';T[30]:='t';
  T[31]:='a';T[32]:='e';T[33]:='h';T[34]:='i';T[35]:='n';
  T[36]:='o';T[37]:='r';T[38]:='s';T[39]:='t';
  T[40]:='d';T[41]:='f';T[42]:='l';T[43]:='m';
  T[44]:='u';T[45]:='w';T[46]:='y';
  T[47]:='a';T[48]:='e';T[49]:='h';T[50]:='i';T[51]:='n';
  T[52]:='o';T[53]:='r';T[54]:='s';T[55]:='t';
  T[56]:='a';T[57]:='e';T[58]:='h';T[59]:='i';T[60]:='n';
  T[61]:='o';T[62]:='r';T[63]:='s';T[64]:='t';
  T[65]:='d';T[66]:='f';T[67]:='l';T[68]:='m';
  T[69]:='u';T[70]:='w';T[71]:='y';
  T[72]:='a';T[73]:='e';T[74]:='h';T[75]:='i';T[76]:='n';
  T[77]:='o';T[78]:='r';T[79]:='s';T[80]:='t';
  FOR I := 1 TO 4 DO
    Write( T[TRUNC( 81.0 * Random() )] );
  END;
  WriteLn;
END PrintWord;
```

Note: There are many other approaches to solving this problem, including the use of the CASE statement with the selector being a random number.

Chapter 15

1. BBB

2.
```
   TYPE Point = POINTER TO Node;
        Character = RECORD
                      Ch: CHAR;
                      Pt: POINTER TO Character;
                    END;
        Node = RECORD
                 P1: POINTER TO Character;
                 P2: Point
               END;
   VAR CharList: Point;
     .
     .
     .
   ALLOCATE( CharList, SIZE( Node ) );
   ALLOCATE( CharList^.P1, SIZE( Character ) );
   CharList^.P1^.Ch := 'H';
```

```
           ALLOCATE( CharList^.P1^.Pt, SIZE( Character ) );
           CharList^.P1^.Pt^.Ch := 'A';
           ALLOCATE( CharList^.P1^.Pt^.Pt, SIZE( Character ) );
           CharList^.P1^.Pt^.Pt^.Ch := 'C';
           ALLOCATE( CharList^.P1^.Pt^.Pt^.Pt, SIZE( Character ) );
           CharList^.P1^.Pt^.Pt^.Pt^.Ch := 'K';
           CharList^.P1^.Pt^.Pt^.Pt^.Pt := NIL;
           ALLOCATE( CharList^.P2, SIZE( Node ) );
           CharList^.P2^.P2 := NIL;
           ALLOCATE( CharList^.P2^.P1, SIZE( Character ) );
           CharList^.P2^.P1^.Ch := 'N';
           ALLOCATE( CharList^.P2^.P1^.Pt, SIZE( Character ) );
           CharList^.P2^.P1^.Pt^.Ch := 'O';
           ALLOCATE( CharList^.P2^.P1^.Pt^.Pt, SIZE( Character ) );
           CharList^.P2^.P1^.Pt^.Pt^.Ch := 'T';
           CharList^.P2^.P1^.Pt^.Pt^.Pt := NIL;
```

3. `.Count( List )`
    `..Count( List^.Link )`
    `...Count( List^.Link^.Link )`
    `....Count( List^.Link^.Link^.Link )`
    `.....Count( List^.Link^.Link^.Link^.Link )`
    `......Count( List^.Link^.Link^.Link^.Link^.Link )`
    `......Return 0`
    `.....Return 1 + 0`
    `....Return 1 + 1 + 0`
    `...Return 1 + 1 + 1 + 0`
    `..Return 1 + 1 + 1 + 1 + 0`
    `.Return 1 + 1 + 1 + 1 + 1 + 0`

4.  ```
    PROCEDURE Count( L: NodePtr ): CARDINAL;
    VAR N: CARDINAL;
    BEGIN
      N := 0;
      WHILE L # NIL DO
        N := N + 1;
        L := L^.LINK;
      END; (* WHILE *)
      RETURN N;
    END Count;
    ```

5. `.InsertElement( 12, Tree )`
    `..InsertElement( 12, Tree^.Right )`
    `...InsertElement( 12, Tree^.Right^.Left )`
    `....InsertElement( 12, Tree^.Right^.Left^.Right )`
    `....Create new node with value 12`
    `....Return`
    `...Return`
    `..Return`
    `.Return`
    ```

6. ```
    PROCEDURE DescendingOrder( Tree: NodePtr );
    BEGIN
      IF Tree # NIL THEN
        DescendingOrder( Tree^.Right );
        WriteInt( Tree^.Info ); WriteLn;
        DescendingOrder( Tree^.Left );
      END; (* IF *)
    END DescendingOrder;
```

7. ```
    TYPE String = POINTER TO Node;
         Node = RECORD
                  Characters: ARRAY [0..79] OF CHAR;
                  Link: String;
                END;
```

12. ```
    PROCEDURE Length( S: String ): CARDINAL;
    VAR N, I: CARDINAL;
    BEGIN
      N := 0;
      WHILE S^.Link # NIL DO
        N := N + 80;
        S := S^.Link;
      END; (* WHILE *)
      I := 0;
      WHILE ( I < 80 ) AND ( S^.Characters[I] # 0C ) DO
        INC( I );
      END; (* WHILE *)
      RETURN N + I;
    END Length;
```

13. ```
    PROCEDURE Length( S: String ): CARDINAL;
      PROCEDURE Count( aNode: String ): CARDINAL;
      VAR I: CARDINAL;
      BEGIN
        I := 0;
        WHILE ( I < 80 ) AND ( aNode^.Characters[I] # 0C ) DO
          INC( I );
        END; (* WHILE *)
        RETURN I
      END Count;
    VAR N: CARDINAL;
    BEGIN
      N := 0;
      WHILE S^.Link # NIL DO
        N := N + Count( S );
        S := S^.Link;
      END; (* WHILE *)
      N := N + Count( S );
      RETURN N;
    END Length;
```

Chapter 16

1.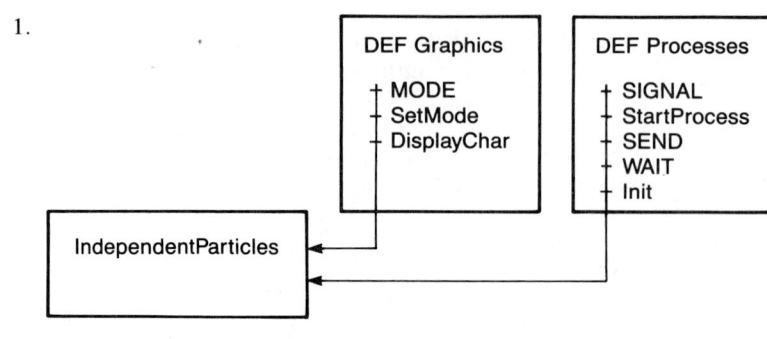

2.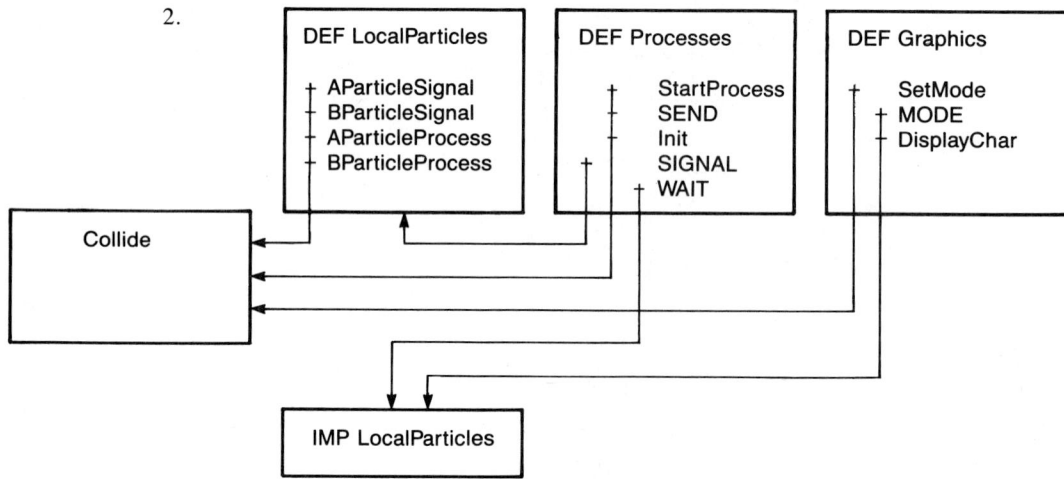

3.  ```
    PROCEDURE MoveParticle( C: CHAR;
                            VAR P, Delta: OrderedPair );
         .
         .
         .
    (* change statements in case of bounce *)
        Delta.X := -0.75 * Delta.X;
         .
         .
         .
        Delta.Y := -0.75 * Delta.Y;
         .
         .
         .
    PROCEDURE CheckCollision;
         .
         .
         .
    ```
    ```

```
(* add after calls to Swap *)
   DeltaA.X := 0.8 * DeltaA.X;
   DeltaA.Y := 0.8 * DeltaA.Y;
   DeltaB.X := DeltaB.X * 0.8;
   DeltaB.Y := DeltaB.Y * 0.8;
```

Index

ABS standard function, 136, A23
Absolute error, 413
Abstract data type, 152, 197, 272, 286, 290, 420
Abstraction, 203
AccumulateSummaryData procedure, 198
Accuracy, 402–404, 413
Actual parameter, 61, 63, 67, 74, 241
Ada, 12, 198, 259, 260, 285, 286, 443, 444, 465–467
Addition, 133, 134
AddPoints procedure, 155
Address, 425
ADDRESS type, A28
ADR function, A29
ALGOL-60, 163, 198, 258, 285, 466
ALGOL-68, 467
Algorithm, 6, 11, 364
   analysis, 373, 381
   complexity, 367, 376, 381
   intractable, 377
Aliasing, 429
ALLOCATE procedure, 426, 430, A28
AlmostEqualRelative function, 415
Analysis of algorithms, 373, 381
AND operator, 141
AngleConversion module, 71
Anonymous type, 149, 233
AParticleProcess procedure, 447, 451
arctan function, 137, A27
Argument, 41
Arithmetic expression, 42, 86, 133
Arithmetic logic unit, 4, 5, 460
Arithmetic operator
   addition, 133, 134
   binary, 134
   division, 133
   multiplication, 133, 134
   subtraction, 133, 134
   unary, 134, 142
Array, 221, 232, 293, 327
   matrix, 238
   open, 244, 293, 337
   vector, 232
ARRAY type, 221, 232, 238, 241
Artificial intelligence, 11, 459, 472
ASCII character set, 222, 294, A1
Assembler, 466
Assembly language, 285, 465, 466
Assertion, 97, 321, 335, 343, 366, 367, 373, 469

Assign procedure, 290, 293, 294, 423, A31
AssignChar procedure, 228, 229, 237, 292, 420, 421, 423, A32
Assignment, 20, 40
   compatible, 149, 234
   statement, 40
Atomic, 345
Automatic range checking, 148
Available function, A29
Average function, 241
AWAITED function, 443, A36
Axiomatic semantics, 469

Backus-Naur form, 466, 468
BarChart module, 65, 66
BarChart procedure, 252
BarScale function, 252
Base case, 107, 365, 378
Base type, 148, 228, 259, 345
Batch processing, 463
BEGIN, 37, 54, 59, 70, 289, 298, 303
Big-O notation, 364, 373–375
Binary
   digit, 133, 285
   number system, 395, 397
   operator, 134
   search, 338
   search tree, 435
   semaphore, 455
   stream, 259
   tree, 434
Bisection function, 415
Bit, 133, 285, 399
BITSET type, 345
Blind search, 478
Block, 163
Block structured language, 163, 167, 175, 466
BNF, 466
Boolean expression, 140, 142, 143, 145
Boolean operator, 141
BOOLEAN type, 39, 139, 226
Bottom-up
   development, 199
   testing, 200, 215
BParticleProcess procedure, 448, 451
Breadth-first search, 478
Buffer, 453, 456
Bug, 48, 101, 202, 208
BusyRead procedure, 266, A27

Index

BY, 83

C, 12, 198, 225, 465–467
Call, 40
CAP standard function, 231, A22
CARDINAL
  type, 39, 136
  type transfer function, 136
CASE, 121, 122, 333, 334
Case
  base, 107, 365, 378
  label, 122
  statement, 121, 122
  variant record, 333, 334
Central processing unit, 5, 461
Change log, 201, 203
Channel, 461
CHAR type, 39, 222
Character
  code, 222, 225, A1
  constant, 223, 225
  set, 222
  string, 23
Chart
  flow, 16, 26, 29
  modular design, 197, 205, 208, 300, 301, 312, 316
  structure, 9, 16, 58–60, 170, 184, 188, 195–197, 204, 244, 305, 313, 350, 383
CheckArea function, 211
CheckCollision procedure, 451
CheckHorizLine function, 212
CheckSideLength function, 211
CheckTitleBox module, 171
CheckTitles module, 69
Chip, 4
CHR standard function, 223, 224, A22
Circle procedure, 287
Classify procedure, 388
Close a file, 53, 268
Close procedure, 272, A35
CloseInput procedure, 54, 264, A24
CloseOutput procedure, 54, 264, A24
CloserThan function, 156
COBOL, 12, 285, 466
Code, 6, 198, 200
Cohesion, 300
Collide module, 452
Comment, 38, 201, 212, 215
Compatible type, 148
Compilation, 35
  error, 48, 49, 52
  separate, 302
  unit, 302

Compiler, 34, 466
Complexity, 364, 367, 373, 376, 381, 390
  big-O, 364, 373–375
  exponential, 376
  polynomial, 376, 377
Computation
  grade average, 235
  Horner's method, 404
  length between points, 236
  rainy days, 236, 239, 240
  series, 401
  trapezoidal rule, 405
Computer, 3
  architecture, 459, 463
  arithmetic, 395, 396
  network, 4, 464
  terminal, 464
Concat procedure, 46, 51, 292, A32
Concatenate module, 46, 51
Concurrent processing, 442, 461–463
CONST, 42, 50, 225
Constant, 38, 42
  expression, 42, 43, 83, 148
Context sensitive, 51, 468
Control character, 223
Control structures, 16, 78
  CASE, 121, 122
  FOR, 82, 83
  IF, 90, 92, 94, 121
  LOOP, 79, 80, 89
  REPEAT, 79, 87, 89
  WHILE, 80, 81, 89
Control unit, 4, 5, 460
Control variable, 83
ConvertAngle function, 71
ConvertAngle module, 43
Copy procedure, 65, 66, 292, 299, A31
CopyFile module, 272
CopyFile procedure, 269
CopyRest procedure, 279
Correctness, 368, 372, 469, 472
cos function, 137, A27
Count function, 434
CountGaps function, 319
CountWords function, 296, 297
Coupling, 300
CPU, 5, 461, 463
Current position, 259, 421
CustomerComp procedure, 359

Data, 12, 199
  flow diagram, 244, 267
  representation, 133, 139, 290, 394, 399, 421
  validation, 13

Data structures, 205
  dynamic, 424, 431, 432
  recursive, 432
Data type, 132
  ARRAY, 221, 232, 238, 241
  BITSET, 345
  BOOLEAN, 39, 139, 226
  CARDINAL, 39, 136
  CHAR, 39, 222
  enumeration, 221, 226
  INTEGER, 39, 136
  LONGREAL, 401
  opaque, 422, 423
  POINTER, 426
  PROC, 407
  procedure, 405, 407
  REAL, 39, 43, 85, 133, 226
  RECORD, 150
  scalar, 83, 148, 150, 226
  SET, 345
  simple, 226
  standard, 39, 226
  structured, 150, 226, 327, 345
  subrange, 148, 226, 241
  transparent, 423
DataInputValidation procedure, 210
Deadlock, 455
DEALLOCATE procedure, 429, 431, A28
Debugger, 53
Debugging, 48, 53, 101, 201, 213, 214
DEC standard procedure, 224, 227, A28
Decision
  table, 147, 276, 277
  tree, 146, 147, 277
Declaration, 34, 39, 162
  constant, 38, 42
  module, 37, 48, 155, 156, 303
  procedure, 58, 61, 70
  type, 148, 226, 345, 407, 423
  variable, 39
Decomposition, 9, 195
Definite iteration, 82
DEFINITION, 155, 287, 288
Definition module, 47, 54, 154–156, 287
Delete procedure, 25, 292, 294, 424, A30
De Morgan's law, 144
Depth-first search, 478
Dereferencing, 427, 432
Design, 9, 195, 203, 243, 274, 311, 349, 382, 411
  detailed, 13, 197
  structural, 9, 195
Designator, 333
Difference, 347

DisplayHorizontalSide procedure, 171
DisplayTitle procedure, 69
DisplayTitleLine procedure, 172
Distance function, 211
DistanceBetween procedure, 156
DistanceToOrigin procedure, 155
Distributed systems, 464
DIV operator, 134
Divide and conquer, 9, 57, 106, 184, 195, 204, 377
Division, 133
DO, 81, 83, 330
Documentation, 13, 202, 215, 254, 281, 323, 360, 390
  external, 202, 216
  internal, 202, 215
  maintenance, 323, 324
  module, 323
  user, 323
DoñaAna module, 355
Done, 261, 263, 265, A23, A26
DrawBar procedure, 65, 66
DrawCircle procedure, 274
DrawFractal module, 181
DrawTriangle procedure, 60–63
Driver, 199, 200
Dummy parameter, 61
Duplicate procedure, 423
Dynamic data structure, 424, 431, 432
Dynamic variable, 427, 429

EBNF, A2
Editor, 34
Efficiency, 112, 113, 120, 125, 327, 338, 342
  big-O, 364, 373–375
ELSE, 90, 121, 122, 333, 334
ELSIF, 120, 121, 127
Emulation, 462
Encrypt procedure, 230
END, 37, 54, 59, 70, 80, 81, 83, 92, 94, 121, 122, 150, 288, 289, 298, 303, 330, 334
End of file, 275
entier function, 137, A26
Enumeration type, 221, 226
Environ module, 163
EOL character, 262, A23
Error, 48, 50, 51, 402
  absolute, 413
  compilation, 48, 49, 52
  relative, 414
  run time, 52
  semantic, 52
  syntax, 48, 51

Evaluation, 135, 142, 143
EXCL standard procedure, 347, A22
Execution, 35
EXIT, 80
exp function, 137, A27
Exponent, 395, 401
Exponential complexity, 376
EXPORT, 288, 289, 303
Export, 288, 301, 302
   list, 288, 293, 304, 344
Expression
   arithmetic, 133, 161
   Boolean, 140, 142, 143, 145
   constant, 42, 43, 83, 148
   logical, 139
External
   documentation, 202, 216
   module, 154, 287, 302

F1 function, 414
F2 function, 415
Factorial function, 107, 176
FactTrace module, 175
FALSE, 139
FetchChar function, 228, 229, 237, 292, 420, 421, 423, 430, A31
Field, 150, 329
   selector, 330
   tag, 333
Figures module, 287
File, 265, 267, 270, 274
   close, 53, 268
   merging, 274
   open, 54
   system, 34, 270
   type, 270, 271, A35
FileConcat module, 268
FileSystem module, 271
FindClientName procedure, 344
FindClientNumber procedure, 344
FindName function, 309
FindNextGap procedure, 319
Firmware, 465
First generation computers, 3
First procedure, 165, 166
Fixed point number, 397
FLOAT standard function, 136, A22
Floating point number, 397
Flow chart, 16, 19, 26
Flow of control, 29, 173, 201
FOR, 82, 83
Formal parameter, 61, 63, 67, 74, 149, 241
FORTRAN, 12, 285, 466
Fourth generation computer, 4

Fractal procedure, 181
FROM, 38, 288, 289, 303
Function procedure, 70, 71
FWriteReal procedure, 43, 44, 67, 87
Fx function, 406

Garbage collection, 428
Generic procedure, 136
GiveInstructions procedure, 322
Global identifiers, 163, 167, 181, 187
Global variables, 66, 167, 187, 321
Grade average computation, 235
Graphics, 273

HALT standard procedure, A22
Hanoi algorithm, 115
Hardware, 5, 460
Heuristic evaluation function, 478
Heuristic process, 11
Hexadecimal notation, 285
HIGH standard function, 241, 299, A22
High-level language, 34, 285
Horner's method, 404

Identifier, 38
   global, 163, 167, 181, 187
   local, 165, 167
   qualified, 150, 263, 267, 288
   scope, 63, 66, 161, 163, 307
IF, 90, 92, 94, 121
Illegible input and output, 260
IMPLEMENTATION, 155, 298
Implementation, 203, 210
   dependent, 258, 273
   module, 47, 54, 154–156, 289
IMPORT, 38, 263, 266, 288, 289, 303
Import, 38, 161, 301, 302
   list, 37, 38, 288, 302
IN, 346
INC standard procedure, 224, 227, 231, A22
INCL standard procedure, 347, A22
Indefinite iteration, 82
Indentation, 201, 212
IndependentParticles module, 447
Index, 229, 328, 336
   type, 232
Indexed variable, 233
Induction, mathematical, 116, 472
Infinite loop, 80
Information hiding, 133, 161, 164, 184, 187, 213, 286, 290, 306, 321, 420, 422, 450
INIT procedure, 443, A36
Initialization, 290, 308

Initialize procedure, 356
InitString procedure, 291, 293, 420, 423, A30
InOrder procedure, 437
InOut module, 38, 41, 47, 260, 264, A23
Input, 4, 43, 461
    data validation, 66, 205
    variable, 17
Input/output, 41, 47, 260, 265, 461, 463
    devices, 53, 54, 260
    illegible, 260
    legible, 260
    redirection, 53, 264, 265
    sequential, 259
InputPoint procedure, 210
Insert procedure, 291, 294, A31
InsertElement procedure, 437
InsertionSort procedure, 371
InsertSpaces procedure, 319
Instruction execution cycle, 461
INTEGER
    type, 39, 136
    type transfer function, 136
Integrate function, 406
InterestCharge procedure, 329
Interface, 197, 199
Internal
    documentation, 202, 215
    representation, 399
Interrupt capability, 461
Intersection, set, 347
Intractable algorithm, 377
Invocation, 28, 29, 40, 58, 162
IrregularSawtooth module, 61
Iteration, 18, 79, 80, 82, 88, 183, 366
    definite, 82
    FOR, 82, 83
    indefinite, 82
    LOOP, 79, 80, 89
    REPEAT, 79, 87, 89
    WHILE, 80, 81, 89

Justify module, 316, 318
JustifyLine procedure, 317, 320

Key, 327, 335
Knowledge-based system, 472

Language
    assembly, 285, 465, 466
    high-level, 34, 285
    machine, 5, 285, 463
Large scale integration, 4, 462
Legible input and output, 260

Length between points computation, 236
Length function, 25, 70, 292, 298, 420, 423, A31
Library module, 36, 47, 54, 287, 302, 343
    FileSystem, 271, A34
    InOut, 38, 41, 47, 260, 264, A23
    MathLib0, 137, A26
    RealInOut, 43, 47, 263, A25
    Storage, 426, 429, A28
    SYSTEM, A28
    Terminal, 266, A27
Line justification, 311
Linear search, 335
LinearSearch procedure, 336
Linked list, 431, 434
Linking, 36
LISP, 12, 466, 474, 476
List, 335
Ln function, 402
ln function, 137, A27
Local
    area network, 4
    declaration, 165, 167
    environment, 162, 163, 177, 307
    identifier, 63
    module, 303
    variable, 66
LocalParticles module, 450
Logic programming, 467
Logical expression, 139
LONGREAL type, 401
Lookup procedure, 271, A35
LOOP, 79, 80, 89
Loop, 18
    body, 80, 83
    control variable, 83
    invariant, 20, 97, 343, 368, 372, 373, 384, 469–471
LowerCase function, 231
LSI, 4, 462

Machine language, 5, 285, 463
Main memory, 5, 270
Maintenance, 13, 202, 217, 254, 324
    documentation, 323, 324
Mantissa, 395, 400
Masking, 167
Mathematical
    function, 137
    induction, 116, 472
MathLib0 module, 137, A26
Matrix, 238
Max function, 469
MAX standard function, A22

Index

MaxDays function, 125
Memory
  main, 5, 270
  management, 462
  read-only, 465
  secondary, 5, 270
  unit, 4, 460
  volatile, 270
  word, 395
Menu, 123, 127, 265
Merge procedure, 279
MergeTest module, 279
Merging files, 274
Microcomputer, 3, 463
Microinstruction, 462
Microprocessor, 462
Microprogramming, 461
MIN standard function, A22
MOD operator, 134
Modula-2, 2, 12, 33, 34, 157, 198, 260, 285, 286, 465, 466
Modular design chart, 197, 205, 208, 300, 301, 312, 316
MODULE, 37, 48, 54, 288, 289, 298, 303
Module, 48, 154–156, 161, 197, 286
  definition, 47, 48, 155, 156
  documentation, 323
  external, 154, 287, 302
  implementation, 47, 48, 155, 156
  local, 303
  program, 36, 48
MoveParticle procedure, 447, 450
Multiplication, 133, 134
MultiplicationTable procedure, 100
Multiply module, 41
Multiprocessing, 442, 462
Multiprogramming, 463
Multitasking, 443
Mutual exclusion, 454
Mystery module, 81

Nest1 module, 173
Nested
  if, 95, 118, 125, 145, 146
  loop, 100, 137
  procedure, 59, 124, 161, 169
NEW procedure, 426
NEWPROCESS procedure, A29
NewStrings module, 423, 430
NIL, 428, 430, 432
Node, 432
Nonlocal identifier, 167
NOT operator, 141

Number
  fixed point, 397
  floating point, 397
  system, 397
Numerical
  analysis, 394
  data type, 39, 133
  integration, 404, 407
  methods, 394

O, 364, 373–375
Octal notation, 222, 225, 285
ODD standard function, 112, 136, 143, A22
OF, 121, 122, 232, 238, 334, 345
One procedure, 168
Opaque type, 422, 423
Open a file, 54
Open array parameter, 241, 293, 337
OpenInput procedure, 53, 264, A23
OpenOutput procedure, 54, 264, A23
Operand, 133
Operating system 5, 34, 459, 465
Operation, 133
Operator
  arithmetic, 133, 134
  binary, 134
  Boolean, 141
  precedence, 86, 135, 142
  relational, 140, 223, 224
  set, 347
OR operator, 141
ORD standard function, 223, 224, 227, A22
Output, 4, 43, 461
  variable, 17
Overflow, 395

Padding blanks, 169
Parallel processing, 462
Parameter, 41, 240
  actual, 61, 63, 67, 74, 241
  dummy, 61
  formal, 61, 63, 67, 74, 149, 241
  open array, 241, 293, 337
  passing, 167
  value, 67, 74, 167, 294, 300, 431
  variable, 72, 74, 110, 167, 168, 294, 436
Partition, 377, 380, 383, 391
Partition procedure, 380
Pascal, 2, 12, 163, 198, 260, 285, 286, 466, 467
Pass, 367, 369, 381, 384, 390
PasswordDemo module, 309

PasswordSystem local module, 309
Pivot, 380, 381, 391
Pixel, 273
PL/1, 198, 285, 467
Point type, 155
POINTER type, 426
Pointer variable, 424, 426, 429, 432
Polynomial complexity, 376, 377
Portability, 348, 462
Pos function, 25, 72, 292, 295, A31
Power function, 112, 126
Precedence, 86, 135, 142
PreferredDay procedure, 358
Print procedure, 165, 166
PrintExpense procedure, 358
PrintInReverse procedure, 109
PrintState procedure, 95
PrintTable module, 225
Probe, 338, 340–342
Problem solving, 6, 8, 195
Problem specification, 195, 467
PROC type, 407
Proc1 procedure, 163, 173
Proc2 procedure, 174
Proc3 procedure, 174
Proc4 procedure, 174
PROCEDURE, 59, 70, 407
Procedure, 38, 58, 161
    call, 41, 58, 162
    declaration, 58, 61, 70
    function, 70, 71
    generic, 136
    heading, 61
    invocation, 40, 58, 162
    parameters, 41, 240
    recursive, 108, 175, 177, 181, 369, 434, 437
    standard, 136, A22
    type, 405, 407
Process, 442
Processes definition module, 443, A36
Processor, 442, 460
Producer-consumer problem, 453
Program, 2, 36, 48
    coding, 200, 210
    documentation, 13, 202, 215, 254, 281, 323, 360, 390
    execution, 35
    formatting, 216
    maintenance, 13, 217, 254, 324
    module, 48
    stored, 3, 460
    testing, 11, 48, 198
    verification, 369
Programming language, 12, 34, 459, 465
Programming style, 200, 201
Prolog, 467, 474
Prompt, 267
Proof of correctness, 368, 369, 372, 469, 472
Pseudocode, 10, 197, 198, 207
PseudoRandom module, 410
Pseudorandom numbers, 408

QUALIFIED, 288, 289, 303
Qualified identifier, 150, 263, 267, 288
Quasi-concurrent processing, 443, 445, 463
Quicksort procedure, 364, 379
Quote, 41, 223

Rainy days computation, 236, 239, 240
Random function, 410
Random numbers, 407
RandomReal function, 408
RandomSentences module, 410
RandomWalk module, 408
Range checking, 148
    error, 227
Read procedure, 261, 266, A24, A27
ReadAgain procedure, 266, A27
ReadandStore procedure, 356
ReadCard procedure, 38, 262, A24
ReadChar procedure, 271, A35
ReadInt procedure, 41, 43, 262, A24
ReadLine procedure, 292, 295, A32
Read-only memory, 465
ReadPcts procedure, 251
ReadReal procedure, 43, 263, A26
ReadScanText procedure, 250
ReadString procedure, 261, 295, A24
ReadWord procedure, 271, 279, A35
REAL type, 39, 43, 85, 133, 226
Real function, 137, A26
RealInOut module, 43, 47, 263, A25
Record
    field, 150, 329
    variant, 332, 333
RECORD type, 150, 327
Rectangle procedure, 287
RecTriangle module, 210
Recursion, 107, 179, 180, 183, 342, 365, 369, 377, 378, 382
    base case, 107, 365, 378
    efficiency, 112, 125
    implementation, 175
    tail, 342, 365, 369, 434
Recursive data structure, 432
Recursive procedure, 108, 175, 177, 181, 369, 434, 437

Redirection, input/output, 53, 264, 265
Referent, 427
Refinement, 196, 197
ReflectOrigin procedure, 155, 156
Relation, 141
Relational operator, 140, 223, 224
Relative error, 414
Rename procedure, 272, A35
REPEAT, 79, 87, 89
Repetition, 18, 29, 78–80, 87, 89
    FOR, 82, 83
    LOOP, 79, 80, 89
    REPEAT, 79, 87, 89
    WHILE, 80, 81, 89
Representation of data, 133, 139, 290, 394, 399, 421
Reserved word, 37
Reset procedure, 272, A35
Response type, 271, A34
Retention of value, 308
RETURN, 70
Reverse procedure, 110
ROM, 465
Root module, 414
RPos function, 292, 295, A31
Run time error, 52

SameSign function, 415
Scalar type, 83, 148, 150, 226
Scale factor, 151, 329, 397
Scope, 63, 66, 161, 163, 307
Scope1 module, 164, 166
Scope2 module, 168
Search
    binary, 338
    blind, 478
    breadth-first, 478
    depth-first, 478
    key, 335
    linear, 335
    tree, 477
SearchForCustomer definition module, 344
Searching, 308, 327, 335, 370
Second generation computers, 3, 462
Second procedure, 165, 166
Secondary memory, 5, 270
Seed, 408, 411
Selection, 26, 29, 78, 90, 91, 95, 117
    CASE, 121, 122
    IF, 90, 92, 94, 121
SelectionSort procedure, 367
Selector, 122
Self-documenting code, 216
Semantic error, 52
Semantics, 36, 469, 474

Semaphore, 453–455
SEND procedure, 443, 444, A36
Separate compilation, 302
Sequencing, 16, 29
Sequential input and output, 259
Series approximation, 401
Set
    base type, 345
    difference, 347
    intersection, 347
    operators, 347
    symmetric difference, 347
    union, 347
SET type, 345
SetJustifiedWidth procedure, 317, 320
SetMinimumWidth procedure, 317, 320
Sharing module, 52
Side effect, 71, 187, 212
SIGNAL type, 443, A36
Simple type, 226
sin function, 137, A27
SIZE standard function, 427, A22
Sketch module, 119
Software, 5, 34, 462
    crisis, 284, 285
    bus, 208, 301
Sorting, 364, 377
    insertion, 371
    Quicksort, 364, 379
    selection, 367
    TriSort, 389
Specification, 195, 197, 467
SpiralGalaxy module, 82, 84
SplitNames procedure, 73
SpruceTree module, 60
sqr procedure, 251
sqrt function, 137, A27
Square module, 16, 44
Standard
    functions, 136, A22
    i/o devices, 53, 54, 260
    module, 41
    procedures, 136, A22
    types, 39, 226
StartProcess procedure, 443, A36
Statement, 34, 39, 161
    assignment, 40
    CASE, 121
    EXIT, 80
    FOR, 82, 83
    IF, 90, 92, 94, 121
    LOOP, 79, 80, 89
    REPEAT, 79, 87, 89
    WHILE, 80, 81, 89
    WITH, 330

Static variable, 424, 425
Stepwise refinement, 11
Storage module, 426, 429, A28
Stored program, 3, 460
Stream, 244, 259, 265
   base type, 259
   binary, 259
String, 23, 46, 421, 430
   constant, 41, 293
STRING type, 39, 46, 221, 228, 237,
   290, 420, 422, 430, A30
StringEqual function, 292, 294, A32
StringGreater function, 292, 294, A31
Strings module, 46, 65, 70, 72, 228, 290,
   291, 298, 421, A30
Strongly typed, 49
Structural design, 9, 195
Structure, 161
   chart, 9, 16, 58–60, 170, 184, 188,
     195–197, 204, 244, 305, 313, 350,
     383
Structured type, 150, 226, 327, 345
Stub, 199, 200, 214, 215
StyleComparison procedure, 251
StylisticAnalysis module, 250
Subproblem, 9, 57, 195, 204
Subrange type, 148, 226, 241
   base type, 148, 228
Subtraction, 133, 134
SubtractPoints procedure, 155, 156
SummaryComp procedure, 359
SumOfIntegers module, 22, 37
Swap procedure, 168, 389, 451
Symmetric difference, 347
Syntax, 36, 467, 474
   diagrams, A9
   error, 48, 51
System
   knowledge-based, 472
   number, 397
   operating, 5, 34, 459, 465
SYSTEM module, A28

Tag field, 333
Tail recursion, 342, 365, 369, 434
Temperature module, 85, 88, 92
TermCH character, 261, A23
Terminal module, 266, A27
Test cases, 11, 198, 199
TestCountWords module, 296
Testing, 11, 48, 198
Testing strategy, 11, 198, 200, 208, 246,
   278, 317, 354, 386
TestIntegrate module, 406
TestJustify module, 322

TestLn module, 403
TestNames module, 73
Text stream, 259
TextAnalysis procedure, 250
THEN, 90, 92, 94, 121
Third generation computers, 3
Throughput, 463, 464
Timesharing, 464
TitleBox procedure, 171
TO, 83, 426
ToChar function, 293, 295, A32
Tomorrow procedure, 125
Top-down
   design, 196
   development, 199
   testing, 199, 215
ToString procedure, 293, 294, A32
Trace, 22
Trace procedure, 176, 181
TRANSFER procedure, A29
Transparent type, 423
Trapezoidal rule, 405
Tree
   binary, 434
   search, 435
   traversal, 437
Triangle procedure, 287
TriSort procedure, 389
TRUE, 139
TRUNC standard function, 136, A22
Truth table, 141
TSIZE function, A30
Turing test, 472
TurtleGraphics module, 44, 45, 273,
   290, A32
Two procedure, 168
Two's complement, 400
TYPE, 148, 226, 345, 407, 423
Type, 38, 133, 221
   compatible, 148
   conversion, 136
   data, 132
   enumeration, 221, 226
   opaque, 422, 423
   scalar, 83, 148, 150, 226
   simple, 226
   standard, 39, 226
   structured, 150, 226, 327, 345
   subrange, 148, 226, 241
   transparent, 423
Type transfer function, 136
   CARDINAL, 136
   INTEGER, 136

Unary operator, 134, 142

Underflow, 395
Union, set, 347
UNTIL, 87
User documentation, 323
User's manual, 13, 216, 217, 254, 361

VAL standard function, 227, 242, A22
Validation, 348
ValidData function, 357
ValidPassword function, 309
Value parameter, 67, 74, 167, 294, 300, 431
   retention, 308
VAR, 39, 72
Variable, 12, 38, 313, 321
   declaration, 39
   dynamic, 427, 429
   global, 66, 167, 187, 321
   indexed, 233
   input, 4, 43, 461
   output, 17
   parameter, 72, 74, 110, 167, 168, 294, 436
   static, 424, 425
Variant record, 332, 333
Vector, 232
Very large scale integration, 4, 462
Virtual
   machine, 465
   memory, 462, 465

Visibility range, 169, 187, 307
VLSI, 4, 462
Volatile memory, 270
Von Neumann machine, 460

WAIT procedure, 443, 444, 445, A36
WHILE, 80, 81, 89
WindChill module, 138
Wirth, Niklaus, 259
WITH, 330
Word, 395, 425
WORD type, A28
Write procedure, 50, 261, 266, A25, A27
WriteCard procedure, 38, 262, A25
WriteChar procedure, 271, A35
WriteHex procedure, 263, A25
WriteInt procedure, 43, 262, A25
WriteLine procedure, 293, 295, A32
WriteLn procedure, 38, 42, 262, 266, A25, A27
WriteMsg procedure, 173
WriteOct procedure, 263, A25
WriteReal procedure, 47, 263, A26
WriteRealOct procedure, 264, A26
WriteString procedure, 38, 261, 266, 295, A25, A27
WriteWord procedure, 272, A36

XSquared function, 406

Standard Functions

ABS(x)	FLOAT(x)	MIN(T)	SIZE(T)
CAP(ch)	HIGH(a)	ODD(x)	TRUNC(X)
CHR(x)	MAX(T)	ORD(x)	VAL(T, x)

Standard Procedures

DEC(x)	EXCL(s, i)	INC(x)	INCL(s, i)
DEC(x, n)	HALT	INC(x, n)	

Standard Types

BITSET	CHAR	LONGREAL
BOOLEAN	INTEGER	PROC
CARDINAL	LONGINT	REAL

Sample Type Declarations

```
TYPE Days = (Mon, Tue, Wed, Thu, Fri);            (* enumeration type *)
     Months = [1..12];                            (* subrange type *)
     HourlyReading =
        ARRAY Days, [0..23] OF REAL;              (* array type *)
     String10 = ARRAY [0..9] OF CHAR;             (* string type *)
     Coordinate = RECORD x, y: REAL END;          (* record type *)
     Figure =
       RECORD
          location: Coordinate;
          CASE shape: (circle, rectangle) OF      (* record with a *)
            circle:    radius: REAL |             (* variant part *)
            rectangle: length, width: REAL
          END
       END;
     SetOfDays = SET OF Days;                     (* set type *)
     FigurePtr = POINTER TO Figure;               (* pointer type *)
     ConvFunc = PROCEDURE (INTEGER): REAL;        (* procedure type *)
```